KOREANS IN JAPAN

Ethnic Conflict and Accommodation

CHANGSOO LEE AND GEORGE DE VOS

WITH CONTRIBUTIONS BY DAE-GYUN CHUNG, THOMAS ROHLEN, YUZURA SASAKI, HIROSHI WAGATSUMA, AND WILLIAM O. WETHERALL

FOREWORD BY ROBERT A. SCALAPINO

UNIVERSITY OF CALIFORNIA PRESS
Berkeley • Los Angeles • London

University of California Press
Berkeley and Los Angeles, California

University of California Press, Ltd.
London, England

Library of Congress Cataloging in Publication Data

Lee, Changsoo.
    Koreans in Japan.

    Bibliography: p. 417
    Incldes index.
    1. Koreans in Japan.   2. Japan—Ethnic relations.
3. Koreans—Ethnic identity.   I. De Vos, George, joint
athor.   II. Title.
DS832.7.K6L43   952'.004957   80-6053
ISBN 0-520-04258-1

Printed in the United States of America

1 2 3 4 5 6 7 8 9

CONTENTS

FOREWORD

Like most societies, Japan is a nation that harbors certain extraordinary paradoxes. In purely political terms, the Japanese polity qualifies as one of the most open systems in the world. The guarantees concerning freedom of speech, press, assemblage, and political activities contained in the 1947 Constitution are not mere rhetoric. They have been scrupulously enforced. Few nations of the world permit the wide-ranging political competition, the complete freedom of expression, and the full organizational rights characterizing present-day Japan. Owing to special circumstances, to be sure, Japan is often defined as a bureaucratic state, reflective of the great power wielded by the civil service in the decision-making process. It cannot be doubted, however, that the ultimate political course of this society is intimately connected with the outcome of free and competitive elections, contests available to all of the nation's citizenry.

Yet Japan can be described as an open society composed of closed units. Japanese social organization is characterized by the importance of the small group, an intimate association carrying with it extensive obligations, hence a proclivity for exclusivism. Whether the ties be those of family, school, business, or political unit, the primary group relationship is an intense one, and by virtue of this fact, any proliferation of the commitments entailed is difficult indeed. In politics, this situation breeds factionalism, and the complex coalition of factions that comprises both the political party and bureaucratic structures has proven enormously resistant to challenge, in spite of the impersonalization that is accompanying rapid socioeconomic change.

Notwithstanding the factional problem *within* Japanese society, however, when one examines the political culture of the whole nation-people, the features that predominate are those of homogeneity and exclusiveness. In a certain sense, the small-group, inner-directed qualities that separate the Japanese among themselves also unite them against any external party.

A homogeneous society has certain very great psychological and political advantages. It is entirely possible that in the course of the coming decades, conflicts having ethnic, linguistic, and religious roots will be the primary sources of disruption at the nation-state level, outweighing class conflicts by a very considerable measure. One of the discouraging aspects of the current scene is that progress in race relations within developing societies is very difficult to discern, and in some instances, retrogression would appear to be taking place. This fact does not augur well for future social harmony and political stability, especially in those states having major ethnic divisions.

The advantages of Japanese homogeneity, however, have a reverse side. Tolerance toward the outsider is extremely limited, as the research presented here demonstrates so clearly. Of course, the sense of being part of a superior or "chosen" race has been of great assistance in abetting individual self-confidence and a collective will to succeed. As the major tradition underwriting Japanese political culture, it has served to bolster the drive toward modernization, hence, the phenomenal Japanese achievements of the past century. In this connection, of course, a minor tradition should not be overlooked: certain Japanese and, at given points of time, Japanese society as a whole have been plunged into extensive self-criticism and self-doubt, seemingly prepared to cast off the indigenous for the foreign. A perpetual hierarchical relation, albeit one shifting from superior-inferior to inferior-superior, has dominated external relations, depending upon mood and perception of status. Equality has been the elusive element and, in this fact, domestic and foreign relations have been interlinked. In an age of increasing national interdependence, a tightly knit exclusiveness will present difficulties of steadily growing significance. Quite clearly, Japan must wrestle with this problem in the years ahead.

The present study focuses upon a truly fascinating subject: the Korean minority in Japan. The work commences with a broadly sketched background. From earliest historical times, the Korean-Japanese relationship has manifested both cooperation and conflict. Korea served as the principal conduit by means of which the Japanese race and Japanese culture came into being. There seems little question that the ancestors of the modern Japanese were predominately Mongol in stock and came to the Japanese islands via the Korean peninsula. Religion, philosophy, literature, art, and political institutions followed a similar route—often originating in China, being modified in Korea, and then being passed on to Japan. Each culture, to be sure, maintained or developed certain qualities that made it unique. The interrelationship was both lengthy and intimate, providing one of the greatest experiences in cultural borrowing that mankind has witnessed.

But conflict entered the scene at an early point and was recurrently interwoven into Korean-Japanese relations. It neither started nor ended with Hideyoshi, although his intrusion was among the most dramatic and tragic. Japanese involvement in Korea in the late nineteenth and early twentieth centuries was at once more gradual and more pervasive. In retrospect, it may also appear to have been inevitable. Historically, Korea had accepted the suzerainty of China, a relation that allowed maximum independence in "normal" times. China, however, was a very sick nation after the Taiping Rebellion, unable to play the historic role to which it had earlier come. The self-appointed heirs were Russia and Japan, and only a strong, modernizing Korea could have preserved its independence against these powers. There were occasional efforts to turn outward, particularly to the United States—a nation unreceptive at that point. The general drift, however, was toward weakness, stagnation, and divisiveness. In this context, Japanese victory in the Russo-Japanese War of 1904-1905 determined Korea's fate for four decades. When formal annexation occurred in 1910, Korea had already lost its independence via progressive Japanese controls.

Japan's dilemma during the colonial era has been well depicted in this and other studies. Tokyo experimented with policies, at times pursuing a very tough line, at times advancing a more conciliatory policy to win the support of the Korean people. The combination was not unsuccessful. As is indicated in the opening section, by World War II, a significant number of Koreans accepted their status as members of the Japanese empire and as subjects of the Japanese emperor, fighting or working valiantly for Japanese victory. Yet although Tokyo's policies centered upon an effort to japanize all Koreans through education, religion (Shintoism), and political indoctrination, the Japanese—officials and ordinary citizens alike—found it difficult if not impossible to accept Koreans as equals. The economic aspects of Japanese colonial policy, moreover, underwrote prejudice by giving it a socioeconomic foundation.

The stage was thus set for the complex, often thorny Korean-Japanese relations of the post-1945 era, and for the painful life of the Korean community now living in Japan. Numbering over 600,000, that community has been subjected to a different type of politicization since 1945. One of the extraordinarily interesting aspects of this study is its description of the contest between North Korea (the Democratic People's Republic of Korea) and South Korea (the Republic of Korea) for the allegiance of the overseas Koreans. Not surprisingly, the Communists took an early lead in this competition, aided by the miserable socioeconomic conditions under which most Koreans were existing in Japan's metropolitan areas.

The Communists paid special attention to education, thereby providing a service badly needed. At first glance, it seems amazing that the Japanese government would tolerate a separate educational system, capped by a university devoted to the glorification of a foreign government and its leader, Kim Il-sung. Yet the old dilemma was still present. Since Japan eschewed the concept of being a melting pot and basically did not want Koreans as citizens, it could scarcely oppose various manifestations of Korean separatism.

Japanese citizenship for Koreans, we discover, is not made impossible but neither is it made easy. And repatriation, once pushed with vigor by

Koreans, has proved to be relatively unpopular. In point of fact, neither North nor South Korea has wanted sizable numbers of expatriates. Economic conditions might have been bad for the Koreans in Japan, but they were generally worse in Korea itself, at least in the initial postwar period. There were also questions of political assimilation. Kim Il-sung preferred that the Koreans in Japan join Ch'ongnyŏn, the political-social organization in Japan controlled by the DPRK, and render their service to the North through this vehicle. Gradually, the ROK also came to appreciate the importance of their overseas compatriots, the overwhelming majority of whom had originally come from South Korea. Thus, through Mindan, they began to compete with the Communists, resulting in an acceleration of political activities and a deepening of divisions within the Korean community.

It is interesting to note that Koreans played a significant role in the early postwar Japanese Communist party, but gradually those whose inclinations were toward the Communist movement were caused to stand apart from the JCP and to uphold loyally the positions of the Korean Workers' party, Kim's chosen instrument in North Korea. Among those whose political proclivities were with South Korea, divisions in Seoul were reflected in divisions within Mindan. Thus, Korean politics in all of their complexity have been implanted in Japanese soil and remain there as troublesome reminders to the Japanese of the price of quasi-apartheid policies.

The latter part of this study contains a series of moving case studies, reflective of the extraordinarily difficult life faced by many Koreans in Japan. Approximately three-fourths of those Koreans have been born in Japan and a number are third-generation residents. But the Korean community displays almost all of the characteristics of segregated, depressed minorities elsewhere. Problems begin with the family: parents with a low level of self-esteem encourage their children to deny their heritage to avoid discrimination; severe economic problems derive in part from inadequate education and low skill levels; broken homes with absent fathers abet the drift into juvenile delinquency. Above and beyond familial conditions, there remains the general feeling of rejection by the larger Japanese community. Hence, an inner tension exists, with many Koreans torn between the desire to pass—to be accepted as Japanese—and the desire to reassert with defiant pride their Korean identification.

The scholars who have undertaken this research are themselves of varied ethnic and cultural backgrounds—Korean, American, and Japanese. They have combined to give us a most illuminating work, representing a pioneer effort in a vitally important field.

Director   Robert A. Scalapino
Institute of East Asian Studies
University of California
Berkeley, California

PREFACE

Ethnic groups, long submerged socially in the multi-ethnic modern states comprising the contemporary world, have begun increasingly to assert the significance of their own distinctiveness and identity. Although most minority groups have never sought total assimilation within a larger cultural and social milieu, today more than ever, ethnic identities have become vital, highly conscious forces for activating new modes of seeking political redress for past social and economic inequities. In recent decades, ethnicity has played an increasing role in the search for political and social change in widely divergent societies, evolving its own forms of political ideology which modify or transcend previous Marxist doctrines of class warfare. New principles have been sought as effective means of advancing group interests.

In presenting this comparative instance of the minority-majority relations of Koreans in Japan, our purpose is both theoretical and practical. Social scientists investigating any problem have two duties: accumulation of relevant data permitting conclusions critically acceptable to dispassionate peers; and communication of the social implications of the research findings to the general reader. We employ various modes of demonstration and illustration because we believe that no one discipline can fully present the social and personal problems of Koreans in Japan. In addition to presenting scientific findings to our colleagues in the social sciences, we address a general audience and also policy-makers concerned with ameliorative change. We hope our attempt provides broad perspectives for future social action and policy-making, both by legislative and administrative means.

This volume summarizes the collective work of many researchers, past and present, who have contributed directly or indirectly. We consider this multiple approach essential to presenting with sufficient scholarly analysis the social and personal problems of Koreans in Japan. The major methods and points of view represented in this book naturally reflect the principal competencies of the authors and editors. Although Changsoo Lee is a political scientist, and George De Vos is an anthropologist and psychologist, whenever possible the approaches of the historian and the sociologist are borrowed. The book is deliberately interdisciplinary, for we firmly believe that work in the social sciences has unitary objectives despite its disciplinary specializations.

The documented materials presented in this volume derive from various social science methods. We have been able to draw on the interested efforts of many Japanese and Koreans who recognize the need to reach a wider audience to raise the general level of concern about the contemporary plight of the Korean minority. We are aware of gaps in our first-hand information and are continuing our investigations, especially with regard to psychological issues. In addition to direct interviews and personal contacts, we have relied on previously published materials ranging from statistical reports to reports in the Japanese daily press. All that we present has been checked and verified, whatever the source. We have not hesitated at times to state our impressions as well as our conclusions, but we have indicated where we judge strong evidence to be lacking.

We are interested in this cultural-historical case not merely for its own sake but for what it can reveal about the effects of social discrimination wherever or whenever it occurs. What we can document and present about the history of social discrimination in Japan is pertinent to the meaning of social discrimination elsewhere. Our generalizations are relevant cross-culturally. Our purpose is not to single out problems of social discrimination in Japan but to document one instance of a worldwide social problem.

Among today's large nation-states, no society is totally free of conflict owing to ethnic differences. We are perhaps more cognizant of the problems faced in the United States than in various Asian societies because American society is based on diversity of origins. But even though the social and ethnic identities of Koreans and Japanese are historically intertwined, separate ethnic identity remains a source of intergroup conflict. We are impressed with the evidence that the consequences of discriminatory practices are strikingly similar whether they occur within a pluralistic America or within a Japan that is relatively homogeneous in its cultural origins. Historical circumstances may be vastly different, but in each instance problems result not only from present inequities but also from a history of ethnic animosity. Today, we learn what we can to ameliorate and perhaps redress our inheritance from a less self-conscious past. No contemporary society can present itself as totally free from a karma of past social, political, and economic injustice.

Americans no longer view total assimilation and complete loss of ethnic allegiance as a foreseeable possibility. In contrast, European societies have sought to hide diversity to foster unified nationalism. Each has had its own history of failure to assimilate, unify, and commit all those within its boundaries to one concept of loyal citizenship that truly transcends past diversity. Today the so-called United Kingdom is restive. Many among the Irish, Scottish, and Welsh minorities seek autonomy and separation. The

United Kingdom may speak the English language, but it is not an English state as far as its minorities are concerned.

Those conversant with social trends in metropolitan France are aware of the resurgence of separatist regionalism there. Old animosities are still felt by the Bretons in the Northwest. Speakers of the *langue d'oc* in the South are reviving the concept of a separate "Occitanie." Modern Germany is still uneasy about its recent barbarous past under Nazism, when attempts at genocide were directed toward gypsies, Slavs, and Jews. Northern Italians today remain contemptuous of Southerners from Calabria and Sicily. But ethnic problems in Europe are minor when compared with those in parts of Africa or Asia. Most present-day African states are artificial amalgams of ethnically distinct peoples where the attendant political and social problems are far from resolution. Throughout Asia, social tensions about ethnic minorities, principally overseas Chinese and Indians, seethe close to the surface.

As we point out in this volume, Japan, seemingly homogeneous to the casual observer, is not an exception. In a previous book, George De Vos and Hiroshi Wagatsuma investigated the problems of "Japan's invisible race," the approximately two million ex-untouchables still covertly branded as biologically unassimilable. The present volume explores the more overt plight of ethnically distinct Koreans caught in the dilemma of identity fostered by present-day legal restrictions as well as by discriminatory social attitudes inherited from the past. Fortunately, Japan today is a democracy capable of converting criticism to constructive self-analysis and social action. Although we write in English, we hope that our readership will include members of the Korean and Japanese communities. We believe the conditions we describe can be ameliorated. Legal remedies are possible, and most modern Japanese have a sincere desire to practice social democracy, rectifying and improving conditions within their society when sufficient public attention is directed to these problems.

To study the topics at issue, we use various means, ranging from statistics to projective psychological tests. Because we believe in the effectiveness of dramatic illustration, several chapters utilize particular case histories to illustrate general social conditions experienced by Japan's Korean minority and to point up the subjective attitudes of Koreans participating in these events or learning about them as part of their heritage. Our purpose in this is to arouse a level of emotional as well as cognitive awareness, a level of total comprehension by which we all can achieve some psychological identification with the Koreans in their plight.

The book owes its existence to many individuals. We would like to extend our sincere thanks to Professors Setsure Tsurushima, Kansai University of Japan, and Kwang-kyu Lee, Seoul National University of Korea, for reading the manuscript in part or in its entirety. They gave us many valuable criticisms and suggestions. We are grateful to Professors Edward W.

Wagner and Richard H. Mitchell whose pioneering works in English on the subject inspired us in a variety of ways. We also like to acknowledge our intellectual debts to Tamaki Motoi, Yi Yu-whan, Chŏng Chŏl, Pak Kyŏng-sik and Pak Che-il whose earlier works on the Koreans in Japan enabled us to study the subject in depth. Also, we give special thanks to Dr. Kim Ki-dae of the Research Institute of Korean Affairs in Tokyo, who helped us locate many valuable data, including his warm friendship. A special debt is acknowledged to Mr. Kim Sam-kyu of *Koria Hyoron*, Chung Kyong-mo, Kim Kun-ba, Bae Tong-ho, Kwak Tong-ui, Kim Chŏng-ju, Kim Whan, Reverend Lee In-Ha of the Kawasaki Korean Christian Church, Cho Il-che, Lee Sung-mok, Chung Ik-wu, Lee Seung-kwon and Han Nok-Ch'un, all Korean residents in Japan, both as informants and hospitable friends during many of our field trips to Japan. We are also indebted to Robert Sakai, Jr., of the University of California, Berkeley. His latest field trip to study community life among Koreans in Japan provided us with invaluable insights and brought to our attention many aspects of important ethnographic problems. Our deep appreciation is also extended to Grace Buzaljko, Stella Dorachee, and Regina Garrick for their skillful editorial assistance. Especially our thanks are due to Gretchen Van Meter of the University of California Press for her able assistance in final editing of the papers. For willing help and research, especially in preparing chapter 1, we thank Alan Kim. Whatever merit this study may possess is owed persons mentioned and to the various contributing scholars. For errors of fact and judgment we alone bear responsibility.

University of Southern California   Changsoo Lee
University of California, Berkeley   George De Vos
January 1981

PART ONE

HISTORY—PAST AND PRESENT

1

KOREANS AND JAPANESE
The Formation of
Ethnic Consciousness

George De Vos and Changsoo Lee

To understand the self-awareness of Koreans in Japan—that is, what comprises their ethnic identity—it is necessary to know something about Japanese and Korean history. Instead of sketching a short chronology, we will place six dramatic scenes in their historical contexts. These episodes are part of the Korean heritage and memory but are either forgotten or suppressed from the consciousness of most Japanese. They summarize, for us, the way that the consciousness of contemporary Japanese differs from the consciousness of those who live in Japan but are aware of their Korean heritage. They mark Korean-Japanese contact, but they serve to keep apart, rather than to bring closer together, these Asian cousins.

GENESIS: THE MYTH OF UNIQUE ORIGIN

Scene One: The Opening of the Takamatsuzuka Tomb

A few years ago a singular event occurred at Takamatsuzuka, on the island of Honshu. An ancient burial site was inadvertently disturbed. The Japanese scientists who entered the burial chamber were astounded by the beautiful frescoes adorning the four walls with images reflecting the social life of a nobility wearing dress indistinguishable from that worn in the ancient states of the Korean peninsula. On the four walls, animal symbols, mythological and real, represented the cardinal directions. The ornamental flourishes all duplicated a culture pattern prominent in Korean burials but previously found in Japan only in the island of Kyushu. Never before had such a pattern, characteristic of the kings of Koguryŏ, been reported in the Kinai area in the present-day Nara prefecture. This area was in the heartland of "Yamato," the place name given to the first self-consciously "Japanese" kingdom.

Whose tomb had been opened? Before its disturbance, this tomb site was thought to be that of the Emperor Munbu, forty-second in the Imperial lineage. But the clothes and frescoes were not comparable with legend. New explanations were necessary. Were these members of an intrusive cavalier culture whose nobility became, for some time at least, the rulers of the land of Yamato? Or were they local nobility whose dress and tastes were at that time totally identical with their Korean counterparts? For many patriotically and pridefully "unique" Japanese, the event was somewhat embarrassing. It was another reminder that cumulative archaeological evidence suggests, as does linguistic evidence, some common origin for modern-day Koreans and Japanese.

This tomb and its contents did more than suggest simple borrowing by an indigenous Japanese imperial line. It gave weight to the contention that in prehistoric times a dynastic complexity had existed which included rulers from the outside—invaders from the peninsula. It added archaeological weight to the assertion that the myth of an unbroken imperium of Japan must give way to increasingly weighty scientific evidence to the contrary. A negative emotional response to the suggestion of a common kinship between Koreans and Japanese, however, has hindered the objectivity of some scholars. A Korean connection from the earliest time of myth and legend is not conscionable to many Japanese.

Gleanings from the Archaeological Record

The interrelationship of Koreans and Japanese symbolized by the Takamatsuzuka tomb dates back to the period when concepts of "Koreans" and "Japanese" did not exist. Present-day inhabitants of Korea and present-day Japanese, as far as contemporary archaeology and linguistics can determine, have a considerable overlap of ancestral stock. It is still not possible to state clearly how and by whom neolithic culture was brought to the Japanese islands. The creators of what is termed Jōmon pottery (pottery of an elaborate style with embellishing rope marks), who were a hunting and gathering population, were abruptly followed by an agricultural "Yayoi" culture, named after an area on the western outskirts of present-day Tokyo where its characteristic pottery was first unearthed.

Geologically, the Japanese islands have taken their present shape only recently. They date by most estimates to approximately the end of the Pleistocene era, an era occurring roughly twenty thousand years ago, subsequent to the last great Ice Age. The first archaeological evidence of inhabitation of these isles after the recession of ice is the presence of large shell mounds. These mounds are the refuse and leftovers of human meals and include many fragments of broken pottery. The Jōmon pottery was low-fired and easily broken. Estimates of the age of this pottery tradition put it back to about 4500 B.C.[1] There are few attempts today to link the Jōmon people directly to modern Japanese. The dental structure does not resemble the scissor-like occlusion that characterizes most modern Japanese. Neither do the remains of Jōmon man resemble the remnants of Ainu populations on Hokkaido. Moreover, there is no evidence that the Ainu spread beyond northeastern Japan. Today, those considered Ainu are, for the most part, so interbred with Japanese that it is difficult to measure differences. Nevertheless, what differences appear do not suggest a Jōmon connection for the Ainu, in the estimate of many archaeologists or physical anthropologists. The Ainu remain an anthropological enigma. They have a polysynthetic language and a culture distinct from the Japanese, with resemblances rather to other northern Asian groups, especially in religious shamanistic practices. The language of the Ainu bears no resemblance to any other linguistic stock.

Whether or not archaeologists suggest some relationship between present-day Ainu and the Jōmon culture, all agree on the abrupt cultural change indicated by the Yayoi artifacts. One can reasonably conclude that the Yayoi culture brought with it to the Japanese islands the Bronze and Iron Ages. In contrast to the Jōmon way of life, based on hunting and gathering, the Yayoi people had already engaged in highly developed wet-rice agriculture. They fired their pottery at high temperatures in closed kilns. They had metal weapons, the crafting of which had already spread throughout continental Asia. Although the coming in of the Yayoi culture was fairly abrupt, human remains show evidence of possible interbreeding with the Jōmon people. Some similarities to the older Jōmon stock in cranial breadth measurements are reported. The general findings are that the Yayoi had greater facial height. In fact, their facial height was greater than the present average for modern Japanese. The tooth structure in approximately one-third of the Yayoi skulls has the scissor-like occlusion of the contemporary population. The average stature, as estimated from the length of femur bones, was considerably greater than either the older Jōmon on the one hand or the modern Japanese on the other.

There is no end to controversy attempting to relate the Jōmon and Yayoi people to modern Japanese. As nonspecialists, we would summarize by saying the Yayoi remains can possibly be considered ancestral to present-day Japanese, but the evidence remains contradictory and offers as yet no certainty of conclusion. The Yayoi culture is dated approximately from the second century B.C. to the third century A.D. It is with this period of Japanese prehistory that controversy about Korean interrelationships becomes a pertinent issue. Today the controversies have shifted from what were formerly problems of religious orthodoxy to matters primarily of archaeological interpretation. Nevertheless, strong emotions persist and give color to present-day partisanship.

Religious Belief vs. Critical Inquiry

Japanese archaeological and anthropological scholarship has faced the same problems in given periods as did Western scholars in the latter half of the nineteenth century. Orthodox religious believers, whether followers of

Christianity or Shintō, have not welcomed any critical examination that calls into question the affirmations of religious mythology. One can here briefly digress, citing parallel experience when Western scholars began questioning their own origin myth. One of the pioneers of modern anthropological theory, W. Robertson-Smith, had in his time a great influence on scientific anthropology, although his general theory of the priority of totemism in the evolution of religious beliefs is no longer seriously considered. This is true, as well, of the other evolutionary reconstructions of human culture that were prominent in his day,[2] but Robertson Smith worked in an area that was considered a direct challenge to fundamental Christianity. Because he had the temerity to examine in some detail the Semitic religions that had preceded Judaism, his research seemed to question the authenticity of the Bible itself. In the late nineteenth century, Great Britain was avowedly a Christian kingdom, and Robertson Smith was removed from his academic post in Scotland. Darwinian evolutionism was as yet, for some, a religious heresy that made its purveyors vulnerable to political and social sanctioning.

In a more retrograde recent period, scientific scholarship during the Nazi rule in Germany fell victim to a military dictatorship that silenced any critical examination. The Soviet Union and China have kept tight controls over what is to be considered official history, past or present.

Such problems faced by scholars elsewhere in the examination of the past are sometimes forgotten when one comments on the fate of Japanese scholars during the prewar militaristic period there. For pious Japanese, their unique origin was also described in sacred scriptures: the Kojiki, first compiled in 712, and the Nihon-shoki, dating from about 720. Many Japanese in protecting religious orthodoxy behave no differently from orthodox Christians. The Christian origin myth in some respects also insists upon uniqueness. In effect, Christianity borrowed directly the origin myth of Judaic culture; Genesis is a religious statement of a particular ethnic group. Through adoption by a revolutionary Christianity, it became transformed into part of a universalist religion. Explanatory legends of the sons of Noah and the Tower of Babel preceded archaeological inquiry into prehistoric human diversity. Conservative Christians today, on the one hand, find it amusing that the Japanese could believe firmly in Izanagi and Izanami, or that the ancient Greeks could believe in a Pantheon inhabiting Olympus; on the other hand, these same Christians consider it heresy to question the Bible or the authenticity of Genesis.

Ethnic problems among Christians may or may not be related to arguments about separate origin, but many Japanese hold views similar to the Jews of an ethnic continuity back to mankind's beginning. They consider themselves a single people whose uniqueness is substantiated by sacred scriptures. Although Japanese archaeology today is relatively free to pursue inquiry into the past, there remains a reluctance to disturb further any imperial tombs. Opening and exploring their contents systematically would, of course, either substantiate or modify the official myths.

Rational scientific inquiry into the origins of humanity in Japan appeared early in the Meiji period, contemporaneous with the questioning of the Bible in Europe and America in the latter half of the nineteenth century. Scientific objectivity and careful scholarship were characteristic of the work of such pioneers as Naka Michio.[3] Naka questioned the traditional chronology of Japanese mythology. By reference to Chinese and Korean sources, he found that the traditional founding date for the Japanese nation (approximately 660 B.C.) was impossible and that Japanese mythical chronology for the third and fourth centuries A.D. was systematically off by two sixty-year cycles or 120 years. Naka's careful scholarship inspired followers, such as Tsuda Sōkichi and others, who were able to establish Japanese archaeology on a firm footing.[4] Dating in rough terms was established for the Jōmon, Yayoi, and Kofun periods, from the second century B.C. to the seventh century A.D.

With the militarism of the 1930s, chauvinistic dogmatism emphasized Japanese uniqueness and made impossible any archaeological work questioning the orthodox beliefs of Japanese origins. In 1942, Tsuda Sōkichi was convicted but not jailed for insulting the dignity of the imperial family by his irreverent use of archaeological fieldwork. Despite present-day freedom to reconsider Japanese origins scientifically, the idea that the composition of the Japanese population was significantly modified by an invasion in the early fourth century from the Korean peninsula still meets with considerable public resistance. This reluctance may stem from an unreadiness to acknowledge a decisive foreign role in the ruling of early Japan. Some of these foreign rulers would in effect have been ancestors of modern Koreans. The fact is, of course, that in this ancient period it is improbable that there was any consciousness of being either "Korean" or "Japanese" in the same way that one thinks about it today. Again, to reach out for a Western analogy, the contemporary Englishman has a different sense of being English than did those living in any part of the British Isles at the time of the Norman Conquest.

Early Incursions and Contributions from the Korean Peninsula

Considerable conjecture surrounds the culture of an "old-tomb" or Kofun period that preceded the advent of literacy and records. Kiley points out very forcefully that the fifth-century Wa kingdom, which was to become the Yamato state, could not have developed except as an integral historic part of northeast Asia. The organization of the nobility suggests a common cultural heritage with other northeast Asian peoples.[5] Kiley notes that the commonality of pattern in all Tungisic conquest states is evidence for incursions from the peninsula into Japan, and he supports Egami's arguments that a group of outsiders using artifacts of Tungisic culture came conquering from the Kyūshū area in the fifth century. Kiley believes that by the end of the fourth century the agricultural population of Yamato was ruled by a military class. The main point of contention among serious historians is not whether there was a conquest by invaders from Kyūshū but whether these invaders themselves were of Tungisic origin. Egami contends that the Wa power was consolidated in the Mimana area, extending from Korea to Kyūshū, before the invaders established a political center in Yamato. Mizuno, who challenges the sacred scriptures, does not commit himself on Egami's thesis of the conquerors as horse riders. But he demonstrates that a critical evaluation of the Nihon-shoki and Kojiki data cannot support seriously a thesis of unbroken dynastic continuity. He demonstrates that this ideology of continuity cannot have antedated the chronicles themselves by more than a few decades. Yamato rulers of the fifth and sixth centuries could not have considered themselves to be members of a permanent unbroken lineage. Some time later, the ideology of dynastic continuity was introduced to strengthen the legitimacy of the imperial line. Kiley states Mizuno's principal conclusion that the archaic Yamato line was ruled by at least three successive lines of kings.[6] First there were ritual religious sovereigns, who reigned during the third and fourth centuries. Next followed a military dynasty of fifth-century kings. And finally, about the year 500, came the installation of the king known as the emperor Keitai. Keitai's dynasty has retained its sovereignty to the present day, technically, if not actually, unbroken.

Gari Ledyard tends to support the contention of Egami that northern Asians pressed down, established rule, and mingled with the inhabitants of Japan prior to the founding of the Yamato state, which marked the inception of a continuous dynastic structure.[7] These nomadic incursions probably extended over considerable time in prehistory. Interspersed with such northern invasions were the movements of agriculturists from southern Asia. The admixture of people of Malayo-Polynesian background as far north as Japan remains questionable. Perhaps it will never be possible for scientific research to distinguish these waves of incursion that imparted distinct differences in racial composition between the people of the Japanese isles and the Korean peninsula.

Written records confirming a sense of ethnic difference and unique origin as support for political legitimacy date from the seventh century. Japanese uniqueness could have become a commonly held belief only because an island location made its people much less vulnerable to the numerous political changes that subsequently characterized eastern Asia, but authors such as Ledyard insist that the Japanese islands must have been susceptible to the earlier convulsions by nomadic people. When Chinese rule weakened, however, the nomads threatened the Japanese islands as well as the more proximate Korean peninsula. Again, in the thirteenth century after the Mongols overran China, it was the Mongol Emperor Kublai Khan whose invasion fleet was wrecked by the sacred wind (Kami Kaze) blowing off the coast of Kyūshū.

When the Chinese state was strong, the nomads could not invade the Korean peninsula. Ledyard, in his discussion, focuses on the fourth century when northern China was flooded with waves of so-called barbarians of every description. The attacks were often so severe that the Chinese rulers left their northern areas and took refuge in the safer South. No Chinese regime ventured north again for two hundred years. The most easterly of these nomadic people influenced societies already established on the Korean peninsula. The invaders probably were illiterate; there were no written records of the incursions visited upon the peninsular and island people. Present legends do not depict resistance to the invasions but are told from the standpoint of the invaders. This suggests that the invaders or their culture became dominant, and it is their legends and myths that pass for history. In effect, then, the identity of those who became "Japanese" and "Korean" was probably borrowed from the invading groups rather than inherited from indigenous groups resistant to outside forces.

Ledyard's reconstruction centers on the Puyŏ as a principal invading group from somewhere in the Manchurian region to the north. They were allies of the Chinese who were left behind after a general Chinese withdrawal from the peninsula. They themselves had moved south and established themselves as the kings of Paekche, one of the major kingdoms to be founded and established with sufficient continuity. The southward movement of the Puyŏ took place, according to Ledyard's reconstruction, somewhere around A.D. 350 to 370.

Ledyard supports the conjecture that the Wa people, as early inhabitants of parts of Japan were termed in Chinese chronicles, may have received considerable cultural stimulus if not population from southern Asia as well as from Altaic groups. There is general consensus as to such a possibility. Ledyard, however, points out that the Wa were not self-consciously either "Korean" or "Japanese." Wa territory stretched from parts of the southern Korean peninsula, across the islands, through Kyūshū, and into southern Honshū. Ledyard describes Wa as a thalassocracy (a sea-state), as were ancient Phoenicia or Minos in the Mediterranean, but he does not cite any strong evidence for the sea-sovereign nature of Wa.

The Puyŏ pushed into this territory and for some time assumed political power. Legends such as those of the conquests of Jimmu Tennō, first emperor (now considered mythical by serious scholars), may be distorted reflections of outside incursions. At some point in the late tomb period, rich burials under huge mounds occurred. According to Ledyard, these mounds may have been built during an abrupt incursion of Puyŏ people, who had previously reigned in Paekche and who brought with them in their wave of conquest a surplus of supporting personnel—slaves and artisans. The labor necessary on these mounds was considerable. The one near Osaka, for example, may not appear as spectacular from the ground as the Egyptian pyramids, but the actual volume of artificially mounded soil far exceeds that of the giant tombs of Egypt.

The old tombs contain the accoutrements of a horse-riding people, artifacts not found previous to this period. There are helmets and armor and many clay statues (Haniwa), including those of horses and armored cavaliers. Ledyard estimates that the period of Puyŏ hegemony lasted at least a century. It too gave way; Puyŏ rule probably weakened, and by the time Japanese protohistory began and legend left off, the Wa emperor Keitai was established as ruler. The less populous Puyŏ were probably submerged and finally assimilated. Although memory of conflict and conquest involving outsiders could not be completely obliterated, there were perhaps deliberate distortions of legend and mythology sanctioned by those who came to dominate. Written records replaced oral transmission. The fact that there had been successful incursions from outside could be hidden, and the surviving written mythology could stress an unbroken imperial line back to the very genesis of mankind itself in the Japanese isles. In effect, from the period of written records, emphasis was placed on what became a Japanese ethnic identity, one based on an established formal mythology of unique, indigenous origin—a single, unmixed Yamato people of divine ancestry. The imperial line itself was directly traced to the paramount deity, the Sun Goddess. Henceforth there was denial of any possible commonality of origin with the people of the mainland. Memories of outside contact were turned around, and the legends made it seem that the Yamato people imposed rule on the mainland area of Mimana on the southern tip of Korea. The reported connection with Mimana was actually a chauvinistic contemporary distortion of a more ancient period in which Wa people, a thalassocratic culture, occupied both sides of the straits of Tsushima.

In Japanese legends, Mimana in southern Korea remained to give the Yamato culture some implicit claim to Korean soil. Here it must be noted that the Korean culture did not foster a myth of unitary origin. Knowledge of the rival kingdoms of Koguryŏ, Silla, and Paekche on the peninsula was a continuum within the Korean heritage. Only the Japanese, who achieved their unification long before literacy, created records in their first writings to support an unbroken dynastic lineage. From its inception, Yamato identity implied uniqueness and apartness from the rest of mankind. In this respect, the Japanese resembled the Jews, whose sense of uniqueness was built around the biblical version of Genesis.

THE GIFTS OF THE BUDDHIST KOREAN MAGI: ART, LITERACY, AND RELIGION

Scene Two: The Kannon of the Chūgūji

In the present-day outskirts of the ancient capital of Nara, in the recesses of the Chūgūji nunnery, once the home of Prince Shōtoku's mother, sits a wooden image, a profoundly moving work of Buddhist piety. It belongs to the realm of universal art—an image of utter tranquillity, the raised arm bestowing peace on a sanguine world. It is dark and shining from the fumes of countless incense burned before it in its place of repose.

Prince Shōtoku's mother, on good evidence, was Korean.[8] Shōtoku, a reformer of the political, social, and religious life of the Japanese state, a man revered by all Japanese for his wisdom and human compassion, was taught by a Buddhist monk named Haeja, from the Korean state of Koguryŏ. The image in the Chūgūji, and many such images created in this period to represent the Buddha and his transformations, were carved by Korean artisans. They are acknowledged by Japanese and Koreans alike to have represented a new cultural wave: the "modernization" of Japan in the sixth century A.D. This statue and its famous counterparts (such as the Kudara Kannon, a tall, graceful wooden figure elongated in a style to be seen much later in the paintings of El Greco) were, for the most part, the work of artisans of Paekche or "Kudara," as Paekche was known to the Japanese. They personify today what Japanese and Koreans alike know well; namely, that Buddhism, although formalized in China, was brought to Japan through a Korean connection—the kingdom of Paekche as well as Koguryŏ and Silla.

Friendly intercourse allowed Japan to become the quiet recipient of medicine, art, and literature as well as religious philosophy. In the Asuka era of the fifth century, around the ancient capital of Nara, occurred the solidification of the imperial dynastic line memorialized in Buddhist architecture. Ironically, the preservation of Shintō as a bulwark of relative social status among the nobility perpetuated the myth of the Sun Goddess and her progeny as an unbroken dynasty. The universal image in the Chūgūji began to coexist peacefully with the particularist, imageless concept of the Kami, the Shintō concept of deity. The universal and the particular were to live henceforth side by side in Japanese conceptions of themselves.

Borrowings and the Reorganization of an Imperial State

There is no denying that from borrowings of the sixth and seventh centuries the Japanese avowedly restructured their state along Chinese cultural lines. The agents of this transformation were for the most part from the Korean peninsula. Cornelius Kiley reports how, even before the formal introduction of Buddhism and writing, mid-fifth-century land and people under royal administration included entire villages of transplanted Koreans.[9] Kiley discusses how the appearance of special crown lands called *miyake* was related to the use by the earliest of the fifth-century kinds of a staff of Paekche clerks and various other craftsmen of Korean origin. Paekche had itself adopted official Chinese writing in A.D. 374.[10] The formation o the so-called *Be* groups of artisans in Japan were on the lines of a general Korean model, and the *Be* themselves were in many instances groups from Korea.

There were times in the seventh century when refugees from Korean wars found asylum in Japan. They were welcome and well received as they were bearers of what was openly recognized as a superior cultural tradition. Nevertheless, Japanese have never been able to distinguish between what the Koreans themselves offered and what was seen as Chinese. The influence of the T'ang dynasty was overwhelming and shaded any awareness of the fact that the Koreans themselves were earlier participants in a then superior culture. As a matter of fact, the few Chinese who appeared were always given greater deference than their Korean counterparts, since they were thought to be the originators whereas the Koreans were carrying a borrowed culture. From early times, therefore, little thought has been given to what the Koreans themselves have innovated or developed.

Richard Miller, in a study of the reform of social status by a carefully designated ranking system devised by the emperor Temmu in the seventh century, comes to the perceptive conclusion that attention to relative ranking performed a number of useful, even necessary, functions for the state.[11] It provided a means of preserving and enhancing the relative status of a number of the traditionally most prestigious and powerful *Uji*, or clans. At the same time, it allowed for a new unified nobility comprised of a graded coalition of older and newer elements. By the end of the seventh century, it became generally accepted that the mythological genealogy that had been created was to be the prime determinant of contemporary status. Miller further comments:

> No scholar today believes that the apical social and political position occupied by the emperor and other scions of the Sun Line derived in ancient Japan from the exalted position of prestige of their ancestress Amaterasu Ōmikami, and yet this idea of feelings still lurks in the emotional recesses of some people who believe or feel that the remarkable survival and continuity of the imperial institution may be so attributed.[12]

Miller concludes that for those of the Heian period (eight century to the tenth century) the religious mythology of ancestry was very much in vogue, and this mythology performed a most practical social role, supporting the emperor and other Sun Line descendants and their claims to positions of social paramountcy within the state.

It is in this regard that one may safely seek at least one explanation for the survival of Shintō practice and belief during the seventh and eighth centuries, when Shintō may otherwise have been lost in the tidal wave of Buddhism that swept over Japan. Ancestral typology was one thing, and played a certain inextricable role in the society of those times, and Buddhism and its beliefs and practices were quite another thing; how else can one attempt a rational explanation of what appears to have been the religious duality practiced in Japan in those early centuries after the arrival of Buddhism?

Buddhism served the spiritual aesthetic appetites of the time, the traditional mythological and ancestral beliefs served as the pivot of the social structure and as a means of calibrating the graduated distinctions of status within the structure. Shintō survived because it performed the service of preserving and symbolizing the mythological ancestral typologies that were socially essential to the highly stratified aristocratic structure of ancient Japan.[13]

In a nutshell, Miller concludes that the function of Shintō and its Sun Goddess has been to preserve until the present time a sense of uniqueness for Japanese ethnicity. The need for a nobility to maintain itself in power led to religious preservation of hierarchy based on lineage. The art of writing brought in by Korean priests and scribes preserved a fabricated mythology that served to erase dim memories of past conflict and diversity of origin. It is this sense of uniqueness, the development of the myth of unbroken imperial lineage, which today still serves unself-consciously to deprecate and exclude from acceptance as full citizens of Japan any whose lineage is "un-Japanese." In this book we will examine various unresolved problems related to the extension of citizenship and social acceptance to others not of Japanese Yamato origin.

In all, this early period of interchange during the time of the Japanese Heian court and the advent of Buddhism has been well discussed by scholars. Contact was peaceful; Koreans were welcomed as craftsmen, priests, and educated professionals, if not as members of an already established and unified nobility. The Kudara craftsmen were part of a Korean stimulus to the Heian culture that lasted for a four-century period preceding the upsurge of a military class, the samurai—a class that became increasingly impatient with the Japanese imperial court and its lack of attention to firm government either in or away from the capital.

The eventual coming to direct power of the military clans in the thirteenth century in Japan had a negative portent for the future of Japanese-Korean relations. From the advent of the so-called Bakufu or military "tent government," the thoughts of the newer, rough-hewn Japanese rulers were no longer about peaceful borrowing. Preoccupations turned gradually to dreams of external military conquest. Portents of Japanese future aggression appeared in the sporadic incursions of Japanese pirates who raided the Asian coast for booty.

HIDEYOSHI'S APOCALYPSE: SAMURAI HORSEMEN RIDE THROUGH KOREA

Scene Three: The Mimizuka of Hōkōji

Near the front gate of the Hōkōji temple on the Yamato Kōji, a street in the Higashiyama ward of Kyoto City, is to be found a memorial stone on a slight rise of ground called the Mimizuka (ear mound). Almost forgotten, it underscores the disparity in what the Japanese leader Hideyoshi means to the Koreans in contrast to the Japanese. It is said that during the attempted conquest of Korea by Japanese troops under Toyotomi Hideyoshi between 1592 and 1598, the ears of killed Korean soldiers and officers were sent back to Japan.[14]

The reason for this shipment of ears from Korea is not clear. Probably they were shipped back as concrete evidence of the success of the Japanese campaigns fought on the Korean peninsula. It had long been the tradition in Japan that when a warrior of high status was killed in battle, the enemy warrior who beheaded him would be rewarded upon receipt of the head in military headquarters as evidence of victory and guarantee of the enemy's death. In a large-scale war, numerous trophy heads were delivered from both sides. The sending of ears from Korea was probably derivative of this tradition. Another version claims that noses, not ears, were brought back from Korea. In 1598, when the Japanese invasion of Korea ended with Hideyoshi's death, this accumulation of ears was buried in a mound at the Hōkōji temple to bring peace to the soldiers' souls. This was done in the tradition of consigning the head of a noble enemy to a grave.

The Hōkōji temple where the ears were buried belongs to the Tendai sect of Buddhism. The temple itself was established in 1586 by Hideyoshi, the second ruler of a unified Japan, who had a huge statue of Buddha (18 meters high) built for the temple. When Hideyoshi died unexpectedly in 1598, Tokugawa Iyeyasu, in consultation with other highest-ranking lords serving under Hideyoshi, ordered the return of all Japanese troops from the Korean peninsula. Although Iyeyasu had sworn loyalty to the Toyotomi family while Hideyoshi was alive, he defeated the Toyotomi two years later in 1600 and had himself designated Shōgun in 1603. In the next year, to wield power more indirectly behind the scenes, he resigned from the Shōgunate, and Hidetada became the second Shōgun. The Toyotomi and their followers, still strong in Osaka, wished to reestablish their power against the Tokugawa. The Tokugawa, however, availed themselves of an opportunity to remove this threat, and the Hōkōji temple was cleverly used by Iyeyasu to bring about the destruction of the Toyotomi family.

Iyeyasu found his chance when Hideyoshi's son, Hideyori, had a huge bell built for the Hōkōji in 1614. Four Chinese characters were carved on the bell, proclaiming "peace and tranquility for the family state." Two of the four characters also stood for *Iye-Yasu* (family tranquility). Iyeyasu claimed that the bell's purpose was to put a curse on him. Iyeyasu himself probably did not so believe, but he used this reason to foment conflicts leading to a series of battles that by the summer of 1615 finished off the Toyotomi clan and its followers.

The significance of the bell and the mound slipped from the consciousness of the Japanese. In Japan, Hideyoshi became a legendary symbol of social mobility. He was a poor samurai who had reached the pinnacle of power. In Korea, Hideyoshi also became a legendary symbol but of Japanese brutality and of a land laid waste. The Korean sense of identity gained strength from tales of heroic resistance to Hideyoshi's armies, a resistance that surfaced again in a general strike in 1919 after Japan had finally annexed Korea in 1910.

The Plundering of Korea

The dominance of the military over the imperial court in the thirteenth century, and the establishment of the so-called Bakufu tent government in Japan, marked the turning point in Korean-Japanese relations. Before this time borrowings had been peaceful and voluntary, but the military mind dreams of conquest and glory. Thoughts of territorial aggrandizement and the possible subjugation of nearby Korea became a fascinating possibility to the Japanese military. Earlier forays had been only preliminary to the campaigns of Toyotomi Hideyoshi. In the fifteenth and sixteenth centuries political anarchy had occupied the Japanese military in internecine warfare. Only after the unification of Japan under Oda Nobunaga and his successor, Hideyoshi, could their thoughts finally turn to external aggrandizement. Hideyoshi's ambitions did not stop with the reunification of the Japanese isles under his centralized power. The nearby Korean peninsula was a temptation to test his military prowess and bring further glory to the Japanese realm. For a period of seven years he battered and subdued. He ravaged the Korean peninsula until it was little more than a scarred, smoldering ruin. With pillage, rapine, and plunder, nothing was left untouched. Even the graves of the Yi dynasty monarchs were opened and their contents removed.

The Korean memory of Japanese brutality has marked all subsequent relationships between the two peoples. The Koreans prided themselves on their resistance, recording how their navy developed ironclad ships. Every Korean child was taught the history of the resistance, a lesson painfully reinforced when Japan occupied Korea in the early twentieth century.

The plunder of Korea by Hideyoshi included conscription of forced labor to Japan. Highly skilled Korean workmen of the time, specialized artisans, were taken prisoner by Hideyoshi's forces. Their techniques of weaving and porcelain manufacture were transplanted to Japanese soil, as was their art of printing with movable type.[15]

Many Korean scholars were also transported to Japan as prisoners of war. We find, for example, that a significant branch of neo-Confucianism following the Sung school was carried to Japan when Kang Hang, a foremost Confucian scholar who studied Yi T'oegye's theory and teaching, was brought in among the other prisoners.[16] It was not the first time a warlike people had taken not only material objects but learned men from among the conquered; the Romans had learned much advanced thought from the Greeks they had captured and enslaved.

The extreme devastation of Korean cities and villages materially impoverished Korea, but ironically the Koreans saw this period of invasion as one in which the Japanese were learning by means of military aggression.[17] The first publication in Japan based on the borrowed idea of movable type appeared in 1614. Koreans had been using this at least since 1403. The Japanese commanders found Korean pottery far superior to that produced by their own artisans. Groups of Korean potters were forcibly removed and set up in special villages near the castle towns of various feudal lords or daimyō.[18] The kilns of Satsuma, Nabeshima, Yatsushiro, and Imari date from this time. These villages in their origin were well protected by the daimyō and the people were well treated. For security purposes ("industrial spies" and the stealing of secret techniques were manifest even in seventeenth-century Japan) the pottery people were kept separate from others. In time, these settlements developed some of the characteristics of other special villages (Tokushu Buraku) already existent in Japan in the form of outcaste settlements. For this reason we still note today some ambiguity about why certain villages in Japan are segregated from their neighbors. In the minds of neighboring communities, a correspondence exists between the outcaste status of the former Eta, based on ritual purity and impurity, and the villages of alien Korean origin.

The inhabitants of special villages have experienced discrimination until present times. It is not an accident, for example, that the filmmaker who exposed the Minamata tragedy of industrial pollution to foreign audiences was himself a Japanese of distant Korean ancestry. As an "outsider" he felt somewhat freer to be critical of Japanese industrial pollution. A tradition of being "different" was imposed upon his pottery village, which was never accorded full social acceptance by neighboring communities.

The writings of the Confucian philosopher Yi T'oegye are known in Japan through the teachings of Kang Hang, a Korean who brought these teachings to Japan as a prisoner of war. They reveal a rather detached, perceptive view of late sixteenth-century Japan. As a prisoner of war, Kang Hang was treated well. He became a teacher of Chinese with a large following of students who supported him so that he could live fairly comfortably. When the wars were finally over, his students bought a boat for him and sent him back to Korea at their own expense.[19] Kang Hang's observations about Japan include comments not only on the social life of the times but on Japanese mythology, history, and geography. He describes the construction used in Japanese towns and castles, and Japanese social organization, including the relationship between feudal lords and farmers. He describes objectively the suffering experienced in Japan as a result of internecine warfare. He makes the interesting observation that, according to his estimate, four out of every ten males had become Buddhist monks for one primary reason: they did not want to be involved in a wartime draft.

Kang Hang wrote to his Japanese colleague Fujiwara, originally a Buddhist monk who converted to Confucianism. In his letters he complained of the sense of military oppression suffered by the Japanese under Hideyoshi. He wrote in his journal as follows:

> It is said to me that never before were the Japanese people more miserable than they are today. If the Koreans with Ming soldiers were to console people and punish war criminals, and if you were to march on the Japanese islands announcing through captured Japanese interpreters that you were waging war in order to free the suffering Japanese, then even Shirakawa Seki, the eastern edge of the island, would not be too far to take. However, if your soldiers were to repeat the Japanese method of killing and looting, you would not even be able to cross the sea to Tsushima.[20]

Kang Hang and many others who were prisoners of war were finally freed by the daimyō, under whose jurisdiction they were kept, in response to the appeal of a Buddhist monk, who said, "There is no difference between them and us in how a man longs for parents and home." It was through this Neo-Confucian scholar, a Korean, that the Japanese received a great deal of Confucian thought, which was ultimately to serve as the basis for Meiji universal education. According to one Japanese scholar,[21] the famous Meiji Imperial Rescript on Education, proclaimed in 1868, is essentially the educational philosophy expounded by Yi T'oegye. Japanese scholarship had, in this fashion, benefited from the "acquisitions" of Hideyoshi.

It is reported also that close to 2,600 volumes were looted from various Korean libraries to become part of the large library of Tokugawa Iyeyasu and were distributed to various daimyō after his death. Hideyoshi's special task force brought back not only pottery craftsmen and other artisans but also priests and women, cows and horses.[22] In consequence of all this, the Korean school child of today, reading of Hideyoshi, is more likely to be made aware of Hideyoshi as a plunderer of Korea than as a unifier of Japan.

THE JAPANESE IMPERIUM AND ITS UNRULY COLONY

Scene Four: National Protest, A Korean Declaration of Independence

The March First movement marks a dramatic scene in the memory of all Koreans who had come to resent the Japanese attempt to obliterate their cultural heritage, to eradicate their language, to change their names, to make them look upon their own past with disdain, to make them embrace the Japanese emperor as their own. On 1 March 1919, thirty-three religious leaders, including sixteen Christians, fifteen Ch'ŏndogyo (members of a Korean nativist religious sect), and two Buddhist monks, gathered to sign a document, a Declaration of Independence, to be publicly read in Pagoda Park, near the center of Seoul. In addition to this public reading in front of thousands of peaceful demonstrators, other demonstrations took place on this date throughout Korea.

After 1910, during their initial suppressive period of colonization, the Japanese conceded one liberality to world opinion. They did not attempt to suppress religious organizations. These organizations have become the focus of Korean nationalism and have served to keep alive for many Koreans the hope of their eventual liberation. Today, however, the Korean sense of ethnic identity is perhaps more closely associated in the public mind with controversy over the political ideology of Marxism, a belief system that was to capture the imagination of many Korean youth. But it is still a moot point whether the religious traditions of Christianity or the political ideologies of Marx will have the most enduring long-term effects. Today in South Korea, one notes that some religious leaders again have mounted protests and are enduring prison out of a firm belief in the ideals of a democratic society. Although Marxism teaches profound truths about the history of social and economic exploitation as a strong determinant in human society everywhere, sometimes to the detriment of other forces, religious belief, in whatever form it takes, seeks to elicit from man some sense of the dominance of love over hate, of the transcendence of brotherhood over the hostilities of the past and the imperfections of the present.

In 1919, after nine years of colonial rule, the Koreans came to a consensus that they were being exploited, oppressed, and degraded rather than appreciated in their wish for modernization. Nationalist feelings in Korea were aroused as part of a global surge toward ethnic independence following World War I. Self-determination became a worldwide expectation with the breakup of large empires. In Korea, the dramatic event of 1 March 1919 brought into focus intense desire for independence which had been totally unrecognized by Japanese administrators in Korea.

The Japanese governor-general of Korea had been extremely suppressive. Shortly after the funeral of the old, deposed Korean King Kojong, in

February 1919, representatives of a number of religious sects gathered, Christian and Buddhist as well as members of the Ch'ōndogyo, a religious sect derived from the so-called Tonghak antiforeign movement. Christianity, in effect, had become a symbol of opposition to the Japanese as well as a symbol of modernity for many Koreans. The religious leaders planned a general strike throughout Korea, centering in Seoul. Everything was prepared in utmost secrecy, and the Japanese officials were totally unaware of what was to happen. On March first the declaration was read in the center of Seoul. The signees then surrendered themselves peacefully for arrest, and thousands of unarmed students and citizens demonstrated in many urban centers throughout the country. Caught totally by surprise, the Japanese did nothing on the day itself. But a vast number of arrests followed with those arrested subjected to torture. Some villages were set to the torch. The movement toward independence was completely crushed, on the surface.

This was one of the first demonstrations in which Korean students became involved in political assertion, with both men and women students taking part on an equal basis. Christianity was being taught in the schools, and Christian churches and schools were centers of organization. The fact that the leaders knew they would be arrested and were resigned to giving themselves up peacefully and with dignity had a profound emotional impact on the whole Korean nation. This event became a memory burned deep into the Korean consciousness. It became part of being Korean to know about and to retell the event.

Religion was also an institution that granted Koreans the integrity of spirit to exercise leadership. As we have indicated, religious leaders could take a leading role in Korean independence and Korean nationalist movements because they had been left alone by the Japanese, who did not wish to incur international criticism for attacking religion directly. The Christian churches, the remaining Buddhist sects, and the Ch'ōndogyo could formulate points of protest and organization. Religious instruction and education fostered a sense of Korean patriotism. Only in the late 1920s, when the Communist movement had gained strong student support, would religious organizations be superseded by more direct political groupings organized around ideology rather than religious belief.

Japan, A Model for Modernization

The brutal lessons of Hideyoshi were to last through the two-and-a-half centuries of the Tokugawa period. The dramatic modernization following the Meiji restoration of 1868, however, gave hope to the Koreans that they might also modernize. By the close of the nineteenth century, some Korean intellectuals turned to Japan only to be brutally betrayed again not only by direct colonization but by deprecation and disdain.

After 1600, once Korea was freed from further Japanese incursions, contact with Japan was broken off. But Japan continued to seek contact with China and could not ignore Korea. In effect, Japan sought Korean assistance. Korea had traditionally turned to China as a protector and had established positive relations with its imposing neighbor. Ironically, Japan at times attempted the role of supplicant to gain Korean support for communication with China.

Korea, already impoverished, became further rigidified, suffering the same stagnation that characterized China throughout the nineteenth century. Korea became a society of rural folk governed by a small elite. Under the aegis of the Yi dynasty, it was poorly governed. Henderson[23] reports that by the end of the nineteenth century a limitless corruption filled the vacuum around the throne. Foreign interests and advisors came in. The most successful of these were the Japanese, who had modernized following the Meiji restoration of 1868 and who informally dominated Korea after 1890.

Restiveness among the untutored Korean masses took the form of a religious movement. By 1894 the Tonghak movement numbered, according to some, over 400,000 members. As a form of religious revitalization, it sought to give some direction to a rudderless, corrupt society. As a mode of reform, it sought to return to a religious past and to eradicate foreign influences. When petitions and delegations produced no results, the movement finally sought release through violence. By 1894 there was a full-scale rebellion in southwestern Korea and an almost simultaneous intervention by Chinese and Japanese troops. The Sino-Japanese war removed almost completely the political and social influence of China, replacing it almost totally by Japanese economic and political power.

The remnants of the Korean revivalist movement became pro-Japanese during 1901 to 1905 and actually supported further Japanese intervention in Korea. Indeed, the sense of hopelessness and drift had become so great that numbers of educated intellectuals, failing in their own movement for modernization and independence, turned to Japan as an obviously successful model of a modern state. Henderson documents the appearance of the Ilchin-Hoe, an antinationalist mass movement that sought large-scale support within Korea for annexation by Japan. Korea, in its sense of helplessness, turned to a progressive Japan, pursuing the innovations of the Meiji restoration.[24] China was hopelessly reactionary; Tsarist Russia autocratic and backward; the United States disinterested; other European states uninvolved. This state of affairs left fuller ties with Japan as the only hope for effective social change.

The Japanese, in the Russo-Japanese war of 1905, demonstrated militarily how modernization could help it surpass a European power. The Ilchin-Hoe was organized by commoners as a national movement. It sought economic development and the development of industry. It sent students to

Japan for education, not on the basis of past privilege but "without regard to class." It brought in Japanese administrators and teachers to set up schools. Ilchin-Hoe, however, showed portents that were not in line with a democratic movement. It arrested people, punished them, used informants, extorted money, forged letters, and employed blackmail.[25] The extremism of its methods caused it to lose popular support, and the Japanese disbanded it after annexation in 1910, although Ilchin-Hoe had advocated annexation.

Japanese Policies of Absolute Bureaucracy and Assimilation

In 1910 after annexation, the aptly named Bureau of Colonization, under the control of a governor-general, assumed absolute authority in Korea. This rule was a result of the triumph of the Yamagata faction in the Japanese parliament over Prince Itō, who was more moderate and sympathetic to Korea. This new policy advocated complete integration of Korea and Japan. It naively assumed that the colonial policy of assimilation could be brought about forcibly and could extinguish the Korean language and Korean ethnic identity. Instead, the assimilationist policy produced a profound sense of humiliation and outrage in all Koreans. Koreans could not be assimilated against their will, but they could be deprecated.

As we shall recount in the following chapter, an enormous number of Japanese immigrated into Korea. By 1940 there were over 700,000 Japanese in Korea, numbering over 3 percent of the population. Of Koreans listed as gainfully employed, 95 percent of the men and 99 percent of the women were listed as ordinary laborers. In effect, rather than modernizing Korea for the Koreans, the Japanese, in colonizing Korea, created for themselves a vast Korean lower class, or more exactly, a lower caste.

Japanese who were too friendly with Koreans were ostracized by their own group and became objects of suspicion. Within the first decade of Japanese occupation, even those most enthusiastic about the borrowing of Japanese techniques of modernization realized that the Korean cause was hopeless. Korea was experiencing castelike colonization as stringent as that exercised by the British in India or in Ireland. To understand why, after the annexation, Koreans emigrated to Japan, one must see how hopeless were the conditions experienced in their own homeland.

HOLOCAUST: 1923

Scene Five: The Aftermath of the Kanto Earthquake[26]

In the early morning of 1 September 1923, a heavy but short rain hit Tokyo. Lions in the Ueno Zoo roared and moved restlessly in their cages. People were still asleep. The downpour finally stopped around 10:00 A.M.,

and by 11:00 A.M. a bright sun appeared in the sky. It was a hot, sticky day.
As the sun climbed higher in the sky, housewives were busy cooking rice
and preparing lunch.

At 11:58 A.M. the earth suddenly trembled. The Japanese wooden
houses swayed back and forth; many crashed to the ground. The first great
quake lasted about seven or eight minutes. A fireman watching the city
from the top of the National Police Headquarters reported that after ten
minutes the ground was still swaying and shaking with aftershocks. He reported seventy fires in the downtown area. By 12:20 P.M., three hundred
buildings were burning. The fire spread so rapidly that he could no longer
count. The whole city of Tokyo was covered with fire. Although the sun
was visible in the sky, it was blurred by gray smoke and ashes. The quakes
and fires lasted for three days and nights (1 to 3 September). People were
dying, crawling about for water. Ueno Park was packed with 500,000 refugees; seventy babies were reportedly born in the park.[27] Eighty percent of
the city was completely destroyed. Transportation and communication
were totally halted. In the major rivers of Tokyo, blackened and swollen
bodies floated. In Kōto-ku, Honjō, and other densely populated areas, the
damage was especially severe. In a plaza of Honjō it was reported that
34,000 refugees had no place to escape when a gusty wind stirred up the fire
and caused it to resemble an oil-tank explosion. All 34,000 died. (This was
near Tsukushima, where many Koreans were later killed.) In Yokosuka
city, oil-storage houses filled with two years' supply exploded. The city was
completely burned down. In nearby Yokohama, 30,000 were killed in the
quakes and subsequent fires.

By the night of 2 September several unfounded rumors spread.[28]
Right-wing fanatics were later proved to be involved in starting rumors that
Koreans were setting fires, throwing poison into wells, rioting against the
Imperial Army, killing Japanese, and raping women. Police headquarters,
the Imperial Theater, the ministry of buildings, the *Asahi* newspaper building, and the Mitsukoshi and Shirokiya department stores were all reported
as burned down because Koreans had thrown bombs. Newspaper reports
carried myriad rumors. For example, on 6 September it was reported that a
Korean riot had been prepared since 2 September when a big rally was
planned for the independence of Korea. The earthquake had been seized
upon as a good opportunity for rape, plunder, and pillage. This report was
a total fabrication, since no large rally had been planned by any Korean
group.

On 2 September a frightened government, believing these rumors,
ordered martial law in the Kanto area. The government issued marching
orders to the Imperial Guard, other regiments, and the police to control the
supposed riot. A total of 70,000 soldiers marched into the city. On 2 September *Tokyo Nichinichi Shimbun* (the Tokyo daily newspaper) carried
headlines that the government had ordered the killing of Koreans. The

article reported that the royal family was safe and that the Yamamoto emergency cabinet had been established that day at 5:00 P.M. The paper stated, "Koreans and Socialists were planning a rebellious and treacherous plot. We urge the citizens to cooperate with the military and the police to guard against Koreans."

Army General Fukuda Masatarō, Kantō district commander, divided the Kantō area into five regions and allocated military forces to each. Two scout planes flew over Bōshu (Chiba prefecture) and the Izu peninsula in Shizuoka prefecture to check the rumor that 20,000 Koreans would land there from the mainland. The Japanese navy sent warships to the Korean Strait. The chief army officer, Abe Nobuyuki, reported that twenty-one infantry, six cavalry, seven artillery, and eighteen corps were guarding the Kantō area against possible attack. The total forces involved were equivalent to five or six divisions. Checkpoints manned by 100,000 soldiers were established in the city to investigate citizens. Any Koreans found were to be immediately killed. The citizens formed a "Jikeidan" (vigilante group) to fight against the Korean "rioters." By 16 September there were about 1,500 Jikeidan in Tokyo, 603 in Kanagawa prefecture, 300 in Saitama, 300 in Chiba, and 450 in Gunma (a total of close to 3,000 in the Kanto area).[29]

During the week after the earthquake, the Japanese in Tokyo went berserk hunting Koreans. They used bamboo spears to stab, clubs to beat, and bare hands to choke Koreans to death. Language was the criteria—any "Korean accent" marked a person for extermination. On the evening of the earthquake (1 September), one hundred Korean manual laborers on their way home had been killed around Shibuya station. On 3 September Ueno police captured seventy Koreans. They chopped off their arms and threw the bodies into a fire. In Kanda, Tokyo, several Korean female students were raped and killed. The Japanese stripped them, tore their legs apart, cut their sexual organs, and stabbed them to death. On 7 September Japanese soldiers arrested 368 Korean students and machine-gunned them on the bank of the Sumida River in Tokyo. During this week, 2,000 or more Koreans in Haneda, 400 in Samida and Honjō, 200 in Kameido, 150 in Ueno, and 1,000 or more in Saitama, Gunma, and Ibaragi were tortured and killed. Several witnesses to the Korean massacre have given the following testimony:[30]

By a Korean who Escaped to Peking:

Jikeidan (vigilantes) were looking for Koreans day and night. When they captured one, they shouted, "Korean!" Many Japanese rushed to the scene, surrounding the victim. They tied him on a telephone pole, scooped out his eyes, cut off his nose, chopped open his stomach, and pulled out his internal organs. Sometimes they tied a Korean's neck to a car and dragged him around until he choked to death. They also captured women, grabbed their legs, pulled them in opposite directions, and tore their bodies. The Koreans resisted till the last moment, begging and insisting on their innocence. But the crowd never listened. The Korean women and children were screaming and crying for mercy in vain. The massacre continued for six days and nights.

By a Japanese Soldier:

The number of military forces involved was not clear. As far as I remember, I can count the Azabu First and Third Regiment, one cavalry, and the Special Police Force. Martial law was ordered not only for all the regiments in Tokyo but also for those in the suburbs. We rushed into the city with open swords and guns, shouting out, "The enemy is in the imperial capital!" The Narashino cavalry, to which I belonged, received their orders just before noon on September 2. We each carried two days' food, extra horseshoes, and sixty ball cartridges. The officers who were commanding us led the charge with Japanese swords. We rushed out of the military camp like a gust of wind, charging toward the capital at full speed. We arrived at Kameido around 2:00 P.M. The place was flooded with refugees. Our first military action was to "attack" trains. The officers checked every car thoroughly. All the Koreans hidden in the crowd were pulled out. As soon as they were pushed out of the car, they fell under Japanese swords and open fire. Loud roars of "Banzai!" were the cheers from the Japanese refugees. They shouted "Traitors! Bandits! Kill them! Kill all the Koreans!" Our cavalry was excited with this bloody ceremony and started the main Korean hunting that evening.

One evening we received marching orders to control a riot of Koreans near Tama River. We ran through moonlit streets to the river bank. We waited and waited, but the enemy never appeared. After a while, we heard water splashing in a thick fog. We saw the dark shapes of men crossing the river. The horsemen opened fire at them. Strangely, there was no resistance from the enemy. They simply fell down into the water, screaming. Some of the enemies who managed to cross the river surrendered unconditionally, lying flat on the ground and begging for our mercy.

By a Member of the Jikeidan:

We saw the explosion of Tsukishima and were convinced that it was done by Koreans. [Tsukishima is an island in Tokyo Bay.] We captured a Korean who was carrying something that looked like a bomb. After a strict investigation, he confessed that the Koreans were planning a riot. We knew that it was he who had thrown bombs in Tsukishima. We immediately chopped his head off. We also captured twenty-four rebellious Koreans. We tied thirteen Koreans and ten Koreans together with wires and struck them to death. We threw them into the sea, but some of them were still alive. We stabbed their heads many times. As we thrust the knives deep, it was hard to pull them out. Meanwhile, three Koreans tried to escape. We grabbed them, tied them together, and threw them into a burning mountain of coal in a charcoal yard.

By a Member of the Jikeidan:

While I was stationed at the headquarters, I was told to go and see the bodies of Koreans in 6-chome Ōhshima-chō. After I finished my night guard duty, I went off to see the bodies. It was a vacant lot (400-500 tsubo) surrounded by walls. There were 250 bodies lying from east to west, most of which were naked. I checked each one of them. There were many whose throats were cut and their veins exposed. One neck was cut from behind. The white flesh was chopped and opened like a pomegranate. There was one body with a neck completely taken off. I guessed that they had pulled the neck with all their force. The flesh, skin, and nerves were intertwined. Many of their eyes were still open. I did not see any sign of agony in their round, dumb-looking faces. Their pubic hair was so thin. Someone said, "They aren't Koreans but Chinese." I felt sorry to see a body of a young woman. This was the only female body there. Her belly was cut open with a six or seven-month-old fetus rolled inside. When I saw a bamboo spear stabbed into her sexual organ, I felt terrified and jumped aside. I did not understand why Japanese had to do this much. I felt so ashamed to be Japanese.

The Political Background of the Korean Massacre

The March First Movement in Korea in 1919 had startled the Japanese. The Russian Revolution had recently brought into being the first Communist nation in history, and although in Japan a democratic ideology had become predominant among liberals and intellectuals, the ideology of communism was starting to attract a number of Japanese youth. Mizuno Rentarō, minister of internal affairs, had become concerned about a possible uprising of leftists. The military thought it important to suppress such left-wing movements that called attention to a widening gap between the rich and the poor. The number of wage workers was increasing yearly. In 1922 (a year before the earthquake) the Japanese Communist party, the Japan Farmers' Union and Zenkoku Suiheisha (the "levelers'" group of Burakumin, or outcastes) were established to bring about social and political change. The labor union movement began to attract larger numbers of workers. Between 1914 and 1916 there were only 232 labor unions with 24,169 workers participating. In 1917 the number increased to 389 unions with 57,309 participants. By 1922 there were 387 unions and the number of members was 137,381. In 1921 Rōdō Sōdōmei (the Federation of Labor) was established to fight in the political arena on behalf of its workers.

The government became increasingly concerned about the rise of the labor movement and the possible appeal of communism in Japan. In June 1923, Mizuno Rentarō ordered the police to arrest a number of communist leaders. The government was waiting for some opportunity to attack left-wing groups on a massive scale. Because Korean intellectuals were prominent in the communist movements, at the time of the earthquake Koreans could be used readily as scapegoats to create "imaginary" enemies and to make credible the rumors of riot. The rumor was spread that the Koreans collaborated with the Japanese Communists and Socialists to incite a riot in order to take over the Imperial government.[31]

On 2 September the Yamamoto cabinet was established. Mizuno

passed his position to Gotō Shinpei. Mizuno was the ex-secretariat general of political affairs in Korea, and Gotō was the ex-governor general of Taiwan. Thus, both had experience in controlling the major Japanese colonies. Using the control of rioting as an excuse, the police arrested or killed many leftist leaders. Sakae Ōsugi, an anarchist, and his wife, Noe Itō, were killed and thrown into the well of their home. Asanuma Ineijirō (later the leader of the Socialist party) and other socialist or labor movement leaders were arrested and tortured. In Kameido police station, nine socialists were killed together with 300 Koreans. The following accounts were given by the socialists, their friends, and the police regarding the Kameido police incident:

By a Friend of the Socialists who were Killed in the Police Station:

On the morning of September 4, I met a few policemen carrying a cart with wood and oil. I saw Mr. Toda Seiichi, a police officer, among them and asked him, "Where are you going, carrying wood and oil?"
"We are going to burn the bodies of those we killed."
"You killed?"
"Last night we stayed up all night killing. We killed 320. Today a foreigner is coming to check the place, so we have to clean up the bodies before that."
"Were they all Koreans?"
"No, there were seven or eight socialists."

By a Socialist (Mr. Yoshio Hirazawa):

I heard that Kitajima, a socialist, had quarreled with Hachisuka, a police officer.... I heard that he was killed on September 5. I could not believe it. But on September eighth when I went to see Mr. Ichirō Kojima, he told me that many Koreans were killed at the First Elementary School. When he went there, those killed were not Koreans but Japanese. The policeman beside him said that six of the bodies were those of Socialists, and that the police had investigated enough about them before they were killed. It was true that Kitajima was killed. On October 17, I went to the factory where Kitajima had worked and asked for his last month's salary. The wife of the president said that a police officer had told them that the police killed Kitajima on September 4, and that it was not necessary to pay anything to his family.

By a Police Chief:

Regarding the Kameido incident in which nine socialists were killed, the chief of the Kameido police station, Mr. Shigetaka Komori, announced as follows:

Around midnight of September 4, a group of prisoners started banging their feet and singing revolutionary songs. Those were the socialists such as Hirazawa and Kawai. I called the military forces to control them. One military officer and several soldiers arrived and pulled them out of the prison. I heard the noise, "If you wanna kill us, kill us!" but I don't know the details. Later, I saw all the nine stabbed to death. We could not keep the bodies in the police station and we burned the bodies with those of Koreans near Yotsuno-bashi Bridge of Ōshima-chō. The reason that we arrested Mirazawa, Kawai, and the others was that on September 1, they sang revolutionary songs loudly on the roof of Kawai's house, which is the headquarters of the Minami Katsu-shika Labor Union, and that we considered them potentially dangerous.

Statistics on the Korean Massacre

It is impossible to get any exact figures of the Koreans who were killed or injured during this period. The Korean governor-general's office (Japanese-controlled) simply reported that hundreds of Koreans were killed by angry Japanese after the earthquake. They estimated that the number of Koreans killed or burned in the earthquake and fire as well as those killed by Japanese was 832. Of that number, about 20 to 30 percent (160 to 250 people) were reportedly killed by Japanese. The Japanese police, however, reported a total of 367 cases of murder or injury of Koreans by Japanese (murder, 303; attempted murder, 24; bodily injury, 25; and others, 15).

These official figures stand in marked contrast to the report by *Tong-A Ilbo*, an independent newspaper. Their correspondents in Japan personally surveyed the deaths of Koreans in the Kantō area alone. In Nara-shina Korean Camp, where Koreans were supposedly "protected," they confirmed 1,052 dead bodies. Newspaper reporters finished their survey on November 25, by which time they had counted a total of 6,661 murders of Koreans. This figure does not include murders outside the Kantō area.

Whatever the numbers, the fact remains that mass hysteria swept the Japanese in the wake of their disastrous earthquake. As in the pogroms against Jews in Eastern Europe, the massacre of Huguenots by Richelieu in France, or the Salem witch hunts in New England, social tensions sometimes find violent outlet in the scapegoating of vulnerable groups.

Scapegoating knows no racial or cultural uniqueness. The victims, however, are not concerned with the ubiquity of what has happened to them. They only ask how humans can so dehumanize others and how anyone can justify such sadistic outbursts. The Japanese have in times past imposed on themselves such rigidity of discipline and severity of expectations that suppressed rage seeks release. Koreans by the early 1920s had come to represent the socially disavowed to the more rigidly controlled Japanese. Koreans by their freer nature had become a projection of anarchy, of the loosening of self-control.

A wave of paranoid fear can sweep a populace. The Jews could represent, to the Germans, forces of dissolution threatening an economically imperiled society. The Slavs could represent, to the self-repressed and disciplined Germans, an inferior people to the east. They could, since they did not manifest virtues equal to the Germans in self-control and discipline, be "justifiably" exterminated or enslaved to create a living space for "superior" folk.

The Japanese could view their Korean cousins as inferior, a people who resisted proper Japanization, which was being bestowed upon them for their own good. Japanese officialdom was frightened by the 1919 March First movement in Korea. It was a direct threat to their strong sense of order. The fear of communist revolution or anarchist upheaval threatened by the spread of Marxist dogma among intellectuals sought some outlet in action. The result was the murder of hapless Koreans, only few of whom represented any revolutionary ideology.

The Japanese fear of radical revolution was not different from the German fear. During a long period before Nazism many Germans thought that a Communist-Jewish conspiracy would undo the German state. During the same period in the United States lynchings of blacks were still widespread, grim events which Americans seek to eradicate from their memory. For Americans, it is easier to concentrate on what happened to Jews and Poles. For Americans, it is easier to peer into the empty cells of Auschwitz, left standing as a mute reminder that it is best not to forget the horrors of the past. Such structures present a graphic image. The hanging of "strange fruit" from trees is being forgotten, if it ever was known by most majority Americans. So too, let us say quickly, very few Japanese know anything about the Korean massacre of 1923. Needless to say, Koreans remember, for it is part of their ethnic identity.

THE GIFT OF FORGIVENESS

Scene 6: The Christian Church of Cheam-ni Village

In southwestern Korea, still far removed from the expressways that bind modern Korea with trucks and automobiles, one can find isolated small villages nestled against hills with farmlands stretching out into paddy fields, brown, waiting for winter, and the cold biting winds that sweep across the Korean peninsula. One recent November, George De Vos visited such a village. He had asked to visit a unique memorial. Set high beside this tiny cluster of old-fashioned houses, overlooking the surrounding fields, is a Christian church built in a peculiar fashion out of rough concrete. Its tower is tall and standing free, like the number "one," and its body is shaped like the number "three." The church was shaped like these numbers to memorialize the first day of the third month, March 1919. A tragic event happened here a few days after the March First movement declaring Korean independence from Japan. This tiny village paid dearly for the collective affirmation of Korean nationality.

De Vos visited this village with a colleague anthropologist and a guide, leaving the easier highways despite the reluctance of the chauffeur to subject the car to the difficulties of dust and gravel. De Vos had heard about the village and the dreadful event. He had also heard that this tiny church might prove to be a symbol of hope.

The group found the church easily. It stood out rather sternly in the late, slanting, afternoon sun. The wife of the minister and her children were at home. When she heard of De Vos's interest she sent for an old woman, over eighty, the last remaining inhabitant who could tell firsthand what had happened to her husband and others.

A nearby Japanese garrison had come to the village. Some of the soldiers had roughed up several male inhabitants believed to have joined in the general active protest. The protestors had been part of the Christian community of this village. Two days after this unpleasant episode, some troops returned. They told all the villagers present to assemble in the church. The villagers did so, thinking they were to hear some word of apology for the brutal behavior of the Japanese soldiers. Once they were all inside, the troops barred the doors, nailed them shut, and poured gasoline about the wooden structure, setting it afire. Everyone inside was incinerated.

In 1969 some Japanese Christians heard this story and sought to send a token of their brotherhood to Korea. They offered to build a church to mark this inhumane act and to say, symbolically, that they would like to acknowledge and to ask some form of forgiveness for this evil instance of colonial suppression. When first the villagers heard this offer they refused. They could not consider participating in an act that would assuage the guilt of those they had learned so deeply to hate. The offer was repeated again and then again. After three years the villagers consented and the church was built. The walls of rough concrete hold two tiny plaques, crudely lettered, telling not only of the horrible events of a past relationship but also of the need for forgiveness and a future of peace among men.

While he was in Korea, De Vos was told of the difficulties in the postwar negotiations for normalization between the Koreans and the Japanese. The Koreans could not gain any ready admission from the Japanese that the colonial period had been marked by indignity and brutality. The Koreans wanted some recognition and acknowledgment of past wrongs. Some of the remaining chapters of this book will describe the tortuous postwar relationship between an independent Korea and a Japan whose military defeat was quickly countered with economic resurgence.

This postwar period has been marked with animosity and distrust. We can make no firm predictions about the relationship between Korea and Japan. In telling this largely unpleasant history, however, we must strongly affirm that every year increasing numbers of Japanese have come to reconsider their facile prejudices and easy derogation. These Japanese, in looking at the past, have come to greater realization of their failure to help Koreans modernize. They have offered them, instead, the bondage of colonization from a position of disparaging superiority.

Contemporary Korea is fast emerging as an economic power, and Koreans are finding in their competitive enterprise a sense of self-respect and of capability. De Vos was much impressed by the emerging sense of a common human understanding. The Koreans may be giving Japan yet another gift, one to be treasured: the gift of forgiveness for past wrongs. Some Koreans and some Japanese have come to realize the need for future interaction on the basis of present mutual respect.

2

THE COLONIAL EXPERIENCE, 1910-1945

George De Vos and Changsoo Lee

The problems of citizenship for the Korean minority do not simply derive from the fact that Korea as a nation was reestablished in 1945 and that Koreans in Japan were no longer necessarily considered Japanese nationals. The problems of citizenship for Koreans, whether in Japan or in their own homeland, started with the annexation of Korea in 1910. Although all Koreans, by the act of annexation, became Japanese subjects, they did not receive full Japanese citizenship. The Japanese maintained a distinction between the "Japanese nationality" bestowed upon their colonial subjects and the "true" Japanese citizenship based on birth and a family lineage legally registered (see chap. 7). To the Japanese, citizenship remained a question of ethnic origin, something which only in very anomalous circumstances would be given to an individual of foreign ancestry. This concept of citizenship was far removed from that developed by the French in Europe after the French Revolution and by the United States as a multi-ethnic nation of immigrants. Societies can be placed on a spectrum between those at one extreme which have a concept of social and national belonging focused on ancestry, and those newer societies at the other extreme which expect people to give up their ethnicity and ethnic loyalties to acquire the citizenship of a new country. Perhaps in the present era Japan still represents the former extreme position, whereas Canada and the United States represent the latter.

Considerable ambivalence exists in many modern states concerning the historical aftereffects of colonialism. This has now forced them to consider their former colonial people as possible full citizens. For example, the United States and West Germany established legal precedents to grant an option to colonial subjects to retain their former nationality upon the relinquishment of colonial territories. The precedents applied only to those already settled in the parent state at the time of the cessation of territory.[1] The United Kingdom has had considerable difficulty in assimilating Pakistani and Jamaican immigrants from former colonies. The Dutch have had problems with the Mollucans from the former Dutch East Indies and with the Surinamers from the former Dutch colony on the northern coast of South America.

In the instance of Japan, the annexation of Korea has meant not simply political control but also the development of an economic symbiosis, with Japanese in large numbers flowing into the industrial and agricultural sectors of the new colony. Korea also has provided a vast supply of unskilled labor that could work in the Japanese homeland itself. The Japanese literally have colonized Korea in that they have not made Koreans equal citizens of an enlarged nation. They have never overcome their ambivalence and initial reluctance to consider Koreans as equals. Periodically, formal government policy has favored total assimilation and the disappearance of a separate Korean culture, but at the same time government has not supported fully the type of integration that would accord respect and status to those of Korean ancestry. In effect, Koreans have remained colonial subjects, exploited economically and despised socially.

Before the annexation of Korea in 1910, there were reportedly only 790 Koreans residing in Japan. Of this number, most were students, eager to learn from a modernizing society. Japan's dramatic victories at the turn of the century over both the Chinese and the Russians had impressed many young Koreans and had stimulated their desire to learn more from Japan as a model in whose image it would be possible to modernize the feudalistic Korean kingdom. For the most part, they very soon became disillusioned. Many joined radical political movements in reaction to Japanese colonial policies. They became the source of a Japanese fear of Korean subversion of the imperial system which culminated in the atrocities of 1923 (see chap. 1).

THE JAPANESE MIGRATE TO THEIR NEW COLONY

The disintegration of Korean society at the time of the Japanese annexation of Korea in 1910 was reflected in the backward state of its almost totally agrarian economy. The old Korean kingdom was plagued by political corruption and a decadence that thwarted any attempts at industrial development. The country was still totally dependent upon its agricultural production.

Just before actual annexation, Korea had been forced in 1905 to sign a "Protectorate Treaty." In 1908 the Japanese Imperial Diet, without consulting the Korean government, passed legislation to establish the so-called Tōyō Colonial Development Company in Korea, whose announced purpose was to introduce modern farming techniques by having Japanese farmers settle in Korea. The company was formed as a joint stock enterprise by both Koreans and Japanese, with a capital of 10 million yen. The Korean government was compelled to set up half of the capital, and since it had no funds, its share was counted in allocations of land. The company was authorized to issue debentures (certificates of debt) up to ten times its paid-up capital, and reimbursement of the debentures to the extent of 20 million yen, together with interest, was guaranteed by the Japanese government.

The Tōyō Colonial Development Company, or Tōshoku, was to handle all business related to farm management, selling, purchasing, renting, and leasing of the land necessary for colonization, and to oversee the recruiting and resettling of Japanese and Koreans, providing them with loans if necessary. Therefore, by the time the Japanese created their administrative machinery for direct political control by annexation, economic colonization was well underway through the Tōshoku. A land survey was undertaken to determine land value and ownership and to classify all arable land. All public lands, including private holdings, the titles of which were obscure, were transferred to the Japanese colonial administration. These lands were turned over to the Tōshoku for control and management. As a result, by the end of 1910, the Tōshoku had acquired more than 31,800 acres of land. Acquisitions increased to 220,500 acres by the following year, creating a land boom in Korea.[2] Through the Tōshoku the Japanese government actively encouraged many Japanese farmers to settle in Korea, and those who responded were heavily subsidized by the company, not only for the land purchases but for travel expenses. Many speculators poured into Korea with "binoculars in one hand and a pistol hanging on the hip."[3]

An enormous number of Japanese emigrated into Korea. By 1940 there were over 700,000 Japanese in Korea, numbering over 3 percent of the population. Forty-one percent of the Japanese were in government service, as compared with 2.9 percent of Koreans. Another 23.4 percent of Japanese were in commerce and 16.6 percent were in industry, compared with 6.5 percent of Koreans in commerce and 2.6 percent in industry.[4] In effect, rather than modernizing Korea for the Koreans, the Japanese, in colonizing Korea, created for themselves a vast lower class. It would be more precise to say a "caste."

It was reported that in 1924 there were a total of 360 mixed marriages, demonstrating that in this castelike atmosphere no integration was taking place, either in sexual or occupational relationships.[5] It was also apparent that a two-way immigration process was occurring: a professional, bureaucratic, and agricultural elite was moving into Korea, and a displaced working caste was moving into the Japanese isles.

Table 1 shows the steady increase of the Japanese population in Korea. When the company relocated one Japanese settler from Japan, about three farm households of Korean peasants had to be moved from where they were living to make room. Many instances were reported in southern Korea in which a whole Korean village was replaced by new Japanese settlers.[6] Andrew J. Grajdanzev's study, however, indicates that population increase was not so much caused by Japanese farmers as by participants in Japanese companies, landlords, and a variety of speculators. Korean ownership of farmland generally passed into Japanese control.[7] Many Korean farmers

TABLE 1

Japanese Population in Korea

Year	Number (in 1,000)	Percentage of increase as compared with preceding period	Japanese population as percentage of total population of Korea
1910	171.5	—	1.3
1915	303.7	77	1.9
1920	347.9	15	2.0
1925	424.7	22	2.2
1930	501.9	18	2.5
1935	583.4	16	2.7
1939	650.1	11	2.9

Source: *Chōsen keizai nenpyō* [Economic Annual for Chōsen] (Tokyo: Kaizōsha Publishing Co., 1939), and Andrew J. Grajdanzev, *Modern Korea* (New York: John Day Co., 1944), p. 76.

were squeezed from the most arable land to less and less desirable land, and were finally forced off the land entirely.

The process was accelerated by the excessive rents and the short duration of lease contracts. All the other conditions and customs of tenancy were so unfavorable to the tenant that his living conditions became truly miserable. When the tenants harvested their crops in the fall, they had first to pay the rent and other debts that had been incurred to meet the bare necessities of life during the growing seasons. Most of them had nothing left. Those who did not become tenant farmers for Japanese landlords were forced to submit as wage earners to the humiliating labor conditions imposed on them by Japanese employers. The problems of surplus farm laborers became worse as they moved to the urban areas. The colonial Korean economy had no program to absorb the unemployed rural migrant. Moreover, modernized Japanese medical practices helped create a surplus population. Koreans became willing to submit themselves to anything just to survive.

KOREANS MIGRATE TO JAPAN

Meanwhile, on the eve of World War I, Japan itself was experiencing an unprecedented economic boom and a rapid industrial expansion that eventually created a labor shortage. Naturally the Japanese industrialists began to cast their eyes on the abundant supply of cheap labor in Korea. In

1911 a textile mill in Osaka pioneered the idea of importing Korean laborers to Japan, and other industries soon followed suit.

It became customary for many industries to dispatch recruiters to Korea, especially to the most depressed agrarian regions, to lure Korean workers to Japan. The recruited workers were brought mostly to industries located in the Osaka and Kobe areas. Initially, all Korean laborers were employed as simple manual laborers performing jobs that needed no special skills, as they were handicapped by language and illiteracy. Japanese employers were content with their Korean laborers, since they seemed willing to work for longer hours and to endure more adverse working conditions than the Japanese workers.

During the initial period of recruitment, Korean farmers were reluctant to respond to Japanese recruiters because of their fear of traveling to a strange other world. Traditionally, Korean farmers maintained a close attachment to their birthplaces and felt a Confucian sense of obligation to safeguard the ancestral graves near which they had lived for centuries. But stories spread throughout Korea about how one could find enough work to support one's family if one were willing to go to Japan.

The first decade after annexation (1910-1920) saw relatively little emigration on the part of Koreans to Japan. A good proportion of those going to Japan continued to be students seeking education and the development of special skills unavailable in Korea. But after World War I there was a truly remarkable expansion of Japanese industry. The impoverishment of the agricultural population of southern Korea grew even more severe. More and more Koreans began to flow into Japan, where they competed with the unskilled stratum of Japanese labor. Just as this flow began to diminish in the latter part of the 1920s, Japan embarked upon its military adventure in China. Again there was a demand for Korean labor to replace the mobilized workers and farmers who were being shipped in increasing numbers to fight on the Asian continent.

Conversely, many Japanese continued to migrate to Korea where they could occupy administrative posts as business entrepreneurs, or even as exploitive landlords supposedly helping to modernize Korean agriculture. An increasingly larger segment of the Korean farmers were reduced close to subsistence level. In the better lands of the south, with its richer soil and fuller sun, conditions became worse for the Koreans. The Japanese administrators consolidated practically the entire countryside under their supervision, if not their outright ownership. The original small landholders were in many instances reduced to the status of debt-ridden tenants. Emigration seemed the only way out for many of them.

According to the figures for 1938, as shown in table 2, 37.5 percent of the Korean emigrants were from Kyŏngsan-Namdo province, 23 percent from Kyŏngsan-Bukdo province, and 20.6 percent were from Chŏlla-Namdo province. Thus, the overwhelming majority of Koreans were from

TABLE 2

Place of Birth of Koreans in Japan as of 1938

Province	Number	Percentage
Kyŏngsang-Namdo	300,163	37.5
Kyŏngsdang-Bukdo	184,651	23.1
Chŏlla-Namdo	165,125	20.6
Chŏlla-Bukdo	48,858	6.1
Ch'ungch'ŏng-Namdo	28,751	3.6
Ch'ungch'ŏng-Bukdo	22,524	2.8
Kyŏnggi-do	14,433	1.8
Kangwŏng-do	8,312	1.0
P'yŏng-'an-Namdo	7,824	1.0
Hamkyŏng-Namdo	5,884	0.7
Whanghae-do	5,643	0.7
P'yŏng-an-Bukdo	4,666	0.6
Hamkyŏng-Bukdo	3,044	0.4
Total	799,878	100

Source: Hōmukenshūsho, *Zainichi Chōsenjin shogū no suii to genjō* (Tokyo: Japanese Ministry of Justice, 1955), p. 12.

those three provinces known to have the best agricultural land in Korea.

By 1920 the pattern had become set. Japanese statistics show between 1921 and 1931 a net emigration to Japan of over 400,000 Koreans, drawn in most instances from what had become a surplus agricultural population.[8] This influx of unskilled Koreans depressed the wages of those Japanese workers who were unfortunate enough to be in the lower ranges of unskilled labor.

In the very early 1920s occurred a short postwar boom. Even though it ended rather quickly and was followed by chronic depression, it did not dissuade more Koreans from finding or seeking a livelihood in Japan (table 3). The year of the Kantō earthquake, 1923, saw the Korean population reaching 80,000. The historical killing of Koreans by the Japanese population, dramatized in chapter 1, was instigated not only by an increasing fear of political dissidence but also by a basic economic fear that this foreign population was competing avidly for available jobs.[9]

THE GROWTH OF MUTUAL HOSTILITY

In competing with the Japanese for jobs, Koreans could utilize neither literacy nor any form of special skills. Most found employment in mining,

TABLE 3
The Migration of Koreans to Japan

Year	Korean population in Japan	Conscripted laborers or military draftees
1909	790	—
1910	—	—
1915	3,989	—
1916	5,638	—
1917	14,501	—
1918	22,262	—
1919	28,272	—
1920	30,175	—
1921	35,876	—
1922	59,865	—
1923	80,617	—
1924	120,238	—
1925	133,710	—
1926	148,502	—
1927	175,911	—
1928	243,328	—
1929	276,031	—
1930	298,091	—
1931	318,212	—
1932	390,543	—
1933	466,217	—
1934	537,576	—
1935	625,678	—
1936	690,501	—
1937	735,689	—
1938	799,865	—
1939	961,591	38,700
1940	1,190,444	54,944
1941	1,469,230	43,493
1942	1,625,054	112,007
1943	1,882,456	122,237
1944	1,936,843	280,303
1945	unknown	160,427

Source: Naimushō, *Keihōkyoku Report*, 1945.

railroad construction, and stevedoring. In 1924, 23 percent were employed in mining industries.[10] In 1929, of 271,278 Koreans, 50 percent were employed as coolies and miners. Later statistics showed little change, but reiterated the fact that most Koreans remained classified as unskilled laborers.[11]

As indicated by table 4, males between twenty and forty-four years of age made up 78 percent of those who migrated to Japan in the 1920s. For both sexes combined, the same age group constituted 68 percent of those who settled in Japan. Again in 1930, 67 percent of males of the same age group dominated the migrant Koreans who settled in Japan. It could be said that the early Korean migrants to Japan were predominantly the prime age group in terms of labor productivity. Also, the imbalance of the sexual ratio during the period would suggest that most of the Korean laborers came to Japan without families and with a "sojourner's mentality." The 1940s figure, however, indicates a relative stability in the sexual ratio and a wider distribution of age groups among the Korean population in Japan.

Japanese governmental policies were not effective in raising the educational level of Koreans, either in their native land or in Japan. Korean children in Japan were subject to compulsory education, as were the Japanese, but little effort was made to enforce the applicability of this provision to Koreans.[12] Even by 1936 only one out of three Korean children was attending school of any kind. Statistics on Koreans in Osaka and Tokyo taken from surveys of 1931 and 1936 classified almost half of them as illiterate.[13] A continuing source of discontent among Koreans was that Korean laborers received considerably smaller wages, sometimes little more than half that paid Japanese in similar jobs. This knowledge created a bitterness that was often expressed toward their Japanese working colleagues.[14] In turn, the fact that they received less pay did not necessarily evoke the sympathy of the competing Japanese.

Mixed in with these unskilled workers in the migrant stream was a small minority comprised of students, Korean businessmen, and intellectuals or professionals. This small element was better able to articulate the resentment of Koreans over their general disparagement. As we shall discuss further, some of these individuals were to become continuing instigators of anti-Japanese radical political activities. The presence of such dissidents produced further anxiety in the general Japanese population, as well as among vigilant police, who were continually on the alert against political radicals.

Many Koreans could not establish a stable place to live. According to a report compiled by the welfare department of the Tokyo prefectural government, many Japanese industries that hired Korean laborers experienced a high rate of turnover and instability among Koreans who did remain on the job. They tended to float from one job to another looking for better wages and security. The language barrier and their illiteracy often prevented their learning skills and securing permanent positions.[15]

TABLE 4
Age and Sex Distribution of Koreans in Japan

Year	1920		1930		1940		1950	
Age	M	F	M	F	M	F	M	F
0- 4	536	494	25,320	24,559	114,180	110,467	40,848	37,817
5- 9	428	347	12,652	11,479	76,098	72,653	33,095	32,200
10-14	1,092	583	11,928	8,593	51,721	43,295	26,626	25,881
15-15	5,313	876	37,836	17,202	78,425	53,810	20,187	18,710
20-24	11,545	917	62,208	19,555	99,419	54,395	19,404	15,657
24-29	8,357	593	53,404	13,699	95,976	48,911	27,118	17,239
30-34	4,997	450	43,639	11,225	78,359	35,488	24,039	13,282
35-39	2,105	187	25,343	5,886	56,812	22,730	21,368	12,137
40-44	1,048	107	15,097	3,470	43,707	17,822	18,078	9,230
45-49	383	65	5,500	1,633	22,356	10,166	13,547	6,318
50-54	160	32	2,487	1,309	13,536	8,483	10,246	4,398
55-59	49	27	1,011	1,036	5,864	5,924	5,383	2,526
60-64			572	893	3,720	5,355	2,758	1,874
65-69	30	34	273	553	2,107	3,684	887	1,093
70			231	416	1,978	3,840	736	1,465
					38	26	87	43
Total	36,043	4,712	297,501	121,508	744,296	497,019	264,407	199,870

Source: Hōmukenshusho, *Zainichi Chōsenjin shogū no suii to genjō* (Tokyo: Japanese Ministry of Justice, 1955), p. 246.

Another preoccupation of the majority of Japanese was the "criminal propensities" of Koreans. There was a tendency to attribute criminal behavior to Koreans, a stereotyping that was encouraged by the attitudes of the police. Newspapers were quick to print stories in which unstable and rootless Koreans were involved in some sort of criminal activity. No doubt there were a considerable number of crimes committed by Koreans who felt no commitment to the Japanese, not an unusual attitude among a discouraged minority that considers members of the majority group fair game. Takahashi states, for example, that there was a common belief that many Korean laborers, once admitted to Japan, refused to go to work at all but instead "wandered around the country, committing every kind of crime."[16] There undoubtedly were some individual Koreans who had little incentive to respect Japanese law. Several Koreans did become part of the traditional Japanese underworld, especially from the 1930s on.

Koreans were exploited continually by labor brokers who exacted percentages of the pitiful daily income casual workers received. Aware of the subjugation of their country and the ruthless oppression practices from 1919 on, they could only feel helpless rage at their condition, finding no recourse. Lawbreaking, for some Koreans, served as a countermeasure to their heritage of suppression. The lower stratum of Korean society did not evidence the highly internalized concern with authority more apparent in Japanese from the lowest rank up. The United States has witnessed a similar attitude arising as a consequence of social discrimination against black Americans. Differential treatment results in a suspicion of all forms of authority, especially of the police, who are seen as agents of harassment. As happened with the blacks in the United States, a readiness to deprecate and look with contempt on Koreans became an interactive process, with some Koreans expressing their hostility through criminal behavior. The Korean population, for the main part illiterate and unskilled, had ample reason for deep hostility felt toward the socially dominant Japanese.

Under these circumstances, the image of Korean laborers was negative. They were characterized not only as rebellious and unruly but also as devoid of a sense of responsibility and less efficient in comparison with Japanese workers. The only assets of Korean laborers were their physical endurance and their willingness to work at lower wages which sustained their survival in hostile surroundings. Occupations such as those of stevedore, coal miner, and laborer, requiring hard physical exertion, were known to be taken up exclusively by Koreans.

Anti-Korean feeling was accentuated by the increased terrorist activities waged by a few Korean nationalists against Japanese officials from the early 1920s on. The uprising of the March First Movement of 1919 had provided a convenient excuse for the Japanese police to place Koreans under constant surveillance. It is noteworthy that most of the data on Koreans during the pre-World War II period were available only from Japanese law enforcement agencies. The Japanese police gave extra impetus to the general antipathy by overplaying stories about Korean revolutionary activities in Japan. The derogatory epithet commonly used by the Japanese characterizing Koreans as *Futei senjin* (rebellious Koreans) is said to have originated in this period.

In the eyes of many Japanese, the alienated behavior of Koreans supported the belief that Koreans were unwelcome intruders incapable of being assimilated into Japanese society. The stereotype of a Korean was related to "badness," not only moral but even in respect to physical comportment. Even today, it is not uncommon to find a grandmother scolding her grandchild by saying, "Don't sit like 'Chōsenjin' do."[17]

There is no question that the Koreans comported themselves in a rougher and more overtly aggressive manner than was customary for the more obsequious and diffident lower-class Japanese. They aroused both fear and contempt among the Japanese, who were accustomed to docility on the part of subordinates. Koreans with greater literacy could express their behavior in more political terms, but the illiterate mass of Koreans could seldom be recruited to perceive their plight in terms of political ideology. And so, the period of migration in the 1920s set a continuing tone of interaction that was to characterize the Japanese attitude toward Korean migrants throughout subsequent periods and into the postwar present.

After the March First Movement of 1919, the Japanese colonial government in Korea began to regard the presence of Korean migrants in Japan as a special security problem. It established a rigorous screening process to weed out any possibly undesirable Koreans. By decree of the colonial administration in 1919, no Korean was allowed to travel to Japan without a permit obtained from the local police station. The rigid screening process was later somewhat relaxed because of the continued high demand for cheap labor by Japanese industries. Travel restrictions, however, remained the same until the end of World War II. Except for students and temporary visitors, Koreans were required to submit a statement from a prospective employer and to prove possession of sufficient funds before filing an application for a travel permit to Japan. When the Manpower Mobilization Act was passed by the Imperial Diet in 1939, such travel restrictions became essentially meaningless because Japan needed an almost unlimited labor supply from Korea to meet the demand of its war effort.

It must be noted that during this period a small trickle of Korean businessmen entered Japan, most of them planning to service the Korean community itself. Among these were some who, despite the handicap of being Korean in a Japanese economy tightly interwoven by personal ties, had sufficiently remarkable entrepreneurial skills to develop important business ventures in Japan itself. These skillful few were to form a thin thread of continuity with those entrepreneurs of the postwar period who also competed successfully on the alien soil of Japan. They were people who tended to put personal gain above group loyalty; they disregarded both the animosity of other Koreans and the lack of social acceptance accorded them by the Japanese.

The group that had the greatest problem of ambivalence throughout the prewar era was the Korean students. The *Japanese Yearbook* of 1921-1922[18] records that there were over a thousand Korean college and university level students in Japan in 1921. These numbers were to show a yearly increase and by 1937 about 8,000 were recorded.

In Korea itself, the Japanese did little to establish facilities of higher learning for those among the Korean youth who, attributing the success of Japanese modernization to their superior educational facilities, wanted more than a high school education. A deep chasm continued in Korean culture between those oriented toward education and the very large uneducated peasant population. Henderson cogently documents the continuity from the premodern period in Korea of this cultural chasm between the capital city and the rural hinterland.[19] Korea only recently has developed a strong middle class of its own.

The Japanese government was highly selective in aiding Koreans who wished higher educational opportunities. It looked favorably only upon the sons of Koreans who cooperated actively with the Japanese regime. These elite were resented by fellow Koreans, but the resentment felt was helpless and unfocused. Well-to-do families were eager to have their children educated in Japan; upon completion of their courses of study, the graduates were expected to assume some official post in the colonial administration. Among those who were not so wealthy but who, by some means, were able to obtain an education, most tended to remain in Japan. They became part of an intellectual contingent of Koreans who found it more possible to express interest in the arts and social sciences in Japan than in a more stringently controlled and traditional Korean society at home. They found a type of minority niche within the more bohemian and dissident segments of Japanese society, some of them exercising a type of creativity that permitted some communality with their Japanese counterparts.

These students and former students formed a contingent of intellectuals who, aware of occurrences in Europe and the United States, were restive in their hope that the concept of self-determination, which was gained for many of the smaller, hitherto subject states of eastern Europe after World War I, could somehow become possible for Korea. Only among the Japanese Communists could Koreans find any sympathy for their desire for independence for their own country. It is not surprising, therefore, to find that many Korean intellectuals came to play a strong role in Japanese radical politics.

Until 1939 the migration to Japan was a voluntary one, although it occurred because of great economic pressures. A survey was made in 1934 by the welfare department of the Tokyo prefectural government to determine the principal motives for Korean migration. Researchers, who interviewed 1,933 heads of households, found that 67 percent had come from Korea as job-seekers.[20] Another 12 percent stated that their initial reason for migration was to gain a superior education, available only in Japan. The remainder gave a variety of reasons. In Kyoto prefecture in 1935, another survey revealed that approximately 88 percent of Koreans residing in Kyoto wished to remain permanently in Japan. Approximately 12 percent desired to return home as soon as they could accumulate sufficient wealth.[21] The surveys determined that most had started as unskilled laborers with very little if any education.

Despite the efforts of the Japanese government to espouse assimilation, the arrival of Koreans simply added a new group toward whom social prejudice could be directed. The Ainu and the Burakumin, and even to some extent the Okinawans, were simply not considered "Japanese." Because Koreans came voluntarily, many felt a counterhostility toward the Japanese. The abject poverty of Korea itself was so great as to preclude for most the idea of returning home. Many Koreans worked for very low wages, but in times of recession large numbers found no work at all. In the large Japanese cities the government sponsored winter relief projects for the unemployed. Takahashi reports that in 1925 Koreans comprised 12 percent of the laborers working on these special relief projects; by 1928 the percentage had risen to an astounding 54 percent of the total. In 1929 the Korean percentage dropped, not because of a decrease in the number of Koreans needing help but because the deepening recession caused a larger number of Japanese to receive relief employment.[22]

Their economic plight was not the Koreans' major discontent. As do poor people everywhere, Koreans placed in their children their hopes for dignity and social acceptance.[23] The government was lax in seeing that Koreans as well as Japanese attended the supposedly compulsory primary schools. The literate Koreans were upset that their more ignorant fellowmen were not encouraged or even constrained to send their children to school. In some cases the reason for nonattendance was the extreme poverty of the children's families. The children were put to some form of work, whatever the pitiful amount they earned.

Going to a Japanese school was not pleasant for Korean children. They were subject to the overt disparagement and contempt of their schoolmates, with teachers doing little to alleviate or prevent such attitudes. The parents at this time, moreover, were still ambivalent about the Japanization implied by formal education. Then as now, some parents did not like to see their children lose their ethnic identity by being thoroughly indoctrinated with a chauvinistic Japanese attitude. By 1936 only 60 percent of the Korean children in Japan were attending elementary schools, in contrast to the almost universal attendance of Japanese. Even more important was the fact that only a handful of the children of Koreans in Japan were enrolled in secondary or higher level institutions. In effect, severe class cleavage continued. Only the small proportion of relatively wealthy Koreans were seeing that their children received a satisfactory education.

The Development of Korean Ghettos

The housing situation of minority outcastes which one witnesses here and there in Japan today—the use of temporary shelters or shacks thrown together out of scraps of iron—was even worse in the prewar period. Then some Korean workers lived in railroad culverts. Even when housing was available, landlords took every opportunity to exploit their ignorant and helpless Korean tenants by overcharging them.

During the 1930s, Korean ghettos began to form around various urban industrial centers. Table 5 indicates the patterns of Korean population distribution in Japan during prewar periods. Early Korean workers in the 1920s were settled mostly in Fukuoka prefecture, where most of the Japanese mining industries were located. Throughout the period, Koreans were scattered around the prefectures that included the seven largest urban areas in the huge industrial complexes, Tokyo, Osaka, Kyoto, Nagoya, Kobe, Yokohama, and Fukuoka. The heaviest concentration of Koreans was in Osaka, where Koreans made up almost 10 percent of the population. The present distribution of Korean population maintains the pattern established during this period.

Because of the unskilled nature of their work, Koreans were the victims of frequent layoffs when economic conditions were bad. The Korean ghettos became the hangouts of many unemployed and uneducated young Koreans. As do the black ghettos in the United States, Korean ghettos produced some individuals who became involved in criminal activities.

Because of the unstable nature of their employment and earning ability, and because of discrimination in housing, many Koreans were compelled to occupy inferior dwellings in what became slum areas on the fringes of factories. Some Koreans built small shacks on vacant lots, using galvanized sheet-iron scraps and other industrial refuse. Chang Hyŏk-chu, a Korean writer known in Japan, reported in a monthly magazine in 1937 on the plight of Koreans living in a slum:

> This is a Korean ghetto in Shibaura Tsukimi-chō. Originally the lot was used as a coal dump by a sugar refinery nearby. A Korean worker employed by the refinery built a small shelter with logs and scrap boards without permission from the owner. Soon he was joined by others. That is how this ghetto was born. The appearance of one wooden shack was so flimsy, with tilted roofs, that one feared the supporting walls would soon give way. But when I took a closer look during the daylight hours, I found another part had been added to make it two stories high with even a laundry-drying rack on

TABLE 5

Geographic Distribution of Korean Population in Japan
(Top Ten Areas)

	1920			1930	
Prefecture	Population	%	Prefecture	Population	%
Fukuoka	7,833	19	Osaka	96,943	23
Osaka	6,290	15	Tokyo	38,355	9
Hyogo	3,770	9	Aichi	35,301	8
Hokkaido	3,462	8	Fukuoka	34,639	8
Nagasaki	2,800	7	Kyoto	27,785	7
Tokyo	2,485	6	Hyogo	26,121	6
Hiroshima	1,173	3	Yamaguchi	15,968	4
Kyoto	1,068	3	Hokkaido	15,560	4
Saga	788	2	Kanaeawa	13,181	3
Ōita	785	2	Hiroshima	11,136	3
Total	40,755	100	Total	419,009	100

	1938			1943	
Prefecture	Population	%	Prefecture	Population	%
Osaka	241,619	30	Osaka	395,380	21
Tokyo	78,250	10	Fukuoka	172,199	9
Fukuoka	64,321	8	Hyogo	135,170	7
Aichi	61,654	8	Yamaguchi	132,526	7
Hyogo	60,105	8	Aichi	126,325	7
Kyoto	53,446	7	Tokyo	123,126	7
Yamaguchi	45,439	6	Hokkaido	82,950	4
Hokkaido	24,878	3	Kyoto	74,079	4
Kanagawa	16,663	2	Hiroshima	68,274	4
Hiroshima	12,063	2	Kanagawa	54,794	3
Total	799,878	100	Total	1,882,456	100

Source: Hōmukenshūsho, *Zainichi Chōsenjin* (Tokyo: Japanese Ministry of Justice, 1955), p. 13.

top. The piecemeal addition must have been necessitated by an increment in the family. I was told that this ghetto is now inhabited by approximately 600 Koreans. It is a dreadful thing to imagine that so many Koreans could possibly live in such small shacks crowded in this limited area.[24]

The poverty-stricken Korean ghettos have always been located in undesirable corners of the crowded urban cities, socially and physically alienated from the mainstream of Japanese society. In the minds of the Japanese public, the poverty of Korean ghettos has resulted from the cultural traits of Koreans, traits also responsible for their destitution. They have considered the Koreans to be intellectually and morally inferior, having different values from the proper Japanese and lacking the ambition and the initiative necessary to advance themselves. The Japanese, more often than not, have refused to accept the fact that their own discriminatory barriers weakened motivation and limited the opportunities for Koreans to acquire skills. The lack of employment opportunities has bound Koreans in ghettos, a situation not unfamiliar to those who have studied the economic and social dead end of the black ghetto in American cities.

As far as the Japanese government has been concerned, the existence of Korean ghettos has never been viewed as a social problem. Instead, ghettos have been treated as seedbeds of subversive activities by rebellious Koreans and left-wing revolutionaries. Japanese officials have been mainly concerned with how to maintain law and order by surveillance of "the undesirables" to be found hiding in ghettos. Koreans living in ghettos have frequently been targets of search and seizure; they have always been kept under the watchful eyes of the Japanese police.

Social Mobility among Koreans in the Prewar Period

In addition to the Korean laborers who formed the core of the Korean ghettos, a substantial number of other Korean businessmen, students, and "intellectuals" played significant roles in Korean minority communities. The Koreans who settled as businessmen were small in number and were mostly minor tradesmen or entrepreneurs running entertainment establishments, such as restaurants, bars, and cabarets. Some were in gambling and prostitution. These were small entrepreneurs, primarily catering to Koreans as their clients. Among these businessmen were a few who, against all odds, became successful but who identified themselves very closely with Japanese interests. Particularly to be noted were prominent businessmen in the rubber goods and textile industries in the prewar period. Nearly all those who achieved success tried to cut their ties with the Korean community, seeking acceptance by passing as Japanese. This phenomenon can be compared with those patterns found in black or Mexican-American minorities in the United States; the black concept of passing relates to the prewar pattern of Korean social mobility taken by a considerable number of Koreans, who placed individual mobility ahead of ethnic loyalty or personal ties.

The result of such occurrences gave rise to considerable strain and enmity among the Koreans themselves. Disharmony and friction within the Korean community was further intensified by the difference in outlook and strategy held by those students and intellectuals who played leading political roles in the community. None of them was able to envision the possibility that many Koreans would eventually become permanent settlers in Japan. Instead, they seemed to seek the solution for the plight of the Koreans in Japan by devoting their entire effort toward a Korean independence movement. Once this ultimate goal of independence for Korea was achieved, they believed, no Korean would find any reason to remain in a hostile Japanese society. Any organized efforts to promote the group interests of Koreans in Japan were invariably linked ideologically with the much broader movement toward independence, which was regarded as a subversive activity by the Japanese authorities. Any group effort of this nature was bound to invite more oppression than amelioration, as far as the Koreans in Japan were concerned.

As a matter of fact, there was a considerable amount of sabotage and violence, incited by students and others in the industries where many Korean workers were employed. Consequently, no simple Korean labor dispute could escape the direct intervention of the Japanese police. Koreans could not express their legitimate grievances but were treated merely as an essential economic commodity whose utilization was administered by strict punitive control.

Korean Political Movements

Organized group activities to articulate the interests of Koreans were generally formed under three broad groupings. One was the Nationalist movement, directed mainly by Korean revolutionaries exiled in China. Another significant program was the International Proletarian Movement, under the banner of the United Front, which was joined to the Japanese Communists. These groups did share to some degree the common goal of obtaining independence for Korea as a nation, but their ideological incompatibility prevented them from organizing any concerted action. By the mid-1930s, most of their organized efforts were suppressed by stringent Japanese police efforts and mass arrests. No significant Korean independent movement became visible thereafter, though minor disturbances and violence continued to plague the Japanese authorities until the end of World War II.[25]

The third group effort was led by a few Koreans who accepted the fate of Japanese colonialism as an accomplished fact and sought to further the interests of the Koreans in Japan by close collaboration and the establishment of harmony between the Koreans and Japanese. They saw the immediate need for articulation of the interests of Koreans in Japan as paramount over any long-term goals of attaining Korean independence. They considered that reliance upon subversive actions could only cause the Koreans in Japan to become the victims of further Japanese suppression. The advocates of this approach tended actively to denounce the Marxist-oriented revolutionaries and the means they used to resist the Japanese establishment. They seemed to think that it was the radical behavior itself that was the source of Japanese hatred and animosity toward Koreans. This sentiment was later fully exploited by the Japanese authorities to recruit informers to help track down Korean revolutionaries in exchange for favor and influence or even for personal gain. For this reason, one historian has termed this group the "anti-nationalists."[26]

Initially this movement was led by a Korean named Pak Ch'un-kŭm, who later was duly elected twice as the only Korean member of the Imperial Diet on the basis of his conciliatory influence among Koreans. He came to enjoy a prestige and power attained by no other contemporary Korean. He had come to Japan in the early 1920s looking for some entrepreneurial activity, but he ended up as a construction foreman for Korean laborers. When he witnessed the mass layoff of Koreans as a result of the economic recession of 1921, he organized a small welfare organization called Sōaikai (The Mutual Friendship Society) to succor distressed Koreans by providing food and shelter out of his own funds. He also helped illiterate Korean laborers to find work. After the Korean massacre following the Kantō earthquake, he was credited with organizing a number of Koreans to assist in cleaning up the shattered city as a means of mitigating the intense hostility between the Koreans and Japanese.

Recognizing Pak's conciliatory role and realizing a need for such services for Koreans, Japanese officials began to provide financial support for Pak's projects. The membership of the Sōaikai in Japan soon reached nearly 100,000. It also began to maintain a close liaison with the Japanese police, passing on information related to allegedly subversive Korean activities. Even though the declared objectives of the Sōaikai were to provide social services and to promote friendship between Koreans and Japanese, it began to function as a control organ over the Koreans in carrying out official Japanese policy.

Many Koreans were aware that the Sōaikai maintained a close link with the Japanese police, but they joined and supported it because it was the sole organization able to represent them with an active spokesman. The Sōaikai often intervened in Korean labor disputes and negotiated with Japanese employers on behalf of Koreans. It is questionable how effective its leaders were in achieving a more favorable outcome in these disputes, but the Korean laborers felt that they at least had some organization on which they could rely and ask for help. As the Korean minority grew in numbers, the Japanese government recognized the need for increased guidance and sought to use Pak to minimize any friction between Koreans and Japanese. The government felt that "reconciliation" was best handled by private Korean organizations and offered financial assistance to any group willing to tackle "Korean problems." Many other Korean organizations in addition to the Sōaikai mushroomed locally all over Japan, competing with each other for public funds but accomplishing very little.

GOVERNMENT POLICIES AS SHAPED BY JAPANESE ATTITUDES

There is no doubt that the attitude of the populace influenced the developing attitude and the policy of the government toward Korean migrants from 1920 on.[27] It was, of course, the lower stratum of Japanese society that viewed Koreans as competitors. The business and commercial men of Japan saw them as a potential source of cheap labor. The influx of Koreans kept Japanese labor costs very low. The lower the level, the greater the impact. A common attitude was that Koreans were crude by nature and were able to adapt to arduous labor. Because they were believed to lack refinement, the abysmally poor hovels they lived in were considered to represent a customary, and therefore an endurable, state of affairs.

Some Japanese became frightened by the fact that the Korean birthrate was appreciably higher than that of the Japanese. Indeed, in one of the early postwar censuses, 37 percent of the Korean minority were children under eighteen years of age. The attitudes of Japanese toward Koreans resembled those of Americans toward Asians in such states as California, where it was feared that the majority population would be inundated by Asians, even if immigration were stopped, because "they breed like rabbits."

Japanese laborers could protest their bad working conditions; Koreans, conversely, felt no such freedom. They were therefore sometimes seen as more "docile" in their work situation. It was quoted in the *Japan Chronicle* of January 1925:

> It is disquieting the crowd of Japanese workers that go to public offices demanding assistance. Tens of thousands of Korean laborers are now in Japan, but they do not take any such improper course. They work very hard at low wages. If Japanese workers worked as hard as the Koreans at as low wages there would always be work for them. It is rather inconsistent for Japanese laborers to be too proud to work for low wages, while making the assertion that if a man shall not work, neither shall he eat.[28]

A rather ruthless capitalistic attitude was openly expressed in the Japanese press of the time, and the Koreans were being used as a means of maintaining a greater docility in the Japanese workers of that period.

The Korean migrants were closely analogous to the European migrants settling in American industrial cities. They were regarded with the same resentment by already established workers and were looked upon as "dirty foreigners" with low standards of living, morality, and honesty. One must note that the Japanese government's sensitivity to possible Korean revolutionary attitudes aided and abetted the hostility of Japanese citizens toward Koreans in general. Wagner points out that the Koreans lacked the historical and cultural tradition common to the Japanese of that time, who were "captives of a powerful inner psychological compulsion which constituted a primary prop to authoritarian rule in Japan."[29] Korean nationalism was in effect based on the idea of a country free from external domination, whereas Japanese nationalism had already been channeled into a concept of competing with the colonial powers of the West, as the Japanese saw the Dutch, British, French, and, to a lesser degree, the Americans, benefiting from their colonial dominance over subject nationalities.

The early Japanese government policy toward the Koreans was a vacillating one. This vacillation reflected the internal struggle for power between the liberals and those inclined toward strong Japanese nationalism. The government made sporadic attempts to limit the influx of Korean labor and to improve the condition of Koreans already present. But no effort of any major kind was made to improve the legal status of Koreans, and any attempt at group betterment from within was rigorously suppressed. Officially, there was a promise of bringing about understanding and harmony, "raising the Koreans to the level of the Japanese," but in actuality, all thoughts were directed toward ways to take advantage of the Koreans in the sustained military effort that had been launched on the continent of Asia. Korean workers continued to be viewed solely from the standpoint of their capacity to contribute unskilled labor, whereas the Japanese were recruited for armed service in ever-increasing numbers.

After the Korean independence demonstration of 1 March 1919, an imperial rescript was issued in which the Koreans were promised equality with the Japanese. This promise was never fulfilled. There was an abiding problem in early Japanese policy: the Japanese in general felt that the Koreans were dangerous and potentially disloyal. They thought that full equality for Koreans would serve to strengthen dissident elements and that if Koreans in Japan were given all the privileges of full Japanese citizenship, it would be difficult for the government to maintain a differential policy in Korea.

On the one hand, the government was somewhat insensitive to the negative national opinion about Koreans. On the other hand, the government was sensitive to international opinion and was aware that, as a representative of a modern Asian colonial power, it was expected to show enlightenment comparable to that developed in the West. The Japanese were careful throughout never to confer full citizenship status on the Koreans.

Nevertheless, when a manhood suffrage act was passed in 1925, it became possible for Korean males in Japan to vote in Japanese elections. Voter qualifications made it unlikely, however, that the vast proportion of Koreans would receive the vote. Anyone receiving relief or government support could not vote; there was a residence requirement of a full year. Through the middle of the 1930s, informal practices remained such that Koreans did not effectively exercise the voting privilege.

In the Japanese tradition, the Koreans were forced to make believe that military service was an honor, but because they were distrusted, Koreans were initially excluded from any form of combat service. Koreans were not permitted to transfer their legal domicile to Japan, a restriction that put them under a number of severe handicaps in the commercial codes practiced. Koreans who migrated to Japan experienced both legal gains and losses. In a number of ways Korean migrants were more favorably treated than those who remained in Korea. Punishment for violating administrative ordinances was not as severe as in Korea, where legal codes were kept stringent to intimidate a restive population. In Korea legal cases might be handled by summary police jurisdiction; but this was not so in Japan. The only advantage for those residing in Korea was that there were some slight modifications in law relative to Korean customs and a person there might be tried before a Korean judge.

It was apparent to all Koreans that there was discriminatory treatment and selective law enforcement. Within the realm of political activities, the government was most stringent and alert; any independent Korean organization was very quickly suppressed. There were frequent reports of terrorist techniques employed by the Japanese toward Koreans. Any efforts to organize Korean workers were met with discouragement, if not outright suppression. In effect the Koreans could make common cause only with leftist unions, since they met with rebuff from more conservative elements in labor. By the mid-1930s any attempts at serious labor militancy were completely stamped out.

As has been mentioned, the privately operated but state-supported and controlled Sōaikai organization became virtually compulsory for Koreans, because it exercised control over the employment of Koreans and over the issuance of travel certificates for return to Korea. It maintained close, continual liaison with the Japanese police and informed on attempted union activities. By the early 1930s the Korean population in Japan was over 400,000, and smaller Korean political and social organizations numbered more than a thousand. The Japanese government, under the control of the military since 1931, felt that the problems of Koreans in Japan could no longer be adequately handled by any private organizations operated by Koreans. What Japanese officials feared most was that some of these organizations might be easily diverted to anti-Japanese activities if they were not properly controlled. In 1934 Korean migrant problems were discussed at a series of cabinet meetings; the resultant stipulations were: (1) integration of all Korean social service activities; (2) solution to the problems of Korean ghettos; and (3) an assimilation policy for Koreans.[30] To implement these policies, the Sōaikai was superseded by the Kyōwakai (Concordia Society), which was established and centralized under the jurisdiction of four government agencies: the Ministries of Home Affairs, Welfare, and Colonial Affairs, and the Colonial Government of Korea. By 1938 local Kyōwakai organizations had been established throughout the thirty-one prefectures where most of the Koreans resided. The prefectural governor served as the head of the local Kyōwakai, and the police chief and the director of educational affairs were usually appointed as deputies.

The publicly announced purposes of the Kyōwakai were to promote understanding between Koreans and Japanese, to raise living standards through social services, and to cultivate the trust and loyalty of Koreans by Japanization. The difference between the Sōaikai and Kyōwakai was that the former was run privately by Koreans although it had government funding, and the latter was operated by Japanese officials. What they intended was to control the souls and bodies of Koreans with a forced assimilation policy. For the Koreans in Japan, Kyōwakai membership was mandatory and every member was required to carry a membership card at all times. The card was to serve as an identification needed to process any government papers. No Korean was allowed to travel anywhere without the identification card. Koreans were forced by fiat to adopt Japanese names and to worship at Shintō shrines. Locally, the Kyōwakai provided employment and welfare services. It also conducted adult classes to teach the Japanese language, sewing, manners, and customs to better assimilate Koreans as "Japanese." Structurally all the important positions of the Kyōwakai, from top to bottom, were staffed by Japanese officials. The organization resembled a paramilitary unit that Koreans were forced to join in the most subordinate positions.

THE SHIFT TO INVOLUNTARY MIGRATION (1939-1945)

As Japan's war on the Chinese mainland expanded after 1937, the government drafted a comprehensive mobilization plan for the entire nation. Under the National Manpower Mobilization Act of 1939, Korean laborers and military draftees were involuntarily brought to Japan to fill the manpower vacuum created by the expansion of the forces and the war economy. The mobilization plan forced Koreans to work in the munitions plants, in coal mines, and at other forms of hard labor.

Coal mining, especially, was failing to meet the growing demand because of a shortage of labor. Traditionally, coal mining in Japan was considered unattractive because of wretched safety provisions, low wages, and poor working conditions. Besides, Japanese mining companies had often practiced a semifeudal form of strict control over coal miners' lives, which added to the mine operators' difficulties in securing permanent labor. The problems of this sick industry were intensified by the exigencies of the Pacific war. The vacuum was filled by conscripted Korean laborers. By the closing years of World War II, Korean laborers constituted 43 percent in the mining industries in Hokkaido, and 65 percent of these were working as miners in the coal pits.[31]

Before 1939 Korean labor recruitment had been handled individually by each private company. Under the Japanese mobilization plan, industries were required to submit requests to the colonial government, which in turn designated areas where their recruiters were to go for mass recruitment. The recruits were thoroughly investigated as possible security risks. After physical examinations for labor, they were taken to Japan in groups led by their respective recruiters who were representatives of particular Japanese companies.

The recruiting process became cumbersome, often taking as long as six months. In 1941, with World War II imminent, the Ministries of Home Affairs and Welfare and the colonial government agreed to organize more effectively the recruiting process in Korea. The colonial government set up labor recruiting stations in each local province, county, and village to administer recruitment. Requests for labor from each industry were to be cleared by the central colonial government, with a recruitment quota then to be assigned to the local recruiting stations. It was the responsibility of each recruiting station to fill its quota. The recruits were grouped together at the regional recruiting stations and were turned over to the appropriate industries. The means employed by the overzealous local recruiting stations to fill their assigned quotas were often questionable. Some localities where the quotas were easily filled were given awards by the colonial government as model villages to exalt their loyalty to the emperor as imperial subjects of Japan.

Korean laborers normally served a two-year tour of duty in Japan; in some instances they were allowed to invite their families to visit them where they were employed. By 1944 the Japanese Imperial Diet finally passed the Korean Labor Conscription Act under which all Korean males were subject to mobilization by fiat. At the same time, Korean youths were compelled to serve under the Japanese military draft. As shown in tables 2 and 3, approximately 822,000 Koreans were brought to Japan as labor and military conscripts between 1939 and the end of World War II. Throughout the war period, the aggregate number of Koreans mobilized by the Japanese government in both Korea and Japan reached almost six million.

With the ever-increasing flow of Korean laborers to Japan after the National Manpower Mobilization Act of 1939, the local branches of the

Kyōwakai served as receiving points for the laborers by providing an orientation program and trying to minimize the attrition rate caused by increasing desertions. If any undesirable Korean were found among the conscripts, the Kyōwakai was to process the deportation. As more and more Koreans were called to the Japanese industrial front to help the war effort, the Japanese government became increasingly concerned about control over Koreans. The Kyōwakai served as an official arm of the government to expedite the war effort. Its stated long-term goals of assimilation became secondary to getting Korean workers to support the industrial requirements of a nation at war.

The Japanese government was never entirely successful in filling its manpower needs. There were many Koreans who evaded conscription. The number of escapees was reportedly very high. According to a Japanese official account, about 220,000 Korean conscripted laborers were missing after being placed in munition industries since the mobilization plan went into effect in 1939.[32] During the early period of postwar repatriation most of these conscriptees returned to Korea as soon as they were free to leave. A high proportion of the present Korean inhabitants of Japan came in the earlier period on a voluntary basis with their families.

Korean Resistance to the Japanese War Effort

Wagner reports that there was considerable difficulty in mobilizing the Koreans to assist in the war effort. Even if they were mobilized, Korean acts of minor subversion and work stoppages occurred, which made the Japanese government feel ill at ease with respect to their draftee labor.[33] To some degree, the Japanese were forced to work at cross-purposes; the more they used Korean labor, the more uneasy the Japanese became because they had less control. The discontent among Japanese workers was obvious. When Japanese authorities attempted some conciliatory measures toward Korean workers, the Japanese workers became upset. The Japanese government, by and large, used the same repressive devices they had found effective in the past. They gained a certain amount in the short run, but they stored up a tremendous amount of hostility that became manifest after Japan's defeat.

In attempting to mobilize Koreans, the Japanese made the mistake of intermingling Korean university students with their labor forces. Wagner reports that there were over 13,000 Korean youths studying at Japanese colleges and universities in 1942. In 1943 there was a special military volunteer service for students, but only about 10 percent of the Korean students enlisted in the Japanese army under this plan. The others were compelled to enter the labor force on a full- or part-time basis and were placed among other Korean workers in the industries for which they had been drafted. These students encouraged their fellow laborers to express openly the latent rebellious attitudes that all possessed. The United States Strategic Bombing

Survey later suggested that Korean labor was stirred up largely by the Korean students interspersed in their midst.[34]

As the Japanese war situation deteriorated, the most active members of the Korean community began to engage in activities detrimental to the war effort. Acts of sabotage became more frequent. Japanese newspapers and magazines complained that Koreans were not doing their part to maintain the Japanese state. While no major incidents occurred until the end of the war, there were many minor actions. One magazine lists 445 separate incidents involving 78,000 Korean workers.[35] Wagner says, however, that Korean acts of overt resistance were related to the underground stirrings of Japanese communism. He cites the fact that there were documents in the files of the "peace preservation" and "thought control" sections of the home industry which recorded the apprehension of the Japanese police about the communist movement in wartime.[36]

The United States Strategic Bombing Survey found that in the late war period the Japanese populace generally were prone to scapegoat Koreans, as was evidenced in the types of rumors that would occur after American air raids on Japanese cities. For example, the police found that Japanese stories concerning Koreans' lack of economic and social scruples decreased, whereas rumors that Koreans were aiding the enemy or had fled in the face of enemy action multiplied. Reports of the negative activities attributed to Koreans increasingly emphasized treasonable subversion. Similar rumors were often repeated by the Koreans themselves, especially by the laborers. For example, it was rumored in the Korean community that Korean immigrants in the United States had formed a volunteer army that was advancing on Japan. There were rumors that most of the airplane pilots who raided a particular area in northern Kyūshū were Korean-Americans.

As Japanese military power waned before the onslaught of the American forces, it became evident in the Korean community that hostility toward the Japanese could be expressed more overtly. Wagner quotes at length from a police directive of January 1943, which attests to the general attitudes in police circles about the unreliability and possibly treasonable activities of the Korean community:[37]

> The character of Koreans is marked by their vengefulness and their "toadyism," i.e., their worship of the powerful. Therefore . . . their ideological activities will in all likelihood be transferred to movements toward their independence, and . . . there is danger that they may carry out subversive practices. . . . In view of this fact, thorough control of the leadership is necessary in regard to these peninsular people.
>
> Of course vigilance and undercover investigation of those who are in Japan for the purpose of study or investigation of Japanese-Korean relationships should be intensified, particularly in regard to students and the members of the educated class. Persons who may be suspected of being in Japan for [purposes] other than study should be watched, particularly in regard to subversive activities.

In view of the fact that demands for independence are beginning to be voiced in some Korean circles, strict watch must be maintained over the actions of the Koreans in general.

As the Pacific war progressed, the importance of Korean laborers on the industrial front was felt keenly by the Japanese authorities. To ensure their loyalty to Japan and their continued work for the war effort, a series of discussions was held at a cabinet meeting during the latter part of 1943. The decision was finally reached to overhaul the Korean position of inequality and inferiority by allowing Koreans to participate fully in the political process. The state-run Kyōwakai, which was primarily used as an instrument for controlling Koreans, was abolished and renamed the Kōseikai (Welfare Society). A "Policy to Revise the Treatment of Koreans and Formosans" was officially adopted by the cabinet in November 1944. Koreans were to be given freedom to travel to and from Japan, a right formerly restricted ostensibly to protect public security; discrimination in wages, employment, and promotion were to be eliminated; welfare payments were to be increased, and many other measures were designed to treat Koreans equally with the Japanese.[38]

One of the far-reaching measures adopted by the cabinet was to permit Koreans to transfer their permanent domicile registration from Korea to Japan. If the measure had been implemented, it would have been tantamount to affording Koreans full-fledged citizenship by eliminating the source of legal discrimination. In addition, the cabinet allocated twelve seats in the House of Peers and seventy seats in the House of Representatives to Koreans so that they would be represented in the Imperial Japanese government. The budget of the Kōseikai was more than double that which the Kyōwakai had had, in an attempt to encourage the active assimilation of Koreans as "loyal Imperial subjects." These cabinet decisions, however, were not put into effect because Japan's defeat was fairly apparent by the spring of 1945.

Meanwhile, a group of Koreans who had collaborated closely with the Japanese banded together and organized an association called Isshinkai (Unity Association). In response to what they saw as the generosity of the cabinet and to demonstrate their loyalty to Japan, they constructed an aircraft factory to assist the war effort and mobilized all the available Korean resources, both in finance and manpower. Practically all those Koreans who supported the Japanese Imperial efforts were listed as either officials or active members in Isshinkai. The irony was that when the war ended, it was these people who were most active in organizing yet another society, the Cheil Chosŏnnin Ryŏnmeng or Choryŏn (League of the Korean Residents in Japan) and sought to act as spokesmen for all Koreans in Japan. Though they obtained almost all the important positions in Choryŏn, they were soon ousted from the organization by the more radical elements when leadership was taken over by left-wing Koreans. As we shall discuss further in chapter 5, the present split in the Korean community in Japan developed when these ousted members then organized the Cheil Chosŏn Kŏryumin-dan[39] or Mindan (Association for the Korean Residents in Japan), while the Choryŏn remained the seat of power of the Korean left-wing throughout the postwar period.

3

THE PERIOD OF REPATRIATION, 1945-1949

Changsoo Lee

When the termination of World War II was announced over the radio by Japanese Emperor Hirohito in August 1945, the heart of a tremulous Japan faltered. It was an incredible and humiliating experience for the Japanese, who had never witnessed defeat, to learn of their country's surrender to the despised *kichiku beiei* (barbarous Anglo-Americans).

The period immediately after the surrender was marked by the most complete breakdown of political and socioeconomic order known in modern Japan. It took several weeks for the Supreme Command for the Allied Powers (SCAP) to establish authority over the defeated nation. Most industries had either been destroyed by American bombing or had been closed down. Millions of demilitarized Japanese soldiers and repatriates began returning to the crowded homeland from abroad. Not only did this create vast unemployment but it also caused a critical shortage of food and housing. The price of goods skyrocketed, leading to an inflation that almost paralyzed the immediate postwar Japanese economy.

For Koreans, however, the surrender of Japan meant the liberation of their homeland from the shackles of Japanese colonialism and a rebirth of their national independence. During the last years of the war, the number of Koreans in Japan had swollen to more than two million.[1] After the emperor's momentous radio announcement, the thoughts of most of these forced migrants turned to home. They were filled with anticipation and hope that a better life would be forthcoming in their own country. What was described as "a spontaneous mass exodus" to Korea began in the middle of August 1945, as Koreans found that they were free to leave Japan if they could find passage across the strait. Hakata, Senzaki, and other ports of embarkation were swamped with homeland Koreans laden with whatever belongings they could carry. All types of seagoing ships, including fishing vessels, were employed in transporting the Koreans to their homeland and the Japanese troops and civilians from their battle stations back to Japan. This uncontrolled mass migration created chaos. Facilities to accommodate the incoming and outgoing throngs at the war-torn embarkation areas were pitifully inadequate. Some Koreans who were unable to arrange their own repatriation were indignant and protested to the Japanese authorities about their lack of assistance. As a result of these protests, a meeting was held at the Ministry of Transportation and Communication on 22 August 1945, and an official repatriation operation was launched despite the limited means of transportation available.[2]

In this initial phase of repatriation, Japanese naval and merchant vessels were mobilized to transport the Koreans. Beginning in November 1945, however, several additional reception centers were opened and U.S. Navy vessels were assigned to the operation.[3] The Japanese Ministry of Welfare was made responsible for the entire repatriation operation, including the expenses, and unauthorized repatriation was forbidden.[4] During the four-month period, from September to December 1945, approximately 640,000 Koreans returned home through official channels.

In early 1946, with better organizations and facilities, the repatriation process became orderly and efficient. Nevertheless, the number of Korean repatriates sharply declined during December 1945 and January 1946. Several factors contributed to discouraging Koreans from returning home. One dominating inhibition was the restriction imposed by SCAP in fixing the amount of property each Korean was allowed to take with him. For the purpose of "control over exports and imports of gold, silver, security and financial instrument," SCAP had issued a directive forbidding any repatriate to take with him more than 1,000 yen or objects of equivalent value.[5] With that amount, one could scarcely buy more than a few cartons of cigarettes in Korea. Any excess money or valued items were supposed to be impounded, with receipts issued by the Japanese authorities pending further directives from SCAP.

The financial regulations were amended in January 1946, allowing Koreans to take their postal savings, bank passbooks, and other financial papers including "checks, drafts, certificates of deposit, drawn on and issued by financial institutions in Japan and payable in Japan."[6] Such a relaxation was, however, insignificant because all financial transactions between Korea and Japan had been suspended for an indefinite period. There were other restrictions limiting baggage to clothing, possessions "of value only to the owner," and goods "limited to the amount each person can carry at one time."[7] The baggage allowance was soon modified to permit personal effects of up to 250 pounds per person.[8]

These restrictions on taking their meager savings and belongings from Japan were not the only factors that caused many Koreans to have second thoughts about returning home. The stories and rumors told by incoming Japanese repatriates from Korea were also disheartening. There were reports of riots, strikes, epidemic diseases, floods, and famine. Not a single description of the situation in Korea was favorable. The uprooted Koreans gradually began to realize that the hope of a better life in their homeland was an unrealistic expectation. They might, in fact, have to anticipate worse conditions than those they had experienced in Japan. Substantiating such reports was the news that many Koreans who had been repatriated were expressing a desire to return to Japan, seemingly having found it too difficult to return home empty-handed and to adjust to life in an impoverished land. To prevent their reentry, SCAP issued a directive to the Imperial Japanese government not to accept returnees.[9] Nevertheless, illegal Korean reentry into Japan became a serious problem. By August 1946 more than 13,000 returning Koreans had been apprehended by the authorities.[10]

With the sharp decline in Korean repatriation to the homeland, it became clear that Koreans were less interested in immediate repatriation. To determine the number of Koreans who wished to return, SCAP directed the Japanese government to have all Koreans registered by 18 March 1946. The Japanese government was also instructed to inform the Koreans that those who wished to remain in Japan as well as those who desired to be repatriated must register; failure to register would result in their forfeiting of repatriation privileges at the expense of the Japanese government.[11] Of 646,932 Koreans who did register, 514,035 expressed their desire for repatriation. It is difficult to determine how many so indicated just to keep their options open. Nevertheless, on the basis of this figure, the Japanese government was instructed to formulate a repatriation program to transport 4,000 persons per day from late April until the end of September 1946 to complete the operation.[12] To encourage more repatriation, SCAP liberalized the baggage and property restrictions, but the number of the Korean repatriates continued to decrease.

The original repatriation plan, which was scheduled to be terminated by September 1946, was extended twice in the hope that more Koreans would return home. But when the official repatriation program closed on 15 December 1946, officially only 72,000 had returned to Korea since the registration began. The rest of the Koreans in Japan had forfeited their repatriation privileges.[13] Though socioeconomic conditions in Japan were little better than in Korea, and though Koreans were faced with hostile and prejudicial attitudes, the remaining Koreans preferred to stay in Japan.

As has been discussed in chapters 1 and 2, ethnic relations between the Japanese and Koreans have seldom been cordial. On 14 August 1945, anticipating a sudden deterioration of Japanese and Korean relations in the face of surrender, the chief of the police bureau in the Home Affairs ministry had ordered all police stations in Japan to take utmost precautions to reduce possible ethnic tensions.[14] Two conditions in the order intended: (1) to provide adequate protection for Koreans' life and property, giving them a sense of security, thereby persuading them to stay at their jobs until further notice, and (2) to try to keep the conscripted laborers separated from the Japanese laborers in each plant to prevent episodes in "word and deed" that would tend to spur racial friction.[15]

Obviously, the Japanese authorities feared that some Japanese fanatics who opposed the surrender might attempt to use the Koreans as scapegoats for the defeat. Rumors persisted that Koreans had helped the "barbarous Anglo-Americans" to win the war.[16] The authorities were trying to avert an incident similar to what had occurred after the Kantō earthquake in 1923, when several thousand innocent Koreans were massacred by Japanese fanatics stirred by racial hatred.

DIVISION WITHIN THE KOREAN COMMUNITY

After the surrender, the future of the Koreans in Japan was obviously precarious. Some Koreans felt the need for an organization that could provide guidance. One result was the creation of a Committee for Korean Community Affairs on 18 August 1945 in Suginami-Ku, Tokyo. Its primary purposes were to minimize possible ethnic uneasiness, to negotiate with the Japanese authorities or SCAP over the repatriation arrangements, and to promote the well-being of the Koreans in Japan. Many other small groups had mushroomed for similar purposes, and on 10 September 1945 they joined together and formed the Korean Association in Japan.

At this time, the situation in Korea was changing rapidly. On 22 August Russian troops had marched into P'yŏngyang in northern Korea, and the Japanese governor-general of Korea had abdicated. It appeared that the independence of Korea was imminent. To establish close cooperation with both a new Korean government and authorities in Japan during the transition period, some expatriate Koreans felt the need for an organization that would represent all of them. A preparatory committee was set up under the auspices of the Korean Association in Japan, with the leadership shared by Cho Dŭk-song, a former Christian minister, Kwŏn Il, a pro-Japanese official, and Kim Chŏng-hong, who had been briefly associated with a Korean communist movement. None of them seems to have used his committee position to further his own political ideology, but each had a unique background and reputation that enabled the committee as a whole to appeal to practically all factions of the Korean population in Japan. A large-scale campaign was begun to organize local chapters. Soon the leaders managed to assemble about 5,000 delegates from all over Japan to open a national meeting at Hibiya Public Hall on 15 October 1945. A proposal to found the Chaeil Chosŏnnin Ryŏnmeng, or Choryŏn was unanimously adopted at the meeting. When the Choryŏn was founded, it was designed to be a nonpolitical organization representing the Koreans in Japan. To accomplish these ends, the Choryŏn collaborated very closely with the Japanese authorities and later with SCAP. The presence of the Choryŏn during these first few critical months was largely responsible for the moderation of ethnic tension and a more orderly repatriation program.[17] The Choryŏn, however, could not long remain merely a social service organization. It could scarcely resist being sucked into a vortex of revolutionary agitation already put into motion by other groups such as the Japanese Communist party (JCP). Several events may have led to this transformation.

As early as September 1945, the "Political Prisoner Release League," organized by the left-wing Koreans, had attempted on various occasions to negotiate with the prime minister, Prince Higashikuni, to secure the release of Korean political prisoners. At first, the Japanese government was reluctant to admit that there were any political prisoners. Their existence became public, however, after a few American and French journalists visited Tokyo Fuchū Prison and reported the miserable conditions in the solitary confinement block, where Communist leaders were being held incommunicado.[18] Following a SCAP directive, in October 1945, all political prisoners were set free.[19]

One of these political prisoners was the Korean Kim Ch'ŏn-hae (Kim Tenkai in Japanese), who had been imprisoned for seventeen years for alleged communist activities.[20] When he walked out of the Tokyo Fuchū Prison on 10 October together with Tokuda Kyūichi, Shiga Yoshio, and thirteen other Japanese Communist leaders, a throng was waiting to greet him. The Prisoner Release League was there with its members. According to an eyewitness account, a crowd of several hundred, mostly Koreans, waved red flags with "flaming enthusiasm." Most noteworthy was the fact that only "twenty or thirty" Japanese were there to greet the Japanese Communist leaders.[21] It was also the Koreans who played a leading role when a welcoming rally for the prisoners was held afterward at the Hikō Kaikan Hall.

The first public statement representing all the political prisoners was prepared by Tokuda Kyūichi and Shiga Yoshio. They hailed the Allied Powers as a force "liberating the world from fascism and militarism" and declared that there would be a new era for "democratic revolution" in Japan with the overthrow of "the Emperor system," thereby creating a "People's Republic."[22] They also set forth what they considered the future party line.[23] During the following few weeks they devoted their entire effort to planning for the reconstruction of the party and recruiting party members. Soon they organized the "JCP Reconstruction Committee," and Kim Ch'ŏn-hae, a committee member, was later credited with reshaping the nature of Korean political activities in Japan.[24]

In the eyes of many Koreans, Kim Ch'ŏn-hae, whose credentials included his seventeen-year imprisonment in the cause of Korean liberation, was an undisputed national leader, and it was appropriate to invite a nationalist hero to speak. When the Korean delegates from all over Japan were assembled at Hibiya Public Hall to organize the Choryŏn on 15 October 1945, the audience was thrilled and overwhelmed by his speech. Although it was not an active official position, he was immediately installed as a "supreme advisor" of the Choryŏn. As a leading member of the JCP's central executive committee, he used his interlocking positions to divert the Choryŏn into becoming a peripheral organization of the JCP. It is worth

noting, when the JCP leaders were released from prison, the JCP as an organization was structurally nonexistent. Its only adherents were less than
three hundred hardcore members, all of whom were held in prison.[25] The
role played by Kim Ch'ŏn-hae in utilizing the Choryŏn's organization and
financial resources to support the JCP was by no means a negligible contri-
bution to the postwar JCP reorganization.

It did not take long for the Choryŏn to come under the complete control of the Left. Those who refused to go along with the radical shift in its
policy were expelled. The left-wing Koreans charged that the moderate
Choryŏn leadership was saturated with pro-Japanese elements, whom they
branded as "traitors" and "war criminals," as they had actively collaborated
with the "Japanese fascists and militarists" in their war efforts.

From its inception the activities of the Choryŏn were wide ranging,
covering almost all spheres of life. Its services included not only an education program to de-Japanize Koreans but also welfare programs for the
needy. To carry out these many programs, the Choryŏn benefited from a
variety of funds from unexpected sources. First, it was able to secure from
Korean repatriates donations of possessions that they could not take with
them because of the financial and baggage restrictions imposed by SCAP.
Included in these were bank savings, war bonds, and other negotiable financial documents. Second, other funds were derived from powers of attorney
delegated by repatriates to the Choryŏn, to claim on their behalf back pay,
compensations, and other benefits that former employers had been unable
to pay before repatriation. The third source was from the reimbursement
paid by the Japanese government to the Choryŏn on behalf of those repatriated at their own expense.[26]

In the early period of the occupation, the Japanese government was
uncertain of the scope of its legal jurisdiction over the Koreans in Japan
because of the unclear nature of SCAP directives. SCAP, in the absence of
any specific guidance from Washington, simply assumed that all Koreans
would eventually be repatriated to their homeland. Hence, it did not bother
to establish any agency to deal with Korean affairs but instead left matters
up to the Japanese authorities.

Meanwhile, the prevailing attitude among Koreans at the time was
that they were "liberated" nationals, whereas the Japanese were conquered
nationals subject to the Allied Powers. This notion was apparently derived
from the Joint Chiefs of Staff directive to General Douglas MacArthur that
Koreans were to be treated as "liberated" nationals if military security were
not involved, as "enemy" nationals "in case of necessity," since they had
been Japanese subjects.[27] A lack of any further clarification, however, as to
when the Koreans should be treated as "liberated" and when as "enemy"
nationals seemed to have caused both Korean and Japanese authorities to
misconstrue the extent of their legal jurisdiction. The Koreans in Japan believed, therefore, that they were entitled to different treatment from the

defeated Japanese. Such notions in some instances led to outlawry and the frequent tendency to claim preposterous legal rights in Japan. In some isolated incidents, Koreans refused to subject themselves to the jurisdiction of the Japanese authorities.[28] The arrogant attitude displayed by some of these "liberated" people derived from their deep contempt for the now-defeated Japanese, which added fuel to the already heated anti-Korean sentiment among many Japanese.

The Japanese policy was rarely conciliatory in dealing with postwar Korean problems. Rather, the Japanese authorities were reluctant if not negligent in providing services to which Koreans were fully entitled. In many instances, Japanese authorities circumvented or evaded "the spirit" of SCAP directives.[29] SCAP also noted that Japanese authorities often purposely delayed the pay of soldiers of Korean descent, although they promptly paid Japanese soldiers.[30] In one instance, a strongly worded SCAP directive was needed to secure the release of a Korean political prisoner being held in Abashiri Prison in Hokkaido.[31] The Japanese government, distorting the spirit of SCAP, commuted the sentence of some Korean criminals as a condition of repatriation and deported them against their will. Under the pretext of implementing the SCAP directive to curtail illegal reentry of Koreans into Japan, police surveillance over Koreans intensified, and they were often subjected to "unreasonable search and seizure."[32] With an increasing number of Koreans wishing to remain in Japan rather than be repatriated, their means of livelihood in Japan became a critical problem. The chances of employment for the Koreans were very slim in the war-torn country, where the unemployment rate was high even among Japanese. Unlike unemployed Japanese, Koreans were not eligible for welfare. Koreans who did hold jobs were thrown out of them in favor of Japanese. Many Koreans became street vendors and engaged in illegal transactions, as did many Japanese. The SCAP authorities were prompted to bring this situation to the attention of the Japanese government, but to no avail.[33]

Under these conditions of despair, hunger, and confusion, the first organized mass rally sponsored by the Choryŏn took place at Hibiya Park on 28 December 1945. Several thousand Koreans gathered to express grievances to and make demands on the Japanese authorities. Their demands were:

1. A full assurance by the Japanese government to guarantee the protection of Koreans' property and their personal safety in Japan.

2. Prompt payment of back wages and allowances for conscripted laborers, including any death disability benefits due.

3. Prosecution of officials responsible for the Korean massacre during the Kantō earthquake of 1923 and proper compensation to those who suffered injuries.

4. Dismemberment of the Kōseikai (see chap. 2) and transfer of its property to the Choryŏn.

5. Permission for the Choryŏn to take over the office of the Japanese governor-general of Korea in Tokyo.

6. An increase in food rations.[34]

After the rally, the Koreans demonstrated in front of the Home Affairs ministry, and a few Korean representatives managed to get into a ministry building to present their demands in person. Almost all the demands were met after a long, persistent talk with Home Affairs Minister Horikiri Zenjirō. As far as the Choryŏn was concerned, the rally was successful in displaying the Choryŏn's strength to negotiate directly with the Japanese authorities. Although Korean suffrage in Japan had recently been suspended,[35] the door seemed wide open for the Choryŏn to plunge into Japanese politics.

Despite the fact that the Koreans were not then considered to have the right to political participation, the rationale for getting Koreans involved in Japanese politics was expounded by Kim Tu-yong, a leading Korean Communist in Japan. In the first postwar issue of *Zen-ei*, the JCP's theoretical journal, he outlined specific issues confronting Koreans in Japan: (1) repatriation; (2) ethnic prejudice; (3) the attempt by the Japanese government to disrupt formation of a united front; and (4) the need to take political action.[36] He reasoned that the early "spontaneous mass exodus" had been ample demonstration of the Koreans' desire to escape from their miserable life in Japan, a desire prompted by the fear of retaliation by Japanese for the brutal treatment of Japanese in Korea after the war.

Despite these reasons for desiring immediate repatriation, Koreans failed to realize, Kim Tu-yong stated, that "our homeland is not yet ready to accommodate us, nor are conditions favorable for our return home." Until that time came, he advised Koreans to remain in Japan. Most of the frictions and disputes between Japanese and Koreans were aroused by racism or perhaps by a lack of understanding between the two peoples. This gap had been skillfully exploited by the "Japanese imperialists" to keep the two peoples apart, thereby deliberately frustrating the Koreans' efforts to cooperate with the "Japanese mass" to bring about a "democratic revolution" in Japan. The demonstration of 27 December may have appeared successful in expressing the Koreans' grievances and demands, but Kim Tu-yong argued, "We must be aware that the fundamental problems of our life in Japan can hardly be expected to improve in this manner." The Japanese policy—the "Go home, if you don't like it" attitude—would never be changed under the Imperial system. "As we have elected to remain in Japan, deprived of suffrage, and with all other adverse conditions, our life and safety can never be assured by our struggle alone." Rather, he urged the

Koreans to form a united front with the Japanese proletariat for the common goal of achieving a "democratic revolution" and establishing a "People's Republic" in Japan.[37]

A similar call for political action appeared in the Choryŏn's monthly journal, *Minshu Chōsen*, under the title of, "The Choryŏn and Its Posture Toward Japan."[38] Im Hun, representing the Choryŏn's viewpoint, declared, "We think the resurgence of the reactionary fascists in Japan no longer remains the concern of only the Japanese people. The matter is of grave concern for everyone," as the remnants of the imperial fascists threaten to endanger "the liberty and world peace" that had just been won by the Allied Powers. "We hold a joint responsibility to overthrow the reactionary forces that stand against democratic revolution in Japan."[39]

An almost identical inflammatory theme was echoed by the JCP in one of seven pamphlets in the JCP's "People's Liberation" series of March 1946 entitled "To Korean Brethren."[40] The pamphlet contained a lengthy presentation of how *zaibatsu* and "military fascists" had mercilessly exploited the Korean workers for their own selfish ends. The JCP not only had championed the principle of racial equality but also had advocated "the liberation of Korea" from the yoke of the "Japanese imperialists." Now that the war had ended, the JCP's pamphlet asked, "What is the Japanese government still doing to you?"[41] It had deprived the Koreans of suffrage in Japan, and it was reluctant to allow even a subsistence level of living for them. It was constantly slandering the Choryŏn's efforts on behalf of the Koreans and deliberately undermining SCAP's image of Koreans, so that SCAP refused to recognize the Choryŏn as the sole representative body of Koreans in Japan.[42]

The Japanese officials may have appeared to listen to the Koreans' grievances and demands in the 27 December demonstration; however, this was merely an expedient face-saving device, the pamphlet said. The system itself was a bottleneck; so long as the emperor system existed, a better life for Koreans would never be obtained. The emperor system was the common enemy; through this medium "the Japanese imperialists" persistently suppressed and exploited both the Korean workers and the Japanese people. To bring about a better society for all, "We, with the Korean Communist comrades, the gallant champions of liberation," fought together well against the common enemy. "It must be remembered that the JCP was then the only ally of the Korean people. The JCP stands for the same goals as it has in the past and will in the future."[43] The writer concluded, "The JCP sincerely hopes that all of you will participate in the Democratic Liberation Front under the JCP's banner and cooperate in the task of overthrowing the Emperor system to establish a People's Republic."[44]

The appeals made by Kim and the JCP had a profound impact upon the majority of the Koreans in Japan, especially upon those whose sense of deprivation and frustration was compounded by their having to remain in a country where they were not welcome. Widespread anti-Korean feeling was openly rekindled by Japanese officials and the mass media. Their charges were directed at black-market activities, smuggling, and illegal Korean re-entry into Japan. In an editorial dated 13 July 1946, the *Tokyo Mainichi* openly expressed the general Japanese dislike of Koreans. Similar cries were heard from all quarters and reached "slanderous proportions," according to Western observers.[45] Shiikuma Saburō, a Progressive party member of the House of Representatives from Hokkaido, made the most inflammatory statement of all. In his speech in the House plenary meeting of 17 August 1946, he blamed Koreans and Taiwanese for the entire postwar black-market operation and the "unspeakable violence" that endangered every aspect of Japanese economic and social life. Consequently, he charged, "one-third of the new yen, amounting to over 50 billion yen, might be in their hands through these illegal transactions." He continued, "Gentlemen, these acts, committed by those Koreans and Taiwanese, which we can hardly bear to watch, make us, who have gone through all ordeals of the defeat, feel as if our blood flows the wrong way."[46]

This prompted the Choryŏn to protest vigorously not only to the Speaker of the House, Yamazaki Takeshi, but also to the Progressive party leadership, demanding an apology and the expulsion of Shiikuma Saburo from the House.[47] Such verbal attacks made the Koreans more receptive to the JCP's call for action.

REACTION TO THE LEFT: MINDAN

As the Choryŏn moved to the left, the presence of dissidents was no longer tolerated. Many labeled as dissidents either were expelled or volun-tarily withdrew from the organization, their major contention being that the focus on "democratic revolution" and the "overthrow of the Emperor system" were not the proper concerns of Koreans in Japan. Rather, they contended, the Choryŏn should concern itself with the promotion of Korean welfare in Japan and the establishment of a Korean government at home.

To counter the Choryŏn's left-leaning tendency, some young dissi-dents from the Choryŏn and other anticommunist groups united on 16 No-vember 1945 to form a rival organization called Chosŏn Kŏnguk Ch'okchin Ch'ŏngnyŏn Dongmeng or Kŏnch'ŏng (Youth League to Expedite the Foun-dation of Korea). The Choryŏn, which had once boasted of being the sole representative body of all Koreans in Japan, began to lose stature. Only a few months after the Choryŏn was officially activated, a fatal division among the Koreans in Japan had occurred. The Kŏnch'ŏng, organized somewhat hastily, was limited in membership to those under the age of thirty, while those over thirty were admitted as supporting members. Thus Kŏnch'ŏng soon became a right-wing youth organization, concentrating its main effort on the destruction of the Choryŏn. Physical violence and terror between members of the two rival organizations became a daily occurrence.

Meanwhile, Pak Yŏl, a political prisoner for twenty-three years, was belatedly released from Akita Prison on 27 December 1945. Pak Yŏl, deeply influenced by a Japanese anarchist, Ōsugi Sakae, had organized the Kokutō-kai (Black Wave Society) in 1922 to lead the Korean anarchist movement in Japan. Later he had been arrested on a charge of plotting to assassinate Prince Hirohito (later emperor) and had received a life sentence.[48] The day he was set free, a huge welcoming rally was held at Hibiya Public Hall, sponsored by the Choryŏn. Acclaimed as a great hero, Pak Yŏl was even more widely known among Koreans than was Kim Ch'ŏn-hae, because of the publicity he had received during his trial in the 1920s. Apparently, Pak Yŏl believed that he was being invited to head the Choryŏn. He thought himself most qualified by virtue of his twenty-three years in prison, assuming that the longer the term one had as a political prisoner, the more prestige one had as a leader.[49]

Pak Yŏl soon realized, however, contrary to his expectations, that the leadership of the Choryŏn was already firmly in the hands of Kim Ch'ŏn-hae's group. His sense of disappointment was well exploited by some anticommunists and other moderate elements in the Kŏnch'ŏng, who asked Pak Yŏl to form another Korean organization under the banner of anticommunism to rival the Choryŏn. Shinchosŏn Kŏnsŏl Dongmeng or Kŏndong (League for the Establishment of a New Korea) was founded on 2 January 1946. In six months, three Korean organizations had come into existence, all declaring the same purpose: to represent the interests of the Koreans in Japan.

In addition to the ideological divisions of Koreans in Japan, other divisive forces were at work on the international scene. The Soviet Union and the United States were occupying separate zones in Korea but had failed to negotiate any definite plan for the future of Korea as a unified nation. To resolve the difficulty, the foreign ministers of the United States and the Soviet Union met in Moscow in December 1945. They reached a tentative agreement, in which Nationalist China joined afterward, whereby a Russo-American joint commission would be set up with a four-power trusteeship for a period of up to five years.[50] When news of the Moscow Agreement reached Korea, the reaction was polarization. Right-wing Koreans denounced the agreement on the basis that trusteeship was too similar to the Japanese rule from which they had just emerged. Instead, they demanded an "unconditional" and "immediate" independence for Korea.

The left-wing group, conversely, hailed the agreement as a true embodiment of the cooperative spirit of the victorious Allied Powers.[51] They argued that the pro-Japanese elements, traitors and fascists who had collaborated actively as the "running dogs" of the Japanese imperialists, were still prevalent everywhere in Korea. The true objective of the Moscow

Agreement was, they stated, to eradicate all "poisonous" remnants of the Japanese imperialistic heritage and its system, which were deeply rooted in Korean society. Korean national culture and economic growth had been seriously impaired and retarded by these elements. "We must reconstruct our homeland," they proclaimed. To these ends, the four-power agreement promised to provide not only technical assistance but also education for the development of true democracy in Korea. Those who opposed the trusteeship were the remaining fascists and traitors who had tried to disrupt the creation of the National Unification Front by engineering dissension between the United States and the Soviet Union over Korea.

The dispute surrounding the Moscow Agreement was also intense in the Korean community in Japan. On 28 February 1946 the Choryŏn called an emergency meeting to decide on its position concerning the Moscow Agreement. After two days of fierce debate and even physical violence, the Choryŏn unanimously passed a resolution to support the Moscow Agreement. The Kŏndong and the Kŏnch'ŏng declared opposition to the agreement. The division between the two sides became intensified when the Soviet-American Joint Commission was dissolved. Moscow issued a statement through *Izvestia* accusing the American delegates of supporting the idea of the trusteeship, which, the party organ declared, violated the spirit of the Moscow Agreement. But the underlying reason for the failure of the Joint Commission was the clash of opposing powers; the Soviet Union was determined to create a Korean government favorable to its interests and so was the United States. The dissolution of the Joint Commission made it clear that the division of Korea into North and South was irreparable. So also was the rift in the Korean community in Japan.

Nevertheless, the Choryŏn dominated the Korean community until it was forced to disband by order of the Japanese government in September 1949, on the charge of being a terrorist organization.[52] Even on a limited scale the Choryŏn had been able to institute educational and welfare programs for the Koreans. The Kŏndong and the Kŏnch'ŏng were as yet solely political, anti-Communist in orientation but devoid of any substantial social program to gain the support of the Koreans in Japan. The anti-Communists did, however, send delegates to study the situation in Korea, who ruled out the feasibility of more Koreans returning to their homeland because of deteriorating social and economic conditions there. The delegates proposed instead the formation of an autonomous organization under the banner of anticommunism, with massive programs to help and to protect the livelihood of the Koreans in Japan. As a consequence, on 3 October 1946 the Kŏndong members dissolved their organization and formed a new organization called Chaeil Han'guk'in Kŏryumindan or Mindan (Korean Resident Association in Japan). Pak Yŏl was unanimously voted head of the new Mindan, which had thirteen local branches throughout Japan. The new organization declared in unequivocal terms that "it will not be a political organization; neither does it intend to affiliate with, nor support on an ideological basis, any political institution in the homeland or abroad." Also, it outlined the Mindan's aims: "To help secure legitimate professions, food, and housing" for needy Koreans.[53]

A few days later, the Mindan issued an "Appeal to the Japanese People," asking for deep understanding and close cooperation to achieve its goals. It stated:

> We, Korean compatriots, have risen up for the founding of a nation. Although we have been obliged to you so long, we have risen, not as Japanese subjects but as your friendly Korean nationals. In retrospect, our two races have been deeply entangled with a cause and effect relationship. Because of it, there have been many unpleasant incidents since the war. We deeply regret it.
>
> We do not intend to demand anything from those of you who are suffering from the bitter misery of defeat. Rather, we should like to ask you to correct your misconceptions, wrongfully molded by the militarists and imperialists, concerning the Koreans, other foreigners, and your outlook on the universe. In other words, please abandon the notion that Japan and its people are the center of the whole universe. . . .
>
> If you had been in our shoes for thirty-six years, you would feel the same way. We fall into sadness when we take a look at our dilapidated homeland. When the Japanese people were contemptuous of us, ill treated us, repressed us, and persecuted us, we do not know how many times we clenched our teeth and shed our tears. . . .
>
> The Japanese people not only took our farmland away from us but forced us to drift from the native land, being deprived of economic means. Subsequently, as you have seen, several million [Korean] laborers were thrown into the Japanese labor market. . . .
>
> Despite many other things which made us hold ill feelings [against Japan], now we are obliged not to return home but to live here for a variety of reasons.
>
> We are willing to drain our bitter memory away in water. From now on let us join hands with the Japanese people for mutual prosperity and coexistence. . . .
>
> We have thereby organized a resident association to make an all-out effort to resolve the problems of our fellow countrymen in Japan.
>
> We sincerely hope that you will extend to us your understanding, cooperation, and support.[54]

The Mindan's statement outlining the future policy was conciliatory and moderate in tone. A similar appeal was later made personally by Pak Yŏl, asking the Japanese people to be more sympathetic and generous in dealing with the problems of Koreans in Japan.[55] At the same time, he cautioned the Koreans that it would be unwise for them to hold hostile feelings or the desire to retaliate against the Japanese people. The *ancien regime* under the imperialists, he said, was "our enemy." He continued, "As Japan shows regret for her wrongdoing by abandoning the imperialist design of the past, and endeavors to tread the path of justice in the future, we must extend our sincere congratulations." Furthermore, he said the two countries were interdependent in every respect. Present industries in Korea were based on Japanese techniques and machineries. If Koreans rejected them, he stated, future industrial growth in Korea would be in jeopardy. Therefore, he urged the Koreans to promote a cordial relationship with the Japanese, because the two groups needed each other's help to build up their countries after the ravages of the war.[56]

Despite these positive beginnings, the Mindan's performance under Pak Yŏl's leadership in practice proved contrary to what it had purported to do for the Koreans in Japan. Although Pak Yŏl's presence might have given the impetus for a new, separate, and rival organization, he failed to provide convincing reasons for the majority of the Koreans as to why they should abandon the Choryŏn. The Choryŏn already had a nationwide organization with good financial backing and programs directed toward the welfare of Koreans in Japan. Only later did it become apparent that, under the cloak of anticommunism and a pro-Japanese government, the Mindan's aim was to destroy the rival Choryŏn and to capture hegemony over all Koreans.

To accomplish his own personal goals, Pak Yŏl, with the aid of his supporters, launched a propaganda campaign to erase his anarchist image and tried to disassociate himself from his old colleagues. Several pamphlets and books were published to idealize him as a great patriotic nationalist who had led the struggle for an independent Korea.[57]

In a rare show of unity, the Mindan members agreed in their unanimous choice of Pak Yŏl as leader. The Mindan was a loose conglomeration, divided on the basis of personal ties, regional origins, and individualistic motives. Constant factional discord and a series of scandals were to follow, seriously impairing the Mindan's activities during the most critical postwar period. After the establishment of the South Korean Interim Government under American auspices in January 1947, Pak Yŏl began to set his eyes on the home country to fulfill his political ambitions. For him, the Mindan was a springboard from which he hoped to vault into prominence in Korea itself.[58] Often threatening to resign as a means of whipping up the loyalty of his supporters, he called special national conventions six times during his two-and-one-half years of leadership.[59] He was able to manipulate various factions by playing off one against the other, but he fell from power in April 1949.[60]

The Mindan's financial base was unsteady because it depended mainly upon black-market activities.[61] When such transactions became less and less possible with increasingly stringent control by the Japanese police, Pak Yŏl appointed a wealthy Korean to be his financial deputy. It soon became the practice to draft wealthy businessmen into important positions in the Mindan as a means of raising funds. The results were questionable, however, as each wanted to utilize the organization as a tool for furthering his own business enterprises. The Mindan resorted to every conceivable means to raise funds. For instance, when the South Korean National Assembly passed the "Overseas Korean National Registration Law" in November 1949, the official Korean mission in Japan delegated some of its administrative work to the Mindan to expedite the registration process of the Koreans. Bitter complaints were heard, however, when the Mindan charged exorbitant fees for the registration on the pretext that the funds would be used to finance future Mindan activities.[62] Consequently, the Mindan in the first few years of existence lost its good name and was never able to win general confidence among the Koreans in Japan. The Mindan gained support neither from SCAP nor from the Japanese government, despite its attempt to appeal on anticommunist grounds. Throughout the American occupation it was predominantly the Choryŏn that continued to be the voice of the majority of Koreans.

4

KOREANS UNDER SCAP:
An Era of Unrest and Repression

Changsoo Lee

Aside from ideological affinity, the desire for cooperation between the Japanese Communist party and the Choryŏn stemmed from practical needs. The most urgent task faced by the postwar JCP was the need to rebuild a party organization that had been shattered completely by the mass arrests in the early 1930s. Seeking support from all conceivable sources, the JCP saw the Choryŏn as a means to broaden its mass base throughout Japan. The Choryŏn, conversely, sought the JCP's backing of its role as spokesman for the oppressed and underprivileged Korean minority. The JCP was able to exert its influence over the Choryŏn through Kim Ch'ŏn-hae's interlocking positions in both the JCP and the Choryŏn. Judging from available evidence, however, the reverse did not happen in the JCP. The scope of Kim's influence within the Central Committee of the JCP seems to have been limited to matters immediately concerning Koreans.[1] It appears that he was installed in the Central Committee so that the JCP could gain Korean members through an alliance with the Choryŏn. In early 1946 Kim began to tour the Korean ghettos in Japan to deliver speeches. At the end of each speech he usually handed out application forms to the audience, exhorting them to join both the JCP and Choryŏn. His eloquence was instrumental in recruiting a substantial number of Koreans as rank-and-file members of the JCP, who were later to be called "Kim's JCP members."

Fraternal solidarity between the Japanese and Korean Communists in Japan was not a new development but had historical roots. In the September 1922 issue of *Zen-ei*, the Japanese Communists had stressed the need for "unity of the Japanese and Korean workers" in their struggle against the "Japanese imperialists and militarists." By 1931 the Japanese Bureau of the Korean Communist party had dissolved as a separate entity and had merged with the JCP.[2] As a demonstration of solidarity, the JCP in 1931 and 1932 adopted as its rallying cry the fight for the liberation and independence of Korea, and subsequently established a "minority section" in every local Communist party committee to accept Korean members.[3]

Although the JCP recruited Korean members, it had little faith in them, always treating them with extreme caution. They were never given any responsible positions in the party hierarchy. According to Japanese police records found later, the JCP was said to have characterized its Korean members as "brutish," "treacherous," and "unprincipled" people of low intellectual sophistication.[4] In comparison with Japanese members, however, it was reported that Koreans tended to possess traits of "daring" and "persistence" once a mission was assigned them; they therefore were best suited to serve as agitators in front-line activities. In view of these expressed prewar views, it was a radical departure for the JCP to elect Kim Ch'ŏn-hae to its Central Committee after the war.

The JCP's initial postwar plan was set forth during its Fourth Party Congress in December 1945. The plenary report indicated a continuity with the tactical line of 1932. Two major themes loomed large: the overthrow of the emperor system and the carrying out of a democratic revolution. These extreme goals, however, were modified by Nosaka Sanzō after his return from exile in Yenan in January 1946. Under his direction, the JCP's strategy and tactics were given a new direction designed to make the party "loved by the Japanese people" by softening its overtly militant posture.

In a joint statement issued by Nosaka and the Central Committee in January 1946, they agreed on the need for abolishing the emperor system. They made a distinction, however, between the emperor as a political institution and the members of the imperial household itself. The overthrow of the emperor system, they stated, referred to the destruction of the monarchy as a political institution; the question of retaining the imperial household should be determined by the Japanese people.[5] This theme was elaborated during the Fifth Party Congress held in February 1946, whose Manifesto declared that the party's immediate objective was "to complete bourgeois democratic revolution by peaceful and democratic means."[6] To relieve any misgivings, Nosaka clarified that "peaceful means" did not mean passivity but refraining from overt violence, such as armed uprising, to capture power. "The Communist party is a revolutionary party," he said. "We have great obstacles and many enemies we must crush. We must be militant to the last degree." To effect the peaceful revolution, Nosaka advocated the unity of all political forces as a "democratic front."[7]

On this basis, the Choryŏn found common ground on which to form a united front with the JCP. Such a front, according to the JCP's scheme, did not require a complete uniformity of views; each group was allowed to develop its own position freely. The task delegated to the Choryŏn was to act as a "vanguard unit," serving to democratize not only Japan but also all other Asian nations.[8] Thus the stage was set for joint action in the early spring of 1946.

This period was marked by continued unrest in Japan, resulting from food shortages and increasing unemployment. Tokyo was plagued by a series of massive demonstrations that placed the blame on the Shidehara

Cabinet. The first was called "the People's Rally to Overthrow the Reactionary Shidehara Cabinet," and it was composed of a loose coalition of left-wing groups, the Choryon supplying 20,000 of the 70,000 people assembled. They made a five-point demand that included a resolution asking for the cabinet's resignation. Later they marched to Shidehara's official residence to present their demands, but they were met by three hundred policemen. In the resulting confrontation several persons were seriously injured. It was the most violent disorder experienced in Japan since the war had ended. Several other demonstrations soon followed, prompting General MacArthur to issue a stern warning on 20 May 1946 that while "every possible rational freedom of the democratic method has been permitted, the physical violence which undisciplined elements are now beginning to practice will not be permitted to continue."[9]

To further control unruly Koreans, SCAP decreed that the legal authority to be exercised by Japanese courts should continue to include jurisdiction over Koreans remaining in Japan, and that the Japanese government would be held responsible for the preservation of law and order, including the control of violent acts committed by Koreans.[10] Once the question of jurisdiction over the Koreans became clear, the Japanese authorities wasted no time in exercising strict control.

Despite more stringent law enforcement, there was no decline in violence. There was an admittedly high rate of illegal activities and acts of aggression on the part of Koreans, who felt liberated and therefore able to express pent-up animosities toward those they considered their oppressors. According to a report published by the Japanese police, there were 128 "violent acts" perpetrated by Koreans by the end of 1945. But the reported frequency increased to 5,336 in 1946, and to 5,681 in the following year.[11] This reported increase of violence and unlawful acts appears to have given the Japanese police sufficient excuse to resort again to the systematic intimidation of all Koreans, as had occurred in the prewar period. Subsequently, Koreans became frequent subjects of unreasonable search and seizure against which they had little defense. Long-held prejudices on the part of the Japanese were again overtly expressed. For example, during an anticrime campaign conducted by the police, a Korean emblem was used as background in posters illustrating a clutching hand reaching out to rob a cringing Japanese woman.[12]

Eventually police harassment of Koreans became so pronounced that Koreans of all political orientations united and organized a Committee for Protection of Korean Rights.[13] The committee issued a statement listing fifteen violent and brutal acts committed against Koreans, mostly by police. An equally serious charge was that the police and government officials were responsible for the death from starvation and lack of medical attention of 272 Korean repatriates between 23 June and 15 September 1946 at the embarkation camp at Sasebo Naval Base in southwestern Japan.

Fig. 1. This Japanese poster, distributed by the Tokyo Ueno Police Station and supported by the Ueno Association of Anti-Crime and Security, appeared all over the downtown area of Tokyo in 1947. It warns the householder to beware of dangerous robbers. With the Korean flag symbol as its central motif, it implies that Koreans are the likely criminals.

PROTEST MOVEMENT OVER LEGAL STATUS, TAXATION AND EDUCATION

In the early days of the American occupation, SCAP made no ruling on the legal status of Koreans in Japan, apparently in the belief that all Koreans would soon be repatriated. But the ambiguous nature of the SCAP policy in treating the Koreans as either "liberated nationals" or "enemy subjects," caused confusion and misunderstanding both for Japanese authorities and for Koreans. The intended implication of the term *liberated nationals* appears to have been merely a means for SCAP to make some distinction between the Japanese and colonial subjects of Japan such as Koreans and Taiwanese. Obviously SCAP never intended to classify the "liberated nationals" in the same category as the privileged United Nations nationals in the occupied country. When SCAP defined the status of the United Nations personnel, neutral nationals, and enemy nationals, Koreans were not even mentioned as nationals of "nations whose status has changed as a result of the war."[14] When special supplementary rations were distributed to most foreign nationals in Japan, Koreans were not included. The SCAP directive of 8 January 1948 on rationing specifically stated that "nothing in this directive will be construed to change the food ration for Korean nationals who have elected to remain in Japan, and who receive the same ration as Japanese nationals."[15] Furthermore, SCAP noted that legal jurisdiction over Koreans was to continue to be exercised by the Japanese authorities. In short, SCAP intended to lump the remaining Koreans legally together with the Japanese without any clear indication of a special future status for Koreans in Japan.

When SCAP made it known in a press release that Koreans who elected to remain in Japan would be considered as Japanese nationals until they were recognized as Korean nationals by a lawfully established government in Korea, the statement became a target for the vigorous protest of Koreans, who felt that it was intended to prolong their enslavement under Japanese rule. "We had suffered enough," they cried, demanding that Koreans should receive different treatment from that accorded to "defeated" nationals. The charge prompted SCAP to make a further clarification on 20 November 1946, stating that it had "no intention of interfering in any way with the fundamental rights of any person of any nationality in regard to retention, relinquishment, or choice of citizenship."[16] Thus for the most part, the question of the legal status of Koreans in Japan was left to the discretion of the Japanese government under the policy outlined by SCAP (see chap. 7).

Rather than giving citizenship to the remaining Koreans, the Japanese government late in 1946 legally classified them as aliens under the Alien Registration Act, and subsequently disenfranchised them from participating in the political process. But when the Ministry of Justice supplied a legal interpretation in April 1952, it stated that the Koreans in Japan would continue to hold Japanese nationality until the Peace Treaty came into force later in 1952.[17] In other words, the Japanese government would regard the Koreans in Japan as retaining Japanese nationality in principle until the official termination of the war. But for all other practical purposes, Koreans were treated as aliens, though still subject to Japanese laws.

Notwithstanding the legal technicalities, the Koreans generally refused to recognize the applicability of Japanese laws, especially some concerning specific taxation. This was illustrated when the Japanese government promulgated the Capital Levy Tax Law, to go into effect on 1 April 1947. This law created a highly progressive property tax applicable to individual assets "valued in excess of 100,000 yen" and retroactive to March 1946. The only people exempted from the tax were United Nations nationals and military.

Although very few Koreans possessed sufficient wealth to be subject to the law, the Korean community as a whole objected to it, not so much on the basis of legal principle as on moral grounds. They argued that such heavy taxation was to meet the reparations resulting from the war waged and lost by Japanese imperialists, for which no Korean was responsible and for which none should share the consequences. The SCAP policy on taxation had specified in a memorandum that taxation for the purpose of reparation or "charges falling upon the Japanese government as a result of the war" should not be levied by the Japanese government upon property of United Nations nationals who bore no responsibility for the war.[18] Those Koreans who had been exploited by the Japanese for forty years argued that Koreans should be exempt from the levy as were United Nations nationals.

Before the official enactment of the law, the Choryŏn organized a mass rally and presented a petition to the SCAP Commander on 13 December 1946, stating, "We petition you to grant us exemption from laws which are applied to Japanese and not to foreigners. We belong to the latter and can never observe such laws as are connected with payment of reparations." Again in March of the following year, the Choryŏn petitioned General MacArthur, stating that "upon the honor of a liberated race, it is not only unbearable but impossible for us to obey such an unjust and humiliating law."

In further protest against the overall treatment of Koreans by the Japanese government, Choryŏn collaborated with the JCP in a "National Mass Meeting for the Security of Livelihood and Overthrow of the Yoshida Cabinet" on 17 December 1946. Three days later the Committee for the Protection of the Livelihood of Koreans, under the auspices of the Choryŏn, called a rally on the Imperial Palace grounds. About 40,000 Koreans assembled and selected ten representatives to present a resolution to Premier Yoshida. While the demonstrators were marching past the premier's residence, the ten representatives went inside to present the resolution. Violence soon broke out among the marchers, seemingly the result of an exchange of unpleasant remarks with the Japanese police.[19] Soon afterward the ten Korean representatives and several others were arrested on charges of inciting a riot.

Despite the Koreans' plea to have more time to prepare their defense, they were tried within a week after the incident by an American military court and were convicted of inciting a riot. One American observer noted that the proceedings appeared to be "going through the legal motions to arrive at a pre-determined verdict."[20] Later, in March 1947, when American lawyers stationed in Korea had occasion to review the trial record, they commented that "insufficient evidence appears indicating beyond reasonable doubt either several or joint activity constituting incitement to riot" on the part of the ten Koreans accused.[21] It had become evident that whatever the Koreans' problems might have been, SCAP's sympathy no longer rested with them.

Nevertheless, another protest movement erupted with the enactment of the Alien Registration Law in May 1947, an act designed to make all aliens register for purposes of easier administrative control. The registration was undoubtedly aimed at the Koreans, who comprised approximately 93.1 percent of all aliens in Japan at the time.[22]

The law required that all aliens were to be photographed and were to be issued a registration card, which was to be carried at all times. For Koreans, it was all too strongly reminiscent of the prewar period. In addition, of course, the registration process might uncover not only those who had entered Japan illegally but also those who might be purchasing double rations by using the ration cards of repatriated persons. Practically all Koreans united against this law, and voiced the following stipulations:

1. The registration should be based on established international procedure.

2. It should be conducted by Korean organizations such as Mindan and Choryŏn.

3. Koreans should be accorded full and conscientious treatment as foreign nationals.

4. The lives and property of Koreans should be properly safeguarded.

5. The Japanese government should take steps to ensure that the Japanese people know and respect the status of Koreans.[23]

If these conditions were not met, both the Choryŏn and Mindan threatened to boycott the registrations. Consequently, during the month-long registration period, only a few Koreans complied. Finally SCAP felt it necessary to issue a statement ensuring the rights of aliens and clarifying the purpose of the registration. Under the pressure of either persuasion or the threat of punishment, however, Koreans became all the more reluctant to register.

Another issue that had a significant impact upon Koreans was the question of Korean education in Japan. Because they had elected to remain in Japan, many Koreans were concerned with how to dejapanize themselves and their children. They argued that the Japanese colonial policy over the years had been designed to drive the Korean national culture into extinction by depriving Koreans of their language and culture. They believed that they had the fundamental right as "liberated" people to recover their lost language and their cultural identity through their own educational programs. Subsequently, most Korean parents withdrew their children from Japanese schools and sent them to Korean language institutes operated by the Choryŏn.

Later the Choryŏn established a Korean Education Committee that established a number of schools and supervised the overall Choryŏn educational programs, expanding courses to include not only Korean language but history, arithmetic, and science (see chap. 9). Although the educational standards of Choryŏn schools generally fell far short of those of the Japanese school system, the Korean community was content with the programs. In some Choryŏn high schools, a course in Marxist doctrine was offered to indoctrinate students with Communist ideals.

In the early days of the occupation, SCAP took no official cognizance of the proliferating Korean schools. After October 1947, SCAP issued a memorandum stating that Korean educational institutions should comply with the rules and regulations established by the Japanese Ministry of Education. But SCAP also stated that "Korean schools would be permitted to teach the Korean language as an addition to the regular curriculum." Similarly, the Japanese authorities at first apparently had no objections to the Korean educational programs. In some instances, local school authorities permitted part-time use of public classrooms for Korean education, since Koreans were taxpayers.[24]

SCAP reforms of the Japanese educational system also affected the Korean educational programs. The Ministry of Education issued a circular note to all prefectural governors in January 1948, informing them that the new School Education Law would be applicable to Korean schools as well, and consequently Korean schools and their teachers were to be accredited by the prefecture governors.[25] All Korean children were to attend accredited schools that met legal standards. Although the Korean language could be taught as an extracurricular subject, other regular classes were to be conducted in the Japanese language.[26] The Choryŏn vigorously opposed these rulings on the grounds that the basic goal of separate Korean education was preparation of future Korean citizens, and the Japanese educational programs were not suited to these ends.

While the Choryŏn opened negotiations with the Ministry of Education to secure accreditation for Korean schools as private institutions within the framework of the School Education Law, Koreans staged demonstrations in Osaka and Kobe.[27] One of the slogans adopted by the Korean demonstrators was the "right to autonomy in Korean education." In the meantime, the Choryŏn organized a Countermeasure Committee on Korean Education, and made the following four specific demands to the Japanese premier.

1. Class instruction to be given in the Korean language.
2. Use of textbooks compiled by a Korean committee under SCAP approval.
3. Administration of schools by parents and teachers.
4. Teaching of the Japanese language as a required part of the curriculum.[28]

In addition, some members of the Countermeasure Committee paid a visit to the Far Eastern Commission of Allied officers functioning with SCAP to appeal the matter. Finally, in an attempt to gain the American authority's sympathy, Choryŏn schoolchildren petitioned the Commanding General of the 25th Division in Osaka. This petition stated:

> We are Korean primary school boys and girls in Osaka. We wish your valuable consideration so that our teachers, whom we all respect, may freely teach us Korean subjects in our own language, inasmuch as it was your great army that liberated our fellow Korean brothers and sisters from the ruthless Japanese oppression. . . . Please give our teachers freedom so that pupils educated under them will be able to assist in the formation of and maintenance of a strong, unified, independent Korea, able to stand proudly with the rest of the independent, peace-loving nations of the world.[29]

The appeal by the schoolchildren, the demonstrations, and the demands of the Countermeasure Committee on the Premier met with no apparent success. On the contrary, the attitude of the Japanese authorities was firm and uncompromising, ostensibly to lessen the mounting tension concerning the issue. Subsequently, prefectural governors began to enforce the law throughout Japan by ordering the closing of all Korean schools that failed to comply with the law by 15 April. Fierce protests sprang up wherever the Korean schools were located. Among them, the Kobe incident is noteworthy because of the violence that erupted.

On 10 April 1948 the Korean schools in Kobe were ordered closed by the Hyogo prefecture governor. The Choryŏn's Kobe office tried to negotiate with the governor and the mayor of Kobe, asking for special consideration on the question of the Korean education. As the basis of negotiation, the Choryŏn stated that the Korean schools would be ready to comply with the law, provided Koreans were allowed to maintain autonomy in organizing curricula and methods of teaching.[30] For several days, starting on 12 April, while a crowd of several hundred Koreans waited day and night outside the prefectural government building, their negotiators tried in vain to secure an interview with the governor, an interview that was denied on the pretext of the governor's absence.

By 14 April the crowd had grown to several thousand, many of whom decided to sit in the building until the governor would meet with them. The protestors were warned by the Japanese police to clear the building or else be arrested. Violence broke out when the protesters ignored the police order. As a result, sixty-five were arrested and the rest were forcibly expelled from the building. After this, the situation worsened, with increasingly more violent confrontations between the protesters and the police.

On 24 April another crowd of about 500 Koreans and some Japanese sympathizers marched together to the prefectural building and again demanded a meeting with the governor, which was again denied under the subterfuge of the governor's absence. This time, the mob stormed into the governor's office and found him in a meeting with the police chief and mayor of Kobe. The angry mob surrounded the governor's office and held governor, mayor, and police chief hostage for six hours, cutting off all communication with the outside, until the governor was compelled to accept their demands. The proclamation he signed agreed:

1. To rescind the order to close the Korean schools.
2. To postpone the return of the classroom buildings to the Japanese rented by the Korean schools.
3. To release protesters who had been arrested by the police in connection with the school issue.[31]

Having accomplished their objectives, the protesters held a brief, triumphant rally in front of the prefectural building and then dispersed. But things did not settle down as they had anticipated. Later in the evening, the local U.S. military commander belatedly proclaimed a state of "limited emergency" and deputized the Kobe police force to act under the direction of the U.S. marshal. He also instructed the governor to nullify the proclamation he had signed under duress and to reaffirm the original school closure order.

The Japanese police, reinforced by the American military police, set up roadblocks and surrounded the Korean ghettos in Kobe at midnight on 24 April to round up all members of the Chōryŏn. By dawn of 25 April, they had arrested more than 1,600 persons, who were in addition to thè almost 3,000 arrested since the beginning of the month-long dispute. During the nighttime roundup, several hundreds were injured and "property damage ran into millions of yen."[32]

Lieutenant General Robert L. Eichelberger, Commanding General of the Eighth Army, who arrived at Kobe to take charge, deplored the incidents as "uncivilized" mob violence, and said he wished he "had the *Queen Elizabeth* here to ship the whole lot of them [Koreans] to Korea."[33] Later, the thirty Koreans and eight Japanese who had led the protest were indicted on a charge of inciting a riot directed against American occupation policy. The occupation authorities believed that "the prime moving force" behind the incident was the Communist party.

Viewed in the light of postwar JCP strategy and tactics, it was undoubtedly the concerted actions of the JCP and the Chōryŏn members which stepped up Korean demonstrations to such an extreme degree throughout various cities in Japan, climaxing in the monster rally in Kobe to build support for their demands and, by this means, to enlarge their following and enhance their power.

Other violent protests that spread to various cities of Japan were not without success. The Ministry of Education moderated its original posture concerning the school issue and decided to negotiate with the Choryŏn officials in Tokyo. After several days of talks, both sides agreed to sign a memorandum on 3 May 1948, affirming the right of Korean schools to have ethnic studies programs with the provisos that:

1. Korean schools shall comply with the School Education Law and the Fundamental Education Law.

2. Korean schools may apply for accreditation, but may conduct autonomous ethnic studies programs within the scope permitted private school systems.[34]

Viewed in the light of short-term objectives, the violent protests and strong-arm tactics frequently employed by the Choryŏn may have had some effect in helping them obtain their demands from the policymakers. In the long run, however, their just causes had suffered more than benefited from tactics that invited not only repressive measures from the authorities but also self-destruction.

DISSOLUTION OF THE CHORYŎN

A number of factors caused the Koreans to choose militant protest to attain their goals, especially in the early years of the American occupation. Koreans were, in general, intensely frustrated and discontented because they were unable to attain the status they thought they deserved as a "liberated people." Furthermore, their hope for a better life after the war turned out to be a false expectation. Their feelings of past oppression and continued deprivation were skillfully exploited to an extreme degree by the Japanese Communists, who benefited from the animosities aroused by direct confrontation.

Limited by their anomalous legal classification as aliens, Koreans had few options through which to channel their demands to the policymakers. Neither the Koreans nor the Japanese had any available past models of ethnic pluralism which would permit citizenship status without sacrifice of ethnic identity. Koreans who wished to maintain their cultural integrity could not become "Japanese," especially when they had just been liberated from what they considered colonial oppression.

After suffrage was suspended for Koreans, Choryŏn members felt a sense of impotency and helplessness in expressing their interests and needs through legal channels. Hence, at the Fifth National Meeting of the Choryŏn, held on 15 October 1948, one item included in the programs of action was to endeavor to secure voting rights and representation from the Japanese government.[35] Acquisition of suffrage by a Korean in Japan meant legally becoming a Japanese citizen. The Choryŏn's justification for seeking suffrage was not because they wished to extend the concept of citizenship but solely because they saw citizenship as a means to achieve Korean goals.[36]

The Choryŏn's lack of overall effectiveness did not go without criticism. As early as the spring of 1947, Kim Tu-yong pointed out the fragmentation and disunion evidenced in actions taken by members who ignored the Central Committee of the Choryŏn.[37] Since most Koreans had little ideological perspective, Kim felt they did not understand the broad objectives of the Korean movement. Their actions, he wrote, tended to be too spontaneous, generated only by emotional outbursts, as if they were engaged simply in retaliatory activities against the Japanese. This sort of action, he warned, would only cause Koreans to isolate themselves from the Japanese mass. Kim suggested that the "task of Koreans was to create cells to build a mass base." Without such support Koreans would be vulnerable. "As things stand now," Kim cautioned, "we would become victims of reactionary forces."[38] Therefore, he concluded that the particular ethnic problems of Koreans ought to be seen as part of the larger picture of class struggle.[39]

Mass meetings and demonstrations openly advocating the overthrow of the government, inspired by the JCP, were ever on the increase. Without fail, the Choryŏn actively participated in such rallies. After the establishment of the Democratic Peoples Republic of Korea in the fall of 1948, the Choryŏn publicly states its support of the republic, and began to display the North Korean flag on all occasions. But when SCAP issued a ban on the display of the North Korean flag in public, the Choryŏn waged another protest, without apparent success.[40] The Choryŏn's persistent display of the flag, and the strict enforcement of the ban by the Japanese police caused numerous clashes everywhere.

To combat the increasing leftist-inspired unrest, the Japanese government, with the consent of SCAP, enacted the Organization Control Law in April 1949. It was designed to outlaw any organization that purposely resorted to violent tactics to influence government policy. In keeping with this act, on 9 September 1949 the Japanese government suddenly deployed about 500 police around the Choryŏn's headquarters in Tokyo and issued an order for it to disband, charging that the Choryŏn was an "undemocratic and terrorist organization." Specifically, the Choryŏn was charged with playing a role in inciting riots over the school issue in Kobe and Osaka. In addition, Attorney General Ueda Shunkichi ordered the confiscation of the property of the Choryŏn. Furthermore, twenty-eight Choryŏn leaders, including Kim Ch'ŏn-hae, JCP Central Committee member, were placed on the purge list by order of Ueda and were forbidden further political activities.

The dissolution of the Choryŏn was a serious blow and was without doubt the opening phase in a campaign to restrict the activities of all leftist organizations. With the mounting tension of the cold war in Europe and the rise of Mao's force in mainland China, this restriction was what the conservative government of Yoshida had long desired, encouraged by the tacit consent of the SCAP authorities. The JCP, represented by Nosaka Sanzō, protested to the attorney general that the action was clearly a "violation of the Potsdam Declaration and the Japanese Constitution."[41] The purged Choryōn officials appealed to SCAP to rescind the order, as well as to the attorney general, but their efforts were in vain. Finally the ex-Choryōn officials brought civil suit against the government on the basis of its illegal seizure of Choryōn property and the unlawful dissolution order.[42]

About ten days after the dissolution of the Choryōn, another order was issued from the attorney general's office which closed all Korean schools operating under the auspices of the Choryōn. The destruction of the Choryōn was thorough and complete, and the repercussions of these events were felt in the two Koreas. Kim Il-sung, premier of North Korea, sent a message to both the JCP and the Choryōn, condemning the Yoshida government's action as a fascist reactionary move to destroy the democratic system in Japan. He advised the Choryōn members to remain calm and not to resist Yoshida's action with physical force, which might jeopardize the position of the JCP as well. In South Korea, conversely, President Syngman Rhee blamed what he termed the "little lieutenants and colonels" of the SCAP staff who had been led to believe by the Japanese that "all Koreans are Bolsheviks, anarchists and gangsters." In addition, he raised the question of why the Organization Control Law was applicable only to the Korean Choryōn and not equally to the JCP. He concluded that this was a clear indication of the Japanese government's intention to "drive the Koreans out of Japan."[43]

Meanwhile, the Mindan, at first disregarding the anti-Korean implications of the Choryōn dissolution, issued a statement praising the Japanese government's action, with the hope that the dissolution would provide a unique opportunity for the Mindan to expand its hegemony over all Koreans in Japan. In fact, several weeks before the dissolution order was issued, a violent clash between the Choryōn and the Mindan had taken place in Shimonoseki on 18 August, and 131 Koreans had been arrested and several injured. After the incident, each organization had accused the other of being a terrorist organization, and each demanded that the Japanese authorities disband the rival organization.

Nevertheless, it did not take long for the Mindan to realize that the Yoshida government's move to dissolve the Choryōn was aimed not only at the left-wing Korean movement but at all Korean activities in Japan. This prompted the Mindan and some former Choryōn members to patch up their differences and to create a "Committee for the Common Struggle" to counter any further repressive measures. This attempt, however, to create a unified Korean organization out of the Mindan and the disbanded

Choryŏn, which would certainly have enabled Koreans to strengthen their positions in Japan, never fully materialized.

THE RIFT BETWEEN LEFT-WING KOREANS AND THE JCP

Yoshida's move to dissolve the Choryŏn in September 1949 came as a total surprise to the JCP. In the early part of 1949, the JCP leaders had been jubilant over their gain of thirty-five seats in the House of Representatives. Nosaka Sanzō reported at the Fourteenth Central Plenum of the Central Executive Committee that the Communist gain was an indication of a fully grown class consciousness of the masses and a sign of their readiness for a democratic revolution. He boasted that the establishment of a people's government was possible even under the American occupation,[44] and in fact he set a target date of September 1949 for capturing political power from the Yoshida regime. Hence, the dissolution of the Choryŏn was an unexpected event that awakened the JCP from the illusion of a possible September revolution. The occasion provided a sufficient warning to the JCP leaders that, if they did not reassess their current policy, they could sooner or later expect a fate similar to that of the Choryŏn.

Bitter criticism of JCP policy came from the Soviet Cominform through a special article published several months after the dissolution of the Choryŏn.[45] The criticism was mainly directed at Nosaka's theory that a peaceful revolution was possible under the American occupation in Japan. The apparent prime objective of the Cominform's attack was to push the JCP into a more militant and radical role in the face of the United States policy to build Japan as a bulwark against communism. On 17 January, about ten days after the Cominform's criticism, the Chinese Communist party also endorsed the main theme of the Cominform's article.[46]

Despite its initial reluctance to accept criticism from abroad, the JCP, after long and heated discussions, decided to admit the error in its strategy and tactics.[47] From the early spring of 1950, the JCP was faced with the problem of planning a new course of action that would eventually meet the "expectation of international proletariats," as pointed out by the Cominform. The problem was complicated by serious divisions within the party over its degree of militancy. Two factions began to emerge: the Mainstream faction, headed by Tokuda Kyūichi and Nosaka Sanzō, and the Internationalist, under the leadership of Shiga Yoshio and Miyamoto Kenji. All four men agreed that the JCP should take a more militant posture, repudiating the United States' occupational policy to convert Japan into its base for further "imperialistic" ventures in East Asia. The Mainstream insisted, however, that the Cominform's criticism was not against the party's basic strategy, but rather it demanded more vigorous and resolute action for the attainment of its goals. The Mainstream saw the immediate task of the party as the intensification of the effort to expand and strengthen the democratic national front.[48] The Internationalists argued that the Cominform called for a complete overhaul of party strategy corresponding with the internationally oriented communist movement. They stressed a more militant stance emphasizing illegal activities, insisting that the main issue was the elimination of American imperialism, an effort that would strengthen the JCP's ties with other international proletariat.

The Internationalists' militant viewpoint was vehemently supported by most Korean JCP members. In fact, the Koreans in the JCP during the early 1950s were a more crucial force within the rank-and-file members of the Communist party than the hardcore ex-Choryŏn members who joined the JCP after the dissolution of the Choryŏn. As a matter of fact, after the dissolution of the Choryŏn, so many Koreans wished to join the JCP in reaction to Yoshida's move that the JCP decided to accept them only on a quota basis. They were not to exceed more than one-quarter of the Japanese communist members of any local branch. The quota system was apparently a move by the JCP to curtail the influx of Korean members lest the party be taken over by the Koreans.[49]

While the Mainstream leaders continued to refrain from a more militant role, they were unable to curb the violent actions taken by some extreme groups of the Internationalist faction. This group, composed mostly of young radical students, Koreans, and day laborers, began to stage violent demonstrations and riots throughout Japan. Finally, when several American soldiers were attacked by anti-American demonstrators in Tokyo on 30 May 1950, SCAP found the episode a convenient excuse for taking repressive action against the JCP.

A week later, on 6 June, SCAP ordered the Japanese government "to remove and exclude from public office" the twenty-four members of the JCP Central Committee and seventeen members of the editorial staff of *Akahata*, the party newspaper. Following the outbreak of the Korean War in 1950, SCAP's pressure on the Communist party intensified. Subsequently the Japanese government and private employers began to launch a large-scale "Red Purge," which resulted in the dismissal of many thousands of Communists and their sympathizers. Furthermore, SCAP ordered not only the suspension of the publication of *Akahata* but the arrest of nine JCP leaders for violating the Organization Control Law, by which the Choryŏn had been ordered to dissolve. The JCP leaders immediately went underground, as they had been anticipating repressive measures ever since the dissolution of the Choryŏn. The time finally had come, they felt, for the JCP to resort to an armed struggle against oppressive forces.[50]

Meanwhile, the outbreak of the Korean War stimulated other scattered and disorganized ex-Choryon members to form another organization to replace the dissolved Choryŏn. In January 1951, after several months of deliberation, they established the Chaeil Chosŏn T'ong'il Minchu Chonsŏn or Minchŏn (United Democratic Front in Japan for the Unification of Korea). It was, in fact, a reincarnation of the Choryŏn, and from its inception it purported to be a political organization. As the North Korean army's situation deteriorated as a result of MacArthur's Inch'ŏn landing and the drive to the Yalu River, the Minchŏn pledged to consolidate all the left-wing Korean efforts in Japan for the defense of the fatherland.[51] To implement this goal, the underground organization, Choguk Bang'ui Uiwonhoe or Chobang'ui (Committee for the Defense of the Fatherland) was placed under the Minchŏn's control as a paramilitary unit.[52] The Chobang'ui, working closely with the JCP's "self-defense unit," was to be developed as a full-scale guerrilla force and eventually to become part of a Japanese Red army.[53] The overall strategy adopted by the Chobang'ui, except for a section that committed itself to the defense of the fatherland, was almost identical to that of the JCP as outlined in the "JCP's Immediate and Basic Action Policy."[54] In short, their strategy was to wage guerrilla warfare against "American imperialism and the Japanese reactionary forces" to bring about what they now termed as a "democratic revolution" for "national liberation."

From the latter part of 1950 to 1952, the Chobang'ui established the "era of the Molotov cocktail." In cooperation with JCP's "self-defense unit," it began to make hit-and-run terrorist attacks, not only throwing fire bombs at police stations but sabotaging factories and American military bases. These terrorist tactics were intended to cause public disorder in Japan. Although the violence was limited to metropolitan areas, the JCP leaders considered creating some guerrilla bases in the countryside as well. The overall result of these actions, however, was a catastrophic failure for the party. The JCP became a symbol of extremism and none of its members was elected to the Diet in the October 1952 election. Moreover, the fear of a communist uprising spurred the Japanese government to enact a law against them which was designed to be even more repressive.

Tokuda Kyūichi, a founding father of the Communist party, realizing the adverse effects of the violent tactics, criticized the party for employing "irresponsible adventurism."[55] He, by now exiled in Beijing, urged the Communists to "learn the art of combining legal with illegal activities" and to refrain from the overt street violence that could only end in self-destruction. Although the principle of an arms struggle has never been abandoned, the JCP's guerrilla tactics of the 1950s, including the Chobang'ui's resort to open violence, had come to an end.

In the meantime, with the cessation of hostilities in Korea in July 1953, the Minchŏn was faced with the need to reappraise its future policy. An argument erupted around two policy alternatives. One faction wished to maintain close collaboration with the JCP and fight for the unification of Korea. Such united action with the Japanese people was necessary if the Minchŏn was to wage a "Three-Anti" campaign (anti-Yoshida, anti-armament, anti-U.S.); as this faction saw it, Japan had now become America's advance base for further imperialistic aggression in Korea.

The other faction emphasized the national consciousness of Koreans in Japan, whose allegiance to North Korea was strengthened by the armistice, which signified to them a successful check against the aggression of American imperialism in Korea; this faction argued that the main task of Koreans in Japan was to devote themselves to the reconstruction of the fatherland after its devastation. If the Minchŏn continued under the JCP's strategic guidance, they stated, the Minchŏn could hardly maintain its autonomy and independent posture.[56]

Advocates of the former position were called the "Pro-JCP" faction, while the latter were called the "Nationalist" faction. The dispute became intensified during the Minchŏn's Fourth National Conference, held in November 1953, wherein the Nationalist faction was stripped from holding any official positions as a result of JCP pressure.[57]

But a gradual breaking up of cold war tension and the peaceful offensive initiated by the communist camp began to affect the Minchŏn's policy. In February 1955, after the end of the American occupation, Nam Il, North Korea's Foreign Minister, declared that his country was prepared to enter into friendly relations with Japan for cultural and trade exchange. Although Japan made no official reply, informal contact between the two countries followed immediately, and a campaign to promote trade with North Korea got underway in Japan.[58] The Minchŏn issued a statement supporting Nam Il's proposal, but the situation demanded an alteration in its Three-Anti policy. It was an apparent contradiction for the Minchŏn to pursue a policy of overthrowing a government with which their homeland government was about to enter into friendly relations.

Finally, the dispute between the Nationalist and the Pro-JCP factions flared up again. Because of this, on 11 March 1955 a Central Committee meeting was hastily summoned to discuss the question, but the result was a head-on collision. Fierce debates took place at the meeting, with Han Dŏk-su representing the Nationalist faction, and Pak Ŭn-chŏl representing the opposing faction. It was at this meeting that Han Dŏk-su made his landmark speech, which eventually led the left-wing Korean movement in Japan to pursue an independent policy without any strategic guidance from the JCP.

In his speech, Han objected to the Minchŏn's policy of functioning as if it were a kind of political party in collaboration with the JCP, which concerned itself solely with capturing political power in Japan.[59] He insisted that the Koreans, as aliens in Japan, should not be directly involved with domestic politics in the host country. Instead, as "citizens" of the Democratic People's Republic of Korea (see chap. 7) their allegiance should be directed to the fatherland and their only political objective should be the unification of Korea by peaceful means. Han argued that the Korean movement in Japan ought to be oriented primarily toward the protection of fundamental rights of Koreans. He stated, however, that protest activities should be orderly so as not to impair the friendly relations between the host government and their home country.

The rising tide of nationalistic sentiment among Koreans in Japan was clearly in favor of the argument advanced by the Nationalist faction. Moreover, some left-wing Koreans began to feel not only a sense of weariness but also doubt as to the effectiveness of remaining within the frame of the JCP's strategy and tactics. The dispute between the two factions was finally settled by the defeat of the Pro-JCP faction at the Sixth Minchŏn National Conference on 24 May 1955, which was convened for the purpose of making a final settlement. The Minchŏn unanimously decided to terminate its status as a peripheral organization of the Japanese Communists and announced that it planned to pursue an independent course by pledging its allegiance directly to North Korea. To create a new image, its leaders decided to dissolve the Minchŏn. On the following day, the National Meeting created a new organization and called it the Chaeilbon Chosŏnin Ch'ongryŏnhaphoe or Ch'ongnyŏn (General Federation of Korean Residents in Japan). At the same time, it instructed its members to withdraw their membership from the JCP. According to the Ch'ongnyŏn's General Policy Statement, "any individual or organization affiliated with the Ch'ongnyŏn shall be neither permitted to join foreign political organizations nor allowed to intervene in any political dispute in a foreign country."

Subsequently, the Ch'ongnyŏn was endorsed by the North Korean regime as the exclusive organization representing Koreans' interests in Japan. At the same time the Mindan was supported by South Korea, which denied the existence of the Ch'ongnyŏn. Thus, the two organizations were pitted against each other, just as were their respective home governments which differed strongly on almost every ideological issue (see also chap. 9).

5

THE POLITICS OF REPATRIATION

Changsoo Lee

It is difficult to determine the precise number of Koreans who repatriated from Japan after the surrender. According to the official report issued
by the Ministry of Justice in 1951, almost one million Koreans repatriated to
Korea within the seven-month period immediately after Japan's surrender.
Many returned home before an official repatriation program was launched
by the American occupational authorities. Moreover, the early stage of the
SCAP repatriation program was a most disorderly and chaotic operation,
and no figures reported were reliable. Many Koreans wished to carry back
goods and money not permitted by the official program, and so some of
these repatriates used illegal routes of passage. Conversely, numbers of
Koreans who journeyed home to Korea found living conditions difficult and
again returned to Japan illegally.

Whatever the means of repatriation used by the Koreans, many Japanese have hoped to rid themselves of the presence of Koreans, whom they
considered to be a source of criminality as well as political unrest. Reflecting
intolerance toward any visible ethnic minority remaining on their soil, the
Japanese government since the beginning of the postwar period has pursued
two conflicting policies with respect to Koreans. One has been to encourage
them to assimilate and disappear by taking a Japanese name, even though
Japanese society remains reluctant to accept fully any individual discovered
to be "passing." Social barriers seriously hinder the effectiveness of any
assimilative policy. Those of known Korean origin, however distant or
however "Japanese" their comportment, are still treated differently.

The other government policy has been to encourage repatriation. The
governmental decision to permit a mass exodus to North Korea in 1959 was
not as reluctant as it sometimes seemed to be on the surface. For many
Koreans, it seemed to provide an opportunity to escape from the misery of
life in Japan and to seek a better life in their newly freed homeland. A mass
exodus to North Korea began in December 1959. It is certainly difficult to
ascertain whether on return to their homeland many Koreans actually found
the better economic and social conditions they sought. Actually, their decision to repatriate should be viewed as prompted more by disgust with their

treatment by the Japanese than by hopes of any improved standard of living. Although some Koreans are still leaving Japan, the yearly number since 1967 has dwindled to a trickle.

However willing many Japanese may have been to see Koreans leave, the decision of the Japanese government on the matter was not a simple one. It could not be separated from the delicate diplomatic maneuvers in which the Japanese government was engaged with the two antagonistic Korean regimes. In theory, although the Japanese government had the final say, a complex triangular diplomatic battle ensued over any Korean repatriation that was to take place. The Korean organizations in Japan, Mindan and Ch'ongnyon, played significant roles in attempting to represent the interests of each home government, South and North Korea respectively. The extensive lobbying launched by both Mindan and Ch'ongnyòn was important, further influencing Japanese public opinion on the policy of repatriation.

When actual repatriation to North Korea began in 1959, the Japanese government had established formal diplomatic relations with neither South nor North Korea. The existence of two opposing Koreas was a complicated diplomatic dilemma which Japan found difficult to resolve. During the American occupation, diplomatic personnel in Japan were accredited to SCAP, not to the Japanese government. The South Korean government had been allowed by SCAP to install what was called the "Korean Mission in Japan," accredited to SCAP, in December 1948.[1] No such recognition was accorded to the North Korean regime.

THE RHEE LINE

Even after the conclusion of the U.S.-Japanese Peace Treaty in San Francisco in 1952, the Korean Mission continued to remain in Japan pending the signing of a separate treaty settling many issues between Japan and her former colony. Under United States initiative, bilateral negotiations between Japan and South Korea had begun in Tokyo in October 1951. The negotiations continued intermittently thereafter, but received an early blow when South Korean President Syngman Rhee announced on 18 January 1952 what was commonly known as the "Rhee Line."[2] It was a proclamation that the territorial waters of South Korea extended an average of sixty miles from the Korean coast rather than a customary three miles at that time. Rhee stated that the boundary was necessary for "safeguarding, once and for all, the interests of national welfare and defense."

Though the declaration was applicable to all nations, it was obviously designed to restrict Japanese fishing activities in Korean waters. Fishing was a vital industry for both Koreans and Japanese as a major source of food. The Japanese government protested vigorously, denouncing Rhee's proclamation.[3] The Rhee Line would have been less provocative to many Japanese had the Korean Coast Guard not enforced it so stringently. In fact, even before the Rhee Line enactment, Japanese fishermen along with their vessels had frequently been seized by Korean authorities on charges of crossing into Korean territorial waters.[4] Each time the fishermen were released through SCAP intervention.

After several months of prolonged talks, the early attempts to normalize diplomatic relations between the two governments failed to yield any satisfactory agreement, and meetings were adjourned in April 1952. Thereafter, enforcement of the Rhee Line by the Korean Coast Guard became tighter than ever before. As seizures of more Japanese fishermen by Korean patrol boats were reported in Japan, tension mounted among the Japanese people. Stirring up already heated Japanese feelings, what was known as the Taihō Maru incident took place on 4 February 1953, when the Korean Coast Guard reportedly used arms to capture two unarmed Japanese trawlers at sea approximately twenty miles west of Chechu, a Korean island. During the capture one Japanese crew member was killed.

Realizing the worsening situation, the Japanese Fishery Association and other groups urged their government to reach an early settlement with the South Korean government. Both governments agreed to resume their talks in April 1953, but the meetings were deadlocked again. In October the negotiating sessions reopened for the third time, but the climate was not cordial. It was at a meeting of this session that the chief Japanese delegate, Kubota Kannichirō, lost his patience and made what were considered derogatory remarks about Korea.[5] As Douglas Mendel has pointed out, nothing could have injured the pride of Koreans more than Kubota's remark that Japan's colonization had actually "benefited" Korea.[6] The indignant Korean delegates walked out of the conference. For the next four-and-a-half years, until Japan agreed to withdraw the statement in 1957, no official dialogue was held between the two governments, and their relations continued to deteriorate. The Rhee regime continued to seize Japanese fishermen and to detain and confiscate vessels, and the Japanese government continued its strict enforcement of the Alien Registration Law of 1947 and the Immigration Control Law of 1951 against Koreans in Japan (tables 6 and 7).

The problem of the Japanese fishermen detained in Korea for violation of the Rhee Line came to be linked in the minds of Koreans with the problems faced by Koreans imprisoned in the Ōmura camp. The Ōmura camp, located on the western tip of Kyūshū, was built in December 1950, exclusively to accommodate those who had violated the Immigration Control Law and the Alien Registration Law. Since a majority of violators were Koreans, the camp was known as a Korean prison in Japan. The treatment of the prisoners was so notoriously inhumane that many prison riots took place there.[7]

A brief explanation is required regarding the provisions of these two Japanese laws. When the Alien Registration Law of 1947[8] and the Immigration Control Law of 1951 were enacted, they were undoubtedly aimed at

TABLE 6

Number of Japanese Fishing Boats and Crewmen Seized (as of 20 August 1961)

Year	Number of boats captured	Number of crewmen detained	Number of boats sunk	Number of boats returned	Number of crewmen returned	Number of crewmen lost
1952	10	132	—	5	131	1
1953	47	585	—	2	584	1
1954	34	454	—	6	453	1
1955	30	498	—	1	496	2
1956	19	235	—	3	235	—
1957	10	98	—	—	98	—
1958	9	93	—	—	93	—
1959	9	91	—	1	91	—
1960	6	52	1	—	52	—
1961 (to Sept.)	9	70	—	5	57	—
Total	183	2,308	1	23	2,290	5

Source: Asian Affairs Bureau, Japanese Foreign Ministry, *Chōsen Benran* [A Handbook of Korea] (Tokyo: 1961), p. 42.

Koreans, since Koreans comprised almost 90 percent of all aliens in Japan. To cite a few examples in the provisions of the Alien Registration Law of 1947: (1) an alien must register a change of address with the mayor of the city or town of his or her new residence within fourteen days after any move; (2) the alien's registration card must be carried at all times, and it must be presented upon request of any proper authority (see chaps. 4 and 7). Failure to abide by the above provisions was punishable by no more than one year's imprisonment or a fine of not more than 10,000 yen (Article 13). As a noted Korean writer in Japan stated, "What a ridiculous thing it was! Everytime I changed my clothes I had to make sure that I had my registration card, even if I just went out for a cup of tea or to the barber shop in the neighborhood."[9]

The Immigration Control Law of 1951 stipulated that any alien falling under the following categories could be subject to deportation: (1) a pauper, vagrant, or disabled person, who had become a charge of the state or any locality; (2) a person who had been subjected to any punishment heavier than imprisonment for violation of the Alien Registration Law.

There was, of course, increased apprehension among Koreans who allegedly had violated any Japanese law. The number of Koreans detained at the Ōmura camp for violation of the alien and immigration laws was at its peak when negotiations between Japan and South Korea were broken off for the third time in October 1953. The worsening relationship between the two governments seemed to cause the Japanese police to resort to much more stringent enforcement of the deportation law (table 7). And the Rhee regime was responding by more vigilant enforcement of the Rhee Line. The hostility between South Korea and Japan intensified with complaints from each side over the arbitrary seizure and detention of the other's nationals.

The North Korean regime did not remain silent during this time. On 30 August 1954, Nam Il, foreign minister of the Democratic People's Republic of Korea (DPRK), protested to the Japanese government for its "outrageous persecution of the Koreans" in Japan.[10] He cited several incidents in which Japanese police raided Korean ghettos and made "unlawful arrests of Koreans." Claiming that all Koreans residing in Japan were citizens of North Korea, Nam Il demanded that the Japanese government stop the forcible deportation of these nationals to South Korea, whose government was nothing but a lackey for American imperialists. The Japanese government ignored his protests.

The Rhee regime, despite its war on Japanese fishing, maintained a Korean mission in Japan to provide diplomatic protection for its own nationals. For all practical purposes, this mission accomplished little. The relief of distressed Koreans in Japan was not the primary concern of Rhee's regime. Rhee repeatedly insisted that the Japanese government must bear the responsibility for the well-being of all Koreans in Japan and should pay

TABLE 7
Koreans Deported from Japan

Year	Males	Females	Total
1950	796	159	955
1951	1,534	639	2,173
1952	1,500	798	2,298
1953	1,733	855	2,588
1954	567	268	835
1955	445	262	707
1956	—	—	—
1957	—	—	—
1958	713	290	1,003
1959	—	—	—
1960	986	445	1,431
1961	375	175	554
1962	462	168	630
1963	336	126	462
1964	428	156	584
1965	465	157	622
1966 (to June)	266	72	238
Total	10,606	4,574	15,180

Source: Zainichi Chōsenjin jinken yōgō tōsō iinkai, *Zainichi Chōsen kōmin ni taisuru danatsu to dairyō tsuihō o mokuromu "Shutsunyūkoku kanri hōan"* [Oppression Against Koreans in Japan and the Immigration Control Law Designed for Deportation] (Tokyo: 1969), p. 13.

due compensation to those Koreans who were forcibly taken to Japan during World War II.

The Rhee regime had no substantive policy for any relief measures of its own. During the first few years of its operation in Japan, the Korean mission was allocated only a bare minimum of funds, just enough to keep its door open in Tokyo. In fact, it became known that the head of the mission sought to solicit funds from a handful of wealthy Koreans to help support the mission. These donors contributed funds to purchase two limousines for the mission and to remodel the Korean ambassador's official mansion.[11]

A more specific instance illustrates Rhee's neglect of the welfare of Koreans in Japan. In 1952 the Mindan president, Kim Chae-wha, made several recommendations to the South Korean government on how it might promote the well-being of its expatriates. Among his recommendations were these:

1. Some portion of the home government's trade with Japan should be through the Mindan and those business firms owned and operated by Koreans in Japan;

2. A fund should be set up at the Bank of Korea's branch office in Tokyo to facilitate financial loans to small Korean businessmen in Japan;

3. A delegate representing Koreans in Japan should be present at the ROK-Japan negotiations;

4. Six observers without voting privileges should represent Koreans in Japan in the Korean National Assembly.[12]

There was no response to this plea. It must be understood that these recommendations were submitted in 1952, at the height of the Korean War. Nevertheless, the lack of any response indicates Rhee's unconcern at that time about the fate of Koreans residing in Japan.

The ultimate blame for this neglect should not be placed solely on the home government but also on the ineffective leadership of the Mindan itself. It is now widely known that Mindan officials, in collusion with the Korean mission in Japan, issued passports to Koreans in Japan for foreign travel only after exorbitant fees had been paid to Mindan officials as a means of raising funds for the organization.[13]

The Mindan therefore never gained the confidence of a majority of Koreans in Japan. Its image became that of an organization that benefited a small number of well-to-do Koreans. Additionally, the president of the Mindan and the minister of the Korean mission in Japan often resisted what each interpreted as domination by the other. A Mindan official sometimes resorted to a petition campaign to appeal to the home government to remove from his post a minister he considered unfit. Conversely, the head of the Korean mission often intervened indirectly in the election of the Mindan's Executive Council by supporting candidates favorable to the home government.[14]

In February 1955, taking advantage of the severed ROK-Japan talks as well as the Hatoyama government's hope to open trade with the Communist bloc, North Korea's Nam Il made a proposal to Japan, expressing his government's desire to enter into friendly relations, starting with trade and cultural exchange.[15]

It is worthwhile to note the strikingly different approaches of the North and South Korean regimes in their relations with Japan. Syngman Rhee was stubbornly unyielding; conversely, the North Korean approach to Japan was quite conciliatory, seemingly willing to set aside many troublesome issues for future settlement.[16] The real objective behind this approach was probably North Korea's intention not only to gain the allegiance of the dissatisfied Koreans in Japan but also to prevent any reopening of the ROK-Japan talks.

Although Japanese Premier Hatoyama Ichiro's government never formally responded to Nam Il's proposal, unofficial contacts between the two countries soon followed. In May 1955 the first Japanese Pacific Mission, led by Hatanaka Masaharu visited North Korea and had a long talk with P'yongyang officials.[17] Following Hatanaka's visit, many organizations to promote trade between the DPRK and Japan mushroomed, including the DPRK-Japan Trade Association in the Ch'ongnyŏn headquarters.

In October 1955, an unofficial trade agreement was signed between North Korea's Kim Che-son, a standing member of the Korean Association for the Promotion of International Trade, and Tanabe Mamoru, director of the Soviet-Japan Trade Association. In the same month a joint communique was issued by Kim Ung-ki, vice-president of the Presidium of the North Korean Supreme People's Assembly, and Furuya Sadao, a Socialist member of the Japanese House of Representatives. They pledged to cooperate in working to: (1) normalize relations between the two countries; (2) establish a permanent trade mission; (3) open a channel for free travel between the two countries; and (4) establish the fishing boundaries between them.[18]

The rapidly nearing DPRK-Japan rapprochement caused the Rhee regime to refrain from further escalation of tension with Japan over the Rhee Line. In November 1956 the Rhee government made a proposal to Japan concerning the detainees held by both governments. The proposal was to include provisions that:

1. Japan would release all detained Koreans who had entered Japan before the date of the Japanese surrender.

2. The Korean government would release those Japanese fishermen who had completed their terms of sentence and would accept Korean deportees who had entered Japan illegally after the date of the Japanese surrender.[19]

But the Japanese foreign minister objected. He insisted on the release of all Japanese fishermen detained in Korea. The Japanese government was, in fact, in a better position to win concessions from the Rhee regime by seeming to incline toward the North Korean government. Several months before Rhee made the proposal, forty-eight Koreans detained in the Ōmura camp had gone on strike, expressing their wish to be repatriated to North instead of South Korea. In July, in response to their wish, the Japanese government sent twenty of them to North Korea aboard a Norwegian ship.[20]

Actually the plan to repatriate Koreans to North Korea was not a new one. Soon after the armistice was signed in Korea, the Minch'on adopted a resolution in August 1953 to send Koreans to North Korea to help reconstruct the war-torn country.[21] But the North Korean response was rather lukewarm because the DPRK's economic recovery was still in the early stages and the country was not ready to accept repatriates. On 29 September

1955, Kim Il-sung stated that "the DPRK will try to arrange repatriation if the Koreans in Japan wish to return." But he also suggested that Koreans should try to establish their livelihood in Japan and work toward the unification of Korea through a close relationship between the DPRK and Japan.[22]

A few months later, on 10 December, the DPRK in a letter to the Ch'ongnyŏn reiterated that it agreed to repatriation in principle but was not overly enthusiastic about immediate action. Even before the Ōmura strike, the Japanese government had made an initial inquiry into the feasibility of repatriation to North Korea through the representative of the Japanese Red Cross (JRC) who visited P'yŏngyang in February 1956. Again the DPRK's response was lukewarm.[23]

In May 1956 the Committee of the International Red Cross (CIRC) dispatched its representatives to Japan as well as to North and South Korea to determine how repatriation could be carried out. It asked the Red Cross organizations of each of the three countries to begin negotiations with its counterparts. But no Red Cross proposals materialized because the South Korean Red Cross refused to participate. For the time being the question of repatriation was tabled.

To further its rapprochement with Japan, the DPRK changed its strategy to emphasize education. In April 1957 it sent a vast sum of money to Japan on behalf of the Korean Education Assistance Fund. The first remittance to the Ch'ongnyŏn was for more than 121 million yen, and another 100 million yen was scheduled to follow in October of the same year.[24] The DPRK's policy was to promote its own image as well as to gain the allegiance of Koreans in Japan, but regardless of its motives, the impact of the DPRK's gesture was profound. It provided Koreans with at least some belief that they were not completely "forgotten nationals." Subsequently some Koreans in Japan began to display a keener interest in the development of North Korea. The foundation for a grassroots repatriation movement to North Korea had been laid.

On 11 August 1958 approximately sixty Koreans gathered at a meeting sponsored by the local chapter of the Ch'ongnyŏn in Kawasaki, Kanagawa prefecture. Having heard reports of the "remarkable economic progress" of North Korea, they wrote a letter to North Korean Premier Kim Il-sung expressing their desire to repatriate. Furthermore, they pledged that:

1. Instead of living in Japan suffering under constant persecution and racial discrimination, let us return to our fatherland and struggle for the peaceful unification of Korea.

2. Let us present our legitimate demands to the Japanese government to make immediate arrangements for our repatriation to North Korea.

3. To accomplish our objective, let us unite and try to seek the support of the Japanese people.[25]

Spurred by the move, the Ch'ongnyŏn headquarters in Tokyo adopted an official resolution on 13 August, when 2,500 local representatives assembled to commemorate the thirteenth anniversary of the Korean liberation from Japanese domination. The official resolution presented four major demands to the Japanese government, which can be summarized as follows:

1. To establish friendly relations with North Korea.
2. To call of the ROK-Japan talks and release Korean detainees held in the Ōmura camp, allowing them to return to the country of their own choice.
3. To demand immediate formulation of a repatriation plan by the Japanese government.
4. To request issuance of entry visas to the North Korean Red Cross representatives to visit Japan, and to grant permission for Koreans in Japan to travel to North Korea to attend the DPRK's Independence Day ceremony.[26]

In the meantime, the Ch'ongnyŏn issued a directive to its nationwide local chapters to wage a massive campaign for repatriation.

Kim Il-sung of the DPRK apparently felt constrained to respond to the repatriation movement at a rally held in P'yongyang on the tenth anniversary of the founding of the DPRK on 8 September 1958. He delivered a lengthy speech in which he stated:

> We must direct our concern to the recent situation of our compatriots in Japan. . . . Suffering under non-rights, national discrimination, and difficulty in living, the compatriots in Japan recently manifested the desire to return to the Democratic People's Republic of Korea. Our people warmly welcome the aspiration of the compatriots who, having lost their means of living in Japan, desire to return to the bosom of their fatherland. . . . The government of the Republic will provide the Korean nationals in Japan with all the conditions for leading a new life after their return to the homeland. We regard this as our national duty.[27]

The Ch'ongnyŏn organized a Central Countermeasure Committee for Repatriation under the chairmanship of Yi Kyae-paek in late September, and they launched a massive campaign to influence the Kishi government. To boost enthusiasm, the United Democratic Fatherland Front (Minchu Choguk T'ong-il Chonsŏn) in North Korea appealed through "Radio Free Koreans in Japan" to the Japanese government. Its members also sent letters in the name of the organization to practically every Japanese public figure who held a favorable image of North Korea, asking for cooperation in the undertaking.[28] The appeal to the Japanese people had an immediate effect. By 2 October twenty-two Japanese "democratic organizations and groups"

manifested in public their willingness to support and promote the repatriation movement. A few days later, Asanuma Inejirō, secretary-general of the
Socialist party, and Fukuda Katsuo, chief secretary of the Liberal Democratic party (LPD) expressed their support of the movement.

About a month after the North Korean premier's speech, the vice-
premier of the DPRK, Kim Il, held a press conference, stating that his government would "bear all the travel expense necessary for the Koreans'
return." He declared that the rest of the matter would lie in the hands of the
Kishi government.[29] From this point on, the repatriation movement gained
full momentum.

Encouraged by the new developments, the Ch'ongnyŏn leaders decided to present a formal request to the Kishi government, which included
these points:

1. Unconditional repatriation for those who wish to return to the
   DPRK.

2. Permission for North Korean vessels to dock at Japanese ports to
   transport Korean repatriates.

3. All necessary procedures by the Japanese government to ensure
   the repatriation.[30]

At the same time, the Ch'ongnyŏn announced that 20 October would
be "Demand Day for the Realization of Repatriation," launching a nationwide campaign that was to include systematic demonstrations and petitions.
The response to the Ch'ongnyŏn's appeal was widespread among many
prominent Japanese, some of whom founded an organization called the Zainichi Chōsenjin Kikoku Kyōryoku Kai or KKK (Cooperation Society for
the Repatriation of Koreans in Japan).

The original members of the KKK were an impressive group of bipartisan national figures. Included were Hatoyama Ichirō, ex-premier and LDP
member; Asanuma Inejirō, secretary-general of the Socialist party; Nosaka
Sanzō, chairman of the JCP; Iwamoto Nobuyuki, former vice-speaker of
the house and LDP member; Oda Kaoru, chairman of the Sōhyō; Hiraba-
yashi Taiko, a well-known woman author; and some ninety others.[31] Furthermore, twenty-eight other organizations affiliated with the KKK, which
set up headquarters in the Diet building and dispatched some 600 delegates
to every corner of Japan to persuade the Japanese people to support the
movement.

As a result of this massive campaign, by the following January, not
more than four months after the North Korean premier's speech, 22 prefectures, 122 cities, 34 village legislative bodies, and 28 governors, mayors,
and village chiefs had adopted various forms of resolutions and pledged to
support repatriation. It was an unprecedented bipartisan movement dis-

playing a unanimity of public opinion such as had not been seen in the past decade.[32]

The mass media was also instrumental in swaying public opinion by reporting candid descriptions of the adverse living conditions of Koreans in Japan. From the beginning of the repatriation movement, lead stories in almost all the Japanese newspapers dealt with Koreans, as did several articles in *Chūō Kōron* and *Sekai*, the widely read monthly journal.[33] The Bunka Radio Broadcasting Corporation carried a weekly program exclusively devoted to the problems of Koreans.

The decision to permit repatriation to North Korea was not an easy one for the Japanese government to make. A major question for the Kishi government was justification of a mass exodus of Koreans from the "free world" of Japan to a Communist regime, while many other people were still trying to flee from Communist rule. Another question which had to be taken into consideration was the reactions of the United States and the South Korean governments.

Under increasing public pressure, the Kishi government was no longer able to remain silent on the issue. On 30 January 1959 Foreign Minister Fujiyama Aiichirō broke the silence by issuing a statement that the Kishi government might soon take up the matter formally at a cabinet meeting. A few days later, on 2 February, Premier Kishi himself stated during a Diet budget committee session that his government would repatriate the Koreans if they wished to return. Not all the LDP members were content with Kishi's intention. Funada Naka, a leading LDP member, warned the Kishi government that "indiscreet disposition of the repatriation problem against the wishes of South Korea will throw the pending ROK-Japan talks into a difficult position."[34] The Kishi government responded that repatriation was an issue based on humanitarian principles and had nothing to do with political questions or the ROK-Japan talks.[35]

The ultimate decision on repatriation was finally reached at a cabinet meeting held on 13 February. The Ministry of Foreign Affairs issued a statement justifying its decision on the grounds that: (1) every individual is endowed with the fundamental right to choose his or her own domicile, as clarified in the Universal Declaration of Human Rights (Article 13, Section 2) and the Japanese Constitution (Article 22); (2) to respect fundamental rights is the basic obligation of all free and democratic nations. The Ministry of Foreign Affairs stressed, however, that its decision should not be construed as an implication of de facto recognition of the North Korean regime. By the same token, the ministry added, it was not a violation of the sovereignty of the Republic of Korea nor did it constitute an unfriendly act against it.

To maintain the unofficial nature of its dealings with the North Korean Communist regime, the Japanese government entrusted the repatriation effort to the Japanese Red Cross. At the same time, the Japanese government through the JRC asked the CIRC to provide an impartial service to determine the free will of those who wished to repatriate to North Korea. In the meantime, JRC delegates opened negotiations with North Korean Red Cross delegates in Geneva on 13 April 1959. It took several months and eighteen official meetings for the two sides to reach an agreement. The final document was signed in Calcutta, India on 13 August 1959.[36]

It is difficult to discern to what extent the decision of the Japanese government to sign the repatriation agreement with the DPRK was truly motivated by humanitarian principles. The decision to permit repatriation served several political purposes as far as the Japanese government was concerned. First, the signing of the agreement constituted a tacit understanding between the two, if not Japan's de facto recognition of the DPRK. It also demonstrated the Japanese government's inclination to pursue a two-Korea policy if it served the interests of Japan. The agreement made it possible for the DPRK to seek a more active role in promoting friendly relations with Japan, and at the same time, the Kishi government was able to mitigate somewhat the mounting pressure of left-wing groups against Kishi's pro-Western foreign policy.

Second, the Japanese government discovered a strong bargaining tool in dealing with South Korea; that is, by appearing to come closer to the North Korean regime, Japan found that it could move the stubborn Syngman Rhee to agree to a resumption of the ROK-Japan talks, which had been deadlocked for eight months. South Korea had received a clear warning that Japan would not hesitate to deal with the DPRK and to embarrass the South Korean government in East Asia.

As for North Korea, the agreement amounted to its greatest diplomatic triumph since the armistice and provided a golden opportunity to boost its international prestige. While many were still trying to escape from Communist rule in North Korea, it was an unprecedented event for the DPRK to receive a reverse flow of population. The prime objective of the DPRK's diplomacy had been to obstruct the successful conclusion of the ROK-Japan talks, and Rhee's unbending and uncompromising attitude had actually helped the DPRK to do so. Most particularly, the successful mobilization of Japanese left-wing groups for the DPRK's cause provided a chance to create a powerful "P'yŏngyang lobby" in Japan. The DPRK was able to enhance its prestige not only in the eyes of all Koreans in Japan but in the eyes of the Japanese. Moreover, the DPRK's success in gaining the allegiance of the Koreans had a tremendous impact upon even those who did not accept the repatriation. Whereas the DPRK promised jobs, homes, and a better life, the Rhee regime offered nothing.

It is difficult to determine the true motives of those who voluntarily repatriated to the North Korean Communist regime. It appears almost certain that they were primarily motivated by socioeconomic reasons rather than political. Actually, almost all Koreans in Japan were originally from

South Korea; few had family ties with North Korea. According to a survey conducted in 1954, only 2.4 percent of Koreans were from North Korea, and the overwhelming majority (96.6%) were actually from South Korea.[37] This was an embarrassing fact for the Rhee regime. The large number of people from South Korea who indicated their desire to go to North Korea constituted a strong vote of no confidence in the South Korean government.

By contrast, the DPRK increased not only its own confidence in dealing with the Japanese government but also acquired much needed manpower on the eve of its Seven-Year Economic Program (1961-1967). Had full-fledged political relations with Japan been the DPRK's immediate goal, the result would have been scored as a failure. For all practical purposes, however, the P'yŏngyang regime must be judged to have achieved a major success.

The only loser turned out to be South Korea. As soon as the decision of the Japanese government was made known, Rhee's spokesmen charged that the Japanese action was an immoral plot to carry out compulsory deportation and that such an action was most unfriendly to the ROK.[38] They protested further that such unilateral action by the Japanese government without consulting the ROK was contrary to international law and morality; the Japanese government was obligated to consult with the lawful government of Korea, which represented the interests of all Koreans in Japan.

Moreover, stated the Rhee government, "the North Korean puppet regime" had been condemned by the United States as an aggressor, and it was an unlawful government.[39] The ROK government said that many Koreans in Japan had been deceived by North Korean propaganda and that the Japanese decision for repatriation was not "humanitarian" but politically oriented. In other words, Japan was trying to use repatriation as a tool for diplomatic dickering on such issues as the Rhee Line.

Virtually all political parties in South Korea voiced support of Rhee's protest in a joint statement. Anti-Japanese sentiment in Korea seemed to have reached a new height. By 23 February 1959, some 4.1 million persons had reportedly participated in antirepatriation demonstrations in South Korea.[40]

In an attempt to stall Japan's repatriation deal with North Korea, Rhee offered unconditional resumption of the deadlocked ROK-Japan negotiations and expressed his government's readiness to accept all repatriates who had been "forcibly taken to Japan," provided the Japanese government paid due compensation to his government for them. Since no favorable response was forthcoming from the Japanese government, the Rhee regime apparently felt compelled to resort to desperate measures. Foreign Affairs Minister Chung W. Cho announced that his government was determined to resist the repatriation plan "with all means and power at its command. This is not a bluff, but a simple statement of fact. To protect our citizens and prevent their enslavement by the Communists, we have no other choice." Rhee elaborated on this point, saying: "We have solemnly informed the Japanese that all ships carrying Koreans from Japan to North Korea will be intercepted by our naval vessels and our planes, which have been placed in the position of alert."[41]

Though the ROK's warning appeared to be deadly serious, it had little actual power either economically or militarily to back up its stance. The South Korean government then appealed to the United States to use its good offices to mediate the dispute. The United States was gravely concerned about the deteriorating relations between Japan and South Korea, two of its most important allies in East Asia. But the United States was reluctant to mediate the dispute lest sensitive feelings in both countries be hurt. A State Department spokesman stated that the United States would not mediate unless Japan also asked for United States intercession.[42] As a matter of fact, by that time the Japanese had given the United States tacit support for repatriation. The South Korean Red Cross also made an appeal to General Malcolm Gruenther, director of the American Red Cross, to block the repatriation scheme, but that effort was futile.[43]

In the meantime, the Mindan had been active in trying to counteract the Ch'ongnyŏn's effort to mobilize Japanese public opinion in favor of repatriation. As early as 9 October 1958, the Mindan had organized a "Countermeasure Committee for the Prevention of Forced Labor Recruitment to North Korea." The committee declared that the repatriation movement to North Korea amounted to no more than a "forced labor recruitment." It pointed out that almost five million people had fled the North to seek freedom in the South since the DPRK was established in 1948. The present repatriation movement, it said, was aimed at filling the manpower shortage incurred by the mass escape. Therefore, the committee stated, "we can hardly stand idle while watching our compatriots being dragged into forced labor. We are determined to smash the plot.[44]

On 14 October 1958 the Mindan issued a directive to all its prefectural and local chapters to take the strongest measures possible to counteract the Ch'ongnyŏn's repatriation campaign. The directive urged all Mindan members to try to gain Japanese public support by exposing the real motives behind the repatriation movement. The Mindan declared that the period between 15 October and 15 November would be set aside as "Preventive Month Against Forced Labor Recruitment," during which time all Mindan members were to participate in a series of demonstrations directed at the Japanese local legislatures. All local Mindan members were instructed to dissuade those Koreans who had already expressed their desire to be repatriated. A Mindan representative even managed to appear himself at the Foreign Affairs Committee meeting hearing in the Diet, which was held on 29 October 1958, and tried to persuade the committee members to vote against repatriation.

TABLE 8

Number of Koreans Repatriated to North Korea

Month	1959	1960	1961	1962	1963	1964	1965
1		2,995	2,303	87	228	68	59
2		4,056	—	141	174	—	—
3		4,079	—	283	123	162	191
4		5,356	2,046	578	190	266	192
5		4,284	4,332	272	290	344	205
6		4,354	5,118	615	311	—	269
7		5,326	2,724	330	296	—	222
8		4,129	2,105	—	278	—	263
9		4,081	1,164	—	236	303	294
10		4,341	1,915	504	223	308	197
11		3,894	816	350	104	182	226
12	2,942	2,141	278	337	114	189	127
Totals	2,942	49,036	22,801	3,497	2,567	1,822	2,255

Grand total: 93,444

Source: *Pukhan Ch'onggam: 1945-68*, pp. 285-286. East Asian Studies Institute, ed., *Buk'han Chŏnsŏ* [Collections on North Korea] (Seoul: Kukdong Munjie Yonkuso, 1974), 3:191-194, and information reported by *Tōitsu Nippō Daily*.

1959-1976

1966	1967	1971	1971	1972	1973	1974	1975	1976
109	49	During						
138	148	the						
210	118	tempo-	At own					
176	162	rary	ex-					
217	168	exten-	pense,					
212	191	sion	after					
117	163	period	17 Sep-					
134	156	be-	tember					
150	216	tween	1971					
155	209	May-						
150	—	October						
92	251							
1,860	1,831	1,081	237	1,003	704	479	379	95

Meanwhile, the South Korean Mission in Japan issued a stern warning to Koreans not to sign any repatriation papers, because they would in effect be forfeiting their legal rights as South Korean nationals in Japan if and when the ROK-Japan negotiations succeeded. At the same time, the Mindan held countless demonstrations and sent petitions to all political parties and to those in positions of power, including the Speaker of the House, the Minister of Foreign Affairs, and the Minister of Justice. Similar appeals were made to the *Asahi*, *Mainichi*, *Yomiuri*, and *Sankei* newspapers to support their cause.

Despite all these efforts, prorepatriation sentiment was already solidly behind the Ch'ongnyŏn and the DPRK. The Ch'ongnyŏn's campaign, in cooperation with Japanese left-wing organizations, was too formidable a force for the hastily organized Mindan. To establish a P'yŏngyang lobby in Japan, the DPRK had worked patiently since 1955 to build strong allies among Japanese left-wing groups. It was reported that the Ch'ongnyŏn, funded by the DPRK, was annually spending some 2 billion yen and was backing Japanese political candidates to win the support of Socialist and JCP members in the Diet.[45] The Japanese government's decision to repatriate Koreans to North Korea was both a practical and a realistic solution to the ever-vexing problem of the Korean minority in Japan. Certainly, the principle of freedom of choice of domicile, on which Japan rested its case, was unassailable.

When the Mindan realized that the position of the Japanese government was irreversible, its sense of bitter defeat was projected onto its home government. On 15 June 1959, the Mindan passed a vote of no confidence in the Rhee government and blamed the failure of the Mindan campaign entirely on Rhee's policy toward Koreans in Japan.[46]

> ...We have pleaded with our home government to provide relief measures for Koreans in Japan for the last ten years. The absence of any sincere reply from the home government makes us lose all our patience. We should like to express our lack of faith in the Liberal Party regime.[47]

The Mindan also denounced its own home government for its total lack of concern for the welfare of Koreans in Japan.

As was planned, the first shipload of Koreans aboard a Russian vessel departed from Niigata for Ch'ŏngchin, North Korea, on 14 December 1959. Almost 100,000 Koreans repatriated to North Korea before the official agreement was terminated in 1967. Since then, with the tacit consent of the Japanese government, a sporadic number of Koreans has been repatriated aboard a DPRK cargo vessel, Mankyŏngbong-ho, which makes frequent stops in Japan. This has been the only means of available transportation between the two countries.

It is difficult to determine the fate of those who repatriated to North

Korea. As there are no formal diplomatic relations established between the two nations, no traveler is allowed to visit friends or relatives in Japan. According to some fragments of information, such as letters by repatriates to relatives in Japan, their lives have not been what they would have hoped. Once there, the repatriates would not experience the harsh discrimination they suffered in Japan. But although some may have found it worthwhile living in their homeland, others may have found difficulty adjusting to the highly disciplined and austere society of postwar North Korea. They certainly would not have as a possibility the material abundance and relative freedom they witnessed in Japan. No repatriate has yet returned to Japan. Perhaps it is more accurate to state that no one has been permitted to return to Japan even if he has so wished. Separated families have no present prospect of reunion. A serious problem remains unresolved for Japanese women who married Koreans and went to North Korea with their husbands. Japanese relatives along with other concerned people have made frequent appeals to the North Korean authorities through Ch'ongnyŏn to permit visits home to Japan. As yet the effort has had no apparent success.

The repatriation movement presents a sad historical episode of neglect and political maneuvering. The South Korean government showed little concern for those who might wish to return; in effect, they forgot them in pursuance of old animosities. The North Korean government saw its political advantage, and the Japanese government was not interested in helping Koreans make a decision about citizenship or in helping them repatriate to a Korean government of their own choice. By not offering Japanese citizenship to them, the Japanese government did nothing to resolve the problem of identity still being faced by most Koreans in Japan.

6

ORGANIZATIONAL DIVISION AND CONFLICT:
Ch'ongnyŏn and Mindan

Changsoo Lee

The social destiny of the Koreans left in Japan as a legacy of Japanese colonization has been determined by the continuing ideological polarization of the Soviet and American superpowers. The Koreans have had little direct voice in world politics, nor could they by themselves have prevented the division of their land at the 38th parallel.[1] With the end of World War II, the Japanese policy of political integration and assimilation of their "Imperial subjects" had abruptly come to a halt. Koreans were now legally classified as aliens and were deprived of suffrage. Their immediate disfranchisement in Japan had acted most effectively to deny them any means to articulate their interests or voice their demands through legitimate political channels. Considering the services rendered by many Koreans in the Japanese war effort, the Japanese government could have given an option for Koreans in Japan to retain Japanese citizenship, if any had so desired.[2] Judging from the prevailing sentiment at the time, however, regardless of citizenship policy, not many Koreans would have desired to remain permanently in Japan. Otherwise, the large-scale exodus of Koreans would not have taken place.

As noted in chapters 3 and 5, many found difficulty in relocating themselves in the chaotic and disaster-ridden homeland in the postwar period. Some Koreans had second thoughts about immediate repatriation. Some thought they would wait to choose the optimum timing of their return with a minimum loss of continuity, reducing the hardships of transition to the new Korean environment. Such expectations were shattered by signs of increasing political tension back home, and then came the Korean War. Even with the end of that war, first-generation Koreans in Japan tended to ignore the reality that repatriation was no longer feasible. Holding to the hope that some day they could return to their homeland, they tended to rationalize their settling down in a society where their presence was no longer welcome. They had adopted a means of livelihood that, although often precarious, still afforded them some sense of security. Even today, many older, first-generation Koreans have not altered their fundamental sojourners' mentality. When the Koreans organized the League of Korean Residents in Japan (Choryŏn) in October 1945, it was the fundamental premise of most that their settlement in Japan was temporary.

As noted in chapter 4, these sojourners became a highly vocal group during the early period of the American occupation of Japan. The better life that Koreans in Japan expected after the liberation of their homeland from Imperial Japan never materialized. To make matters worse, SCAP was ill-prepared to handle Korean problems and relegated the whole question of the remaining Koreans to the Japanese authorities.

A majority of politically active Koreans responded to Choryŏn's call for organizing, which appeared to be the best answer to their dilemma. Actually, according to some, Choryŏn was originally intended to be a non-political and temporary social service organization acting until all Koreans could be repatriated to their homeland. But following the sharp decline of repatriation and the increasing desire of many Koreans to postpone their journey home, Choryŏn's expressed functions were rapidly reoriented to more than social services. Its leadership was taken over by Korean leftists, whose objectives were closely linked to those of the Japanese Communist party (JCP). They believed that there was little chance of improving the lot of the remaining Koreans, so long as the Japanese political establishment persisted. Hence Choryŏn members joined the revolutionary ranks of the JCP and began to advocate the destruction of the emperor system with a "people's liberation" movement. In fact, Choryŏn played a very decisive role in broadening JCP's mass base throughout Japan. It is noteworthy that when the JCP was reorganized by the leading Communists just after they were released from their Japanese prisons by SCAP, the membership was composed of approximately 150 Japanese and 100 Koreans.[3] Under the JCP's postwar strategic guidance, Choryŏn became a front organization and its members served as JCP's functionaries, rarely hesitating to combine legal with illegal activities and legal with illegal organizations employing mass agitation and violence aimed at an eventual mass uprising. These disturbances were climaxed by the Hanshin Riot of 1948, which provided a convenient pretext for SCAP, together with the newly reconstituted Japanese authorities, to take suppressive measures. Finally in 1949, Choryŏn was charged with being a terrorist organization and was ordered to disband by the Japanese government, a prelude to the subsequent "red purge" against the JCP leaders.

When the Korean War broke out, the remnants of the ex-Choryŏn core members formed an illegal underground organization and engaged in hit-and-run guerrilla warfare in close coordination with the JCP's Self-Defense Unit, sabotaging railroads and United States military bases in Japan. They planned to develop a full-scale guerrilla force and eventually to become a part of the Japanese Red Army. But, as noted, such militant tactics were later condemned by Tokuda Kyūichi, then in exile in Beijing, as "irresponsible adventurism" that could only end in self-destruction. As a result of Tokuda's warning, the era of overt violence came to an end in 1952.

CH'ONGNYŎN

After the cessation of hostilities in Korea, the left-wing Koreans felt a need to reappraise their strategy. One group sought to remain under the JCP's guidance as part of an international proletarian movement. Others sought to dissociate themselves from the JCP to pursue an independent line pledging allegiance to the Democratic People's Republic of Korea (DPRK). The present Ch'ongnyon is the outgrowth of the latter viewpoint, which eventually triumphed over the former.

The latter-day Ch'ongnyon differed from its leftist predecessor in several aspects. First, it was no longer under strategic guidance from the JCP but followed an independent policy. In fact, however, it pledged allegiance to North Korea as an agent representing the interests of North Korea in Japan. It also became an agent of North Korean foreign policy. Second, the Ch'ongnyon declared in its platform that it would refrain from direct involvement in the internal affairs of Japan. The Ch'ongnyon pledged that it would not function as if it were a political party solely concerned with capturing political power in collaboration with the JCP. Rather, as an organization composed of North Korean nationals, its primary effort would be to protect the fundamental rights of Koreans in Japan.

In the platform adopted at the Ch'ongnyon inaugural meeting in May 1955, delegates specified that their major goals in Japan were: (1) to help strengthen the "democratic base" of North Korea in achieving the peaceful unification of Korea; (2) to protect the rights of Koreans in Japan; and (3) to promote friendly relations between North Korea and Japan.[4] The core of the Ch'ongnyon is composed of four major organs that represent the highest echelon in a rigid chain of command. These are the Ch'ongnyon National Convention, the Central Committee, the Central Standing Committee, and the Control Committee.

National Convention

This constitutes the supreme authority within the Ch'ongnyon's hierarchy. Delegates to the convention are elected by Ch'ongnyon members through the local organizations. The delegates formulate overall policy, discuss governing regulations, appropriate the annual budget, and lay down the principles of action. They elect all the members of the executive organs: the Central Committee, Board of Chairmen, and Control Committee. But with increasing stress on the concept of "democratic centralism," the National Convention has functioned less and less as a supreme policymaking body, a trend reflected in the decreasing frequency and importance of its supposedly annual conventions.

Central Committee

In reality, the Central Committee is the authoritative organ of the Ch'ongnyŏn, replacing the functions of the National Convention. The Central Committee meets at least once every four months and is often called the "little convention," as it is composed of some 200 members. It is headed by a Board of Chairmen consisting of one chairman and five vice-chairmen. In 1963, seven Central Committee members, including four members of the Board of Chairmen, ran as candidates for the Supreme People's Congress of North Korea, and were officially elected.[5] Currently, Han Dŏk-su, Chairman of the Board, and several other Central Committee members are duly elected members of the North Korean People's Congress and are actually representatives of North Koreans in Japan. Han Dŏk-su, Chairman of the Board of Ch'ongnyŏn, also serves as head of a quasi-diplomatic mission representing the DPRK in Japan. Nearly every year he invites diplomatic officials from Communist nations accredited to Japan to a party to celebrate North Korea's national holiday, and he is in turn treated reciprocally by other Communist diplomatic missions in Japan.

For all practical purposes, the Board of Chairmen has become a self-perpetuating group whose authority is limited only by the DPRK. All important decisions on strategy and general policy are made by this group, which always meets in closed session. Although the Central Committee retains the final authority in regard to formulation and implementation of Ch'ongnyŏn policy, it has delegated the daily execution of these tasks to the Central Standing Committee, which is staffed by Central Committee members.

Central Standing Committee

Membership of the Central Standing Committee is composed of the six members of the Board of Chairmen and, subordinate to them, thirteen bureau chiefs of the following bureaus: General Affairs, Organization, Public Relations, Political Affairs, Education, Social Welfare, International Affairs, Industrial Affairs, Cultural Affairs, Printing, Planning, Economics, and Finance. The Central Standing Committee, summoned by the Chairman of the Board, meets twice every month. Actually, it is the Central Standing Committee that manages and operates the entire Ch'ongnyŏn activities in Japan.

Control Committee

Members of the Control Committee are elected by the National Convention. The Control Committee is responsible for preventing and detecting infiltration from the outside and for carrying on its own intelligence activities. It enforces absolute discipline among its members as prescribed by the Ch'ongnyŏn. In addition, it conducts auditing and other miscellaneous investigative duties within the organization.

Local Organizations

Local organizations form the echelon directly below the central organs in the Ch'ongnyŏn chain of command. Japan is divided into eight regions following traditional geographic boundaries, each region having a regional council. Each region is subdivided into prefectural areas, with at least one Ch'ongnyŏn headquarters in each. These areas are further broken down into districts, branches, and units. The size and number of districts and branches varies in accordance with Ch'ongnyŏn membership and the Korean population in the areas. There are 49 prefectural headquarters, 419 districts, 2,700 branches, and 246 units throughout Japan.[6] This huge organizational web in Japan is run by some 5,600 full-time staff members paid by the Central Committee of the Ch'ongnyŏn.[7] On the basis of the alien registration figures published by the Japanese Ministry of Justice in 1974, it is estimated that Ch'ongnyŏn has approximately 250,000 members.

The structure and operational procedures of the Ch'ongnyŏn outlined here give us only a glimpse of the organization's overall activities. The Ch'ongnyŏn draws much of its strength from a host of peripheral organizations as well as from Japanese left-wing organizations over which the Ch'ongnyŏn exercises varying degrees of influence and control. Ch'ongnyŏn leaders feel that no segment of the population is too insignificant, no group too small, no field of interest too remote for cultivating support. Since Koreans in Japan do not have direct access to the Japanese political system to articulate their interests, the Ch'ongnyŏn tends to seek support from Japanese sympathizers. It is for this reason that the Japan-DPRK Society needs careful analysis.

JAPAN-DPRK SOCIETY (Nitchō Kyōkai)

The Nitchō Kyōkai is very closely associated with the Ch'ongnyŏn, and its role can hardly be underestimated. It has 37 local prefectural chapters and 170 branch offices in Japan. Some of its 15,000 members are nonpartisan but many are prominent left-wing leaders, Diet members, prefectural governors, and mayors.

Originally, the Japan-DPRK Society was intended to be a "nonpolitical organization for the promotion of cultural exchange between the two countries." Its founders, both Korean and Japanese, were mostly religious leaders, writers, educators, and artists. Organized in 1951, in the midst of the Korean War, the society first actively engaged in a relief program for war victims, both North and South Koreans. The Nitchō Kyōkai took a leftist position after the "Ethnic Study Revival Campaign," which it conducted in cooperation with the leftist Minchŏn (chap. 3) in 1952. The society's leadership came under the total control of Hatanaka Masaharu, a Nitchō Kyōkai leader who went to North Korea for a series of talks with Kim Il-sung in 1955. Upon his return to Japan, he immediately assumed the chairmanship of the society's board of directors and called the first national convention in November 1955. Attending were many delegates representing twenty-nine prefectures as well as leaders of the Japanese Communist party, the Socialist party, labor unions, and educators who pledged support to the Japan-DPRK Society.[8]

Hatanaka stated in his keynote speech at the convention, "the fundamental policy of the Japan-DPRK Society is that Japanese people will demonstrate initiative in establishing friendly relations with Koreans as nationals of an independent nation. To this end, the society will support the Ch'ongnyŏn's Platform of Action and cooperate closely with the Ch'ongnyŏn."[9] Various resolutions were adopted by the convention to launch new programs, including helping Koreans in Japan to repatriate and expediting the mutual release of Japanese fishermen jailed in Korea and Koreans imprisoned in the Ōmura prison camp (chap. 6). Since then, the society has attempted to strengthen ties between Japanese and North Koreans, providing full support to the Ch'ongnyŏn in safeguarding the interests of Koreans in Japan. Today, the Japan-DPRK Society has become the most powerful P'yŏngyang lobbyist organization in Japan, and many of its leaders have been awarded the DPRK's Second Class National Flag medals by Kim Il-sung for meritorious service.

THE CAMPAIGN AGAINST THE ROK-JAPAN NORMALIZATION TREATY

Ch'ongnyŏn's close collaboration with the Japan-DPRK Society is essential if it is to articulate its demands. Certainly, the Ch'ongnyŏn could not have succeeded in obtaining the accreditation of Chosŏn University and the agreement on Korean repatriation to North Korea (chap. 6) without the society's support. This support, however, does not always ensure Ch'ongnyŏn's success, as the campaign against the ROK-Japan Normalization Treaty indicates.

There was a plethora of arguments against the Normalization Treaty. Opposition to the treaty can be classified into two broad categories, one originating from left-wing ideology and the other from general dissatisfaction with the substance of the treaty. Those who held the former position were mostly Ch'ongnyŏn members and Japanese leftists, who denounced the whole idea of normalizing relations between South Korea and Japan. They argued that Japan's attempt to normalize relations only with the ROK would jeopardize the possibility of Koreans achieving a unified Korea, thereby perpetuating its division into two political entities. Japan's action, they said, would constitute a denial of the DPRK's existence and also an explicit manifestation of an unfriendly posture against the government of the DPRK. They predicted that the ROK-Japan Treaty would eventually lead to a military alliance against the DPRK, which might draw Japan into a war in Asia. Furthermore, they argued, normalized relations between the two nations would provide an opportunity for Japanese capitalists to penetrate the South Korean market for further economic exploitation.[10]

Nonideological opposition to the treaty came from elements of the Mindan forces opposed to the Park regime in South Korea, who criticized the low posture maintained by the ROK government in the treaty negotiations and its obsession with obtaining economic aid from Japan. As a result, they alleged, ROK officials made excessive concessions to the Japanese in all other important matters. They charged that all the agreements signed by the ROK government were products of this humiliating diplomacy.[11]

During the first ten years of ROK-Japan negotiations, starting in 1951, there was little organized opposition in either country because the chance of success in the talks seemed quite remote. But the military coup of 1961 in South Korea and the willingness of the junta to come to an early conclusion of the treaty with Japan changed the whole situation. As the negotiations between the two countries progressed, forces opposing the talks gradually built up strength within left-wing groups, especially the Ch'ongnyŏn. On 3 December 1964 the organization convened a meeting of its Central Committee and drafted a protest note against the Japanese government's resumption of negotiating sessions with the ROK government delegates. On 7 December the protest was officially adopted by some 1,800 local Ch'ongnyŏn delegates assembled at the Bunkyō Hall in Tokyo, where they deliberated strategy for their antitreaty campaign.[12] Later, the Ch'ongnyŏn delivered the protest note to the Japanese Minister of Foreign Affairs. The Ch'ongnyŏn declared that 1965 would be the decisive year to crush the ROK-Japan talks, which it would do by strengthening its ties with the Japanese people. This announcement marked the beginning of its fervent antitreaty campaign.

For two weeks in early January 1965, the Ch'ongnyŏn mobilized some 14,000 demonstrators in twenty-eight different locations throughout Japan to protest resumption of the treaty negotiations. A distinctive feature differentiating this campaign strategy from others was that the Ch'ongnyŏn strongly urged its members to refrain from any violent action and to limit the protest movement to the legal framework prescribed by Japanese law.

The thinking behind this strategy was that the Japanese government might take oppressive measures against the pro-North Korean elements in Japan upon the successful conclusion of the normalization treaty with the ROK. Anticipating the worst and recalling the red purge of the early 1950s, the Ch'ongnyŏn was reportedly preparing to go underground to carry on its activities.[13] In the attempt to block the treaty, the Ch'ongnyŏn was reported to have received 50 million yen from the DPRK, and another 100 million yen was raised among Koreans in Japan. With these funds, the Ch'ongnyŏn pledged to aid both "materially and morally" the Japanese left-wing groups involved in the campaign.[14]

The Ch'ongnyŏn decided to place its emphasis on mobilizing the Japanese people and dissident groups within the Mindan to participate in mass action in the streets and to join opposition forces in South Korea in an all-out campaign against the treaty. The task of mobilizing the Japanese left-wing groups was to be performed by the Japan-DPRK Society, because the left-wingers were ideologically opposed to Premier Eisaku Sato's attempt to normalize relations only with South Korea. In mobilizing the Mindan dissidents, the Ch'ongnyŏn lured them with promises of financial rewards for participating in the campaign.[15] As a matter of fact, many dissident elements within the Mindan were looking for a chance to express their frustration against their home government. The situation was aggravated by the ROK government's refusal to allow a Mindan representative to participate in the negotiations with Japan on the question of Mindan members' legal status in Japan.

The major strategy for the Ch'ongnyŏn members was to participate in only peaceful protest rallies and petition assemblies while placing greater emphasis on propaganda activities. In early July 1965 many leading members of the Ch'ongnyŏn were sent on speaking tours around the country to explain to the public why the Ch'ongnyŏn opposed the treaty. By September, the Ch'ongnyŏn had dispatched 863 of its members to 249 different cities in Japan to distribute propaganda materials in the streets. Sometimes the materials were stuffed into daily newspapers distributed to subscribers through regular delivery channels. On the twentieth anniversary of the DPRK's Independence Day, the Ch'ongnyŏn actively exploited the occasion for propaganda purposes. Various art and music festivals were also sponsored throughout Japan by the Ch'ongnyŏn, always designed to suit its propaganda purposes.[16]

Meanwhile, the first wave of street demonstrations against the treaty had begun in Tokyo in early March 1965. The Mindan dissidents, including students instigated by the Ch'ongnyŏn, staged demonstrations in front of the office building of the South Korean mission in Japan and at hotels where the delegates were staying. The dissidents protested the humiliatingly low posture maintained by the ROK delegates during the negotiations and their failure to secure from the Japanese government a more favorable legal status for Koreans residing in Japan. On several occasions, demonstrators broke through police cordons, and nineteen of them were arrested by the Japanese police.[17] Despite this series of demonstrations staged by Mindan members, the official position of the Mindan was to discourage demonstrations and to support the ROK government policy.[18]

As for the mobilization of Japanese left-wing groups, it is difficult to ascertain how much influence the Ch'ongnyŏn actually had in its treaty campaign. There is little doubt that the Japan-DPRK Society played as active a role as possible in appealing to the Japanese people for support. To this end, it had established a detailed play in early December 1964 for enlisting the support of other Japanese left-wing organizations.

In early February 1965, Japanese involvement in the campaign against the ROK-Japan Treaty began to pick up momentum and spread throughout the country. The series of demonstrations that followed, staged by both Japanese left-wingers and some of the Mindan's dissident groups, were particularly violent and were accompanied by massive civil disobedience. Notable were the demonstrations to block the Japanese Foreign Minister's visit to South Korea on 17 February; the demonstration to oppose the signing of the initial draft treaty on 20 February; the demonstration against the signing of the draft agreements on fisheries, properties claims, and the legal status of Koreans in Japan on 3 April; and the demonstration against the official signing of the ROK-Japan Treaty and other related documents on 22 June.[19] From April to August 1965, the effect of the demonstrations appears to have been eroded by the sudden increase in the United States bombing raids and the escalation of the ground war in Vietnam. But following the opening of the fiftieth Diet session to consider approval of the ROK-Japan treaty, the demonstrations resumed their ferocity, reaching a climax between early October and the middle of December 1965.

During the year mass demonstrations took place in 2,900 localities throughout Japan, in which nearly two million people participated. These figures represented only 33.7 percent of total numbers of demonstrators the left-wing claimed they could mobilize. The arrest of 889 people was reported, 607 in the Tokyo area alone, indicating the intensity of the demonstrations in this area. It must be noted again that Ch'ongnyŏn members were conspicuously absent from direct involvement in the demonstrations. Instead, each time they sent a handful of representatives to the rallies to express their appreciation to the Japanese people.[20]

During the sixty-eight-day peak season from 5 October to 11 December 1965, the Japanese left-wing was able to mobilize more than one-and-a-quarter million people in nationwide demonstrations. The Japanese police estimated that the demonstrations were the largest ever held in the country, rivaled only by the anti-Security Treaty demonstrations of 1960.[21]

Despite the impressive mobilization of the masses, the Japanese left-wing and the Ch'ongnyŏn failed to accomplish their objective: blocking the ROK-Japan Normalization Treaty. Before considering several possible reasons for the failure, it is necessary to make one thing clear. It would be an unwarranted assumption that the massive involvement by the leftists in the treaty campaign was solely the result of Ch'ongnyŏn influence. On the contrary, the Japanese Socialist and Communist parties had their own interests at stake in participating in the campaign. They found common cause with the campaign for the purpose of enlarging their base for future political maneuvering. For both JSP and JCP, the campaign provided a perfect chance to protest and display their strength in preparation for the forthcoming battle against the renewal of the Japan-United States Security Treaty in 1970.

Early in the antinormalization campaign, the JCP proposed to the JSP that the two groups create a united front by reinstituting the defunct Joint National Council to Fight Against the Security Pact (Anpo Kyoto Kokumin Kaigi), a key element in the 1960 demonstrations. While the Mainstream faction of the JSP supported the proposal, the non-Mainstream faction opposed it. Since 1960, the JSP and the JCP had been at odds with each other because of their fundamentally different views on the questions of the Sino-Soviet dispute and the sponsoring of annual ban-the-bomb meetings. Moreover, the non-Mainstream faction of the JSP, including the Sōhyō labor federation, frequently disagreed over the question of the militant tactics employed by the JCP in demonstrations.[22]

The JCP reportedly sensed from the start the impossibility of blocking the ROK-Japan Treaty because of the prevailing political climate in Japan and Sato's firm determination on the issue, supported by the United States. To build and strengthen the JCP's local organizational structure, some pretext was needed in the mid-1960s to stir up and mobilize the public as a prelude to the 1970 struggle against the renewal of the Security Treaty. As a matter of fact, the JCP later claimed to have boosted its membership from about 150,000 to 200,000 and the circulation of its official newspaper, *Akahata*, from 620,000 to 900,000 during the hectic period of antinormalization demonstrations.[23] Despite inflammatory polemics emphasizing the significance of the campaign in *Akahata*, the JCP urged its members to avoid "extreme adventurism" in the protest movement. Hence the number of arrests of JCP members throughout the campaign was relatively small in proportion to the nearly two million people participating in the demonstrations. Even among those arrested, JCP members were fewer than those of the JSP, Sōhyō, and non-JCP organizations.[24]

As for the JSP, it selected the year 1970 as its target date for the establishment of a JSP government. By assuming the leading role in the antinormalization campaign, the JSP's scheme was to gain public support by exposing the military implications inherent in the ROK-Japan Treaty and

sharpening its criticsm of Sato's pro-United States foreign policy. By alien-
ating the public from the Sato regime, the JSP expected to influence Japan to
repudiate the Japan-United States Treaty in 1970.

Thus the major concern of each left-wing group was to compete with
the others and to display its ability to mobilize the masses in the campaign.
Therefore, the leftists saw no practical need for organizing one united front.
It was only with the official announcement of the successful conclusion of
the ROK-Japan talks that the left-wing leaders hastily convened a meeting
to discuss joint action. The only thing they could agree on was to work
together on a daily basis in participating in the antitreaty campaign.[25] With
this temporary coalition, they were able to carry out sensational wavelike
demonstrations five times within a one-month period. But the united action
by the left wing in attempting to block Diet approval of the treaty came too
late. In the Diet, it was an unequal contest from the outset. Sato's Liberal
Democratic party enjoyed not quite a two-thirds majority in both the House
of Representatives and the less important House of Councillors. Hence the
outcome of the Diet deliberation was predictable, and indeed the treaty was
ratified by both houses.[26]

For the Ch'ongnyŏn the success of the campaign was heavily dependent upon unity among Japanese left-wing groups. The issue of the ROK-
Japan Treaty alone was insufficient to arouse the interest of the entire Japanese public, unlike the 1960 protest movement. Besides, the real issue of the
Normalization Treaty was somewhat blurred by other equally salient issues
of the time, such as the anti-Vietnam War movement, the campaign against
the visit of a United States aircraft carrier and a Polaris submarine, and the
campaign to expedite the withdrawal of United States troops from Japanese
bases. Nevertheless, the LDP was adamantly determined to pass the treaty
and launched a well-organized counter campaign through the mass media
urging the need for normalization. With the support of the Democratic
Socialist party, the LDP was able to outweigh the influence of the Ch'ongnyŏn.

A few words should be added concerning the contemporary relations
between the Ch'ongnyŏn and the JCP. Viewing them in terms of their ideological affinity and their past cooperation, one would expect that the
Ch'ongnyŏn would derive most of its outside support from the JCP. On
many occasions in the past, *Akahata* referred to the People's Workers Party
of North Korea as a "fraternal party" to indicate their ideological solidarity.
The Ch'ongnyŏn could always count on the JCP's support on crucial issues
such as Chosŏn University accreditation or the repatriation of Koreans to
North Korea. In 1955, the JCP and the Ch'ongnyŏn jointly produced a film
entitled *Ch'ŏllima* (Flying Horse) to promote the public image of North
Korea in Japan.[27]

The relations between the two began to show signs of strain after a
visit of Miyamoto Kenji, secretary general of the JCP, to North Korea in

1968. He was reluctant to endorse the North Korean campaign to deify Kim Il-sung as "Sun of the Nation." The discord became irreparable after *Akahata* ran an anonymous editorial on 2 March 1972, the tone of which was acrimonious throughout. Though it did not mention Kim by name, it warned fellow Japanese to refrain from endorsing a "personal cult" in support of the leader of a foreign nation. By implication, the charge was directed against the Japan-DPRK Society, which had supported the North Korean deification campaign. Until then, the Ch'ongnyŏn seems to have wielded some substantial influence over the formulation of policy in the Japan-DPRK Society, keeping it congruent with the DPRK's objectives. As the JCP gradually began to disassociate itself from Japan-DPRK activities, the Ch'ongnyŏn could no longer count on its support.[28] Currently, the Ch'ongnyŏn seeks support from some Socialists who organized the Association to Support the Unification of Korean People (Chōsen minzoku no tōitsu o shiji suru kai), headed by Den Hideo, and the Japanese Committee to Support the Autonomous and Peaceful Unification of Korea (Chōsen no jishuteki heiwa tōitsu shiji Nihon Iinkai), headed by Iwai Akira. In this, as in other matters, the Ch'ongnyŏn has openly become a semiofficial organ of the North Korean government.

The basic posture of the DPRK was outlined by Kim Il-sung in his address to the Fifth Party Congress in 1970,[29] when he indicated that his primary goal was the unification of Korea on his own terms. According to his view, the Park regime was a puppet of the "United States imperialists" and had built a military base in Korea to expand into North Korea. The chief hindrances to Kim's goal of unification were the Park regime and the United States troops in South Korea. One way to achieve unification, he stated, was to drive out the Americans from Korea and to liberate the people of South Korea by overthrowing "Park's fascist regime" through revolution. He further noted that the proper role for Japan would be to assist its neighbor to attain this goal, but the Normalization Treaty with the Park regime constituted an unfriendly act toward the DPRK.[30] He made a distinction between the Japanese people as a whole and its regime by saying that the Japanese regime refused to cooperate with North Korea, although the Japanese people were friendly to the DPRK.[31]

In responding to Kim Il-sung's address, the Ch'ongnyŏn convened its own Ninth National Convention in January 1971, at which members pledged to comply with the DPRK's policy. The Ch'ongnyŏn adopted the Action Policy Program at this time, a program that included, among many other things, support for the anti-Park campaign in South Korea and the goal of the eventual unification of Korea.[32] It also stressed the need for strengthening friendly relations with the Japanese people.

A Committee to Expedite the Unification of Motherland (Choguk T'ong-il Ch'okchin Uiwŏnhoe) was created within the Ch'ongnyŏn in 1974 to carry out these aims. It has begun a lobbying campaign to mobilize Japanese sympathizers, using two other Japanese groups serving as front organizations—the Committee in Japan to Support the Peaceful Unification of Korea (Chōsen no jishuteki heiwa tōitsu shiji Nihon Iinkai), headed by Iwai Akira; and the Committee to Support the Unification of the Korean People (Chōsen Minzoku no tōitsu o shijisuru kai), headed by Den Hideo. To maintain close contact between the DPRK and Ch'ongnyōn, *Mankyōnbong-ho,* a DPRK cargo vessel, makes a regular stop in Japan at least once a month. In recent years the Ch'ongnyōn has been functioning more as a political organization under direct control of the DPRK than as a simple overseas Korean community organization in Japan.

Despite the impressive achievements of its twenty-year history, the Ch'ongnyōn seems to have entered a new era, a transitional period of great importance. The end of the long years of Han Dok-su's leadership of the Ch'ongnyōn appears to be in sight and the struggle for succession has begun. This was manifested when his heir apparent, First Vice-Chairman Kim Byōng-sink, was purged in 1972.[33] Han's autocratic and unyielding personality and his intolerance of any criticism have been the main cause of the proliferation of dissenters within the Ch'ongnyōn hierarchy. The more intellectual members of the Ch'ongnyōn are increasingly skeptical and cynical about the growing emphasis on the deification of Kim Il-sung and his *chuch'e* (independence and self-reliance) idea, which demands absolute loyalty and unbending dedication to the North Korean regime. Some writers, scholars, and activists, like Kim Tal-su, Pak Kyōng-sik, Kang Chae-ŭn, and others who contributed a great deal to the founding of the organization, have left the Ch'ongnyōn. A number of other seemingly high-ranking members have also defected after publicly criticizing Han's authoritarian leadership. They organized a separate organization called Chominryōn (the Federation of Koreans in Japan for the Promotion of Democracy) in January 1975 and for a brief period maintained an underground status, as many of them wanted to remain anonymous. The Ch'ongnyōn denounced the existence of the Chominryōn in public, saying that it was a phantom organization fabricated by the Korean intelligence agency in Japan to embarrass the Ch'ongnyōn.[34] Actually the emergence of Chominryōn as a splinter group has had little effect in the overall structure of the Ch'ongnyōn. An interesting thing is that the Mindan has also experienced such a split within its own organization, the Hanmint'ong being the Mindan offshoot.

In September 1975, Han Dōk-su was summoned to P'yōngyang by the DPRK to attend the thirtieth anniversary of the founding of the North Korean Workers' party. At the banquet, he made a speech admitting some of his errors in leadership, as if implying that there was actual or impending stagnation and degeneration of Ch'ongnyōn activities in Japan.[35] While he was still in P'yōngyang, several hundred rank and file members of the Ch'ongnyōn accepted an invitation from the Park regime to visit South Korea. It amounted to a mass defection from the Ch'ongnyōn organization.

At a meeting of the Tenth Central Standing Committee of the Ch'ongnyŏn on 28 November 1975, Han was said to have expressed his firm determination to prevent any further erosion and to set up a new policy to revitalize the organization. The Ch'ongnyŏn from then on was placed in a defensive position, and the Mindan has more recently undertaken offensive action challenging its hegemony in the Korean community in Japan.

MINDAN

Currently the membership of the Mindan (the Korean Resident Association in Japan) is limited to those who have officially registered as nationals of South Korea. Without holding such nationality, no Korean is allowed to acquire permanent resident status in Japan under the provisions of the ROK-Japan Normalization Treaty of 1965. Though the size of Mindan membership is unknown, it can be estimated, from the number of those who acquired permanent resident status under the treaty, that there may be approximately 350,000 members. Its organizational structure and functions are actually very similar to that of the Ch'ongnyŏn. It also has four central organs that are the highest in the hierarchical organization. They are the National Convention, the Central Committee, the Central Standing Committee, and the Control Committee. The function of each organ is almost identical to that of the comparable Ch'ongnyŏn organs.

Despite its similarity to the Ch'ongnyŏn in formal organizational structure, the Mindan has been until recently a loose organization seriously lacking in discipline and unity among its members. Except for its general anti-Communist stance, the Mindan has had no strong ideological force to bind its members together. Successive Mindan leaders have blamed its shortcomings on a poor organizational structure and have tried periodic reforms without much success. Moreover, the image of Mindan's leadership has been seriously tarnished by a series of scandals about money changing hands ever since the period of the American occupation of Japan. As a result, the Mindan has been unable to gain much grassroot support from the Korean community in Japan until recently.

The Mindan was organized in October 1946, a year after the Choryŏn. Its original members were mainly anti-Communists, including some who had been expelled from Choryŏn or who had come to disagree with Choryŏn policy. Many of the current active officials in the Mindan had some past affiliation with the Choryŏn before its demise. The major objection raised by Choryŏn dissidents was that involvement in Japanese politics, by advocating "democratic revolution" to overthrow the Japanese emperor system, was not the proper concern of Koreans in Japan. Their primary interest, they argued, was to promote the well-being of resident Koreans. The Mindan therefore adopted an anti-Communist policy in direct opposition to Choryŏn Marxist-Leninist dogma. The emergence of these two ideologically opposed organizations helped deepen the split within the Korean community which has weakened the efforts of Koreans to aggregate their interests against Japanese government policy.

From the beginning, the Mindan was unable to convince the majority of Koreans that another organization was needed. The abstract ideological arguments used were almost incomprehensible to many Koreans. The visible and immediate actions taken by the Choryŏn seemed adequate to protect their interests in Japan. The Mindan leaders assumed that the Japanese government would eventually come to their aid because of their anti-Communist position, and that the Japanese would abolish the Choryŏn in reaction to the series of violent protests sponsored by left-wing groups. The Mindan was correct in its second assumption but not in its first. The Japanese government was indifferent to the Mindan's political stance, deciding that, like the Choryŏn before it, the Mindan was to be placed under the surveillance and control of law enforcement agencies. Japanese antipathy toward all Koreans had intensified with the demise of Choryŏn, and the Mindan could not capture the leadership of the Korean community. It remained a loose conglomeration of small groups of individuals related by regional loyalties, personal ties, or special interests. Constant factional strife and disunity among the leaders have marked the history of its thirty-odd years of existence. A lack of faith in Mindan's leadership was the factor that most hindered any growth toward cohesion during its critical early period.

One of the most persistent patterns among its leaders was their attempts to use the organization as a base for personal political leverage or economic advantage. Few leaders in the Mindan had any social vision or set of convictions justifying Koreans to continue residence in Japan. Self-interest seemed to be the prime motive governing their activities. As the Mindan failed to elicit any grassroot enthusiasm, it had no means of enlisting financial support. At the national level, it resorted to the practice of drafting wealthy businessmen into prestigious positions in the organization to raise funds. This practice was not very successful because, once recruited, the businessmen tried to manipulate the organization to enhance their own interests. At the local level, the leadership fell to those who had some ability to finance the organization. In many instances, the head of a regional Mindan organization acted as if he were semiautonomous, creating friction and disharmony between his local groups and the central organization.

The Mindan resorted to almost every conceivable means to raise needed funds. Toward the end of the occupation period, when some goods were set aside by general headquarters for Mindan members, these goods were often resold for profit on the black market. When the South Korean mission in Japan delegated to the Mindan some of the administrative work of processing the registration of South Korean nationals in Japan, the Mindan charged exorbitant fees for the service. Some Koreans could not avoid paying, since registration as a national of South Korea was a prerequisite for a passport to travel outside Japan or to visit the homeland.

The irreconcilable ideological differences between the two rival organizations have frequently led to acts of violence. After the Choryŏn was forced to disband, the Mindan hailed the Japanese government action, hoping that Choryŏn's demise would provide a unique opportunity to take over leadership of Koreans in Japan. But the Japanese government policy was aimed not only at left-wing Koreans but at all Koreans to restrict their political activities. This move prompted members of Mindan and of the ex-Choryŏn to open up a dialogue to explore the possibility of forming a unified Korean organization, but the effort was futile because of the outbreak of hostilities in Korea between South and North Korea.

The Mindan's effectiveness was further incapacitated by lack of support from the South Korean government. Syngman Rhee's position was that the Japanese government should bear the responsibility for the well-being of all Koreans in Japan and pay due compensation to those who had been forcibly taken to Japan during World War II. The Rhee regime itself had no substantive policy for providing any assistance for the Koreans in Japan, although from late 1950 on, Mindan officials had appealed repeatedly to the Rhee regime for it. Once they realized that no support was forthcoming, the Mindan leaders denounced the Rhee regime and proclaimed a vote of no confidence in the home government.[36] Rhee's lack of concern for the Korean residents contributed to a general alienation that turned many of them toward North Korea.

Even when it was negotiating the Normalization Treaty with Japan, the Park regime failed to obtain adequate concessions for the Korean residents in Japan. The final outcome of the 1965 agreement determining their present legal status was left almost entirely to the Japanese government. Since that time, however, the Park regime has appropriated "Supplementary Funds for Overseas Koreans" to expand pro-South Korean education in Japan as well as to strengthen the Mindan organizational structure. Meanwhile, starting in 1957, the North Korean regime began to send funds annually to support the Ch'ongnyŏn, which had resumed the activities of the Choryŏn disbanded in 1949. After the signing of the DPRK-Japan Repatriation Agreement of 1959, the DPRK successfully lured some 100,000 Koreans to repatriate to North Korea. (What their fate has been there has not been adequately reported.) With the DPRK's support, Ch'ongnyŏn has been generally successful in arousing and retaining "ethnonationalism" among those pledging their allegiance to North Korea.

In retrospect, the Mindan has had to struggle strenuously in four directions. They have had to combat internal strife and disharmony, to contend with the Japanese government, to enlist support from the home government, and to compete continuously with the rival organization, the Ch'ongnyŏn. Disunity was not limited to the Mindan itself. Frequent feuding occurred between the Mindan and officials of the South Korean embassy in Japan, who often meddled in the internal affairs of the Mindan under the pretext of extending diplomatic protection to the Koreans in Japan. When the time came to elect Mindan officials, the Korean embassy would lend support to one candidate over the other. In some instances, the Mindan officials resisted such intervention by appealing directly to the home government and asking for recall of the ambassador.

Perhaps the most serious shortcoming of the Mindan has been the absence of charismatic leaders who could bind the members together. During the first thirty-three years of its existence, the Mindan had to call for a national convention thirty-nine times to elect leaders, with terms of office varying from three months to two years. Too many candidates competed with one another, spending several million yen in campaign funds. Election irregularities, vote buying, and corruption were very common practices during national conventions. After the elections the affronts suffered by rival candidates were seldom mollified, widening the rivalries between the factions. To reward its main supporters, the Mindan created many unnecessary posts with important-sounding titles within the organizational hierarchy, resulting in a top-heavy organization with too many leaders and too few rank-and-file members, especially among the younger generation.

The Mindan maintains its own ethnic studies schools, but the student enrollment is far less than that of the Ch'ongnyŏn. It has also its own credit union systems, organized nationwide to help promote the small businesses owned by its members. And yet the Mindan has not provided ideological solidarity to bind its members together. Instead, they remain too sensitive to a variety of political issues prevailing in South Korea, and are split between antigovernment and progovernment elements. The split widened irreparably after the Kim Dae-jung kidnapping incident in 1973. Since then, the splinter group from the Mindan called the Hanmint'ong (National Congress for the Restoration of Democracy in South Korea and Promotion of Unification) has spearheaded the anti-Park movement in Japan. This splinter group has been nicknamed the "Vietcong group" of the Mindan.

The assassination of Madam Park in 1974 compelled the Park regime to reassess the importance of overseas Korean problems, particularly in Japan. Her assassin was a Korean youth who had grown up in Japan with a deep sense of hostility toward the South. The South Korean government wasted no time in formulating a new policy to strengthen the Mindan organization. It stepped up its program to indoctrinate the entire Korean populace in Japan. The South Korean government now actively encourages the children of Mindan members to visit the home country, offering them various scholarships to attend schools in Korea. A training institute under direct control of the Mindan headquarters in Tokyo provides regular courses to train future leaders of the organization. Some staff members are occasionally sent to Korea for further training. The Mindan is keenly aware of the need for interesting younger members, as the leadership is still too firmly held by the older generation. The Mindan is in fact becoming a highly centralized and disciplined organization staffed by professionals seeking to meet the challenge of the Ch'ongnyŏn.

To infuse a stronger ethnic identity, the Mindan has launched a fifty-hour compulsory ethnic studies program for all its members.[37] It has also since 1975 taken decisive measures to solidify its membership and to reorganize its structure under the slogan of "harmonious collaboration" and the "se-Mindan" (New Mindan) campaigns.

The current invitation to all Koreans in Japan to visit their families and relatives in South Korea is part of this new program. The Park regime now believed that winning the minds of presently pro-North Koreans in Japan can be considered a sort of victory in the South-North Korean confrontation. South Korea therefore had opened the door to all past and present Ch'ongnyŏn members, allowing them to visit South Korea regardless of their left-wing political involvement. At the same time, their safe conduct and return to Japan are fully assured. Since the offer was first made in the spring of 1975, several thousand rank-and-file members of the Ch'ongnyŏn have responded to the invitation. Encouraged by this response, the Mindan has pledged to set up a fund of one billion yen to subsidize Ch'ongnyŏn members' trips to South Korea.

CONCLUSIONS

The division between the two antagonistic organizations—Mindan and Ch'ongnyŏn—is so wide that it has seriously reduced the likelihood that Koreans in Japan can integrate their demands to overcome the various discriminatory policies of the Japanese government. Each Korean organization as a pressure group is bound to divert its attention to three different fronts. First, each has to mend its fences with the home government. Second, each has to compete with the rival organization. Third, each has to face the Japanese public and policymakers. These concerns are closely interwoven in formulating action policy.

In turn, the shortcomings of the two Korean organizations are well exploited by the Japanese government to keep the Korean problem under control. The immediate disenfranchisement of the Koreans in Japan after World War II was an effective means to incapacitate them and prevent them from becoming politically potent as an ethnic voting bloc in postwar Japan. By so doing, the government used a legitimate subterfuge to segregate Koreans in all aspects of life.

Two persistent patterns are used by the Japanese public in dealing with the Korean minority problem: one is to try to reduce the number of Koreans in Japan through repatriation and deportation. The other is to compel Koreans to assimilate behaviorally to Japanese cultural norms while refusing to accept them into the mainstream of society. The present Japanese society does not tolerate the presence of a different ethnic, cultural, or linguistic group in Japan.

The Ch'ongnyŏn has firmly demonstrated its determination to preserve its members' ethnicity, culture, and language through the establishment of its own educational system from kindergarten to university. Mindan members and their children, however, have generally been more amenable to assimilation, hoping that through acquiescence they may escape discrimination and persecution. It is a widely accepted practice for non-Ch'ongnyŏn members to use two names: one is in Korean as it appears on the "alien registration card"; the other is a Japanese name commonly used in daily social contact, in school, or in business transactions. The children in such families have often shown eagerness to be accepted by the Japanese to secure a feeling of attachment and of belonging to a majority.

The inability of the Mindan in the past to serve as an effective Korean interest group in Japan has caused the South Korean government to step in through its embassy on behalf of the Korean community. In fact, the South Korean embassy and eight other regional consulate-generals located throughout Japan are more capable than the Mindan in helping with the problems of Korean residents. Consequently, the Mindan is not in a position to dispute the authority of the Korean embassy on matters of grave importance when it may be necessary to put pressure on Japanese government policy. Until the Mindan can develop as an effective pressure group to protect Korean residents' interests, intervention by the South Korean government seems likely to continue. Neither Mindan nor Ch'ongnyŏn can be said to be nonpolitical organizations. It is apparent to everyone that both are heavily subsidized and under the firm control of their respective home governments.

Like Ch'ongnyŏn and the P'yŏngyang lobby formed by Japanese left-wing groups, South Korea has strengthened the Seoul lobby among the conservative Liberal Democratic party members. Two groups, among many others, should be noted here. One is the Japan-South Korea Friendship Association (Nikkan Shinwakai), and the other is the League of Japan-South Korea Parliamentary Members (Nikkan Giin Renmei), which was organized in 1975.[38] These are counterparts of Ch'ongnyŏn's support organizations, the Japan-DPRK Society and the League of Parliamentary Members to Promote Friendly Relations between Japan-DPRK (Nichō Yūkō Sokusin Giin Renmei).

In their efforts to influence the Japanese people and policymakers, both Mindan and Ch'ongnyŏn are now aligning themselves with Japanese sympathizers. At the official level, the links are between South Korean parliamentary members and Japanese Diet members of LDP, and between North Korean parliamentary members and the left-wing parties in Japan. In the complicated networks of both lobbying groups, the Mindan and Ch'ongnyŏn are likely to function as subsidiary agents of the respective home governments rather than as merely overseas Korean community organizations representing the interests of the Korean residents in Japan.

PART TWO

CONTEMPORARY ISSUES

The three chapters of Part II deal with issues interrelating Japanese citizenship with the persistent myth of Japanese ethnic homogeneity. Chapter 7 examines the legal status of Koreans in contemporary Japan, considering from a legal standpoint, as well as the standpoint of ethnic identity and pride, the reasons why many Korean Japanese have not become Japanese citizens.

Chapters 8 and 9 examine the complex issues that have shaped policies of formal education. These policies are crucial when one considers why present-day Koreans do or do not assimilate into Japanese society. Chapter 8 traces the attempts to utilize ethnic studies to maintain or even revitalize an ethnic conscience in Korean children born in Japan. Chapter 9 discusses the possibilities of success of the ethnic studies presently attempted by various Korean groups.

What are the reasons for the maintenance of a separate Korean identity? What is the role of formal education in respect to these questions concerning the diversity of identity as it now exists within Japanese society—a society that does not yet distinguish between ethnic heredity and citizenship? Can a modern society refuse to make this essential distinction?

7

THE LEGAL STATUS OF KOREANS IN JAPAN

Changsoo Lee

According to a generally accepted principle of international law, each state is the sole judge of the extent to which aliens may enjoy civil privileges and other substantive rights within its jurisdiction. For Koreans in Japan, however, legal status and subsequent privileges were determined formally by international agreement and informally by social attitudes. The difficult process of attaining Japanese citizenship was not simplified by the international agreement signed by the Republic of Korea and Japan in 1965. Although the Japanese government acknowledged the peculiar historical circumstances under which Koreans came to Japan before World War II, the legal privileges granted to Koreans under the treaty agreement were severely restrictive in scope. To date, the whole array of Korean problems in Japan has been complicated by legal discrimination against those with ascribed alien status despite their long years of residence in Japan. In effect, there is still no sufficient distinction in present Japanese legal thought between ethnicity and citizenship.

The present Korean residents in Japan include those who elected to remain there after World War II and their descendants born in Japan. By the end of 1974, 643,000 nonnaturalized Koreans were recorded in Japan, a figure that represents 86.1 percent of all aliens registered in the Immigration Control Bureau of the Ministry of Justice (table 9). And of these alien Koreans, 75 percent were born in Japan. Therefore, whenever any amendment to the Immigration Control Laws is discussed in the Diet, Koreans usually become a focal point in the minds of many Japanese legislators.

According to the birth registrations of those born in Korea, the majority were registered in the three southern and southeastern provinces of Kyŭnognam, Kyŏngbuk, and Cheju. It is for this reason that the Kyŏngsang provincial dialect is most widely spoken. Whereas the older generation speaks Japanese with a Kyŏngsang accent, Japanese-born younger Koreans who can speak Korean, speak a Kyŏngsang Korean with a heavy Japanese accent.

According to a report published by the Japanese government, 75.6 percent of present-day Koreans are "Nisei" and "Sansei," second and third generations respectively, in Japan; Koreans born in Korea now comprise less than 25 percent of the total (fig. 2). Most of the former have never seen Korea, nor do many speak Korean to any degree. Their age distribution in 1974 is shown in figure 3, which indicates that a majority were between the ages of twenty and thirty and thus were born during the postwar baby boom. Although the older generation, with its memories of the Japanese colonization of Korea, will gradually disappear, there is little sign that the younger generation will be more readily accepted by the mainstream of an affluent Japanese society.

According to a report published by the Ministry of Justice, an intermarriage rate of 42.4 percent between Koreans and Japanese was reported in 1969, increasing to 43.4 percent in 1970, 46.9 percent in 1971, and up to 48 percent in the following year. This trend will undoubtedly grow in the future. It is an indication that the traditional antipathy between the two nationals is on the wane among the young. While such exogamy is still strongly frowned upon by many older-generation Koreans and Japanese, the number of ethnically mixed children born will increase. It is difficult to determine how many of these intermarriages are with Burakumin who live in adjacent neighborhoods.

Naturalization and intermarriage take place among the second and third generations and are related to their assimilation, an indication that Korean organizations in Japan cannot confine the younger generations. Those youth affiliated with the Mindan more readily assimilate because they are socialized in Japanese schools, whereas Ch'ongnyŏn youth are usually more limited in their peer contacts with outsiders, since their activities at school and in voluntary organizations are ideologically dogmatized. Many of these youth drop out of most group activities after they graduate from senior high school. Interested in their immediate, contemporary world, many consider the values and norms of both Mindan and Ch'ongnyŏn organizations too much oriented to the native land.

In instances of intermarriage, most young Japanese who have developed an intimate relationship with a Korean think their partner is different from the stereotyped image the Japanese hold of Koreans. They believe that the Koreans with whom they are associating are basically "Japanese" in race and culture. Accordingly, young Japanese who plan marriage with a Korean are not sensitive to the cultural, social, and political differences that may be raised by their own families when they become aware of impending marriage.

Two significant trends are noticeable among the younger Koreans in Japan. One is the increasing number of second- and third-generation Koreans who become naturalized. The other is the increase in intermarriage between Korean and Japanese young people. It is estimated that this number exceeds the number of intragroup marriages between youths related either to the North Korean or the South Korean political factions. Marriage across

KOREANS IN JAPAN
PLACE OF BIRTH

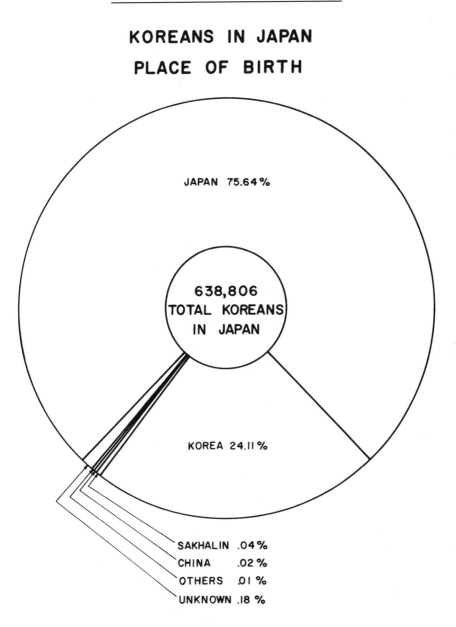

Source: Ministry of Justice *Zairyūgaikokujin Tōkei,* 1974.

Fig. 2. The slight discrepancy between this figure and table 20 in chapter 10 derives from different closing dates. Table 20 is as of April 1974, and this figure is as of December 1974.

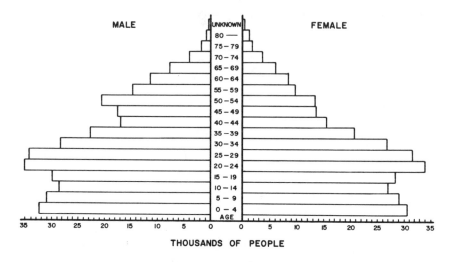

Source: Ministry of Justice *Zairyūgaikokujin Tōkei*, 1974.

Fig. 3. Koreans in Japan.

ethnic lines has been, generally, socially tabooed for both Japanese and Koreans. There are numerous reported episodes of love affairs broken up by family pressure. Contrary to this tradition, among the 7,450 marriages reported by Koreans in 1972, 3,576 were mixed marriages between Koreans and Japanese. The number of Japanese males marrying Korean females is slightly higher than the number of Korean males marrying Japanese women.

COLONIAL NATIONALITY

After the official transfer of Korean sovereignty through annexation in 1910, Koreans were legally considered to be under Japanese jurisdiction and thereby to hold Japanese nationality. The Japanese Ministry of Justice, however, noted that the old Japanese Nationality Law enacted in 1899 was inapplicable to colonial subjects, even though they were considered Japanese nationals. Then, ethnicity determined citizenship. Colonial subjects were not to be accorded the same respected status as Japanese citizens. The Imperial Japanese government maintained a rigidly segregated *koseki* system (family registry) to differentiate those of Japanese ancestry (*naichijin*) from nationals of colonial origin (*gaichijin*). A child born in Japan of Korean parents was to be registered according to parental lineage in Korea and could not be registered in any Japanese *koseki*.

The place where a family registry was initially recorded was to be officially regarded, for purposes of identifying national origin, as a person's permanent address. Although the Japanese government undertook very extensive cultural assimilation politics to Japanize all its colonial subjects, it never intended to integrate them fully nor to accord them full-fledged citizenship. Suffrage was never extended to Koreans in Korea by the colonial government. The Japanese government relented, however, in respect to Korean voting privileges in mainland Japan.

By declaration of the General Election Law of 1925, all male Imperial subjects were enfranchised for the first time in Japanese history. As Imperial subjects, 38,912 Korean men were eligible to vote in the election of September 1931.[1] The turnout was so low, however, that their votes were considered insignificant. But in 1932 and 1937, several Koreans were elected to the Japanese Diet and served full terms as Diet members, and several hundred Koreans were given appointments in the Imperial Japanese government. Many of them had graduated from the Japanese Military Academy and had served in the Japanese Imperial Army.

LEGAL STATUS OF KOREANS UNDER THE AMERICAN OCCUPATION

In the early days of the American occupation of Japan, the Supreme Commander for the Allied Powers (SCAP) made no clarification regarding the legal status of Koreans in Japan. SCAP authorities apparently believed that all Koreans would soon be repatriated to Korea. The American Joint Chiefs of Staff sent a directive to General Douglas MacArthur that Koreans were to be treated as "liberated nationals" if military security were not concerned, since they had been Japanese subjects.[2] A lack of any clarification as to when Koreans should be treated as "liberated" or as "enemy nationals" caused both Koreans and Japanese to misconstrue the possible extent of Japanese legal jurisdiction. The Koreans believed that they were entitled to treatment different from that of the defeated Japanese, and in some isolated incidents, Koreans refused to subject themselves to any jurisdiction by Japanese authorities.[3]

The term *liberated nationals* had been a means for SCAP to distinguish between the Japanese and their former colonial subjects but at the same time to exclude the Koreans from the category of the most privileged United Nations nationals serving in the occupied country. Koreans were not even mentioned as citizens of "nations whose status has changed as a result of the war."[4] As stated in chapter 4, this thinking was clearly symbolized at the time when supplementary rations were distributed to foreign nationals who had been residing in Japan. Koreans were not included. The SCAP directive on rationing specifically stated that "nothing in this directive will be construed to change the food ration for Korean nationals who have elected to remain in Japan, who are to receive the same rations as Japanese nationals."[5]

Finally some fifteen months later, SCAP made it clear to the public through a press release that Koreans who elected to remain in Japan would be considered Japanese nationals until they were recognized as Korean nationals by the lawfully established government of Korea.[6] Therefore, legal jurisdiction over Koreans in Japan would continue to be exercised by Japanese authorities. Koreans immediately protested, demanding legal treatment different from that accorded "defeated" nationals. The protest prompted SCAP to declare on 20 November 1946 that it had "no intention of interfering in any way with the fundamental rights of any person of any nationality in regard to the retention, relinquishment, or choice of citizenship." But SCAP stressed that to exempt Koreans from the observance of Japanese laws might create a form of extraterritoriality that was against occupation policy.[7]

The Japanese government had suspended the suffrage of Korean residents with passage of the Amendment to Election Law No. 42 of the House of Representatives on 17 December 1945.[8] In 1947 the Japanese government, with the tacit consent of SCAP authorities, enacted the Alien Registration Law, by which Koreans were legally classified as aliens. The Japanese Ministry of Justice, however, held that Koreans in Japan would continue to retain Japanese nationality until the peace treaty with the United States became effective in 1952.[9] Thus the Japanese government's policy was contradictory, recognizing Koreans' retention of Japanese nationality in principle while treating them as aliens, restricting their legal rights in the areas of public housing, social welfare, taxation, food rationing, and business.

The Immigration Control Law of 1952 (Art. 24, par. 4, items e and f)[10] stipulated that anyone who violated the provisions of the Alien Registration Law (slightly amended the same year) was subject to deportation. The practical effect of these laws was frequent abuse by prejudiced Japanese police officers, who began to harass many innocent Koreans. It allowed for a police surveillance system conducive to extortion as well as harassment and subjected many Koreans to unreasonable search and seizure. The inability of a Korean to produce a registration card upon interrogation by an officer often gave rise to suspicions of illegality. From the early 1950s, the Japanese government began to invoke these laws to prosecute many left-wing Koreans once affiliated with the Choryŏn, which had been ordered to disband because of its militant activites.[11] Throughout the fifteen-year period after the enactment of the Alien Registration Law, a total of 182,700 violations by Koreans resulted in indictments, fines, and other forms of prosecution for violation of various portions of its provisions.[12]

It is a generally accepted principle among nations that each state is free to decide who shall be its nationals, under what conditions nationality shall be conferred, and who shall be deprived of such status and in what manner.

TABLE 9
Korean Violators of the Alien Registration Law, 1947-1961

Year	Number
1947	882
1948	1,074
1949	2,499
1950	10,193
1951	9,253
1952	9,451
1953	19,377
1954	19,898
1955	24,993
1956	13,897
1957	23,167
1958	9,725
1959	10,333
1960	18,407
1961	9,511
Total	182,700

Source: Zainichi Chōsenjin no jinken o mamorukai, *Zainichi Chōsenjin hōte-kichii* (Tokyo: Zainichi Chōsenjin no jinken o mamorukai, 1965), p. 91.

Therefore, the action taken by the Japanese authorities to reclassify the legal status of Koreans in Japan was technically within the sphere of Japanese sovereignty. Viewed from the standpoint of ethnic discrimination, however, it is clear that Koreans who once had rendered service, willingly or otherwise, to Imperial Japan were now stripped of legal rights on the basis of ethnicity. The Japanese government failed to provide even a minimum standard of justice for Koreans remaining in Japan by not offering them the freedom to select citizenship, which is customary upon the transfer of sovereignty.[13]

The emergence of two antagonistic Korean regimes added to the legal confusion over nationality. In accordance with the Alien Registration Law of 1947, every alien was required to identify his or her nationality in the column provided on the registration form. The Koreans simply noted their nationality as "Chosŏn," or Korean, as no legal government was yet established in Korea. But when it was necessary for aliens to renew their registration, the Mindan demanded a change from "Chosŏn" to "Han'guk." They argued that the name "Chosŏn" had been established by Imperial Japan after its annexation of Korea, and that only those who pledged their loyalty

TABLE 10

Detailed Breakdown of Korean Violators of the
Alien Registration Law, 1955-1961

Violations of provisions	Total number of arrests	Remarks
Failure to register birth of child	10,528 (10.7%)	Tardiness in birth registration of more than 30 days after birth of child
Failure to reapply for registration	4,232 (4.3%)	Applied for reissuance of registration card more than 14 days after loss or theft of card
Failure to renew registration	44,075 (44.8%)	Applied after expiration date
Failure to notify of change of address	9,948 (10.1%)	Failure to notify of change within 14 days after move
Failure to carry registration card	26,329 (26.7%)	Unable to produce card upon interrogation
Other	3,371 (3.4%)	False information and perjury
Total	98,479 (100%)	

Source: *Sangi'in Hōmu Iinkai Kaigiroku*, 20 December 1962.

to North Korea still adhered to it. As "Han'guk" was used by the legitimate government already established and recognized by the United Nations, the continued usage of the old name would constitute dishonor to the legal government of the Republic of Korea.

The Japanese Ministry of Justice responded that filling the space in the registration form had no binding legal effect upon the determination of one's nationality, and that the legal question of nationality would be settled after the conclusion of the peace treaty in 1952. But persistent demands by the Mindan forced the Japanese government to accept the name change upon the presentation of a certificate duly registered by the ROK government. Thus the alien registration system intensified the polarization of Koreans in Japan by giving rise to questions of nationality and of allegiance to one or the other of the two regimes in Korea.

THE IMMIGRATION CONTROL LAW OF 1952

Since restoration of Japan's full sovereignty by the San Francisco Treaty of 1952, the legal status of Koreans in Japan has been regulated by Japan's Immigration Control Law. This law has been amended more than a dozen times. Immediately after the law went into effect, Koreans were required to establish their eligibility for continued residence and to designate the length of time they intended to stay in Japan.

Article 4, paragraph 1, of the Immigration Control Law states that "no one is permitted to land in Japan without having registered in his passport a specific category of legal status." Included under the sixteen categories are: diplomat or other foreign government official, transient, tourist, businessman, student and researcher, sportsman, artist, entertainer, clergyman, correspondent, technician, special laborer employed by a Japanese firm, permanent resident, and so on. The conditions of admission and the length of stay permitted in Japan vary according to the category under which an alien is admitted.

Most Koreans, however, had already established residence in Japan without having been issued passports. Therefore, most Koreans had no legal status. What the Japanese government had intended to do was to classify Koreans under certain stipulated categories so as to control and restrict their activities as aliens in Japan.

Because no provision in this law was applicable to the Koreans in Japan, the Japanese government enacted supplementary Law No. 126 of 1952.[14] It specified that those who entered Japan before 1 September 1945, and their descendants born from that date until the peace treaty went into effect on 28 April 1952 were exempt from the applicability of this law. It further stipulated that Koreans who established their residence during the period mentioned would be given special consideration for "humanitarian" reasons to maintain their residence in Japan until their legal status could be determined by further legislation. Since this privilege was granted by Law No. 126, Article 2, paragraph 6, those Koreans falling under this provision were usually referred to by the Ministry of Justice as 126-2-6 aliens, and this designation was recorded on their alien registration cards.

The last of the sixteen categories covered by the Immigration Control Law is a residual one for "special resident aliens," whose stay is to be limited to a period between thirty days and three years in length. This category is widely used to cover all Korean residents who were not in Japan before 1952.

A child born after 28 April 1952 to parents of 126-2-6 aliens is required to obtain a legal determination of his or her permitted period of residence in Japan. As this type of case is covered by Article 4, paragraph 1, item 16 (2), of the law, the alien is generally referred to as 4-1-16-2 alien. The child's alien status is acquired at the time of birth registration within thirty days after birth, when the period of its stay in Japan is officially limited to three years. The child's continued residence in Japan is contingent upon a renewal of the registration every three years and is subject to approval by the Ministry of Justice (Art. 22, par. 2, items 1 and 2).

Confused bureaucratic problems have arisen over these provisions. The diversity of status within a single family creates many complications. In effect, the Japanese government deprives the child of the legal status of his or her parents. The implications are very clear; by setting up the deadline of 28 April 1952 the Japanese government intended to limit the number of Koreans given privileged alien status in Japan. Such status would be phased out as the number of 126-2-6 aliens gradually declined until the last of them died. The legal status of the special 4-1-16-2 aliens is uncertain because this status must be renewed every three years subject to approval by the Ministry of Justice. Under the law, any parent who fails to renew a child's application on time is subject to fine, imprisonment, or deportation on the grounds of "illegal presence" in Japan.

Furthermore, once an alien juvenile reaches the age of fourteen, he or she is required by law to appear in person to renew the alien registration (Art. 14, par. 1). Any alien above age fourteen who violates the Alien Registration Law is subject to a maximum punishment of 30,000 yen in fines or a one-year imprisonment (Art. 18, par. 1). It should be noted that the Japanese Civil and Criminal Codes normally accord juvenile status to anyone under the age of twenty years, which protects an adolescent from criminal prosecution. This is not so, however, for Korean aliens above fourteen years of age, who are required by law to carry a registration card at all times (Art. 13, par. 1). Failure to carry the card makes one subject to arrest and subsequent indictment for prosecution and results in a criminal record. Therefore, the card is nicknamed by some Koreans as a *"kae p'yo"* (dog tag). It was reported that during the six-year period between 1955-1961, 26.7 percent of the Koreans arrested for violation of the Alien Registration Law were cited for failure to carry the card. The statistical breakdown of Koreans arrested for violation of the Alien Registration Law is shown in table 10.

The 126-2-6 alien status seems to grant permanent residence to older first-generation Koreans in Japan, but holders of this status remain subject to deportation on the grounds specified in Article 24 of the Immigration

Control Law. Not all Koreans who have resided in Japan since 1945 are entitled to this relatively privileged status. The privilege is reserved only for those who have maintained their residence "continuously" in Japan since World War II. Anyone who at any time returned to Korea and then rejoined his or her family in Japan is not entitled to this status. For example:

> Mr. K. migrated to Japan with his family in 1938. He was employed by the Mitsubishi Shipyard Industry and lived in Kawazaki city. He was exempt from the military service, as he was working as a technical welder at a dry-dock located near Tokyo Bay. As the B-29 saturation bombing intensified, he was forced to evacuate his family back to Korea under order of the Japanese Manpower Dispersion Plan, which was intended to minimize bombing casualties during the war. After Japan's surrender, he remained in Japan and brought his family back from Korea. Under the "continued residence in Japan" clause, his wife and children were not qualified to obtain the 126-2-6 status.

The 4-1-16-2 alien status is granted only to children of 126-2-6 aliens, and their stay in Japan is limited to three years and subject to renewal thereafter. If a 126-2-6 alien loses his status as a result of criminal conviction or any action punishable by deportation, his child is not entitled to retain the 4-1-16-2 status. Instead, the child is reclassified as a 4-1-16-3 alien, as are all grandchildren of 4-1-16-2 aliens. As of 1974, there were 21,700 Koreans holding the legal status of 4-1-16-3 aliens, whose period of stay ranged from thirty days to three years (table 11), with the possibility of remaining longer if granted special approval by the Ministry of Justice. The main difference between the 4-1-16-2 and 4-1-16-3 status is that the latter has more grounds for deportation and is more restrictive in terms of social welfare benefits.

Finally there is a special category for permanent residents specified in Article 22 of the Immigration Control Law, which provides that any alien may apply for permanent resident status to the Ministry of Justice, provided the applicant satisfies certain conditions: (1) that his permanent residence is in accord with the interests of Japan; (2) that his behavior is good; and (3) that he has sufficient means or the ability to make an independent living. The advantage of 4-1-14 status is that a person may reside for an indefinite period in Japan and is free to change his profession without acquiring other resident status. The holder of this status, however, is not entitled to the National Health Insurance Program, livelihood protection, and educational opportunities that are accorded to others with permanent resident status.

A person with 4-1-14 status is subject to deportation if he or she commits an act that falls under the provisions of Article 24 of the Immigration Control Law. According to the Ministry of Justice, permanent Korean residents with 126-2-6 status are not subject to deportation. But the 4-1-14 status was finally established as an alternative measure to relieve some Korean residents who failed for one reason or another to qualify under the permanent resident status afforded by the treaty agreement. The new cate-

TABLE 11

Population of Koreans in Japan by Status Classifications (as of 1 April 1974)

Status designation	Status description	Period of stay	Number
4-1-3	Transient	15 days	11
4-1-4	Tourist	60 days	1,068
4-1-5	Business	up to 3 years	13
4-1-6	Student	1 year	540
4-1-7	Teacher or researcher	3 years	23
4-1-8	Academic or cultural activities	1 year	30
4-1-9	Entertainer or sportsman	60 days	222
4-1-10	Clergyman or missionary worker	3 years	40
4-1-11	Correspondent or journalist	3 years	25
4-1-12	Engineer or technician hired by Japanese firm	3 years	8
4-1-13	Skilled worker hired by Japanese firm	1 year	10
4-1-15	Unmarried dependent children of aliens with 4-1-5 through 4-1-13 status	same as guardians	395
4-1-16-1	Short-period residents with 4-1-5, 4-1-10, or 4-1-11 status	180 days	234
4-1-14	General permanent residents	permanent	1,712
4-1-16-2	Descendants of 126-2-6 status aliens	3 years	121,217
4-1-16-3	Special resident aliens approved by the Minister of Justice	Ranges from 30 days to 3 years	21,700
4-1-16-4	Descendants of residents of the Asumi Islands after 25 December 1953	3 years	1

Permanent resident aliens by treaty agreement	342,366
Status unknown	149,076
Status pending clarification	115
Total	638,806

Source: The Immigration Control Bureau, *Zairyū gaikokujin tōkei*, 1974. According to the 1978 report, the total Korean population in Japan is 659,025. As of this writing, the above table is only available statistics classified by each legal status of Koreans in Japan. The latest report published in 1978 by the Immigration Control Bureau does not indicate any detailed breakdown of the figure. Although the 1978 figure shows a slight increase of the Korean population over the 1974 report, the overall outlook on the legal status patterns has no significant change. For details, see the Immigration Control Bureau, "Shōwa gojūnen ni okeru shustunyūkoku kanri no gaikyō" [The Current Situation of the 1978 Immigration Control], *Hosōjihō*, 31, no. 7 (1978): 37, 57.

gory was confirmed by a joint communique issued by both South Korean and Japanese Ministers of Justice on 24 August 1969. As a result, the scope of eligibility for permanent residence for Koreans was broadened to include: (1) Koreans who resided in Japan until the end of World War II but visited Korea briefly and returned to Japan before the Peace Treaty went into effect in 1952; and (2) persons who had never resided in Japan before or during the war but had entered Japan before the Peace Treaty went into effect.

Under the current Immigration Control Law, the door to permanent resident status is still closed for the holders of the 126-2-6 and 4-1-16-2 status. A bill is pending, however, in the judicial committee of the Diet to amend the law to accommodate these people under the category of permanent resident. It should be noted that Koreans who pledge their loyalty to North Korea are not entitled to permanent resident status by the treaty agreement, since proof of South Korean nationality is required for that.

Consequently, there is a substantial number of Koreans who still hold the 126-2-6 status who have descendants with 4-1-16-2 status. As to the number of the 126-2-6 status aliens, the Ministry of Justice refused to reveal the exact figure in the report, except to state that the figures were recorded under "unknown" (table 11). It can be assumed, however, that almost all figures designated "unknown" refer to 126-2-6 status aliens. Viewed from the "resident status by treaty agreement" classification (discussed below), it is generally estimated that there are a little over 350,000 pro-South Koreans who hold membership in Mindan, as compared with approximately 250,000 who are reported to hold membership in Ch'ongyön, the pro-North Korean organization.

It must be noted that the complicated web of status classifications and the subsequent legal treatment accorded aliens are equally applicable to all other aliens residing in Japan. The presence of a large number of Koreans was the most important factor taken into consideration when the Japanese Diet legislated the Immigration Control Law and the Alien Registration Law, the two primary laws governing aliens. Since the end of World War II, Koreans have continued to comprise about 85-90 percent of all aliens residing in Japan.

THE ROK-JAPAN NORMALIZATION TREATY

The ROK-Japan Normalization Treaty was signed on 22 June 1965 and went into effect on 18 December 1965. The agreement accompanying the treaty covered fisheries, property claims, and economic cooperation; art objects and cultural cooperation; and the legal status of Koreans in Japan. Most important of all, as far as Koreans in Japan were concerned, was the agreement defining their legal status and rights, and the subsequent treatment to be provided by the Japanese government.[15] The significant factor is that the legal status of Koreans in Japan was determined by an international treaty, even though Japan as a sovereign nation had exclusive jurisdiction over aliens. The agreement on the legal status of Koreans in Japan consisted of three major parts: scope and eligibility to apply for permanent residence, grounds for deportation, and subsequent legal treatment.

KOREAN ELIGIBILITY FOR PERMANENT RESIDENCE

Until the ROK-Japan Normalization Treaty, Korean residents in Japan had been generally classified into three categories: 126-2-6, 4-1-16-2, and 4-1-16-3 status aliens. As stated in the Preamble to the treaty, the Japanese government recognized officially the long years of Korean residence in Japan. But the eligibility of Koreans to apply for permanent residence was to be limited to: (1) those who had been resident *continuously* in Japan since 15 August 1945, up to the time of their application for permanent residence (Art. 1, par. 1*a*, emphasis added); (2) those who were born in Japan after 16 August 1945 as lineal descendants of persons in category 1 and who applied for permanent residence within five years of the effective date of the agreements (Art. 1, par. 1); and (3) children born after 16 January 1971 of parents who received permanent residence status under categories 1 and 2, provided that application for the children's permanent residence was filed within sixty days from their date of birth (Art. 1, par. 2).

The important factor to note here is that the agreement makes no mention of any future generations born to parents in category 3. But under Article 2 Japan agreed, if requested by South Korea, to hold consultations regarding the matter after a lapse of twenty-five years. The Japanese government was reluctant to grant permanent residence to successive generations of Koreans in Japan lest their privileged alien status be perpetuated forever. During the negotiations, the ROK government representatives insisted that permanent residence be granted to all future descendants of Korean residents in Japan. But even after years of negotiations, the Japanese government refused to consider the proposal.

The agreement also stipulated that continued residence in Japan was a condition for permanent residence. If anyone left Japan, however briefly, after the war, he or she was not eligible to apply for permanent residence. Moreover, the applicant was required to produce a record of evidence to prove continued residence in Japan.[16] At a glance, this might not appear to be much of a problem. But those who had lived through one of the most chaotic eras in Japan's history might be faced with an insurmountable task in attempting to produce a satisfactory record of some twenty years of continued residence. To illustrate:

> Mr. L. left his wife behind in Korea when he was conscripted as a forced laborer in a mine in Hokkaido. After Japan's surrender, he opened a small business in Japan and established himself there. Eventually he visited Korea and brought his family to Japan through an illegal route. His illegal exit from

and reentry into Japan were discovered by the Japanese immigration authorities. He and his family served about a year at the Ōmura camp and then were released. They had acquired "special residence status" which was subject to renewal every two years by the Ministry of Justice. They were not qualified to apply for permanent residence under the terms of the treaty.

Mr. P. was brought to Japan as a forced laborer during the war. However, he escaped from a coal mine in Niigata prefecture and changed his name several times to hide his identity while he was drifting around the countryside. After the war ended, he began to use his real name, but when the time came to produce evidence of his continued residence in Japan, he was unable to present a residence record with his real name on it. Hence he was ineligible to apply for permanent residence.

In addition to proving continuous residence, the applicant was required to present proof of nationality as a citizen of the Republic of Korea. Those who failed to acquire acceptance of nationality by the South Korean government were not eligible for permanent residence in Japan. Therefore, the Koreans who had pledged loyalty to the DPRK were not qualified for permanent residence. Hence, they might become stateless persons, as the DPRK had no diplomatic relations with Japan. Many Japanese jurists were critical of this legal point on the grounds that the agreement left no alternative for Koreans in Japan except to take the nationality of the South. It was a provision that could be construed as a denial of freedom of choice, which would contradict the principle of Article 15 of the Universal Declaration of Human Rights and Article 22 of the Japanese Constitution.[17]

Another important provision in the agreement was that permanent residence was to be granted only if applicants filed their requests within five years from the date of the agreement. It meant that the Japanese government was prepared to grant permanent residence to Koreans not as a matter of right but as a privilege regardless of their long years of residence in Japan. Up to the deadline for application, 16 January 1971, there were 351,262 Koreans who filed applications for permanent residence. Of these, by 1974, 342,366 Koreans were granted permanent residence by treaty (table 11). The Koreans who obtained legal status by this means were called "permanent resident aliens by treaty." It can be assumed that some 250,000 Koreans did not attempt to apply for permanent residence because of ineligibility, allegiance to North Korea, or other reasons.

GROUNDS FOR DEPORTATION

The permanent resident alien status does not necessarily assure Koreans of permanent residence in Japan. They are subject to deportation to the country of their origin if they fall into one of the following categories: (1) persons who are sentenced to imprisonment for a crime against the head of a foreign state, or a diplomatic envoy, which may be prejudicial to the interest of Japan; and (2) persons who are sentenced to imprisonment for

TABLE 12

Korean Deportation Orders and Deportations

Year	Deportation orders issued to Koreans	Koreans deported
*1952	35,952	29,677
1953	2,561	2,713
1958	1,703	1,802
1963	959	928
1968	1,172	870
1973	737	633
1977	936	793
1978	744	748
Total	44,764	38,164

*Aggregated number until 1952.

Source: The Immigration Control Bureau, *Hōsōjihō*, 31, no. 7 (1978): 54-55.

more than three years for violation of narcotics control laws or are charged with crimes more than three times or are sentenced to more than seven years imprisonment for the violation of any Japanese law (Art. 3, pars. *a, b, c,* and *d*).

Despite the assurance given by the Japanese government that the agreement is designed to reduce the possible grounds for deportation, it still contains enough provisions to encompass almost any forms of repeated misdemeanor. Ogawa Masaaki, a leading Japanese jurist, for example, argued that in the absence of a clear definition of insurrection or acts prejudicial to the interest of Japan, there would be a danger of arbitrary application of this provision, so that misdemeanors committed by Koreans could result in deportation.[18] Furthermore, the agreement enables the Japanese government to deport any Korean to South Korea, including those who claim their nationality to be North Korean, because the South Korean government is obligated by the agreement to accept all Korean deportees from Japan.[19] As indicated in table 12, the total number of deportation orders issued to the Koreans by the Ministry of Justice until 1978 was 44,409. Of these, actual deportation was imposed on 38,164 Koreans as of 1978.

TREATMENT OF KOREANS

The treatment of Koreans in Japan subsequent to the determination of their legal status is spelled out in Article 4 of the agreement, which states: "The Government of Japan shall pay due consideration to . . . the matters concerning education, livelihood protection and national health insurance in Japan" for those granted permanent residence.

Originally, the National Health Insurance Law did not specify that nationality was to be a determining factor for eligibility in obtaining insurance benefits. However, according to the administrative rule established by the Welfare Ministry (Art. 1, par. 2) to implement the Health Insurance Law, a person who did not hold Japanese nationality (including his family) was ineligible for the insurance unless eligibility was granted by an ordinance of his city, county, or village government. As of 1965, just before the agreement went into effect, only 40 percent of the city, county, or village governments had passed ordinances to provide health insurance for Koreans in their locality. Hence, if a Korean family happened to live in a locality where the local government had failed to extend its insurance coverage to Koreans by ordinance, they were excluded from health insurance benefits.

The Livelihood Protection Law of 1950 provides that "*all people* who suffer from destitution are entitled to protection from the state" (Art. 1, emphasis added). Later the Ministry of Welfare gave the interpretation that "all people" meant only Japanese citizens; that the law was not intended to provide protection to aliens residing in Japan; and that the law could be extended to aliens for public safety and for humanitarian reasons, but not as a matter of legal right. In other words, according to the Ministry of Welfare, Koreans are entitled to welfare not by right, but as a privilege bestowed upon them by the Japanese government. The Ministry of Welfare implied that Koreans had no right to file a motion of formal complaint if they were aggrieved by any irregularity in the benefits and any disposition of the standard remuneration.

Because of this capricious interpretation, Koreans are likely to be excluded from other social welfare benefits, such as Child Welfare, Old Age Assistance, Aid to Handicapped Children, and so on, even though they are subject to equal taxation.[20] For instance, Koreans were excluded from the benefits of the Public Housing Laws of 1951, which provided housing for low-income families residing in congested metropolitan areas. In 1954, it was clearly stated by the Director of Public Housing that no alien had the right to demand such benefits, regardless of the amount of taxes he or she paid in Japan.[21]

The most serious problem not covered by the 1965 agreement was the question of Korean veterans who had served in the Japanese armed forces during World War II. It was estimated that more than a million Koreans had served in various capacities in the Japanese war effort,[22] but the exact number still remaining in Japan is unknown. None were covered by the Special Relief Act for the Families of the War Dead, Disabled, and Wounded. The Japanese government's position was that financial compensation was included in the $300 million paid to the Park regime when the Normalization Treaty of 1965 was signed.

The only provisions for Koreans enumerated in the agreement were the Livelihood Protection and the National Health Insurance programs, which amounted to no more than a mere fraction of the possible social welfare benefits. In fact, neither of these enumerations constituted additional benefits for Koreans but simply affirmed what already existed. What would happen to Koreans who refused to apply for permanent resident status, since the acquisition of South Korean nationality was an absolute condition for granting such legal status? Would welfare benefits be denied them? Japanese government officials reiterated that minimum social welfare benefits could be extended to needy persons on humanitarian grounds regardless of their legal status.[23] As far as legal treatment was concerned, therefore, in actuality there was only a slight difference between a person who acquired the status of a permanent residence alien and one who did not. The only real difference was that it was more difficult to deport permanent resident aliens than those who were not so classified.

Another item in the 1965 agreement was concerned with education. Japanese government obligated itself to take such measures "as it deem[ed] necessary" to see that children of Koreans with permanent resident status were permitted to enter Japanese public schools and universities, provided they met all qualifications. This amounted to a restatement of what the Japanese government had been offering to the children of Koreans in Japan even before the agreement was signed.

Also included in the agreement was a provision that permitted Korean permanent residents to take along property and personal effects should they decide to return permanently to Korea. The cash withdrawal, however, was limited to no more than approximately $10,000 per family at the 1965 exchange rate.[24] This provision is what prevents some Koreans from taking their property out of Japan, should they wish to return to Korea.

It is worthwhile to note that these provisions in the final agreement were almost entirely the work of the Japanese side. During the negotiations, the ROK government either made no serious effort or was incapable of exerting its influence to obtain better legal status for its nationals in Japan. As stated in chapter 5, the primary concern of the Park regime at the negotiating table was to secure financial concessions from Japan. It placed less importance on questions of the legal status of Koreans in Japan.

NATURALIZATION

According to a Japanese judicial interpretation, Koreans in Japan lost Japanese nationality with the signing of the San Francisco Peace Treaty on 28 April 1952. For all practical purposes, however, Koreans in Japan had ceased to exercise rights as Japanese nationals since 17 December 1945, when Japan disenfranchised them. Under the old Japanese koseki or family registry system, a woman marrying a Korean had to transfer her koseki to her husband's registry. When the Alien Registration Law of 1947 was enacted to classify Koreans as aliens, she was also subject to alien registration as she no longer retained her koseki registry in Japan. Conversely, a Korean woman might acquire Japanese nationality by marrying a Japanese and would not need to register. If those who lost Japanese nationality wanted to reacquire it, they had to go through a naturalization process in accordance with the procedure prescribed by law.

The current Nationality Law, enacted in 1950, recognizes acquisition of Japanese nationality on the basis of the principle of jus sanguinus: a child of Japanese citizens is also a Japanese citizen. Birth in Japan per se has no legal significance in determining Japanese nationality. The current Nationality Law is much more stringent than the old Nationality Law of 1899, which recognized acquisition of nationality by marriage, acknowledgment of paternity, or child adoption. Under the present law, an alien man or woman marrying a Japanese citizen is not automatically entitled to Japanese citizenship; the alien must file an intent of naturalization in person, and it must be approved by the Ministry of Justice.

Filing of the application and declaration of intent by proxy is permitted only to a person under age fifteen. There are qualifications to be met as specified in Articles 4, 5, and 6 of the Nationality Law of 1950. Under Article 4, the general qualifications for naturalization are spelled out:

1. A person who has continuously resided in Japan for more than five years.

2. A person who has attained the age of 20 and possesses legal personality in accordance with the law prescribed by the previous nation in which he or she held nationality.

3. A person of good behavior.

4. A person who has sufficient means or ability to make an independent living.

5. A stateless person, or a person who pledges to renounce his or her previous nationality when Japanese nationality is accorded.

6. A person who has never attempted or advocated the overthrow of the Japanese Constitution, nor organized or been affiliated with any subversive organization for the same purposes.

If the above conditions are not all met, consideration can be given to the following categories, under Article 5:

1. The husband of a Japanese citizen who has continuously resided in Japan for more than three years.

2. A child of a person who was once a Japanese citizen residing in Japan for more than three years.

3. A person who was born in Japan and has continuously resided there for more than three years, or a person at least one of whose parents was born in Japan.

4. A person who has continuously resided in Japan for more than ten years.

Even when a person qualifies under the provisions of the law, the application for naturalization is subject to approval by the Ministry of Justice. As a matter of fact, almost all Korean residents in Japan are technically eligible for naturalization. One of the major obstacles, however, that prevents Korean residents from being naturalized is the "good behavior" clause in the provisions. In the absence of a clear definition of what constitutes "good behavior," anyone with a simple police record is unlikely to pass the rigorous scrutiny by the Ministry of Justice.

It has been the policy of the Ministry of Justice not to make figures available regarding the number of Koreans being naturalized. An estimate can be made, however, from the Annual Report of the Ministry of Justice, which shows the total numbers of aliens naturalized each year. Since the end of World War II, Koreans have consistently constituted approximately 85-90 percent of the total number of aliens in Japan. Therefore, the trend shown in table 13 provides a rough estimate. According to an unofficial report, the average annual rate of Koreans being naturalized amounts to less than 1 percent of the total Korean population in Japan.[25]

As shown in table 13, the yearly number of naturalized aliens seems to be increasing, although the proportionate rate from the total Korean population in Japan still remains very small. If naturalized, a Korean is legally entitled to the rights and privileges accorded a native-born citizen of Japan, as are his minor children. Naturalization, however, does not guarantee that the Korean-Japanese will be socially accepted by the majority of Japanese people.

It is difficult to ascertain the real reasons why some Koreans have or have not become naturalized. A common rationale for naturalization seems to be a hope that naturalization will provide some means of escape from ethnic discrimination in business or employment. There is also concern for future marriage plans of offspring as well for the future legal status of their descendants. It should be noted that the current permanent resident status by treaty agreement does not apply to successive generations of Koreans. Under the prevailing law all Japan-born future generations of nonnaturalized Koreans are to be treated as ordinary aliens with severely restricted privileges and without any social welfare benefits, even though they are subject to the same taxation as are Japanese citizens.

Some Korean parents are also extremely concerned about the identity crisis they witness among young Korean youth born and raised in Japan, especially those who have been assimilated into the majority society. A fourteen-year-old girl whose parents had not yet been naturalized expressed her candid feelings in a poem sent to a Korean community newspaper published in Japan. Her sentiments may be considered typical of many young Koreans in Japan (see also chaps. 13 and 14).

"I Want to be a Japanese"

by Omura Akiko

Until this moment,
I have been hating myself being Korean.

When I was little,
I was really shocked to learn myself to be Korean.

Korea is a beautiful country.
My father, brother, and sister have been there several times.
I was told that the air is much cleaner, and things are much
   cheaper, too.

But, I can't help disliking Korea.
I don't think I can love it as my motherland.

When I was little, how many times was I insulted by my peers
   and ridiculed about Korea?

When they said, how lucky they were to be born as Japanese
   I wish I could have said the same.

By all means, I want to be a Japanese.
When I am 15*
I must do my alien registration in person.

What shall I do, how shall I behave, at the local district office?
I just hate to think of myself going to that office.

Nevertheless, my 15th birthday is coming soon . . . [26]

Akiko desires acceptance into the majority society, and yet she gives no thought to naturalization. She simply anticipates her registration as an alien. Hostility and denial of her Korean identity result in self-hatred. Such hatred leads to negative attitudes directed toward Korea and Koreans. She defends the beauty of Korea but cannot love it as her motherland. She has

---

*She apparently figures her age in accordance with the Japanese custom of adding a year.

TABLE 13

Number of Naturalized Koreans in Japan: 1952-1977

Year	Total naturalized aliens	Koreans naturalized
1952	282	232
1953	1,431	1,326
1954	2,608	2,435
1955	2,661	2,434
1956	2,547	2,290
1957	2,582	2,312
1958	2,594	2,246
1959	3,076	2,737
1960	4,156	3,763
1961	3,013	2,710
1962	3,614	3,222
1963	4,100	3,558
1964	5,445	4,632
1965	4,088	3,438
1966	5,409	3,816
1967	4,786	3,391
1968	3,501	3,194
1969	2,153	1,889
1970	5,379	4,646
1971	3,386	2,874
1972	6,825	4,983
1973	13,626	5,769
1974	7,393	5,000
1975	8,568	6,323
1976	5,607	3,951
1977	5,680	4,261

Source: *Tōitsu Nippō,* 29 September 1978.

been born and reared in a Japanese society but this has not automatically qualified her for citizenship, as it would have in the United States.

The agreement on legal status by treaty was primarily designed by the Japanese government to encourage future Korean generations to be naturalized and assimilated. Paradoxically, although the government encourages Koreans in Japan to assimilate, the social attitudes of the Japanese populace reject any thrust toward assimilation.

To naturalize is to identify with the Japanese, who despise Koreans. It means capitulation to negative attitudes toward parents, kin, and ultimately toward oneself, as if born of tainted origin. Becoming a naturalized Japanese citizen does not make one more Japanese. One's sense of self-worth is threatened by the continual knowledge of how much Koreans are despised.

Although Koreans are physically indistinguishable from the Japanese, once they are recognized as Korean, whether naturalized or not, they are likely to be considered inferior. They seldom gain acceptance as "true Japanese." It is still a widely accepted practice in Japan to include a copy of one's koseki when applying for a job, for school admission, or for membership in any group. Even when applying for a golf club membership, one sends his koseki, and at such times one's country of origin is revealed. Naturalized Japanese are often socially stigmatized as *pan tchok ppali* (half-Japanese) and are alienated from both communities. They exist on the margins of two societies. To avoid social alienation, naturalized Koreans occasionally organize clubs of their own, such as the *Seiwa kurabu*, set up in March 1973 nationwide to promote friendly relations among Korean-Japanese.[27]

Unlike the fourteen-year-old girl who sought acceptance by the majority society, some people, tragically, can perceive no way out of the identity dilemma. One Korean youth who resented the naturalization of his parents committed suicide by self-immolation. He noted in his diary:

> . . . My father decided to be naturalized after years of painful deliberation and agony. It meant that we became legally Japanese. But for Koreans, legally becoming Japanese does not necessarily assure them equality. . . . If I were not then nine years old, I would have refused to be naturalized. My parents' rationale for the naturalization was to avoid having us in a disadvantaged position in the future when applying for school admission and employment. For that reason alone, however, can they renounce their own fatherland? . . . Instead of becoming a "half Japanese," I strongly wished to live as a Korean. When I visited my fellow Korean students who were struggling hard to keep their own ethnic identity in an alien land, they were reluctant to greet me by shaking my hand, because I was a naturalized Japanese. . . . Frankly, in their view, I was a turncoat who gave up his fatherland. I am neither to be Japanese nor Korean but the one who has abandoned his fatherland. . . . Where is my place to live and rest myself?[28]

Unable to resolve the inner conflict centering on his identity, the young man resorted to self-immolation. In effect, he was protesting the rejection he experienced both from Japanese and Koreans. In the minds of most Koreans the question of naturalization lies somewhere in the broad spectrum that separates these two instances.[29] Naturalization by itself does not contribute to a resolution either of the internal dilemma or the social problems faced daily by Koreans. These dilemmas will intensify once Koreans as a group acquire a Korean consciousness, even if Japanese society itself should be ready to modify its fundamental attitudes toward other ethnic minorities. Most Koreans feel that Japanese prejudice toward them has not diminished even some thirty years after the end of colonialism.[30] By now their bitterness is a deeply rooted social attitude that will not be easily changed (see chaps. 13 and 14).

Recently, however, a few concerned Japanese and Koreans have increasingly sought to test the issue of the fundamental human rights of Koreans in Japan through the judicial system. The legal cases discussed in chapter 11 result from these concerted efforts to test how one can retain one's Korean identity without suffering discrimination in a modern Japanese society dedicated to becoming a genuine democracy.

The current problems of the Korean minority in Japan have arisen from the legacy of Japanese colonialism and from the by-products of its modern nation-state system. Japanese "racist" attitudes have not been exclusively aimed at Koreans. More than a century has passed since Japan opened its doors to the outside world, but many traditional social attitudes are still retained. The intensity of feeling about a "closed" Japanese society has been augmented by the strong nationalistic movement existing from the Meiji period until approximately the end of World War II. This nationalistic sentiment was clearly present when the old Nationality Law of 1899 was amended in 1950 to uphold the principle of jus sanguinus. The fact of being born in Japan to permanent residents of the country was not sufficient to confer Japanese citizenship on a child of Korean ancestry.

The immediate disenfranchisement of Koreans in Japan after Japan's surrender was the most effective means of preventing any politically potent legal action on behalf of Koreans. By disenfranchisement the Japanese government deprived Koreans of their fundamental right to remain permanently in Japan and founded a legal ploy for segregating Koreans in all aspects of social life.

At the present time, three persistent social patterns underlie Japanese laws and the legal status accorded to the Koreans in Japan by treaty agreement. First, the number of privileged permanent resident aliens is to be kept at a minimum so that they will eventually be phased out by attrition. Second, the Ministry of Justice reserves a broad range of discretionary powers to invoke the deportation clause under the law, which may be used contrary to the "spirit" of granting permanent settlement to Koreans in Japan. If and when the Japanese government considers the presence of some Koreans a case of "clear and present danger" to official policy, there is no adequate mechanism available to Koreans under the existing laws to protect their fundamental rights in Japan. Third, future descendants of Koreans in Japan are denied the right to inherit the privileged alien status of their parents. By applying rigidly narrow provisions under the laws, the Japanese government seeks to screen out those they consider "bad" Koreans. Koreans who seek to become naturalized Japanese citizens find their lives closely scrutinized by officials.

Each state as a sovereign nation is the final arbiter in deciding how aliens are to be treated within its own jurisdiction. The precarious legal status accorded to Koreans by the Japanese compounds a problem of social and psychocultural origin. Unresolved moral and humanitarian issues derive from a past history that did not start with Japan's colonial adventure in Korea. The maintenance or discarding of ethnic identity is the paramount issue. Legal inequity can complicate the problems, but even achieving legal equality or justice will not completely resolve how Koreans in Japan feel about their roots. They cannot simply ignore their own origins in what is for them an alien soil, nor can they ignore their lack of acceptance by Japanese society as persons without Japanese blood lineage.

8

ETHNIC EDUCATION AND NATIONAL POLITICS

Changsoo Lee

After the annexation of Korea in 1910, the urgent task faced by the Japanese government was to moderate its policy of heavy-handed military rule, seeking to placate the national consciousness of the Koreans through a more subtle and conciliatory posture. To accomplish this, an ambitious long-range program was launched by the colonial government to assimilate the indigenous people to the Japanese culture. The assimilation policy of the colonial government was criticized by many Japanese. One outspoken critic was Aoyanagi Nammei, a prominent professor of history at Tokyo University.[1] Aoyanagi made a personal plea to Katsura Tarō, the prime minister, objecting to the assimilation policy and citing past efforts of the Japanese to assimilate the Korean minority in Japan. He pointed out that there were about 5,000 Koreans living in the area of Koma village in the Saitama prefecture. Despite hundreds of years of residence in Japan, this minority had maintained its traditional communal life and cultural heritage.[2] Aoyanagi cited their strong individualism, contending that Koreans were unassimilable, but his arguments against the assimilation policy went unheeded.[3]

Conversely, those who favored an assimilation policy argued on the grounds of: (1) the racial affinity of the Korean and Japanese people; (2) their geographic proximity; and (3) the Japanese understanding of Korea and her culture. Above all, it was argued that the assimilation policy was necessary to neutralize the ethnic consciousness of Koreans, thereby minimizing any potential unrest and thus perpetuating colonial rule over Korea. Therefore, the colonial government decided to uproot the separate cultural heritage of the Koreans. Subsequently, the Korean language and other subjects that had a direct bearing on ethnic identity and national consciousness were strictly forbidden to be taught in the schools of Korea. These subjects were eventually replaced by the Japanese language and history, with emphasis on loyalty to the emperor. This policy was carried out by: (1) creation of the Education Affairs Bureau under the colonial government; (2) specially trained cadres to oversee the policy; (3) direct management of the Korean school system; (4) compilation of textbooks by Japanese officials; and (5) censorship of publications by the colonial government.

JAPANESE ASSIMILATION POLICY IN KOREA

The forty years of Japanese colonial rule and the attempts at assimilation through education can be divided into three phases. The first phase was the "paternalistic protection" period, from the signing of the Protectorate Treaty of 1905 to the formal annexation of Korea in 1910 (see chap. 2). Criticizing traditional Korean education as "primitive," Itō Hirobumi, one of the chief architects of Meiji government policy, introduced the "civilized" Japanese educational system to Korea under the pretext of modernizing it.[4] Korean schools soon became the focus of oppressive vigilance by Japanese officials, who suspected the schools of being seedbeds for a national resistance against the presence of the Japanese in Korea. The first governor-general of Korea, General Terauchi Masatake, went even further by instructing the local provincial governors to outlaw any popular songs or folklore that might encourage an independence movement.

The second phase started with the annexation of Korea in 1910 and lasted until around 1938, when the Japanese government began to mobilize Korean labor to meet the manpower shortage incurred by Japan's continued military expansion into Manchuria and China. During this second period, the colonial government introduced a slogan for the Japanization of Koreans as "imperial subjects of Greater Japan." Hence, in accordance with the Imperial Rescript on Education, the fundamental goal of Korean education, as in Japan proper, had to be based on *Isshi Dojin* (universal benevolence), by which the absolute loyalty of all subjects was to be directed to the emperor. After the March First Movement of 1919, the colonial government became especially anxious in its attempts to destroy the national identity of Koreans. Yūge Kōtarō, then director of the Education Affairs Bureau in the colonial government, wrote that the source of the March First Movement was the Koreans' continuing desire for independence. He argued that the only way to eliminate this desire was to make Koreans realize that they were no longer Koreans but Japanese. To infuse this notion, he said, Korean education needed to develop "a sense of rationality" in its students, by which Yūge meant an appreciation of the benevolence of Japanese colonial rule, an ability to perceive colonial rule as an inevitable outcome of the prevailing world situation, and the knowledge that it would be futile to engage in any rash actions against colonial rule.[5] It was around this period that numerous scholarly studies appeared attempting to justify the annexation of Korea and Japanese colonial rule. The recurring themes of these studies were that the Japanese and Koreans had a shared ancestral origin, that paternalistic relationships had existed between the two races in the past, and that therefore the annexation of Korea was justified as the restoration of their ancient status as a single entity.

The final phase of the assimilation attempt, from 1938 to the end of

World War II, was not confined to the sphere of education but was extended to the entire life-style of Koreans. Korean-style clothes were forbidden in public, and Korean names were required by law to follow the Japanese style. Koreans were even forced to convert from Buddhism to Shintoism, and visits to Shintō shrines were made compulsory. Koreans were encouraged to make ceremonial obeisance in the direction of the Imperial palace every morning. All governmental directives, newspapers, and public or private documents had to be written in the Japanese language. Only Japanese was to be spoken in public. Every Korean was required by law to recite the "Oath of Imperial Subjects" at all public and private gatherings. Two types of pledges of allegiance were to be recited at all public occasions, one designed for elementary schoolchildren and the other for adults.

Pledge for Schoolchildren

1. We are the subjects of the Empire of Greater Japan.
2. We, by uniting our minds, pledge our allegiance to His Majesty the Emperor.
3. We, by perseverance and training, will become good, strong subjects.

Pledge for Adults

1. We are Imperial subjects and pledge our allegiance to the Empire.
2. We Imperial subjects, by mutual faith, love, and cooperation, will strengthen our union.
3. We Imperial subjects, by perseverance and training, will cultivate our strength to exalt the Imperial Way.[6]

This system of compulsory conformity, expressed in an ideology of emperor worship, was to be the formative force that would mold and shape Koreans toward an acceptance of colonial rule. Many Koreans, indeed, seemed to have converted to Shintoism, believing that they were truly loyal subjects of the emperor. Some Koreans volunteered to serve in the Japanese Imperial armed forces and pledged to die in the name of the emperor. A few Koreans published books in support of the colonial policy.[7] As Japan became more deeply involved in China, the Japanese government proclaimed the National Manpower Mobilization Law in April 1938. Koreans, as subjects of the emperor, were also subject to the manpower mobilization program. From the inception of the program until the end of World War II, more than six million of the aggregate number of Koreans were reportedly mobilized and many of them were involuntarily taken to Japan to work for the war effort (see chap. 2).

ASSIMILATION POLICY IN JAPAN

In contrast to the stringent policy of assimilation applied in Korea, resident Koreans in Japan were ignored until after the depression of the 1930s, which caused severe unemployment among Koreans. A rising crime rate and left-wing agitation among the Koreans stirred Japanese officials to action. The Social Welfare Bureau of the Ministry of the Interior undertook a study and recommended instituting an assimilation policy similar to that in Korea. As a result, a substantial amount of money was set aside in the 1936 budget to initiate an assimilation program, officially designated as Kyōwa jigyō (Project for the Japanization of Koreans).

To implement the program, the Kyōwa Association was organized under the direct supervision of the Ministry of the Interior in 1939, with branches in each prefecture and smaller units in cities and towns. All Korean residents in Japan were compelled to hold membership in the association and were required to carry their membership cards at all times. In reality, the creation of the Kyōwa Association had a dual purpose. One was to assimilate the Koreans, and the other was to control any potential subversive activities among them. The first Kyōwa National Conference, convened in Tokyo in December 1940, adopted the following pledge:

1. In accordance with the wishes of Emperor's universal benevolence, we pledge to become loyal Japanese subjects.
2. In accordance with the principle of the Imperial way, we pledge to devote ourselves to public service.
3. In accordance with the principle of unity, we pledge to reform and improve our life style.[8]

The Kyōwa project was literally designed to restructure the souls of Koreans to conform to an Imperial Japanese society. Included in these programs were the changing of Korean names, compulsory Shintō worship, and the learning of Japanese language and customs. Adult classes were established in local areas to teach not only the language but also the "Japanese way" of family life. Especially for Korean women, classes were conducted to teach Japanese cooking and sewing and even Japanese marriage and funeral ceremonies. Korean children were already attending Japanese public schools, in which it was assumed all children were "Japanese" in cultural heritage.

By the end of the war, many Koreans had become "quasi-Japanese" as a result of the systematic and thorough indoctrination to which they had been subjected. Therefore, the primary goal of the Korean ethnic studies programs that Koreans established immediately after the war was to dejapanize the Koreans and their children in Japan. These programs were a reaction to the past assimilation policy and were motivated by a sincere desire to regain what Koreans considered their lost language and suppressed customs. Korean language courses began in improvised classrooms set up in war-torn houses, and a separatist Korean educational movement spread spontaneously throughout Japan. A slogan was introduced to encourage effort:

> Those who have money, use money;
> Those who can give labor, use labor;
> Those who can give wisdom, use wisdom.
> Let us build our schools together.[9]

Other courses were added, such as Korean history, geography, and arithmetic, primarily designed for teaching Korean children. Only a year after the Japanese surrender, there were almost 550 Korean schools with 44,000 students.

The main efforts behind the increased number of schools should be credited to the Choryŏn (chap. 3), which had been organized in October 1945 to protect the interests of Koreans in Japan. Within the Education Bureau of the Choryŏn, a Committee for the Compilation of Elementary School Textbooks was organized to edit a good quality of textbooks suited to the education of Koreans in Japan. In the early stages of preparation, many well-known Japanese educators and intellectuals, such as Hatano Kanji, Kokubun Ichitaro, and Gotō Teiji, provided professional advice. Meanwhile, in accordance with a recommendation submitted to the Japanese government by the American Education Mission in April 1946, the Korean schools agreed to conduct coeducational programs in the 6-3-3 pattern (six elementary grades, three middle grades, and three high-school grades).

By the summer of 1947 the Korean Educators' Union and the Korean School Management Union were organized to oversee and improve not only teacher training but school management as well. Despite many difficulties in the midst of confusion and chaos immediately after the defeat of Japan, remarkable progress was apparent.[10] By April 1948 there were 58,000 students in 600 schools (table 14), which had been established with little financial help from the Japanese government. As private institutions, these schools were relatively free from stringent governmental regulation of their curricula, but the situation was beginning to change.

At first, the SCAP authorities took no official cognizance of the mushrooming of Korean schools in Japan. SCAP's primary concern was directed toward reforming the undesirable chauvinistic aspects of Japanese curricula. In October 1947, however, SCAP's Civil Information and Education Section issued a directive on the education of Koreans, stating that the Japanese government be directed "to ensure that Korean schools comply with all

TABLE 14

Number of Korean Schools, Students, and Teachers
in Japan: 1946-1952

		Month and year			
		10/1946	10/1947	5/1949	4/1952
Elementary	Schools	524	541	288	154
schools	Students	42,182	46,961	32,368	14,144
	Teachers	1,022	1,250	955	327
Middle	Schools	4	7	16	17
schools	Students	1,180	2,761	4,555	2,914
	Teachers	52	95	165	110
High	Schools	—	—	3	3
schools	Students	—	—	364	570
	Teachers	—	—	50	54
Youth	Schools	12	30	unknown	unknown
schools	Students	750	2,123	—	—
	Teachers	54	160	—	—

Source: Fujishima Udai and Ozawa Yūsaku, *Minzoku kyōiku* (Tokyo: Aogi shoten, 1966), p. 43.

pertinent Japanese directives, with the exception that Korean schools would be permitted to teach the Korean language as an addition to the regular curriculum."[11]

A few months later, on 24 January 1948, the Japanese Ministry of Education directed local prefecture governors to accredit Korean schools that complied with the legal standards of the School Education Law of 1947.[12] What irritated most Koreans about the ministry directive was the fact that Korean schools were also told to conduct classes in the Japanese language, teaching the Korean language only as an extracurricular subject. The Koreans protested immediately, charging that the directive was actually intended to deny the right of Koreans to maintain an autonomous educational system. The Koreans felt that it was reminiscent of their past experiences, when the Japanese government tried to regulate every aspect of Korean life. The protest movement spread quickly throughout Japan. On 6 March 1948 the Korean Parent-Teachers Association met in Tokyo and adopted the following demands, to be submitted to the Ministry of Education: to recognize the autonomous nature of Korean education in light of the special circumstances of Koreans in Japan, and to defray expenses of the Korean schools. No response came from the Ministry of Education. By 23 March the Countermeasure Committee on Korean Education was organized under the auspices of the Choryŏn. This committee submitted a list of four demands to Premier Yoshida, covering:

1. Instruction in the Korean language.
2. Use of textbooks compiled by a Korean committee and censored by SCAP's Civil Information and Education Section.
3. Administration of Korean schools by the Korean School Management Union.
4. Teaching of the Japanese language as a required subject in the curriculum.[13]

Representatives of the committee also made a direct appeal to SCAP headquarters. SCAP's only response was to repeat the Japanese directive, and the Japanese began to close nonaccredited Korean schools in April 1949. The Koreans were determined to resist the closings, insisting that it was an act of oppression to deprive them of the right of an autonomous Korean education in Japan. They argued that because the Japanese government classified them legally as Koreans, it was natural for the Koreans to operate and manage their own schools.

The uncompromising attitudes of both Koreans and the Japanese authorities eventuated in violence. The protests lasted a full month in Kobe, in Osaka, and in other places where Korean schools were located. Many thousands of Koreans were arrested and imprisoned on charges of inciting riots and resisting the government's order to close the schools.[14] The dispute was settled by negotiations on 3 May between the Japanese Minister of Education and representatives of the Choryŏn. The two sides signed a memorandum agreeing that Korean schools were to comply with the school education law, and to be subject to accreditation, but were to maintain autonomous ethnic studies programs within the limits accorded private school systems in Japan.[15]

The agreement, however, lasted little more than a year. As a result of the government's order to dissolve the Choryŏn in September 1949, 92 schools out of the total of 337 schools operating under the direct supervision of the Choryŏn were ordered to close. The closed school buildings were confiscated by the Japanese government, since they were regarded as Choryŏn property, and the students were told to attend Japanese public schools.

Schools that were ordered closed in Hyogo, Aichi, Hiroshima, and Osaka prefectures were firmly determined to ignore the closing order. Feelings ran especially high in Hyogo prefecture and its city of Kobe, where about 40,000 Koreans assembled almost every day in front of the prefectural governmental office, demanding that the school closing order be rescinded. On 27 November 1949 the Hyogo governor mobilized about 4,000 armed police officers to arrest more than 30,000 Koreans, putting an end to the continuous demonstrations. Seventeen Korean schools were allowed to remain open in the prefecture but were told to change their curricula and educational system to conform to those of the Japanese schools. In fact, the "compromise" amounted to no more than a restatement of the January 1948 order that had sparked the initial protests. This time no protest followed, as the Japanese government and the police were obviously well equipped to deal with any further violence.

The Tokyo prefecture issued its own directive to limit the scope of Korean ethnic studies as follows:

1. Korean students were to be transferred to Japanese public schools.

2. Class instruction was to be conducted in the Japanese language. But in schools with large Korean enrollments, the Korean language and history could be taught as extracurricular subjects.

3. Only Japanese were eligible to be principals. Koreans, however, could be appointed as regular teachers if the principals approved and if the Koreans met the teacher qualifications prescribed by law.[16]

As a result of stringent control by the Japanese government, the number of Korean schools and students began to dwindle, as shown in table 14.[17] During the heyday of the schools in October 1947 there had been 541 elementary schools with 47,000 students; by May 1949 the schools had decreased to 288, with some 32,000 students; by April 1952 there were only 154 schools with 14,000 students (table 14).

Obviously, the Japanese government intended to limit Korean ethnic studies to discourage further ferment. For many Japanese, ethnic diversity was intolerable in a land proud of its mythological founding as a homogeneous culture. The mounting tension of the cold war provided a convenient excuse for the Japanese government to suppress political and educational diversity. No doubt the curriculum in schools operated by the Choryŏn was heavily slanted toward Communist doctrine as advocated by the North Korean regime. Schoolchildren were taught to pledge allegiance to North Korean Premier Kim Il-sung and to embrace a revolutionary spirit against the United States and the "element of reactionary forces" in Japan. Ethnicity was politicized and exploited as a political weapon.

Following the government's dissolution of the Choryŏn in September 1949, all Korean schools were ordered incorporated into the Japanese public school systems under the direct supervision of the prefectural government.

Korean schools were to be headed only by Japanese principals appointed by the prefectural governor, and Korean ethnic studies were to be taught only as extracurricular subjects. School expenses were to be defrayed by the Japanese public treasury, as Korean children were included in the compulsory education system. After the Japanese Peace Treaty went into effect in April 1952, however, the Japanese government refused further financial responsibility for Korean education. The government argued that Koreans in Japan were no longer considered to be Japanese nationals in accordance with Chapter 2, Article 2, of the Peace Treaty, since the Japanese government had abandoned its claim of sovereignty of Korea. Because of strong Korean protests, the government later modified its stand, saying that the program would not affect Korean students who were already enrolled in public schools. However, new students from then on would be admitted to the public schools:

1. Only if space and facilities were available.

2. If the parent or student made a pledge not to disturb public order.

3. If the student did not demand Korean ethnic studies.

4. If the student agreed to receive the education prescribed by the Japanese government.[18]

Besides these attempts of the national government to limit the number of Korean children educated at public expense, the Tokyo prefecture on 8 December 1953 issued six additional restrictions to which Korean public schools had to adhere.[19] The Tokyo restrictions were later elaborated into thirty, ranging from curriculum programming to the management of school administration. Japanese educational inspectors were regularly dispatched to check any violation of provisions. Again, the purpose was to control the entire Korean educational program and eventually to eliminate it.

The Japanese government soon found it too difficult to eliminate Korean ethnic studies and to enforce its complex provisions. Instead, education officials decided to eliminate the Korean schools from the Japanese public school systems. In the Tokyo prefecture, it was announced that all matters concerning Korean education would be transferred back to the hands of Koreans effective as of April 1955, and that the expense of Korean schools would no longer be defrayed by the prefecture. The Koreans immediately protested the move, arguing that they were entitled to public education because they were taxpayers. Finally, a compromise was reached between Japanese government officials and the Korean community in Tokyo. The Tokyo prefecture agreed to pay 120 million yen per year for five years, beginning with the school year 1955, to permit Korean students already enrolled in the public education system to complete their education. But the Japanese government announced that it would bear no financial responsibility for new Korean students who enrolled in Tokyo public schools in the school year of 1955.

As a result, permission was granted by the Tokyo prefecture for the legal incorporation of the Korean Education Institute (Tokyo Chōsen Gakuin). As a kind of board of trustees, this institute would oversee all Korean schools in the Tokyo prefecture. Other prefectures soon followed suit in cutting off public education funds to beginning Korean students. Now that Korean schools existed as private institutions, ethnic studies programs again flourished, especially after the formation of the Ch'ongnyŏn in 1955.

THE CH'ONGNYŎN'S EDUCATIONAL OBJECTIVES

Prior to the formation of the Ch'ongnyŏn in 1955, there were two fundamentally differing views as to how the interests of the more radical Koreans in Japan could be protected. One view was based on belief in world communism and proletarian internationalism as the way of obtaining common goals. Advocates of this view identified their goal with that of the Japanese Communist party. They believed that it was in their interest to participate in the task of overthrowing the Emperor system and establishing a "People's Republic" in Japan. The other left-of-center view grew out of awareness of the Korean national consciousness. Members of this group gave their primary allegiance to their fatherland, disassociating themselves from involvement in JCP's cause and pursuing an independent line.

With the triumph of the latter view within the Ch'ongnyŏn, the primary goal of Korean education in Japan became that of educating Korean youths to be loyal to the fatherland and instilling in them national pride as citizens of an independent nation. More specific details of the educational objectives were spelled out in the Decision Papers at the Inaugural Meeting of the Ch'ongnyŏn in 1955. The Ch'ongnyŏn openly declared its intent to carry out Korean ethnic education in accordance with guidance from North Korea and from the North Korean educational system.[20] Thus it was obvious from the outset that the Ch'ongnyon intended to continue communist education in line with the DPRK so that Korean students in Japan would be able to devote themselves to the construction of a "democratic fatherland."

It should be noted that the Mindan has also developed its own school system in opposition to the Ch'ongnyŏn's more extensive education scheme. Not only does the Mindan have fewer schools but its program and scope are fundamentally different from those of the Ch'ongnyŏn. Although the Ch'ongnyon in the early 1970s operated about 180 schools with almost 35,000 students, the Mindan had only 18 accredited schools throughout Japan with fewer than 4,000 students. The Ch'ongnyŏn emphasizes the enhancement of nationalistic sentiment and pride, and the equation of individual well-being with the collective interests of the state—North Korea. By contrast the Mindan's orientation is toward adaptation to Japanese surroundings by promoting individual welfare while living in Japan.[21] Consequently, the children of Mindan supporters are usually sent to Japanese schools to learn together with Japanese children and to compete freely with them. As a result, Mindan supporters are less enthusiastic about developing separate school systems, although in the late 1970s the organization launched a minimum fifty-hour ethnic studies campaign, to encourage all its members to send their children to Mindan schools. It is not uncommon to find many Mindan supporters who use Japanese names in public with the hope of being treated like any Japanese. In contrast, Ch'ongnyŏn members are motivated by a strong sense of nationalism to preserve their names and ethnic identity under the slogan "Korean children should be taught in Korean schools."[22] It is precisely by appealing to this sentiment that the DPRK is skillfully attempting to induce absolute allegiance of Ch'ongnyŏn members to its regime.

SUPERVISING AND FINANCING "DEMOCRATIC ETHNIC EDUCATION"

The final responsibility of supervising North Korean-style "democratic ethnic education" is entrusted to the Korean Education Association in Japan, or KEA (Chae'il Chosŏn'in Kyoyuk'hoe), which is under the direct control of the Ch'ongnyŏn. Two other organizations assist in the work of the KEA. One is the Korean Teachers' League, organized not only to promote fraternal relations among its 1,500 Korean teachers but also to improve the quality of teaching. In accordance with Ch'ongnyŏn guidelines, the Teacher's League often conducts workshops and seminars during summer vacations to exchange information and to evaluate the progress of ethnic education. The second subsidiary organization, the Korean Student League in Japan, was originally intended to promote the welfare of Korean students who came to Japan for study. Since 1955, however, it has become an organ of the Ch'ongnyŏn and distributes scholarships and financial assistance to Korean students attending Japanese schools, for which it seeks their allegiance in return.

As stated above, the KEA manages the entire Ch'ongnyŏn school system. In addition, the KEA is responsible for allocating the educational funds remitted from North Korea to needy schools. Thirty-two regional education associations are affiliated with the Central Education Association for a total KEA membership of approximately 22,000 individuals.[23] One duty of the KEA is to provide all possible support to upgrade the Ch'ongnyŏn schools to meet the legal standards for accreditation prescribed by the Japanese School Education Law. It is reported that the KEA is considering becoming an incorporated foundation to acquire a legal personality.

To maintain the entire Korean school system, the KEA derives its

financial support largely from tuition, association membership fees, donations, and the Korean Education Aid Fund, which has been remitted regularly from the DPRK. According to a KEA report in 1963, only twenty-
seven schools were financially able to support themselves; the remaining
schools relied heavily on financial aid. As a matter of fact, the remittance
from the North Korean government comprises more than 50 percent of the
total budget needed to carry on the "democratic ethnic education" in
Japan.[24] Understanding this high degree of financial dependency on the
DPRK may help indicate the true nature of the Ch'ongnyŏn's educational
program and its goals.

The funds began to arrive from North Korea in April 1957, about a
year after four representatives of the Ch'ongnyŏn visited Premier Kim Il-
sung in P'yŏngyang and appealed for aid. Direct remittance of funds from
the DPRK has continued since that time (table 15). Since the fiscal year of
1963, the DPRK has included the item in its national budget and has annually appropriated funds to support the education program in Japan. As of
April 1977, the total amount of funds that had been received by the KEA
was about 23 billion. It is important to note that the DPRK spent approximately seven times more than the ROK government for the purpose of
Korean education in Japan during the ten-year period between 1957 and
1967 (see table 16).[25] In addition to the Education Aid Fund, the DPRK
sends books, Korean musical instruments, and other teaching aids and
materials. Furthermore, the DPRK awards meritorious service medals to
teachers who have distinguished themselves in Korean education and also
honors certain faculty members teaching at Chosŏn University as "DPRK"
professors.[26] Thus, it is only through the DPRK's financial support plus the
strenuous efforts of the Ch'ongnyŏn that a significant ethnic education is
available to Koreans in Japan.

THE FOUNDING OF CHOSŎN UNIVERSITY

With the expansion of the Korean elementary and secondary education program, the Ch'ongnyŏn felt the need for an institute of higher learning. The decision to support a university-level school was announced at the
Inaugural Meeting of the Ch'ongnyŏn in May 1955. In the following year a
two-year college was established on the campus of one of the Korean high
schools in Tokyo. In October 1957 a remittance of 100,510,000 yen per year
(about $300,000) from the Education Aid Fund of the DPRK enabled the
Ch'ongnyŏn to look for a building site for the construction of what was to
be called Chosŏn University.[27] An initial attempt by the Ch'ongnyŏn to
purchase farm land covering 10,000 tsubo (33,100 square meters) in Ita-
bashi-ku and Nerima-ku, Tokyo, was denied by the local agricultural committee without a stated reason.[28]

TABLE 15

Remittance of Korean Education Aid Funds from DPRK
(as of December 1973)

Number	Date	Amount (yen)	Number	Date	Amount (yen)
1	4-57	121,099,086	34	2-70	313,121,100
2	10-57	100,510,000	35	9-70	297,000,000
3	3-58	100,000,000	36	9-70	297,780,000
4	9-58	100,210,000	37	10-70	302,850,500
5	2-59	176,382,500	38	1-71	302,365,000
6	9-59	114,654,090	39	4-71	301,940,000
7	2-60	202,100,000	40	9-71	301,910,000
8	9-60	217,392,231	41	10-71	289,340,000
9	3-61	411,060,000	42	12-71	302,827,800
10	3-62	558,470,000	43	2-72	300,820,110
11	3-63	401,440,000	44	4-72	318,060,000
12	6-63	202,770,000	45	7-72	342,270,800
13	9-63	186,852,644	46	10-72	363,425,000
14	4-64	303,930,000	47	12-72	351,225,000
15	7-64	302,940,000	48	2-73	350,925,000
16	11-64	201,400,000	49	4-73	374,176,500
17	3-65	302,940,000	50	7-73	334,725,000
18	8-65	202,020,000	51	8-73	321,420,000
19	11-65	303,450,000	52	12-73	369,684,700
20	2-66	303,570,000	53	3-74	362,020,000
21	8-66	201,860,000	54	4-74	395,170,000
22	11-66	303,210,000	55	5-74	601,425,000
23	3-67	303,420,000	56	10-74	697,150,000
24	7-67	201,420,000	57	10-74	703,450,000
25	10-67	301,950,000	58	12-74	752,580,450
26	12-67	194,246,300	59	4-75	1,060,122,500
27	2-68	305,025,000	60	5-75	608,265,000
28	6-68	347,305,400	61	12-75	613,350,000
29	10-68	345,783,600	62	4-76	700,000,000
30	2-69	299,754,000	63	9-76	633,204,000
31	4-69	350,960,000	64	12-76	500,928,500
32	8-69	298,261,240	65	4-77	500,000,000
33	10-69	247,950,000			

Sources: Institute for East Asian Studies, *Bukhan Chŏnsŏ* (Seoul: 1974), p. 178; *Tōitsu Nippō*, 12 May 1977.

TABLE 16

Expenditures for Korean Education in Japan
by Republic of Korea and Democratic People's Republic of Korea
(in U.S. dollars)

Year	ROK	DPRK
1957	$ 22,000.00	$ 615,580.00
1958	74,800.00	556,136.11
1959	186,000.00	808,432.00
1960	367,200.00	1,165,256.40
1961	160,659.50	1,141,854.00
1962	214,238.70	2,197,396.30
1963	115,486.30	844,250.00
1964	119,294.91	2,844,026.76
1965	120,054.64	843,250.00
1966	321,121.00	842,833.33
1967	405,532.00	
Totals	$2,196,387.21	$14,210,320.73

Source: Kim Sang-hyŏn, *Chaeil Hangug-in* (1969), p. 231.

Anticipating further difficulty in obtaining a school site, the Ch'ong-nyŏn, in cooperation with the Japan-DPRK Society (Nitchō Kyōkai; see chap. 5), established a dummy business firm called the Kyōritsu Industrial Company. The company, incorporated under the names of Japanese who were members of the Japan-DPRK Society, was officially registered with a capital investment of 3 million yen on 25 November 1958.[29] The Kyōritsu Company was, in fact, to serve as an agent of the Ch'ongnyŏn to procure a building site and to file an application for a construction permit. It was through this arrangement that Chosŏn University was able to secure its present location in Kodaira city, Tokyo.

In filing for a construction permit with the Kodaira city government, the officers of the company stated that the proposed building would be used for transistor radio research and to train engineers and technicians. Finally, when the building neared completion in May 1959, the Kyōritsu Industrial Company simply pretended to have arranged a lease agreement with Chosŏn University to rent all their structures and facilities.[30] For the Ch'ong-nyŏn this arrangement served a dual purpose. First, by processing all the necessary legal matters in the name of a Japanese firm, the Ch'ongnyŏn was able to circumvent any existing legal obstacles to the construction of university buildings. Second, since Chosŏn University was listed merely as the leaseholder, the buildings and other facilities could not be subject to confiscation as the Korean schools had been in the school shutdown of 1948.

The official announcement of the opening of a new university campus at Kodaira city was made on the final day of the Ch'ongnyŏn's Fifth National Convention on 10 June 1959. As the plan had been carefully concealed until the completion of the buildings, the announcement came as a total surprise even to the delegates assembled at the convention. The formal opening ceremony was held at the new campus site on 13 June with all the Ch'ongnyŏn delegates and some Japanese guests present at the campus, which covered an area of 66,000 square meters and had four newly erected school buildings. At this ceremony Han Dŏk-su, chairman of the Ch'ongnyŏn and president of the university, declared in his opening speech that

> This university is completed by the kindly aid given by the DPRK, and the courses offered will be the same as those offered in a university in the fatherland. In the near future, we are planning to invite foreign students from all over Asia to receive a communistic education. If this plan materializes, this university will become the sole international university in the non-Communist world.[31]

The long-range goals of the university encompassed not only giving an ethnic education to Koreans but serving as a training base to spread its political ideology throughout Asia.[32] Further clarification of the university's educational goals was made by Han Dŏk-su in his speech at Chosŏn University on 11 April 1964:

> We must arm ourselves with the thought of Kim Il-sung and an ideology of socialistic patriotism to strengthen the revolutionary transition. The students must prepare themselves to be the future national leaders in order to expedite the independent and peaceful unification of the fatherland.[33]

As the ultimate goals of Chosŏn University became clearer, the question of how to deal with the avowedly communistic education of the entire Ch'ongnyŏn educational system became a controversial public issue in Japan. The Japanese government had always frowned upon the Korean's insistence on ethnic education lest a minority culture be nurtured in Japan. The Ministry of Education, however, had no legal administrative control over the public school system in postwar Japan, since the system had been decentralized by the School Education Law of 1947. As a result, jurisdiction over Korean education rested not with the Minister of Education but with the prefectural governors.[34] Thus authorization for establishing Korean schools had been granted by local governments, which classified them as "miscellaneous schools" as specified in Article 83 of the School Education Law.[35] Accordingly, Korean schools did file applications for the approval of their institutions by each prefectural governor. There were several advantages to securing approval: acquisition of a tax-exempt status and the privileges of purchasing teaching-aid materials and commuter passes for students at discount rates. There was no uniform policy among the prefectural governors about granting the approval because of the decentralized nature of school supervision and jurisdiction. Where prefectural governors did not grant prompt approval, Korean schools nevertheless continued to operate.

Although the Japanese Education Ministry lacked direct control over Korean schools, on many occasions its suggestion not to issue approvals was made clear to prefectural governors,[36] some of whom disregarded the suggestions. As a result, unapproved Korean schools continued to flourish in some areas, especially in Osaka and Tokyo.

THE FOREIGNERS' SCHOOL SYSTEM BILL

In an attempt to bring about more effective control over Korean schools, the Ministry of Education organized a Special Committee for Foreigners' Education to study the problem. The chairmanship was held by the education minister, and its members were drawn from the Liberal Democratic party's Education Committee and Public Security Committee. The special committee finally came up with a proposal to revise the School Education Law and to submit a bill called the "Foreigners' School System." The draft of this bill was officially endorsed at the fifty-first session of the Diet later that year. No sooner had the proposal been announced to the public than the opposing forces rallied solidly behind the Japanese Socialist and Communist parties in the Diet. These forces were almost the same as those that had just previously led the attempt to block the passage of the ROK-Japan Normalization Treaty of 1965. The Foreign Minister of the DPRK also issued a strongly worded statement criticizing the pending bill, and so did the Ch'ongnyŏn.[37] Their ears still ringing from the noisy confrontations over the treaty ratification, the LDP members decided to postpone the school proposal to a later date.

The ultimate objective of the Foreigners' School Bill was doubtless to restrict the "democratic ethnic education" provided by the Ch'ongnyŏn. In fact, the aim was clearly spelled out in a provision of the draft that foreign schools were to be forbidden to offer education considered prejudicial to the national interest of Japan. The final authority to determine the question of what kind of education was in the Japanese national interest was to be exercised solely by the Minister of Education.[38] For this purpose, the Minister of Education was to be given the authority to license or close foreign schools and to investigate foreign school administration and textbooks. Furthermore, teaching staffs of foreign schools were to be approved by the Minister of Education. Had the bill passed the Diet it would have afforded the most sweeping power ever granted to the Minister of Education, giving him almost unlimited control over Korean education in Japan.

Opponents of the bill, especially among the leading Japanese jurists, argued that the Koreans' right to provide ethnic education was one of the fundamental rights guaranteed not only by the principles of international law but by the Japanese Constitution as well. The jurists affirmed that although Koreans were legally aliens, they were endowed with certain rights, both as to person and to property, according to the principles of international law.³⁹ Second, since the continued presence of Koreans in Japan was due to the involuntary servitude forced on them by the Japanese government during the war, they must be viewed differently from other ordinary aliens.⁴⁰ The right to receive education is fundamental, as noted in the Universal Declaration of Human Rights (Art. 27, par. 1). This declaration upholds the principle that such "education shall be free" and that "parents have a prior right to choose the kind of education that shall be given to their children" (Art. 27, par. 3). Even the Japanese Constitution guarantees fundamental rights and freedoms (Arts. 11 and 14) and stipulates: "*All people* shall have the right to receive an equal education" (Art. 26: emphasis added).

Nevertheless, an important question raised at the symposium was whether these constitutional guarantees were applicable to aliens residing in Japan. On this point, Yamazaki Masahide contended that the fundamental rights, except political rights, should not be construed to extend only to Japanese citizens but to "all people," as is clearly stated in the Constitution. The words "all people," according to Yamazaki, implied no distinction of any kind, such as race, color, or national origin. The nature of Korean "democratic ethnic education" was in line with the educational policy of their fatherland. It would be unconstitutional, concluded Yamazaki, to deprive some people of their fundamental rights because their education happened to be communist-oriented.⁴¹ Yamazaki's arguments carried weight among leading jurists. Public attitudes also shifted toward support of ethnic education, and a campaign to obtain signatures on a petition to assure the right to a "democratic ethnic education" was waged throughout Japan. The bill was finally killed at the committee stage and failed to reach even a plenary session of the lower house. This was probably a significant crisis in Japanese civil-rights history. The failure of a bill to pass was perhaps less dramatic but bore equal importance with other more stirring events. It was against this civil rights crisis that questions concerning the accreditation of Chosŏn University received close public attention.

THE CAMPAIGN TO ACCREDIT CHOSŎN UNIVERSITY

In April 1965, Chosŏn University had just filed its first application for accreditation to the Tokyo prefectural governor.⁴² In previous years, successive Tokyo governors had rarely bothered to regulate it, since the education it offered was not provided at public expense.

After the application was filed, Azuma Ryūtarō, the Tokyo prefectural governor, consulted with the Ministry of Education and withheld his decision for more than a year. He did so to comply with guidelines issued by the Ministry of Education on 28 December 1965. By delaying the governor's decision, the Ministry of Education hoped that it would eventually take over control of Chosŏn University, if and when the Foreigner's School System Bill passed the Diet. The minister's secretariat, spokesman of the Japanese government, publicly indicated on many occasions the undesirability of accrediting Chosŏn University.[43] Opposing the ministry's stance and in support of the Anti-School System Bill campaign already being waged by Japanese jurists and educators, another organization was founded, called the Liaison Council for the Protection of Democratic Ethnic Studies of Koreans in Japan (Zainichi Chōsenjin no minshushugi minzoku kyōiku o mamoru Renrakukaigi). In November 1966, the Ch'ongnyŏn itself organized a committee to expedite accreditation of the university.

As part of a public relations effort as well as to present a new image of Chosŏn University, a grand ceremony was held at the school on the occasion of the tenth anniversary of its founding in April 1966. Many thousands of prominent Japanese, as well as the ambassador from the USSR and other foreign dignitaries in Japan, were invited to celebrate the occasion. Hundreds of congratulatory messages flowed in from university presidents and scholars all over the world.[44] It was a perfect opportunity to strengthen the image of Chosŏn University as a school enjoying international recognition. The guests and dignitaries who visited Chosŏn University on this occasion reportedly numbered more than 10,000. Beginning in early spring 1966, a series of round-table discussions with prominent Japanese university presidents were held at the invitation of Han Dŏk-su, the Chosŏn University president, in an attempt to enlist their support.[45]

In April 1967 the movement to expedite the accreditation of Chosŏn University gained a formidable new ally when Minobe Ryūkichi, an economics professor in Tokyo and a Socialist, won the Tokyo prefectural governorship. His victory was made possible by the unprecedented coalition of the JSP and JCP to support a single candidate to defeat the LDP-endorsed candidate. The adroitly coordinated efforts of both the Ch'ongnyŏn and its Japanese counterparts began to gain public support for Chosŏn University. The Kodaira city assembly, where the university was located, adopted a unanimous resolution on 23 June 1966 in support of its accreditation. On 10 November of the same year the Tokyo prefectural assembly followed suit.[46]

On 21 August 1967 Minobe stated that he would examine the Chosŏn application "purely on an administrative basis" without any political prejudice. His justification to take up the matter much delayed by his predecessor was that:

1. Attempts to legislate the Foreigners' School System Bill had failed fwice in the Diet.

2. The Tokyo Prefectural assembly had twice passed a resolution demanding immediate approval of Chosŏn University.

3. Many other local legislative assemblies and mayors either adopted resolutions or declared their support for the University.

4. In July 1967 Minobe himself had received a petition signed by more than 2,000 scholars and literati in Japan demanding prompt accreditation.[47]

Minobe stated, therefore, that he found insufficient grounds to delay a decision any longer, and he referred the matter to Tokyo's Private School Council for further study and recommendation.[48]

Minobe's statement drew immediate reactions from various right-wing groups, including the Ministry of Education. Kennoki Toshihirō, then minister of education, commented that even if accreditation were granted it would not mean anything because he believed that, sooner or later, the Diet would pass the Foreigners' School System Bill. In other words, he implied his readiness to cancel the accreditation, once the bill became law. In the meantime, the Ministry of Education showed its determination to block Governor Minobe's move.

Outright opposition came mostly from extreme right-wing groups, such as the Pan-Japanese Patriots Organizational Conference, the Association for National Compatriots, the Shōwa Restoration League, the Committee for the Reconstruction of Great Imperial Japan, and the Anti-Communist Volunteer Unit. They condemned the university because it was financed and ultimately controlled by a country hostile to Japan. The university, they said, would provide communistic education disguised in the name of ethnic studies, which was not only incompatible with Japanese educational goals but was harmful to the national interest of Japan. If unmonitored, they argued, Chosŏn University would become a breeding ground for a communist attempt to overthrow the Japanese government.[49] They denounced Governor Minobe's pro-communist attitude and at the same time criticized the LDP for irresponsibly allowing accreditation to become an issue.

For nearly eight months, while the matter was under study by the Private School Council, Governor Minobe was the target of pressure from all quarters. The ROK government, too, joined the protest against Minobe's action, as did the Mindan. While right-wing groups along with the LDP and the ROK government led the protests, the supporters of Chosŏn University organized a group called the Society to Encourage Governor Minobe (Minobe Chiji o Hagemasukai). As a matter of fact, during the eight-month

period of deliberation, hardly a day passed without a crowd of either protestors or supporters appearing at the governor's office or residence. But the
protest movement waged by the various right-wing groups was fragmen-
tary in nature; it was unable to mount any concerted action because of its
lack of unity and horizontal coordination. Furthermore, the motives of the
right-wing groups appear to have been mixed. Some felt bitter toward
Minobe because of their defeat in the Tokyo gubernatorial election, and
they hoped to embarrass the Minobe administration.[50] It was reported that
some even threatened Minobe's personal security.

Generally speaking, these right-wing groups were usually advocates of
the supremacy of the Yamato race (as they perceived "true Japanese" to be)
and held a strong bias against Koreans being created citizens (chap. 1). The
relations between the Japanese right-wing and the ROK government,
including the Mindan, could not become amicable enough to form a united
front, despite their common goal in the protest movement. In contrast, the
DPRK, through the unflagging efforts of the Ch'ongnyŏn, was able to
muster the solid support of the Japanese left wing.

Soon after Governor Minobe referred the Chosŏn accreditation case
to the Private School Council, the Japanese left wing stepped up its activities in support of Chosŏn University. On 6 September 1967 the Assembly of
Scientists Demanding Accreditation held a meeting in Tokyo and decided to
launch a nationwide petition campaign to obtain signatures of all sympathetic university professors. They also adopted a manifesto warning education ministry officials to refrain from exerting any undue pressure on Governor Minobe. Similar warnings were signed by more than 300 nationally
known literati in Japan and by the Petition Signer's Association to Expedite
the Accreditation of Chosŏn University.[51] Representatives of the JSP and
JCP met with the Minister of Education and demanded a stop to the harassment of Governor Minobe. Attempts by the education ministry to interfere
in a matter within the jurisdiction of the Tokyo governor, they argued,
would constitute a serious violation of the principle of local autonomy specified not only in the Japanese Constitution (chap. 8) but also in the School
Education Law of 1947 (Art. 84).[52]

The DPRK also charged that the Sato regime's outspoken opposition
to accreditation was a deliberate attempt to oppress Chosŏn University.
Thus the supporters of accreditation tried to shroud the real issue in the
principle of local autonomy. The LDP's response to the charge was that the
Fundamental Education Law and the School Education Law of 1947 were
enacted not for aliens but in the interests of Japanese education. The existing
laws were inadequate to regulate education that might be contrary to the
objectives of Japanese education conducted by aliens. The Foreigners'
School System Bill was designed to meet this purpose, they asserted, and
they asked Governor Minobe to withhold his decision until appropriate
action could be taken by the Diet.[53]

On 6 April 1968, after eight months of careful study, the Tokyo Private School Council submitted its report to Governor Minobe for final action. But the report did not make any specific recommendation as to whether accreditation should be granted. Apparently council members wished to avoid involving themselves in the controversy. Instead, they left the matter to the governor's discretion, merely pointing out eleven questions that he might take into consideration in making a final decision.[54] The report concluded that the school possessed adequate educational facilities and financial resources to run as a university. The council stated, however, that it was unable to determine the true objective and scope of Chosŏn education, as the fundamental concept underlying ethnic education was ambiguous. The issue, according to the report, was a matter of national educational policy associated with political questions as well as with relations with other countries. Hence it was beyond the capacity of the council to pass judgment. The council, however, did go so far as to suggest that if accreditation were granted under the "miscellaneous schools" clause in the School Education Law, Chosŏn should not be permitted to use the university title but should be required to change the name of the school to one that would differentiate it from a regular university.[55]

Several shortcomings were noticeable in the council's report. First, despite its awareness of its incapability to pass judgment on the case, the council suggested that Chosŏn University not be permitted use of the university title. Yet the council recognized that the facilities and financial resources of the school were adequate for a university. Second, although the council was concerned about national education policy, it failed to take into consideration the unanimous resolution of the Tokyo Prefectural Legislative Assembly demanding immediate accreditation. Third, to judge from the overall content of the report, it was negative in tone and it avoided the crucial decision on whether to accredit.

Upon receiving the report, Governor Minobe commented to the press that although he had read it only cursorily, he had noted that the council's opinions were not entirely relevant to the matter in question. Because the report was silent in regard to the advisability of accreditation, he stated, he alone would assume responsibility for the decision.

In an attempt to assist the governor in the situation, five professors, represented by Yūkura Ryōkichi, professor of Administrative Law at Waseda University, handed in their scholarly analyses of the council's report to the Governor. Analyzing the report strictly from the legalistic point of view, they advised the governor that not a single provision in the report could be construed as restraining him from granting the accreditation, even the council's suggestion to disallow use of the university title by Chosŏn.[56] In the meantime, Chosŏn supporters held an assembly in the first conference room in the Tokyo Prefectural Legislative Assembly building to encourage the governor and to hasten his decision. There were about 190 representatives from approximately 100 different left-wing organizations, including the Sōhyō, Nikkyōso, JSP, and JCP. Three other groups visited Governor Minobe on separate occasions to express their support for prompt action. These were the representatives of 141 university presidents and professors; representatives of 480 writers, columnists, actors, and actresses; and jurists agreeing with Yūkura Ryōkichi's analysis on the council's report. Governor Minobe, before his final decision, met with the Minister of Education on 11 April to make clear his decision in favor of accreditation. The Minister of Education acknowledged that the jurisdiction concerning Chosŏn University legally resided with the governor but urged him to use utmost prudence in his final decision. However, Governor Minobe's meeting with the Minister of Education was undoubtedly designed to warn ministry officials and thereby clear the way for his forthcoming announcement.

On 18 April 1968 the day finally arrived for Governor Minobe to announce his decision to grant accreditation to Chosŏn University, an announcement that elicited front-page headlines in every major newspaper in Japan. Minobe stated at his press conference that the Constitution of Japan and the subsequent statutory laws were the only elements he had weighed in the balance in making his decision. To grant accreditation, he stated, was an administrative matter, and his decision had nothing to do with political questions. Thus it took almost two years of strenuous campaigning by the Ch'ongnyŏn and its Japanese counterparts to obtain accreditation.

We have presented the fight for Chosŏn accreditation in some detail because it illustrates a number of issues in Korean-Japanese relationships, and because it underscores the fact that, regardless of the general atmosphere of prejudice toward Koreans, many Japanese today seek sincerely to respect minority rights.

The death of the education bill in 1966 perhaps marked a high point in the continual right-wing effort to reintroduce that control over education they had exercised prewar. This control had sought to maintain the myth of Japanese homogeneity. The left/right polarization of political philosophy is extreme and continuing. This struggle is complicated by the essential issue of a person's right to an education that supports his maintenance of a separate "ethnic identity." A large number of individuals in Japan are cognizant of this fact. Many individuals who supported the accreditation of Chosŏn University did not agree with the university's political orientation, but for them the overriding issue was the right of ethnic maintenance. Many Koreans continue to suffer from discrimination in Japan, but it must be noted that many members of contemporary Japanese society are struggling to develop and maintain democratic institutions governed by law. The legislative process is functioning in Japan. It is possible to arouse the Japanese public to support just causes and to put pressure on political figures so that, despite the continuance of a conservative majority, repressive legislation has not been passed in the critical area of education to the degree espoused by those who would return education to its prewar functions.

Another point to be emphasized in this detailed review of ethnic studies is the difficult position of the political moderate who would like to espouse a Korean ethnic identity within the existing Japanese society. Given the lack of structure supporting a dual identity of being Japanese and yet being Korean, the Mindan (chap. 5) cannot develop a viable type of education that satisfies those suffering problems in ethnic identity. The organization cannot muster from the Korean communities sufficient internal resources to offer special education. In this context, it must be noted that it is only because the North Korean government finances ethnic studies that a separatist Korean education continues. Since our direct contacts with students attending North Korean school facilities have been made impossible by conditions of political militance, we are in no position to judge whether the education in a Korean school resolves internal identity conflicts to any satisfactory degree.

9

EDUCATION: POLICIES AND PROSPECTS

Thomas Rohlen

The key question today concerning the education of Koreans in Japan is whether the future points toward gradual assimilation or revived ethnicity. This is no mere academic question, since it lies at the heart of most of the issues raised between Koreans and the Japanese government, and between the various political groups representing the Koreans themselves. The formal education afforded young Koreans is a central factor in determining whether young Koreans further abandon their "Korean" ethnicity or participate in conserving it. Both alternatives are closely tied to their prospects for advancements in Japanese society.

So that the reader may be alert to the direction of my arguments and the relative strengths of the facts supporting them, I wish to state my conclusions in advance. I cannot envision much future for the revived ethnicity approach. Direct inquiries have convinced me that:

1. The popularity of Japanese schools is growing, whereas Korean language schools are declining in popularity and strength.

2. Although Korean educational attainment falls short of the Japanese average, it is not a question of barriers existing within the school system itself. Barriers to advancement are encountered later—when Koreans seek employment in the Japanese labor market.

3. The home life of most Korean resident families does not reinforce an ethnic education, although such efforts are visible in certain aspects of family life (see chap. 15).

4. The recent increase of interest in ethnic education in some quarters is not likely to prevent further loss of the cultural content supporting Korean ethnicity.

5. Korean ethnicity is increasingly important as a symbol for the minority civil rights movement, which, if successful, will encourage, ironically, greater social assimilation.

I have set forth these rather controversial conclusions to underscore the analytic issues involved. To date, despite a growing polemical literature on the question of education for Japan's Koreans, little empirical research has been done and little objective consideration has been given to the key questions.

The ethnicity versus assimilation issue is framed by a fascinating set of related questions. First, will the Koreans in Japan ever return to their homeland? The kind of education they select and the practicality of Korean language education in particular are related to this question.

Second, can Japan, as a closed, culturally homogeneous society, become pluralistic enough to accept a Korean minority as different but equal? The Japanese (especially the intellectuals) working to support the civil rights of the Korean minority have this sort of new Japanese society in mind; recent fledgling efforts to supplement the Japanese public school curriculum with ethnic studies for Korean students point in the same direction. One can find close parallels here with the ethnic studies efforts in American education.

Third, will the present contradictions in Japanese government policy continue? Presently, public educational policy encourages cultural assimilation, but contravening government policies in virtually all other areas (such as employment and welfare) prevent rather than encourage actual social assimilation. Above all, there is the high wall built around the sacredness of Japanese citizenship. Will these contradictions continue in the face of increased civil rights pressure? And if change comes, what direction will it take?

Fourth, setting aside the question of official policy, what social forces are presently at work in Japanese society as a whole that may influence the outcome? Compared to other advanced nations, Japan remains much more closed to the entry of outsiders. Can it resist the general forces found in most modern societies that are bringing an end to ethnic isolation? To some extent, public education, forms of modern employment, and the universal application of law all hasten this tendency in a modern society.

It seems fair to say that the education of minorities in advanced societies presents many common problems. The pressures of daily life in any urban situation emphasize at least outward conformity and assimilation. To look, speak, act, and even think like the majority is not only a matter of survival; over time it can also mean opportunities for advancement and social acceptance. Such opportunities are not trivial if, as with the Koreans, the minority group is low in status and material well-being. Two aspects of advanced societies are directly relevant to opportunities for advancement: education and employment. Typically, the modern state offers universal education even to aliens, and in this regard Japan is no exception. It is also typical for advanced societies to have large and expanding sectors where recruitment for employment is strongly affected by educational qualifications. The ideal of recruitment by objective standards, often protected by laws prohibiting various forms of discrimination, is one that becomes influential not only in education but also to some degree in employment. The situation in Japan regarding Koreans is that although the ideal and some of the legal underpinnings are present, and although education is inclusive, employment practices (both public and private) retain a strong discriminatory inclination. Compared with the ideal, and also compared with European and North American democracies, Japanese society appears notably closed to Koreans, and yet this observation should not obscure the fact that as a highly bureaucratized and democratic society, Japan has undergone an opening up, however slow and unintentional it has been. It is my impression that education, and more precisely the government policy of offering Korean aliens Japanese public schooling, is the cutting edge of eventual change as it creates a group of educationally well-qualified Koreans who constitute a significant source of pressure on the discriminatory aspects of the employment system.[1] (This is not to deny that Japan's prewar policy was to educate Koreans but at the same time to keep them as second-class citizens. There is, in effect, no real postwar policy.)

In Japan as elsewhere, modern mass media and popular leisure bring the allure of the majority culture directly into the center of family life of ethnic minorities, creating, especially among the young, a strong emotional current toward identification with majority popular culture. Generation by generation the minority is thus progressively dissociated from its parent culture. The gap between generations, a reflection of this, assumes special prominence. Minorities may always have spoken of first, second, and third generations, but the degree of cultural differentiation between each generation is much greater now than in the preindustrial past. Minorities lacking enduring qualities, such as racial or religious distinction, quickly become invisible behaviorally, if fully accepted by the larger society. Japan, of course, has not accepted the Koreans. The point here that relates directly to education is that assimilation in a modern society is not simply a matter of what kind of school young people attend. The language of the home, peer group life, and continual exposure to popular culture are probably more powerful in combination than formal education per se. In Japan, these influences are also steadily pushing the Korean minority toward cultural assimilation and thus are reducing the cultural content of Korean ethnicity.

For many minorities, furthermore, cultural assimilation is not accompanied by as rapid social assimilation. Typically, the early generations, despite their adoption of majority culture, gain a toehold only at the bottom of the social ladder. Certainly for Koreans in Japan, becoming culturally "Japanese" has not been accompanied by equality in economic, legal, or social status. Still poor and treated as outsiders by the Japanese, many Koreans of the second and third generations cannot count on a personal resilience that comes with a clear sense of belonging to a different, equally proud tradition.

The school-age children of Korean residents total approximately 125,000. More than three-fourths of them are enrolled in Japanese schools, both public and private. A significant but much smaller group attend Korean schools supported either by Ch'ongnyŏn or Mindan. All but a handful of the latter schools belong to the Ch'ongnyŏn organization, discussed in chapters 4, 5, and 8. There is some question about the reliability of the figures for Ch'ongnyŏn-affiliated schools, and the years represented do not match perfectly, but the latest figures available are given in table 17.

There is much to be said about these figures. Obviously the most significant point is that the great majority of Korean children—about three-fourths—are attending Japanese schools. Published figures indicate that the percentage in Japanese schools was fairly constant between 1960 and 1975.[2] Japanese schooling is understood by Koreans as contributing to their integration into and their upward mobility within Japanese society, whereas Ch'ongnyŏn schools promote retention of a strong Korean identity built upon patriotic feelings for and service to the North Korean government. No sharper contrast of intentions and philosophy of education can be imagined than that between Japanese and Ch'ongnyŏn schools. Mindan schools (see chap. 5) attempt a compromise solution that accepts Japanese residence as permanent but aims at preserving Korean ethnicity while emphasizing the centrality of a Japanese language curriculum and a set of skills oriented to life in Japan.

If we look at the figures for specific levels of schooling, we find the percentage of Koreans in Japanese elementary (76%) and junior high schools (76%) to be higher than for senior high schools (69%). Several explanations for this difference exist. Although the numbers are small in terms of the total, a comparably larger percentage of the Korean graduates of Japanese junior high schools reportedly take jobs rather than continue on to high school. Second, a number of the Korean graduates of Japanese junior high schools transfer to Korean high schools, largely because for academic reasons they cannot gain acceptance into a public Japanese high school.[3]

More to the point in reading these statistics, however, is the fact that Koreans do not easily cross the line between the two school systems except at the point of high school entrance. Movement out of Korean and into Japanese schools is complicated by the reluctance of school officials on both sides to approve the transfers, and the small movement the other way is limited largely to the time of high school entrance. The Japanese and the Korean school systems operate essentially in isolation from one another, and entrance into one means a strong probability of continuing with it to the end.

Let us briefly review the central social characteristics of the present

TABLE 17

Types of Schools Attended by Korean Students in Japan
(1974 and 1975)

Japanese public schools (1974)	Number of students	Percentage of total
Elementary	50,297	
Junior high school	26,516	
High school	15,893	
Technical college (*senmon gakko*)	45	
Junior college	356	
University	3,797	
Total	96,904	75.2
Schools belonging to Ch'ongnyŏn (1975)		
Elementary (90 schools)	14,811	
Junior high school (54)	7,701	
High school (11)	7,054	
University (1)	1,000	
Total	30,566	23.5
Schools affiliated with Mindan (1975)		
Elementary (3 schools)	558	
Junior high schools (4)	405	
High school (4)	703	
Total	1,666	1.3

Source: Mindan unpublished compilation of statistics (May 1976) including their own, those published by Ch'ongnyŏn, and official Japanese government statistics.

Korean student population in Japan. Virtually all have been born in Japan. Very, very few of their parents are wealthy, and only a small portion are middle class. There is high unemployment among their parents, and the jobs Koreans do hold are characterized by low social status, low pay, and little security of employment.[4] Many small Korean enterprises eke out an existence on the fringes of the Japanese economy. These companies are undercapitalized, dependent on very low labor costs, and reliant on insecure sources of income. Nevertheless, as Japan has prospered, many of these tiny firms have survived and have even gained a modicum of security. Koreans connected to them are undoubtedly better off today than twenty years ago.

The overall educational level of Korean parents is low by Japanese standards, and the percentage in manual and factory labor is high. Compared to the Japanese population as a whole, there is more poverty, more broken homes, and a higher crime rate. About half of all Koreans live in the poorer sections of some Japanese city. Whether a student is Korean or Japanese, such environmental factors are likely to affect school performance. In fact, we can see many similarities between the statistics on educational performance of Koreans and other students in poor urban areas.

Korean parents are well aware that they are part of a highly dependent minority, economically speaking. Their businesses and jobs depend on the Japanese economy. In hard times, Koreans' small businesses are typically the first to suffer. Economic security comes with gaining a foothold in the Japanese economic world, whether as the employee of a secure Japanese company, as a professional, or as a small businessman with reliable connections to the larger Japanese system. Unlike overseas Chinese communities in Asia which have developed firm economic positions that provide considerable security and influence except in unusual political circumstances, the Koreans in Japan are near the bottom of an economic pecking order. The desire for greater security for their children is understandably strong among Korean parents, and this desire is very influential when educational choices are made.

Geographically fragmented and split by deep political divisions, the Korean residents have very few sources of unity other than their national past, their common history as migrants and labor conscripts, and their alienated position in Japanese society.[5] No single religious affiliation unites them. Their common language is generally Japanese. Only small segments of the population interact socially as Koreans by doing such things as wearing native dress, eating native food, and celebrating Korean holidays. Furthermore, the emphasis on the individual family and the persistent fact of competition among Koreans in business constitute further sources of division. Some young people wish to avoid being known as Korean even among other Koreans. There are residential concentrations of Koreans in places like Kobe, Osaka, and Kyoto, but in these places community cohesiveness is sporadic at best.

To summarize, young Koreans today know only Japan and most speak only Japanese at home; typically, they come from families low on the socioeconomic scale, and their parents' education is considerably below the Japanese average. From these few but critical characteristics we would expect their academic performance to fall below the Japanese average; we would also expect the goal of assimilation represented by Japanese schools to receive general reinforcement, since Korean aspirations for security and success are great and they center on making a living in Japan.

SCHOOL POLICIES AND KOREAN EXPERIENCES: KOREANS IN JAPANESE SCHOOLS

Only about two in every ten Korean students use their Korean name when they register for Japanese high schools.[6] Looking the same, having the same school uniforms, speaking Japanese exactly like their Japanese peers, Korean students are indistinguishable to the casual visitor to Japanese schools, and even a moderately prolonged inquiry turns up only hints of the Korean presence in many schools. My previous fieldwork was in Japanese high schools, and I remember vividly my surprise when at one school, the student council president, named Suzuki, whispered that he was Korean. We were alone at the time, and he switched to faltering English to convey this message. His clandestine manner gave me the impression that very few others were privy to the fact. As it turned out, the faculty was generally aware of his nationality (as we would expect, since all students of foreign nationality are registered in schools as foreigners), but they did not discuss it among themselves and showed signs of discomfort when I asked if they knew he was Korean. Most students apparently did not know (as the job and status of student council president carries little significance in Japan, his election to this job defies interpretation in terms of the Korean/Japanese distinction). His closest friend was also Korean, however, and the two of them visited my house several times to discuss the possibility of going to college abroad, as both dreamed of starting new lives in some country other than Japan or Korea.

In Suzuki's high school, there were 17 Koreans out of 1,220 students. The proportion of Korean students in Japanese schools varies considerably from school to school, city to city, and prefecture to prefecture. In Osaka, about 4.3 percent of the students in public schools are Korean,[7] but in some rural prefectures Korean students constitute only a tiny fraction of 1 percent. One public elementary school in Osaka has a student body that is 57 percent Korean,[8] and a few other elementary schools in that city have an enrollment at least 20 percent Korean. Some Osaka elementary schools, however, have few if any Koreans. The situation in neighboring Amagasaki and Kobe is not too different, but the concentration of Korean students is, on the whole, less. My impression is that in the rest of Japan, including Tokyo, it is rare to find even 10 percent Koreans in a public school. Residential concentration is highest in Osaka, Amagasaki, and Kobe.

Even in those Osaka elementary schools with many Korean students, the use of Korean family names is far from universal. Recently, officials of liberal persuasion in one Osaka school have encouraged parents to register their children using their Korean names (as part of the ethnic education movement). Many parents have complied, but not all. About one-third still insist that their children use Japanese names, something school officials had typically encouraged (and even insisted on) in the past. This has led to such unlikely situations as a Korean child (using a Japanese name) teasing another Korean child (with a Korean name) for being a Korean.[9] The epithet "Korean, Korean," is well known in Japanese schoolyards and neighborhoods. Even very young Korean children, not clear about their own identity, use it as a term of opprobrium. A Japanese name obviously offers some protection for little children facing this sort of hostile environment. Parents typically help their children learn how to hide behind a Japanese public identity.

Upon entering junior high school, students, both Korean and Japanese, begin to show considerable independence from teachers and parents. This age group in Japanese society has recently come to be regarded as especially troubled. For example, although Japanese crime rates for most ages, including the high school years, are static or declining, the crime rate for junior high school students has been rising rapidly. Discipline in some junior high schools is now a serious problem. A recent rash of assaults on junior high school teachers is one illustration. The relevance of this situation to Koreans in Japanese education lies in the fact that the urban junior high schools where the delinquency rates are highest and discipline problems most acute are often schools with an above-average percentage of Korean students.[10]

Does this mean that Korean students are the cause of the problems? Not necessarily, but Japanese opinion typically connects them to such problems in a facile manner, and many Japanese public school teachers complain of the difficulties of teaching in schools "with many Koreans" or "many Burakumin." In Kobe, demonstrably more behavioral difficulties and teacher complaints characterize those junior high schools that have a relatively high percentage of minority Burakumin students. Crime and delinquency rates among Korean juveniles are notably high—reportedly about six to seven times higher than among Japanese.[11] Prejudices about minority students are not totally unfounded.

The fundamental character of this syndrome is obvious and is hardly limited to minorities just in Japan. Not only do a large proportion of Korean students experience the collective disadvantages of attending such troubled schools, where learning rates are low and peer pressure is negative, but the syndrome has sustained the basic character of anti-Korean prejudice.

In cities like Kobe, where the Korean population is large, anti-Korean prejudice is a recognized educational problem. Not many, but some middle-class Japanese parents will move their residence or send their children to private schools to avoid troubled public junior high schools "with many Koreans." Because students usually come to school already having learned to think of Koreans as aggressive and untrustworthy, school campaigns are directed as countering such opinion. Although other students only very rarely express such prejudice openly, covert attitudes to this effect ominously shadow Korean students throughout school and later life.

The school board in Kobe, a city run by a progressive political coalition, has attempted by various means to counter the majority prejudice against Burakumin and Korean minorities. Official pamphlets and other locally generated materials for classroom use have been produced centering on the inhumanity, unneighborliness, and injustices of prejudice against Burakumin and Koreans. It is hoped that high school and junior high school students will read these tracts and then discuss prejudice in their homeroom classes.

The most powerful organization exercising continual pressure against discrimination is the Kaihōdōmei, a Burakumin organization. Since the Burakumin are more numerous and possess full Japanese citizenship, they can exert more political pressure with the Koreans riding their coattails. The Burakumin therefore receive most of the attention in educational programs, but the results for both groups are much the same.

What actually happens in the homerooms of the Kobe schools is the responsibility of the individual teachers. I have found some teachers to be keen on the notion of confronting prejudice in the classroom, but more privately confide their discomfort with it. Most teachers are concerned about discrimination, but they are reluctant to discuss prejudice openly and, in some instances, they refuse to examine frankly their own feelings. In my judgment, uncertainty as to the efficacy of teacher-led discussions of discrimination characterized most teachers in 1977.

The programs do succeed at least in introducing students to a conscious consideration of the problem of discrimination in Japan. A vocabulary of awareness, such as the frequent use of the term *sabetsu* ("discrimination"), is introduced and probably has lasting influence. It is too optimistic, however, to assume that such a program ends discriminatory attitudes among students. Students no doubt learn to be more cautious in offering their private opinions (much as their parents and teacher have learned). They also come to have suspicions about minority groups based on a sense that behind any such insistent denials of difference must lie some hidden, unmentionable realities. Teachers find discussions of discrimination difficult to lead, and students rarely get beyond the expression of idealistic truisms. But sometimes a minority student stands before the class and for the first time publicly reveals his or her identity or tells of the experiences, fears, and hopes that are the common secrets of minority students. The class is transfixed, and a lifelong memory is formed that cannot but positively affect future attitudes. Most often, however, minority students do not want to go before their peers in this dramatic fashion. Teachers recount instances of minority students virtually begging to be allowed to remain anonymous.

The split among Japanese teachers, between activists who adamantly insist that minority students and their parents proclaim their minority identity and those who favor continued silence and a facade of uniformity, represents two fundamentally different views of Japanese society. One group encourages Korean students to use their Korean names and urges them to express their problems and bitterness to the class. The other and much larger group, however, sympathizes with the individual's wish to remain indistinguishable from the majority—a normal (if almost pathologically well-developed) inclination among Japanese in general. If Japanese schools are microcosms of Japanese society, then the activists hold a vision of a future pluralism not shared by the majority of teachers or, for that matter, the Korean students themselves. The ideal is not criticized as unattractive but rather as unrealistic.

Kobe's board of education has another program worth a brief note. Junior high schools with more than 10 percent Korean students are given one extra teacher. This teacher's duties are not formally specified, but the intention is to lighten the workload and improve the teacher-student ratio. It is impossible to say whether this policy is intended primarily as a countermeasure to the discipline problems associated with those junior high schools or as an expression of concern for the special problems of education and guidance for Koreans. Both perspectives were mentioned by teachers and both are germane to the affairs of any school.

Given the usual invisibility of Koreans and the official disregard they typically receive at school, only two kinds of data are really of much help in delineating the experience of Koreans in Japanese schools: anecdotes and overall statistics. The following three anecdotes were garnered during my own visits to Japanese schools.

In the first instance, during a two-month visit to one of the best high schools in Kobe in 1975, I was told that several Korean students wished to see me after school. We met in a small room reserved usually for faculty use, and the Japanese teacher discreetly disappeared after making introductions. The two boys began by asking me what I thought of the Japanese. I stumbled around, concocting an interpretation neither too pejorative nor too complimentary. They smiled and asked if I thought Japanese were at all strange or funny. I replied that by normal American standards they certainly seemed to have some strange aspects to their character. They immediately wanted to know what Americans would see as strange. I listed the group orientation, the constraints on expressive behavior, and the extreme attention to courtesy and politeness.

It was as if a dam had broken. Both boys started talking eagerly about how Koreans see the Japanese as strange in the same ways, how they could discuss this sort of thing only with other foreigners, how at home Koreans are more expressive than Japanese, and so forth. Once this subject was exhausted, they let me ask about their future plans and their relations in the school. Both wanted to enter medical schools because, as they explained, medicine offers one of the few good careers for well-educated Koreans. Both said they had never experienced open discrimination at school, but they preferred their close friends to be Korean.

The second example quotes from a junior high school student's essay, entitled "Prejudice":

> One boy who was quite an outstanding member of our class and another, a Korean, known as a troublemaker, were standing around the room during lunch period. I asked them to help me with something, and the troublemaker made an excuse and left. "Koreans sure are lazy," I said to the boy helping me. "I'm Korean, too," he replied matter-of-factly. I was shaken, and at that instant I understood my own prejudice.

In the third instance, a junior high school coach told me that Yoshio was the biggest kid in his ninth grade class. He was not much at school work, but no one could beat him at judo. Yoshio's junior high school judo team was the city's best, and he was its hero. He and half the others on the team were Korean, and the coach took the team to Korea once a year on a goodwill visit as representatives of Kobe's school system.

One day some of the Korean boys in Yoshio's neighborhood who went to the Ch'ongnyŏn school challenged Yoshio to an after-school fight. They prided themselves on their karate ability, and it was Yoshio's reputation that led them to make the challenge—that and the fact of being from different schools. Yoshio went alone, but five showed up from the other side. Their leader stepped forward, and Yoshio, forgetting all his judo, charged straight at the fellow, hitting him one big haymaker. He knocked his opponent unconscious and ended the fight right there. But his troubles had only begun. His opponent was diagnosed as in critical condition at the hospital, and Yoshio was arrested.

Every day for two weeks, one of the Japanese teachers from his school (no doubt disliking the task), visited the hospital to convey the school's regrets to the injured boy's parents. An investigation was made by the school with the cooperation of the Korean school's teachers, and finally Yoshio's relative innocence was brought to light. Still, he had to go to a juvenile home for a few months. His coach arranged for his release a few weeks early so that he could go with the team to South Korea one last time before graduation. As the coach told me, "Behind the statistics of Korean juvenile arrests are many stories of individuals who usually don't intend to get into any trouble at all."

Can we generalize from illustrations such as these? We know already that most Korean students avoid revealing their Korean identity among Japanese students. Teachers know they are Korean, but the use of a Japanese name may prevent other students from knowing. The fears of discrimination that lie behind the mask and the secret itself no doubt cause anxiety, create barriers to friendships, and leave the student vulnerable to shock when Japanese casually drop prejudicial remarks.

When visiting Japanese schools I spoke to Japanese teachers for the most part. I therefore heard largely positive and encouraging examples. I was told time and again of Koreans befriended by a dedicated teacher, of successful Korean students going on to universities, and so forth. This is also part of the story, for there are many successful Korean students in Japanese schools. Obviously, generalizations at a certain point falter, so complex and varied is the Korean experience of Japanese schooling, not to mention the variety of Korean students themselves.

The replies of 164 Korean students in Japanese high schools to a questionnaire sent them by the Korean Scholarship Society in 1975 reveal the complex ambivalence that generally characterizes Koreans in Japanese education:

Are you using your Korean name at school?
Yes	23.7%
No	76.3

Did you use your Korean name in junior high school?
Yes	5.0%
No	95.0

Are your closest friends Korean or Japanese?
Japanese	71.2%
Korean	26.6

Of those seeking a close friend, which would you prefer?
Korean	54.6%
Either	42.4
Japanese	3.0

Do your parents wish you to live as a Korean?
Yes	49.0%
Don't know	31.0
As Japanese	2.4
Other or no reply	17.6

What do you think about being born Korean?
Proud	27.4%
Rather be Japanese	20.1
No answer	46.9

Who would you prefer to marry?
Korean	40.4%
Japanese	6.0
Either	26.2
Any nationality	27.4

These answers convey a general sense of ambiguity among Koreans receiving Japanese education. At home, although parents may not speak Korean, growing up to be a Korean is stressed by about half of the parents; among Japanese friends and Japanese peers at school, being Japanese is emphasized. The development of an uneasy balance between a self that is publicly Japanese and privately part-Korean would seem to be the typical result. After graduation, employment and the choice of marriage partner determine further shifts in this pattern. It is notable that today one-third of all Koreans are marrying Japanese.

Educational Achievement

Although it would be an overstatement to say that the fate of Koreans in Japan depends totally on their success in Japanese education, few considerations are more important, because the Korean minority is a highly urbanized population with few capital resources. For most Japanese, to get ahead today means to enter a profession or to get a good job in an economically secure company or government office. Young Koreans face the same basic social situation, one that underlines the importance of education, but their prospects for good jobs in Japanese organizations are dim by comparison and their chances for promotion are darker still. Compared with the uncertainty, the long hours, poor working conditions, and low wages of Korean-run small businesses, the professions and employment in the Japanese corporate system are highly attractive. Koreans in Japanese schools cannot help but view education as most Japanese do—as the key to future social position and security.

Two questions come immediately to mind: How well do Koreans do in Japanese schools? And do they obtain jobs commensurate with their educational achievement? Recently, statistics have become available which allow us to answer the first of these questions with considerable exactitude, for Hyogo prefecture at least.[12]

In Japan a complex set of distinctions exist which serve to sort students into an elaborate educational hierarchy. These distinctions are created at two points of school transfer: from junior to senior high school; and from high school to university. Graduation from junior high school is the terminal point of compulsory education, and before high school, school attendance patterns are entirely a matter of residence.

Entrance into public high schools is strictly by competitive examination. The number of public high schools in urban areas is sufficient to enroll from half to three-fourths of the total graduates of junior high schools. A bottleneck exists, in other words, and here the sorting of students by tested educational ability begins. High schools, as a result, are ranked according to the academic ability of those who get in. College entrance, jobs, and future income differences follow from this ranking. Like public school sys-

tems everywhere, the professed intention of equal opportunity is thus ultimately accompanied by the fact of differentiation and ranking, and the hierarchy of status and qualifications that emerges is persistently significant for
the social life of the school generation.

A small number of students (8% in 1975), those with the least academic ability, go directly to work upon graduation from ninth grade. At the
bottom of the school hierarchy, night schools or private schools of low
quality admit those students least qualified in terms of academic performance. In the middle rank, two basic distinctions serve to characterize the
hierarchical order: public high schools are more desirable than private
schools; and academic high schools, with rare exception, are more desirable
than vocational high schools. At the top stand the elite public and private
high schools that produce candidates for Japan's top universities.

How do Korean students face this educational watershed? Do more
Koreans go to work following ninth grade? The evidence is that they do. In
1976, 88.2 percent of the Koreans graduating from Hyogo junior high
schools went on to high school, whereas for the total student population of
the prefecture, the figure was 93.7 percent. If the comparison had been with
only the urban portions of the prefecture, the contrast might well have been
larger.

Only since the late 1960s have the country's poor in general begun to
attend high school as a matter of course. Prosperity has brought Japan to
the point where very few students are not going to high school, and this
means that most Koreans, along with the rest of Japan's lower and lower
middle classes, now expect their children to go to high school. Today the
more critical question is: "What kind of high school?" Family socioeconomic levels and the student's future social status are definitely reflected in
the answers to this question.

The students who enter high schools where an academic or university-
entrance oriented curriculum is offered are those with the better junior high
school records and the best prospects for higher education. Here, too, we
find a difference between the Korean entrance rate and the population as a
whole (see table 18). Although 74.8 percent of the total prefectural high
school student population attend academic high schools, the rate is 68.0
percent for Koreans. Furthermore, the percentage of Koreans attending private high schools (36.0) is greater than for the student population as a whole
(28.9%), indicating that Koreans are (a) paying more than average for high
school education but (b) generally getting less out of it, since private high
schools are, with the exception of a handful of elite schools, lower in academic caliber.

Koreans also enter public night schools, the lowest rung on the high
school ladder, at twice the average rate (8.2% for Koreans compared with
4.0% for the whole population). If we realize that in the public/private
school comparisons presented above, public night schools are included in

TABLE 18

Comparisons Between Korean and Buraku-Area Students at the Point of High School Entrance (1976)

1. Percentage of junior high school graduates going on to high school:

	High school enrollment	Employment plus high school enrollment
Total prefecture	93.7	1.8
Korean students	88.2	4.2
Buraku-area students	88.8	2.7

2. Percentage of high school entrants in public and private high schools:

	Public	Private
Total prefecture	71.1	28.9
Korean students	62.0	36.0
Buraku-area students	69.6	30.0

3. Percentage of high school entrants going to public night schools:

Total prefecture	4.0
Korean students	8.2
Buraku-area students	4.7

4. Percentage of high school entrants going to academic and vocational high schools:

	Public academic	Private academic	Public vocational	Private vocational
Total prefecture	74.8		25.2	
Korean students	38.0	30.0	24.2	7.2
Buraku-area students	36.6	20.6	33.5	9.5

Sources: *Shinrō Hoshō*, nos. 7 and 8 (1976). Kobe, Hyogo-ken, *Shinrō Hoshō* Kyōgikai. Kihon Gakko Chōsa (1976). Kobe, Hyogo-ken Kyōiku Iinkai.

TABLE 19

Comparisons Between Prefectural Totals and Korean Buraku-Area Students at the Point of University Entrance (1976)

1. Percentage of high school graduates going on to higher education:

Total prefecture	45.8
Korean students	26.3
Buraku-area students	32.1

2. Percentage neither taking employment nor going on to higher education:

Total prefecture	21.6
	(29.0 of all males; 14.3 of all females)
Korean students	26.2
	(28.4 of all males; 24.1 of all females)
Buraku-area students	14.6

3. Percentage of higher education entrants attending university as compared to junior college:

	University	Junior college
Total prefecture	64.2	35.8
Korean students	48.3	51.7
Buraku-area students	58.3	41.7

Sources: *Shinrō Hoshō Kyōgikia*, 1976; *Hyogo Kyōikuiin-kai*, 1976.

the otherwise preferred public school category, we can grasp the point that Koreans do even less well than the statistics indicate.

To summarize, when it comes time to go to high school, Korean students are (1) more likely not to go to high school at all, (2) only half as likely to enter the most desirable public academic high schools, (3) twice as likely to go to night schools, and (4) more likely to attend private and vocational high schools.

The whole sorting procedure is repeated at the time of university entrance (see table 19). In 1976, 45.8 percent of all Hyogo prefecture high school graduates went on to universities or junior colleges as compared with only 26.3 percent of the Korean graduates. Part of this reflects the fact that fewer Koreans attend academic high schools. In addition, those Koreans who went on to higher education were more likely to enroll in junior colleges than the average (51.7% compared with 35.8%). In Hyogo, in 1976, 64.2 percent of all those seeking higher education went to a four-year university, but among the comparable group of Koreans, only 48.3 percent proceeded to a four-year university.

Students in Japan who do not succeed in entering the university of their choice often opt to study independently for a further year in hopes of passing the examination the next time. Since these students neither go on to higher education nor take jobs, they constitute a particular official statistical category of their own. This category also includes such exceptions as those who work in a family business, are ill, or are attending schools for occupational training (like beautician's school). The prefectural total in this category represents about one-fifth of all high school graduates; categorized according to sex, however, the group is predominantly male. Much greater emphasis is placed on higher education for males than for females, with particular emphasis on entrance into the right university. The Korean percentage in this special category is higher than that for the Japanese average. Analyzed according to sex, it is higher because of a much higher than usual rate for females. The likely explanation is that after graduation many more girls stay at home helping in the family business. They may also take jobs in bars and night clubs, occupations they prefer not to report to the school.

The educational situation of Koreans in Hyogo can be readily compared with that of residents of designated Buraku areas in the prefecture. The educational patterns that emerge for the two groups are strikingly similar. As table 19 illustrates, both minorities obtain lower than prefectural averages at every critical point. By my calculations, the chance of entering a four-year university is approximately 17 in 100 for Koreans and 19 in 100 for Buraku area residents, but for the prefecture as a whole (including these minorities) the rate is approximately 36 in 100.

Although Koreans today have statistically less than half the average chance of going to a university, I found little evidence that this difference in outcome stems primarily from discrimination in the educational and matriculation process itself. School district differences are small and entrance criteria are not in the least discriminatory against Koreans. Rather, family background factors seem responsible, coupled with the negative effects of anticipated job discrimination. The high level of competition in the Japanese educational system makes family factors, such as parental education, important; the average Korean family is unable to provide the degree of support for academic achievement that the average Japanese family provides. Lower levels of income and aspiration figure as elements of a single complex recognizable among impoverished minorities in many modern nations.

Given this factor of disadvantaged social conditions, the question is how much weight in the educational imbalance it bears in comparison with explanations that emphasize the barriers and psychological harm created by minority status and Japanese discrimination. Empirical evidence at this time is insufficient, so answers become speculative. More to the point for comparative purposes is the fact that Japanese educators are not inclined to influence actively these educational statistics. There are some special programs for Burakumin but precious few for Koreans. The vast machinery of public education works away with impersonal regularity. It must also be noted that although the statistical averages show Koreans doing poorly compared with Japanese, some Koreans are doing very well. Among the small number of Koreans going on to higher education are some who enter Japan's top universities.

Employment

The educational achievements of many Korean students have little significance if they are not recognized at the time of employment. The conversion of "value" achieved in the educational system into long-term personal benefit in the social system is the basic (if rather inelegantly stated) goal of the parents and most of the students. It is at this point that Koreans in Japan encounter the sharpest discrimination and frustration. If the educational outcome for Koreans in Japanese schools seems molded more by the family's socioeconomic circumstances than by any overt discrimination, the same cannot be said for employment. Korean graduates face serious employment barriers at almost every level of society and in almost every form possible. The remark of one teacher that his Korean students are "children without a tomorrow" was directed to this fact. As Korean students reach adolescence, their awareness of employment discrimination is likely to separate them from their dreams of a future career and their hopes of attaining stature in Japanese society. The fact that many Korean students persist and do well in the Japanese educational system is all the more notable in light of their knowledge that their chances of gaining recognition for scholastic achievement are low in comparison to their Japanese classmates. Statistical data are not available on the progress of Koreans and Japanese who go to work after junior and senior high school in Hyogo prefecture. We must depend here on information gleaned from adult Koreans and Japanese career advisers in the schools.

There is a definite structure to employment discrimination and its resultant frustration patterns. The higher the educational achievement of the Korean student, the less likely will he be to gain a job in a Japanese institution commensurate with his education. Yet it is the better student who is most culturally assimilated and who has the highest ambitions and hopes for a future in Japanese society. The reasons for this situation and its consequences for Korean life in Japan are important.

From the early 1960s to the early 1970s, Japan enjoyed a very low unemployment rate. This put a premium on the lower-paid, younger worker with less than average education, especially as the numbers of junior high and high school graduates entering the work force had been steadily declining. Companies of all sizes in the late sixties had trouble finding enough junior and senior high school graduates. As a result, many companies became more willing than in the past to employ young Koreans with low levels of education. Such Korean workers were not expected to take significant supervisory posts during their careers. This does not mean that Japanese companies stopped their discrimination against Koreans, but it is widely agreed that economic factors, the work of high school teachers, and the progressive Japanization of the Korean population all combined to loosen the once very rigid resistance of Japanese companies to employing Koreans.

The Hitachi case described elsewhere in this volume (see chap. 11) is illustrative of many instances of discrimination that continue to occur; but it is important to note that the court ruled in Pak's favor and that a significant number of Koreans are taking jobs in large Japanese firms. Teachers advising Korean high school graduates, however, sometimes suggest avoidance of Japan's largest companies, despite an increasing possibility of acceptance, because in the largest firms the Korean's chances for promotion are not good. Japan's largest companies can choose the top Japanese high school applicants, and talented young Koreans are less likely to get the recognition they might earn in medium-size firms where ability is at a premium. Teachers can cite many instances to illustrate their impressions, but no actual statistics exist.

The labor market for graduates of higher education presents a different story. The growth of higher education has paralleled a declining job-to-applicant ratio. Some college graduates in Japan are taking jobs that in the past would have been taken only by high school graduates. Since 1973, a small but growing number of male college graduates has not been able to find jobs upon graduation. No economic reasons compel Japanese companies to employ Korean university graduates. Some exceptions might be found in expanding areas of technology, where recent graduates with special skills are in short supply. Bright Korean high school students have sought to anticipate such shortages; nonetheless a university degree places a young Korean male in a very competitive situation in the market for good jobs.

Employment for minority Koreans in the world of Japanese business is greatly influenced by laws of labor supply and demand, with Koreans generally given low priority within each educational skill category. Koreans, for example, who have earned an architectural degree, expect to find reasonable jobs after graduation when or where architects are in short supply. But should their skill turn out to be in excess supply when they leave the university, the fact that they are Korean is almost certain to work against them. It is for this reason that bright students are urged to avoid the liberal arts and to pursue skills that can be put into private practice should they encounter employment or promotion barriers. Desirable professions in this respect are medicine, architecture, and engineering, and a large proportion of the most talented Koreans seek to train in these specific professions, eschewing such courses as economics, law, and the liberal arts, which produce generalists.

A large bank in Hyogo prefecture exemplifies one aspect of the present hiring situation. Not having hired any Koreans until recently, the bank has in the last few years begun to hire a few Korean high school graduates from academic high schools, including some males. The bank does not, however, hire any Korean college graduates. With most talented Japanese going on to college now, the bank has found Korean high school applicants (typically those from good schools who cannot afford college) to be superior.

Public employment options for Koreans are governed by an absolute prohibition against the hiring of non-Japanese citizens. Japanese law is interpreted as prohibiting Koreans from being hired by national and local governments, including Japan's many public corporations, public schools, and national and public universities. There are a few exceptions, such as the ten part-time Korean "lecturers" teaching Korean ethnic education in Osaka elementary schools. Korean residents can become students but not teachers in public universities. No higher barrier to Korean employment in Japan can be found than the one erected and maintained by the government itself.

The knowledge that government employment and government-licensed occupations are prohibited prevents Koreans from considering jobs such as schoolteacher or policeman. Occasionally, only after extensive training has already been completed does it become clear that a Korean cannot enter an intended occupation. A Korean high school graduate working at Haneda (Tokyo) airport, pumping aviation fuel, offers one instance of this unfortunate situation. He had always wanted to be a pilot and went through a special vocational high school in Hokkaido to qualify as a commercial pilot, only to discover that Japanese law prohibits non-Japanese from taking the pilot's qualifying exam. He still hopes someday to be given a chance to train as a pilot.

Government-created employment barriers are under criticism today. Their abolishment would constitute a significant progression in the opening up of Japanese society to Korean residents. Mindan-led activities in a number of cities in the Kansai area have resulted in local government promises to end discrimination in future hiring.

The role of teachers in the effort to lower employment barriers is worthy of note. Fighting the discrimination levied against Burakumin job applicants is a major activity of some leftist teachers in the high schools of the region, an activity consonant with the ideal that teachers should help their students find satisfactory work upon graduation. Recently, at the local level, some teachers in this group have become keen to help Koreans as well, publicly protesting discriminatory hiring practices, using methods of detection and confrontation developed by the movement to aid Burakumin job applicants. It is also true, however, that the national teachers' union has avoided involvement with the issue of discrimination against Korean job applicants. Many politically neutral teachers have opposed radical practices in favor of unobtrusive persuasion, believing open confrontation between teachers and employers to be ultimately counterproductive. In any event, the role of the teacher has been critical in the hiring of Koreans by Japanese firms. Eighty-five percent of those Korean graduates of Hyogo Japanese high schools in 1975 who took jobs were introduced to their employers by their schools.[13]

Most Japanese university professors feel little obligation to help graduating seniors find jobs. Therefore, a Korean who advances to a Japanese university cannot count on help from his teachers unless he has worked closely with a particular faculty member who has noted his ability and has assumed a personal interest in helping him find employment. Highly trained Koreans, particularly those with advanced degrees, depend heavily on strong recommendations from their university professors to find work in institutions with which the faculty members maintain close ties. This pattern is also said to dominate in the medical profession and in the academic world. The most highly educated Koreans have a special need for a Japanese academic patron.

For both university and high school graduates, gaining a job in a Japanese organization is but the beginning of employment. In Japan, the larger companies and other private institutions generally observe the practice of lifelong employment, meaning that Koreans hired as regular employees are not likely to be summarily fired or laid off. But according to many Koreans with whom I spoke, Koreans who do get jobs in large Japanese organizations (the most desirable by Japanese standards) leave at some point in the first decade of their employment, often to return to their family's small business. Why do they leave? Secondhand accounts suggest disappointment over promotion prospects, a sense of hostility aimed at them, and feelings of loneliness as an outsider. Personal relations in Japanese companies are very important, and being left out or slighted in small ways is exceptionally hard to bear. Even educational achievement coupled with acceptance by a large Japanese firm is no guarantee that the benefits such success brings to Japanese will be enjoyed by Koreans.[14] The efforts of teachers who help their Korean students obtain desirable jobs in Japanese organizations are thus fragile achievements easily erased.

To summarize, the basic influences of Japanese education on the emerging place of Koreans in Japanese society requires the balancing of a number of perspectives. Viewed historically, Korean achievement in Japanese education certainly advanced in the 1960s and 1970s, and some increased employment opportunities in Japanese organizations have been obtained. Many Koreans are going to universities, and some are entering professional ranks. A Japanese-trained intelligentsia of young Koreans is emerging, able to claim high status on the basis of education. They represent a form of pressure, or potential pressure, on the closed doors of Japanese employment.

There are, however, hundreds of formal, legal barriers to Korean employment in Japanese public institutions. In addition, informal discrimination resulting in interpersonal difficulties in Japanese work places prevent many of the Koreans who succeed in school from assuming satisfactory positions in Japanese society. Even those Koreans who have no intention of working in Japanese-run institutions are likely to consider Japanese education important. Korean life in Japan today is based on skills related to Japanese language and learning. Most Korean newspapers, banks, companies, and other organizations tend to employ Koreans who have achieved success in the Japanese educational system, with the obvious exception of members of the Ch'ongnyŏn and its affiliated organizations.

An almost totally Japanese cultural existence and the necessity of earning a living within the Japanese context create a situation in which Japanese education continues to grow in importance in the lives of the Korean residents, despite the disappointments and frustrations that await most young Koreans at the time of employment. Increasing numbers of well-educated but often frustrated Koreans, Japanese educated but unassimilated in terms of work, represent the cutting edge of pressure on the closed doors of Japanese society. In my opinion, their perspective and situation is the crucial one to understand if we are to grasp the essential character of the civil rights movement in Japan as far as Koreans are concerned.

KOREAN SCHOOLS

Hundreds of Korean language schools sprang up across Japan immediately following World War II. These schools were for adults and children alike. All ages intending to return to the Korean homeland, especially those who needed language training, were encouraged to enroll as part of their preparation for their new life on the peninsula. These schools were initially set up to serve the goal of repatriation, and most Koreans at that time expected to return to Korea. The great era of repatriation came and went, leaving many more Koreans in Japan than had been expected by the Japanese, the Americans, and even by the leaders of the Koreans themselves. Political events in Asia moved rapidly in a direction that all but closed off the opportunity for repatriation and ended the era of liberal policies toward Japan's Korean minority. Occupied Japan was soon part of the massive cold war confrontation, represented in Asia by such momentous events as the

Chinese revolution and the Korean War. As described in chapters 4 and 8, the Japanese government from 1948 to 1954 acted to close Korean language schools and to inhibit the power of Korean organizations affiliated with the North.

Some Korean schools loyal to the DPRK managed to survive the purge era,[15] reemerging as independent entities by the mid-1950s and strengthened in their political resolve. These became the building blocks for a stable and highly integrated Ch'ongnyŏn school system, a system much larger and better organized than its Mindan-supported rival. Subsidies from the DPRK to the Ch'ongnyŏn system are large, and support is also strong from other organizations affiliated with the Ch'ongnyŏn. Ch'ongnyŏn schools offer an education explicitly designed to support the North Korean government, the Ch'ongnyŏn itself, and the idea of contributing to the unification of Korea through DPRK leadership. The schools receiving subsidies from the South, by contrast, are independent of one another and are less directly political. Their curricula are built around the common assumption of continuing residence in Japan, but in fact they do not constitute a unified school system. Only a common dependence on Mindan for extra funds, a non-Communist perspective, and a concern for maintaining a Korean education in Japan unite them. Thus, despite the common labels of "Korean" and "ethnic" (*minzoku*), these two sets of schools are very different, and it will help to consider them separately.

Ch'ongnyŏn Schools

The organization that established most of the Korean schools in Japan after World War II was a parent of the present Ch'ongnyŏn organization. Both that organization and most of its schools were suppressed by the Japanese government beginning in 1949. The Choryŏn organization and its descendant today were and are explicitly allied to North Korea and the North Korean version of communism. It is important to note that a few Korean schools in Japan not affiliated with the Choryŏn survived the events of 1948 and gained recognition from the Japanese Ministry of Education; these schools are among those supported by the Mindan today. This fact indicates that a political position rather than simply ethnic discrimination lay at the heart of the government's suppression of the Korean schools. This point is often ignored by Japanese scholarship, which tends to see the suppression as anti-Korean. Few politically nonaligned Korean schools survived, but their survival had little impact on the total Korean population of Japan. The events and policies of 1948 forced nearly all school-age Koreans to enter Japanese public elementary and junior high schools, and most Korean students have continued in that system. In a clandestine manner, however, Ch'ongnyŏn influence in the education of Koreans remained after 1948.

Japanese local school officials, faced with the nearly impossible task of immediately integrating the Korean students into Japanese public education, compromised with the realities they faced. Many Korean schools, for example, were being conducted in Japanese public school buildings, and forcing them out would not have been easy. Furthermore, wherever there were many Korean students, integrating them into Japanese schools was a large problem, given the intense mutual hostility, the language barriers, and other related circumstances. Japanese officials in many large cities opted to permit the Korean teachers and students to remain together in the same school while formally annexing it to the Japanese public school system.[16] Thus, despite the arrival of a Japanese principal and a small group of Japanese teachers, Korean schools remained essentially Korean with a facade of Japanese official control.

Historical research and the personal recollections of one Japanese teacher in such a school support the fact that Korean teachers were able to continue in much the same educational vein after the Japanese takeover. The emphasis continued to be on North Korean communism, with a well-developed program of instruction in Korean language, history, and geography. Such anomalous institutions were bound to have a limited lifespan, but from 1948 until the latter half of the 1950s these schools constituted an underground Korean school system. Japanese education officials at the local level publicly ignored the existence of what was in effect an educational program in support of the Japanese government's political and ideological enemy, and officials in the national government apparently also went along with this self-deception. The Korean teachers also apparently tacitly agreed to refrain from public actions that might jeopardize the arrangement. This implicit "live and let live" approach is the other side of the story of Japanese suppression of Korean schools.

Following the end of the Korean War, the Korean teachers and the Ch'ongnyŏn began negotiating the withdrawal of their schools from the Japanese public school system. Korean faculty and students began moving into newly built Ch'ongnyŏn schools. With the beginning of direct North Korean aid for the Ch'ongnyŏn educational system in 1957 (chap. 6), new schools were constructed at a steady pace and the present shape of the Ch'ongnyŏn system emerged.

Before discussing the Ch'ongnyŏn school system today, I must indicate the limits of my knowledge. I have walked by but have never been permitted in one of their schools. I have talked to Japanese and Koreans with acquaintances who are teachers in these schools. I have read the few written accounts available and have looked briefly at Ch'ongnyŏn textbooks, but as an American with no special credentials or contacts I have been unwelcome in schools fiercely loyal to a nation that has considered the United States its greatest enemy. Several Japanese leftist intellectuals in contact with the Ch'ongnyŏn told me that their own requests to visit the organizations' schools had been politely forgotten, and several warned that I could cause

Ch'ongnyŏn teachers great trouble by trying to make personal contact with them. The point is that these schools are quite isolated even in Japanese society and my knowledge of them must therefore depend on secondhand and incomplete sources.[17]

Ch'ongnyŏn elementary and middle schools are now located in all regions of Japan, so that even some of the geographically more remote Korean residents may send their children to them. Many high schools also now have dormitory facilities to accommodate boarding students from outlying regions. With Chosŏn University in Tokyo (see chap. 8) now capping off the Ch'ongnyŏn system, it is fair to say that the Ch'ongnyŏn school system is geographically inclusive, vertically integrated, and physically well endowed. Most of this achievement must be credited to the financial support of the North Korean government.

What of the family background of the students who attend Ch'ongnyŏn schools? Clearly they come from families belonging to the Ch'ongnyŏn organizations and thus they hold DPRK citizenship. A great deal of pressure is reportedly applied to Ch'ongnyŏn members not to send their children to Japanese schools. Enrollment drives are conducted by the organization every year with national goals and quotas of first-graders to be recruited by each local Ch'ongnyŏn chapter. The close interdependence of Ch'ongnyŏn and its school system is obvious in this and in other matters soon to be touched upon. They prosper and suffer together.

As we might expect, the content of Ch'ongnyŏn education is patterned closely on North Korean educational practice. The textbooks come from North Korea. North Korean national holidays, such as Kim Il-sung's birthday and Independence Day, are observed in the schools. The North Korean flag and pictures of Premier Kim are displayed in classrooms. Efforts are made to introduce into Ch'ongnyŏn schools those national political campaigns that are taken up in North Korean schools. In other words, the highly politicized perspective of North Korean education is to be found throughout the curricula and activities of the schools. The theories of Kim Il-sung are taught in math courses as well as in history and language courses.

Given the basic educational assumption that Ch'ongnyŏn schools are to serve the DPRK, this curriculum makes sense. It is also consistent with the large amounts of North Korean financial assistance received. The needs of the Ch'ongnyŏn for a system of thorough political training to preserve organizational discipline and continuity is also a central consideration justifying the curriculum. Classes and textbooks are, of course, in Korean, and until recently the level of standard educational achievement was widely regarded as high compared with that of Koreans in Japanese schools.

Some comic moments have been connected with the rather strict adherence to North Korean educational policy. One such instance was the decision (later reversed) to ban baseball, Coca-Cola, and chewing gum among Ch'ongnyŏn students as part of an anti-American campaign announced in the North. The general affection in Japan for these things and the fact that baseball is the national sport of Japan, not to mention of Communist Cuba, apparently caused big headaches for school officials trying to enforce these prohibitions.

Mindan is quick to ridicule such subservience to DPRK ideological extremism. A more basic problem in the curriculum, in the eyes of many resident Koreans, is the impracticality of an education aimed at returning to Korea. Like other Koreans, Ch'ongnyŏn parents realistically expect their children to grow up, make a living, and probably see the end of their days in Japan. The repatriation premise is no longer seen as a very important support for Korean education. Japanese language skills and knowledge of practical value to working in Japan are now viewed as more important than DPRK politics and the Korean language training.

The situation is far different from that which gave rise to Korean education in the 1940s and 1950s. Unification remains but a distant hope. The roots of the Korean population are sinking deeper and deeper into the soil of Japanese life. The chances of fitting back into North or South Korea have progressively diminished. As a result Ch'ongnyŏn's educational approach has experienced increased pressure to adapt to this set of realities. The challenge may prove to be more difficult to meet than the Japanese political suppression of 1948.

There are benefits, of course, in learning to read and speak Korean as well as those connected with ethnic identity and pride, but communication among Koreans in Japan is now almost entirely in Japanese, and with the passing of the first generation this will be even truer. Ch'ongnyŏn students going to and from their Korean schools chatter away together in Japanese, not Korean. In fact, the entire Korean-centered curriculum offers them little help in preparing for life in Japan. Compared to Korean students educated in Japanese public schools, Ch'ongnyŏn graduates are at a disadvantage. They are relatively uneducated about Japan and are likely therefore to suffer inconvenience, embarrassment, and disadvantages in work. In partial acknowledgment of these problems, Ch'ongnyŏn schools are said to have recently increased by a small amount their regular instruction in the Japanese language.

The related matters of jobs and higher education are also closely linked to this general issue. The Japanese Ministry of Education has never allowed the Ch'ongnyŏn schools to be accredited as regular academic institutions. They have only the status of "special schools" (*tokushū gakkō*), which means they do not qualify for any kind of Japanese government support and their graduates may not enter any Japanese public institutions of higher learning. Furthermore, a stigma is attached to the schools because the category of special school is associated with beautician and other low-status vocational training. Undoubtedly, this treatment reflects the political hostility of the Japanese government toward the Ch'ongnyŏn. It is also true that all foreign schools in Japan with foreign textbooks and curriculum have the same status and limitations. The difference is that most other foreigners have no intention of remaining permanently in Japan.

Graduates of Ch'ongnyŏn high schools may attend Chosŏn University, which is accredited by Tokyo prefecture. They may also gain admission to one of the relatively large number of Japanese private universities that accept graduates of Korean schools. They may not apply directly to the less expensive but more prestigious and better equipped Japanese public universities unless they are willing to undergo a second education in a specially accredited Japanese preparatory school. For the bright and ambitious, Ch'ongnyŏn schools thus carry a handicap, as they limit the opportunities both to join a profession and to enter the world of Japan's intelligentsia.

The best jobs in business and public administration also typically go to graduates of the public universities. Even job discrimination cannot undermine the high personal status achieved by Korean graduates of public universities in Japan. Ch'ongnyŏn students are cut off from this source of prestige.

What sort of work are graduates of Ch'ongnyŏn schooling likely to find? Reportedly many are the children of middle-class owners of small factories and shops, who, lacking other prospects, can always succeed to their parents' work and status. Those from less established families may find jobs as employees of businesses owned by members of the Ch'ongnyŏn organizations. Most small Japanese companies will not hire graduates of Ch'ongnyŏn schools, and the same holds for many Korean employers not affiliated with the Ch'ongnyŏn. Many of the best job prospects are thus to be found within the organization itself. The Ch'ongnyŏn school system is said to employ about 1,000 teachers (new teachers now come from Chosŏn University), and there are office positions in the organization throughout the country. The bank operated by Ch'ongnyŏn is also a source of relatively secure, high-status jobs. Even so, the total number of annual openings in the organization cannot be too large and any diminution of Ch'ongnyŏn strength is likely to result in problems of shrinking employment possibilities in the organization itself—a matter of no small consequence to the Ch'ongnyŏn school system. A particular dynamic exists within inclusive organizations like the Ch'ongnyŏn. In times of expansion, schools, jobs, and membership levels all thrive and reinforce one another, but a reversal of fortunes causes the opposite effect.

Such a reversal seemed to be occurring in the late 1970s. Those with whom I spoke in 1977 referred to a serious crisis in the Ch'ongnyŏn school system. Enrollments, they thought, were down more than the official Ch'ongnyŏn figures showed, especially for the lower elementary grades. The reasons included declines in the number of Ch'ongnyŏn member families, the decreasing attraction of the Ch'ongnyŏn educational approach, and the lower birthrate among Koreans in the last decade. Despite the rumors, there are no hard figures to prove that of late the Ch'ongnyŏn has been receiving less than its usual one-fourth to one-fifth share of all resident Korean students. As many as 100,000 Koreans in Japan are said to have switched their allegiance from North to South Korea since 1972. The degree to which this figure represents defections from the Ch'ongnyŏn or stands as a portent of Ch'ongnyŏn decline is also a rough measure of the problems the Ch'ongnyŏn schools face in maintaining enrollments.

The problem of numbers has been compounded by a recent shift in the school system's financial situation. Thanks to almost twenty years of North Korean assistance, totaling (by 1977) 23 billion yen or about $65 million (see table 15), the Ch'ongnyŏn developed many new and well-furbished schools, and employed a large and well-qualified teaching staff. The high overhead generated by expansion was not a serious problem as long as Ch'ongnyŏn prospered and DPRK aid for education continued. But inflation, coupled with higher costs owing to increasing seniority of staff and the growing costs of maintaining buildings, have become major problems for education in Japan, and the Ch'ongnyŏn system can be no exception.

In 1957 the DPRK sent over 200 million yen. The figure grew steadily until 1974, when the annual total was 3,700 million yen. But in 1975, the figure suddenly dropped to 2,280 million yen, a 40 percent reduction (see table 15). Despite the official announcements that no decrease had occurred, something very serious was happening. In 1976 DPRK aid to the Ch'ongnyŏn school system fell further. North Korea at the time was clearly having serious international balance-of-payments problems, and the sudden decline in aid to Ch'ongnyŏn's schools was seen as tied to this predicament.

Loss of this aid has hurt the Ch'ongnyŏn school system, but it is difficult to gauge the extent of the damage. Some observers doubt that the North Korean money was ever used exclusively for educational purposes.[18] Furthermore, educational budgeting is flexible and any financial problem would probably be spread throughout an organization to lessen its effects. I asked people close to Ch'ongnyŏn schools about rumors that a few teachers had been laid off. No one confirmed the rumors, but it was certain that things were getting tighter. The increased emphasis placed on recruiting among Ch'ongnyŏn families to keep up school enrollments may have been spurred by fear that the money crisis would undermine parental confidence and would encourage the tendency to send children to Japanese schools.

The quality of students attending Ch'ongnyŏn schools may have declined somewhat, according to the impressions of a number of Koreans (admittedly not close to the Ch'ongnyŏn). They suggest that the restricted prospects facing Ch'ongnyŏn school graduates have served to dissuade some parents of bright boys from placing them in the Ch'ongnyŏn system. At the high school level, Koreans who fail in the entrance exams to Japanese high schools may apply late and may be accepted into the Ch'ongnyŏn schools. Cumulatively, these trends spell a gradual erosion of academic

quality. Each may represent no more than a tiny percentage of total enrollment each year, but the long-term effect is one that will slowly bring down
the reputation of Ch'ongnyŏn schools. As we shall see, Mindan-related
schools are most certainly experiencing this pattern, one that underscores
the magnetism of Japanese schooling among Korean residents.

As the possibility of repatriation to a united Korea decreases and as
North Korea itself experiences economic troubles and a poor press, the
Ch'ongnyŏn organization and its schools suffer. Today, of the two Koreas,
South Korea is the more dynamic nation. After years of ignoring the Koreans in Japan, the South Korean government through Mindan has recently
become actively concerned with their welfare. By most accounts, this
general shift in the fortunes of the two rival nations has not so much infused
Mindan with new strength as it has caused the Ch'ongnyŏn to weaken.
Unless these general circumstances change, the future of the only large and
viable Korean school system (and thus of the option for a Korean language
education which it represents) appears anything but promising. Many
observers are waiting to see whether future Ch'ongnyŏn enrollment statistics admit a change. At present, no conclusive evidence of a shift is available, and much of the change is more anticipated than certain.

Mindan Schools

On the other side of the political fence, a handful of Korean schools
not in the Ch'ongnyŏn system now receive modest financial support from
South Korea, funneled through Mindan. They are also suffering financial
and enrollment problems, probably at more serious levels than are the
Ch'ongnyŏn schools. Unlike their Communist counterparts, they use Japanese textbooks and follow the Ministry of Education's curriculum, teaching
Korean (about five hours per week) as a foreign language. The assumption
of continued residence in Japan is an explicit part of the curriculum.
Although each of these schools is somewhat independent, they all follow
Mindan and South Korean policy toward overseas Koreans. Since the early
1950s these schools have been accredited and their graduates have been permitted to enter Japanese public universities.

The political content of the education is, of course, slanted to favor
the ROK, but its place in the curriculum is small. There is little pressure on
Mindan members to attend these schools. My general impression, gained
from interviews and a visit, is that this variety of school will have great
problems in the future despite the prosperity of South Korea.

We can best appreciate the character of these schools by briefly considering Hakuto, the best known of the group. The school is located on the
outskirts of Osaka on land donated after World War II by a wealthy
Korean. The buildings are not much different from those of older Japanese

schools, but the facilities seem especially cramped. Hakuto offers classes from first through twelfth grades. In addition to five hours of Korean language instruction per week, Korean identity is fostered through the use of Korean names, the presence of a totally Korean faculty, homeroom discussions and general assemblies, a visiting teacher from South Korea each year, the learning of Korean songs, and study of Korean geography and traditions. All this is squeezed into the few free hours left in a weekly schedule dominated by a Japanese curriculum.

Let me paraphrase the principal as he spoke of the problems facing his school:

> Twenty years ago we had excellent students, some of whom entered top Japanese universities. There was great pride in the school. That is no longer true. The best Korean students tend to go to Japanese schools now, and those who come here following Japanese junior high represent those Korean students who have done so badly in the Japanese system they cannot get into any Japanese high school. As a last alternative they come here. The students with us from first grade on are better qualified, but their numbers are declining, especially as the school's reputation declines because of the presence of the more mediocre students at the high school level. Part of the problem, of course, is money. We had to agree to accept support from the South Korean government, even though it caused a big split within the faculty, simply because without it we had no means of resisting the pressures to accept virtually any student who applied regardless of how unqualified. I made the decision to trade the school's former political neutrality for a degree of leverage in the matter of enrollments, in the hope that over the coming years we can regain our former good reputation. Frankly, it is a gamble that many teachers oppose.
>
> The most unpopular subject for many students is Korean language study. I am constantly trying to find ways to justify what seems to them a needless subject, especially among those who enter from Japanese schools at the secondary level.

Thus, despite an educational approach that assumes a future in Japan for the Korean minority and increased financial aid from South Korea, schools like Hakuto are also experiencing considerable difficulty attracting students, particularly good ones. Can we conclude that Korean schools in Japan are in the process of a gradual decline? I think so. Much depends on the fortunes of the Ch'ongnyŏn and Mindan, of course, since their support is vital. Just how far the Ch'ongnyŏn will decline or how successful Mindan will become in the years ahead is not easy to predict. But at present, there can be little doubt that the Korean language schools in Japan are in a troubled state. They probably will not disappear, but it is hard to imagine them assuming a more significant role in the future, despite their symbolic importance among proponents of the growing movement for greater Korean ethnicity.

ETHNIC EDUCATION IN PUBLIC SCHOOLS

The decline of the Korean language schools is occurring, ironically, just as intellectuals and educators, Korean and Japanese, have been awakening to a new enthusiasm for the idea of ethnic education (*minzoku kyoiku*), especially as an attribute of a more open and pluralistic Japanese society. The realities of the Korean schools and the new movement for greater ethnicity constitute fundamentally contradictory trends in education for the Korean minority. As organizational support for and popular commitment to formal language education wane, the beauty and necessity of ethnic education is being proclaimed among scholars, young Koreans, and some Japanese schoolteachers. To read the recent literature is to gain the impression that ethnic education is about to become a vital new trend, but to investigate the actual public school situation is to conclude the opposite. Somewhere in between lies the likely future pattern. Let us first consider a few recent developments in Japanese public schools.

In ten of Osaka's public elementary schools, classes in Korean culture are conducted after school by Korean teachers. The city and prefecture have recently begun to support these classes by supplying the classrooms and paying the teachers' salaries (as Koreans they are employed only on irregular status). Korean parents of fourth-, fifth-, and sixth-grade students are encouraged to enroll their children in the program, with each child receiving between two to four hours weekly of supplementary classes (known as *minzoku gakkyū*). Considering the fact that there are approximately twenty elementary schools in Osaka with enrollments of more than 10 percent Korean children, the number of schools with supplementary ethnic education courses is not yet particularly impressive. According to the Korean teacher who serves as the unofficial dean of this project, a more sympathetic school board and a growing number of Japanese teachers supporting the idea of ethnic Korean education within Japanese public schools has led to recent improvements. I have not heard of similar classes being conducted in the Japanese public schools of other cities and, as of 1977, Osaka appeared unique.

I visited one of these classes in an elementary school in Ikunoku (the "mecca" of Koreans in Japan) in which the enrollment was about one-fourth Korean. After school some fifty bright, noisy students crowded into the ethnic studies room. Not enough desks were provided, and many students stood around the sides of the room. It was early in the new school year, and the teacher planned a short lecture on being proud to be Korean. He emphasized the importance of using their Korean names and studying hard to bring respect to themselves. "Don't let Japanese do better," he said in conclusion. The lecture was presented in a stern, forceful, and fatherly manner, the teacher tolerating no interruptions from the children. At the end, he asked them what it means to be Korean. Faltering answers came from several he called on, and then a girl replied, "To be proud and do our best." Students later pointed the girl out as a serious and very good student, the kind who would take ethnic education seriously.

After class the other students gathered around me and gaily volunteered that it did not seem too important to them whether they were Korean or not. They were not very certain what the class was all about, they said, everyone giggling, but they liked it anyway. What they preferred to discuss with me was American singing stars and sports heroes, all prominent in the Japanese media. The teacher observed afterward that most children at this age do learn a good deal, though not in a consciously integrated fashion.

The usual content of these classes includes brief introductions to Korean history and geography, music, the Korean alphabet, and rudimentary Korean conversation. Sixth-graders are able to read simple sentences in the language. Classes, however, are conducted completely in Japanese. The room set aside for ethnic studies in this school is decorated with many pictures and items of interest, like musical instruments, chosen to reflect the beauty and accomplishments of Korean civilization. Because this is a Japanese school, and because the local Korean community is politically divided, the subject of politics is strictly taboo.

The children's parents are organized into an association that supplies supplementary funds and offers other support to the ethnic studies teacher. I was told that some Korean parents have little interest in sending their children to the special class, preferring to have them attend Japanese private tutoring academies (*juku*) after school, since they are more helpful in gaining future academic success. Some children also do not want to attend, and some parents are bothered by the teachers' insistence that the children use their Korean names. Such resistance to the ethnic education idea within the local Korean community is disheartening to the teacher, since after many years of effort he has finally achieved considerable support from the Japanese teachers of this school. In many of Osaka's other elementary schools, teachers are not so cooperative and no ethnic education classes have been created. No such classes exist at the public junior high school level. Thus, the embryonic ethnic studies program in Osaka seems yet of little consequence, despite the fact that it is conducted with a positive outlook.

At the high school level in numerous prefectures one finds a movement to create after-school clubs for Korean students. Known as *chōbunken* (Korean Culture Study Clubs), they typically involve such activities as learning conversational Korean, studying Korean history, practicing Korean dancing (among female students), and discussing minority problems. Usually these clubs meet once a week. In the Osaka-Kobe area a Korean teacher specializing in leading these clubs visits public and private Japanese high schools with chōbunken on a regular basis. His salary is paid by the Korean Scholarship Association (discussed below).

A survey of 212 high schools, public and private, in Hyogo prefecture reveals that approximately 10 percent have these clubs.[19] Since schools with sufficient numbers of Koreans to support a club tend to be mostly vocational and lower-level private high schools, chōbunken appear largely in such schools. At most academically strong Japanese high schools in the Kansai, the attention of teachers and students, including Korean students, is concentrated on preparation for examinations. Ethnic studies is less likely to catch on at these high schools. We might note once again that a significantly larger number of Koreans in vocational and other low-level high schools are using their Korean names.

Even at schools where clubs are in existence, a majority of the Korean students do not join. The reasons for this are numerous, but parental opposition and membership in another after-school club are central factors. Parental opposition often arises because clubs led by activist teachers have generated pressure to get the students' families to use their Korean names. These clubs are at a particular disadvantage because no such clubs exist at the junior high school level, so recruiting new members is always difficult. Most members each year are seniors, who presumably have developed enough security and ethnic consciousness to "come out" openly as Koreans. The result is that, at the beginning of each new school year, the club must recruit heavily to continue in existence. This situation compares unfavorably with most sports and other clubs that inherit a flow of freshmen recruits from junior high schools. The fact that only after several years in the school are some Korean students confident enough to enter into an experiment with an open ethnic identity strikingly illustrates the powerful tendency toward assimilation in Japanese schools and the revolutionary role played by chōbunken for the minority of Koreans who join.

Using one's Korean name, learning a bit of spoken Korean, meeting exclusively with other Korean students, and perhaps even making a public presentation of Korean entertainment to a Japanese audience are activities that most Korean students in Japanese public schools are likely to approach with great anxiety, for they mark a reversal of the usual inclination to act and feel as Japanese as possible. Yet those who enter and become active often express an accelerated sense of having discovered a new identity and cast off an old burden. They find friends with whom they can frankly discuss being Korean. As they begin to learn about Korean civilization, they sense pride in its accomplishments, maybe even to the point of criticizing Japanese culture in the light of Korean perspectives. It is common knowledge, for example, that the cultural roots of several key eras of Japanese history can be readily traced to influence from Korea, and yet Japanese education is prone to forget this fact. The influence of chōbunken learning serves to reverse the Japanese bias in textbooks, for example, so that a more resilient Korean identity can begin to develop. I have no doubt that attitudinal rebirth occurs in many high school students who join these clubs. The numbers are not yet large, however, and since most of the students involved cannot be expected to go on to university (because of the kind of high school they attend), their exposure to *minzoku kyōiku* is brief.

University-bound Korean students are likely to attend high schools without chōbunken activities, and thus those who join one of the variety of Korean student organizations on Japanese campuses may be encountering such activities for the first time. In other words, extreme discontinuity between the different levels of Japanese schooling characterizes the present efforts at ethnic education. There is a high probability that Korean students involved at one level will not be involved at any other. This situation stands in strong contrast with the persistent and pervasive Japanese influences to which Koreans are exposed in the course of Japanese schooling.

On Japanese university campuses Korean student activities often assume a political quality less evident at lower levels. Reflecting the fragmented political world of Korean residents, a number of Korean organizations are likely to be found competing for the allegiance of students. Often there are two organizations focused on South Korea, one favoring and one opposed to the Park government, and sometimes one focused on North Korea can be found. The future Korean leadership in Japan will consist largely of university graduates, so their recruitment to a political perspective is viewed as a serious matter by all parties to the political scene. Chosŏn University takes many of the students oriented to the North, and therefore the student groups on Japanese university campuses are more preoccupied with South Korea. It is the antigovernment, pro-South Korean group that seems most dynamic at present. The dream of Korean unity has always held enormous appeal to most Koreans in Japan. A political position between both the North and the South, but focused on eventual unity, has the strongest attraction for today's Korean students. This marks a trend toward criticism of all established political authority and a subsequent weakening of connections to "practical" political organizations. Idealism and independence are marks of the Japanese intelligentsia and, of course, of the opposition in South Korea. That this trend is strongest among Koreans in Japanese universities forecasts a trend away from the polarization of Koreans in Japan between Mindan and the Ch'ongnyŏn and toward a more complex pattern with various new centrist positions emerging. These centrist positions are expressions of the particular position of overseas Koreans, unencumbered by the weight of the circumstance in either North or South Korea. It is also a perspective close to that held by most Japanese intellectuals. The strong emphasis on Korean ethnic identity in these clubs is linked to a political perspective grounded in independence. The two together mark a significant change in the meaning of Korean ethnicity. The direct links to Korea are less important now, but Korean ethnicity, as a means to foster pluralism in Japan, has become more important. What assimilation means in light of this perspective is problematic for the educated individual who takes employment.

Both Mindan and Ch'ongnyŏn also have some educational activities that take place outside of regular schools. Mindan's big educational effort of late has not been focused on children but rather on adults. Backed almost totally by financial aid and educational materials supplied by South Korea, it has established classes at Korean cultural centers in Japan designed to teach the basics of the Korean language along with the rudiments of history, culture, and geography. Clearly what is being offered is introductory, the assumption being that the adults attending will be graduates of Japanese public schools and thus unacquainted with the history of Korean civilization and with its language.

In Nagoya it was recently decided that all Mindan members must take a compulsory fifty hours of this special schooling. This decision, remarkable for Mindan in its firmness, may have been initiated as much because of the disappointing response to those classes before the requirement was set as because of Mindan's new optimism and energy. At any rate, the Mindan people with whom I spoke in Kobe, although enthusiastic about the new program, admitted that they were not satisfied with the response from members. They saw the Nagoya requirement as perhaps the only way to maintain an extensive program.

The South Korean embassy now publishes a slick news magazine reporting on Korean cultural center activities, and it sponsors trips back to Korea for some of the people involved in such programs. The South Korean government has also set up a university-level school near Seoul, specifically for overseas Koreans. This special school is interesting because it represents the closest thing to repatriation that the South has instituted, and yet repatriation is not encouraged. Since most overseas Korean students cannot speak Korean at first, the government gives them an education separate from the regular South Korean universities, a point of profound disappointment to many of the overseas young Koreans, who attend the school thinking of it as an opportunity to "go back home." Overseas Koreans and native-born Koreans are pretty much kept apart, and a cold reserve on the part of the native-born is often felt by those coming from abroad. As one student returning to Japan said in an interview, "We quickly came to feel different, and despite being Korean it was clear we were not being encouraged to move back to Korea." Many of those from Japan go with this possibility in mind and hope that once the language barrier is surmounted they will finally find a home where race, culture, and national identity match. This dream, however, very rarely materializes. Koreans in Korea are in some instances no more receptive to Japanese-speaking Koreans than to regular Japanese.

Both Ch'ongnyŏn and Mindan also conduct brief summer camps for high school and college-age Korean youth. The programs appear to be popular. To find themselves only among other young Koreans is an unusual experience for many. Undoubtedly it serves as a counterweight to the usual sense of almost total immersion in Japanese culture.

In my opinion these various extracurricular efforts will become more prominent for they are more consistent with the present condition of Koreans in Japan. I see them as parallel to Hebrew, Japanese, and other language schools and ethnic clubs among American ethnic minorities—instructional efforts aimed at essentially assimilated youth reflecting an otherwise weakening ethnicity among a population that has settled into its foreign home.

Ethnic education, whether extracurricular or part of a full-time language school, is involved in a fundamental paradox that is now readily discernible in Korean education. With the passage of time, what is lumped together as ethnicity undergoes certain fundamental changes. On the one hand, succeeding generations of a minority group living abroad experience a decreased exposure to the language, customs, and basic cultural patterns of thought and feeling of their forebears. On the other hand, in the process of growing up they experience virtually the full magnetic pull of the majority culture.

The home is, of course, the center of ethnic conservatism, where the language is taught as a living language and where the emotional content of parent-child relations is wed to the basic behavior, symbols, and wisdom of the traditional culture. What happens in the home is in general much more important than what is taught in school, but schooling can be an alternative means of preserving or reviving ethnicity when the home no longer serves the purpose. The two kinds of ethnic education are, however, very different.

Perhaps the single most deeply rooted item in the whole vast assemblage of culture is food. In most Korean homes in Japan, food is one of the last remaining aspects of ethnicity with "home-grown" vitality. Second- and third-generation Koreans having little command of the Korean language and little knowledge of Korean tradition, having no spontaneous sense of Korean forms of politeness, humor, or interpersonal relations, often talk about food when they try to express their ambivalence about their basic ethnic affiliation. One third-generation man in his mid-thirties working for Mindan remarked:

> It's a matter of which do I like better, *kimchi* (Korean pickles) or *takuan* (Japanese pickles). Frankly, I prefer *takuan*. When I was growing up my father wanted me to like *kimchi* and I ate it at home, but despite my efforts I couldn't change from liking *takuan* better. Now I'm a parent and I have gone through a period in which I struggled to find the meaning of being a Korean in Japan. I've come to understand better my father's wish that I like *kimchi*, and I've started thinking about my own children's education in this regard. But frankly I must admit I still like *takuan* better, and I don't think I know what being or feeling Korean really is.[20]

Food here is obviously being treated as representative of ethnicity. The problem of ethnic commitment has two aspects for this man, one intellectual or moral, and the other emotional. An awakened sense of the importance of Korean ethnicity (essentially intellectual) has not changed this man's preference (essentially emotional) for Japanese food. He feels he should be more Korean, but things Japanese, even food, have been more familiar from childhood. He is Korean in name, in work, and by Japanese legal definition, but by his own confession, his sensibilities—those things of cultural identity learned earliest and retained longest—remain essentially Japanese. Self-conscious efforts to sponsor and conserve ethnicity among Koreans in Japan must contend with the basic fact that the great majority of young Koreans today share a socialization experience that is fundamentally grounded in Japanese daily culture.

As already mentioned, few of the third generation speak Korean and most of these have learned it at Korean schools, not at home. With this as a rough yardstick of the general state of Korean ethnicity, it is apparent that ethnic education aimed at increasing the awareness of ethnic identity of Korean students, whether in Japanese or Korean schools, is an effort largely counter to the general socialization experience of most young Koreans today. Ethnic education, when it is significant, comes late and meets considerable resistance among Koreans young and old. Resistance is owing not only to the fact that many doubt its practical value but also that many people are uncomfortable with the heightened personal sense of polarity that is generated. Troubling questions are raised.

What seems intellectually correct and what feels emotionally correct are often different. If Japanization can be considered a surrender to an empty promise, ethnic education is open to the criticism that it is now artificial and too intellectual in origin. The need to survive and the fear of discrimination in a closed society were, no doubt, basic motives behind past assimilation to Japanese society, but today the great majority of young Koreans have a well-developed feeling for the Japanese life-style that stands in profound contrast with the efforts in ethnic education to create a familiarity with Korea. No wonder that just using one's Korean name is the key watershed point at the present time.

Among persons most keen about ethnic education are small groups of Japanese educators and intellectuals. For them the history of Japanese colonialization of Korea, the forced migration of Korean labor, and the strict governmental control of Koreans in postwar Japan are unforgettable and unforgivable injustices. Oppression of this sort still continues, they feel, and Koreans should not take it lying down. Ethnic education, in the light of this perspective, is a form of resistance to the Japanese establishment.

Ethnic consciousness is the foundation for personal resolve in this fight. The importance of this idea, in political, moral, and intellectual terms, is likely to keep ethnic education significant as part of modern Japanese thought, despite the fact that its intellectual interest exceeds its vitality among the majority of Koreans living in Japan. The principles and enthusiasm involved in a self-conscious ethnic education program are different from simply "growing up Korean." All this goes back to basic issues raised in the metaphor of Korean versus Japanese pickles.

CONCLUSIONS

Ethnicity is potentially many things to the people who have or claim it. Its qualities range from complete immersion and participation in the culture of an ethnic group to a tenuous grasp of a few remnants of an otherwise lost culture. For analytic purposes we can construct a scale that runs from total immersion through stages of cultural loss to the point where ethnicity is represented by almost nothing more than the name of the ethnic group as an identity label. Ethnic minorities experiencing assimilation in a foreign cultural environment typically find their ethnicity passing along this scale, from "thick" to "thin." Typically, families at first, then institutions belonging to the minority (such as religious, fraternal, commercial and other organizations) attempt to preserve the mother culture. Efforts to reverse the direction of assimilation are not uncommon, but the difficulties involved are great; short of almost revolutionary zeal and social isolation, success is rare. It seems that as ethnicity becomes "thinner" and its expressive elements fewer, the elements that do remain become more important or stronger in their symbolic content because they must stand for much more than before and because they mark the impending loss of all value associated with the ethnic heritage. Eventually a threshold is passed for many, beyond which the very question of ethnic identity is rarely important.

Obviously, language is a key element of ethnicity for minorities, and one of the easiest to scale in terms of the relative degree of assimilation that has occurred. Clothing, food, celebrations, intermarriage rates, employment, and many more elements of life, perhaps all of life's culturally discrete qualities, are at least potentially relevant to the "measurement" of assimilation, not only to social scientists but to people themselves. Among the numerous traits counted as expressing ethnicity, some are easily moved along from one degree to the next in either direction whereas others are changed much more slowly and are much more difficult to revive.

Consider clothing, festivals, and language in this regard. One can change from the costume of the minority to that of the majority and back again several times in the same day. Community festivals belonging to a minority group, on the other hand, require much cooperation, resources, and work to organize. The necessary skills can be learned and revived, however, as long as there is enough energy and commitment among at least some portion of an ethnic group. The language of the mother culture is not so readily revived once it is lost, as it takes years of effort and dedication to learn, reinforced by the presence of those to whom the student can speak. When a language is lost, it is not lost overnight but between generations, and only under conditions of supreme effort and dedication can it be revived as the daily language of a minority. The three items thus differ greatly as to their role in the overall process of change involved.

Social institutions obviously play an important role in the retention of ethnic qualities in a minority; organized efforts are required to preserve traditions and to educate new generations in the context of a foreign culture. The family is the first line of defense, and public organizations are the second. Typically, as the family becomes less and less effective because of the assimilation of the parental generation, ethnic organizations must assume a heavier burden. The learning of ethnicity then begins later in the lives of the minority's young and occurs in an organizational and therefore somewhat self-conscious context.

Some interesting ambiguities arise in the relationship between the family and organizations over the question of ethnicity and its conservation. Ethnic organizations have a natural self-interest in the conservation of ethnicity, and their leaders share this self-interest. The leaders' elevated positions rest, in part, on the retention of the group's ethnic identity. The rub comes from the fact that, typically, leadership also rests on foundations outside the ethnic group. Education or business success or political skills acquired in the majority society are often critical to high position within any ethnic community. The children of leaders are often among the most thoroughly assimilated for this reason. Nowhere is the issue of ethnicity more complex and paradoxical than in the families of its leadership. Among Koreans in Japan it is the highly educated who are both proudest of their ethnic background and the most assimilated.

In families lacking high position and material resources, the matter of ethnicity is less complicated. Survival and upward mobility are central concerns, and most often this goal governs the families' perspective on questions of assimilation versus ethnicity. The economic costs of preserving the heritage from one generation to the next are clearest where the less assimilated are concerned.

Clearly, there is much variation on the question of ethnicity to be found within any ethnic group, and the Koreans in Japan are no exception. Yet this does not prevent us from drawing a set of conclusions about the Korean minority in the light of the above framework. Korean is still spoken in some families, and some 20 percent of the Korean young are attending schools where the language is taught. Young Koreans do not, however, speak Korean among themselves. Korean organizations are now actively attempting to fill the culture gap left by second-generation parents who cannot offer a very rich ethnic education at home; other tentative efforts at ethnic revival are beginning in Japanese public schools. The revival aims at such things as using one's Korean name, being able to speak a little Korean, and knowing something of Korean music and dance—items rather far along the scale from full participation in the mother culture. There is no zealous effort for complete revival, and it remains to be seen whether, having learned a small vocabulary of Korean things, the new generation will find opportunities to use them in their adult lives. This is a problem that the Korean organizations must tackle if assimilation is to be arrested.

I expect the process of assimilation to continue. It has now progressed a very long way indeed, and if tomorrow the Japanese government were to change its policies and sincerely welcome the Koreans to citizenship and equal status, I would predict the slow but progressive absorption of most of the Korean minority into the legal Japanese population. Some might disagree, but the value of Korean citizenship to Korean residents in Japan is not great, while full Japanese legal rights would indeed be valuable.

For these reasons I look upon much of the ethnic education movement as well intended but historically limited. The forces producing cultural assimilation seem far more powerful. I have no doubt that education to foster a sense of Korean pride is valuable, but where successful it will result primarily in furthering social assimilation as the young Koreans it inspires find the strength to force open particular areas of Japanese society and to do better in them.

Here the distinction between cultural and social assimilation proves quite valuable. So far assimilation has been largely cultural, not social. The next stage is likely to be marked by progress in gaining social acceptance and position. The opportunities provided by Japanese public education, the activism created by the young Korean leadership, and the vision of a plural Japan held by some Japanese intellectuals may all be complementary ingredients in a formula that will combine slowly to open Japanese society to Koreans. Ethnicity will become increasingly an intellectual and symbolic commodity, its vitality being in reverse proportion to the degree that it is closed and hostile. The remote possibility exists that an ethnic revival beginning in this way could with time become much deeper, richer, and more significant. The role of the Korean language would be critical, however, and so far there has been little indication that a revival of language among the second and third generation is going to occur. The shape of Korean life in Japan, in fact, seems on the verge of a new formulation. Related to the tendency for some Koreans to attain real educational success in the Japanese school system, a generation of leadership is emerging that is less tied simply to either Ch'ongnyŏn or Mindan. This group and the generation they represent assume a future living in Japan, and therefore they feel independence from Korea itself. Furthermore, they are conversant with Japanese life and are confident of their talents. Similar to (and actually part of) the Japanese intelligentsia, this group has no organizational base, but its voice is growing in the media, the literary world, and the Japanese intellectual community. It also parallels the activist stance of the Korean Christian churches in Japan.

Mindan reflects this to a degree by its new spirit of activism oriented to helping the Korean minority gain greater rights in Japan. A shift away from activities tied to and focused on the Korean homeland is occurring.

I see the Japanese public school system and the Japanese universities as actually playing a central role in producing the type of Koreans who lead and support this transformation. The key focus from now on will be Korean rights in Japan. If the rights movement is successful, the greatest remaining barriers to social assimilation will begin to come down. There is recent evidence to indicate that this process is now underway. The fundamental issue raised by these new tendencies is whether ethnicity and ethnic identification will remain a viable resource for Korean organizations (and ethnic education efforts) beyond the time when Koreans gain equal rights in Japan.

Other factors are also at work on the Japanese side of the equation. The increasing economic strength of South Korea has impressed the Japanese with the necessity of taking a more complimentary attitude toward all Koreans. In the media a subtle shift toward a less chauvinistic attitude is occurring (the NHK year-long historical drama, "Ogon no Wibi," portrayed Koreans sympathetically and had as its protagonist a Japanese who supported them in resisting Hideyoshi's invasion). The Koreans say publicly that they do not share their parents' hostility to Japanese. It "was the product of an imperialism we do not know."

Other chapters in this book are largely about the past injustices Koreans have suffered in Japan, but the contemporary scene, especially in education, contains much that points to continued assimilation as the future trend.

PART THREE
THE ETHNIC EXPERIENCE

With Part III, our method of approach shifts. We turn to the methods of the psychological anthropologist, seeking the inner experiences of Koreans and their own expressions of what it means to be a member of a minority group in Japan. In chapter 10, after a general demographic introduction, we present briefly the social environment, the daily life, as well as the thoughts of those living in a Korean ghetto. In chapter 11, we use the case history approach, utilizing court testimony as well as newspaper and journal accounts of some recent trials occurring within the Japanese courts. These trials illuminate how Koreans have protested, by legal or by illegal means, against their discriminatory social and occupational experiences. Chapter 12, through case history and anecdote, describes how some Koreans "pass" in the contemporary world of mass entertainment, and why they choose or do not choose to do so. Chapters 13 and 14 present what is perhaps our most poignant material. Here we focus specifically on problems of alienation experienced by minority youth, and we learn their sometimes tragic consequences.

10

COMMUNITY LIFE IN A KOREAN GHETTO

George De Vos and Daekyun Chung

DEMOGRAPHIC DISTRIBUTION OF KOREANS IN JAPAN

The geographic distribution of Koreans in Japan is shown in table 20. They are mostly scattered in seven of the largest metropolitan areas, namely, Osaka, Tokyo, Kobe, Nagoya, Kyoto, Yokohama, and Fukuoka. The largest concentration is found in the Osaka metropolitan area, where 188,720 Koreans were well established in 1974. Of these, 39,404 Koreans were heavily concentrated in the northern section of Ikuno-ku, Osaka city, which forms a "Koreatown," often nicknamed "Kimchee town," famous for its Korean market streets. For any outsider, Ikuno-ku is the area where one can often hear elderly persons speaking loudly in Korean; many speak a broken Japanese with a heavy Korean accent. This is a stronghold of the Ch'ongnyŏn, whose local members pledge absolute loyalty to the Democratic People's Republic of Korea. The assassin who killed Madam Park Chung-hee in August 1974 came from this area.

The 1974 statistics of the gainfully employed Koreans in Japan, when compared with approximately 200,000 males between the ages of 20 and 64, would suggest that about 30 percent of the adult male population is unemployed. Only a small percentage, about 3,700 individuals, is listed in what could be considered the professions. About 26,000 are listed either as simple manual laborers or as building and construction workers. Another 31,000 are technical workers in manufacturing. An interesting listing indicating some specialization shows nearly 13,000 Koreans as "drivers of vehicles." From our observations, the number of women listed under "entertainment business" is totally unreliable, since there are fewer than a thousand so listed. Women who work in bars and cabarets are probably among the many unreported in table 21. We would consider such work the most prevalent occupation of Korean women.

These statistics reveal what is very apparent to the observer: Koreans

TABLE 20

Population of Koreans in Japan
(as of 1 April 1974)

Area*	Numbers
Hokkaido	7,540
Prefectures north and east of Tokyo	25,686
Saitama	8,895
Chiba (suburb of Tokyo)	9,171
Metropolitan Tokyo	74,404
Yokohama, Kawasaki city, and surroundings	29,569
Central Japan (10 prefectures)	52,647
Nagoya city and Aichi prefectures	53,657
Kyoto city and surroundings	43,881
Osaka city and surroundings	188,720
Kobe and surrounding prefecture	67,044
Southwestern Japan (11 prefectures)	56,672
Fukuoka-Kita city area and surrounding Fukuoka, Kyushu	25,786
Other prefectures of Kyushu and Okinawa (7 prefectures)	11,035
Total	638,806

*To, do, fu, and prefectures, including the seven largest metropolitan areas.

Source: Ministry of Justice, Zairyū gaikokujin tōkei, 1974.

tend to have unskilled jobs or to be unemployed. For the most part, they comprise an unskilled labor market. By a certain age, many of the men become unemployable because of various forms of personal debilitation. It is hard to estimate how many of the unemployed are alcoholic or show other forms of emotional or social debilitation. In the brief glimpses of the ghetto community reported in this chapter, one can see the further meanings of these statistics as far as the personal and social lives of many Koreans is concerned.

Two significant trends are noticeable among the younger Koreans in Japan. One is the increasing number of second- and third-generation Koreans who become naturalized. The other is the increase in intermarriage between Korean and Japanese young people. We estimate that this number exceeds the number of intragroup marriages between youths related either to the North Korean or the South Korean political factions. Marriage across ethnic lines has been, generally, socially tabooed for both Japanese and Koreans. Numerous episodes are reported of love affairs broken up by family pressure. Contrary to this tradition, among the 7,450 marriages reported by Koreans in 1972, 3,576 were mixed marriages between Koreans and

TABLE 21

Gainfully Employed Koreans in Japan, 1974

Classification	Total number of Koreans	
	Males	Females
	336,787	302,019
Engineers	615	16
Teachers	756	283
Doctors and medical workers	544	323
Clergy	204	70
Writers and authors	108	8
Correspondents	162	21
Scientists	320	81
Artists and entertainers	457	246
Other professionals	568	99
Managerial workers	4,595	202
Office workers	16,796	3,973
Traders (import and export)	181	4
Scrap iron and ragpicking workers	7,112	382
Other sales workers (retail and wholesale)	19,041	4,058
Agriculture and forestry workers including farmers	2,737	962
Fishery workers and fishermen	243	130
Miners and stone cutters	463	21
Transportation and communication workers	804	22
Builders and construction workers	10,681	134
Other technical workers and manufacturers	31,051	3,858
Simple manual laborers	15,177	1,744
Chefs	1,422	116
Barbers and beauticians	470	576
Receptionists in leisure industry	697	98
Restaurant, cabaret, and other service workers	2,069	956
Drivers	12,794	67
Housewives	—	724
Students	2,735	1,792
Total employed	155,929	218,711
Unemployed		
Unclassifiable	492	209
Unreported	47,564	62,133

Source: Hōmushō, *Zairyū gaikokujin tōkei*, 1974, pp. 42-49.

Japanese. The number of Japanese males marrying Korean females is slightly higher than the number of Korean males marrying Japanese women.

K MACHI, A CONTEMPORARY KOREAN COMMUNITY

The large area on Tokyo Bay lying between the cities of Tokyo and Yokohama, centered on the city of Kawasaki, became by 1938 (after the Sino-Japanese war) the largest intensive industrial complex in Japan. One of the principal industries of this area has been NKK (Nihon Kōkan, the Japan Steel Pipe Company). Initially, during World War I, a number of Korean peasants were shipped to Japan to work in the mills and armament plants of NKK. In one corner of the land owned by the company, a number of Koreans set up a squatter community, which has been continuously occupied since that time. By the end of World War II about five hundred workers and their families were located in what we will term here "K" Machi. What follow are excerpts from the ethnographic notes of Daekyun Chung, who lived in the area for some time and interviewed many of its inhabitants.

Between 1938 and 1940, the city of Kawasaki and its surroundings included about 25 percent of all the factory workers in mainland Japan. Today, Kawasaki city as a whole is known as a city of working-class people. It is considered by outsiders to be dirty and polluted. The area of the city known as Tajima Chiku, in turn, is looked down upon by those living in other areas of Kawasaki, who consider it a "Korean town." K Machi is the most "Korean" part of Tajima. In 1973 the population of Kawasaki was reported to be 1,026,119 Japanese and 10,170 "alien," or Korean. The population of Tajima was 59,268 Japanese and 3,192 alien. The population of K Machi was 1,576, with approximately 600 Japanese and 900 Koreans. Tajima has the highest reported concentration of Korean population in the Kanto area.

Japanese as well as Korean children from Tajima Chiku are viewed as particularly rough and tough and are feared generally. Some of these children, Japanese as well as Korean, learn there are certain advantages in assuming the stereotypes directed toward them.

History of Growth

At present, K Machi has a population of approximately 1,500 people. It is an island of tiny houses surrounded by railway sidings, an industrial road, and an expressway running between Tokyo and Yokohama. On the south and west the village borders on the huge NKK steel company with its large stacks piercing what is generally a leaden gray sky.

At the turn of the century, Tajima village was established on newly reclaimed land, covered with reeds, adjacent to the city of Kawasaki. The area first developed as an industrial site during World War I. After Japan Steel (NKK) built its first plant there, other heavy industries followed, mainly plants for electricity, ship construction, and cement. The once small village turned quickly into a working-class town.

Many of the original inhabitants of Tajima were Korean laborers, peasants from the southern part of Korea who came alone (see chap. 2), fleeing the poverty of their country in search of employment in an industrializing Japan.

In 1920, Tajima village had a population of 12,561 in 2,611 households; in 1923, 10,001 in 2,997 households; in 1925, 20,063 in 4,559 households. The present K Machi developed out of part of Tajima. In 1931, NKK bought this adjacent site. As an adjunct to its munitions factory, the company built some dormitories to house several hundred laborers who moved in to work in the plant. Most were Koreans of peasant heritage.

During the ensuing war with the United States, 4,180,000 general laborers were recorded in 55,000 munitions factories throughout Japan. About 360,000 were brought involuntarily from Korea and Taiwan. The 500 inhabitants of K Machi in 1945 were mostly Korean factory workers as well as day laborers who engaged in construction work in the vicinity. Housing for the most part was abysmally bad, usually a series of cramped, tiny rooms constructed out of refuse wood. Many of the hovels were periodically flooded. When it rained there was no sewage system beyond some primitive ditches dug beside the paths between the houses. There was no running water; people had to carry it in heavy buckets from elsewhere. Some were accustomed to carrying buckets on their backs, as was done in the Korean countryside. But the air they breathed in K Machi was quite different from that of rural Korea; it was laden with soot and smoke. The ground was glazed in many places with a black sheen composed of iron particles.

With the postwar disruption of 1945, the numbers found within this already cramped community swelled with homeless Japanese as well as Koreans, who could still find employment in the surviving Kawasaki industries. The Japanese came from all over Japan; some of the Koreans came from mines in southern Japan, which were being closed with the wiping out of war industries. The once homogeneous Korean community became a mixed neighborhood.

The housing shortage in Kawasaki became acute. K Machi, with its jerry-built hovels, reflected the first upsurge of Japanese postwar industry. In 1950 the population was approximately 900. It peaked, according to records, in 1961, when more than 2,700 inhabitants were recorded for the village. From 1962 on, housing facilities elsewhere in Kawasaki began to catch up with the population influx, and there was a gradual decline in K Machi to the present residual population of approximately 1,500.

Census records in 1970 reveal a 2.2 ratio of households to household members, whereas in Kawasaki city as a whole, the ratio is 3.24 and the overall ratio in Japan is 3.7. These averages suggest a large number of single-person unmarried households in K Machi. The age distribution, however, shows comparatively fewer young people between the ages of twenty and forty, suggesting that younger people of this community leave to go elsewhere; the unmarried are in effect an older group. We shall discuss this situation later. Among present-day inhabitants, 23 percent were born in K Machi; another 32 percent have lived there for more than ten years; 17 percent have been there from six to ten years; 20 percent from one to five years; and 8 percent are newcomers. The percentage of those born in the area is somewhat less than that in many residential areas in Japan.

Living conditions have gradually improved since the early 1960s. Initially, many Koreans, coming from a rural background, kept pigs near their houses in small sites as an economic survival technique. Almost all the pig-pens have disappeared, nor are there any remaining traces of the illicit stills that produced low-grade spirits from the lees left over from the sake manufacturers in the area. The older hovels have been upgraded, rebuilt, or repaired. About half the present dwellings have tiny second-story additions. Some of the very newest even have flush toilets with septic tanks. Generally, however, the sewage system is still primitive and is in part dependent on the ditches found crisscrossing the area. Some lower ground has been filled in where flooding was most severe. Nevertheless, the environmental situation is far below contemporary Japanese standards elsewhere. Ninety-two percent of the houses do not meet present construction criteria, and there are very narrow passages between them. They remain unmarked, without the numbers that are now making it more possible to locate residences in the Tokyo area. Many of these mazelike passages remain unpaved and become puddled with mud in the rain.

There have been some efforts to raze the area. Municipal officials point out that they cannot improve the environmental situation because this is a squatters' village built on the private land of the NKK and the TEP (the Tokyo Electric Power Company) property. The residents resist periodic attempts to move them to comply with legal, sanitary, or health statutes. NKK made some efforts to get rid of the squatters after the large influx in the early 1950s, but it has never brought the issue to court because it is generally known that the company encouraged squatters before the war when it found it convenient to utilize cheap Korean labor. In 1957, when a large fire burned down thirty-four houses, NKK attempted to prevent any rebuilding, but municipal officials mediated between the residents and NKK with a compromise plan permitting rebuilding by those who had lived there continuously for a long period before the fire.

In 1971, the polluting iron works of NKK were removed to other reclaimed land. Many present residents point out the improvement in the atmosphere since then. Some informants reported how bad it was in the past, several mentioning how iron particles, some as large as hailstones, fell on the village area. One mentioned how he had looked up once and an iron particle had fallen into his eye. He could not remove it and had to go to an eye clinic. Women reported how hard it was to keep a clean room and how many hours they worked cleaning and washing clothes, which often would be dirtied as they dried. One put it poetically: "Here it snowed in summer and the glow of the factories gave us sunset at midnight."

To the outside observer, Kawasaki city remains one of the worst possible areas of atmospheric pollution, and yet the residents seem to express little concern. They are aware of improvement compared with the even more horrible past. They are not aware that whereas the more noticeable smell of sulfur dioxide has decreased, less obvious toxins such as nitrogen oxide are on the increase. A number of the residents suffer from chronic bronchitis and complain of asthmatic attacks.

The Green Belt Project

The municipal government of Kawasaki city has been planning to build so-called protection zones to separate industry from human habitation to prevent accidental pollution or some industrial mishap from killing any of the neighboring population. For example, the Keihin industrial area is a petrochemical complex which could, given the circumstance of a major earthquake, lead to many deaths in areas such as K Machi. A "green belt" project was started in 1972 to build a green area along the major industrial road. As a second stage, a 50-meter wide green belt is to be built around the northern part of K Machi. If this green belt project materializes, probably half the present residents of K Machi will have to move elsewhere.

So far, most of the residents seem indifferent to this possibility, as if they do not really believe that it will happen in the near future. The expressed attitudes of village leaders tend to be critical, the present head of K Machi saying that the municipal government is corporation-oriented. He insists that the factories, not the residents, should be moved. The interviewer was not certain that the attitude of the head represented the general opinion of the residents. Some residents said to Chung that if they were given a reasonable substitute dwelling, they would move. This problem cannot simply be resolved between the residents and the government. K Machi is the property of NKK and TEP. Therefore there will be a struggle before a solution is reached among the four parties. Chung predicts that a serious problem will arise when some of the residents resist. The result may be an influx of outsiders utilizing this potential struggle for political purposes.

The Social Image of K Machi

K Machi is known in the surrounding area as a Korean village of construction laborers. It is considered by others in Kawasaki as dirty and polluted. Those living on the other side of the tracks share the general Japanese stereotypes about Koreans, and all the children are sensitive to these attitudes when they go to school. Some parents in K Machi have managed through one technicality or another to send their children to more distant schools. By so doing, they hope to avoid the disparagement of those nearby. Some Korean youths cluster in delinquent-prone gangs and live out the stereotype of being "tough" and intimidating toward others (see chap. 13).

We have recorded some concern expressed by mothers who find that their children are being influenced negatively by their peers and are beginning to act tough. Nonworking mothers have more opportunity to supervise their children and to concern themselves with whom their own children are associating. Some others consider themselves unfortunate because they are fully occupied with economic survival and are not able to give their children sufficient supervision. One often hears the complaint that living in K Machi is detrimental to the proper upbringing of children. Many say that they would like to leave for this reason. Not only do they see baleful influences in growing up there but they feel that living in this village will make it difficult for their children to make good marriages.

As we see from the statistics of population by age, a great many youths over twenty leave the area, characteristically after finishing high school, to seek opportunity elsewhere and perhaps to escape the stigma attached to their ghetto. The eldest son often remains to help in the economic activities of the family, whereas the other children are freer to depart. Those staying behind usually seek their intimate associations outside K Machi. Some of the departees are replaced by older single male laborers from elsewhere who have been somehow forced by circumstances to come and live in this community.

Looking at inhabitants' attitudes about their village, one obtains a range of positive and negative evaluations. There are those who would like to leave if circumstances would allow. Others rationalize their living in the village as economically cheaper. Some even state that it is a more relaxed place to live "because you don't have to care about how you look living here." Some point out how the environment has improved, and some state, of course, that there is no place like one's home. If we were to generalize from our informal interviews, we would state our impression that youth and second-generation villagers express the strongest negative feelings about the image of their village. Those who have grown up in it and afterward come to associate with people outside are more sensitive to the disparaging attitudes directed toward them from the outside. Schoolchildren especially have ample experience with the freely expressed negative attitudes of outside children. These same attitudes may be felt by the neighboring adults, but it is the majority Japanese children who freely express disparagement directly toward the children of K Machi. To live in K Machi is to be branded as dirty, tough, and probably delinquent.

In K Machi one can perceive on the part of the Japanese residents a certain level of acculturation into Korean culture. For example, most acquire some simple Korean words. Some say they have come to prefer eating Korean rather than Japanese foods since they have moved to K Machi.

Economic Life

In effect, this area is an economic as well as a social ghetto. The remaining residents, as well as those newcomers who still arrive, are people who cannot readily move for one reason or another. Most are presently incapable of finding better living circumstances. Nevertheless, a few are kept by the sentiment attached to long residence. They are aware of improvements compared with the dreadful past. However substandard their environment may be when compared with that found elsewhere, some of the residents feel themselves to be comparatively well off.

A third of the residents receive some form of social welfare assistance. Of these, 80 percent are Korean. A number of elderly remain who are afflicted with a number of diseases, many of them attributable to the hardships of their lives. Practically everyone in the village works in some activity close by. According to the 1970 census, 60 percent of the women in K Machi have outside jobs, in addition to their work as housewives. Among those classified, 42 percent are in some form of manufacturing or factory work, 25 percent are in wholesale or retail merchant activities, and 13 percent are in some form of service industry. In effect, about 50 percent of the women are factory workers or are doing hard physical labor. Most of these classified in wholesale or retail are actually store clerks. Those in service industries work in restaurants, bars, and coffee shops.

Among the men in 1970, 15 percent are out of work; 20 percent drive vehicles, either trucks or taxis. Of those classified, 84 percent are employees and 13 percent are self-employed. More than half the self-employed are owners of small construction companies with fewer than ten employees, operating subcontracting establishments that received periodic work. Other self-employed men are in effect junk dealers, recycling scrap iron; a few are proprietors of small stores or fishing boats, boat rentals, or restaurants. Those working in boat rentals take out customers who want to fish.

Most of the self-employed are Korean, both Mindan and Ch'ongnyon (see chap. 3). When they hire others, they hire both Japanese and Korean. Chung, however, reports one Korean head of a small construction company who will not hire any Koreans.

Mujin

Those who are better off financially in K Machi usually join a *Mujin*, a society for mutual financial assistance. When a family faces some unusual financial expense, such as supporting a child's entry into a professional school, a marriage arrangement, or a funeral, they can draw on this mutual assistance society. The Mujin are not limited to financial matters but also serve as social clubs. Meetings are held at various restaurants, and members go on group tours together. The Mujin in K Machi are divided along political and ethnic lines. Some are loyal to North Korea and the Ch'ongnyŏn, some favor South Korea and the Mindan and, of course, the remainder are the Japanese. Some residents complain that the South Korean or Mindan adherents tend to form more questionable types of Mujin, called *Kenka* "quarrel" groups.

Political Cleavages

All forms of social participation in K Machi, not only the Mujin, are divided by ethnic and political cleavages. The Japanese inhabitants generally keep to themselves and stay out of Korean political issues. Among the roughly 600 residents classified as being of "Japanese" nationality are some Koreans who have become naturalized Japanese. Of the roughly 900 classified as Koreans, 400 are considered loyal to North Korea, the remainder to South Korea.

The formal village association for the area, which nominally involves all residents, consists of an elected headman, two vice-headmen, and five chiefs of sub-ward areas. Among these, the headman is legally required to have Japanese nationality, since citizenship is necessary to be officially recognized by municipal government agencies. At present, one of the vice-headmen is a naturalized Korean. Two chiefs among the five subheads are Korean citizens; the others are native-born Japanese. The village meeting-house, or *Kaikan* is formally open to any residents, but it is characteristically used by the Japanese rather than by the Koreans. The Ch'ongnyŏn, however, have their own small meetinghouse, and the Mindan have recently seen to it that they have a somewhat larger one than the Ch'ongnyŏn.

The Japanese, of course, attend Japanese public school. Nearly all the South Korean-oriented families also send their children to Japanese schools. About half of the Ch'ongnyŏn children attend a local primary and high school that is operated by the Ch'ongnyŏn. The others attend ordinary Japanese schools.

A number of personal relationships cut across these cleavages, and some individuals do not closely associate with what would seem to be their appropriate group. There are not infrequent instances of intermarriage that create ambiguities in allegiance. For example, some Japanese women are married to Korean men. In a number of these instances, the Japanese woman does not have her name entered into the husband's Korean register. Instead, the children are entered into the mother's family registry. We have been unable to ascertain the frequency of this type of arrangement.

It has been very difficult to gain much straightforward information about the relative number of naturalized Japanese living in this area. It is not a topic on which one can survey people too directly. One must establish a certain degree of confidentiality before such topics can be freely discussed. There is even some ambiguity about actual loyalty to either North or South Korean groups. In some family situations, one family member will belong to one group and one to another, simply as a matter of economic and social expediency. Belonging to the Mindan usually assures having "Kankoku" (South Korean nationality), but Mindan membership does not always relate to the actual ideological opinions of individuals. There are expedient reasons for belonging to the organization as well as ideological ones. Since 1966 there has been a great deal of ambiguity as to where loyalties lie. From 1966 to 1971, the Japanese government offered permanent resident status only to those who had Kankoku nationality. Some of those who were of North Korean conviction changed their affiliations, in spite of attempts by the Ch'ongnyŏn group to prevent such defections. A number of individuals were concerned that they might not have any opportunity to leave the country or to receive welfare benefits if they did not change their official affiliations.

The actual relationships among the residents of K Machi are far more complex than their nominal division into three groups. It is hard to generalize how a Japanese woman who has married a Korean, for example, will maintain and develop individual and group relationships. Chung, in reviewing his interviews about social participation, has noted that whereas some Japanese wives of Korean husbands have friendships with other Koreans, no Japanese wife involves herself in organizational activities within a Korean group. Despite the split between North and South, a number of Koreans maintain relationships on an individual basis with those of the opposing group. They carefully avoid any meetings or situations of a political or ideological nature.

According to informants, from 1959 through 1963 there was a great deal of discussion and activity about the issue of repatriation to North Korea (see chap. 6). At that time, according to retrospective reports, the number of individuals affiliated with the Ch'ongnyŏn exceeded the number of those active in Mindan. The Ch'ongnyŏn held classes on socialism, Korean history, and the Korean language for both youth and adults. At that time most of the children whose parents were affiliated with North Korean groups attended Korean schools, and even some Mindan parents enrolled their children in these schools. During this time the Mindan group was almost totally inactive. The main activities espousing Korean causes came from the Ch'ongnyŏn.

The very success of North Korean repatriation, however, changed the balance of adherents toward the South Koreans, since many of the more active North Korean affiliates repatriated. Also, the economic advantages of nonrepatriation went to those who could somehow achieve permanent residence status. Despite such shifts in population, the North Korean group still comprises almost half the Koreans in K Machi. Until 1975, the Ch'ongnyŏn organization remained better organized than the Mindan. Since then, supported financially by the South Korean government, the South Koreans have gained in strength. The Mindan has attempted to emulate some of the Ch'ongnyŏn activities, such as holding Korean lessons for children once a week. One may judge that this language activity is actually minimal and the amount of learning that takes place is fairly slight. Though the effect of such activities is symbolic more than practical, it does carry the message of increased concern and a willingness to lend support to Mindan activities. On 15 October 1970 *The Daily Asahi* newspaper reported that a South Korean visitor who had come to see his relative hid himself when some Ch'ongnyŏn members arrived to present to a South Korean their "Northern" point of view. The South Korean, who had been strictly warned by his government not to have any contact with Ch'ongnyŏn members, was so frightened that he hid himself behind a sewing machine, so as not to be found by them and not to be reported as having had any contact. One notes in such incidents that there is also a general fear of spying activities, so that individuals who are not familiar with personal affiliations in a particular area will be very circumspect about expressing any attitudes or seeing anyone who might compromise them.

Since 1975 the South Korean government and the Mindan have put funds forward to invite people with Ch'ongnyŏn affiliation to go for group tours of South Korea, stressing that there need not be any change of membership, but that they are free to see how South Korea is progressing socially and economically. In some instances such tours are a temptation for Ch'ongnyŏn affiliates, especially the more elderly who have close relatives still living in South Korea. In K Machi, as perhaps in other Korean neighborhoods, one finds cars with loudspeakers carrying on a propaganda war of words, seeking to change allegiances.

What we have observed in microcosm in this village is a reflection of the more general struggle for power between the two organizations. But a group of Koreans living as closely together physically as the residents of K Machi avoid as much as possible any open expression of their factional affiliations. They do not wish to arouse others to any state of excitement that may move from the psychological to the physical. They must maintain a daily face-to-face contact within a small, confined territory. Sometimes when outsiders come in to proselytize for one side or the other, the inhabitants become resentful, even if the representative is of someone on their own side. One woman who had strong anti-Communist feelings, for example, pointed with a frown at the loudspeaker of a Mindan organizer and said, "I can't understand why they are doing such a stupid thing. They don't at all put themselves in our position or concern themselves with the consequences of what they're doing."

Organizations for Social Reform

Other reformers are also to be found in K Machi, motivated more by social or religious than by political concerns. Let us briefly mention three such groups. During the Hitachi trial (see chap. 11), a number of activists (both Japanese and Korean) moved into the area around Tajima, which was known to have the largest concentration of Koreans in the Kanto area around Tokyo. Mostly university students or graduates, they found jobs in the area (as factory workers, truck drivers, or in some service role), uniting in a program of community action.

Some sympathetic Japanese had started a group called the Kawasaki Dōhō Jinken O Mamoru Kai (Association to Protect Korean Civil Rights in Kawasaki City). Frequently they have been successful in demands for juvenile allowances to assist poor families and for freer admission to municipal facilities for Koreans (a demand pressed in July 1974 and agreed to by local government in January 1975). Among these were two university students as well as a university graduate who had moved into K Machi in 1974 as group leaders motivated to raise local ethnic consciousness. They helped initiate the Sakuramoto nursery, or kindergarten, in April 1975 as an informal school for ethnic education. Members of the Sakuramoto Gakuen also functioned as a community action group uniting local Hitachi action groups with some members of a Korean Christian Church located near K Machi.

The Sakuramoto Gakuen runs both a preschool and an after-school program as a means of fostering ethnic pride. But programs on ethnic background have caused some confusion. For example, at the nursery school, Korean children were encouraged to use their Korean instead of their Japanese names. They were taught Korean songs and some Korean words and phrases. Some of the children's parents, however, preferred to have their children use Japanese names and discouraged interest in their Korean heritage. The teachers at Sakuramoto Gakuen thus found themselves in conflict with some of these parents. They were sending their children to the nursery school solely because they appreciated the care and daytime supervision given their youngsters, not because they wanted tutoring about their ethnic background. It is interesting to note that the after-school elementary program has twice as many Japanese children (65) in attendance as Korean (33). Therefore, the program has certain unresolved issues about what is involved in raising consciousness and about the meaning of Korean ethnicity for those in attendance. Is it an acknowledgment of origins and the respect that should be paid by mature Japanese to Japanese of Korean ancestry—or is it aimed at maintaining some actual elements of Korean culture in the young?

This program has been meeting with a mixture of acceptance and rejection on the part of both North-affiliated and South-affiliated families. The Gakuen group at first obtained permission to use the South Korean Mindan *kaikan* and started a number of activities, both educational and recreational. Children of both Ch'ongnyŏn and Japanese families were also invited. Unfortunately, the Mindan organization decided to refuse further use of its *kaikan* after January of 1976. Although their reasons for refusal were not clearly stated, their decision seemed based on political considerations. Nevertheless, afterward, a large number of Mindan members continued to send their children to the Sakuramoto nursery, which had moved into its own quarters. Because Mindan members do not have a kindergarten of their own, they generally are positive toward the ethnic program founded by Sakuramoto nursery. A principal advantage of the nursery is its low tuition fee. Nevertheless, leaders of the Mindan are suspicious of what they perceive as the "radical" orientation of the group, believing that this new group is basically affiliated with the so-called anti-Park dissidents among Kankoku nationality holders, such as Hanchŏng (see chap. 6). Actually, the Gakuen group has sought to avoid any political affiliation, focusing instead on specific issues of discrimination. They expressly avoid taking any stand on the Korean problem in Japan which might throw them into the ongoing conflict between the Mindan and the Ch'ongnyŏn over the political relations of North and South Korea. On the contrary, the Gakuen group believes that one has to work at the microscopic level rather than attend to the broader issues of conflict. The attitudes of Mindan members toward Sakuramoto Gakuen and its nursery are mixed. Small numbers of active Mindan members are very skeptical about the group's political stance. Some Mindan members are suspicious about the religious affiliation of the Gakuen group, and yet others of the Mindan support the new group enthusiastically. These supporters are either Christians (four families in K Machi) or relatively young mothers who have experienced an "ethnic rebirth" through participation in the PTA at the nursery. Mothers of this group voluntarily work on the camping activities and special events put on by the Gakuen.

Overall, the majority of Mindan residents of K Machi regard these activities instrumentally: What benefits are to be gained? They are skeptical about the ethnic revivalism that motivates the Gakuen group. They ask why the group has to focus narrowly on ethnic problems instead of seeing more practically to the improvement of the schoolwork of their children.

The Sakuramoto Gakuen group is not the only one to have tried to bring improvement to K Machi. A group of Japanese university students, many of them members of Minsei (the youth organization of the Japanese

Communist party), tried organizing settlement activities. Most of the children they succeeded in contacting were Japanese, although they attempted to involve Korean children too. Some of the K Machi children have at one time or another been involved in the Minsei's Kodomo Kai or "Children's Group," which held meetings at the Mindan *kaikan* or later in the Sakuramoto Gakuen. The children who attended often expressed the attitude that the settlement activities of this group were more enjoyable because the leaders did not mention ethnic problems.

Sōkagakkai, a new religious group, has also attempted active organizational work. Not only has it involved Japanese families but it also has worked to gain membership among Korean families. These activities are typical of Sōkagakkai activities elsewhere, although it is Chung's impression that Sōkagakkai has not been as successful among Koreans in K Machi as has been reported in some other areas. There has also been a local attempt to form a strong, cohesive Buddhist church membership sometimes utilizing rather aggressive recruitment techniques. And many village residents have become active in the Kōmeito political party, an increasingly powerful minority party in Japanese politics.

Informal Social Life: The Restaurant

The local restaurants are a center for much of the local social life. Let us illustrate: There is one Korean restaurant called Rika En in K Machi, run by a 50-year-old Korean widow. Rika En opens at 8:00 A.M. and closes at midnight. Mrs. Kim, the restaurant owner, usually works continuously, with one woman assistant. Mrs. Kim, who gives the impression of energy and well-being, says that she "hates to play" but enjoys her work.

The restaurant can seat nearly thirty customers. Usually there are five to ten customers present. When the place becomes very crowded, some of the customers voluntarily help with the orders. The interior and its equipment are relatively poor. The restaurant is equipped with air conditioning for the summer and a somewhat primitive-appearing heating stove for winter cold. The color TV is on constantly.

Restaurants such as this are among the few places for relaxed social communication. The customers are principally men during the day. Rika En is then frequented by unemployed men, some who have become chronic alcoholics and others who have failed to find daily labor for that day. Housewives come together to gossip between household chores. In the evening, laborers who have finished their work come by to drink and eat snacks. A few of the frequent customers are local Japanese on good terms with certain Koreans. Also found here are bachelors or unemployed men from outside K Machi who are visiting with long-time friends.

On the weekends the customers are more diverse and include many Japanese customers who rent the commercial fishing boats and stop at the restaurant after fishing for some convenient refreshments. The usual small talk is about life's cares, the good old days, sex, sports, and sake.

The alcoholics appear in the late morning, two or three of them being continuous occupants. Most are more than fifty years old; many have no hope of future work. Most are receiving some form of financial relief. Mrs. Kim is reluctant to serve these older men, since they very often come without any money in their pockets. She says, "While I hate to serve them, when I see them I feel something like pity. So often I give them something to eat for free." She is torn between her natural generosity and a need to keep her business solvent.

Some evenings there is singing started by a group of local residents and lasting until midnight. The flow of beer and sake is continuous. Sometimes those already drunk can persuade Mrs. Kim to join them. She apparently offers little resistance to participation. If one listens to the content of the songs, one will notice some variety among them. Most often they are Korean folksongs or Japanese popular songs that are elegiac and nostalgic. Chung was surprised to encounter one of the Japanese residents whose father used to be a policeman in Korea. The son was brought up in Korea and later married a Korean woman. He too loved to sing Korean sentimental folksongs with a sense of nostalgia. In the same circle, one Korean daily laborer in his early forties liked to sing Japanese lyric songs, French chansons with Japanese verses, and part of Beethoven's Ninth Symphony, as well as Korean songs. He was a dropout from a college in Tokyo.

Cycle of a Day in K Machi

On a weekday by 5:45 a.m.: Several small boats leave the waterway to pick up iron scraps from the foreign ships lying at anchor near the port. A few years ago, when Japan Steel had its iron works there, about twenty boats and one hundred men were engaged in this activity.

By 6:00 a.m.: Most housewives get up and prepare breakfast for their families. Physical laborers leave, some in minibuses and trucks owned by small construction companies.

By 8:00 a.m.: High school students and company and factory workers (mostly youth, more women than men) leave home.

By 8:30 a.m.: Elementary schoolchildren leave; some housewives leave to work in small factories nearby.

From 9:00-12:00 a.m.: K Machi is quiet. Some older women take care of their small grandchildren and visit their neighbors. In some houses, housewives work on cottage industry jobs with their neighbors. A few alcoholics loiter here or there.

1:00 p.m.: Elementary schoolchildren return home. The boys play catch, spin tops, ride bicycles, set off fireworks, or simply hang around. The girls play, eat ice cream, play with infants, ride bicycles, or hang around.

5:00-7:00 p.m.: Workers return home. High school students return to watch programs on TV.

7:00-10:00 p.m.: Housewives prepare supper, and the families eat. Voices scolding children drift out into the alleyways, as do sounds of quarreling children. Sounds of TV are everywhere.

10:00 p.m.: K Machi becomes quiet.

12:00 p.m.: The restaurants in K Machi close, to open again at 8:00 A.M.

2:00-3:00 a.m.: Women who work in bars return home by taxi.

On Sunday: In the morning, everyone starts later. More than one hundred customers from outside of K Machi come to the two shops that rent fishing boats in the waterway. Children go outside to play. Several young women leave home to spend the day outside K Machi. By 12:00, all the men have finally gotten out of bed. Rika En has more customers than usual. In the afternoon, men begin playing mah-jong with their friends. Some start to drink. Some fathers and children go someplace where the children can play outdoors, or to a movie or baseball game. The evening scene in K Machi is not much different from that of weekdays. The noise of TV.... If the Sunday is rainy, the men get up by noon. If they do not go outdoors or do not meet others, they may sleep again after eating a meal. They may play mah-jong or have a banquet with friends at the restaurant. Some take care of their children.

The Unemployed: Alcoholics

There are several unemployed alcoholics in K Machi. There are many more chronic drinkers who keep on working. Those considered serious alcoholics have lost their capacity to work, and Mr. Yim is one of them. Sometimes he can be found sitting on the side of a narrow street with his head in his hands. At other times he will be lying on a bench by a restaurant. He always keeps a small bottle in his pocket. People say he will not live long.

Mr. Yim is forty-eight years old. He is separated from his wife, aged fifty-three, who returned to Korea eight years ago. A rural peasant, he married when he was fifteen years old. His first daughter, who is thirty-one years old, is also living in Korea at present. His two other children, now eleven and nine years old and both sons, are in a Japanese child-welfare institution. He receives a welfare payment on the third of every month. He usually manages to spend all his money before the tenth of the month. He first pays off debts he has incurred during the previous month and then spends the rest for liquor. He often shows up at the Rika En to eat but mostly to drink. He is suffering from chronic bronchitis and a variety of other complaints. He can obtain free care at a community hospital nearby, as he has been made eligible for social welfare medical benefits, but often he refuses to see a doctor. He is ashamed because he smells of alcohol. It has been noticed that he has been indulging even more heavily since his closest friend (also an alcoholic) died last year. Many remark how deeply he was grieved by his friend's death.

Chung (the interviewer) visited him in his dark back room, for which he pays a small rent. The room is decorated by a colorful calendar illustrating a Japanese woman in a bright kimono. He has a black-and-white TV that he picked up in a junkyard. One corner is strewn with empty bags of instant *ramen* (noodles) and copies of *Akahata* (Red Flag), the Communist daily paper he receives from the community hospital nearby, which is run by Japanese Communists. He claims he reads the paper every day.

Chung reports part of a conversation between Mr. Yim, Mrs. Kim (of Rika En), and himself:

MR. YIM: (turning his face to Chung rather than to Mrs. Kim), I used to meet my children once a month. But recently I cannot go so often. Sometimes I call them to phone. It's a shame. However, I try to be a man as usual. It is not so easy. I married when I was fifteen years old in Korea. I have a 31-year-old daughter there. We have been separated for thirty years. Somehow I don't feel like going to see her. What a pity for her!

MRS. KIM: Oh, my goodness! What is pitiful? Chikusho! [Japanese expletive meaning "Beast!"]

MR. YIM: I know manners. I am the oldest son in my family. I have to protect my family until I die. So I feel I have to do something for my family. Thirty years is not a short time.

MRS. KIM: I have never seen such a damn person as you. Why can't you clean your room and work by yourself? It's OK to receive money [social welfare], but how are you spending the money? You know Japanese are not stupid. They all know how you are spending the money.

MR. YIM: You say I am unkempt. Damn. But I think everybody here is the same.

MRS. KIM: What? What a fool you are! Who else is drinking from morning to night? Ah?

MR. YIM: I feel somehow lonely. . . .

MRS. KIM: Who else is not working at all just because he feels lonely? Look at Mr. Kim and Mr. Chi!

MR. YIM: Oh, no. They don't have a child and. . . .

MRS. SUNG: If you have a child, you have to work more. Even if you can't get full-time work, you should work at least part-time work.

MR. YIM: Yes, that's right.

MRS. KIM: You must have become crazy from alcohol.

MR. YIM: I think I have to study. . . . I think I can start to work if I wish. But sometimes I wonder why I have to.

MRS. SUNG: Listen. Don't say "Give me a glass of drink" if you don't have money. OK? You should not drink if you don't have money. You always drink without eating food. You know what you are doing?

MR. YIM: I am made miserable by the situation.

MRS. SUNG: My goodness, how have you become like this? You had better die. Ah.

MR. YIM: No, no. To kill yourself is no good. Why do you say such a thing? If I can kill myself, I will do anything instead. I don't have the energy to kill myself.

MRS. SUNG: Why don't you die now? Do it!

MR. YIM: (mumbles)

MRS. SUNG: What makes it worthwhile to live? You are damned by everybody, even by your kids.

MR. YIM: I don't mind that. But I can't die. It is determined that a human being is born once and dies once. Everything ends if I die now, you know. Please don't say such a thing. . . . The only way is to change my mental situation, I think.

MRS. SUNG: Why don't you spend your social welfare little by little? Ah? Why don't you buy rice first?

MR. YIM: Please don't say such a thing.

MRS. SUNG: It's a shame to have you at our restaurant. Don't come anymore. I have been sympathetic with you just because you are Korean, but I found it's useless. There are people who can understand what they have done. But you can't. So I'm angry with you. How will you live tomorrow? Ah? If you come and say "Give me a cup of sake," I will give you one. Ah? Of course I don't give you free. That's not a problem. I mean you have to change yourself.

The Aged

According to Chung's informal observations, most of the very elderly in K Machi are women. Some still do daily labor through so-called unemployment relief work, provided by the municipal government, until they are no longer able. Chung describes one of the aged he interviewed in the following excerpt:

Lee Sanyo, age 71, was born in a southern province of Korea in 1905. At age nine, her mother died when a younger sister was born. Two years later her father died. The father had three younger brothers, all of them very poor. She and her only sister were taken care of by the father's youngest brother. She received no education. The family worked very hard, but whatever they did, they could not get enough food. Sanyo became a maid for a merchant when she was thirteen years old. She cooked, washed, and cleaned the house until her twentieth year, when she married a farmer.

One year later she gave birth to a daughter. By the daughter's first birthday, her husband had left her to go to Japan with another woman. (She did not know he had left with another woman until she met her husband again in Japan.) About eighteen months after he left, he finally sent Sanyo money for her and her daughter's passage to Japan.

All four of them lived together in a laboring section of Yokohama. The husband's mistress mistreated Sanyo, as the mistress was jealous of her. Sanyo felt helpless but thought she could not find any other place to live, and so she endured the abuse of the mistress. One night, however, she left for Toyohashi in Aichi-ken, having learned that she could get employment there in a silk-goods factory. Upon her arrival she was amazed to find so many other Korean women. After a while, she was fired when the factory force was cut back owing to a depression period. She went back to rejoin her husband. They all moved from Yokohama to the Yokosuka Naval Base area. But Sanyo and her young daughter soon rented a separate room. Meanwhile, she had conceived a son (with whom she is living now in K Machi). Her husband died when her eldest son was about six or seven years old.

Sanyo remarried when she was in her late thirties. She had another son by her new husband, born in 1945. She has lived continuously in K Machi since she remarried. Her new husband, also a Korean, bought a small truck in an attempt to start a small transportation business. Unfortunately, he died two or three years after her remarriage.

After her husband died, she supported her family by obtaining daily unemployment relief work in neighboring Kawasaki city. She used to leave home early in the morning with her younger son on her back, traveling on foot to the hiring hall. If she could not get there early enough, she would not be employed for the day. On her way back home, she used to buy little cakes. Her elder son would wait for her return with boiling water ready to make tea. He would always clean his half-brother's hands and feet with some of the water. Once on the way to work she slipped and fell to the ground with her small son on her back. She seriously sprained one knee and still has periodic attacks of neuralgia in this leg.

At this time of contact she was doing relief work, but she also finds odd jobs around K Machi. Residents of K Machi know her well. She is generally well liked, but she associates little with K Machi people, remaining quiet and withdrawn. Her only real pleasure now is to attend the nearby Christian Korean church every Sunday. She has been a Christian since her youth in Korea.

Group Relations Among Children

To the casual observer, children at play do not demonstrate any great degree of tension. Casual activities cross the social division between Japanese and Korean. For example, Chung's notebooks contain several observations of a typical Sunday afternoon. In one instance, Chung met three school-age girls eating ice cream and candy at a small general store owned by a Korean. Two of the girls were of the North Korean faction; the other girl was of a mixed marriage between a Japanese mother and a father who had South Korean affiliation. All three of these young girls attended the nearby Japanese elementary school. Nearby, Chung also observed two preschool boys, who were cousins, killing worms with lighted matches. Both boys were of families in the South Korean faction; one of the boys attended a Korean church (Christian) kindergarten. There was a third little group consisting of a preschool boy and a woman with a baby. The boy, who was of the South Korean faction, was playing with a toy steam locomotive at the side of the road. The woman and the baby were Japanese. Two other boys playing catch in the road were of the South Korean faction and went to the Japanese school. All these children were familiar with Chung's presence and greeted him casually.

In general, Chung observed that the friendship patterns of preschool children in K Machi cut across factional divisions. In many instances, this is because people live next door to one another and the children very often form groups on the basis of proximity. But as Chung's observations gained depth, he found that there were many signs of periodic tension which could arise upon provocation.

According to Chung's informants, general attitudes about the "toughness" of older Korean children have not changed. Both the leaders and followers of juvenile gangs in this area, now as before, tend to be Korean. Japanese children fear these tough Koreans. Nonetheless, the Japanese children continue to feel themselves socially dominant, if not as physically assertive as the Koreans. It is interesting to note that open ambivalence about one's identity is found even in smaller children. Each of the children described by Chung in his notebooks, even the younger children, have a Japanese name in addition to their Korean name. When relating to one another, as well as when relating to outsiders, they are more likely to use their Japanese rather than their Korean name.

In effect, smaller children provide a more direct and obvious reflection of the adult society. They manipulate what they see as their social advantage or disadvantage whenever possible. Children are not so concerned about the insulting vulnerabilities of others. Proximity and contact lead to mutual play, but at times of frustration or anger, mutual vulnerabilities will be exploited.

Many adults have retrospective reminiscences about the negative relations between Koreans and Japanese children at the time when many Japanese and Koreans flowed into K Machi just after the war. Many derogatory songs are reported to have been popular among children up to the 1960s.

Japanese children, for example, would sing, "You said your Korean school is good, but one finds that it's only a dirty shack" (paraphrase). Korean children would sing back, "You said the Japanese school is good, but one finds that it's only a dirty shack." Another example is difficult to translate: "That Korean is so miserable that his shack was burned down by yesterday's fire," or, "Koreans are so miserable. They claim to have won the war but run away with pigs on their backs." The Korean children in turn sing out, "The Japanese are so miserable. It is they who were defeated in the war." Today one no longer hears such songs.

At present, there are few chances for communication, let alone camaraderie, between the North Korean Ch'ongnyŏn and Japanese youth in K Machi. Both at the grade school and the high school levels, Ch'ongnyŏn children are mostly confined to their own school and to separate organizational activities even after school and on holidays. One does not find them playing casually in the streets or lots of K Machi. They are generally antagonistic toward others when they meet, and sometimes violence breaks out between the two Korean groups. Mindan and Japanese children going to the same schools congregate with one another. It is to be noted that Korean children tend to assume a dominant role over the less aggressive Japanese children. The Japanese children may feel prejudice against Koreans but usually do not express it because they fear the tough Koreans. Korean children, however, are defensive about their own negative ethnic images, of which they are well aware.

After leaving high school, many youths also leave the area to seek opportunity elsewhere or perhaps to escape the stigma attached to their ghetto. Those youths who remain usually seek intimate associations outside of K Machi.

Most of the Korean children and adults (but fewer of the Ch'ongnyŏn members) are likely to use Japanese names and try to pass for Japanese among strangers. Children in K Machi, as elsewhere in Japan, are given status ratings according to their school, not according to the afterschool lessons to which they are sent by their parents. K Machi children have less opportunity than other children in Japan to attend abacus classes or to take piano lessons. But even those not enrolled in these nonformal classes take part in the afterschool program at Gakuen or a few of the classes held at the village meeting house. The reason for their lower attendance is the parents' lack of income. Rather than indicating lack of interest, parents state that they cannot afford such extras for their children. Accordingly, the informal associations of K Machi are governed by economic considerations. Children are aware that they are not given the extras such as considerable sums for extra tutoring which middle-class parents can provide.

What one notes today among the Ch'ongnyŏn families in K Machi is their reluctance to consider repatriation. It must also be noted that more than 75 percent of those with a North Korean affiliation were born in Japan. They do not feel that it is realistic now to consider a return to their ancestral land. Therefore, increasing numbers are attending Japanese schools rather than continuing in separate Korean schools. They are aware that graduating from a Korean school ill prepares an individual for finding jobs, which are in any event difficult for Koreans to secure. Not attending Japanese schools sometimes can prevent one from acquiring the Japanese literacy necessary to obtain a driver's license. Less than half the children of the Ch'ongnyŏn faction still go to a Korean school. Stimulus toward higher education within K Machi is relatively low. The attitudes of Korean parents toward education are more characteristic of attitudes found in lower-class Americans than in Japanese, including the residents of Arakawa ward studied previously by Wagatsuma and De Vos (1977).

A considerable number of the Korean parents themselves are functionally illiterate. Although they are hopeful of their children's betterment, and express generally positive attitudes about the economic and social benefits of education, they feel that their own children could not possibly succeed through academic study. Chung gathered remarks such as "I don't really hope that my son will get good marks in school. It's really not useful for a Korean who lives in this society. I just hope he is physically tough and strong." Some children see school in terms of athletic achievement. They hope somehow to excel in sports. A number of the children have obviously negative attitudes toward school. Some of the latter are considered to be juvenile delinquents both by their teachers and by the parents of other children.

Teen-Age Tensions

We present here in disguised form some sketches of Korean youth whom Chung interviewed in their family context. One notes that the parents express considerable concern about the possibility of their children becoming delinquent.

Dong Soo was nine years old when his family moved into K Machi. He is now thirteen and goes to the local public junior high school. His family consists of his mother and younger brother, two years younger. His father died several years ago; his mother was born in Japan and speaks no Korean. Relatives living in K Machi arranged for the widow and her family to have a tiny residence of their own. They are of the North Korean faction and all associate frequently with one another. Dong Soo's mother does not wish to develop relationships with other residents in the village. She herself works in a Kawasaki bar as a hostess.

It was not too long after the family moved into K Machi that Dong Soo was initiated into stealing by some older boys. His mother broke off the association when she discovered what was going on. Dong Soo has not adjusted well at school. His teacher teases him as a pupil who needs a lot of individual attention, which she cannot always provide. He is generally rejected by his peer group. He has two nicknames, "Cockroach" and "Vampire." He explained to Chung how he acquired the nickname "Vampire": he sees himself as excitable. He gets angry when others call him something like "Chibi" (roughly, "Shorty"). He is one of the shortest boys in his class, actually shorter than his younger brother. When a schoolmate calls him a name, he jumps on that person and holds him down. Short as he is, he is proud to be tough. Once, when the classmates of a boy he was subduing came to the other fellow's rescue, he fought back by biting his adversaries.

His mother is very aware that her son has problems. She attributes them to the fact that when he was younger she had to work and was forced to leave her child under the supervision of acquaintances, some of whom she felt were inadequate. More recently, she has become concerned that her son is more acceptable to his delinquent peers than to more conforming children.

Chung observed that the mother herself tends to deprecate her son, noting that the mother compared Dong Soo with his younger brother, saying, "You are inferior to your brother." When Dong Soo approached his mother once, she reacted, "Why are you so pushy? That's why you're hated by everyone." Nonetheless, Dong Soo's mother maintains strong aspirations for him. She wants him to get ahead. She bought him a small Hammond organ that she hoped he would learn to play. At one point she hired a tutor to help him with his schoolwork. Dong Soo was not interested and resisted the discipline imposed.

Recently the mother seems to have given up ideas of improving Dong Soo. She says, "As he's so poor at everything, I've decided to provide him with more practical skills like learning the abacus." She has ordered Dong Soo not to attend the Korean church school run by Korean and Japanese young volunteers who are interested in overcoming ethnic discrimination. Rather, she wants him to practice the abacus. "You will not become a good adult if you can't master the abacus. You don't have to go to the church school because they are talking too much about things like discrimination and being a Korean."

Byung Chull is fourteen and also attends the local junior high school. His family consists of his mother and his younger sister. His father died in 1974. His mother runs a small general store that sells candies and necessities.

Their tiny house consists mostly of the store plus a back room. The family used to be an affiliate of the North Korean group but has recently switched to the Mindan to have Kankoku nationality.

At school Byung Chull uses a Japanese alias. He is tall and tough. He does not participate in any juvenile group but maintains a tense aloofness. Others do not quarrel readily with him. In his own neighborhood he assumes a leader's role with his peers, mixing with both Korean and Japanese. At home his mother trusts him and does not pressure him in any direction. He is allowed to take the initiative in his activities. At times he helps his mother with the store. His dream is to become an airplane pilot, so he is considering Japanese naturalization, since he recently learned that such a position would require Japanese citizenship. He now shows resistance to any attempt to call him by his Korean name. His mother's attitude is, "If he really wants to become a pilot I won't oppose his idea to take on Japanese citizenship, but I will never do that for myself. . . ."

Yun at sixteen is considered an adult by many. He works now as a daily laborer. At one time he was considered a "big shot" among the juvenile groups in the area. The family consists of his father, mother, older brother, and older sister; another older brother died in infancy. The family maintains a North Korean affiliation but is not active in political affairs. As a family they periodically attend music festivals and athletic meets held in neighboring Kawasaki. His father owns and manages a small construction company employing several Japanese and Korean laborers who live in K Machi.

Yun went to the Ch'ongnyŏn elementary school and later was transferred to the local Japanese high school. He was not a good pupil at either school. He used to cut his Korean classes and was known as a frequent truant. Despite the opposition of his Korean teachers, his parents transferred him to the Japanese school hoping that he would find it more difficult to be a truant. In his new setting, however, he quickly established himself as a leader among those resistant to school. He was recognized for his physical prowess. Despite some halfhearted attempts to learn, he could not overcome the disability of having an inadequate primary education in Japanese.

It is interesting to note that most of his followers were Japanese who were not located in K Machi. Although he used his Japanese name, he made no attempt to disguise his Korean background and was accepted by the Japanese because they recognized his leadership qualities. He took advantage of the fact that being Korean made him an object of fear by many of the Japanese school pupils.

Hostility developed between his group and a juvenile gang from the Korean school. Gang hostilities leading to violence between Japanese and Korean groups are reported with some frequency. As a leader of the juvenile gang at the Japanese school he experienced a crisis of loyalty. In one fight he reported to Chung that he heard one of his close Japanese friends say, "Let him fight alone with them." He fought on by himself and was seriously hurt by a gang of twenty-four Korean students who were armed with wooden swords. He maintained his relationship with his Japanese schoolmates after the event but said to Chung, "Since that time I cannot believe a Japanese." At present most of his friends are Japanese school dropouts who also work as laborers in the immediate area. He has several Korean friends who graduated from the Korean school. It is to be noted he has almost no acquaintanceship with anyone on the Mindan side. . . .

Kil Ho is twenty-six years old. In the spring of 1976 he started his present job at a plastics shop run by relatives of the North Korean faction. Since starting his present job, he has given up the Japanese name that he had used for some time before. His family consists of his father, mother, and two younger sisters, who are also members of the North Korean faction.

He went to Korean schools and stayed until graduation from junior high. At school he had a good academic record and was considered an able athlete. He was, however, a loner. He did not participate in informal group activities and remained generally isolated from his peer group. As he recalls it, "The education at the Korean school was terrible. I hated school every day. They taught me too much about socialism."

He decided to transfer to the Japanese high school, a desire opposed by many in the Ch'ongnyŏn school and complicated by the reluctance of the municipal school officials to encourage any transfer from a Korean school to a Japanese school. Finally, Kil Ho entered what was considered a third-rate private high school in Tokyo, commuting every day. In Tokyo he used his Japanese name, disguising from others his ethnic background and his residence. He could not adjust well in the different environment of the new school. He commented, "Teachers were less strict there and the atmosphere was much freer than that which I experienced in the Korean school." Nevertheless, he was positively stimulated but found he could not follow the classes well because of his deficiency in Japanese. After one semester he quit and transferred to a Mindan institution in Tokyo. He had a couple of classmates with whom he previously had attended the Korean school. They became fast friends and spent their free time together when in Tokyo.

After graduation he went to Seoul, South Korea, having gained entry into a university there. It is relatively easy for Mindan-affiliated youth to enter a Korean university because of the special consideration they are given. Kil Ho was dubious, however, about the academic career in Korea, questioning whether the course work would be accepted by a good Japanese university. Halfway through his courses he quit, finding it impossible to follow the classes conducted in Korean. Finally, he returned home to K Machi in 1975, starting his work as a laborer in 1976.

In the past, Kil Ho's family associated for the most part with people from the Ch'ongnyŏn faction both in and outside their local area, but Kil Ho's family decided to drop out of the Ch'ongnyŏn, since they hoped to gain permanent resident status in Japan. They were motivated by a desire to visit their remaining relatives in South Korea. The family's relationships today are limited mostly to Ch'ongnyŏn people. Kil Ho's mother, for example, belongs to a local Mujin affiliated with the Ch'ongnyŏn, and his younger sister has recently married a youth active in the Ch'ongnyŏn. The family does not officially participate in any meetings of the organization but attends those of the Mindan when it is unavoidable.

Kil Ho is unhappy with his present job. He feels that he was committed to it by his family before he had made up his own mind. His present associations are limited to other employees of his workshop. He is rather reluctant to associate with any Ch'ongnyŏn members, although he has many acquaintances in the area with whom he studied at both the Ch'ongnyŏn and the Japanese schools. These relationships seem to him to be all in the past.

He once reflected that the best time in his life was his first year in Seoul. He earned some pocket money there teaching Japanese to Korean girl students. Contrasting that freer life with his present existence he says, "I had a lot of fun with Korean women then. Maybe that's why my present life seems so unbearable."

11

ON BOTH SIDES OF JAPANESE JUSTICE

Changsoo Lee and George De Vos

A number of cases in the Japanese courts involving minority Koreans dramatically illustrate the effects of discrimination. We have excerpted biographical materials from three cases covered in the daily press and in weekly journals in styles ranging from crass sensationalism to thoughtful discussion of the sources of delinquency and crime in contemporary social conditions. Discrimination can become a serious inducement toward a criminal career. Or discrimination can temper the character of an individual, strengthen his resolve, and induce him to take up a cause that results eventually in the support of others in the slow but firm establishment of enduring democratic institutions.

These cases not only provide glimpses into the positive and negative features of Japanese law enforcement but present the positive and negative features of contemporary Japanese journalism. On the one hand, the daily press can expose petty discrimination and arouse genuine sympathy for an oppressed person. On the other hand, a sensationalist press with crass monetary motives can manipulate the news, using shock tactics rather than educating its readers. Minority Koreans, both as defendants and plaintiffs, have tested the functioning of the Japanese court system. The results have been increasingly encouraging. Although the specific laws about citizenship for Koreans have not yet been altered, the court interpretations of existing general laws are tending more and more toward procedural fairness and respect for human rights. Discrimination among some Japanese police officers is another issue, as the following case illustrates:

THE MAKING OF A DEVIANT—JAPANESE STYLE: THE CASE OF KIM HI-LO[1]

The place was Shimizu city, Shizuoka prefecture; the date was 20 February 1969. A forty-year-old Korean, Kim Hi-lo, entered a cabaret carrying a rifle. He walked up to a table and shot two men. Subsequently, these men were reported to be part of the Inagawa gang, a local *yakuza* (or Japanese-type gangster) group controlling prostitution and gambling in the area. They also were known as loan collectors hired to intimidate those who did not pay up in time. Kim left the cabaret, drove quickly to a friend's home, called the police, and reported the killing to them. In a desperate, crazed state, he then drove his car to a nearby mountain resort area, entered the Fujimi Inn, and asked for a room.

What transpired afterward was clouded by a variety of interpretations of the actual events. Clearly, Kim was armed with sticks of dynamite, a shotgun, and a rifle. He again called the police to tell them to come and take custody of him. The police claimed that he held thirteen others hostage for eighty-eight hours. During the negotiations Kim made two demands and pledged to kill himself when he released the hostages.

His first demand was for a public apology from a local detective named Koizumi. Kim had witnessed a street fight between a Japanese and a Korean. Koizumi, a detective known for his anti-Korean attitude, broke up the fight, shouting at the Korean in a disparaging way, "You Koreans haven't done one damn worthwhile thing since you've come to Japan!" The form of "you" (temaera) used in Japanese was one of the lowest derogatory forms of address possible. This event witnessed by Kim symbolized for him the bitterness of his entire life.

His second demand was for a public announcement through the mass media that the killing of the two yakuza was part of his plan to end once and for all the unbearable harassment to which he had been subjected by underworld figures.

The press coverage of this dramatic eighty-eight hours was turned into a spectacle, a circus of excitement for the Japanese public. The television cameras were there, continually panning the surroundings of the inn with its large cordon of police. Utilizing Kim's request for direct contact with the press, the police finally captured him by disguising twenty officers as reporters who entered, supposedly to interview him. Indicted on several criminal charges, Kim was sentenced to life imprisonment by the Shizuoka district court after a series of dramatic trials lasting eight years. The Japanese Supreme Court, reviewing the case in 1975, upheld the lower court's decision. Kim is now serving a term of life imprisonment.

Kim Hi-lo's court testimony and his interviews with reporters illustrate forcefully how discrimination helps shape the direction of an individual's life. Throughout his contact with the public media, Kim was exploited to the fullest by those aware of the commercial value of sensationalism. His ordeal, however, also aroused the attention of thoughtful Japanese who saw beyond the particular events and the personal limitations of Kim's character. Some could understand Hi-lo's crazed but cogent protest. At times almost incoherent, it could nevertheless be interpreted as a poignant commentary on the effects of Japanese racism on a vulnerable and yet defiant man. During the ensuing trials, Kim's life was probed by the press from every angle. He willingly expounded how his accumulated bitterness had sought an avenue through public display. The shooting of the two yakuza was done during a climactic and explosive paroxysm of rage. Having gone the limit, he could expose freely what he felt about a society that could not grant acceptance and respect to those of Korean ancestry.

Like many Koreans in Japan, Kim Hi-lo has been called by more than one name. At various times he has answered to two Korean and three Japanese names. When Kim Hi-lo was only three years old, he suffered the loss of his biological father in an industrial accident. His dead father's family name was Kwŏn. His present family name, Kim, is that of his stepfather. At various times he has taken for himself the Japanese names of Kaneoka, Kondo, and Shimizu, just as at various times he has tried desperately to assume a Japanese identity.

There are conflicting reports as to the exact date of his birth. His oldest sister indicates he was born on 25 February 1927. The record kept at the Shimizu elementary school, however, reports that he was born on 29 October 1928. According to his *koseki* or family registration, he was born on 1 January 1927. Kim himself stated that the koseki was refiled after the war, since the records kept at Shimizu City Hall were destroyed by bombing. He himself claims that he was born on 20 November 1928, one of three children.

His father worked as a stevedore. One day while he was unloading lumber from a ship, the crane chain broke and his father was injured by falling timber. He died a few days later at a hospital. Together with three-year-old Hi-lo and her two other children, his mother soon settled in a small barrack-type house at the edge of town. She had moved away from her mother-in-law as soon as possible after her husband's death.

Koreans share with Japanese the tense mother-in-law/wife relationship. But the Korean woman is reported to feel more capable of moving out of an unhappy home situation, keeping her children with her rather than surrendering them to her husband. Korean migrants could not establish the solidity of patrilineage in Japan to the same degree as in Korea itself. Also, most Korean migrants, being of lower social status, were less motivated by strongly held concepts of lineage.

To eke out a living, Hi-lo's mother bought a small cart and traveled about as a ragpicker. Some of Hi-lo's early memories are of the teasing he endured from other children. When he was about five or six he often accompanied his mother as she pushed her cart through tiny alleys, looking for refuse. She still wore her Korean-style dress, and small children would taunt them about his mother's odd dress. Sometimes they threw pebbles or stones at them, along with ridicule about "dirty Koreans." Surrounded by poor Japanese, they had little social contact in their own neighborhood. Though also impoverished, their neighbors looked down on the sprinkling of Koreans living among them.

His mother had come to Japan when she was eighteen. She had known

Hi-lo's father before his signing up on a work crew to dig the long railroad tunnel at Tanna that was to become part of the main Tokaido line between Tokyo and Osaka. He worked on one of the many Korean labor crews recruited to help build the Japanese railroads. Attitudes held toward these Korean crews were not too dissimilar from those held by Americans toward the Chinese coolies recruited to build the Union Pacific Railroad.

When his father died, Hi-lo's paternal grandmother wanted him to stay with her, but given the choice he preferred to stay with his mother. Taken periodically to his grandparents' house, he would sometimes run away to his mother's home. When Hi-lo was seven, his mother was remarried to an old acquaintance of his deceased father. His Korean name was Kim Chong-sŏk, but he was known as Shimizu Fujitarō to the Japanese. Hi-lo well remembers crying at his mother's remarriage, fearing that he would lose her. He was reported to have said over and over, "Give me back my mother." His memory of his stepfather was that he was quiet but had an explosive temper. From the first they did not get along well.

Hi-lo remembers times when his stepfather would come home with angry complaints to his wife of how "Koreans are always getting paid less than Japanese, even for the same work." Periodically he would come home drunk; then his temper would be explosive. Hi-lo remembers his stepfather bitterly drunk and angry, venting his rage at his mother by overturning the small Japanese dinner table, or on another occasion throwing his cup of rice in her direction. Frightened by his stepfather's temper, the boy grew actively to dislike him. He withdrew from all but necessary contact with the stepfather.

Kim joined his older sister, Mieko, at elementary school. He had imagined that school would be a pleasant place to play with other children. He noticed, however, that his sister disliked school and would often come home crying. He did not realize why. When he was in the third grade, however, an incident occurred that he could never forget.

Much is said of how Japanese disguise competition whenever possible within their society. Japanese children, nevertheless, know full well that everything is subject to scrutiny and comparison. Impoverished, Hi-lo's mother economized on what she provided for school lunch. The price of polished rice was high. Hi-lo took with him a ball of barley packed around a pickled plum in an old, battered lunch box. The children at school carefully compared who received what for lunch and made covert observations to each other. One day two boys from obviously well-to-do Japanese families sat by Hi-lo as he ate his usual fare. They used the occasion to make cutting comments about Hi-lo's lunch box and its contents. Angered, Hi-lo struck back, beating at the two with his fists. The classroom teacher intervened but scolded only Hi-lo in front of the assembled class. Nothing was said to the Japanese boys about their provocation. Hi-lo felt severely deprecated and unfairly treated. After that incident, he was reluctant to go to school. His mother, hearing of the incident, tried to spend more on his lunches to encourage him, but his active dislike for the school and what it represented was permanent. If his mother provided money to buy school equipment, he would go with it to a candy store. He began to play truant. The teachers, noticing his frequent absences, called upon his mother. No one was able to persuade Hi-lo to continue. By the fifth grade he had dropped out.

Koreans, as a socially disparaged group, to survive will take on activities that are deeply despised by ordinary Japanese. Just as Japanese outcastes have taken on ritually impure tasks, Koreans in Japan have sometimes engaged in such noisome activities as raising pigs to enhance their incomes. Hi-lo's mother kept a dozen pigs in the tiny area in which they lived. It became Hi-lo's task to forage food for the pigs and periodically to clean out the pigsty. He and his sister scavenged leftover food behind local restaurants or went to the produce markets to pick up rotten and unusable vegetables. Coming home with their buckets of scraps, they were accosted by the children in their neighborhood with derogatory remarks about their savage and dirty natures. The neighbors knew well that the mother would sell the more acceptable parts of the pig but use the feet and other unappetizing parts for home cooking. Allusions were made to Hi-lo about his eating habits.

There is no way to transcribe directly the emotional impact of derogatory terms used toward Koreans. The word *Chōsenjin* sounds as strongly derogatory to Japanese and Koreans as does the term "nigger" in white/black relationships in the United States. It is often the intonation, not the word itself, that creates the derogation.

It is to be inferred that Hi-lo's mother had little time to supervise him. She was out daily with her ragpicking cart, eking out a living for her family. We do not get any direct impression from his testimony about his mother's reaction to his failure in education. We may presume that the mother herself felt some ambivalence about the school situation and what it represented; at any rate she did not force him to continue. She seemed totally unable to cope with any of Hi-lo's decisions by the time he was eleven or twelve. During the period of his increasing truancy, he went fishing or simply stayed about the house. Sometimes, however, he went with his mother, helping her with her ragpicking. An atmosphere of chronic family dissension was punctuated by increasingly frequent fights between his mother and stepfather, fights that Hi-lo did not enjoy witnessing. Home life became so unpleasant that whenever possible he would spend his nights at the home of someone else.

Hi-lo's family pattern strongly resembles that of many families with a delinquent child.[2] The child's strong sense of social resentment is not solely owing to the presence of external discrimination or, at least, is not simply a direct reaction solely to external events. Social discrimination deepens the sense of difficulty some children feel as a result of family tension and family supervision. The force of social degradation influences home life and, through its effects on parents, compounds their difficulties. Parents are less apt to maintain a socially cohesive household or to have the time and energy available for consistent supervision and discipline of the children. Tensions caused by their own impoverishment are reflected in anger and resentment that are sometimes displaced upon another. The child in such circumstances does not experience the consistent love of a parent; he is more likely to see the parent as inconsistent, angered, and antagonistic, if not self-destructive.

Hi-lo could feel no love or respect for his stepfather, nor could he feel that his mother exercised a consistent supervisory role. He certainly could find no model of mutual love and respect in the constant disharmony between his parents. All these family experiences combined with periodic sadistic teasing by his Japanese peers caused Hi-lo to develop antagonistic attitudes toward society. These attitudes were continually reinforced by an unfeeling, disparaging adult society that could see nothing but a negative destiny in store for its minority Koreans.

When he was about twelve, Hi-lo had a brief experience as a grocer's apprentice in Tokyo. A man who owned a greengrocery in Tokyo happened to visit Hi-lo's neighborhood in Shimizu. Learning of the idle youth, he offered him a job as a live-in shopboy at his market. This suggests that the old-fashioned Japanese custom of using apprentices from the countryside was still in existence in some *shitamachi* or merchant areas of Tokyo, where youths were characteristically brought in at age twelve and, in exchange for food and lodging, were required to work several years for a master. If the arrangement succeeded, the master had some implicit obligation to see to the welfare of his apprentice, including, perhaps, even inheritance of the business, should marriage take place with an eligible daughter. It is interesting to note that this shitamachi dweller was willing to undertake this type of arrangement with a Korean lad. As events unfold, however, his attitude toward the boy appears exploitative rather than directed toward making the boy a genuine apprentice.

It was Hi-lo's first time away from home. His life in Tokyo was strange and he found himself ill at ease with the people he met and the type of food provided him. One day his boss found him nibbling a piece of garlic that Hi-lo had picked up from the vegetable shelf. Like other Japanese mentors, the boss found no reluctance in chiding his apprentice. He pinched Hi-lo's cheek but went beyond a simple scolding for picking at the produce, saying by way of insult, "No wonder you Koreans always stink." Hi-lo felt betrayed and hurt. Accustomed from his early years to periodic wandering, he decided to run away. Managing to find his way through the complexity of the Shinjuku railroad station, he returned to Shimizu.

It should be noted that it is expected that Japanese youth will put up with some scolding on the part of mentors. A delinquency-prone youth, however, is less tolerant of frustration and may quit his job more readily out of a well-developed sense of resentment. With any minority youth, the provocations are more frequent. He has an easily justified sensitivity to unfair treatment that may go beyond simple resistance to authoritarian paternalism. The feeling of being not only unacceptable but unaccepted makes it easier for minority youth to resist authority and to rebel against those in charge.

It is characteristic of delinquent youths that they may try several jobs in rapid succession, finding none to be satisfying. Hi-lo obviously found it difficult to sustain himself through any adverse or frustrating situation. He worked in sequence at a furniture store, a candy shop, a dry-cleaning establishment, and a printing shop. He was only thirteen but had already started to drift about, staying away from home frequently, living a vagabond existence, finding places to sleep in railway stations or parks.

When he was about thirteen, he was picked up at the Shimizu railroad station by the police and taken for interrogation. The police, suspecting that he might be a delinquent, contacted his mother and requested that she come to the police station to take him home. Listening to his mother's Korean-accented Japanese and seeing her dress, the police knew she was Korean. Their attitude hardened. In his episode with the police, Hi-lo was to remember how their treatment changed for the worse once his minority identity was revealed.

As it is true of many individuals with low social status when thrown upon their own resources, Hi-lo was quick to identify himself as an adult wanting to take on an independent career. Not yet fourteen, Hi-lo decided to move away from home permanently, to go to some distant place where nobody knew him. We gain the impression that he wanted to pass, to give up being known as Korean, and to see what it would be like to pretend to be Japanese. He headed for Shimonoseki on the southern tip of the island of Honshū.

He got as far as the town of Ōmichi in Hiroshima prefecture on the Inland Sea. There he landed a job as a kitchen helper in a supply depot that served the Kure naval base. His job was on a small boat that transported food to the cruisers, battleships, or submarines lying offshore. The captain of the boat became fond of Hi-lo and wanted to take him on as a regular member of the crew. He therefore asked Hi-lo to send home for his koseki (family register) so that he could be formally registered. At that point the captain found that he could not legally hire him, since Hi-lo was not yet fifteen. The captain, with reluctance, had to ask him to leave. He paid him a back wage which was somewhat over the amount expected. Hi-lo had genuinely loved his job and had experienced for the first time genuine paternal affection from an older man. It was, most of all, an acceptance that transcended the fact that he was a "Korean" boy. He had enjoyed the intense, close relationship with the ship's crew and the fact that they considered him one of them. Had he been able to stay on, his life might have turned out differently, or so Hi-lo has felt in retrospect.

Hi-lo started back north. He arrived at Nagoya, where he chanced upon work as a porter in the railroad station. He had no formal lodging and was soon picked up for sleeping in the waiting room and was taken to the police station for questioning. He refused to reveal his home, since he remembered well what had happened when his mother was summoned to the station by the police. The Nagoya police searched him and found a cheap wristwatch. They would not believe that he had bought it with the wages he had received while working in Hiroshima.

Finally the police forwarded his case to the local juvenile court. He was placed in a juvenile home in Seto for temporary custody. While confined there, he reports, he was beaten by the custodians because it was discovered that he knew beforehand of the plotted escape of a fellow inmate and had not informed the authorities of it.

World War II had commenced by this time. All the inmates of the juvenile home were suddenly mobilized for work in the Nagoya shipyard as part of the "Youth Service Corps." They joined the inmates of prisons who were sent there under rigid surveillance. Despite the presence of many guards, Hi-lo managed to run away from the shipyard during a rest break and went back to Shimizu, where he was quickly informed that the police had been notified and were looking for him. His mother and stepfather had meanwhile moved to Kumamoto on the southern island of Kyūshū to work as laborers in airfield construction. His aunt suggested that he would be safe if he joined them there. She prepared some clothes and gave him sufficient money for the trip.

The Korean laborers in Kumamoto lived in barracks. He was quickly given the task of carrying lunch boxes, distributing them to the laborers in the field. He also worked pushing carts of dirt away from the leveled airstrips. Hi-lo considered himself an adult in every respect and became interested in women. He had met a pretty girl two years his senior who was of Burakumin (outcaste) origin. They often went to movies together.

One night, while coming back from a movie, the young woman was stopped in the street by three burly men who seemed to know her quite well. She later told Hi-lo that they were hoodlums who had escaped from the conscripted labor camp at the Yahata Steel Company in Kumamoto. When they began to harass her for going to a movie with a stranger, Hi-lo tried manfully to intervene and to explain that he and the girl were good friends. One of the men suddenly struck him over the head with a bike chain. He returned home with a bloody forehead, which his mother treated with a home remedy made of bean paste as a means of preventing infection. No doctor was called since they were hard to find, even for those financially able, because medical personnel had been conscripted for the war effort. He still retains a scar because no surgery was performed to close the open wound.

Otherwise, Hi-lo found life at Kumamoto boring. He could not escape involvement in the intense and frequent quarrels between his mother and stepfather; sensing that by now he would be safe from the police in Shimizu, he returned to his old home.

At this point Hi-lo for the first time began activities that would classify him as a true delinquent. Entering a candy store, he noticed that a woman's purse had been left unguarded. He picked it up and left, but he had been observed. The police quickly apprehended him and he was placed in a juvenile home. He was kept there from 1943 to August 1945, when World War II came to an end. Even within a juvenile institution, Hi-lo was to be reminded of his Korean minority status. He had first been placed in a home that was only for Japanese. When his identity was established, however, he was quickly sent to a segregated institution, the so-called Mutual-Love Educational Institution (Sōai Gakuin) located in Tokyo.

There were about eighty Koreans and three Taiwanese inmates in the juvenile hall, which had no rehabilitation program. Instead all were put to work. They wove canvas cloth to cover aircraft and worked on lathes to manufacture tiny screws used in the fusilages of Zero fighters. Hi-lo remembers the intensification of the B-29 bombing of Tokyo, when work was periodically suspended so that the inmates could take refuge in air raid shelters. When Hi-lo saw the Japanese interceptors shoot down a B-29, he was overjoyed, and so were the other Korean inmates. They too hated the Yankee red devil. The irony was that Hi-lo felt himself to be part of the Japanese war effort, no matter how much he was discriminated against as a Korean. When the Emperor announced the nation's surrender over the radio, Hi-lo, like many others, cried with chagrin at Japan's loss.

By this time Hi-lo was eighteen. Set free after the surrender, he returned to Shimizu. He joined his family at nearby Kakegawa, the site of a tunnel construction built to house a huge underground factory for the Nakashima Industry Company. The Korean conscripted laborers dispersed after Japan surrendered, looking for whatever jobs they could find in the economic disarray that followed the surrender. Hi-lo was not reluctant to enter the burgeoning black market. As did many others, he went out to the countryside to buy rice to resell at illegally high prices. Subsequently, Koreans were charged with carrying on the black market, as if there had been no Japanese involvement.

During this time, he met a young woman named Itō Sawako, three or four years older than he. Again, this memory of the young woman was later associated with his masculine intervention in a conflict: she was being troubled on the street by a drunken Japanese. Hi-lo drove him off, and he and the girl became close friends. Hi-lo, throughout the telling of his life history during his trial, liked to take the role of rescuing people from bullies. It must be noted that the dramatic episode that brought him to public prominence was his demand for an apology from a police officer, not for something that had been said to him directly but to another Korean who was being disparaged by an offensive remark. Hi-lo liked to see himself as protecting others. He saw this trait as distinct from that of retaliating for injuries that he had suffered.

Hi-lo and Sawako's friendship deepened into love. He went to his mother, requesting her permission to marry. His mother was against it, citing that the young woman was older than he and that he was not yet twenty himself. It must be noted that neither Koreans nor Japanese feel free to marry without parental approval; but in lower-class groups, a young couple may set up living arrangements together. In this instance, Hi-lo and Sawako began to live together. In his autobiographical remarks, Hi-lo stated that with Sawako he tasted the sweetness of life for the first time. He spent on her everything he made from his black-market activities, but overreaching his means, he fell into debt.

Short of ready money, he began to swindle his steady clients. He took money without the ability to deliver the promised goods, and it was not long before someone informed on him and he was picked up by the police as a swindler. He was indicted and tried by a local court and sentenced to two years for embezzlement, with four years of additional probation. Again, it must be noted that the social attitudes and character of Hi-lo led him into difficulty. One must distinguish between delinquency and the compounding of a delinquent career by the natural resentments stimulated by discrimination. Not every Korean who experiences discrimination also manifests what can properly be termed delinquent attitudes. Hi-lo found it hard at this point of his career to set limits that would prevent his getting into difficulties with others. It must be noted that those he swindled were not only Japanese but also fellow Koreans. In effect, Hi-lo was heading toward a criminal career in which he felt it possible to dupe others or to keep their money without repaying.

Even faced with a criminal term, Hi-lo reported that his outlook on life was brightened by the assurance that his girlfriend would be waiting for his return. They promised each other to marry immediately upon his release. For a time she kept in close touch with him, but after he was transferred to a more distant prison, her visits became progressively less frequent. Through another inmate he learned that his girlfriend had married another man. This news was so shocking that he refused to believe it for a considerable time. To confirm or disprove the story he began to plot escape. The authorities, sensing his attitude, transferred him repeatedly from one prison to another. He was finally set free in November 1949, after having served three years and three months in prison. His sentence had been prolonged by his uncooperative attitude.

As soon as he was released, he set out to look for Sawako. No one seemed to know her whereabouts. He finally located her and found that she had married a policeman. The marriage had been arranged by a police detective who was working at the station where he was first arraigned. As she was visiting Hi-lo frequently while he was detained, the police detective had become interested and arranged a marriage for her with another policeman after Hi-lo was finally sent away.

Furious at the discovery, Hi-lo decided to kill her. He hid a kitchen knife in his clothes and approached her house. He saw her from a distance sweeping the ground and cleaning up about the house. She looked happy and contented. He felt deep pain and self-pity, but his hatred had evaporated. Instead of externalizing his anger, he became depressed. He decided to take poison and end it all. He was found unconscious by his sister and taken to a hospital. Given antidotes, he recovered. This incident occurred only forty days after his release from prison.

Not long after leaving the hospital, he was picked up again by the police on a charge that he had failed to return an overcoat borrowed from a neighbor. It is uncertain whether he was framed, but it was obvious that the police had kept him under surveillance and were looking for an opportunity to arrest him. He gave open expression to his bitterness—so much so that the police were taken aback. All the staff at the Kakegawa police station knew what had happened with his girlfriend. According to Hi-lo's story, the police chief there actually became sympathetic and even tried to calm him down, saying, "But now it is too late: she is already married. What can you do? Try to forget it!" Even though detained on a formal charge, he received special treatment. The police saw to it that he received meals from home instead of the ordinary food for detainees. During the day he was allowed to walk freely inside the police station. Hi-lo reported that the police felt that he had no intention to escape. He was even allowed to leave the jail and to go out to a nearby restaurant upon his promise to return in the evening.

His truce with the police was broken, however, during the investigation when the chief criminal investigator remarked that, "After all, it was you who took someone else's girl." Deeply incensed by the remark, he did not return to the police station the next time he was let out.

It may seem to the reader a curious type of interrelationship here between the police and Hi-lo. It may well be that the police suddenly felt touched by the unfairness of the situation, and once this attitude prevailed they began to treat him differently. Japanese are personally very concerned with "sincerity." In Japanese law, equity is important. Despite what we see here of discriminatory attitudes toward Koreans generally, individual Japanese may be so touched by the intensity and sincerity of a person that they may permit relaxation of the usual security measures at a police station.

This incident has some further interesting aspects to it. After Hi-lo left the police station, he visited an old Korean friend who had also served some time in prison and was part of a local Choryŏn left-wing political organization. When Hi-lo told the friend that he had left the police station, his friend arranged for him to stay overnight at a house of prostitution and paid for the female company he was provided.

The police waited until morning to surround the house and asked for his quiet surrender. He was taken back to the police station without handcuffs or any other form of coercion. On the way they passed the barber shop whose owner had accused him of not returning his overcoat. Hi-lo smashed the window of the shop, shouting at Nakamura, the owner, "You liar! You framed me!" The man rushed out, stating, "That's not true! It was the police who stopped by and asked me to sign a paper. That's all I did. If I had known, it would not have turned out this way. I would not have done it."

By now the police were thoroughly embarrassed by the whole episode. The police chief told Hi-lo, "When you go to the prosecutor's office, don't tell anybody that you were allowed to go in and out of jail while you were detained. Just tell them that you tried to escape when the guard left his sentry post momentarily. We'll take care of everything else later." All charges surrounding the incident were later reduced to that of simple escape.

As Hi-lo continued to recount his special relationship with the police, one could begin to question the truth of much of his story. It became at times quite fanciful and one could begin to see it more and more as a demonstration of bravado, at least the parts dealing with his relations with the police. Hi-lo wanted others to view him as a somewhat daring, forceful person, and he wanted to give the impression of the Japanese police as unfair or, if friendly, somewhat devious in their relationships with him.

In the course of these stories about his relationships with the police, Hi-lo described other scenes in which a friendly policeman tipped off his mother about the coming of a tax inspector. The mother, at the time, was engaged in illegal candymaking and was also brewing a bootleg white rice wine, called in Japanese slang *doburoku*. He cited this friendliness as part of the reason for his silence about police activities that eventuated in a two-year prison sentence.

On 20 March 1950, Hi-lo, aged twenty-three, entered Hamamatsu prison to begin serving his sentence. He soon got into trouble with three Japanese yakuza, who ridiculed him for being Korean. As he described it, he grabbed them and threatened to kill them with a razor blade. The fight came to the attention of the authorities, and Hi-lo was given an extra four months' time. He was sent to Fuchū and later transferred to Niigata prison. At Niigata he first met members of the Inagawakumi, a yakuza group, two of whose members he later killed.

After his release, Hi-lo returned to Shimizu and began frequenting a sake bar called Osato. It was a typical, small Japanese bar with two or three hostesses serving drinks to men. One day he ran into an old friend who had served time with him at the same juvenile detention institution. This old crony had previously told him that his girlfriend had married the police officer. The two had a nostalgic reunion and went on a drinking binge that stopped only when they ran out of money. Realizing they were dead broke they decided to rob a taxi. Hi-lo had obtained a gun from another friend. Use of a handgun is highly illegal in Japan, and Hi-lo's use of a weapon attests to the fact that he had taken a thoroughly antisocial stance. His crony asked for the gun. They stopped the first taxi passing by, got in, and held up the driver. They were soon picked up by the police.

This time Hi-lo was given eight years for armed robbery and illegal possession of a weapon. In September 1952, he entered Chiba prison. As he described it, for the first year and a half he was belligerent, but then he underwent a change of heart. He began to reflect on the fact that it was his own ignorance that had caused the Japanese to look down on him. He had an urge to improve himself. He obtained from the prison library a dictionary and spent his free time learning to read rather intellectual journals, such as *Chūōkōron*. During these seven years in prison he claimed he even learned to write poems. He was released from prison in February 1959 at the age of thirty.

The Ise peninsula had just been damaged heavily by a typhoon. Many Korean laborers were employed for reconstruction, and Hi-lo also found work. He met a young woman, Kanemoto Junko (*Kane*moto, written with the same character as "Kim" in Korean names, is frequently used by Koreans who Japanize their names). His mother again objected to a possible marriage, since the young woman had been divorced by her previous husband after only six months of marriage. Such a rapid divorce is a highly disgraceful act, but as Hi-lo described it, knowing full well that he himself bore the stigma of an ex-convict, he was not one to worry about what was considered "disgraceful" by others. Despite his mother's objections, he determined to marry and had a Korean-style ceremony performed. The couple moved into a rented room Hi-lo had found.

An aunt who was the sister of Hi-lo's dead father ran a small grocery in Shizuoka city, and the newlywed couple started to work for the aunt in her grocery store. It was not long before trouble developed. His wife and aunt both had strong personalities and could not avoid quarreling. As Hi-lo described it, they attempted to drag him into their quarrels, which he avoided as much as possible. From the description he gave of his wife, she was not in the least interested in domesticity. She liked ballroom dancing and began to frequent a dance hall during the day while Hi-lo worked.

When he warned her to refrain if she cared anything about saving her marriage, she quickly responded that she did not concern herself about his attitudes; if he did not like what she did she would find another man. Soon thereafter they had another serious argument, whereupon he told her to leave. He also took his own belongings and moved to Hamamatsu, where he met Katō Kazuko, a young woman who had run away from home and had just been stopped from a suicide attempt by the innkeeper of a small hotel where she had taken a room. Hi-lo attempted to cheer up Kazuko. He so successfully cajoled her out of her depression that they began to live together.

Hi-lo described dramatically how one day she reached into his pocket and found his alien registration. With tears in her eyes, she said in a dismayed tone, "You are Korean!" Surprised and disappointed, he said, "If you dislike Koreans so much, let's split." She said, "Well, since we're already involved, how can we?" She announced to her parents that she was in love with a Korean and that they should try to understand the situation. They settled into life together.

It was not long before Hi-lo got in trouble again with the police. The young son of a wealthy contractor, driving a sports car, ran over the elderly father of a friend of his. Hi-lo was angered to hear that the young man refused to take any responsibility or pay compensation for the injuries incurred, claiming that the old man had jumped in front of the car and therefore it was not the driver's fault. Hi-lo intervened and "persuaded" the car owner to pay 7,000 yen compensation.

Meanwhile, Hi-lo had begun to go hunting with a friend and had borrowed a double-barreled shotgun, which he carried in his car for a few days. He happened to stop by the police station to see about some money he had lost out of a wallet. The chief criminal investigator recognized him and told him he was under arrest because a charge had just been filed accusing him of intimidation. Hi-lo tore up the warrant and said, "You can't arrest me for that." The police replied, "We'll arrest you for the destruction of an official document." Hi-lo impulsively took a small jackknife out of his pocket, which somehow had not been confiscated by the police, and as a means of protest he cut into his stomach and then slashed his wrist. His blood poured out upon the floor of the police station.

According to Hi-lo, suddenly the police investigator said, "OK, we understand you. Let's not talk further about arrest." But Hi-lo challenged the police to arrest him. The police chief appeared and told him not to be emotional. "We'll call all the parties concerned and settle the matter tomorrow. For now, go home." After Hi-lo had his cuts patched up, the police returned the shotgun, which they had confiscated on the charge of illegal possession of arms. Hi-lo did not reveal to his mother his problem with the police when she asked about the patch on his stomach. He told her he had been in a fight and had been stabbed.

Not long after this, Hi-lo was charged with intimidation and was incidentally found to be in illegal possession of a shotgun, which he had borrowed from a friend for a hunting trip. According to Hi-lo, the police dropped the second charge, which seems improbable in the light of Japanese attitudes about firearms. Through his long recounting of this and other incidents we shall not repeat here, one sees that Kim Hi-lo had developed a personal relationship with some of the police, so much so that they were indulgent with him on relatively minor transgressions. One might almost infer that Hi-lo wanted to believe they had developed a liking for his open style and "gutsy" behavior. If so, it was a rather peculiar relationship based on such continuous contact that, in a sense, he had developed immunity from minor harassments. But he found himself in one large difficulty after another. It almost seemed impossible for Hi-lo to stay out of trouble for more than a few months. He repeatedly got into difficulty and ended up in prison. This kind of criminal career has psychological meaning and has been reported with some frequency among American prisoners. Certain individuals cannot tolerate staying outside prison but become habituated for one reason or another to a type of prisoner role. Kim Hi-lo, by his own recounting, continually became involved in illegal acts. He made it impossible to continue a stable relationship with a woman. He challenged fate as well as society and its police. He flaunted activities that he knew would cause imprisonment.

After he had been convicted of intimidation and sent back to prison for two years and six months, Hi-lo asked himself, "What am I becoming? What am I living for? I claimed to be a self-taught man pretending to know something, but did I have any skill that would allow me to make an honest living?"

This time while in prison he determined to become an auto mechanic. He learned that to be qualified as a mechanic he would need a minimum of junior high school education and that he would have to pass a national certifying examination. Developing a burning desire to learn, he contacted the proper officials and had himself placed in a special program to receive education bringing him up to a junior high school level. The prison even agreed to create a special course in auto repair.

The prison authorities, noticing Hi-lo's diligence, reported him to be a model prisoner. He himself had the thought, "I can be rehabilitated." He studied every spare moment in his cell. He described how nervous and scared he was before taking the exam. Because of repeated truancy and dropping out of school early, he had only the equivalent of two or three years of grade school education. He managed to pass the national examination and was issued a certificate by the Ministry of Transportation. He quoted himself as thinking at that time, "I shouldn't be discouraged by being a Korean. Anybody can do it if he tries hard."

Released from prison in September 1965, he opened a restaurant with Kazuko. She ran the restaurant while he sought a job as an auto mechanic. He also attempted to get a license to drive a truck van and enrolled in a truck-driving school. He had taken the precaution in prison to have a clerk record his permanent residence as Japan rather than Korea because he had anticipated difficulty in finding work if it were known that he was Korean. On his mechanic's certificate issued by the Ministry of Transportation, however, his Korean name had been set down. When he tried to find a job he discovered, as he put it, that "no one seemed to be interested in hiring me." He did not know whether it was because he was known to be an ex-convict or because he was Korean. After a few months' failure he gave up the idea of a mechanic's job and from then on worked behind the counter in his restaurant.

Fortunately, a number of his Japanese friends and some neighbors began to patronize the restaurant. Business picked up. It became a known place, so much so that a few local yakuza showed up to throw their weight about. One of the Inagawagumi asked, "Aren't you Korean?" Hi-lo replied, "You are here for a drink, aren't you?" The yakuza did not respond to him but instead turned to a guitar player nearby and shouted at him, "It's too noisy. Stop playing." A woman listening nearby responded, "He's playing for us. Don't disturb him." The yakuza grabbed a glass of beer and threw it in her face. The beer splashed over the man playing the guitar. The guitar player clenched his teeth and was about to explode. Hi-lo came from behind the counter, grabbed the neck of the yakuza, and dragged him off to the police station, where he was released the following day since Hi-lo had not pressed any charge.

A few days later several other yakuza came by. Interestingly enough, they attempted no intimidation. Some others that Hi-lo knew told him how the yakuza would come to a store and extort money, suggesting that if they received no payment they would cause trouble and spoil the owner's business. Hi-lo suggested that they go to the police. They replied that the police would do nothing in these cases. It seems likely that the yakuza saw that Hi-lo was not to be easily intimidated and attempted no further pressuring. Instead they came and would meet at his restaurant for a snack. In effect, they decided to become friendly.

At this point in his story, Hi-lo describes how as a small child he had read stories of premodern yakuza like Shimizu no Jirōchō. For the Japanese, Shimizu no Jirōchō is a romantic figure, a Robin Hood who protected the weak and took from the strong. Such figures are periodically seen as heroes in the modern Japanese cinema, but as Hi-lo put it, "The yakuza nowadays only exploit the weak and kowtow before the strong. They blackmail those who are vulnerable. Since I knew the yakuza world well, I hated them."

Once, while a yakuza group were drinking at his bar, one of them asked Hi-lo to pick up a package from his car, parked not far away. When Hi-lo reached the car, which was unlocked, he noticed that a rifle and shotgun were lying inside it. For safekeeping he brought them back to his restaurant. The yakuza thought of this as a considerate act, became very friendly, and began to patronize his restaurant regularly. Both his wife and mother warned him not to get involved as the visits became more frequent. Often when the yakuza came they would not have sufficient cash and would ask for credit. Sometimes they even asked Hi-lo to fix them up with girls. Hi-lo now and then witnessed them brawling at some other place, episodes that would bring in the police.

The yakuza became so friendly with Hi-lo that they would stop in at his home, where he had a tiny bar set up with a few bottles of Western whiskey. Now and then they finished a bottle together. Then they were always noisy and boisterous, and Hi-lo would put them up if they got too drunk to navigate. He would then go and notify their families that they would return safely in the morning.

Hi-lo does not suggest it directly in his reminiscences, but one certainly gets the impression that he was ingratiating himself with this group and seeking some kind of camaraderie with them. The details of his story belie his statement that he continued to hate and despise them throughout. Soon he was hunting with them. Hi-lo himself did not own a rifle, but he would be loaned one to go on trips for wild boar or birds. Hi-lo enjoyed the sport and decided that he too would seek permission to own a hunting rifle. He went to the local police chief, who knew him well by now, and asked for an application for a hunting gun. The police chief responded that since it was so soon after his release from prison, he should wait a bit. Some months later he again approached the chief, who assured him he would issue a license provided Hi-lo passed a qualifying examination. He signed up for a class and submitted a certificate showing that he had completed a course in firearms. He had already illegally bought an American-made .22 rifle under the name of an acquaintance who had the necessary license. Hi-lo states he assumed that it would be all right, since he had been assured that he would eventually get his own license. But after he submitted his formal application, several days went by without any response. He then went to see the chief, who told him that a license now looked unlikely because the report had gone out that Hi-lo had become too closely associated with local yakuza since his release from prison. The application remained pending. Hi-lo then told the police chief, "Well, I've already purchased a rifle." Whereupon the police chief, according to Hi-lo, said that he would unofficially acquiesce to his going hunting, but that he would have to wait a bit longer for the official license. In his account, Hi-lo explained at length how he cultivated the acquaintance of the police chief by giving gifts such as pottery, Korean ginseng (a medicinal root), and other goods.

Hi-lo began to experience domestic difficulties. His common-law wife evidently had some physical defect that prevented her from bearing children. (He mentioned en passant that he had made another woman pregnant and that she had had an abortion. It seems likely that he mentioned this other impregnation to affirm that he was indeed virile and that it was not his fault there was no issue from his common-law relationship.) As a consequence of this concern, they decided to break up. The thriving business was sold and his wife went back to her mother, taking with her all her belongings. What remained of their joint household was sold for whatever price they could get.

As he put it, ten years of effort to straighten out his life went down the drain. He became depressed, felt hatred for the world in general, and bought potassium cyanide. Determined to kill himself at some distant spot where no one knew him, he set out for the island of Kyūshū with a few clothes and the bottle of poison. (He stated in an aside that he did not have a driver's license.) For ten days he drove about trying to work up the courage to kill himself. He failed, finding that he still had some deep attachment to life. He drove to Shimizu, dropping into a cabaret owned by a fellow Korean. On the stage a girl was singing a song called "Stepsisters." The sad melody remained in his mind. Although he usually avoided drinking, that night he had several drinks. He requested several songs from the singer. Finally she sat down at his table for a personal talk.

Here Hi-lo digressed to say that he really hated drinking; that the image of his drunken stepfather had been a lifelong deterrent. He also mentioned how just a glass of beer or two so reddened his face that he was embarrassed. (This is a common Japanese concern; indeed, it is noticeable that there is an immediate capillary reaction to alcohol in many Japanese or Koreans.)

He learned the young woman was from the rural north and had landed the job as a cabaret singer through a friend. She was already being harassed by the Inagawagumi yakuza. Hi-lo at first felt just friendly concern, but then he began to visit her apartment, where he noted the contrast between her shabby little place and the attempted glamour of the cabaret. Feeling pity, he bought her new bedding, an electric fan, and a few articles of furniture. Soon he was living with her.

At this point, Hi-lo's life approached its tragic climax. It was July 1967, around 8:00 P.M. He happened to pass by a large crowd and witnessed police intervention in an altercation. A police officer shouted in crude, disparaging Japanese, "You Koreans haven't done one damn worthwhile thing since you've come to Japan." Hi-lo turned around and saw in the crowd a distant cousin of about seventeen or eighteen and another acquaintance, a young man of twenty-two. He asked them, "What are you doing here so late? Why don't you go home?" The policeman glared at him. Hi-lo asked one of the young men leaving the crowd, "Who's that detective?" "He is Koizumi." Hi-lo recognized the name of a detective notorious among Koreans for harassment. He left the scene with his Japanese friend, Aogi. They stopped at a small Korean restaurant-bar, where Hi-lo decided to call the police station.

He asked for Koizumi, who was called to the phone. Hi-lo told him that he had overheard his remarks and felt they were inappropriate. Hi-lo described how his own tone of address was polite, but the response by Koizumi was simply to state as crudely as possible, "You beastly Koreans deserve what I said." An argument developed over the phone, and Hi-lo reminded Koizumi that the Koreans had been brought involuntarily to Japan during the war. The quarrel escalated and challenges were issued to talk it over face to face. Hi-lo was invited to the police station by Koizumi. He countered, "You talk big things, but you're scared to come out alone." He overheard laughter in the background at the station. Hi-lo threatened to "make a big issue of this. You just wait and see." Koizumi laughed and replied, "Do it. Do it by all means. I'll wait for you at any time with pleasure." Hi-lo hung up.

He was thoroughly inflamed and his sense of self was wounded by the disparaging treatment. He remarked that the police sneered at the Koreans as if they were animals. His patience was at an end. He felt like taking drastic action but, thinking of his mother and the girl with whom he was living, he also felt frightened and cowardly. He chided himself, "Why don't you do something against the police? How can we take such insults, as if all Koreans were subhuman?" Later he wandered about the vicinity of the police station, having put his rifle in the back of his car. He did not do anything.

He continued to feel tense and distraught. He had lost hope for any future. He had lost wife, home, and business. Wherever he went people called him "Korean" (chōsenjin). He remembered how his girlfriend had reacted with disappointment when she discovered he was Korean. With the detective's disparagement he had hit rock bottom. He felt that if he stayed in Shimizu any longer he would commit some irrevocable, desperate act. He talked it over with his new girlfriend. They packed their few belongings at his friend Aogi's home. Then he loaded his car with his rifle and about seven hundred rounds of ammunition hidden in a golf bag, and they took off for the north. He knew of a cousin who ran a *sushi* (rice topped by raw fish) restaurant in Akita. When he arrived with his girlfriend, he was made welcome. His girlfriend was put to work as a helper in the sushi restaurant, and he and his cousins looked about hoping to start a second enterprise.

Soon, however, he felt that the Akita restaurant was not for him and moved on again, going to Numazu and renting a tiny apartment. His girlfriend found a job at a local cabaret, and they spent about a month there. He was obsessed continually with detective Koizumi, whose image taunted him. Deciding that he should break up with his girlfriend, he told her that he was worthless, that he must leave her to do something important, and that he needed seclusion from the world. Instead of agreeing with his plans for separation, she said, "Why don't we go to the mountains together?" Having grown up in a rural area she felt ready for such hardship. They found a hut on a mountainside above Numazu, where they cooked their meals over a brazier and washed their clothes in a stream.

He described how they carried water together, he managing the heavier loads, and how he hunted for game with his rifle. After about two weeks he was visited by three acquaintances, who informed him that the Japanese forestry police were searching for someone who was hunting illegally. They warned him, "If the police find you you'll get into heavy trouble." They asked him to give up the rifle. Instead he decided to move out before he could be found by the police.

They went to his girlfriend's brother's place in Chiba, east of Tokyo. On the way there, his girlfriend lost her purse containing her brother's address. They spent a number of restless and indecisive weeks trying to settle down in a succession of towns. Hi-lo remained obsessed with detective Koizuma. His girlfriend found work in restaurants and cabarets, but Hi-lo, again hunting for a job as a car mechanic, again found only rejection. His girlfriend comforted him when he was depressed, and he began to feel that she was serious and really cared about him. As he put it, "Our relationship had developed to a point where I could not desert her without good reason. I found that she needed me as much as I needed her for my survival." In Yokohama, he placed a long-distance call home. His younger brother answered the phone and said, "Where have you been? Something serious has happened at home. Father killed Mitsubō [his grandson] and committed suicide."

Hi-lo had placed his call about ten days after the stepfather's suicide. It was 10 November 1979. He rushed back home with his girlfriend to find his mother in a state of shock. He offered incense to the portrait of his stepfather. He told his mother he was trying to reestablish himself in Yokohama. When he returned to Yokohama he found that his acquaintance there, Okumura, and four others had stormed into his tiny apartment looking for him in the middle of the night. They were angry about a check that had bounced. Hi-lo called back long distance to Okumura and found that he had cashed a promissory note before it was covered in the bank. This bank had requested that it not be cashed until the date posted. Okumura had cashed in to pay his debt to some yakuza. Immediately, when the yakuza heard about the bad check, they raised the amount they wanted from him from 100,000 to 150,000 yen. The yakuza found out who owed Okumura and said they would collect the debt for him. In this way they now saw Hi-lo as vulnerable to pressure. Negotiations ensued in which a yakuza named Soga entered the scene. The debt began to escalate. By this time Hi-lo was pressured to pay back 380,000 yen, and he signed a promissory note under duress.

Unexplained in Hi-lo's account is how this fairly small sum of 100,000 yen—then approximately $350—could become such an issue. What is evident, however, is that by postponing payment the promissory note escalated. This is a frequent occurrence in the loan shark business, which is one of the principal sources of income for Japanese hoodlums, as it had been for American gangsters.

There is no need to go into Hi-lo's very detailed account of subsequent events. Suffice it to say that he attempted counteraction against the yakuza. At one point, during an altercation, he shot his rifle in the home of one of the yakuza. They mollified him, asking him to talk it over. In an attempted reconciliation, Okumura was blamed for everything that had transpired.

Hi-lo's account does not clarify the ultimate extent of the debt, nor why the bill was not paid off. But after considerable action and reaction he signed another promissory note, this time for the 380,000 yen with no fixed date for repayment. Both sides sealed the agreement by eating sushi together. Okumura told Hi-lo that in the sixteen years he had known one of the yakuza in question, he had seen him pick up the tab only two previous times. In this instance it seems that the others were in some way also placating Soga.

On the way home Hi-lo began to reflect on what had happened. He felt somehow that he had been duped. Why had he signed another promissory note? At this point he fled to Aomori in the North with his girlfriend and lived there on some money he had taken with them. He had to send for additional money, since they were soon penniless. In February 1968 he received a letter from Soga, saying that he knew where Hi-lo was and demanding immediate repayment of the debt. The letter contained direct threats. Hi-lo saw no possibility of further retreat, so he determined to return and kill Soga. Along the way he equipped himself with some dynamite sticks.

Before the final confrontation, he stopped at his uncle's place in Shimizu. Hi-lo's uncle had also been harassed by Soga. The uncle's son had actually lost some of his fingers. Cutting off a finger or two is a disciplinary action taken against subordinates who for some reason are sanctioned by the gang. Another son of the uncle had been stabbed by the yakuza. Hi-lo did not provide details to explain how or why his relatives had become deeply involved with underworld activities, but we may infer that such involvement is common in parts of the Korean community.

The final showdown was in a cabaret. Soga was not aware that Hi-lo had armed himself for a final, desperate encounter, with dynamite sticks, a lead pipe, and his hunting rifle stashed in the rear of his car. When Soga met Hi-lo he evidently thought he was going to be paid. Two of his henchmen sat in a nearby booth; Hi-lo had told them before the meeting that someone was going to help pay off the debt.

Hi-lo and Soga both went into the toilet of the restaurant where, from a neighboring urinal, Hi-lo told Soga that unfortunately the money would not be available that day. Soga shouted in anger, "What do you mean, you beast? You talk like any other Korean!" Hi-lo remained quiet, but went out to his car and got his loaded rifle and thirty rounds of ammunition. He covered the rifle with a piece of cloth and carried it into the cabaret. A noisy band was playing on the stage as Hi-lo approached Soga's table. When he pointed the rifle at him, Soga showed no sign of fright. He shouted some expletives and reached for something at his waist. Hi-lo pulled the trigger twice. As Soga tried to stand up, Hi-lo shot him with the third and fourth rounds. He shot a fifth round as Soga fell dead to the ground. Two of Soga's henchmen, full of arrogance a moment ago, were cowering, seeking cover. Hi-lo stated that he had no intention of killing them, but he fired two or three rounds in their direction to wound them and scare them off.

As he left, approaching the cashier's counter, he realized that someone had already dialed police emergency. When several in the cabaret seemed to be trying to follow him, he shot some warning rounds and rushed out. He turned his car toward the nearby police station, not to surrender, but to have a final shootout. But realizing that the police had been notified, he did not want to be trapped in the middle of town where innocent people might be hurt if further shooting occurred. Instead he stopped at Okumura's house long enough to call the police himself, and then he headed out of town, listening to the radio reports of the deaths of two yakuza and bulletins of his supposed whereabouts. After a number of dramatic episodes, he finally arrived at the inn.

Hi-lo's account of the siege and his capture provides a clear picture of how the Japanese mass media used this traumatic situation for commercial purposes. Hi-lo documents how particular commentators and professional writers sought contact with him to exploit his story for their own financial gain. He depicts the police as self-protective and deceitful. A few honest individuals were genuinely concerned, but most betrayed any trust Hi-lo placed in them by rushing out sensational stories. Hi-lo is particularly bitter about a Christian minister by the name of Choe Ch'ang-sŏp, whom he cites as a typical example "of a Korean who sells his soul to the Japanese colonialists to advance himself for his own selfish ends." Korean publishers advised Hi-lo of the minister's plan to publish a book in Korea entitled *The 86-Hour Battle with Kim Hi-lo*; he did not hear about the plan directly from Choe. Hi-lo reports that Choe also accepted donations amounting to four or five million yen by setting up a letter campaign soliciting support and sympathy for the cause of Kim Hi-lo. Kim received little benefit from this campaign, although Choe periodically brought him some presents.

During Hi-lo's siege at the Fujimi Inn, the press reported his stated determination to kill himself after receiving the demanded apology and the media announcement. His mother sent him clean underwear. She expressed the hope that he would not blow himself to pieces in a messy manner but would try to die gracefully with a neat appearance. Kim was sincerely prepared to die. He made out his will in favor of his mother and his common-law wife. He gave his watch to the owner of the inn by way of apology for the trouble he had caused.

Kim was not to succeed either in obtaining an apology or in committing suicide. He was captured when the police, disguised as reporters, were let in, ostensibly for an interview. Handcuffed, he nevertheless managed to bite his tongue severely, hoping thereby to kill himself. In the court trial he described the scene immediately after he was captured:

The police forced me to open my mouth and gagged me with a police notebook. I heard somebody yelling to bring a big wooden bar, which they tried to put in my mouth. I was swallowing the blood. I hoped to die by excessive bleeding by the time I arrived at the police station. While I was handcuffed and gagged, someone kicked me several times. It must have been the police officers, not the reporters. I was thrown into a car like luggage. When the car started to move I noticed a man outside the car yelling, "Hey, Mr. Kim!" Someone in the car yelled, "Keep it moving! Keep going!" Then the man outside threw a stone. Someone shouted, "He threw a rock at us! He must be a damn Korean! Stop the car and let's get him!" I thought I should not let the police stop the car to arrest him, so I tried hard to loosen the handcuffs with wild motions so they would not try to stop the car to arrest this other guy. The car kept moving without a stop.

Later he states:

There is something I forgot to mention. After I bit my tongue to kill myself my mouth was so swollen I was unable to talk, and yet the police dragged me out of the jail cell and continued to interrogate me. According to the paper, it was reported that my wound was minor. However, I received medical treatment from three doctors. My chief defense attorney had a doctor's statement from the Shimizu hospital about my wound.... Despite the seriousness [of the wound] I was interrogated by the police throughout several days and nights, and yet it was reported by the police that the wound was minor.

Kim was quite aware that his siege at the inn had attracted worldwide attention. He was to receive letters, telegrams, and packages from all over Japan and Korea, and even from the United States. Many letters and telegrams were expressions of understanding and sympathy.

In part of Hi-lo's final testimony before the court, close to the end of a long account of press exploitation and police perfidy, he delineated his own character in idealized terms. He viewed himself as an aggressive, volatile, virile man, but above all as a human being sympathetic to the plight of others. His image of himself was closely modeled upon romanticized versions of the Japanese hero outlaws of the past, not those forming groups but the loners fighting oppression whether from the social establishment or from other yakuza. Hi-lo quoted Kazuko as saying, "He always stood by the weak and helped a lot of girls who were troubled by the yakuza. Helped by him, many girls fell in love with him or had sexual relations with him. But anyway, Hi-lo has done a lot of things to help poor girls. He always rebelled against the strong." He saw himself as having taken a heroic stand against majority oppression:

Having suffered from the misery of life in the past, I am glad I have loved people. Because I have been receiving letters from all over Japan almost every day, it reflects the feelings of the Japanese how they have had a distorted image about Koreans. It could be easily understood from the volume of letters arriving in the past two months.

Regardless of the reason I killed the yakuza, I admit that I've done wrong. There's no excuse for that. As I've said many times I'm willing to take the consequences. I'm ready to take full responsibility. I deserve to be punished. By so doing it is the only way the honor of Koreans and their pride can be restored. There are some Japanese, especially among police officers, who are still prejudiced toward Koreans. When I was interrogated by prosecutor Narita I asked him whether he knew how many Koreans were massacred during the Kantō earthquake. He said he did not know. Rather, he asked me whether such a thing had actually happened.

In effect Kim Hi-lo numbered himself among Koreans sharing collective memories of past Japanese atrocities. In his final moments of testimony he expressed the hope that this sad history could be reconciled through present understanding:

Some time ago there was a special issue in the *Asahi Shimbun* commemorating "Our One Hundred Years." One headline read, "Graveyard Without Name: The Massacre of Koreans in 1923." The number was estimated to be three or four thousand.

Another thing I did not learn even when I was at school was that Itō Hirobumi [the Japanese Prime Minister] was the man who engineered the annexation of Korea by Japan. I saw a picture of Itō dressed in a Korean costume, with the caption that a Korean had killed him, even though he tried to be friendly to Koreans by wearing their native garb. The prosecutor [Narita] was not aware that Japanese prejudice against Koreans had not been diminished. Many Japanese still think of it as natural. Even in this court, I'm sure so many of our Korean compatriots have had similar experiences.

I came to wonder about Japanese and why they look down on us. I have thought of what kind of people they are. I have almost come at times to feel hatred. But I have repeatedly denied myself this hatred. Even though I was insulted by a policeman, I would think I should not hate the Japanese because not all Japanese are like this policeman. Ever since childhood I thought somehow that Koreans were disliked. However, reading a variety of books recently, I could find of no wrongdoing by our people against the interests of Japan. I must tell you there is no reason for Japanese to hate Koreans or to discriminate against them as subhuman beings. . . .

If the Japanese were in our shoes, how would they think? Perhaps they can hardly understand our feelings, since they have never had the same experiences. It would be too much to ask. The long years of our hardship in Japan— I doubt whether they can understand it. Korea is physically the closest country to Japan. There should be some better understanding between our peoples.

Once I cried in my prison bed. It was after reading the special issue carried by the *Asahi Shimbun* commemorating "Our One Hundred Years." The pictures were shown in the newspaper—so many of my compatriots being killed by the police, just like pigs and cows slaughtered at the stockyards. I could hardly understand why *Asahi* carried such terrifying pictures.

Among the final words of Kim Hi-lo's statement were these:

Japan is my birthplace. I know no other language but Japanese. I don't know much about the history of my own country. My elders used to scorn me for not knowing proper etiquette and Korean manners. I am not Japanese but speak better Japanese than the ordinary Japanese. I am merely the deformed victim resulting from Japanese policy. I feel strongly about it lately. Just think of how they have treated us. Not long ago I received a piece of paper from the Minister of Justice, Okama. It was a "permit" for residence in Japan.... The document is a good illustration of how arbitrarily we are treated here from a legal standpoint. It is as if the piece of paper allows me to stay here. It is a legacy of the Japanese government which brought my parents to Japan as forced laborers. I certainly have a legal right to live here permanently.

In the case of the Chinese in Southeast Asia and many countries there, they enjoy citizenship just like any other native people. But in Japan we don't have any right of participation in elections. Because of a difference in nationality we cannot buy insurance. Neither are we able to establish credit to buy a home. We are discriminated in all means of livelihood. However, I don't want to bow my head down begging the Japanese government to allow me to stay here, because we have a wonderful country to which we can return.

But then I would like to appeal to the Japanese government, please give me back my national language. Dear Japan, please make me think and feel as a Korean. I would like to appeal to all of Japan. No one wants to go to jail leaving behind all his loved ones. But this is the time; I should be judged by the Japanese court. At the same time I would like to appeal to the Japanese conscience and place them under trial for their prejudice and bias in the same manner I am tried here at this court.

Our Korean people are a very thoughtful people. It was reported by a paper the other day [that] a Japanese who took care of war orphans died in Mokpo, Korea. Some forty-thousand people gathered to mourn his death. I was really moved. Despite hardship suffered at the hands of Japanese, the Koreans still appreciated the efforts of an individual Japanese who did something for humanity. I am very proud of our people.

Among those things said before this court are many events perhaps beyond anyone's comprehension. They may seem unbelievable. But I've given evidence to support my allegations. My intention has been to straighten out everything and present it as it happened, leading to what I have done. Finally, I must say that I admire my mother and that I am really proud of her. Thank you.

THE PRESENT LEGAL SEARCH FOR "HUMAN" RIGHTS

One of the genuine advances of the postwar period in Japan has been the development of a liberal tradition within Japanese law. The postwar Constitution promises civil rights and human rights to all in the nation. Family law has been altered to give equal rights to women. A Supreme Court has been established and the entire judicial branch of government has been strengthened. Genuine advances toward greater equity have been made through a series of significant court decisions. Among these have been decisions in cases involving Korean plaintiffs. To the credit of the Japanese press they have been reported in great detail and have gained sympathy for Koreans caught in dilemmas as they seek to preserve their ethnic identity with dignity. Much more briefly stated and not so dramatic as the case of Kim Hi-lo, they nevertheless illustrate how minority Koreans by their individual courage and integrity can effect permanent change in the direction of democratic equalization of opportunity. While all three cases in this chapter involve Koreans pleading for justice, the two less dramatic cases that now follow will have the more enduring impact on national life.

PAK CHONG-SŎK v. THE HITACHI COMPANY (1974) [3]

Pak Chong-sŏk, the plaintiff in this case, was born in Japan of Korean parents who migrated to Japan in 1929. Until he finished high school, he used his Japanese name, Arai Shōji, like many others hoping to advance occupationally through educational means. He neither speaks nor reads a word of Korean. In 1970, he responded to an employment advertisement by the Hitachi Company and applied for a job. He successfully passed the company's examination and received an official notice of hiring. As is customary in Japan, to complete his personnel file the Hitachi Company asked him to submit a certificate showing his koseki. It was then that the company learned of his Korean nationality. When Pak initially filed his application he had used his Japanese name and had put down his place of birth as Japan. He had intended to disguise his nationality, for he thought the Hitachi Company would not even accept his application if they knew of his Korean nationality. Legally, he should have used his Korean name as it appears on his alien registration card and the permanent address of his koseki to identify his national origin. A few days later, Pak received a letter of rejection from the Hitachi Company on the ground that he had committed perjury by providing false information.

Pak insisted that the perjury charge was merely an excuse for the company's discriminatory hiring policy. He decided to file a suit against the Hitachi Company, charging discriminatory hiring practices and the violation of his fundamental human rights. His suit was supported by a few mindful Japanese and Korean civil libertarians. Many young people began to gather around Pak in support of his lonely battle against one of the biggest business giants in Japan. They organized a group called the Committee to Support Pak Chong-sŏk and conducted an extensive campaign to mobilize public opinion to influence the judicial decision. During the three-year legal battle, this group was able to organize a very successful boycott campaign against Hitachi products by sending out letters to practically every known human-rights commission in the world. Hitachi and its subsidiary companies were extremely concerned with their image abroad, especially in Southeast Asia and Korea, where they had substantial investments. What Hitachi feared most was that the boycott, which had spread from Japan to Korea, would spread to other areas as well.

While the trial was still in progress, Hitachi privately made an offer to settle the dispute out of court. The company agreed to reinstate Pak with all back wages plus the monetary compensation he had demanded as retribution. Pak, however, rejected the offer, arguing that Hitachi had refused to acknowledge in public its discriminatory hiring practices against Koreans.

The dispute was finally settled by the court in June 1974. The judge read the decision that "the court finds no apparent reason, other than the factor of ethnic discrimination, why the defendant rescinded the contract to hire the plaintiff in the case." As to the plaintiff's use of his Japanese name, there was neither malignant motive nor any harm inflicted upon the contending party. Rather, "the court's sympathy rests with the motive of the plaintiff," because it was Japanese society that compelled him to act in the way he did to escape from discrimination against Koreans. Therefore, stated the judge, "the rescission of the initial hiring notice should be construed as an arbitrary breach of the labor contract, which was a violation of Article 3 of the Labor Standard Act and Article 90 of the Civil Code of Japan."

KIM KYŎNG-DŬK AND HIS PETITION TO THE SUPREME COURT

Kim was born in 1949 of parents of Korean nationality living in Japan. He graduated in law from Waseda University in 1972. Among several thousand applicants, he successfully passed the judicial examination given by the Ministry of Justice in October 1976. The passing of this examination is merely an initial step to becoming an attorney in Japan. The successful candidate is then required by the Lawyers' Law to complete a two-year training period at the Judicial Research and Training Institute operated under the Ministry of Justice.

The old Lawyers' Law was amended in 1955 to eliminate the "Imperial subject" clause formerly included in the list of qualifications for being an attorney in Japan. As there was now no specification regarding nationality, an alien technically had the right to become an attorney, provided that he or she followed the proper procedures prescribed by law. But the Judicial Research and Training Institute had since 1955 been admitting aliens only if they declared an intent to become a naturalized Japanese citizen. For Koreans in Japan, therefore, the question of nationality had been the factor precluding most from entering the law profession (see chap. 7).

Kim Kyŏng-dŭk, having successfully passed the examination, applied for admission to the Judicial Research and Training Institute. His application was summarily rejected because he refused to declare an intent to become a naturalized Japanese citizen. Kim considered the Institute's grounds for rejecting his application to be legally untenable since the Lawyers' Law, as amended in 1955, did not specify naturalization as a requirement for becoming a lawyer. The rationale for excluding aliens had been that during the two-year training period a trainee was paid by the Japanese government like any other regular government employee. Furthermore, trainees were required to serve apprenticeships under the close supervision of judges and public prosecutors. According to the official view, such an apprenticeship for a noncitizen would have been equivalent to appointing an alien to a Japanese government position.

Kim was determined not to declare an intent to naturalize even if it meant not becoming an attorney. To defend his cause, he decided to submit a petition to the Japanese Supreme Court in November 1976. He appealed to the conscience of the Supreme Court Justices, requesting that they accept him without forcing him to renounce his Korean nationality. He stated that he wanted to become an attorney to defend fundamental human rights, "I do not want to be a judge or a public prosecutor in Japan."

As the Korean population constitutes more than 85 percent of the aliens in Japan, there is an acute need for Korean attorneys to handle a wide range of litigation as well as issues of human rights. Kim argued, "Had I considered the issue as only my personal concern, whether or not I should become a judicial apprentice, I could have simply resolved it by declaring my intent of naturalization." He believed, however, that the issue at stake was the fundamental human rights of his 650,000 fellow Koreans in Japan; therefore, it was an "unthinkable" idea for him to resolve the issue by declaring an intent to naturalize. According to Kim, Japanese society had failed to ensure fundamental human rights for Koreans in Japan. Their human dignity and worth had been constantly threatened by deeply entrenched prejudice and systematic discrimination. He continued:

> Throughout the years of my life in Japan, I have hated myself for being a Korean and always tried to pretend to be Japanese. I don't know how often I have trembled with fear of having my real identity discovered by my peers. It has been an agonizing experience to go through. As I grew older, I began to realize what a fool I had been; my endeavor should not have been directed toward hiding my identity but [toward] fighting against discrimination and helping to protect the rights of Koreans in Japan.

His desire to become an attorney in Japan was, Kim said, an attempt to achieve these ends. Forcing him to declare an intent of naturalization as a condition for acceptance to the Institute was tantamount to demanding that he compromise his very reason for wanting to be an attorney. Kim doubted whether his fellow Koreans would have trust and faith in him, allegedly the protector of their fundamental rights, if he forsook his own identity to become an attorney. He also wanted to provide an example for many Korean youth who were undergoing identity crises similar to his, encouraging them to take pride in being Korean. As long as prejudice and discrimination against Koreans persisted, he stated, "I find no justification for declaring an intent to naturalize into a society in which my own rights are frequently denied."[4]

When the petition was filed on 20 November 1976, the Japanese Supreme Court was greatly surprised. In the past, there had been ten alien applicants to the Institute, eight Koreans and two Taiwanese, all of whom had accepted the condition of naturalization without protest. The Supreme Court hastily solicited legal briefs from various agencies, including the Ministries of Justice and Foreign Affairs and the Japanese National Bar Association. In the meantime, concerned civil libertarians rallied behind Kim Kyŏng-dŭk and supported his cause. It took four months for the Court to deliberate on the matter. On 23 March 1977, the Supreme Court finally issued a very short statement, "In the case of Mr. Kim, nationality would not be a factor to deny admission to the Judicial Research and Training Institute." The Court refused to elaborate any further, however, as to whether its ruling would apply to all aliens in Japan. Later the president of the Japanese National Bar Association stated that the ruling should be construed to apply only to the case of Mr. Kim as noted by the Court. The legal question concerning the general eligibility of aliens to become attorneys has not been resolved but awaits further clarification in the courts.

Nevertheless, these two cases are landmark decisions, as the judicial authorities have now admitted the existence of legal discrimination against Koreans in Japan. Such judicial action has long been overdue. It has provided an impetus for the civil rights movement in the decades ahead. There is now legal sanction for arguing that the clause in the Japanese Constitution "all people . . ." refers literally to all people who establish legal residence in Japan.

12

PUBLIC FIGURES IN POPULAR CULTURE:
Identity Problems of Minority Heroes

William Wetherall

If you want to see a good cockfight, observe the vicarious participation of the audience, rather than the action in the ring. Racial aggression continues to motivate much of what passes for healthy spectator sport in interethnic competition. Ethnologists have even argued that athletic rituals may serve to express the same kinds of psychosocial and psychobiological tensions that find release in warfare. The popular cult of Rikidōzan Mitsuhiro (1924-1963), an outstanding champion wrestler of postwar Japan, would seem to support this view.

CLOSETED ETHNICITY AND MACHISMO

In the Preface to Rikidōzan's 1962 autobiography, Ōno Banboku has written: "In a nation laid waste by defeat in war and in the milieu that prevailed under the occupying army, by knocking large-bodied *gaijin* [foreigners][1] around the ring and beating them to the mat, Rikidōzan vented in proxy the pent-up emotions of the Japanese people at that time. We must not forget his meritorious service in thus imparting courage to the postwar Japanese."[2]

Chin Shunshin (Ch'en Shun-ch'en), a popular novelist of Chinese ancestry who was born and reared in Japan, writes of an incident he observed as he entered the lobby of an Osaka hotel. A television set was tuned to a wrestling match between Rikidōzan and a gaijin opponent. Rikidōzan was hurting his opponent with damaging karate chops. When the gaijin fell to the mat, an ardent viewer in the lobby stood up and shouted in delight, "Beautiful! Give it to him! Show him some Japanese strength!"[3]

Journalist Ōshima Yukio reports, in a biography of baseball star Harimoto Isao (Chang Hun), that Rikidōzan's ability to withstand the brutal rule infractions of American wrestlers and ultimately to pin them in victory in their own sport made him a bona fide Japanese hero.[4] Harimoto, born in 1940 when Rikidōzan was training for national *sumo* (traditional Japanese wrestling) competition, was among the many youths of postwar Japan who idolized Rikidōzan and sought to emulate his masculinity in athletic achievement. But interests unrelated to their common fame in sports later led to a close friendship between the two athletes.

Rikidōzan's home, on the eighth floor of a Tokyo apartment building he had bought with some of his earnings, had a private room into which no one was allowed but relatives and intimate friends. Harimoto, whom Rikidōzan treated like a younger brother, became one of these privileged few. Ōshima relates the following episode:

> One day Harimoto was invited into the room. Harimoto took one step inside, and his eyes widened in surprise. The other rooms were done in a Western manner, but this one was decorated ethnically, including several pieces of old Korean ceramics. For Rikidōzan, who didn't reveal his origins to his fans, this room was an oasis for a heart irrevocably steeped in ethnic nostalgia.
>
> "Hey, Hari, let's listen to some music!" As Rikidōzan said this to Harimoto, he locked the door and put on a record of folksongs from his mother country. Apart from his elation at having been invited into Rikidōzan's private room, Harimoto found the ethnic consciousness of the terribly reserved wrestler disconcerting.
>
> "Why do you have to lock the door before you listen to the music of your own country?" It was the first time Harimoto had challenged Rikidōzan. Rikidōzan snapped the phonograph off, his mood suddenly soured. Paying no heed, Harimoto continued his remonstration. "Why can't you say the name of your ethnic group with dignity?"
>
> Rikidōzan's facial expression hardened. "Look, I'm an idol of children around the world, and I'm living in Japan. I can't say such things."
>
> Harimoto stood up and retorted, "What are you ashamed of?"
>
> "You're a fool!" Rikidōzan exploded in anger, jabbing at Harimoto. Harimoto, equally excited, knocked a glass from the table to the floor, breaking it.
>
> "What'd you say?"
>
> "Okay, okay, sit down!" The tone of Rikidozan's voice had changed. You've been talking big, saying you've got ethnic pride, but you don't know our generation!"
>
> "What if I don't?!"
>
> "In our generation, if you said you were Korean [*Chōsenjin*], it didn't matter that you were the same human being, you were treated no better than an insect. You have no idea what a man like me had to do, with nothing but my big body, to overcome that thick wall."
>
> "What if I don't?"
>
> "Don't push it! You're always so proud!"
>
> "What's wrong with that?"
>
> "You're still a young punk and don't understand. When you grow up more, you'll come to know what it means for people like us to be in the limelight in Japan."[5]

Only one of the three major Japanese dailies, in reporting Rikidōzan's death in 1963, touched upon the question of ancestry.[6] Only one of the several magazine articles reviewed for this chapter openly questioned the ethnic origins of the man who did his best to conceal them. The article simply commented in passing:

> There is no riddle like that of Rikidōzan's birth. We have it that he was born on November 14, 1924, in Ōmura city of Nagasaki prefecture, the third son of Momota Minosuke; but another account has him born in Korea. Moreover, it is commonly said that his father Minosuke died when Rikidōzan was two, but there are people who say that his biological father is still living in Korea. It may be a case of having parents who bore him and parents who raised him.[7]

The typical Rikidōzan nativity story has the hero born in Japan to a farming family, as Momota Mitsuhiro, the third child and third son of Tatsu, wife of Momota Minosuke. The wrestler is said to have lost his father at the age of two or three. His mother seems to have died in 1943, shortly after he made his debut in national sumo competition. Biographies that give details of his childhood commonly portray conditions of extreme poverty. The adult Rikidōzan is often quoted as recalling the figure of his mother bent over piecework late into the night, making straw sandals and other small products so that her youngest son might eat and be warm. The rambunctious, quarrelsome, marginally delinquent Mitsuhiro is at first insensitive to the suffering he causes his mother, but eventually he comes to feel an enormous sense of guilt in having failed to return her nurturing devotion.

In the midst of a war that ended in defeat, Rikidōzan fought on the home front, serving the cause in sumō, the ritually symbolic, almost sacred native sport. His mother died as poor as ever, but one imagines that she passed in peace, knowing that her least settled son was embarked on an honorable career and that her final years had not been in vain. Entering the stable of a known sumō champion, training for the day he would compete before the nation, became Rikidōzan's way of expressing both his physical restlessness and his awakened sense of filial piety.

These are the tender emotions that give meaning to the rough exterior of the Japanese warrior. Macho lust is seldom, in any culture, sufficient to make one a hero. What may be needed in addition to machismo will vary with the culture but will usually involve human compassion. In Japanese popular culture, the masculine hero must live and die for his mother to qualify as a true "Son of Nippon." The tears must be real; those in the audience who participate in their shedding have need to believe that they well from a childhood nostalgia imbued, like theirs, with guilt concerning filial ingratitude toward maternal suffering, particularly concerning failure to achieve in accordance with maternal expectations. Dynamic psychocultural themes like these characterize the many book-length biographies that bill Rikidōzan as a classic popular Japanese hero.[8]

After World War II, Rikidōzan left a moderately successful career as a sumō wrestler to help introduce American-style professional wrestling to Japan. He trained under Asian-Americans in Hawaii and competed on the American continent before returning to Japan. The Japanese tabloids were not large enough to contain the excitement he generated as a promising Japanese contender in the new sport. Rikidōzan encouraged Japanese youth who had all the qualifications to compete except confidence by pointing out that if Japanese-American wrestlers like Great Tōgo, Great Yamamoto, Mister Moto, Harold Sakata, and Tommy Kono could wear championship belts in competition with generally larger whites and blacks, so could Japanese yellows. Rikidōzan went all over the wrestling world to promote yellow competitors, importing such athletes as Brazilian-born Antonio Inoki, of Asian-Japanese ancestry, called by Muhammad Ali both a "Pelican" and a "Jap" in verbal exchanges preceding their 1976 boxing vs. wrestling exhibition. Ironically, in the early postwar years in Honolulu and San Francisco arenas, Rikidōzan often heard the word "Jap" in the noisy ringside frenzy and became sensitive to what his Japanese-American wrestling peers had experienced from birth.[9]

Life for Rikidōzan was ultimately rougher outside the ring than in. Few who knew him well, and who knew of his use of bodyguards and of the gangster connections and rivalries that surrounded him, were totally surprised to read in the papers on the morning of 9 December 1963, that their friend had been stabbed the night before by a young hoodlum in the course of an argument in the toilet of the New Latin Quarter, a large nightclub in the Akasaka district of Tokyo. Unable to catch his assailant, Rikidōzan mounted the stage of the club in the midst of a show and announced, in Japanese mixed with English, that he had been stabbed and that an armed man was loose.[10] Released after treatment at a nearby hospital, Rikidōzan appeared to be making a good recovery, but an acute relapse, apparently provoked by his stubborn refusal to recognize his need for total rest, found him back in the hospital a few days later and dead of peritonitis on 15 December.

The fatal flaw of many a hero is his reluctance to acknowledge that he is mortal. This flaw enables the hero to be heroic, which often involves dying under tragic circumstances. No one knows why Rikidōzan chose to ignore medical advice. No one wrote in obituaries that the champion of postwar Japanese machismo wanted to die. But another face of the gusto for life that laughs at death is the silent wish that one will die when least expecting to, for to sense that the end is near is to know, if not to admit, that one is mortal. Rikidōzan did not seem the type who would want to die of a knife wound incurred in a drunken brawl. Death in the ring, the result of an illegal assault by a gaijin opponent, might have been tolerable. Thus one can only think that Rikidōzan failed to fight for his life because of delusions of indomitability. In the manner of the true human hero, he was vulnerable only to himself.

Rikidōzan died only weeks after John F. Kennedy was assassinated. Japanese women's magazines at the time focused on the problems that beset widowed mothers with young or unborn children, like Jacqueline Kennedy and Momota Keiko, Rikidōzan's wife. Magazines read mainly by men raised the question of whether the high audience ratings of professional wrestling broadcasts and telecasts—not only higher than baseball but most entertainment programming at the time—would continue at such levels without their principal attraction. The sports tabloids were thrown into a state of shock in fear of circulation drops on the lucrative commuter runs. Few commentators on Rikidōzan's death failed to observe what the wrestler had meant to postwar Japanese fans. As one Tokyo sports programmer expressed it: "Rikidōzan can be called a hero of the age, given birth by a Japan defeated in war. His flinging of the giant bodies of gaijin wrestlers was a hit with the Japanese, who had been shocked by the defeat. No matter what the mass media may do now, it cannot create a hero like this a second time."[11]

It is probably true that the specific climate in which Rikidōzan became a popular hero is past, but media mongers can hardly be said to have "created" Rikidōzan. At most they gave him time and space, reporting his achievements in the belief that they held profound meaning for their audiences. That Japanese listeners and viewers found his demeanor to their liking cannot be attributed to media technology or methods. If Rikidōzan was a product of exploitative marketing, he was a product that largely sold itself.

In any event, the apprehension that the Japanese wrestling world and sports media expressed about their future has proven unfounded. Professional wrestling, featuring mainly Asian Japanese versus non-Asian foreigners, continues to command several hours of prime-time television every week. Commuter tabloids have multiplied, showing as much as possible of the pulpy gore of battered bodies in color gravure with sensational captions. The continued and possibly increased interest in professional wrestling in Japan since Rikidōzan's death may be credited in part to subsequent developments in media knowhow and related changes in social behavior, but the media did not create such interest, much less the behavior that attracts or attends such interest. The need to display sexual power, the capacity to ritualize such display for the benefit of vicarious participants, and the potential for such ritual to extend to interethnic competition, have existed in human cultures throughout history.

In the instance of Japan, one has only to refer to any of the widely available reproductions of Japanese erotic art, particularly of the premodern periods, to understand why "cockfight" is more than a Freudian double entendre when applied to professional wrestling and other gladiator sports. Some of the great masters of *ukiyoe* (floating world pictures) and *shunga* (spring pictures) have left dramatic portrayals of males fighting one another with exaggerated phalli, or otherwise engaged in overt phallic competition. Also of interest are the classic depictions of sumō matches between male and female sexual organs. In early Japanese sexual humor, as well as in caricature art, one finds considerable evidence of concern over intra- and intersexual rivalry placing importance on organ size. It was therefore not a new obsession but simply a modern extension of an ancient one that inspired Asian Japanese to challenge gaijin in the ring. From early sketches and caricatures of such interethnic matches, one imagines the enormous crowds that gathered and the keen interest they took in the rivalry between "Japanese spirit" and "gaijin might."

Contemporary Japanese weekly magazines often feature articles on marriages between large athletes, like sumō and professional wrestlers, and women of normal stature. Interviewers of these spouses all but ask directly for details of their sexual life. Similar interest is shown the subject of interracial sexuality, particularly between smaller yellows on the one hand, and larger blacks and whites on the other. Rikidōzan escaped none of this, although in his day the media was less explicit. He exposed his body with obvious pride to both sexes and all races. What this exhibitionism meant to Rikidōzan cannot be known. More important, perhaps, is what it meant for his fans. For not a few Asian Japanese who watched his explosions of machismo, he symbolized ethnic hope. During the early postwar years, he made more bearable the street parades of yellow women on the arms of black and white soldiers.

DEBUNKING MYTH

Decades after such racial embarrassment, some majority Japanese continue to suffer an apparent inferiority complex from documentary and fictional flashbacks of occupied bars and beds. The weekly magazines continue to churn out the conventional warnings to their Japanese female readers against casual liaisons with gaijin men, while ironically baiting them in others. But since the late 1960s and early 1970s, a new genre of lurid story has begun to appear, featuring Asian Japanese male conquests of gaijin womanhood in Japan and abroad, suggesting that the proverbial "number-one economic animal" of the 1980s will sport a new coat of sexual confidence, to warm its neonascent pride in national achievement in the face of increasingly chilly alien winds.

The aura of Rikidōzan is never too remote from such currents in Japanese popular culture. Between mid-1971 and mid-1972, the most widely read ring magazine revived the cult in a feature series on Rikidōzan's life.[12] In late 1972, Rikidōzan's youngest son (the wrestler left two sons and two daughters) followed his father into the ring, and the more vicarious older son became a ringside announcer.[13] In late 1976 and early 1977, the image of Rikidozan's muscular body was recalled to duty, helping to sell Nikka whiskey in display ads that capitalized on the "Yesterday Once More" television specials by NHK (Japan's national public broadcasting network) and on commercial networks celebrating their twenty-fifth year. The special programs gave great tribute to the "gaijin conquerer" who had helped so much to boost the spread of Japanese television in the early 1950s. And in mid-1978, billing himself as Rikidōzan II, the older son traded his microphone for trunks and boots, claiming that it was in his blood to be where the action was.[14]

The myth of Rikidōzan as a "Japanese" ethnic hero, however, has finally begun to be viewed with considerable skepticism. This is not to say that the myth will die as easily as the man who became its central character, but that the abutments supporting the myth are showing signs of erosion from undercurrents of criticism. Rikidōzan researcher Ushijima Hidehiko, for example, has disposed of practically every element of the fable of Rikidōzan's origins as found in most popular biographies.[15] An exhaustive search of the records of the Ōmura schools supposedly attended by Rikidōzan have produced no evidence that the wrestler lived in Japan before his midteens. And Ushijima has interviewed people with documents making it clear that Rikidōzan acquired his Japanese nationality through being adopted by Momota Minosuke, who was anything but an impoverished farmer. Nor was Rikidōzan such an obedient son.

One of Ushijima's principal informants was Ogata Toraichi, who claimed to have scouted Rikidōzan in the late 1930s while serving as a border patrolman with Japanese military police in Korea. Ogata was the son of a relatively wealthy Ōmura merchant who died of cancer. Ogata's widowed mother became a common-law wife of Momota Minosuke, who thus became Ogata's stepfather. Not a farmer but a foreman, and then a promoter and geisha-house operator, Momota was an avid sumō fan and became the benefactor of Tamanoumi and other local sumō contenders.

When Ogata discovered Rikidōzan, the wrestler's mother and older brothers were running a rice mill on the outskirts of Seoul. The family name Kim became Kanamura in 1939, when all citizens of the Imperial Japanese territories of Korea, Taiwan, and Karafuto (Sakhalin) were ordered to Japanize their names.[16] Rikidōzan had attracted Ogata's attention when he and the oldest of his two brothers won a sumō tournament in Seoul. His mother, however, is said to have been strongly opposed to her sons participating in a sport that made them naked spectacles, and she was so adamantly against Rikidōzan pursuing a sumō career in Japan that she pressed him to marry in the belief that he would never want to leave Korea if he slept with his bride even one night. Rikidōzan conceded to the wedding, but not looking forward to spending his life milling rice, and possessed by dreams of becoming a sumō champion of Imperial Japan, the fifteen-year-old youth abandoned his bride and sought Ogata's shelter and patronage.

Imperial subject Kim Kwangho, alias Kanamura Mitsuhiro, was a citizen of the Imperial Japanese territory of Korea, and not of Japan proper. Thus he required a landing permit to enter Japan. Such a permit would have been difficult to obtain had Ogata not been a veteran of many years on the military police in Korea, as well as the nominal stepson of an influential Kyūshū sumō promoter. The only additional passes required on the road to becoming a competitor in Japan were Japanese nationality and training in the stable of a proven competitor, and both were granted by Momota Minosuke, who adopted Rikidōzan and apprenticed him to Tamanoumi.[17]

Ushijima describes the postwar wrestling scene as one which found Asian Japanese and Koreans concerned not only about whether yellow competitors could beat blacks and whites, but who would win in competition between Japanese and Koreans. Apparently Rikidōzan was not a favorite among those ethnically open Koreans who suspected or knew of his Korean ancestry and of his willingness to identify with Japanese who felt that Japanese machismo was superior to that of Koreans.

Rikidōzan did his best to maintain his image as a "Japanese" ethnic hero (which he definitely was, although he had once been Korean). He was irritated whenever the media alluded to his Korean origins, as it did on the occasion of his January 1963 visit to the Korean peninsula. Some papers had reported this visit as "the first to his mother country in two decades," instead of simply saying that he had gone to play golf. But Rikidōzan himself seemed to have found his "Japanese" mask too heavy to wear on this visit, during which he once said "thank you" in Korean, when welcomed as a "Korean" hero by bouquet-bearing Korean girls. He then apologized that two decades of speaking only Japanese had left him unable to speak his mother tongue very well.

Korean wrestler Kim Il so admired Rikidōzan for his "Korean" machismo that in April 1958 he smuggled himself into Japan to seek out his idol and make his acquaintance. Later arrested in a Yokohama brothel, the illegal immigrant appealed to Rikidōzan, who prevailed upon the political ties of Ōno Banboku to secure Kim's immigration status in Japan as one of Rikidōzan's ring disciples. But Rikidōzan forbade Kim to use his Korean name, assigning him the ethnically Japanese ring name of Oki Kintaro.[18]

Rikidōzan's confusion about his identity is further reflected in a comment he once made to a ring referee, reported by Ushijima, in which he referred to himself as a "Japanese-Korean halfbreed" (Nihonjin to Chōsenjin no haafu). In this variation of the Rikidōzan nativity story, his father is said to have been a Japanese soldier, stationed in Korea, who abandoned his Korean family when he returned to Japan. But questions of Rikidōzan's parentage aside, in Ushijima's words, "He lost no time endeavoring to become completely Japanese."

ETHNIC DEFINITIONS AND STEREOTYPES

But what would majority Japanese have thought had they known that their wrestling hero was a Japanese whose parents had been garlic-eating, conniving, dirty, arrogant Koreans? Ōshima understates the potential sense of ethnic betrayal when he writes: "The heroic story of Rikidōzan performing in the midst of the fanatic cheering and applause of Japanese fans should really be called the grand fiction of Japanese popular nationalism. For Rikidōzan was not a Japanese [*Nihonjin*] but a Japan resident Korean [*Zainichi Chōsenjin*]."[19]

But if contemporary kings of Japanese machismo (such as pulp-story writer and sports biographer Kajiwara Ikki)[20] are irresponsible or even deceitful when they capitalize on Rikidōzan's image as a Japanese national hero uncompromised by tabooed questions about his ethnic ancestry, then Ōshima would seem to be equally guilty of betrayal. Indeed, the greatest betrayal of all may be the manner in which Ōshima denies that Rikidōzan was a *Nihonjin* (Japanese) and labels him a *Zainichi Chōsenjin* (Japan-resident Korean). For the moment Rikidōzan's name was entered in Momota Minosuke's domicile register, the wrestler became a Japanese national and therefore Japanese. Examples of ethnic majority Japanese and others reserving the word "Japanese" for those who are thought to be of Japanese racial pedigree are ubiquitous. Even in scholarly writing, which is supposed to be objective in the most humanistic sense of this word, the term "Japanese" is almost invariably used to connote a mythical race of people, rather than to denote people who in reality are bona fide members of Japanese society and who may wish to be considered as such.

Ethnocentric sociolinguistic conventions also make it difficult for majority Japanese and many others to entertain the notion of a Japanese of Korean or other non-Japanese ethnic ancestries. But psychocultural identity includes not only nationality and the emblems acquired from the society in which one is living, but also emotional ties to earlier years that may have been passed in other societies, or an ethnic heritage acquired through a lineage that may include immigrant ancestors. Thus another kind of betrayal is the betrayal of the individual by society, as seen in the reluctance of critics like Ōshima to consider Rikidōzan a person who was both Japanese *and* Korean, rather than simply Japanese *or* Korean; a person who may have had both a Japanese side and a Korean side, the former propelling him into a public career, the latter moving him to nostalgia for things he kept locked in a room and comfortably shared only with those he felt he could trust with his secret; a person who was ethnically proud but both expected and feared social discrimination if he tried to be ethnically honest.

If Ōshima's report of Harimoto's encounter with Rikidōzan's locked ethnic closet is an accurate representation, then the wrestler's motive for passing as a majority Japanese would seem to have included the wish that he did not have to. Whatever the law may tell us about Rikidōzan's nationality, and whatever journalists or scholars may say about his identity, it is clear that he had reasons to identify with Japanese *and* Korean culture and society, whether his Japanese and Korean connections were biological, cultural, social, linguistic, legal, religious, psychological, or even delusionary. It is reasonable to suppose that he would have been elated to feel free to acknowledge the Korean and Japanese parts of himself as an integrated whole. But his ego was divided by the tyranny of limited labeling choices in a multi-ethnic Japanese society most of whose members, and even outsiders, prefer to regard as mono-ethnic.

Common to all betrayals of the pressing desire to express one's ethnic self without division or hiding—essential factors in the psychology of closeting and passing—is the social pathology induced by conventional ethnic labels. Labeling traditions imprison users of language in conventional categories that tend to disallow racial and cultural mixing, to nourish obsessions with purity, and otherwise to help condition visceral ambivalencies about belonging to a disparaged group. Traditional ethnic labels thus discourage the formation of attitudes free of the need to resolve real or fictitious multiple identities into one favored identity.

If Rikidōzan was unable to be both selves at once, it was because he grew up with people who insisted, in accordance with their labeling traditions, that he be only one self, preferably Japanese. But equally tragic, though etiologically telling, is that even in death his identity should remain the object of an ethnic tug-of-war that labels him one or the other, but not both Japanese and Korean. It is this general absence in human cultures of the spirit of ethnic accommodation, multi-ethnicity, and pluralism that made Rikidōzan an ethnic schizophrenic. That the causes of his symptoms were social more than personal is reflected in the manner in which his biographers, and others who use his life to serve their own purposes, continue to divide the whole person that Rikidōzan would probably have been had prevailing cultural linguistic categories been less ethnocentric.

WHAT'S IN A NAME

The language of Harimoto Isao's culture inspires him to remain a Korean national while being both Korean and Japanese in terms of his actual life. Derogatory jeers like *ninnikubara* (garlic belly), *kimuchi kutabare* (kimch'i, i.e., Korean, go to hell!), and *Chōseni kaere* (Korean go home!)[21] have followed Harimoto from his youth in Hiroshima, where an older sister died from effects of exposure to the atomic bomb, to his present life on the ballfield, where ethnic gibes from the grandstands and even from opponent players keep him busy defending his pride with his bat if not with his mouth or fists. Unlike Rikidōzan, Harimoto wants it known that he is of

Korean ancestry, and also that he is Korean and does not wish to be Japanese.

The one accommodation Harimoto has made is to continue to be known by his ethnic-majority Japanese passing name, which he has used since childhood. Koreans in Japan and Korea, and persons of Korean ancestry who are no longer Koreans but who continue to bear witness to their ethnic heritage, know Harimoto by his legal name, Chang Hun. This name also appears, with no objection from Harimoto and usually on his recommendation, in much of the mass-media coverage of his life and career, including television programs, book-length biographies, and magazine and newspaper articles.

NHK television, for example, once featured a prime-time documentary on Harimoto as a Japan-resident Korean superstar who had refused to naturalize. The program was telecast nationwide on 6 February 1976, when NHK was fighting a lawsuit filed by legal scholar, Christian minister, and civil-rights leader Choe Chang-Hwa (Ch'oe Ch'anghwa) for alleged discrimination in its policy of reading all ethnically Korean personal names—for which Chinese characters are known—in Sino-Japanese rather than in Japanized forms of Sino-Korean.[22] The title of the NHK program, "Chan Fun," was based on Harimoto's Korean name. It consisted of the Chinese characters for the name Chang Hun, followed by (in parentheses) the Japanese syllabic transcription for the Sino-Korean pronunciation of the characters. The Korean name Chang Hun was pronounced on the program in the Japanized form, Chan Fun, rather than Chō Kun, the Sino-Japanese reading of the characters.

This represented an unusual NHK deviation from an otherwise totally ethnocentric attitude toward ethnically Korean and Chinese names. NHK, arguing in court that to render Korean names in Korean or in Japanese based on Korean would invite "confusion and misunderstanding" among Japanese viewers, makes concessions only in cases of superstar performers and other Korean minorities in Japan who are known to have the courage to place their self-proclaimed ethnicity before their personal careers and paychecks. Less distinguished Korean and Chinese minorities have little hope of having their ethnic names recognized by majority institutions, a situation reminiscent of the colonial period when Koreans, Taiwanese, and indigenous peoples of Karafuto were ordered by Imperial Japanese administrators to Japanize their names. But NHK is only one of the pillars of majority Japanese culture and society that practices systematic discrimination against ethnically non-Japanese names expressed in Chinese characters. Reflecting but also perpetuating the strong tendency of Japanese to ignore the languages of their nearest Asian neighbors, practically all Japanese institutions responsible for the dissemination of information in the Japanese language systematically ignore the ethnic readings of Korean and Chinese names, even when their bearers make personal requests that their names be read as they read them, or clearly indicate the readings they prefer in press conferences or commercial publications.

Freedom in the choice of names when naturalizing in Japan is another area of controversy in maintaining ethnicity via ethnic names. Andrew Horvat, a freelance writer residing in Japan, writes under the subheading "Not One Person in Japan Has a Foreign Name," as follows:

> Japan is a strange country. It is a rule that Japanese nationals [*Kokumin*] must have a characteristically Japanese name [*Nihonjin koyū no namae*]. If I, Horvat [*Horubaato*], acquire Japanese citizenship, I would have to change my name to something like Horikawa, Horie, Horibata, or Horibato [as written in Chinese characters]. So long as I am Horvat, city hall will refuse to establish my domicile register.
>
> In Hungary I was Horvat, and I was Horvat after moving to Canada. Only when becoming Japanese would I be forced to discard the name Horvat. In other words, the basis for preventing the assimilation of Japanese with other ethnic groups is clearly provided by law.
>
> Lafcadio Hearn, in order to become Japanese, changed his name to the Japanese name Koizumi Yakumo. Persons with names like Pak or Kim, or with other names that convey non-Japanese ancestral origins, are not recognized as Japanese. Is there nothing that can be done about this?
>
> There are blonde, blue-eyed people who like me are saying that if possible they would like to become Japanese. But we are told, "If that's how you feel, then take a name like Yamamoto."[23]

Horvat, like Ōshima, is sincere in his criticism but hasty in his use of ethnic labels. To state that no one in Japan has a foreign name is to ignore the nearly one-million foreigners, including himself, who are not only in Japan but who comprise a vital part of Japanese society. Most of them are life-long residents who have been born and raised in Japan, are native speakers of Japanese, and are psychologically at home in Japanese society. Foreigners in Japan who came to Japan as adults include, for example, a Canadian whose name is Ishikawa, and he—not she—is "a white-skinned, gaijin-esque male with blond curly hair and blue eyes that shine in the dark" —with not a trace of "Japanese" blood in his veins.[24] But because he is a foreigner, Ishikawa must be a foreign name—for only foreigners can have foreign names, and all names of foreigners must be foreign. And if Hamamoto is the name of a Japanese American in Japan, then it is also a foreign name, for its owner is not Japanese but American, and Americans in Japan are foreigners. But to suggest that no Japanese in Japan has a foreign name is ludicrous, for no Japanese in Japan is a foreigner, and so no name of a Japanese in Japan can be a foreign name, whether the name is Hamamoto (the name retained by the above-mentioned Japanese American when he naturalized and became not only Japanese, but a Japanese-American Japanese), or Wagana (Wagner, the name of a Japanese sculptor who naturalized from Hungary), or Chin Jukan (Sim Sugwan, the name of a Japanese potter who traces his Korean roots fourteen generations back to 1604, and continues to be in touch with relative potters in Korea).

In fact, Japanese naming laws and their administrative interpretations place not a single restriction on the *ethnicity* of the legal name elected by a naturalizing alien or naturalized citizen, or the name assigned to an infant native-born citizen. The laws require only that a name being entered in a Japanese domicile register, as the name of a member of the register (which is tantamount to being a Japanese national), must be written in one of the three officially approved scripts: that is, Chinese characters selected from a standard list of about 2,000, or one of two standard syllabic Japanese scripts. It is not even required that a name be written in characters; either of the syllabic scripts can be used to transcribe names from other scripts, including *hangŭl* (the Korean alphabetic script) and Roman letters. Thus Horvat could be written Horubaato (as his translator did in his book), and Kim and Pak could be written Kimu and Paku. For that matter, the Chinese characters for Kim and Pak are included on the official lists, and there is nothing in Japanese law to prevent a naturalizing foreigner from becoming Japanese as Kimu or Paku—if not Kim or Pak.

This is not to say that there is not considerable discrimination regarding names. Instructions in the guidebook for nationalization applicants state that, in principle, the applicant is free to choose any name. But it is immediately added that, as far as possible (*narubeku*), the name used as a Japanese citizen should be a "Japanese-style name" (*Nihonfu-na namae*). And because all examples of entries on forms show only so-called Japanese-style names, the field is wide open for quasi-legal discrimination on the part of officials who receive and process naturalization applications. Applicants are given the impression that their application will be refused if the name to be used as a Japanese citizen is not "Japanese" in the ethnocentric sense of this word. But it must be noted that the legality of refusals to accept "non-Japanese" names has never been tested in court.

Some Koreans, Chinese, and other foreigners in Japan may avoid naturalizing because they fear they will lose their ethnic names. But it seems that most who naturalize are inclined to want to give up their ethnic names and to establish a so-called Japanese name. Available breakdowns of naturalization statistics, by former nationality and by other cohorts, show that most foreigners who naturalize in Japan already have a foot in the door of majority ethnicity, through either their own or their parents' international marriage.[25]

Sensitivity about one's ethnic name may vary with national minority. Unofficial statistics compiled in 1971 on Koreans and Chinese living in Kawasaki show that of 4,944 Chōsenjin (North-Korean-affiliated Koreans), only 2,087 (42%) had registered passing names, compared with 2,555 (58%) of the 4,390 Kankokujin (South-Korean-affiliated Koreans) in the city. In sharp contrast with both Korean groups, only 61 (14%) of the 449 Chinese in the city had registered passing names.[26] These figures suggest that members of some minority groups may attach more importance to ancestral ethnicity than those of other groups, particularly as regards the desire to assert one's ancestral ethnicity by using an ethnic name, and to use this name despite expectations of unwanted attention, if not discrimination.[27]

Significantly, the stigma that a Korean may attach to one's ancestral name in Japan does not necessarily abate when going abroad. Japan-resident Koreans who go abroad to study or work respond in various ways to the "ethnic freedom" they tend to discover. Those going to America, for example, may begin to express their Korean selves by attempting to gain acceptance in a Korean immigrant community. If they fail to marshal the ethnic emblems required for admittance, they may fall back on the comforts of their familiarity with things Japanese, including passing. Others are known to continue passing when around "Japanese"—with no more assurance than when in Japan that the "other" Japanese are not also passing Koreans.[28]

The subject of naturalization is so highly politicized that it is difficult to separate fact from fiction. There are no naturalization quotas, and although naturalization requirements are strict and are subject to quasi-legal interpretation, it would seem that the majority of Japan-resident Koreans are technically able to naturalize. But so great is the feeling that becoming a Japanese national amounts to betraying one's Korean ethnicity, and the fear that one might be found unqualified, that only a few thousand Koreans per year take out their papers. Those who naturalize seem to feel that being a Japanese national with a majority name would make life easier, and given the discriminatory structure of Japanese society, assimilation through naturalization is easily rationalized.

Foreign nationals in Japan are disadvantaged in opportunities for employment compared with Japanese nationals. Blatant discrimination is even found in the classified ads of the major English-language dailies published in Japan, which are mainly read by Japanese nationals learning English in order to "internationalize" their view of the world. The editor of The Japan Times, for example, has publicly defended the paper's use of the phrase "Japanese only" in some of its help-wanted ads by writing that, "There may be exceptionally qualified non-Japanese individuals, of course. But they are, statistically speaking, very few."[29] If opinion leaders like the editor of Japan's most influential journalistic link with the rest of the world can so facilely reduce the human problem of discrimination in Japan to a numbers game (despite editorials in the same paper advocating early implementation of the United Nations Human Rights Covenants that the Japanese Diet ratified in 1979), then optimism about the future of Japan as an open, humanistic society is best entertained with considerable reservations.

Although refusal to employ on the basis of nationality is illegal for most kinds of jobs, any number of quasi-legal means are available to the Japanese employer who wishes to hire only Japanese. These problems tend to affect most greatly those who have not established themselves economically and those whose skills are not sufficiently in demand to neutralize barriers of discrimination. But such problems are found also among minorities ostensibly best able to hurdle discriminatory occupational barriers. Even the most qualified and reputable foreign scholars, and other foreign professionals, have been systematically barred from regular posts in national universities, although Korean and Chinese doctors are welcomed in rural areas avoided by citified Japanese medics. And being a star ballplayer or sumo wrestler does not necessarily ease a resident foreigner's anxiety over post-retirement employment. Kaneda Masaichi, who holds most of the major pitching records in Japanese baseball, naturalized in 1959, shortly after Harimoto Isao made his debut. Kaneda, privately but never publicly known as Kim, was also a friend of Rikidozan. Kaneda is said to have told Harimoto of his apprehension that Korean nationality might be an obstacle to his becoming a manager of a Japanese ball club.[30] Ironically, Kaneda became manager of Lotte Orions, which is owned by Lotte Incorporated, Japan's largest chewing-gum and candy company, founded and developed by Sin Nak Ho alias Shigemitsu Takeo, one of the successful postwar entrepreneurs of Korean ancestry in Japan who have found it convenient to be known by different names in different worlds.

Few successful Koreans in Japan are as direct about their use of passing names as movie maker Yoo Jinshik (Yu Chinsik), whose business card also carries the name Ryu Shinnosuke, the name he used as director of a documentary movie released in 1980 on Koreans in Japan. The film attempts to show how well Koreans have succeeded in Japanese society, and otherwise supports the ROK-affiliated Mindan policy of minimizing the problem of discrimination in Japanese society while holding apparently unsuccessful Japan-resident Koreans individually responsible for their failure.

Although Japanese nationality is no longer required to compete in national sumo, the Sumo Association continues to regard sumo as an "indigenous" sport to be protected from foreign incursions. Thus Japanese nationality is required of all association officials, including retired wrestlers who wish to open training stables. Takamiyama became a Japanese national in June 1980, only one month before he set the all-time record for the most consecutive matches in the senior division. Known as Jesse Kuhaulua when an American, he is now Watanabe Daigoro. Takamiyama long protested that he should not have to become a Japanese national in order to be a stable boss in Japan when he retires from competition, but the Sumo Association refused to change its "Japanese only" policy.[31]

THE SOUND OF MUSIC

Ethnic minorities who pass as majority Japanese unwittingly do racially sensitive majorities an incalculably great psychological favor. If one is an ethnic majority who deeply believes that race determines ability to speak the Japanese language, or appreciate Japanese food, or compose a Japanese poem, or sing Japanese songs, then nothing can be more disturbing than to find a racial outsider speaking Japanese as well or better than insiders, or eating Japanese food with as much or more relish, or writing Japanese literature and rendering Japanese music with equal or greater facility and feeling.

Admitting the heterogeneous reality of the Japanese population and its culture would reduce the level of enjoyment for those who subscribe to the myths of ethnic purity and homogeneity that bolster majority identity, and for those who feel that arts labeled "Japanese" can best be performed and appreciated only by "Japanese" artists and audiences. To encourage outstanding minority artists to perform under their ethnic names would subvert that profoundly religious sense of otherworldly uniqueness that not a few majorities and even some outsiders have the need to attribute to things Japanese. The ethnic minority who is able to pass feels pressured to assume a "Japanese" name and present oneself to the public as a "genuine" son or daughter of Nippon. Younger minority performers may be finding it easier to acknowledge their ethnicities, but trends in this direction are anything but clear. Pressure not to present oneself as Korean, for example, comes in part from parental and managerial desires not to risk a promising career in the name of ethnic pride. Once established as a "Japanese" performer, it is all the more difficult to "reveal" one's closeted self without the sense of having deceived not only one's ethnic peers but also one's fans.

Japanese popular culture reflects the same racial concerns that are found at other levels. Whether one is "Japanese" is almost invariably a matter of blood, in the genetic sense, and rarely a matter of culture or nationality. The tendency to regard blood as the ultimate ethnic emblem is epitomized in the caption to a magazine picture of an American talent in Tokyo who happens to be of Japanese ancestry. It reads: "She was born in Japan but raised in Hawaii. Her nationality is American, but no foreign blood [gaikokujin no chi] flows in her veins. She's a third generation [something] of Japanese ancestry [nikkei sansei].[32]

Another issue of the magazine reports that promoters of a popular Japanese singer's Las Vegas appearance "hoped to draw mainly gaijin [foreigners], but 80 percent of the turnout was nikkeijin [people of Japanese ancestry]."[33] The singer, Itsuki Hiroshi, is best known for his renderings of enka (popular ballads), which are thought by many to be the "soul" of popular Japanese musical expression.[34] But not a few critics regard the enka genre to have been inspired by Korean songs, largely owing to the fact that Koga Masao (1904-1979), the late god of enka scores, spent the formative years of his youth (1912-1922) in Korea, although in his autobiography he fails to attribute his musical inspiration to Korean sources.[35]

The "roots" of enka became an open issue in Japanese journalism in late 1976 and early 1977, when Korean enka songstress Yi Sŏng-ae toured Japan and impressed enka lovers with her moving renditions of Japanese and Korean ballads. One of her best-selling albums bore the subtitle "Enka no genryū o saguru" (Seeking the Source of Enka), and it was inevitable that review articles compared her with Miyako Harumi (b. 1948), who won the Best Singer of the Year award in 1976 for the enka ballad "Kita no yado kara" (From an Inn in the North). The "enka-roots debate" was especially interesting because Miyako's father is known to be of Korean ancestry, although this fact is rarely acknowledged in entertainment magazines.[36]

Miyako, who has been a top-billed enka singer since the late 1960s, was apparently not aware that her father was Korean until she saw how her name was listed on her junior high school diploma. Given the highest award of the Japanese popular music world in late 1976, she and her mother mounted the stage in tears that stopped a show accustomed to tears on such occasions. In magazine interviews and personal appearances over the weeks that followed, her mother told the familiar story of maternal suffering and how she had bet everything on her daughter's success. And she did so without referring to her estranged husband, much less to his Korean ethnicity. An anonymous reporter, in an article criticizing the taboos that prevent ethnic honesty in Japan's entertainment world, quoted Miyako on her reaction to discovering that she had been raised under her mother's family name Kitamura (Miyako is her stage name) rather than her father's name of Yi, as follows:

> I remember seeing my junior high diploma, and asking why the name was not Kitamura Harumi. But I immediately forgot all about it, and now it doesn't concern me in the least. After all, we're all the same human beings. I think it is really something that my father came alone to Japan from Seoul at the age of twenty-one, and then struggled to establish his business [in textiles]. It may have been a big decision in my mother's day [to marry a Korean], but it's different in mine. . . .[37]

Rikidōzan in myth, and Miyako Harumi in reality, achieved their glory with strong mothers at their backs or sides. Their fathers were either deceased, missing, or absent. Baseball star Harimoto Isao, raised in Japan as the youngest of three surviving children by a Korean mother who tolerated only a minimum of passing, is another model of maternally inspired achievement. Shortly after the end of the Pacific War, when his mother was thinking of returning to Korea, she received notice that her husband had died of sickness. She therefore resolved to raise her family in Japan.

Harimoto is proud at the bat, but he is prouder still when with his mother, who is frequently pictured in Korean garb. The athlete states that it was largely his mother's counsel that inspired him not to comply with requests that he naturalize so that his ball club could meet the Foreign National Player Quota and hire an American player. Unable to have their way with Harimoto, team owners sponsored the change in baseball regulations limiting the number of foreign national players allowed on one team. The law was changed so as to exempt from the quota Korean or Chinese nationals who held Imperial Japanese nationality at the end of the war or who were born in Japan to former colonial subjects.

In mid-1976, Harimoto's mother, Pak Sunbun, was recognized as "Mother of the Year" by an organization in the Republic of Korea that wished to cite her undaunted devotion, while living in a foreign land and bereaved by the death of her husband, "in raising her children to be proud Koreans, and in raising Harimoto Isao to be an ethnic hero and not to succumb to the various allurements that would have had the athlete Harimoto become a naturalized Japanese citizen."[38] And in 1979, a Korean film company came to Japan to produce a move on Harimoto's life.[39]

Harimoto cuts a spectacular figure wherever he goes. He walks with a certain swagger that is probably more the result of his large trunk and macho character than an ethnic chip on the shoulder. Nonetheless, as an eligible bachelor he attracts considerable female attention, particularly in the watering spots he is known to frequent. Harimoto is said to have contended that one in five bar and cabaret hostesses are of Korean ancestry, and that some of them reveal their ethnicity to him. Ōshima reports the following anecdote:

> For example, a hostess at another table gets up for some reason. When passing Harimoto she whispers in his ear,
> "I'm a sister."
> "You're kidding!"
> "Follow me if you want proof."
> The hostess goes to the entrance of the toilet and flashes Harimoto her Alien Registration Certificate.
> "Keep it quiet."[40]

TRAGIC PATHWAYS OF ALIENATION

Although one may find some refuge in hiding secrets from others, trying to hide realities from oneself can be fatal. Yamamura Masaaki (1945-1970), a Korean-Japanese college student who aspired to be a writer, committed suicide (see chap. 7). Yamamura doubted his worth as a naturalized Japanese in a society that seemed to require the total ethnic surrender of its minorities. His older brothers were moved to publish a posthumous collection of his diary entries, essays, poems, and notes, including the following lines:

> *Youth.*
> *I do not regret my youth!*
> *Literature, religion, politics,*
> *   ethnic problems, student movements.*
> *I drove myself in everything*

to the limits of my ability.
And though it didn't last,
I even fell in innocent love.
I do not regret it!
At least I have to tell myself this.
It is just that I am extremely fatigued.
I am exhausted
and can no longer walk on.[41]

These words are quoted from a long stretch of very fragmented and gloomy prose reflecting mainly on suicide and death. On the whole, Yamamura's writing tends to be very disorganized and hostile. Much of the content is clinically "schizoid" in the manner in which he dwells upon problems concerning Christianity, politics, and "blood" ethnicity. Yamamura represented a case of cognitive incapacity to resolve a psychological problem common to those who obsessively struggle with ethnic labels that stress "purity of blood" over "sincerity of culture." He applied all the conventional labels to himself, and even a few of his own invention, including *kika Chōsenjin* (naturalized Korean), *han-Nihonjin* (half-Japanese), and *sokoku sōshitsu sha* (person who has lost one's country of ancestry). He found that none of these fit, and he knew of none that would be acceptable not only to others but to himself. But he was Japanese and Japanese only. Moreover, he was entirely Japanese, for there is no such thing as being partly Japanese. One is either a Japanese national or not, and questions of ethnic ancestry have absolutely no bearing on whether one is Japanese. The problem that Yamamura faced was that neither he nor the vast majority of those he came in contact with were aware of this. In a society that made adequate allowances for ethnic diversity, Yamamura might have survived the consequences of his private obsessions and those of others. As ethnically convoluted as Rikidōzan but of more fragile fiber, he became another strand in the rope of individuals strained in the tug-of-war between racists on both sides of the Korean/Japanese ethnic barrier.

MYTHS OF HOMOGENEITY

Ki no Tsurayuki (ca. 868-945), compiler of the *Kokin wakashū* (905), Japan's first anthology of *waka* (31-syllable poems), cites in his preface a poem he praises as the archetype of waka, and he atttributes its authorship to an immigrant Korean scholar named Wani.[42] That the "father" of Japanese poetry was possibly an immigrant is seen by Watanabe Shōichi as evidence that there was little discrimination in early Japan, where he claims that all people were equal before waka in the sense that, in some Euro-American societies, all people are said to be equal before the law.[43] Watanabe, a professor of English who argues that the spirit of Japanese language and its poetic expression is all but genetically transmitted,[44] stops short of saying that there is discrimination in present-day Japan, but he observes that although some Japan-resident Koreans have won literary awards for their Japanese fiction or prose, he knows of no foreigner who can write good waka.[45]

Using an "immune reaction" metaphor, Watanabe has advocated that "a country like Japan, which from the beginning has been strongly aware of the pure blood [of its people], must regard this [aspect of] its character seriously and be stringently cautious about suddenly admitting [into its body] large amounts of alien substances."[46] He has also advocated that Japanese should racially discriminate against foreigners of Japanese ancestry by employing only white native speakers of English to teach English to Japanese. He reasons that because Japanese have such an enormous "gaijin complex," they would not feel comfortable learning English from native speakers of Japanese ancestry.[47] Watanabe's rationalization for racial discrimination in Japanese society is not without persuasiveness, especially for those who find discrimination convenient, desirable, or profitable.

The appreciation of insect sounds also tends to be the peculiar province of Japanese, according to Tsunoda Tadanobu, an otolaryngologist who has experimented with the differential reception of insect sounds and other sounds in the two hemispheres of the brain. Tsunoda's best-selling book on his research constitutes an incredibly deceptive blend of presumably scientific biometric data with cultural observations that constitute mere preconceptions and stereotypes rather than conclusions logically arguable from the data.[48] Although Tsunoda occasionally warns his reader that sensitivity to insect sounds is a matter of language and not genetics, his use of nationality labels in his small-sample comparative studies is thoroughly racist, and the impact of his book has been to strengthen the popular view that "Japanese" are racially unique.

Tsunoda writes, for example, of the Japanese spoken by two white subjects who showed the predominately "Japanese" pattern of sensitivity, that "if you listened to their Japanese as it came over the curtain [of the experiment booth they were sitting in], it was so perfect that you would have thought that they were Japanese."[49] In calling his book *The Brain of Japanese People* rather than *The Brain of the Japanese Language*, Tsunoda would seem to emphasize race rather than language. The title, like most of his research, ignores the existence of the hundreds of thousands of Koreans in Japan who are native speakers of Japanese, and the similar number of Japanese of recent Korean ancestry, not to mention Japanese of other ethnic ancestries. His "ethnic clinging" to foreigners of Japanese ancestry is tellingly ambivalent, for so-called Nisei and Sansei are always vaguely *nikkeijin* (people of Japanese ancestry) or *Nihonjin* (Japanese); never are those born in American said to be Americans.[50] For Tsunoda, being "Japanese" is a matter of race and little else.

Another example of how such obsessions with "blood" pervade human thought and make it exceedingly difficult for multi-ethnicity to emerge as a healthy alternative to extremism, schizoid paranoia, and self-destructive psychosis is found in a book published in Japan in 1976 by an international businessman and essayist, Sakamoto Uichirō, stylishly entitled *Gansō to Nihonjin: Anata no senzo wa nanizoku ka* (Facial Physiognomy of Japanese: What Ethnicity Were Your Ancestors?). The book epitomizes the kind of verbal categorization and expression that one can find innocently embedded in practically all contemporary commentaries on Japanese ethnicity: by Japanese and non-Japanese; in Japanese and other languages; and in pulp, popular, vernacular, journalistic, and even most scholarly publications—in short, in all the media.

A paragraph ten pages into the book directs the reader to a black-and-white photograph on the facing page, said to have been taken at a big-league baseball game, with a legend reading "Blonde girl and Korean-ancestry girl" (*kimpatsu shōjo to Kanminzoku-kei shōjo*). The author discusses the photograph as follows: "In the center of the photo is a blonde girl of Anglo-Saxon ancestry [kinpatsu no Anguro-Sakuson-kei no shōjo]. She probably came to cheer Dave Johnson,[51] who batted well that day. Even if the rather Korean-like girl to her left is Japanese, there can be no visual confusion of taking a blonde girl for a Japanese."[52]

What makes these and similar comments throughout the book innocent travesties of ethnic sensitivity is the conventional manner in which the author uses common words with their most ordinary meanings to express impressions that most of his readers probably share without hesitation. Not only has Sakamoto emphatically stated that naturally blonde, phenotypically Caucasian people *cannot be Japanese*, but he seems to imply that white blondes go to baseball games in Japan to watch gaijin batters triumph over "Japanese" pitchers. Moreover, after labeling an unidentified Asian face *Korean* in the caption, he admits in the text that the person may be *Japanese*, thus also using these labels with a degree of racial arbitrariness that utterly ignores the only criterion by which one can ever tell who is Japanese and who is not: bona fide nationality.

Not surprisingly, the same book includes other examples of reductionist cliches. Discussing the distribution of categorically white skin tones among apparently Asian-ancestry Japanese, the author does three very interesting things. First, he observes that better than 80 percent of Asian-Japanese (my term) have skins with yellow tones, while about 10 percent have darker, brownish skins typical of Polynesians and other South Pacific peoples. Second, he implies that the remaining few percent have "clear white skins that in whiteness seem to differ little from those of the peoples of northern Europe; or smooth, lustrous skins like *tamanegi* [round onions]; or beautiful skins translucent enough to faintly transmit the red tones of capillaries."[53] Third, and most significantly, Sakamoto writes in conclusion that:

It is very regrettable that recently there are many examples among the many caricaturists and artists who in portraying our masses uniformly render the faces of these masses in the same yellow skin tone. But there are also examples of calling us Japanese things like "Yellow Yankees" [Ieroo Yankii] or "Yellow Americans" [Kiiroi Amerikajin]. And [so] I feel that caricaturists and artists should more closely observe that which relates to white Japanese and emphasize this "white" existence.[54]

What one fails to write often provides the best clue to the meaning of what has been written. For example, a very competent journalist specializing in Japan once wrote, in a widely distributed pamphlet, of Japan's "well-known cultural homogeneity (one language, one race, one common historical experience)."[55] Having thus reduced Japan to a simple, mono-ethnic society, it is understandable why the reader was told nothing of the mutual unintelligiblity of some Japanese dialects, or nothing of the suppression of Okinawan, Ainu, Chinese, Korean, and other minority languages found in Japan or nothing of the dozen definitive ethnic groups that comprise a sizable fraction of the resident population, or nothing of the regional contrasts in historical experience that continue to diversify Japanese physique, personality, and culture.

Sakamoto does not seem to believe that "Japanese" origins are monogenic. Indeed, the point of his book is that "Japanese" origins are ethnically diverse. He simply fails to praise darker skins while admiring lighter skins. And he fails to ask that artists begin to emphasize the "dark existence" in the Japanese population, which might make it easier for darker, racially-mixed Japanese to be accepted as full Japanese, which they are if they are Japanese nationals.[56] And he fails to ask artists to represent Japanese of Korean, Chinese, Okinawan, and Ainu ancestry in their portrayals of the Japanese masses, and Japanese with black and white faces, and blonde hair and blue eyes.

To ask that Japan be portrayed as a multiracial, multicultural society is only to ask that the artist, journalist, and scholar be objective and humanistic. For Japan has never been a country for which the description "homogeneous" or "mono-ethnic" would be appropriate except as a reductionist, holistic caricature. During the one-and-a-half millennia for which we have reasonably accurate historical accounts of Japanese society and its population, it is clear that Japan has never been without ethnic minorities and ethnic conflict.[57] The tendency to deny that Japan is a complex, heterogenic, multi-ethnic society is the major source of anxiety and anguish for passable minorities who wish to be members of Japanese society without submitting their ethnic souls and acquiescing in the myth that they, if they pass, become as pure as those who would reject them if they did not. For those who cannot pass, there are constant reminders, verbal and nonverbal, that they lack the ethnic, usually racial emblems deemed essential to "Japanese" identity. But studies of popular heroes like Rikidōzan and others like him clearly show the extent to which "Japanese" racism can be self-deceptive. The fact that some disparaged outsiders can pass as majority Japanese, and be cheered and acclaimed as Japanese ethnic heroes, is the best reminder we have that majority Japanese are not as unlike the rest of humankind as popular self-images and stereotypes would have it.[58]

13

PROBLEMS OF SELF-IDENTITY AMONG KOREAN YOUTH IN JAPAN[1]

Hiroshi Wagatsuma

Korean youths born and raised in Japan may share potential problems of self-definition and pride. I say "potential" because I do not know how many individuals actually suffer from such problems, which may appear as acute and painful identity crises or may persist as chronic and vague states of self-doubt. From time to time, some young people may work out tentative solutions. Others may try to avoid facing the problems and may indeed be successful in such avoidance.

Several major social and psychological factors contribute to the formation of identity problems among Korean youth, generating negative emotions of self-hate and self-doubt. These factors include: (1) Social discrimination and prejudice against Koreans, and negative stereotyping of Koreans by the Japanese; (2) an unfavorable reality among the Koreans, in consequence of existing social injustice, that is used to justify further prejudice and discrimination; (3) Japanization and de-Koreanization of those Koreans born and raised in Japan; and (4) a Japanese citizenship based upon jus sanguinis, which makes it difficult to acquire the status of a naturalized citizen of Japan. These factors affect the most vulnerable lower classes with their full force. They may be mitigated for those who are more protected and fortunate. Individuals may be exposed to different combinations of these factors with varying degrees of intensity. A number of individuals have articulated their inner struggles with the problems.

DISCRIMINATION, ANGER, AND SELF-HATE

Koreans are exposed to strong prejudice and institutionalized discrimination from many sectors of Japanese society. Negative stereotyping of Koreans is readily available and is frequently utilized. It has been amply proven that, in the socialization processes of a minority-group member, exposure to the majority society's negative attitudes and stereotypes may result in the formation of a negative self-image.[2] Disparaging treatment may become internalized in a child's mind, resulting in a negative self-attitude.

In 1972 a magazine published the results of interviews with one-hundred individuals[3] who had experienced discrimination and prejudice.

These individuals included Burakumin,[4] Koreans, Chinese, Ainu, children of mixed parentage, and people from Southeast Asia. To avoid repetition, I will quote from only a few interviews. It should be remembered that incidents of individual and institutional discrimination against Koreans are numerous, and that discrimination leads not only to anger and resentment against the discriminators but often to shame and a wish to escape from one's disparaged identity.

> *Kumiko Takayama* (a maid, age 22, who used her Japanese pseudonym): It was when I was in elementary school. I was walking hand in hand with my close friends along a street in a shopping district. We were on our way home from school. Suddenly I saw an old woman in a white *chokoli* [Korean dress] walking toward us. My heart began beating fast. What should I do if that was my own grandma? If they found out that I was a Korean they would all walk away from me! I felt I was blushing. I was no longer holding my friends' hands. Step by step the old woman approached us. As I saw her face more and more clearly, my heart was beating faster and louder. There was only a 100-meter distance between us and the old woman. There was absolutely no doubt that it was my own grandmother. I prayed that she would not notice me. I prayed that she would not talk to me. I had gained all my close friends by hiding the fact that I was a Korean. Should I lose them nobody would talk to me any longer. Other children already had known what I was. They had laughed at me and called me a dirty Korean. I could no longer lose my friends. I prayed desperately. I walked along the edge of the street, keeping my face downward, looking at the surface of the road. But my prayer did not work. "Kumiko!" My grandmother called my name loudly and happily. She was greatly fond of me. I felt as if I had lost my eyesight! As if frightened, my friends quickly moved away from me. I brushed my grandmother's hand away and went home running and crying. . . . The next day, I wished I could stay home. I had to force myself to go to school. Nobody talked to me any more. The children who had been my close friends until that day, watched me from a distance without a word. . . . Why did I, alone, have to be laughed at, stoned, and spat at? After all we were the same humans, the same children. . . . I loathed my fate. Why was I singled out to be treated like that? Now that I am an adult I no longer wish I were a Japanese. I am satisfied with my being a Korean. However, I keep wondering why we cannot build a society without discrimination, a society in which everybody, regardless of race, color, and nationality, can live harmoniously together?

It seems almost universal that at times parents play an active role in tainting their children's minds with ethnocentrism and prejudice. The following premed student notes the difficulty Koreans have in getting a good job.

> *Ryu Kil-sang* (a university student, age 24): I have decided to become a doctor because the medical profession is necessary and valuable regardless of what happens to a society. It deals with human lives. I would like to believe that as long as I become professionally qualified it will make no difference whether or not I am a Korean. When I was a high school student I had a closest and best friend from my junior high school days. Until that time neither my friend nor his mother had known of my citizenship. When they came

to know I was a Korean, his mother suddenly changed her attitude. I was suddenly an unwelcome guest in their home. She was suddenly cold, indifferent, and inhospitable. Eventually my friend moved away from me, although I had long trusted him as my real friend.... In my neighborhood was a Korean woman, several years senior to me. She was bright, kind, and very attractive. Her school records at high school were excellent. However, she could never pass the examination for getting a job at big companies. She would always pass the written test but after an interview no company would offer her a job, while all the Japanese applicants who did poorly on the written examination were employed.... She asked her school principal and her teachers to help her. However, the wall of discrimination was too thick to break through. She gave up and is now working as a maid....

Some parents have sought to improve their children's lot by contriving to have them pass for Japanese.

Pak Ch'i-nam (print setter, age 21): I was born in October 1950 in Arakawa ward of Tokyo. My parents were Koreans. When I was born my parents were in the depths of poverty. They were eking out their scanty livelihood as day laborers. Their wages were very low. They worked as hard as the Japanese laborers, but as Koreans they were able to receive only half of the regular wages. Since my childhood I was taught to pretend to be a Japanese, throwing away Korean pride. Otherwise, my parents said, I would be discriminated against and exploited just like they were.... My parents were so poor that I could not attend a kindergarten. I went to an elementary school in the school district adjacent to mine, so that nobody knew I was a Korean. My parents registered me at this school as "Fukuda Masao." They wished that I would "pass" as a Japanese child. I did not quite understand why this had to be done. "Why do I have to pretend to be a Japanese, while I am actually a Korean?" However, I never expressed my question to anybody. I finished my elementary school as "a quiet and obedient Japanese child." My parents wanted me to enter a second-rate private junior high school far away from home. My parents were working hard to send me to school. and I had no choice. Everyday it took me nearly two hours each way to commute to school. At the end of my third year there, the final examination scores were announced on a board. My scores were ninety points out of a hundred for English, but forty-five for Japanese. Looking at them, the teacher of Japanese said, jokingly but loudly, "Fukuda, your scores make you look as if you were a foreigner, doing so well in English, while rather poorly in our own language!" And then he murmured as if to himself, "Well, after all, you are a Korean, aren't you?" Some of my classmates overheard him. For the following few months until the day of graduation almost every classmate hissed me. Even those I had thought of as my closest friends blamed me. "Why did you deceive us? You are a liar!" "So, you are a Korean, eh? No wonder you stink!" It is difficult to believe that the teacher of Japanese meant ill. None of my classmates who changed their attitudes toward me was particularly an evil person. All of them were average, normal Japanese. It is among those average, normal citizens of this country that strong exclusionism and discrimination exist. Unlike some leftist ideologues, I would not differentiate between Japanese imperialists and Japanese common people. The Japanese are discriminators and oppressors as a group, all of them. I intend to fight them, keeping in mind all the memories of humiliating experiences in my past....

As long as one resents discrimination enough to fight it, one's self-attitudes may not incur many negative consequences. Once a person succumbs to discrimination, however, and wishes to hide what he really is, his self-image ultimately suffers. The following is a statement by a young man with remarkable insight into himself:

Cho Ryong-whan (high school student, age 19): I am a Korean but I am hiding it from my classmates. I would not willingly choose this hiding, and so it hurts me a great deal. It is only because I am a Korean that I cannot open up my own amateur radio station. I have to carry an alien registration card all the time. When I was smaller I could not receive any innoculations at school. However, I am not bothered so much by such visible discrimination. Every time that somebody sneers at me saying "Ha! You are a Korean!" my self-awareness as a Korean becomes strengthened. What I fear most is the formation of discrimination inside myself, as the result of my long exposure to discrimination from the outside. There happened once an unforgettable event. I was a seventh-grader then. It was in an English conversation class. The teacher was asking questions in English and we were answering them. Suddenly, his question was "Are you a Japanese boy?" Each student was to answer it repeating him, "Yes, I am a Japanese boy." What should I say to answer the question, if the teacher asked me? I almost panicked. I wished that the teacher would not ask me that particular question. But what if he did? All of a sudden, I realized that I did not know any English word for Korean. It was a great relief. It gave me an excuse. I told myself that I did not have to answer the question honestly because I did not know the word to use! The teacher was approaching me, repeating his question to other students. It was my turn. "Are you a Japanese boy, Mr. Tanaka (which was my pseudonym)?" I heard myself answering him, immediately and clearly, "Yes, I am a Japanese boy!" My mind was quickly filled with humiliation. I had cheated. I had lied. I had deceived my own self. Instead of resisting against and fighting discrimination, I had given in. People still make fun of me, calling me a dirty Korean. It is nothing, however, compared with that humiliating experience of self-deception.

Kim Kyong-dŭk, the Korean law student who fought with institutionalized discrimination in the judicial field, as reported in chapter 11, admitted in his statement that he, too, hated himself because he was Korean: "Throughout the years of my life in Japan, I have been hating myself for being a Korean. I have always tried to be like a Japanese. I do not know how many times I have trembled with fears of having my real identity discovered by my peers."[5]

NEGATIVE SELF-IMAGES AND THE SEARCH FOR A POSITIVE IDENTITY

It is a widely recognized social and psychological phenomenon that stereotypical images of a minority group are eventually absorbed and believed by the members of that very group. I was once discussing anti-Semitism with a Jewish student. Responding to my question, "But how could people tell that you are Jewish?" she pointed to her nose and answered, "With this nose?!" as if the question were so naive that she could not help but smile. When I once visited a juvenile prison in Hokkaido, the northernmost island of Japan, I learned that two inmates were Ainu. In response to my question about possible problems between the Japanese inmates and the members of this minority group, the superintendent answered, "No, they are getting along well with each other. However, both of the Ainu boys refuse to take a communal bath with the other Japanese boys. The reason for their refusal is that as Ainu they are hairier than the Japanese and they are afraid lest they should be laughed at for their hairy bodies." The Ainu, a Proto-Caucasoid group, are *believed* to be hairier than the Mongoloid Japanese, in spite of the fact that through generations of mixing with the Japanese many Ainu individuals have lost their original physical characteristics. The requested physical examination by a doctor of these two Ainu inmates at the juvenile prison revealed that they were neither more nor less hairy than any Japanese. It is worth noting, therefore, that Lee Hoe-sŏng, a well-known Korean writer who published his work in the Japanese language, implies in one of his apparently autobiographical novels that he believes in such physical stereotyping of the Koreans: "... As if punishing himself, Joang suddenly slapped his calf. It was *almost completely hairless as is common to many Koreans. Speaking of the physical characteristics of the Korean, the back of his head was flat, too*"[6] (italics added).

Such internalization by minority individuals of the majority society's negative attitudes toward them may create a self-image inseparably associated with a negative image of their own group as a whole. Social discrimination has actually created an unfavorable reality among the Koreans. Many of them live in poverty, engaged in undesirable or disreputable occupations, and many display deviant behavior. Such a reality may support and perpetuate negative images of the Koreans as a group and may be used not only by Japanese but by Koreans as well to justify prejudice and discrimination. Self-contempt and self-hatred may fuse with contempt and hatred directed against other members of one's own group. The ideas of impoverished, dirty, violent, disreputable, or outright improper ways of life in a ghetto, real or imagined, are at times utilized by individuals almost as an excuse for negative feelings toward one's own group and eventually one's own self. Such inner conflicts are also described by the novelist, Lee Hoe-song:[7]

> His father was angry at the Japanese who were contemptuous of and discriminating against the Koreans. His father was protesting against the Japanese. He was also contemptuous of the Japanese. Nam-su [the protagonist] understood to a degree, at least, his father's resentment. However, he looked down upon his father for different reasons. Looking at his father at home, Nam-su felt contemptuous of his father. It was a different contempt from the contempt his father felt toward the Japanese. At home, Nam-su's father was a feudal lord, a

tyrant. Nam-su felt ashamed of his father, who spoke loudly, shouted at everybody, and displayed physical violence. He felt contemptuous of his father and ashamed of the Koreans as a whole. This also meant, however, that he hated himself, because he too was a Korean. He felt that the longer he stayed home the more he disliked the Koreans and the stronger became his self-denial. He also felt that the real way to be a Korean existed somewhere else outside his home. He forced himself to think that he had to leave his home no matter what. In order to become a real Korean, he had to deny his own father's home.[8]

It is highly significant that for this young Korean his father's behavior and home symbolize a "negative identity" for the Koreans, and that in his attempt to find—or create in himself—a "positive identity" (which he calls "a real Korean") he must leave his father's home. His mother does not understand her son's inner struggles and becomes sad, not knowing why her son has to leave her.

. . . when his father beat him, his mother protected him with her own body, crying, *"Aiko! Bulsangt'a!"* On her son's behalf, she avoided no trouble and no suffering. However, she was totally ignorant of her son's problems, his suffering and painful attempts to become a [real] Korean. She never doubted that she was a Korean. Therefore, her son, to whom she gave birth, could be none other than Korean. It was that simple, and she never understood why her son had to suffer from "problems" . . . . "It must be," thought Nam-su, "that Chŏn-ya's mother, too, was at a loss when her son looked down upon the Koreans and asked her why she had given birth to him as a Korean. However, no matter how sad and disappointed the parents may become, their sons could not become Koreans unless and until they found something they could be proud of as Koreans."[9]

In the attempts to find a positive self-identity for Koreans, the negative image of their own group is not the only obstacle. Perhaps more unmanageable is their inner sense of "Japaneseness." Born and raised in Japan, most of the second and third generation Koreans are more or less Japanized. Not only must they rid themselves of every association with negative images of their own group but they must replace Japanese qualities in themselves with what is positively Korean.

Japanization can take place as a consequence of over-identification with Japanese culture. When a member of an oppressed minority group wishes to escape from his own social status and to be accepted by the majority group, he may attempt, consciously or unconsciously, to incorporate the behavior patterns of the majority group while totally rejecting what characterizes his own.

Before the era of ethnic consciousness in the United States, many middle-class blacks were said to be more "middle-classy" in their dress, speech, values, and life-style than their white counterparts. In their attempt to be assimilated into the dominant white culture, many Japanese-Americans in the past liked to claim that they had totally lost the knowledge of the Japanese that had been their first language in childhood. Individuals may overdo in attaining such optative identities, becoming almost caricatures. I once knew two student leaders of a black action society at an Eastern university. They were very militant, spoke almost exaggerated "soul language," and presented themselves as more-than-typical black young men in their dress, gestures, and mannerisms. One of them had a German mother. The other had a Japanese mother. Nonetheless, they had seemingly persuaded themselves that they were totally black and had no trace of German or Japanese elements in themselves. Koreans may have done the same in rejecting things Korean.[10]

Japanization is not necessarily caused by over-identification. It may simply be an unavoidable consequence of growing up in Japan. The majority of the Korean children go to Japanese schools. It is only natural that they learn Japanese as their first, and often *only*, language. When a child grows up in a society, enculturation in that society is a natural consequence. The child may grow up on an island of foreign culture in the midst of a dominant culture. The child may somehow be insulated, but it is usually extremely difficult to shield the child completely from outside impact. Koreans in Japan do not live on a well-shielded island of Korean culture. They are exposed to surrounding Japanese. It should also be remembered that, for a Korean child, the learning of Japanese culture often brings a special reward. The child can pass as a Japanese and as long as such passing is successful, even temporarily, he is safe from discrimination.

Either through over-identification or natural enculturation, many Koreans have become more or less Japanized. Such Japanization may cause an individual to become *less Korean* as his or her Korean identity is internally eroded. A derogatory term, *Pan Tchokppali*, designates a Japanized Korean or a half-Japanese, "Tchokppali" being a very derogatory word meaning Japanese. A Japanized Korean may not only suffer from loss of Korean identity or from inner erosion but may also experience self-hatred. If one hates prejudiced and discriminating Japanese, such hatred and anger can be directed to the Japanized aspect of oneself. To the extent that one desires to be like the Japanese, while simultaneously hating the Japanese, ambivalence toward oneself is unavoidable.

To develop a positive attitude toward oneself, one must undertake not only to *de-Japanize* oneself but, conversely, to *Koreanize* inwardly. A number of Korean intellectuals, themselves considerably Japanized, have expressed the need for such a task. Novelist Lee Hoe-sŏng characterizes a young Korean, Kim Mun-ho, who tried very hard during the war to be assimilated into Japanese society. He became known in his class as a "commendable boy," loyal to the country and always obedient. Simultaneously, he developed the "detestable character trait" of servility. He was satisfied to be second-best, although he could have been first in the class, "because he calculated his disadvantages as a Korean and also because he had been somehow convinced that he could not really do better than the Japanese children." After the war, Kim Mun-ho realizes that he has become Japanized and de-Koreanized. Now he must somehow restore his Korean identity:

> He had frequently fallen into a situation in which he had to prove that he was a Korean. When Japan was defeated in the War, he vaguely thought he would return to Korea. However, it was not so easy as he had thought for an assimilated boy" to become a Korean. How difficult it was for somebody who was originally a Korean to prove to himself and to others that he was still really a Korean! It was a task that needed years and months. It was not like going to a city ward office and looking at one's own family registry. The task of restoring one's national awareness that was once lost was almost like finding the soul of an individual.[11]

Another Korean author, O Im-chun, also writing in Japanese, talks about himself:

> I am a Korean. I am supposed to have said good-bye to all the Japanese sword-fighting films so popular among the mass of Japanese. Yet, somewhere in my mind, I cannot forget them. I cannot stop liking them. . . . Stab my body, now, and I still bleed the blood of a half-Japanese. . . . Kim Hi-lo [see chapter 11] shed tears when Japan was defeated in the war. Such feelings of Japan-born Koreans should certainly be buried. In order to restore Korean pride, we shouldn't speak Japanese language among ourselves but speak it only to the Japanese. If one does not speak Korean fluently, one should master it, even if it means not speaking Japanese meanwhile. . . . Such a handicap, that one cannot speak one's own language, is the poison which Japanese Imperialism forced us to take. However, the poison does not completely and thoroughly permeate our systems. At least those who survived poisoning and escaped death will know from their experiences how to be careful about poison and will never take it again. . . . By the same token, the poison I took—the establishment of a half-Japanese inside myself by ignorance and the choice of wrong experience—has turned into a strange benefactor who reminds me of how contemptuous an individual I once was.[12]

Another author, Kim Hak-Yŏng, also writing in Japanese, expresses his hope for restoring a new Korean identity in himself:

> "If you resent the discrimination, why don't you go back to your own country?" He read it in a letter to the newspaper editors from a housewife. When he read it he momentarily wondered if he had read it accurately. It was the most indifferent, most ignorant, and most cruel remark he had ever read or heard. Wouldn't an elementary school child be ashamed of saying such a thing? Who was responsible for the fact that the Koreans left their own country and began living in Japan? Who deprived the Koreans of their land and life? Who forced millions of them to wander around in Japan and in northeastern China? Could this be a remark made by a Japanese to the Koreans? He

felt both strong anger and terrible disappointment. He wondered why such a letter had been chosen and printed in the newspaper. If such an opinion were expressed only in one single letter, such a letter would not have been selected. The fact that it was selected and printed probably meant that several other similar letters had been received by the editors who, therefore, judged that such an opinion was shared commonly by many Japanese. The letter from a housewife was chosen as expressive of the voice of an average Japanese.... What makes the Japanese entertain such an opinion? He said to himself, "I was born in Japan. I have received a Japanese education. I have lived and will live in the Japanese climate. I will never be able to escape from the 'Japanese' in myself. I will never be able to escape from my fate of being neither a Korean nor a Japanese, or of being both a Korean and a Japanese.... However, through understanding and accepting myself as such, I may perhaps be able to understand the Japanese nation better. I may even be able to think of humanity more deeply. There might even be a true liberation for me in my efforts to learn and understand all about this."[13]

THE TRAGIC ENDING OF A SEARCH FOR IDENTITY

The three social and psychological factors discussed above may be observed among many ethnic minorities in various societies, including those in the United States. They are not limited to the Koreans in Japan. A fourth factor, however, is unique to the Koreans in Japan and is related to their citizenship status. Every hyphenated American, regardless of disadvantaged or privileged status and psychological problems, or of color, creed, and culture, is entitled to be an American citizen if born in the United States. American citizenship, like that of Canada, Australia, and several other countries, is based on jus soli. Anyone born on the soil of the United States is entitled to American citizenship. In contrast, however, Japanese citizenship is based on jus sanguinis, the rule that a child's citizenship is determined by his parents' citizenship. A child may be born and may grow up in Japan, speaking only Japanese language, behaving in the same way as any other Japanese child. But if the child's parents are not Japanese citizens neither is the child.

A simple legal fact is that a majority of the Koreans born and raised in Japan remain aliens. This simple legal fact may have more complicated psychological implications. Although it is no more than a hypothetical proposition, difficult to test empirically, it is possible that the citizenship based upon jus soli and that based on jus sanguinis have somewhat different meanings for an individual's self-identity. When one can become a citizen of a country only when one's parents are already the citizens of the country, such a citizenship, based upon blood ties, may be felt as something closely integral with one's self-identity. In contrast, however, when one can become a citizen of a country simply by being born there, and especially when one's parents or grandparents are aliens, or naturalized citizens, such citizenship may be felt as less integral with, and as a somewhat loosely attached part of, one's identity. In countries like the United States, Canada, and Australia, a permanently resident alien can relatively easily become a naturalized citizen. It is not easy at all for an alien to obtain Japanese citizenship. This difficulty may mark the Japanese citizenship as something special. When citizenship is felt to be an integral part of one's self-identity, newly acquiring such citizenship by naturalization may be felt to affect one's identity. By becoming a citizen of Japan, an individual may lose a previous alien identity.

In contrast, however, when citizenship can be felt as a more loosely attached part of one's identity, the acquisition of such a citizenship may not so seriously affect one's identity. One may be able to become a naturalized citizen of the United States while inwardly remaining a Korean, a Japanese, or whatever one originally was. The naturalization can remain more or less a legal change, without involving much change in the sense of identity. Admittedly, such a difference may very well be a matter of degree. And yet the difference seems to have some important psychological consequences. A number of Korean youths raised in Japan have remarked that the idea of becoming a Japanese citizen is felt to be a betrayal, although the idea of becoming an American citizen is not felt in the same way. "It can simply be a legal procedure almost for the sake of convenience."

It is also possible that their anger and hatred toward Japanese society can make the Koreans feel that becoming a Japanese citizen is "selling oneself out." Even when they have an opportunity to become naturalized citizens of Japan, many Koreans have refused to do so. The aforementioned law student, Kim Kyong-dǔk, refused to acquire citizenship as the condition for his acceptance into the training institution after passing the governmental examination (see chap. 11). He stated: "Forcing me to declare the intention of naturalization is . . . to negate my own ethnic identity. . . . As long as the prejudice and discrimination persist against the Koreans, I find no justification to declare my intention to naturalize myself into a society in which my own human rights are frequently denied."[14]

Among those who have been able to become naturalized Japanese citizens, some feel comfortable with their changed identity. Others may insist that they remain inwardly Korean in spite of the change in their legal status. Still others may feel guilty for having "betrayed" their fellow countrymen and themselves. Worse still, some feel that they have become neither Korean nor Japanese. One young man ended his life in the middle of his attempt to find his new positive identity. He had become a naturalized citizen because his parents had decided to do so when he was still a small child. It was not his own choice. He felt he had betrayed his fellow Koreans. He was Yamamura Masaaki, or Yang Chǒng-Myǒng, born in Yamaguchi prefecture of southwestern Japan in June 1945 as the third son among seven brothers and sisters. He was an excellent student throughout his elementary, junior, and senior high school years. In June 1955, his entire family became naturalized citizens of Japan. But Yamamura was unable to feel that he had become a "real Japanese." Instead, he felt he had become neither a Korean nor a Japanese. Actually, he was rejected with scorn by some young Koreans who saw him as a "traitor" despite his desire to join them in the fight against discrimination. Upon finishing high school, he found a job at the Tōyō Manufacturing Company in Hiroshima city. But he had long wished to become a literary writer, and he could not give up his wish. Six months later he resigned from his job and moved to Tokyo. He prepared for an entrance examination while supporting himself with a variety of menial jobs. In April 1967, he passed the examination and became a student in the Department of Letters at Waseda University, one of Japan's leading private institutions. Influenced by a Japanese woman whom he admired as his own elder sister, he converted to Christianity. He published poems and novels in the campus literary magazines. More and more, however, he became interested in political activism and joined the student movements. He was continuously tormented with identity problems and doubts about Christianity. Financially, too, he was pressed. He was wounded in one of the fights between two subgroups among the student activists. His love for a Japanese woman ended in unhappiness because he was a Korean. From all this he became totally exhausted. Early on the morning of 6 October 1970, he soaked himself with gasoline and burned himself to death. He was twenty-five years old. Left behind were letters to his parents and a statement protesting racial and ethnic discrimination among the Japanese. His notes, letters, and poems were posthumously published in a book entitled *Even if My Life Ends in Flame*[15] (Inochi moetsukiru tomo). The following selections from his writings reveal his inner conflicts and his anguish over the problems of social injustice, hatred, anger, identity crises, and loneliness.

Like others before him, Yamamura experienced the loss of his friendship with his Japanese peers and even of his love for a Japanese woman when he revealed his Korean heritage. He wrote:

"Destiny"

When I confessed it
With great determination and
With great anxiety,
She looked down and remained silent.

Our conversations were buried forever
And she disappeared from my life
As if running away.

At that time I told myself
Never again to have a dream....

On 21 August 1965 in his letter to a Japanese woman he confessed that he was a "stateless" person, being neither a Korean nor a Japanese. Although he was a naturalized citizen he could not fully identify himself with the Japanese, whom he hated for their discrimination and prejudice. As a good Christian he tried to forgive them, but he was not consistently successful in his attempt. He could not feel inwardly Korean, not only because of his citizenship status but probably because he had become too Japanized:

> Have you ever reflected upon the fact that you are a Japanese? It is not the home country or patriotism that I am talking about. I think I would not have become a man of such a character if I had been born as a real Japanese. I have no home. I have no country of my own. My parents are Koreans. Fate, beyond human control, decreed their birth in Korea and yet led them to Japan to settle, to live and, in the end, to die. The Japanese judge them to be members of an inferior nation. However, I have contempt for the Japanese. Although I have acquired Japanese citizenship, I am not at heart a Japanese. Neither am I a Korean any longer.... There must be tens and hundreds of thousands of unfortunate people like myself. It is not that I am the only miserable one. There are also many people who are well adjusted to Japanese society and successful in their work and life, without being bothered by such an inner conflict as I have (although I am sure nobody can avoid thinking about it deep in their mind...).

He expressed his statelessness in a poem:

"Loss of Homeland

In my body runs
The blood of a group long exploited and humiliated.
Under the oppression and difficulties of living in
       this country
I finally found real friends, I thought.

When I told them what had been hidden in my mind
With my own determination,
Their hands, too, became cold toward me.

True, it is
That I can no longer be
Their real friend....

On 5 April 1968 he wrote in a letter to his elder brother,

> ...in my case, my complex as a Korean is more specifically an inferiority complex about myself toward the Japanese. Once you said you may marry a Japanese woman while pretending you are a Japanese. I do not understand

why you have to lie like that. I am afraid that such an attitude reveals your own prejudice against Koreans. Why do you have to hide your being a Korean? Why do you have to run away from this fact? Why are you ashamed of it? There is absolutely no reason why we have to be looked down upon by the Japanese. It is the Japanese who ought to feel ashamed of their mean despoilment. . . . In any case, you are doing quite successfully as a member of this society. You are more capable than average Japanese people. Unlike myself, you are goodlooking, too. If she still likes you, you should tell her the truth. If she were to leave you because you are a Korean, should such a woman deserve your affection? You should turn her down. Anybody with sympathy, with an insightful and broad mind, should accept a Korean as a Korean. You don't have to worry about people around you. You are not going to marry a house or a piece of property. Any person with a normal mind will understand your moral character and accept you eventually. I think it is too sentimental and infantile to withdraw without telling her, so that no one will be hurt and the memory [will] remain happy and peaceful. It is not an adult's love. I think I am right. I think this is the best solution.

He tried to "forgive" and even to "love" the Japanese with the help of God's love in Christian teachings. When he thought he had reached that state of mind he published a tract on 17 February 1969, entitled *The Confession of a Soul: Memoir of a Second Generation Korean in Japan*. A selection from this essay follows:

I have long hated the Japanese because through my body runs the blood of the Koreans who were trampled down by the Japanese. . . . My parents moved to Japan in the mid-1920's, leaving behind their mother country which had been totally exploited by the ruthless conquest of Japanese Imperialism. My parents do not like to talk about their past. It must be beyond my imagination how much they suffered in the pre-war Japan when prejudice and contempt toward the Koreans were by far stronger than they are now. . . . When I began playing with neighborhood friends, I learned that we were to be discriminated against, that we were different from all the other children in the neighborhood. They called me and my brothers and sisters "Chōsenjin! Chōsenjin!" (Koreans) with contempt and sneers. I was simply sad and angry without truly understanding the meaning of the situation. . . . It was when I was in the fourth grade. I was caught on my way from school by children in upper grades. They called me, "Chōsenjin! Chōsenjin!" I became angry and tried to stop them. But I was overwhelmed by them. I had to run. Three big boys chased me, and I was pushed down into the soft mud in a rice paddy. Trampled down in mud, I cried. Several adults were watching us, but nobody tried to stop my enemies. . . . My parents tried to escape humiliation once and for all. As they could not find a way to move back to their home country, they decided to become naturalized citizens of Japan. I remember seeing them visit and bow in front of the town's leaders, presenting gifts they managed to buy even in their poverty. I felt sorry for them. I felt angry at them. Later I learned that there are roughly two types of Koreans in Japan. The first group does not give up their pride as Koreans while living in a foreign country. The second group desperately tries to be assimilated into Japanese society. To my great sadness, my parents belonged to the second group. They had experienced enough pains. They had struggled hard to survive. Probably I should not blame them for their wish to be assimilated into Japanese society. However, I was unable to respect my own parents because they had tried to forget their own country and countrymen, and because they had tried to be accepted by the Japanese. . . . Why do we have to be so humiliated and held in contempt? Are we really an inferior ethnic group: Have we lived in any way that deserves disdain? No! It is the Japanese who should be held in contempt for what they have done to the Koreans. . . . I chose a high school that was far away from my own town where people knew what I was. I spent two hours on a train commuting to school. It was a totally lonesome life. On the surface I must have been an excellent student. I always remained at the top of my class. I was the vice-president of the students' self-governing body. I was also active in the student newspaper. At the time of our graduation, my teacher said to me that I was the "hope of the school." Inside, however, I was always lonely and miserable. No matter how well I might have done at school, I never experienced real joy. Conflicts remained unresolved in my mind. . . . I detested all human beings. I looked down upon everybody—neighbors, classmates, teachers, and my own parents. Humans are all ugly. Often I was tormented by my own self-hatred. Is this society really worth living in? Or is it myself that does not deserve life? What is the use of human life? What is its real value?

Yamamura became a Christian, although in the beginning he could not believe in God's love because, "if justice and fairness are God's attributes, why does God allow evils and injustice in human societies? The strong torture the weak. The whites torment the blacks. The Japanese slight the Koreans." Exhausted from financial worry and internal conflicts, Yamamura once decided to commit suicide. He wandered around in the Japanese Alps for ten days looking for a place to die. Unable to make up his mind, he returned to his room in Tokyo and opened the Bible.

> I felt the sentence I read had been meant for me. "Cast away from you all your transgressions, whereby ye have transgressed; and make you a new heart and a new spirit: for why will ye die, O house of Israel? For I have no pleasure in the death of him that dieth, said the Lord God: wherefore turn yourselves, and live ye" (Ezekiel: 18: 31-32).
> Christ's blessing brought me many things. Peace of mind, an eternal hope, joy of life, strength to live, and above all, God's love. I learned to love. I learned to love people. My hatred turned into love. . . . My Japanese friends! Please understand this. The Koreans did not choose of their own accord to lead a miserable life in this foreign land. So many Japanese say so easily and so quickly, "If you do not want to be slighted, why don't you go back to your own country?" These Koreans have the foundation of their lives only in Japan. . . . Let me end my essay with quotations from the Bible.
> "Hereby perceive we the love *of God*, because he laid down his life for us" (1 John 3:16). "There is neither Jew nor Greek, there is neither bond nor free, there is neither male nor female: for ye are all one in Christ Jesus" (Galatians 3:28). "For our conversation is in heaven; from whence also we look for the Saviour, the Lord Jesus Christ" (Philippians 3:20).

He could not consistently live as a Christian. Instead, breaking the Christian's rule, he took his own life by turning himself into a human torch ablaze.

"Fate"

Fate.
I am too weak to carry its heaviness.
I tried to run.
I tried to deceive.
I tried to forget.
I tried to forgive.
At last, I learned that I must fight.

But, alas!
I wish I could have avoided
Having been born in such a land. . . .

RESTORATION OF NATIONAL PRIDE: A SOLUTION

In the worldwide trend toward an increased ethnic, racial, and national awareness, the Koreans in Japan have found a solution to their identity problems by being fully Korean, proudly knowledgeable of their own language and culture, and by struggling to obtain fair and equal treatment by the Japanese. This approach is complicated by the political and military situations in the Korean peninsula. Some Koreans in Japan are capable of firm identification with and loyalty to North or South Korea as a nation, looking at it with pride as their "home country." But many others are bothered by the division of their homeland into two antagonistic states and by the division of the Koreans in Japan into two opposing groups—Mindan and Ch'ongnyŏn (see chap. 6). The name of the Japanese language newspaper widely circulated among the Koreans reflects their wish: *Tōitsu Nippō* (the Unification Daily News). A short-lived magazine carried the name of *Madang*, meaning "a plaza" or "a public meeting place" to be used for conversation between or among peoples of different ideologies and viewpoints. Koreans are seeking a unified homeland with which they can proudly identify. Until and unless such a political change is brought about, the identity problem cannot be fully resolved.

For example, in regard to an increasing number of intermarriages between Japanese and Japan-born Korean youths, a writer expressed his concern with the loss of national identity among such youths, emphasizing the importance of a unified Korea for the maintenance of national pride:[16]

What matters after all is the loss of national identity among the second-generation Korean youths and their attitudes which do not resist marriage with the Japanese. Unless we somehow stop the Japanization among them we cannot prevent all these tragedies resulting from the inter-marriages. In order to stop Japanization and to establish among them national pride, many methods are conceivable. The expansion of ethnic education is one. However, the most important and decisive means for it is the establishment of a unified Korea as a state. Korea, split into halves, filled with repeated political confusions, economic misery, social oppression, is nothing more than an object of repulsion for the Japan-born Koreans. The solidified efforts among the Koreans in Japan to establish a unified Korean state is the only premise for solution.

It is true, however, that regardless of the problems of a split homeland, this new nationalistic trend has yielded positive consequences, especially for younger Koreans. The following report describes three such attempts to restore in children a national pride. The first attempt was made at a kindergarten in Kawasaki city near Tokyo. The second and third attempts took place at schools in Osaka city.

It should be noted that the restoration of national pride begins with the use of Korean names. A name is one of the most important factors in identity.[17] Prevailing reluctance among parents to let their children use their Korean names suggests not only how harshly they have experienced discrimination but also how intensely they fear such social injustice. Many Koreans have protected themselves behind Japanese pseudonyms and wish to continue thus. It takes courage to walk out of a hidden shelter into an open struggle against discrimination. Nonetheless, numerous Koreans are so doing. They are restoring their pride, which must be further fortified by identification with their language and culture.

Approximately nine thousand Koreans are living in Kawasaki city of the Kanagawa prefecture, embedded in the so-called Tokyo-Yokohama Heavy Industrial Zone. More than half of these Koreans are concentrated in four districts of the city. In April 1969, the Kawasaki Korean Christian church established a new nursery school in one of the four districts. The main purpose was to help the working mothers in the neighborhood. Many Japanese working mothers had been pleased with the news about the establishment of a new nursery, but when they learned that the nursery was to be run by the Korean church, most of them wanted to withdraw their advance applications. The potentially drastic reduction of clients would have had serious financial implications. The nursery administrators asked a Canadian missionary to teach the children English conversation. Lured by this rare opportunity, the Japanese parents agreed to send their children to the nursery. When it first opened, the nursery school had three governesses and thirty children.

In spring of 1970 the nursery school administration decided to register all the Korean children by their Korean names. It also began teaching the Korean children Korean songs and elementary Korean conversation. The children happily learned the language. They were comfortable with their Korean names, by which each was identified. But most parents were very much upset. In a variety of ways they expressed their concerns: "We are living in Japan. Why not use the Japanese names?" "We have suffered from discrimination against the Koreans. We would like to protect our children from the same experiences. For doing so, we must make them use Japanese names." "Why is it necessary to make such a big issue out of names? What matters is that our children themselves know that they are Koreans. They need their Japanese names to protect them from prejudice and discrimination." "Our children are still too young to understand such a difficult problem. Leave them alone until they become older. Please call them by the names they are accustomed to."

To overcome such parental opposition, the school governesses met with the parents, discussing the situation at length in hopes of persuading them. One of the governesses, Miss Chūng, admitted the difficulty. "I was afraid to propose the use of the Korean names. I myself was unsure of its effects. The parents said to me that I was too much of an idealist to realize how important it was for them to hide their Korean background and thereby avoid discrimination. It was a matter of survival for them. I did not know how to counter their arguments. However, I believed that the use of the Korean names would give ego support to our children. It wakes them up to the fact that they had been overly Japanized, and it protects them from further assimilation. This is the only way to make them strong enough to fight discrimination. Otherwise, they will repeat the same sufferings we went through. I did my very best to persuade the parents."

Finally the parents agreed to the use of the Korean names. To the great disappointment of the schoolteachers, however, the children switched back to their Japanese names as soon as they left the nursery school and entered grade school. Making the parents agree to the use of the Korean names at school was far from sufficient. The school teachers wanted to do something more—such as conducting ethnic studies (*minzoku kyōiku*), and teaching Korean language and culture. But no teacher could speak Korean fluently. Nobody knew any appropriate teaching materials to be used. They were also afraid lest the Japanese parents might resent an emphasis on the Korean culture and withdraw their children.

In February 1974, four years after the school was established, it became a corporate body under the administration of a social welfare organization called Ch'ŏngku Association, Inc. (Ch'ŏngku, or Blue Hills, is the nickname of the Korean peninsula.) It had six Korean governesses, one Japanese governess, two kitchen workers, and eighty children. With separation of the Korean and Japanese children into different classes, the school began emphasizing Korean education. The name plates at the lockers for the Korean children were all spelled with the Korean alphabet. The school also encouraged the mothers to organize themselves into a study group for discussion. The teachers attended the mothers' meetings and taught them the importance of ethnic studies at home. Language and history classes were offered by the youth group of the Kawasaki church and many mothers attended them. The parents gradually became convinced of how important it was for them and their children to be proud of being Koreans.

Today at this nursery school the Korean children are all called by their Korean names. They greet each other and their teachers in Korean. They sing Korean songs. Teachers incorporate Korean words into their predominantly Japanese conversation with the children. The number of Korean words is gradually increased to enrich the children's vocabulary. Although the children bring rice from home, the rest of their lunch—including hot Korean pickles—is provided by the school.

A school governess, Miss Mun, was educated at Japanese schools. She had been using her Japanese pseudonym until she began working at this school. "Since coming to this school," said Miss Mun, "I have continuously suffered from conflicts. I have wished to quit a number of times. When we proposed the use of the Korean names, a Korean child said to me that he was not a Korean. At that time I was still using my Japanese pseudonym. How could I have forced the children to use their Korean names? Finally, I decided to use my real Korean name, although I had to hide it from my mother who opposed it." Miss Mun still wavers. "On the one hand, I think that the basis of our education is sound and that the use of the Korean names is the right thing to do. On the other hand, however, I am not so sure at times. Honestly, I often lose my self-confidence."

The overwhelming majority of the children leave the nursery school for Japanese schools. While at the nursery school, they say proudly, "I am a Korean." At the Japanese schools among the Japanese children, however, they become less and less sure of themselves. Many children decide to use their Japanese pseudonyms again. Mrs. Lee, age 31, the mother of a second-grader, says, "I knew I should give my child a Korean name. But after wondering for a long time I chose the name that can pass both as a Japanese [Kei-ichi] and a Korean [Kyŏng-il]. Six months after he entered an elementary school, my son came home and said to me, 'Ŏmoni [mother], I wish to become a Japanese.' I asked him why but he would not tell me. I told him that he is a Korean and that he cannot become a Japanese. I said that both his parents are Koreans and it is a good thing. He remained silent. Some time later he came back to me and asked me to change his name from Korean to Japanese. He is the only Korean child in his class and other children bully him because his name is different." Mrs. Lee went to school and talked with the teacher. The teacher discovered that the mother of a child in the class had told her child not to play with the Korean and this warning had spread among other children. Mrs. Lee asked the teacher to stop such discrimination, but the teacher did not give her a very encouraging answer. Mrs. Lee found her own answer to the problem. "I decided to think this way," said she, "that the experience of discrimination and prejudice should help my child grow up strong. I wish him to be a tough person who can fight and overcome discrimination. Exposed to discrimination and injustice, he perhaps will become a man who is more understanding and sympathetic toward others than the child who grows up without such experiences."

Another mother indicated somewhat different attitudes. Mrs. Kim is the mother of a girl in the eighth grade. Her daughter used her real Korean name at the nursery school, but since leaving the school she has been using her Japanese pseudonym. Mrs. Kim admits that she is letting her daughter use her Japanese name:

> But I keep telling my daughter that she should live with pride, without fearing prejudice and discrimination. After all, humans are humans and they are all equally important. She does not say anything, though. She just smiles and listens to me. When there are Japanese around, my daughter calls me and my husband, "Mama and Papa" like many other Japanese children do. When no Japanese are around, she says "Ōmoni [mother in Korean] and Abōchi [father]." She must be self-conscious about being Korean. I understand the importance of using real Korean names. I must admit, however, that it is extremely difficult to do it. When my daughter finishes high school I wish to send her to Korea for a college education. Then she will use her Korean name. Until then I do not wish to think about it, because I cannot decide one way or another. I was born in Japan, and I know no Korean language. I hope my daughter takes a real interest in learning Korean. Then I will also attend language classes and learn my own language.[18]

The use of their real names began among the Korean children at a school in a ward of Osaka city with a high concentration of Koreans. At this school in 1974 approximately 20 percent of its 620 children were Koreans. On the morning of 13 December 1974 a Korean child read his announcement in the school auditorium to the children gathered for the morning meeting. "Since last November, I have been using my real name, Lee T'ae-sik, in my class because I wanted to have self-confidence in my being a Korean. From now on I would like to feel proud of my being a Korean, to talk with each one of you, to fight discrimination, and to restore our history, our name, and our language that were once taken away from us Koreans by the Japanese. I would like to ask all of you, both Japanese and Koreans, to call me always by my real name." This announcement by the sixth-grader greatly impressed the children in every grade. Many of them expressed their admiration in their composition classes. Many Korean children also followed T'ae-sik's example. Teachers at the school supported these decisions and continued discussions in their classes regarding effective ways to remove prejudice and discrimination against the Koreans. They were aware that anti-Korean feelings were strong among the children and especially strong among the parents. They sent a letter to PTA members soliciting their support for a campaign against discrimination. The Korean parents also held their own meetings. A first step toward improving the situation has thus begun, although efforts will have to continue for a long time.

When T'ae-sik made his announcement, his mother was upset. "I was really surprised to learn that my own child had decided to use his Korean name," said Mrs. Lee. "I tried to stop him. I said, 'What are you going to do? What are you talking about? People will call your mother *Mrs. Lee.* Don't you mind? We have been always hiding the fact that we are Koreans. Why do you want to disclose it? Why do you want to be a hero?' Every time my child told me about the history of the Koreans and said that we were forced to move to Japan I told him not to say such things. I told him not to talk ill of the Japanese, to whom we should feel grateful for their allowing us to stay in their country. After all, this is their country. There are all kinds of Koreans and I did not want my child to do something wrong to the Japanese."

Mrs. Lee, trying to stop her son, said to him, "Don't use your real name! People will reject you. You are publicizing the fact that you are a Korean. Do you know what I have gone through only because I am a Korean? Why do you want to be known as a Korean? Your Japanese name is also your name. Why don't you use it?" Her son's answer was, "It is better to use the Korean name from the beginning because I can avoid the disappointment I must experience later if I use my Japanese pseudonym first and am later discovered to be a Korean. If I must lose my friends when I tell them I am a Korean, they are not my true friends anyway. I have told my friends that I am a Korean, and they have not left me. They are still my friends! Mother, you are wrong, wishing to hide your being a Korean. Mother, I don't mind being called a Korean. I am a Korean. If I cannot get a good job because I am a Korean, I will work as a daily laborer like my father." Mrs. Lee also said, "If you act so big while you are a Korean, the Japanese may say, 'OK, Korean, if you act so big, you'd better go home!' Then what? That will end the whole thing, won't it?" Her son answered, "No, mother! You are wrong, mother! You must become stronger. We did not come to Japan on our own accord! The Koreans were deceived and forced to come here!"

"Now I think I was wrong," said Mrs. Lee, "I think I should be like my own son. He announces his own name and feels proud of using it. It was not so with us, you know? Like my child, I suppose, I too should feel proud . . . although I do not know if a person like me has anything to feel proud of. I have gone through so many things that nothing significant is left to me."

Mrs. Lee was born in 1939. Now she is the mother of three children in the sixth and fourth grades and in kindergarten. Her parents came from Chechu island, but she was born and raised in Japan. Her mother lives in the neighborhood, but she never taught Mrs. Lee Korean history, culture, or language. She studied at Japanese elementary and middle schools and then got a job. She had to change her jobs frequently because, "I could never get a job at a large company. They would look at my family registry, which indicates that I am a Korean, and that was always the end."

She had to work for small factories that did not require the submission of family registry. After she married her husband, Mr. and Mrs. Lee began their own small workshop, manufacturing plastic caps for lotion bottles. "It is hard work. We have a machine at home and we work from 8:00 A.M. to 9:00 P.M. It is not that we like this work but what else could we do?" Large manufacturing companies will not directly subcontract with the Korean workers, and therefore the Lees must sub-subcontract with another factory. Their income is small and the recent economic recession has reduced their work load to half the previous one.

"We are second-generation Koreans, born and raised in Japan. We do not understand the meaning easily when we are told that the Japanese took away from us our history and our name." Mrs. Lee seems to believe that she is representative of many Japan-born Koreans of her generation. At times she uses the term "we." "When I was a child I did not wish my parents to come to school. I did not want my friends to find out that my parents were Koreans. Anyway, my parents were too busy with their work to come to my school. On my way to school and back home, I often saw my grandmother walking in a white Korean dress. I wanted to say 'hello' to my grandmother, but as I was always with my friends I could never do it. I was so ashamed of myself that I covered my face and walked home."

Recently, Mrs. Lee took her youngest child to a nearby kindergarten. Seeing that they were Koreans, the man in charge of admission refused to admit her child. Mrs. Lee asked why, and the man said, "Korean mothers show no interest in their children's education. When it rains, for example, all the Japanese mothers come to take their children home, but no Korean mothers come with an umbrella. The Korean children have to remain here until it stops raining. Or we have to worry about them. It is a nuisance." Mrs. Lee insisted and finally had her child accepted into the kindergarten.

Her son and many of his Korean friends are happily learning the language and history of their country and proudly announce their Korean identity. Mrs. Lee, however, is not absolutely sure. The political situation back on the Korean peninsula bothers her:

> Some people suggested that I send my children to a Korean school, but I decided to send them to a Japanese school. After all we are living in Japan and I thought it better that they receive a Japanese education. Our country is split into two. People argue about the North and South. People in our generation, however, do not wish to get involved. After all, we do not hear very encouraging things about our country. We learn nothing about the North, and the South is a different country. After all it is not in very good shape—you know —split into two. So we say we do not want to be involved. People in my mother's generation are much more excited about the Mindan and Ch'ongnyŏn issues. Old ladies in my neighborhood went on demonstration the other day! They came home and complained that their legs hurt! People in my generation do not want to do such things. We feel ashamed of doing such things about our country while living in Japan. After all, we are halfway about

everything, thinking about both Korea and Japan. My country is split into two. Here are the Mindan and Ch'ongnyön fighting with each other. Such is our country. I wonder how we could really be proud of it.[19]

The Korean population is also highly concentrated in another ward of Osaka, Ikuno-ku, with the majority said to be from Chechu island. Accordingly, numbers of Korean children are relatively high at schools in this ward. In 1975 at one school more than 50 percent of the children were Koreans. At four elementary schools, Korean children constituted 30 percent. At three other schools they constituted 20 percent, at seven schools 10 percent, and at four others less than 10 percent. In November 1972, teachers at one of these schools with a large number of Korean children told the children to write an essay regarding Japanese attitudes toward the Koreans. The teachers found that the Japanese children had been discriminating against the Koreans in many different ways. Having been alerted to the problem, an eight-member investigating committee was formed during a teachers' meeting. This was the beginning of the campaign against discrimination. The teachers decided to spend thirty hours per months for education designed to eradicate discrimination. At another meeting, it was proposed that the real Korean name of each child be written on the certificate of completion of elementary education handed to graduating children. There was opposition among the teachers. An opinion was expressed that a Korean name should be written only at the specific request of the children and their parents. Other teachers thought it was necessary to persuade the Korean parents first. Many teachers talked to the parents and eventually the Korean names were written on all the certificates, except for some children whose parents did not agree. The next step was to register all the entering children with their Korean names and to call them by these names at school. This proposal met with very strong opposition from the parents. Most parents wanted their children to be called by their Japanese pseudonyms, because "they had been known as such at kindergarten and at home as well." The teachers felt that they had to continue their efforts to teach the parents the importance of ethnic pride.

Meanwhile, the teachers continued teaching children special classes designed to remove discrimination. Korean folktales were read to the first-graders by a teacher who emphasized the similarities between Korean and Japanese tales. The children were taught the importance of friendships among people with different backgrounds. Second-graders were encouraged to think of other people's feelings, to understand and to help their friends regardless of their background. The importance of group discussion and decision to solve conflicts was emphasized. Third-graders were taught that both Japanese and Korean cultures have their own merits and that it is important to be proud of one's own country. They were taught to have a strong will to tackle problems and to express their own opinions regarding the solutions. Fourth-graders were encouraged to identify the children who were excluded by others and to discuss their problems so as to increase their group solidarity. An emphasis was placed on the importance of humanity and the commonality of people regardless of race and culture. Fifth-graders were taught to compare Japanese and Korean folklore and to understand the life, customs, traditions, hopes, and sorrows of peoples in the past. They were encouraged to compare and to understand the differences and similarities of the Korean and Japanese histories. Discussions focused on the efforts of people who fought against discrimination and exploitation. Sixth-graders were taught that fundamental human rights, guaranteed by the Constitution, were violated in reality, and that human rights must be won by every individual. The historical relationships between China, Japan, and Korea were taught, and understanding of the Chinese and Korean cultures in relationship to Japanese history was emphasized.

Beginning in 1951, Korean teachers were hired to teach language and culture to Korean children participating in ethnic classes (*Minzoku kyō-shitu*). The enrollment was on a voluntary basis, and it gradually increased. A booklet entitled "For the Removal of Discrimination and the Formation of Proud Cha cter" was prepared and distributed among the members of the PTA. In March 1974, all the Korean children graduated from the school using their Korean names. The teachers then tried to register the entering children with Korean names. Only 25 percent of the parents agreed to do so. The teachers visited the parents in their efforts to persuade them. The number of children using their Korean names slowly increased. As is shown in table 22, the proportion of the Korean children who use their Korean names is increasingly greater in the higher grades. The major reason seems to be the fact that the Korean children in the fourth, fifth, and sixth grades attend the ethnic classes after their regular classes are over. In the ethnic classes every child is identified by his Korean name.

Not every child is willing to participate enthusiastically in the ethnic classes. Some of them dislike being identified as Koreans. Others complain that they have to continue to work when the Japanese children can go home. "A few days after I became a fourth grader, the teacher said that he would read the names of the children who should go to the ethnic class," wrote a child. "My name was among them. I was very unhappy. After the class my friends came to me and said 'I did not know that you are a Korean.' I felt very sad." As they continue attending the ethnic classes their attitudes gradually change. "When I was a fourth grader, I hated learning the Korean language," wrote another child, "The Japanese children can go home or play after school is over, while we had to continue studying. I disliked the class especially in summer. It was very hot, and Japanese children could go swimming at the pool or go home and take a nap while we had to work. Now I feel very happy about the ethnic classes. Only the Koreans get

TABLE 22

Korean Children in Japanese Schools Using Korean Names

Grade	Number of children	Number of Korean children	Korean children using Korean names
1	113	32	8 (25%)
2	118	41	20 (49%)
3	127	32	15 (47%)
4	125	39	30 (77%)
5	145	41	33 (80%)
6	143	32	28 (88%)
Total	771	217	134 (62%)

together in a classroom and we learn our own language and history. I am glad that I did not quit."

Regarding the use of Korean names, the opinions of the parents vary greatly. Some say it is natural for the Korean children to use their Korean names with pride. Others are worried in the beginning but become happy to see their children use their real names with pleasure. Others wish their children to be prepared to meet with discrimination and fight it. Some are opposed because they do not believe the use of their Korean names will improve the situation as long as political discrimination and social prejudice are not removed. Others wish to spare their children any risk that use of the Korean name may increase the discrimination and prejudice to which they are exposed. Thanks to the efforts of the schoolteachers, the trend is toward an increased number of children who proudly use their Korean names.[20] Such trends have been greatly facilitated by the ethnic education system, requiring fifty hours, that originated in Aichi prefecture. This system has been adopted by almost every school with Korean children. Now the Central Education Bureau of the Mindan is working toward publication of textbooks to be used in these ethnic classes. Availability of such well-edited textbooks will certainly help the ethnic education programs.[21]

Korean national identity among the Japan-born youths is strengthened by various other means. Participation in the New Community movement (*Saemaul*) in the Republic of Korea is one such example. Since 1972 the Korean youth groups have been annually visiting South Korea to plant saplings. They also attend lectures and visit villages. The Korean Government Fellowship is another example. Since 1977, about thirty young men and women who pass an examination receive an all-expense government grant to attend universities in Seoul.[22]

Resolution of the identity problems is perhaps easiest for the Korean youths who attend the Korean schools (*not* Kankoku but Chōsen—namely, North Korean and Ch'ongnyōn affiliated). National pride is much more strongly emphasized at Ch'ongnyōn-affiliated schools (from elementary school up to the Korean University) than at Mindan-affiliated schools (elementary, junior, and senior high schools, with no university). As the school uniform, the girls wear *Ch'ima* and *Chokori* (traditional dress). Teaching is done entirely in the Korean language. Students whose language ability is inadequate are required to take supplementary classes.

Students are politically indoctrinated in Kim Il-sung's thoughts. A strong sense of loyalty toward Kim Il-sung as a great, benevolent leader, is cultivated in the youthful mind, almost to the point of personal admiration and affection, if not cultism. The teachers also believe in their cause. The classroom atmosphere tends to be generally stoic, austere, and intensely committed. If the student is able to identify strongly with this country, ambiguity about identity or self-doubt is resolved into the clear consciousness of the Overseas Public Citizen of the Democratic People's Republic of Korea. But problems of self-identity among the Japan-born Korean youths are often highly complicated and complex—too much so to be resolved by a political ideology and allegiance. The following excerpts from a discussion among five Korean youths will illustrate this point:

> *Kim Ye-cha* (born of a Korean painter and his Japanese wife, attended Japanese elementary and junior high schools, then attended a North-affiliated Korean high school to learn the language): I do not agree with those who say that every Korean in Japan is discriminated against, thus generalizing the problem. . . . In order that a Korean can assert himself on an equal basis, with the Japanese, the Korean must try much harder than the Japanese. We cannot avoid this fact. We cannot be excused from it by saying that we are Korean. There are many Koreans who do not seem to understand this simple fact. When they fail to accomplish something, they seem to give up very easily, thinking that the discrimination prevents them from success. This is wrong. They should try harder. If we have no way of establishing ourselves in our own country, we must find a way to do so in Japan. This, I think is the most serious problem we are facing. . . . I am certainly against discrimination. However, I also think that we should improve and train ourselves and become strong enough to fight discrimination. It is also important that we remember our parents' pride. . . . When one feels that one's future is limited both in Japan and in Korea, one may feel tempted to give up and become a "stateless person." It is then that our parents' ethnic pride prevents us from succumbing to such temptations. . . . There should be two tasks for us. One is the unification of our home country. The other is to change the negative and distorted images of ourselves in the Japanese mind.

> *Chang Sŭn-ho* (28 years old, attended a Japanese elementary school up to the fifth grade, then finished North-affiliated Korean elementary, junior, and senior high schools): For us Koreans, born and raised in Japan, the division of our country is a serious problem. However, there is another problem.

That is the gap between us and the Koreans in Korea. I have the feeling that they are different from us. I cannot say anything definite until our country is unified and we actually live with them in the same place. But at present, there are too many differences between us and them—social structure, life style, and many other things.

Sin Yŏng-ch'ŭl (senior at Tōkai University, attended North-affiliated Korean elementary, junior, and senior high schools): I know I am a Korean [*chōsenjin*] but I do not feel a true yearning toward my own country, in spite of the fact that I went to the Korean [*chōsen*] schools.... What bothers me really is the problems of future for the Koreans in Japan. We will inherit the Korean blood but as we continue to live in the Japanese environment, the awareness of our being Korean will inevitably become less and less intense. We will remain Koreans, no doubt. However, will we not become different from the Koreans living in Korea?

Lee Ŭn-cha (sophomore at Wako University, attended Korean primary and junior high schools, but went to the Japanese senior high school): My father belongs to Mindan, while my mother belongs to Ch'ongnyŏn. When I decided to go to Japanese high school rather than to Korean school my father supported my decision but my mother was against it. I insisted upon my own choice. I kept my Korean name while at the Japanese high school, although I did not feel as natural with it as I did while at the Korean schools. When I finished high school, I decided to see my own country, which had long been on my mind. I went to a school in Seoul and consequently I think I found myself to some extent.... The school I went to was called *Kyōhō no Kenkyūjo* (Learning Center for the Overseas Koreans). All the students there were from Japan. We used to take a bus to our school and we were often with the students at the Seoul National University. As we could not speak Korean we were talking in Japanese among ourselves. The Seoul National University students did not understand this. They would blame us, saying, "Why do you have to speak Japanese when you are back to your own country?" Conflicts often arose. I explained to them in Korean language that most of us could not speak their own language, and that it was the fact, although regrettable, that happens to those who were born and raised in a foreign country. However, they would say, "Chinese speak their mother tongue no matter where they live. Why can't you do the same?" Those students also talked ill of Japan very often. While in Japan I used to get angry at those who talk ill of Korea and Koreans and used to defend them [Koreans]. And yet, when I heard the Koreans criticize Japan and Japanese I found myself defending them [Japanese]! Looking at myself in such a position I wondered what on the earth I am! I went to Korea to become fully Korean, but I felt as if I had been rejected by my own country and countrymen. That's how I returned to Japan.

Kim Si-in (33-year-old psychiatrist, trained at the University of Tokyo): Until I was a sophomore at the university I had used a Japanese name and then I decided to use my real name. Currently, at the University of Tokyo Hospital, I am using my Korean name. People may say that it is a trivial matter whether or not you change your name. However, for the Koreans in Japan, or at least for me, it has a very important essential significance.... For me, using my own name means a spiritual independence, the establishment of my own identity.... When I was a medical student, I wanted to see my own country. I also wanted to know if I could by any chance work there so that I could contribute to my own country. My field is neuropsychiatry. I visited a number of well-known Korean psychiatrists. When I was talking with a professor at a university, he said to me, "No matter how much you may study in Japan, we could not put you on a teaching career here. If you really wish to work in this country, go to the United States, study there, and then come back." They would not accept any returnee from Japan. I have a feeling that the country called the Republic of Korea, or the people who live there, look at us and treat us as guests. They would not accept us even if we should wish to join them and work with them. . . .

In my daily life, I do not have many opportunities to realize that I am a Korean. No restaurant refuses to serve me because I am a Korean. However, discrimination hits us when it is totally unexpected. A best friend of mine, a Korean, was graduated from the University of Tokyo with excellent records. He received a Ph.D. in engineering. Supported strongly by his professor's recommendation, he applied for a teaching position at a national university as an assistant professor. The administration of this university quoted the Ministry of Education regulations and said that they could not hire any foreigner above the rank of a lecturer. My friend had already published books and been very well known in his field. As long as he was doing research at a university, he met no discrimination. Once he reached the stage of becoming a full-fledged member of the society, the discrimination blocked his career. . . .

A Japanese friend of mine said to me the other day, "You must be a Japanese, although your name is unusual for a Japanese." I told him that I was a citizen of the Republic of Korea. He was really surprised. He asked me with all seriousness, "You were born and raised in Japan and why do you have a Korean citizenship?" I did not know how to explain, where to begin. He did not mean any harm. He was simply ignorant. The young Japanese are going abroad and their world is getting somewhat open, but ignorance of this kind is very prevalent. . . .

I feel a definite gap between the first and second generation. Their thinking patterns and their language are different from ours. They like to think that we are not different from them. I think it is better that we fully recognize these differences and then start looking for a way to bridge over the gap between the generations.

PROBLEMS OF INTERMARRIAGE: COMPLICATION FOR IDENTITY

Interracial, interethnic, international, and any other kind of intergroup marriages may complicate and confuse individuals' identity problems, self-definitions and self-feelings, and intergroup attitudes. Such marriages sometimes occur as a product of unconscious prejudice and discrimination, of unconscious guilt, or of an unconscious desire for assimilation into another group.

In the past as well as at present, Korean youths fall in love with Japanese and their love may lead to marriage. Romances may disintegrate when a Japanese finds out that the partner is a Korean. Marriages may fail to work out because too much comes between a Japanese and a Korean. A Korean waitress, age 28, recalls her failed marriage with a Japanese:

My husband and I made a brief trip to Enoshima in August 1965. My parents were Koreans, but I, having been born in Japan, was not clearly aware of my being a Korean. Since our marriage in the previous year, it was our first relaxing and enjoyable experience together. On the Enoshima beach, my husband said to me, "In our life together, let's overcome the difference of our nationalities. You are a Korean; I am a Japanese. But we both are humans." I loved my husband. He was considerate and affectionate. I was even proud of him as my husband. Three years passed. We did not become parents. It was not for any financial reasons. My husband did not want to have a baby. I did not know why but I trusted him too much ever to question why. I suggested a number of times I wanted a baby. Every time the answer was the same. "There is no need to hurry. We are still young. First we should secure the financial basis of our life. Then let us have children." Perhaps things would have been different if we had ever had children. It was in May 1971 that my husband began coming home late. By June he began staying out overnight occasionally. When it became more frequent, I asked him where he had been and why he had not come home. He would reply, "Don't worry about it. It does not happen very often anyway." His voice was gentle and his attitude was affectionate, but almost instinctively, I sensed the other woman. Late one night toward the end of the last year, I was waiting for my husband. From the window I saw two dark figures passing. I recognized one as my husband. Quickly opening the window, I saw the back of my husband as he disappeared into the darkness. The next morning he returned as if nothing had happened. I tried to control my anger as I greeted him, but the coldness of my voice surprised me. My husband's face stiffened. "What kind of attitude is that?" Then he said, "I knew from the beginning that it would not work, not with you. That's why I did not want children. After all, my blood and your blood are different (*chi ga chigau*)." I stood there without words. All of a sudden, I realized why he had never wanted me to have a baby. When I heard him say "Our blood is different," I immediately decided to get divorced from him. We broke up. After all, I was a Korean and he was a Japanese.[23]

A Korean man, a graduate student of comparative literature at a prominent private university was living with a Japanese student of dentistry at the same university. The woman's parents did not know that their daughter was living with a Korean man. The Korean man was very proud of his Japanese girl friend and introduced her to his Korean friends and relatives. At times she wore a Korean dress. She began learning Korean. They vacationed together in Korea. However, when they finished their study they broke up. A Korean writer, mentioned before, visited the Japanese woman and asked why. She said,

An immediate reason was that I had to go back to my parents' dental clinic. However, he could have lived in my house and continued his work on literature. Such a technical problem could have been solved, had we been able to solve the mental problem. Frankly speaking, I had had no interest in Korea until I met him. While living with him, my lack of knowledge about Korean culture and Korean problems became an increasingly serious obstacle between us. At first he helped me understand them. However, he began saying that I did not understand Korean problems because I am a Japanese. I could not respond to such a remark. I had choices—either to forget about the whole issue of Korean problems or to become an expert on it. I could do neither. I could not handle the Korean-Japanese problems. It was too much for me, and I could not bear its weight. I had to flee. I neither dislike nor hate him. We did our best and it did not work. Historical facts are too heavy for an individual to ward off.[24]

Another Korean man, at age 21, lived with a Japanese woman. They had a baby girl. His mother and elder sister insisted that he break up with his Japanese common-law wife. They even arranged a marriage with a Korean woman for him. He would not listen to them and to avoid further argument he disappeared with his Japanese wife. Then his mother died. Some years later, the aforementioned writer saw him. He was then married to a Korean woman. He had broken up with his former Japanese wife. The young man, talking to the writer, admitted that when he was living with a Japanese woman, he could never be really free from "tension and anxiety," feelings he never experienced with his Korean wife.[25]

The older Koreans who experienced exploitation and humiliation at the hands of the Japanese in the past naturally hate the Japanese. Out of hatred they reject the idea of intermarriage with the Japanese. A writer, Kim Yang-ki, captures the situation in the following description:

> The Koreans in Japan stubbornly refuse any marriage with the Japanese, regardless of individual ideologies or thoughts. Their refusal springs from their past experience in this country. They firmly believe that any intermarriage between a Korean and a Japanese leads to only one ending: tragedy. Even a person who idealizes and adores romantic love and love marriage cannot rationally deny this firm conviction. Among Koreans who move from Korea to Japan, a marriage between a Korean and a Japanese is a taboo. Among them, this taboo is strictly observed.... [This refusal] is [also] the product of the self-protective instinct of the Koreans who were forced to come into Japanese society and somehow managed to survive in the midst of prejudice and discrimination. When they were young, they had no financial or spiritual freedom to entertain dreams, hopes, and ideals, let alone affection. Trying to survive on the verge of death, they were too busy to feel anything. For them the Korean community and Korean home were the only place for momentary rest and refuge from oppression. They were the place where mutual trust existed and where national pride could be maintained. The more valuable such a sanctuary was, the stronger was their desire to protect it without letting any outsider in.[26]

The older Koreans' rejection of intermarriage may also reflect their habitual resistance to the "phony" assimilation policies of the past imperial Japan, which aimed at crushing Korean nationalism while continuing discriminatory practices against them. When a Japan-born young Korean falls in love with a Japanese and wishes to marry, it is natural that many elderly Koreans become upset. When they cannot stop such a marriage, they refuse to attend their child's wedding. Kim Yang-ki, writing about such marriage problems, thinks that this stubborn refusal, although natural and understandable, should be stopped. "In these days when there is no longer any Japanese Imperialism," he writes, "we must acknowledge that there is a danger that such an attempt to maintain our ethnic-cultural identity can very easily transform into nationalistic chauvinism." Kim went to Korea and talked with the young Koreans about the international marriages. Japanese young men go to Korea for study, for work, or even for sightseeing, and some of them marry Korean women. Kim knew more than ten such couples personally. The youths in Korea he talked with said that they had known something about the discrimination and prejudice in Japan. They also said, however, that discrimination and prejudice were one thing, but marriage with a Japanese was totally another thing. For them, intercultural marriages were no subject of serious concern. Kim said to the youths that if his own daughter wished to marry a Japanese man, he would probably refuse to accept it. The young Koreans did not understand the writer's feelings. They did not understand such a refusal reaction so prevalent among the older Koreans. Upon returning to Japan, Kim reported to the Koreans in Japan the results of his interviews with Korean youths. "It is hard to believe it!" was a general response. This experience taught him that there was a "widening gap at a gut level" between the Koreans in Korea and those in Japan.

His comments on this point seem to suggest something profoundly significant for the problems of identity among future Koreans in Japan. It may be that, in spite of the apparent success of recent emphasis on national pride, becoming a "proud" Korean permanent resident in Japan may not be the whole answer.

> For the second and third generation Koreans born and raised in Japan who have never known their home country through direct experiences, their home country is not real but an image. When all the first-generation Koreans are gone, such an image of Korea, in the mind of the younger Koreans, can and will become increasingly more idealized, abstract, and unreal. This has to be prevented. The only way to prevent it is to change the structure of awareness (*ishiki kōzō*) among the young Koreans. A new way of establishing and sustaining the bond with Korea must be found and worked out. We must prevent the present emphasis on ethnic purity from becoming chauvinistic nationalism *that has no realistic function for the Koreans in Japan* (italics added).[27]

14

NEGATIVE SELF-IDENTITY IN A DELINQUENT KOREAN YOUTH

Yuzuru Sasaki and Hiroshi Wagatsuma

In the previous chapter we presented a number of illustrative instances of identity problems among Koreans in Japan. Here we intend to examine one such problem from its inception in childhood to its tragic conclusion. The interweaving of negative social attitudes and other causal features of early life leading to deviancy is complex. Nevertheless, we attempt to illustrate them here with a particular instance—the personal history of a Korean youth who, after a short delinquent career, committed suicide.[1] This situation well illustrates how a minority identity compounds adolescent problems and how, in effect, a sense of degradation is passed on from one generation to the next.[2]

We have no direct case history relating to the dead father of this young man. It would certainly teach us a great deal if we could learn why he also ended his life in a drunken stupor at a relatively early age, having followed the self-destructive path of alcoholism.

The boy used either his Japanese pseudonym or his real Korean name, depending on with whom he associated. He was known among his Japanese peers by his Japanese pseudonym but among his Korean friends by his Korean name. To avoid confusion, we will use a fictional Korean name for him throughout this report.

THE "VITA" OF A DELINQUENT CAREER

Han-il was born of Korean parents in Japan in April 1952. In March 1966, at age 14, he finished junior high school and enrolled in a barbers' training school and a night high school. He began associating with a group of older Korean boys who were oriented toward delinquent behavior. In January 1967, at age 15, in the company of his Korean friends he stole money from a candy store. In September, at age 16, he dropped out of both schools and began working. With the group of Korean boys he "resisted and injured an arresting police officer." He was tried at a family court and placed on probation. In December he was one of a group of five Korean youths who burglarized a drive-in restaurant. They were not caught. He soon dropped out of contact with the Korean boys and began associating with a group of Japanese youths. In January 1968 he was arrested for "proneness to crime" with his Japanese group for sleeping-pill play. The family court again placed him on "probation supervised by a family court officer." In March, with a Japanese friend, he attempted to avoid payment for a meal at a restaurant. He was arrested and again placed on probation by the family court. In May, at age 17, his December burglary was discovered and he was arrested. He was tried at the family court and once again placed on probation. In August he was arrested for "proneness to crime" for sniffing glue, but he was released untried. He began isolating himself from his Japanese peer group. In November he was arrested twice for "proneness to crime" for sniffing glue and for violent behavior. He was kept on probation by the family court officer. In December the probation was terminated. In March 1969 it was discovered that he was continuing with glue-sniffing and he voluntarily entered a mental hospital for therapy. Discharged after a month's therapy, he immediately resumed glue-sniffing. In April, not yet age 18, Han-il Kim committed suicide.

LIFE HISTORY NOTES FROM THE FAMILY COURT

Officer's Report of Interviews with Han-il and his Mother

As of May 1968, when Han-il was tried for the burglary of the drive-in, his family consisted of: his mother (age 39, a janitor at a factory, with primary school education only); his sister (age 20, a factory worker with one year of high school education); his older brother (age 18, an apprentice at a barber shop and a third-year student in a night high school); Han-il (age 17, a factory worker with a junior high school education); and a younger brother (age 15, in the ninth grade).

The father of the family had died five years earlier, at age 43. The family lived in a two-room unit in a so-called long house (*nagaya*).[3] The home was neatly kept but extremely small, consisting of two tiny rooms, one 9 x 9 feet and the other 9 x 12 feet. A few hundred yards from their home was an area exclusively inhabited by Koreans. Among their more immediate neighbors, however, most were lower-class Japanese and a small number of Korean families. Han-il's mother avoided associating with the other Koreans. The family had been using a Japanese name since the 1950s.

Han-il's father, the third of four brothers, had finished six years of primary school in southern Korean before World War II. He had two older brothers who died in young adulthood. He lived on a farm with his parents until age 21. He voluntarily migrated to Japan in 1939 as an unskilled factory laborer and stayed at the house of his paternal uncle. His younger brother, whom he never saw again, continued to live with his parents. When Japan entered World War II in 1941, Han-il's father was not drafted but continued to work in various factories as an unskilled worker. After the war ended in 1945, he remained in Japan as a construction laborer. In 1946, at age 28, he met his future wife, age 17, and married her.

Han-il's mother had come to Japan from Korea at age 6 with her parents. Her father, a construction laborer, was described as quick-tempered and strict with his children, hitting them frequently. Her mother worked at home as a seamstress to supplement the family income. Han-il's mother recalled her own mother as a "careful and thoughtful woman." She herself had four elder brothers and sisters, but they all died young. She described her two younger sisters as resembling their mother in character. She described herself, however, as "just like my father," strong-willed and quick-tempered.

Han-il's parents were married in Kobe, but soon afterward they moved to a small Korean ghetto of about forty households in a neighboring small city. With their relatives in the same community the couple became engaged in a variety of "businesses," ranging from making Korean candies, through illegal brewing, to raising pigs. Initially they worked very hard and their income gradually increased.

Since his youth, Han-il's father had liked to drink. As the family income increased, his drinking became progressively heavier. Once he began drinking he would continue uninterrupted for several days, moving from one bar to another. When sober he was a timid person (*ki ga yowai*), but when drunk he would become indiscriminately generous, buying drinks for others whom he befriended at bars. Eventually his drinking bout would end when he fell into a drunken stupor. His wife would have to go find him to bring him home. More and more the family affairs were left to Han-il's mother, who had to devote herself to hard work from early until late at night. This situation still persisted at the time of Han-il's birth in 1952, when his older sister and brother were being taken care of by their maternal grandparents, who lived with the family. Han-il's mother had "very little time to take care of the newborn baby." His mother could recall only "feeding the baby when I had some time to spare" and "putting the baby to bed." The rest of her memory from these days is that of working to the point of exhaustion.

As a small child, Han-il remembers how afraid he was of his father, who was a moody person. When he was in a bad mood, he would hit Han-il "so hard that I fell down to the floor." He also remembered his father getting drunk and arguing with his mother. She would cry and shout, blaming her husband for being "a lazy drunkard who did not live up to the role of family head." Han-il was afraid of his father and his mother as well. When they were engaged in a wild argument, he would sit in a corner of the room, silently siding with his mother. Han-il described his mother as a "woman with guts" (*konjō ga aru*), but she was prone to quick anger when she could not have her own way. His mother admitted her short temper. Often she "exploded" while arguing with her son when he repeated his delinquent acts. But she also seemed to have a passive, socially submissive side to her personality. She said, for example, that even after her husband became a drunkard, she continued to rely on him as the family head. After her husband's death, she wished her son "had a strict man like his father around who could control his delinquent behavior."

Since his early childhood, Han-il had participated in peer group activities. As the family lived at that time in a small Korean community, his friends were all Korean children. Never a "leader type," he recalled, he was, however, "an active boy" in the group and "fought often and well with other children." (It should be remembered that he liked to recall himself as "aggressive" as part of the manly image he sought to present to others.) In primary school he did poorly. His school records placed him in the lowest third of his group. His teachers recorded that he lacked concentration and was restless in the classroom, showing "no initiative or composure." Apparently he was neither bright nor studious.

In 1961, when Han-il was a fifth-grader, the family businesses were in serious decline. His father considered repatriation to North Korea, telling his wife that he believed that there people could find a secure job under the Communist regime. The mother was unwilling but eventually agreed to repatriate for financial reasons. The family sold the house and their other remaining business assets and were ready to go, but Han-il's father's uncle (who had long been a "father surrogate" for Han-il's father) learned about the plan. He was strongly opposed, and Han-il's father had no choice but to obey the older man. Rather than attempt to reconstitute some form of business, the family moved to Kobe, where the father began working as a construction laborer. The mother found a job as a janitor at a nearby factory. The father continued his heavy drinking.

In May 1963, the father left home for a relative's house and did not return. Three days later he was found lying on the street not far from home in a stupor produced by a mixture of shōchū (cheap but potent liquor of low quality) and sleeping pills, which he had used in order to increase the intoxicating effects. It was an unusually cold day for May, and he was frozen almost to death. Taken to a hospital, he died without regaining consciousness. Twelve years old at the time, Han-il recalled that he had felt "relieved" (hotto shita) at his father's death. "I shouldn't say such a thing about my old man who is dead," said Han-il, "but I really felt relieved and freed." At the funeral Han-il could not weep although "everybody else was crying," and he became very self-conscious. Rather than reacting to his father's death, he was much more frightened and shocked at his mother's behavior. "She would cry and shout loudly like she was crazy, and then she would remain absent-minded for hours like a fool." After the father's death, Han-il's sister quit high school and began working at a chemical factory.

Han-il felt sorry for his mother. After the father's death she became more and more "peevish and grumbling" (*guchippoi*) and often complained how difficult it was for her to raise four children all by herself. He felt angry at his elder brother, who seemed to lack sympathy for their mother. Han-il was the most worried and upset when his mother became ill.

One month before his father's death, Han-il had entered a junior high school known for its large number of Korean students and its relatively high delinquency rate. He became closely associated with delinquency-prone boys, and his school behavior became progressively worse. Always a poor and unmotivated student, he now began coming to school late and leaving early. This tendency was especially noticeable during his last year at the school. After finishing junior high school in March 1966, he entered a barbers' training school and a night school, following the strong urging of both his mother and sister. His elder brother, while studying at night high school, had attended the same school and was already an apprentice. The mother believed that becoming a barber provided a secure job ("people always need haircuts"). She looked forward to seeing her two sons open their own barbershop, but her dream was never to be realized.

Han-il was interested neither in barber training nor in the night school classes. He attended only because "that's what my mother wanted me to do." The barber school was over by early afternoon, and classes at the night high school did not begin until five o'clock. Han-il had nothing to do in the several hours between. He described how one day he wandered into an entertainment area of Kobe "to kill time" in the afternoon. He ran into a group of Korean boys whom he had known at junior high school. These boys were all older than he and had left school some time before. He was accepted by the group and began "hanging around" on streets with them.

All those in the group had some kind of income from minor jobs, which they spent on clothes and "fun." Han-il envied their fashionable clothes. He imitated their hairstyle and bought some new clothes, but he was envious of their leather boots and high-fashion jackets, which he could not afford. He looked up to the older boys, following them to bowling alleys and even trying to "seduce women," something which they were wont to brag about. He could not help feeling inferior because he could not keep up with them, either in "having enough money" or in "making women like tough guys."

When Han-il began coming home late and missing his classes at both schools, his mother confronted him about his lack of diligence. He began arguing and quarreling with her in a way he had rarely done before. When his mother would not give him enough money to keep up with his Korean friends, he began using abusive language. In August, during one such argument, his mother shouted at him, "I no longer need a good-for-nothing like you!" He thereupon left home for Tokyo. Through a friend he found a job there at a leather-goods store. He soon felt very lonely away from home and he did not like his job. He returned home after two weeks. This experience gave him the idea, however, that if he earned money himself his mother would not be able to interfere with the way in which he spent it.

Summer vacation ended, but he did not return to any classes. Instead, he got a job at the chemical factory where his elder sister was working. His mother was very unhappy with this development, but she could not make him change his mind. He found the work at the chemical industry to be "too hard" and he soon was frequently absent from work. He often took off to be with his Korean friends at a bowling alley or bar. Frequently he would join in a fight with other groups. He recalled that in the beginning he enjoyed his Korean company because he "felt he was becoming stronger and tougher."

In January 1967, still only fifteen years of age, Han-il was walking with three of his Korean friends. They entered a candy store and bought some cookies. Leaving the store, they noticed that the storekeeper kept small change in a basket hung by a string from the ceiling, as is done in some small retail shops. The four boys decided to steal the money from the basket "just for fun." They flipped a coin, and it was decided that Han-il and another boy would watch outside the store while the other snatched the money. The basket held about 2000 yen (about $7), which they divided equally. Han-il spent his part on food. The boys were not caught at that time, but the incident came to light when Han-il confessed it after a subsequent arrest on another matter.

In the spring of the same year, Han-il quit his job and went to work in a metal factory for about a month, but he quit to take a job in another factory where he could work "on and off." He worked only because he felt he needed money that he could spend without interference from his mother. He believed that "nobody liked work for its own sake." He worked only "in order to play." His mother and sister both told him he was "lazy and disliked work like his father." Han-il agreed.

One night in September 1967, Han-il was wandering with eight of his Korean friends. After some drinks, one of them began a fight with a passerby, beating him severely as the others watched. When a police officer arrived and tried to arrest the culprit, the others immediately intervened, injuring the officer. More police arrived and two of the youths were arrested, one of them being the leader of the group. The others, including Han-il, ran away.

Those who had escaped began to plan some way of gaining their leader's release. Han-il volunteered to give himself up, telling the police that it was he who had actually injured the officer and not those arrested. As he recalled later, he "did not really lay a finger on the policeman," but he wanted to be a hero to his peers. He wanted to show his older friends that he too could act tough (*ii kakko o shitakatta*). He also considered that since he had never been arrested before, he could gain his release without penalty.

The boys went together to the police station, where Han-il "confessed." He was booked and allowed to return home. Han-il was later called into the court, investigated, tried, and placed on probation.

In December 1967 Han-il quarreled with his mother, who continued to disapprove of his "playing around" and "wasting money." He left home and stayed at a friend's apartment. During the day he sometimes returned to his house while everybody was out at work and ate whatever he could find in the kitchen. Later in the same month, he was walking with the leader of the Korean group and met another boy who was a good friend of the leader. This young man had a plan to burglarize a drive-in restaurant for which he had previously worked. He knew that no one was on the premises at night, and it would be easy to take the cash from the previous day's sales, which was kept in the office. He rented a car and invited the leader, Han-il, and two others to join him. All five then drove to the restaurant, where Han-il and two others were told to stay in the car as lookouts while the leader and the chief planner of the burglary broke into the restaurant. They actually found 600,000 yen ($2,000) in the office, but told those outside they had found only 100,000 ($333), giving each 10,000 ($33). The leader gave Han-il an extra 10,000 yen to express his appreciation for Han-il's having rescued him from the police station.

Shortly after the burglary Han-il became acquainted with a small group of delinquent Japanese boys and girls who frequented another entertainment district of the city. Members of this group were younger and were attracted to Han-il, who responded to their appreciation of him. Han-il felt he could not keep up with the Korean group, all of whom had much more money than he had and would not lend or give money to him.

In contrast, the Japanese group had much less money; most of those in the group had no jobs but were school truants who had run away from home. They shared whatever they had with one another in an atmosphere of mutual help. The Korean boys, in contrast, emphasized their individual masculinity and toughness, and Han-il could not overcome his feelings of inferiority toward them. They were interested in bowling, fighting, and contacts with women. In contrast, the Japanese group, whose members included many girls, was not machismo-oriented but was interested in go-go dancing and sleeping-pill play (*suiminyaku asobi*). This was a popular form of drug taking among delinquency-prone minors, as sleeping pills were then available in various brands without prescription. The resultant drowsiness produced a state of semidelirium. They would take the pills in a coffee shop and then would walk around the streets until midnight. Such behavior constituted an illegal act, termed "proneness to crime" (*guhan*) in Japanese juvenile law. One night the police picked up the group. Han-il was arrested and again tried at the family court. His earlier probation period was prolonged.

In March 1968 Han-il met one of his Japanese friends on the street. This boy had run away from home, had no money, and was very hungry. Han-il felt sorry for him and wanted to help, but he was too broke. Nevertheless, he took his friend to a restaurant. After a meal they tried to sneak out without paying, but the restaurant owner had become suspicious of them and had already called the police. The boys were immediately arrested, and for the first time Han-il was detained for several days at the juvenile classification center (*shōnen kanbetsu sho*). He was tried and placed on probation.

In May 1968, two months after the restaurant incident, Han-il's part in the previous December's drive-in burglary was discovered. One of the Korean boys had been caught for another criminal act, had confessed the burglary, and had informed on the other participants. Han-il was arrested and detained at the juvenile classification center again. He was diagnosed as "lacking any control over his egocentric and impulsive needs." The family court research officer, who visited his home on more than one occasion, judged the home as "inadequate in supervision or discipline." The psychologist at the center recommended that Han-il be placed in a child welfare facility. In contrast, the court research officer, the *hogoshi* (volunteer probation supervisor), Han-il's mother, and his elder brother all wanted him to be returned home. The judge decided that he should be placed on "probation by the family court research officer."

While in the classification center, Han-il had written in his diary (the practice of keeping a diary was required) that he was so lonely he felt he was losing his mind. "I am all alone. I wish my mother would come for me." He also wished to "die and live happily in the other world (*ano yo*)." He felt fed up with himself and wondered why he alone among his siblings was getting into trouble. He wrote, "Why only me in my family, like some kind of 'mutant' (*totsuzen hen-i*)?"

Upon being returned home, he began working regularly at the metal factory. He no longer contacted the Korean group, and he ceased quarreling openly with his mother, although mutual dissatisfaction continued to exist. He did not run away as he had before. He was allowed to spend Saturday afternoons go-go dancing with some of his Japanese friends. In July the Japanese group that had been involved in sleeping-ill play planned a dance party to raise some money. His mother learned about it and reported it to the *hogoshi*, who advised Han-il against participating. The boy agreed but became angry and resentful that his mother was "spying on him." His work habits quickly became irregular, and he began being absent from his job. He also began missing the required appointments at the family court.

In August he went swimming, encountered his Japanese group, and resumed his meetings with them. The group taught him a new enjoyment— sniffing glue. It was possible at that time to go to a toy or stationery store

and buy a tube of glue used for making plastic airplane models. The volatil-
ized ingredients produced a kind of drunkenness. It was not long before he
was arrested by a policeman who saw him sniffing glue in a coffee shop. He
was released after receiving an admonition. He indulged more and more in
glue-sniffing, missing work, staying home, and becoming isolated and
withdrawn.

In September Han-il finally quit the metal factory and found a job at
the chemical factory at which his sister was working. He had worked there
before, but had quit after a short time. This time he intended to "stick with
the job." He was readily rehired because the husband of his maternal aunt
was an executive of this small factory. Most of the factory's hundred-odd
workers were Koreans, many of whom wore their Korean names on their
name tags and "walked around proudly," self-consciously assertive about
their Korean identity. Han-il felt envious of them. He had been in the habit
of using his Japanese pseudonym, although he was known among his
Korean friends by his real Korean name, and his expressed attitudes about
Koreans had been very negative. Although his opinion of his fellow Koreans improved somewhat, he could not find any new friends among his co-
workers. Instead he remained a loner, continuing to sniff glue in secret.

On a rainy night in late October he walked along a street, sniffed glue,
and lost consciousness. He fell down but was helped home by a policeman.
In early November he again sniffed glue and became so violently aggressive
toward a neighbor that the police were called in and he was arrested. These
two incidents caused him to be sent to the family court and to be charged
again with being a "crime-prone juvenile," but he was released without trial.

In December the probation period under the family court officer was
terminated. In March 1969, his mother went to the family court and reported that he was still sniffing glue and missing work. He was examined by
the family court psychiatrist, who recommended that he be admitted to a
mental hospital to cure the habit. Both he and his mother agreed, and he
stayed in the hospital for about a month. There was no observable sign of
problems during this period, and accordingly he was discharged. He returned home, only to resume glue-sniffing immediately. His mother scolded
him, but seeing no effect, called the family court officer. The officer promised to visit him at home the following week. Han-il remained at home and
continued to sniff glue.

Four days later, in the morning before leaving for work, his mother
became very angry with him and chastised him for sniffing glue and doing
nothing. She told him to leave home because "she felt so totally fed up with
him." The mother, sister, and older brother all left for work, and his
younger brother went to school. Han-il was alone in the house. When his
younger brother returned home after school that afternoon, he found Han-il
hanging from a beam, dead. It was three days before the promised visit of
the family court officer. Han-il was not quite eighteen years old.

Late in the day of the wake, after the funeral, the family court officer visited Han-il's home. A tiny altar had been placed at the wall of one of their two rooms. The mother and elder brother were sitting in front of the altar with heads bowed. The sister was washing dishes in the kitchen. The younger brother was watching television in the other room. Gathered in the middle of the room were several older people, relatives, lying on the *tatami* mat and talking. It was evident that they all had been drinking heavily. One was asleep, red-faced and snoring. The court officer recalled that Han-il, while making negative comments about Koreans, had once said, "Koreans are impolite and impudent, so much so that they, for example, go to a relative's funeral, drink a lot, and fall asleep in front of the altar."

Two years after Han-il's death, the family court officer again contacted the family. Han-il's elder brother had quit the barbershop and was working "on and off" while wandering around with a group of Korean youths. He quarreled frequently with his mother. Han-il's younger brother was becoming very much like Han-il—disliking work, spending money, and arguing often with the mother. Only Han-il's sister was stable and helping her mother. The mother lamented, "It must be all my fault and my failure as a mother, but I do not know what I did wrong and why all my boys have to make me suffer like this."

THEORETICAL IMPLICATIONS AND OBSERVATIONS

This tragic case represents a number of issues related generally to the genesis of delinquency formation and more specifically to problems of negative social self-identity. The case also illustrates how Japanese agencies and personnel work within the Japanese family court system as it is now constituted.

Procedures Within Japanese Correctional Facilities

Understanding of the case may be aided by discussion of how agencies operate with youths who commit deviant activities to the point of being classified as delinquent. The Japanese juvenile justice code classifies problem juveniles into three categories depending upon their age and the nature of the act. First are those actually classified as "criminal juveniles" (*hanzai shōnen*). These are individuals over fourteen and under twenty years of age who have committed what is legally defined as a crime. Second are "law-breaking juveniles" (*shokuhō shōnen*), those under fourteen who have committed a crime but cannot be held accountable. They tend to be put under the jurisdiction of welfare agencies rather than the family court system. Third are "crime-prone juveniles" (*guhan shōnen*), who have not technically committed any crime but are considered to manifest improper behavior suggesting that character factors in their environment are leading them toward criminal behavior. Truancy, running away from home, frequenting what-is considered undesirable places, lack of proper behavior, and lack of proper guidance and supervision by the legal guardian or parent can cause a juvenile to be classified as "crime-prone." All three forms of classification are collectively called in Japan "juvenile delinquency," and those youths coming in contact with the police are considered "delinquent juveniles" (*hiko shōnen*).

There are three main forms of police discretion after arrest and interrogation. First, youths whom the police judge not to be seriously delinquent or those not proved to have been involved in any lawbreaking act are released or handed over to their parents. Second, those who are at least fourteen years old and are suspected of serious offenses are sent to the family court for jurisdiction. They may be sent directly to the court or through the public prosecutor's office. Third, those under age fourteen are sent to a child-guidance clinic. The clinic in turn may have the discretion to send the individual to family court. In addition to cases brought to them by the police, the family court also receives juveniles directly upon complaints by parents or other responsible adults and through the reports of family court research officers.

In the family court itself, a judge interviews the juvenile and decides whether he or she should be returned or should be detained at a juvenile classification center, as happened to Han-il in May 1968. At the classification center the individual is interviewed and psychological tests may be administered. The judge of the family court makes use of materials presented to him by the psychologist and by the research officer of the family court, who also conducts interviews and testing. The juvenile and the parents are called into the court for interviews, and the judge then renders a judgment regarding the treatment to be administered in the case. The judge has five possible alternative decisions to choose from:

(1) No trial, or dismissal without hearing. When the judge so decides, he can dispense with any official trial and, without having the case brought before him, can refer it back to the family court research officer, who then interviews the juvenile, admonishes him, and, when necessary, works out some program for rehabilitation by giving advice or making other educational and family arrangements.

(2) No court action or dismissal after hearing. When the consequences of a trial prove the juvenile to be not guilty, or when the judge decides from his assessment of the juvenile's character or from environmental factors that there is no necessity for inflicting a penalty, the court takes no action. Instead, the judge and research officer admonish the juvenile, give advice, and make some educational arrangements, such as suggesting regular consultation with schoolteachers or employers.

(3) Court actions. These are divided into three main categories: First,

probation or, as it is known in Japanese, "protective observation." The juvenile is allowed to remain in the community under the guidance and supervision of a probation officer, who in turn works with a voluntary probation supervisor (*hogoshi*). The hogoshi is usually a person of status within the juvenile's immediate community who takes responsibility for direct supervision. The government probation officer has very little direct contact with the delinquents but works with the hogoshi assigned to him. Second, commitment to a child welfare facility. When the juvenile is under eighteen, and his environment is judged to be harmful to his welfare, he can be committed to a welfare facility, which is to be distinguished from a correctional institution. Third, commitment to a correctional institution. Such institutions are classified into primary (for younger juveniles), secondary (for older juveniles), and special (for the more seriously delinquent). There are also special medical facilities for physically ill and mentally retarded individuals.

(4) Handing the juvenile over to the prefectural governor or the director of a child guidance clinic. If the juvenile is under eighteen, the judge may decide to place him or her under the supervision of a child welfare officer.

(5) Sending to the public procurator's office. This is the most serious possible decision on the part of the judge, made in cases of very serious criminal activities. The juvenile is sent to the public procurator's office, from which the case may be sent to a district court for trial. After the trial, the juvenile may be given a suspended sentence, or may be made subject to probation, or may be sent to a juvenile prison. The district court sometimes sends a case back to the family court for reinvestigation.

As in the case of Han-il, a more frequent procedure is to place the juvenile on probation, technically under the competence of the family court research offier. The juvenile is then allowed to return home under the intermittent guidance of a hogoshi. The court officer can, upon his later observation of the juvenile's behavior, recommend action that ranges from no trial to sending a case to the public procurator's office.

In observing the handling of Han-il's case, we note that the general tendency of court officials is not to overreact to his behavior but to attempt some kind of rehabilitative procedure within the home. Generally speaking, the family court officers are sufficiently trained to be free of prejudice in the case of minority youngsters. It is the general observation of the most compassionate commentators on the system that problems of discrimination in Japan do not arise out of personnel within the family court. In contrast, there are reports periodically of police officers who may show some prejudicial behavior, though this is by no means widespread. In the present instance, a careful examination produced no evidence of prejudicial behavior on the part of any police or professional personnel coming into contact with Han-il. The problems he experienced as a minority youngster did not stem from the types of correctional intervention he experienced. The case instead

represents issues more related to the question of why Han-il acted delin-
quently and how his minority status contributed to self-concepts that
helped bring about his tragic end.

Generally speaking, there is much more police vigilance in Japan than
in the United States. Police are more likely to intervene if they see what
looks like delinquency-prone behavior. Usually, however, the police exercise fairly objective judgments, and by and large their vigilance is not resented by the Japanese public in the way that similar vigilance might be
resented by the American public.[4] The attitudes toward the police displayed
by Han-il and his family are fairly typical of those in Japan. One does not
find any expressed resentment of the police; on the contrary, the mother
several times sought the assistance of police intervention in impossible situations with her son. This is not to say that the Koreans in Japan do not have
greater animosity toward police than do the majority Japanese. But the
degree to which this animosity manifests itself in individual instances is
much less than would be noticeable with many black or Chicano families,
for example, in the state of California.

Possible Causes of the Delinquency and Death of Han-il

Some interpretations of Han-il's situation can be made in reference to
other studies of Japanese families. As in the United States, more delinquents
in Japan come from broken homes than from intact families. The absence of
a parent during significant years is an important variable. We must note,
however, that the death of Han-il's father occurred only after Han-il had
reached twelve years of age. The statistics on broken families indicate that
the more significant period of a father's absence is between four and eight
years of age. Direct information on the interaction of Han-il's father and
mother is lacking because the reported material comes solely from the
mother and the sons. The father's version of what happened to the family is
not obtainable. The impression is of a father who was feared, who was periodically ill-controlled, and who manifested several forms of weakness best
symbolized in his alcoholism.

Previous studies of Japanese families, comparing socioeconomically
matched samples that produced delinquent and normal boys, demonstrated
that some of the American literature on the genesis of delinquency is equally
applicable to Japanese scenes. In considering differential socialization experiences in delinquent families, the interrelationships of insufficient or vacillating love, discipline, and family cohesion seem to influence a child toward
some expression of deviant behavior. These are repeatedly discussed as
major factors in the research literature, although there is not complete unanimity in assessing priorities. Researchers differ considerably in assessing
the relative weight to be given to maternal or paternal care and family cohesiveness. There is also considerable difference of opinion as to whether

delinquent attitudes arise from direct, conscious experience or from less accessible, unconscious layers of personality shaped by family patterns.

The Gluecks[5] considered statistically a number of social factors present to a significant degree in delinquent youths in many societies as compared with nondelinquents. According to their Japanese data, the Gluecks' method of predicting delinquency is applicable to Japanese youth. Numerous items finally reduced to five basic factors most effective in differentiating delinquents from nondelinquents. First among these factors is the quality of discipline exercised by the father—whether overstrict, erratic, lax, or firm. Discipline considered erratic or unreasonable, and discipline considered harsh or oppressive, exacting obedience through fear, were highly correlated with delinquency in contrast to a firm discipline considered reasonable from the child's perspective. Han-il noted that he could not express any feeling of loss when his father died but instead manifested a sense of relief to be free from what he felt was the erratic, oppressive discipline of his father.

A second factor is supervision by the mother. The delinquent child is often left alone to his own devices. Well-adjusted children have a history of close, continual supervision by and interaction with their mothers. Han-il's mother, from his birth on, had very little time to devote to her child, given the exigencies of poverty. In attempting to keep the family business solvent, the mother put the child for a time in the hands of his grandparents. It is obvious from the later social history that the boy was not sufficiently supervised at home to prevent his involvement with older individuals who induced his first delinquent acts.

A third important criterion is the expression of fatherly affection toward a normal child in contrast with its absence toward a delinquent child. It seems clear that Han-il never received and enjoyed his father's affection. The father, no matter what he may have thought of his child, did little but alienate his son. He achieved no closeness nor any influential form of personal contact but manifested continually a type of drunken behavior that the son found abhorrent. The father offered him no adequate role model. If anything, he deepened his son's sense of negative identity. The paternal relationship, therefore, until the father's death in a drunken stupor, must be evaluated as having been almost a totally negative influence.

A fourth crucial criterion, highly differentiating between delinquents and nondelinquents, is the affection of the mother for her child. In Han-il's case, this criterion seems to have been a complex issue. It is obvious that his capacity to internalize to some degree was influenced by some feeling of warmth coming from the mother, even though the mother felt ineffectual and unable to cope with the problems evidenced by her child. The mother was concerned and, it seems, was not without affection. This affection may have enabled Han-il to attempt to internalize—to incorporate within himself—social expectations rather than to flout them. He did not succeed, however, in managing himself or in maintaining sufficient self-control to meet work expectations. His ultimate suicide was an uncharacteristic step for a delinquent. Han-il, in effect, did internalize his conflicts and partially, at least, could not identify with or justify his own behavior. He became intrapunitive, deepening his own sense of unworthiness. More and more he felt himself to be in an impossible personal and social situation.

A fifth essential factor is lack of family cohesion, a lack very apparent in Han-il's situation. The home was unintegrated. Although initially the parents strove to operate some forms of business together, as time went on one does not sense any pride in the home, any expression of mutual affection, or any kind of sharing of experience. Self-preoccupation, except perhaps for the mother with her children, exceeded family group interest. As in many families of this kind, Han-il sought an outside reference group among his peers for some form of affiliation and a sense of belonging. He attempted to belong to an older group of Korean youths with a type of masculine bravado, but he never felt adequate among "tough guys." He shifted to a younger Japanese group. The seeking of outside group relationships in this instance, as with many so-called social delinquents, stemmed directly from the lack of any satisfaction within the family itself. In spite of his attempt at masculine bravado, the main feature of Han-il's delinquency was his search for social contact with a group. His behavior toward the outer world was not characteristically aggressive. He fit very clearly into the pattern of a "socialized delinquent" rather than an "antisocial aggressive delinquent," as distinguished by Hewitt and Jenkins[6] and as found in a number of subsequent research reports.

The factor of neglect rather than active rejection characterizes Han-il's socialization experiences. Except for the last period before his suicide, when glue-sniffing became an act of social withdrawal rather than a group activity, he never committed a criminal act by himself but always followed the lead of his peers or acted "for the sake of his friends." It is clear that his delinquent activities were based on a need to find affiliative group relationships. The fact that they led to antisocial behavior was in some sense secondary. He first sought the friendship of those older than himself in the Korean group; he was basically a follower. A shift from the Korean to the Japanese group was in a sense a shift in the nature of his deviant behavior from a more aggressive type to a less aggressive type. Han-il was struggling with role models of what it was to be a Korean and what it was to be a Japanese; he was caught in an identity conflict based on certain role expectancies common in his "cultures."

Let us turn to some personality characteristics that are not uncommonly found in delinquents. The first is a pleasure or "now" orientation as opposed to one that assumes some self-discipline and the realization of goals at a future time. Han-il became completely pleasure-oriented in contrast to the normative directives of Japanese society, which emphasize working toward long-range goals. He was interested in flashy clothes, a type of self-presentation for which he found himself inadequate perhaps both financially and personally. He was simply not a "tough guy." Many of his acts with the Korean group were attempts to demonstrate externally what he did not feel internally.

Han-il's difficulties in school relate again to his incapacity to sustain himself in discipline. It is here that the inadequate role model of the father and the lack of intensive supervision by the mother was perhaps most influential in his character formation. Given the atmosphere of Japanese schools, Han-il must have seen himself as a somewhat inadequate person who could not sustain himself as well as the ordinary child in his class. Rather, he was restless and given to more impulsive and uncontrolled behavior. He probably disliked these traits in himself to some degree, or at least conflicted with them. In other words, he must have had periodic thoughts to the effect that he was "no good." He therefore sought out deviant groups, feeling ill at ease with any conformist peers who put positive value on being a good student or on following the social directives expected.

The features mentioned so far, in terms of family interaction patterns and perhaps in terms of personality features, are sufficient to produce delinquent behavior in a sizable proportion of majority Japanese. When interwoven with problems of being a minority Korean among majority Japanese, they become even more telling.

We have no records of Han-il's early attitudes about himself or at what period of his childhood he became aware of the special problems of being Korean. What is apparent, however, is that he shared many of the negative attitudes toward Koreans held by ordinary Japanese. One gains a strong impression that he attributed to his father many of the traits of aggressiveness, unpredictability, and drunkenness that he found in other Korean men, and found potentially to be within himself. He could not develop any positive attitude toward work. He felt himself incapable of diligence or of internalizing any kind of sustained achievement values. He found himself quitting any jobs he started. Control over his impulses was weak and inadequate and he was captured by a pleasure orientation; deep down he found himself filled with an inner sense of inadequacy and weakness. The one trait of Korean males to which the Japanese accord a grudging regard is that they see them as tough and aggressive, and hence very masculine in comportment. Han-il sought a relationship with an older peer group that provided a "Korean" image toward which to aspire. Clothes and flash became important; in effect they became a motive for work. Despite his love for his mother, he began to manifest toward her open aggressiveness.

The group he joined had lived in the same Korean community since childhood and had attended the same junior high school. They knew each other thoroughly and evidently had a strong sense of solidarity. We do not know why they accepted Han-il. Perhaps their own self-images were enhanced by his eagerness to join and his willingness to be led. The group manifested the behavior of young "machos"—drinking, going to bowling alleys, betting, and periodically fomenting fights with members of other delinquent groups. They displayed, perhaps more in fantasy than in reality, their ability to "make it" with women. From the court records we note that most of the group with which Han-il had contact had police records for aggressive, antisocial behavior. In short, group members emphasized the value of being tough, masculine Koreans in a world of what they perceived to be more conformist, less aggressive Japanese. Han-il looked up to these boys and sought to identify himself with them, thereby gaining some sense of strength. In this way, Han-il tried to become his "true" self. He began fighting and quarreling and using foul language, even to his mother. His mother was, however, no passive foil; as she described herself, she was quick-tempered, shouting back at him and calling him a lazy good-for-nothing.

The fact that he was seen as "worthless" by his mother was something, as we note in his tragic end, that he could not dismiss or avoid. It penetrated and deepened his own inner sense of worthlessness. Han-il admitted, "I secretly regretted what I did, but I did not want to show it either, and therefore I never said I was sorry." Outer heroism was an attempt to overcome an insistent sense of inadequacy. He decided to give himself up to the police so that the leader of the group could be released. He wanted to show not only loyalty to the leader but also his capacity for heroism. He could, however, never make himself believe he was indeed tough. The attempt was, in a sense, self-defeating, because Han-il was ambivalent toward Koreans, whom he defined as tough. Not only did he not *feel* tough but he never fully wanted to *be* so.

Turning from the Korean group, Han-il found a group of younger Japanese delinquents who accepted him for reasons that are not clear. Han-il never told them that he was a Korean—an indication of his confusion over identity. He explained that he was attracted to this particular group because it was almost "the opposite of the Korean group." The Korean group emphasized toughness and a display of wealth that made him feel inferior, whereas the Japanese group emphasized sharing, indulging in passive activities with drugs and in go-go dancing, where active heterosexual contact was unnecessary. Han-il felt more at ease and secure with the Japanese group. He stated to the family court officer who interviewed him, "I think I never really fit into the first group. I was cut out more for the second group."

The closer he came to the Japanese group, however, the more he became self-conscious about being Korean. Evidently his parents, or at least his mother, were ambivalent about being Korean. But as a small child he had always played with Korean children, and in junior high school he had been among Korean classmates. Until then, according to Han-il, he had thought nothing of being Korean and not Japanese. But now he joined a group of Japanese and wanted to belong. Yet he heard his Japanese friends speaking ill of Koreans.

He complained, according to his mother, of "the misfortune of having been born a Korean." His mother said she replied, "You dislike the Koreans, but what can you do about it? After all you are a Korean, too. Everybody wishes to have been born into a nice family, but no one can avoid his own fate. It is your fate that you are a Korean." She also stated to him, "Instead of complaining about your bad luck, you should cooperate with the rest of the family to improve our living conditions. You try to improve what you can. You don't complain about what you cannot improve." But Han-il came to criticize his own mother for "being a typical Korean woman who did not know how to cook and serve refined food." Having noted that his mother had avoided associating with Koreans in the nearby community, he wondered "why she had not stopped behaving like a typical Korean." He said to the family court officer that Koreans and Japanese were very different from each other. He said, "A Korean has an impudent and imprudent look on his face, while a Japanese has a polite and courteous look on his face." In Han-il's mind, the Koreans were demanding, exploitive of one another, and ready to take advantage of anyone. The Koreans had many bad habits; for example, "they would walk into somebody's house without greeting or receiving permission" and "they would get drunk and laugh at somebody's funeral ceremony." He believed that the Japanese disliked the Koreans for these bad habits and characteristics. "The Koreans lack strength and they are impolite, and that's why the Japanese hate them." But he was not simply negative about his fellow Koreans; he was ambivalent. He also voiced positive opinions about Koreans. When he was talking about his mother he said, "My mother is a typical Korean woman—faithful to her husband, faithful to her duties, and full of guts." He said the Japanese women did not have such strength of character and therefore were not as reliable as Korean women.

As we have noted, Han-il's attempt to identify with the Korean group and become a tough guy himself was not very successful. It is possible that this attempt was strongly counteracted by pressures from his mother and siblings as well as from the family court officer and the probation officer he was seeing. It is likely that Han-il formed some feeling for the family court officer with whom he was in contact, that was sufficiently positive to enable him to voice some of his own ambivalence about who he was. One can imagine that this step would only have been possible given sufficient rapport; otherwise, and more characteristically, a delinquent will hold back from giving any inside view of a sense of inadequacy.

When Han-il enumerated the negative traits of Koreans, he was not only voicing stereotypes about Koreans but was also attempting to describe his Korean friends as he observed them. He seemed to oscillate between the two possibilities of a Japanese or a Korean identity, but he seemed to need one that would afford him sufficient leeway to be delinquent. He did not feel within himself the capacity, perhaps, to reenter a more conforming atmosphere. He did nevertheless periodically seek work. Perhaps what he felt on the job was his incapacity to work for a purpose in the ordinary sense. The sustained day-to-day commitment to a job was somehow alien to him. He could not maintain motivation. At work he saw the possibility of identifying positively with Korean workers who, conscious of their minority status, wore badges proclaiming their Korean identity. This minority identity was being acted out not in the negative sense of a delinquent gang but in the positive sense of workers who felt a common social purpose. Han-il's identity problems might have been solved if he could have identified with these workers. He evidently was not sufficiently mature to do so. He could only fall back on a more immature delinquent identity, seeking out some deviant group or, given his inner turmoil, falling further back within himself.

Failure of Identity and Retreat

Han-il retreated further and attempted to escape his sense of despair and confusion through the use of drugs. Through glue-sniffing, he took to a form of isolated self-destructive behavior. At this point the mother's attempt to chastise him or make him become active only deepened his own sense of worthlessness. We have no idea of the degree to which the problem was compounded by the psychological and organic effects of the glue-sniffing on his brain. We do know that chronic exposure to the effects of the glue tends to produce damage to the central nervous system and can induce mental disturbance. His mother reported that he was failing to eat properly and looked rather sickly toward the end.

Suicide among youths in Japan is not uncommon. It attests to the severe internal conflicts that can arise between an internalization of directives on the one hand to work hard, to be responsible, and to meet one's obligations, and on the other hand, a gnawing sense of personal worthlessness. With Han-il, this pattern was compounded by his own unresolved ambivalence about being Korean. For him, being Korean was a negative destiny. He had witnessed at age twelve the drunken, stuporous death of his father, a father who had become a failure because of drink. We do not know what was inside the father's mind. It is very possible that the father himself had similar ambivalence about being Korean.

It is too easy to presume, however, that Han-il's failure can be attributed solely or in good part to his Korean minority status. What is obvious is that the minority status made positive possibilities more difficult for him. There were some role models of a more positive nature available for him at the factory, where many Koreans were capable of uniting in their identity, proclaiming it and finding in it a focus for pride. Han-il's sense of personal worthlessness made impossible for him this type of resolution. Generally speaking, therefore, in problems of identity confusion, certain features of early socialization make a mature solution of minority status less likely. Every group manifests both mature and immature responses to discrimination. Han-il was an instance of a tragically immature response.

15

CONCLUSIONS:
The Maintenance of a Korean Ethnic Identity in Japan

George De Vos and Changsoo Lee

In the course of this volume we have in its first section looked at the persistence of a Korean ethnic minority in Japan as a social, historical aftermath of the Japanese colonization of Korea. One can readily relate these segments of our presentation to parallel ethnographic or sociological studies of the economic and social effects of European colonization of other nations or peoples over the past two centuries. Much more can be said on this plane of discourse—but this is not our purpose. We have another theoretical task in mind: namely, a more psychocultural examination. Why and how does an ethnic identity develop? How do the social attitudes of the majority and the ethnic minority toward one another interact to create social conflict? What forms of psychological and social accommodation occur? Why is it likely that a modern state such as Japan must eventually learn to accommodate to the abiding social situation, giving formal legal recognition to the inevitable continuity of some form of ethnic pluralism? This is the only foreseeable course, as we have been arguing. In a modern state, one must distinguish between the legal status of full citizenship and the historic or even mythological claim of any given ethnic majority to discriminatory legal rights. This process of history is still unfolding in some parts of the world. For example, irreconcilable disputes continue in the Middle East and Northern Ireland, where deep religious cleavages rather than racial mythology are the basis of continuing conflict.

Conversely, looking at the situation from the standpoint of the minority, why is it likely that a process of *cultural* assimilation is inevitable in most instances? Not to mention the degree of *social* assimilation that occurs within the various ethnic segments of any modern state. The Japanese example is an extreme instance. Of the large modern industrial states, Japan comes closest to a pretense that it represents a single ethnic constituency. We have sought to dispel this misconception by pointing out that at least 4 percent of the inhabitants of Japan hold some form of minority status (chap. 12). Koreans, aliens or naturalized, are the largest group self-consciously considered to comprise an ethnic minority in any usual sense of the word. We shall not enter here into any discussion of whether the Buraku-min are, in effect, an *ethnic* minority.

We have illustrated in some detail the economic and social consequences not only of formal, legal discrimination but of informal types of discrimination experienced by Koreans. How do these circumstances lead to ethnic persistence? What are the possible effects of legal changes or of educational policies, whether aimed at the majority to dispel discrimination, or aimed at the minority to maintain their ethnicity?

In examining the current social and personal problems of Koreans in Japan, it is obvious that the larger issue includes the basic problem of what it means to be "Japanese" as well as what it means to be "Korean." As our introductory chapter indicates, Korean and Japanese cultures are related by more than a language of common origin and by geographic proximity. What came to be the "Japanese" population, whether nobles or commoners, was a blended population drawn from the Korean peninsula as well as from agricultural communities already located within the Japanese islands. Despite recent archaeological and linguistic findings, many modern Japanese still cling to a firm conviction of genetic uniqueness. Until the end of World War II, their sense of origin was embedded in an official mythology that affirmed an autochthonous origin, teaching that the Japanese race was descended from indigenous gods.

The problem of Korean minority status in Japan is still rooted in a deep-seated social conviction that the "Japanese" are and should remain ethnically homogeneous. The Japanese still pride themselves on their uniqueness and resist the idea of assimilating or accommodating any ethnic minority fully within a concept of citizenship that remains almost identical with a concept of racial purity.

This emphasis on Japanese uniqueness is apparent if we contrast the situation in all other modern industrial states, perhaps with the exception of Germany to some degree. Certainly France today deemphasizes racial or ethnic origins in its concept of French citizenship. The United States is avowedly pluralistic, as is the Soviet Union. The five-star red flag of China has four stars for its larger minorities in addition to the major one signifying the Han people. Italy is pluralistic, at least in terms of its strong remaining regionalism and its acute awareness of subcultural variations. The British and Dutch have been struggling to assimilate individuals from various parts of their former empires.

Admittedly, none of the large pluralistic states of the world have achieved even their present level of ethnic accommodation without accompanying social tensions. But the Japanese have as yet not overcome the implicit pattern of secondary nationality accorded to Koreans dating from before World War II, when Imperial Japan sought to absorb the Korean peninsula and, with some ambivalence, to assimilate its inhabitants. We have noted how Koreans in Japan today are still under constraint to use

Japanese names and to deny their origins to obtain even marginal acceptability as "Japanese" citizens. In effect, many Japanese would not mind that
Koreans pass and assimilate by becoming totally invisible. But this form of
assimilation is impossible. It overlooks the continuing pull exerted by an
inner sense of Korean integrity as well as by Korean counterreactions to discriminatory attitudes, as is true for the former outcastes or Burakumin,
reported on in a previous volume.[1] Many Koreans insist on maintaining for
themselves a separate ethnic identity. We shall presently summarize the
complex motives that help explain why most do not choose to pass, whatever the expediencies of becoming "Japanese."

The Korean problem is part of a greater issue as yet not faced by Japanese society. To become a leading industrial state with true international
perspective, Japanese social structure must develop some mechanism for
absorbing talented individuals from outside the traditional society. Every
other modern culture reaching preeminence has found a means of assimilating foreign-born talent. The Japanese so far have found no means of crossing what is conceptually a racial as well as a cultural barrier to social assimilation. No other Asians, let alone those of European or African ancestry,
can become really "Japanese." Not only are Japanese incapable of assimilating those of obviously different physical strains but their racism is so strong
that they cannot readily assimilate even those who display no physiological
differences.

Although most Koreans are physically indistinguishable from Japanese, they nevertheless continue to be considered racially distinct by Japanese. Whether they avow it openly, many Japanese consider Koreans biologically inferior to themselves. They do not consider that observable
behavioral differences are owing to differences in cultural heritage.
Although intermarriage with Koreans is legally tolerated, most Japanese do
not like to see it. Indeed, many express more ready acceptance of intermarriage with Caucasians if they are of suitable social status.

The children of marriages between Korean and Japanese are called
"mixed-blood children." The same term is used for children born of a Japanese and a Caucasian, or of a Japanese and a black American. We have
noted also (chap. 12) that Koreans are rated just above Africans as among
the most disliked "foreign" groups. Koreans living in Japan, therefore, are
faced with an insoluble dilemma. On the one hand, Japanese policy advocates assimilation. On the other hand, many officials as well as the ordinary
public continue to evidence a profound disparagement that conveys a message that Koreans can never become true Japanese.

Just as the so-called black problem in the United States is really a problem of developing an inclusive American identity, even so the Korean problem in Japan, of much smaller numerical proportions, is a Japanese problem
related to a continuing myth of racial superiority. As long as such racism
remains inherent, it is socially and legally difficult to extend the option

of citizenship, at least to those who are born in Japan or to some resident aliens who would like to become Japanese. The presently operative restrictions are personally demeaning to those who seek naturalization (chaps. 7, 12, and 13).

The day is not yet near when a Korean-Japanese or an American-Japanese or a French-Japanese identity will be socially as well as occupationally acceptable. The recent court cases discussed in chapter 11 are but a first step in this direction. The concept of according full citizenship to a person who elects to preserve his foreign heritage while participating in Japanese occupational activities is not yet clearly established in the Japanese legal mind, let alone in the common perceptions of the ordinary person in Japanese society.

Today, those of Korean background are reinforced in their separate identity by an awareness that the Japanese are reluctant to acknowledge their cultural debt to Korea. Before the tenth century, the Japanese were appreciative of Koreans who came to Japan, but in subsequent centuries they attributed cultural superiority to China and political inferiority to Korea. By the time of Hideyoshi at the end of the sixteenth century (chap. 1) and again at the beginning of the twentieth century, Koreans had to withstand brutal Japanese incursions that permitted them no sense of dignity and self-esteem, either culturally or politically.

Brought to Japan involuntarily, many Koreans repatriated after World War II. Many, however, found it difficult to do so because of economic uncertainties. Most of those now in Japan are a new generation. They are not simply Koreans who may choose to go back to Korea. They are largely third-generation inhabitants of Japan who, despite their continuing Korean identity, are familiar only with life in Japan. In most instances they speak no Korean. Even when they do, they think more spontaneously in the Japanese language. What keeps them "Koreans"? The processes that maintain a Korean ethnic minority in Japan are, in effect, little different from those that contribute to the persistence of distinct ethnic enclaves elsewhere.

From the standpoint of social science, the issue of Korean ethnicity can be approached on several levels. On the level of sociological-historical analysis, one looks at social processes as they relate to those social structures that maintain some continuity, whatever the subjective interpretations of the changing ideology of their members. On another level, no matter how such structural analysis is or is not divorced from the consciousness of the members of a society itself, one cannot dismiss underlying psychological motivations.

These are, in turn, on two levels. Much human behavior is rational in the sense that individuals seek personal advantage, either individually or as members of a group. Such "instrumental" motives are well understood and are usually fully considered as part of economic or sociological theory.

What is less well considered is how or why an individual's motives remain unconscious and irrational. Present cultural behavior, therefore, remains "expressive" of past social vicissitudes, as we shall presently illustrate in an analysis of why and how Korean minority status is maintained in Japanese society.

Why is it not sufficient to consider the basic processes still at work to be simply the aftermath of a recent history of colonialism and class exploitation? We have well documented the history of Korean exploitation, especially in chapter 2. Koreans provided cheap labor for Japanese capitalists who, emulating Western colonial powers, annexed Korea and, as part of the resources thus acquired, reduced the illiterate masses of Koreans to economic thralldom.

This form of analysis, succinctly stated, encompasses much of what can be said, but it leaves out much that may be unique in the given historical circumstance. For example, basic differences exist in how exploitation can be structured in a culture that psychologically supports caste segregation as compared with a culture organized by class segregation. A class society exploiting its own depressed occupational segments does not operate in quite the same manner as a colonial society or a racially segmented society. In caste situations especially, other psychological processes besides simple instrumental exploitation are at work. These create a true difference in the historical aftermath. Stratification in a caste society endures even after the economic advantages of exploiting a particular group have come to be outweighed by the disadvantages, economic and social, of maintaining a segregated society.[2]

It is therefore important to understand that the present plight of Koreans is not simply a result of "class exploitation," despite all the features of economic exploitation we have documented. It is equally important, in this instance, to consider the plight of Koreans in Japan historically as a reaction to racist-caste thinking of a type peculiar to the Japanese as they interrelate with individuals socialized in a "Korean" psychocultural milieu.

Koreans in Japan have responded to their present conditions by an ethnic consolidation not dissimilar in some modes of social adaptation to those that have been occurring in the black American population. In each instance, group members have come to recognize that their submerged, exploited condition occurs within a racist society. Many Koreans are ambivalent about espousing a Marxist explanation for their own plight, although Marxist militancy has indeed been a most active unifying force through which Koreans have sought redress. It is not that a Marxist explanation lacks cogency; it is that it does not explain fully the Japanese inability to accept the Korean people or their culture. Marxist "worker solidarity" does not readily cross racial barriers in Japan. The racism that has affected northwestern European states has much in common with the situation in Japan, despite independent cultural-historical origins. Class attitudes in

Europe and Japan, however, are different in intensity and structure. The Japanese are not alienated by class differences in a manner true of Europeans.

Nathan Glazer and Daniel P. Moynihan, in the theoretical introduction to *Ethnicity*,[3] offer several major reasons for the growth of ethnic social movements in modern industrial cities. Glazer and Moynihan are also against the idea that ethnic conflict in the United States is simply reducible to an understanding of class conflict. They deny that such conflict is simply a variety of colonial or postcolonial conflict, an uprising of the internally colonized, and so on. They too seek a more complex series of causes.

They rightly note that ethnic identity among minorities has become a more salient focus of political mobilization because of the growing ethnic heterogeneity of most modern industrial states, which have recently taken advantage of widespread labor migration. As an internal dynamic evident in such heterogeneous populations, Glazer and Moynihan cite the conclusions of Ralf Dahrendorf (1969) as to how an unresolvable conflict arises between equalitarianism and the differential achievement of norms by different class or ethnic segments of a population.[4]

Dahrendorf clearly states that "selection of norms always involves discrimination, not only against persons holding sociologically random moral convictions but also against social positions that may debar their incumbents from conformity with established values."[5] In other words, his thesis is that every society emphasizes norms and established values selected from a diverse set of possibilities. Once the selection is made historically of what is "good" and what is "bad," individuals and ethnic groups come to have different levels of success in attaining desired status conditions. These norms may define physical traits, characterological traits, or particular talents that are differentially socialized within different groups. Therefore, a conflict occurs between the idea that all people should have equal opportunity and the differential possibility of achieving the norms of that society.

This form of analysis certainly pertains to the relationship between Koreans and Japanese, as we have documented. Koreans are disadvantaged by their particular socialization experiences within a racially disparaging Japanese society. The intensity of feeling on the part of Japanese must be considered a part of personality variables resulting from strongly felt internal problems about being socially acceptable. Koreans are considered to exhibit various traits disavowed by Japanese, and they are therefore easily used as scapegoats.

As noted by Dahrendorf, countering the forces leading to inequality of status are those forces noted in most contemporary societies, related to humanitarian ideals of acceptance and the bestowal of welfare benefits on the needy and the disadvantaged.[6] We have mentioned how such processes are at work in Japan as well, although programs broadening welfare in Japan remain ambivalent about a "foreign" ethnic minority. Here the question of citizenship becomes a critical issue. Koreans by and large have not become Japanese citizens. For the reasons we have noted, the situation of Koreans in Japan has come to resemble the situation faced by noncitizen migrant laborers in Europe. Koreans are treated in racist terms, as are certain segments of European migrant labor. In France, for example, Arab and Senegalese workers are the focus of attitudes more racially discriminatory than those expressed toward Spanish and Portuguese workers.

A final reason for the recent appearance of ethnicity, according to Glazer and Moynihan, is the rapidity of international communication now possible.[7] Techniques of confrontation used in one part of the contemporary world are quickly transmitted to other places, particularly the strategies used in ethnic conflicts. Although more apparent now, such rapid communication was by no means absent in the past; since the turn of the century political ideas have traveled quickly. But the ideological messages after World War I were different. Hopes for ethnic self-determination or the development of government by an international working class quickly spread through Asia as well as Europe.

Intellectuals among the Koreans in 1919 were moved by the possibilities of national self-determination. Aware of the breakup of the Austro-Hungarian empire into independent countries based on ethnicity, Koreans were aware too of the effects of the Russian Revolution and the independence of the Balkan states freed from Imperial Russian domination. But the Wilsonian efforts successful in parts of Europe were not to be extended to Asia. We have documented in chapter 1 the brutal suppression of the Korean uprising of 1919 by the Imperial Japanese, who were still bent on Japanization of Koreans. The message of international Communism was quickly espoused by many Koreans as well as by some Japanese intellectuals. A general nationalist Japanese fear of such a spread, as we have documented, found fanatical and hysterical expression in the massacre of Koreans in Japan following the Kantō earthquake in 1923.

Today too, Koreans in Japan are promptly aware of social movements occurring elsewhere. They are aided and strengthened in their own ethnic identity by the knowledge that now ethnic minorities in other countries are expressing themselves more openly. The historical reasons for this recent resurgence may be somewhat different from place to place, but the fact that such movements are occurring throughout the world is a mutually reinforcing spur to action. Korean-Japanese are well aware that ethnic minorities in the United States and elsewhere have been able to press their interests not as a depressed class but as a minority citizenry seeking to redress grievances of past political suppression.

In effect, the Koreans, who have always been aware of their minority status in Japan, have taken new heart in the knowledge that movements elsewhere seem to be gaining privilege and acceptable status when group members assert themselves in concert. The international political climate is such that there is no ideology under which any modern state today can suppress an ethnic minority without drawing upon itself severe international sanctions. It is now more possible to work through ethnic groupings, since liberal governments have generally been responsive to active groups using confrontation techniques.

In American cities, a style of ethnic voting has found new political power. In this instance, circumstances differ in Japan; the Koreans are relatively too small a force, and their general lack of citizenship is a principal handicap. Although Koreans recognize that some form of solidarity is necessary, they are presently split by irreconcilable political differences. The Japanese labor movement, in its emphasis on class conflict, tends to ignore the fact that the Koreans comprise interest groups with more than class-specific considerations at stake.

We are in general agreement with contemporary sociological thought about the present saliency of "instrumental" activities of ethnic groups within the contemporary social climate of modern states. But we contend that it is also incumbent on psychocultural analysis to reexamine and analyze in detail what Daniel Bell has simply summarized as "primordial feelings."[8] Noting that such feelings are operative in ethnic groups but are presently absent in the labor movement, Bell rightly states that "ethnicity" has become more salient because it can combine an "interest" with an "affective tie." In an analysis similar to ours, Bell sees ethnic groups, whether racial, linguistic, religious, or communal, as past-oriented units that, with the rise of industry, have been crosscut by economic and class interests. There is "an emergent expression of primordial feelings chosen by disadvantaged persons as a new mode of seeking political redress," he notes.

Thus, as a sociologist, Bell recognizes the role of emotional needs, but he does not think it within the province of sociological analysis to delve into either the psychological or historical reasons for the "how" or "why" of psychological processes. Suffice it for him to examine how ethnic minorities attempt to actualize instrumental goals and how these movements are powered by strong emotional forces.

We must disagree. The ingredients of these "primordial feelings" cannot be left unanalyzed simply because a sociological framework by itself is not equipped to deal with them. Indeed, any understanding of ethnic identity demands an understanding of how deep psychological structures operative within the individual have profound social consequences, differing from one culture to the next despite similar sociological forces at work in modern societies. In our terminology, we must understand how ethnicity is a complex combination of "instrumental" *and* "expressive" motivations that operate within and, in turn, influence historical-sociological processes operative within any conflict-ridden, changing social structure. Let us therefore add another dynamic dimension to what has already been said about processes of economic and social exploitation operative in Japan as elsewhere.

Utilizing our dual framework of analysis as we have applied it previously,[9] we shall draw some complementary psychocultural inferences from our findings about the various intrapersonal and interpersonal "internal needs and external presses," in the language of Henry A. Murray,[10] to understand some of the principal features of a Korean ethnic identity problem and its consequences in contemporary Japan.

INSTRUMENTAL MOTIVATIONS: PROS AND CONS OF MAINTAINING A SEPARATE ETHNIC IDENTITY

We have listed, for purposes of analysis, five main ordering concerns in instrumental, goal-directed intrapersonal and interpersonal motives. First, concerns with *achievement;* second, *competence;* third, *responsibility;* fourth, *social control;* fifth, questions of *cooperative* or *competitive interaction* in problem-solving or goal realization.

It must be noted that the analytic use of categories of instrumental and expressive concerns is difficult, since the categories in effect refer to elementary concerns which in actuality are seldom found in their pure state. That is to say, most human motives are complex, and all human behavior is multi-determinant. Hence, in the following discussions, we have at times focused on particular interpersonal concerns under one category, when in effect they could be discussed with equal pertinence under another. For purposes of clarity, one must make a linear presentation; in reality, one finds no such ready separation of human motives.

Concern with Achievement and Alienation

Definitions of social, occupational, economic, and political success or achievement are found in every society. In any pluralistic society that emphasizes the ascendancy of one group, the achievement of social success may well require one to disguise one's minority origins. In chapter 12, Wetherall has noted examples of "passing" in which Koreans have changed their behavior and appearance to obtain what is defined as success in a variety of occupations in present-day Japan. The term "passing" first appeared in social science literature, borrowed from its common usage by black Americans to describe a light-skinned person of African ancestry who, as a means of avoiding the consequences of American caste relationships, passed himself or herself off as white. It is obvious that passing is not limited to racial mobility. Passing is practiced in moving from one class to another or in moving out of an ethnic minority. In racial situations, passing depends on physiological acceptability as well as an assumption of proper behavior patterns. In passing from one class to another, the individual who passes must disguise behavior patterns, linguistic usages, and patterns of social participation that would betray his past affiliations. In class societies such as those of the British or French, certain individuals delight in exposing pretenders who betray themselves by the use of improper verbal expressions.

To be known as Korean in Japan today is still to court possible failure in many business or professional careers. It is dangerous economically to "surface" even after gaining recognition. Only in given instances can a Korean make direct public avowal of his ethnic background.

Japanese may evidence transitory interest in foreign entertainers or foreign professionals who come to their country as visitors or guests, but they make no attempt to incorporate them into any Japanese group. A Korean-Japanese entertainer therefore remains a social anomaly (chap. 12). Whether he or she is or is not technically a foreigner makes little difference. Third-generation Korean youths growing up in Japan, knowing no other social atmosphere than Japan, gain little acceptance as Korean-Japanese. To gain full acceptance one must pretend to be of Japanese ancestry. Some Koreans find it more expedient to live as if they are totally Japanese, avoiding the perplexity and partial withdrawal that would be accorded them if they were known to be Korean. Many in public life, such as entertainers or business and professional people, find that it is not only simpler to pass, but that the need to consider passing to become successful is paramount.

Among Koreans there is continual ambivalence about the acceptability of passing. There exists an awareness that others of one's group indeed may need to pass; at the same time there is an insistence that the person who is passing must somehow maintain, at least covertly, allegiance with Korean causes. A great deal of distrust is directed toward fellow Koreans who desert, and much bitterness is expressed about those who totally turn their backs on their Korean origins. Some "successful" individuals experience subsequent crises in identity at moments when they must choose between conflicting group loyalties.

Frustration of a need for achievement in a particular minority has four common results: first, active political dissidence, some of it illegal and violent; second, goal-oriented criminal activity; third, unresolved ambivalence about future purposes; and fourth, withdrawal from society and its goals. The choice of these alternatives has to do, of course, with personality components as well as with available social possibilities. Our field work in Japan to date has given us impressionistic evidence, if not statistics, that demonstrate the prevalence of each of these modes of response to discrimination.

First, the history of social protest, including violent political radicalism, past and present, has been discussed in various contexts in the above chapters. Koreans have been motivated to take a wide variety of means to redress their social plight. Religious sects still vie with Marxist parties as rival ideological commitments. In turn, the total Korean community has been feared by majority Japanese as a wellspring of political violence and therefore as a continual threat to their society.

Looked at psychologically as well as socially, social protest displays a broad spectrum of adjustment patterns ranging from infantile destructiveness rationalized as social purpose, to mature espousal of a political cause deriving from a sense of common humanity and compassion. By and large the social adaptions involved in political commitments cannot be reduced to particular psychological patterns. Suffice it to say that in some instances the use of protest is a psychologically healthy response on the part of individuals with a secure sense of social self. The proper means to effect change is a question not yet securely answered by modern history. Suffice it to say that in Japan open social protest jeopardizes an individual's occupational success. Political commitment takes energy and dedication; it also antagonizes employers. Active political dissidents are forced into marginal occupations and careers.

Second, it is similarly difficult to generalize about Koreans in Japan who pursue criminal careers. Robert Merton, in his seminal volume, *Social Theory and Social Structure* (1957),[11] first discussed Durkheim's concept of "anomie" from the standpoint that deviant criminal careers are actually very often alternative patterns of achievement for the socially marginal. One finds that the Koreans in Japan amply demonstrate the fact that individuals who have a strong achievement motivation will resort to criminal careers if ordinary avenues of advancement within the society are not opened to them. Numerous Koreans of an intelligent, energetic nature have found that they can actualize themselves only in marginal occupations, since they are looked upon with animosity by the majority society. In a situation of mutual hatred, many find themselves psychologically free from the constraints and restrictions that ordinary Japanese might feel about entering criminal activity. Koreans have found acceptance in the Japanese underworld among the yakuza or Mafia-type Japanese gangs. In fact, their "toughness" exemplifies the type of bravado traditionally favored by the Japanese underworld. This pattern is well illustrated in the case of Kim Hi-lo, reported in chapter 11.

The findings of our previous work[12] have been supported by the continuing relatively high rate of juvenile delinquency among Korean youth. It is evident that the social environment generally experienced by Korean youth is more conducive to delinquency than is the environment of majority Japanese. One can also document psychological and attitudinal determinants contributing to internal stress as they are selectively experienced by youth growing up in discontented or broken families. These negative features of family life are more likely to be experienced by Korean youth than by majority Japanese. The fact is that discrimination has an internal effect on the stability of family life, causing children to experience the consequences of its deleterious impact on parental roles. Chapters 13 and 14 discuss the complexities of socialization within a Korean-Japanese family: expectations about "tough behavior," the disparagement of peers, the availability of deviant gangs, and other factors that interact to produce a high rate of juvenile delinquency in Korean youth. Delinquent behavior, although seemingly activist and possibly instrumental in producing some forms of immediate material gratification, is at the same time expressive. It can be testimony to a sense of alienation and lack of social purpose. It can be rebellion against inconsistent parental authority. It can be evidence of self-disparagement, of social violation, of a sense of emotional as well as economic deprivation, and of a blind need to express destructive feelings. Juvenile deviancy, in summary, tends to be more expressive than instrumental. Whatever the patterns of motivation in a given youth, only those individuals who successfully *instrumentalize* their behavior go on to successful criminal careers.

Our small sample of psychological testing to date supports another impression: even more prevalent than actual behavioral deviancy is a deep sense of alienation and uncertainty about future goals, resulting in various forms of social apathy. Rather than holding to the fantasy of future success which sustains most youths on all socio-economic levels of Japanese society, Korean youth have a sense of conflict and uncertainty about their own purpose, their goals in life. They cannot naively project a happy future. They tend to feel more conflict about committing themselves to any purpose. They are aware of the unemployment rate among fellow Koreans. They have witnessed failure in family and kin. It has often been stated that American minorities suffer similar forms of alienation. Our evidence from Japan certainly supports this view of the social cross-purposes faced by many ethnic minorities when family or community cohesiveness is insufficient to insulate the individual against social disparagement.

Competence

Ethnic identity may determine, to a large extent, the varieties of self-confidence or self-doubt among various groups in a competitive, achievement-oriented society. Wagatsuma and Sasaki (chap. 14) have cited several instances, including the pathetic case of one juvenile delinquent who committed suicide, in which there is evidence of self-disparagement or of worthlessness and incapacity partially self-attributed to the individual because he finds himself to be "Korean." The individual's own negative life experiences, especially those he has witnessed afflicting his parents, keep demonstrating to the individual, before he has the capacity for mature judgment, the social inadequacy of his group, family, and self. The readily available negative attitudes of the majority are used to explain the failures he witnesses about him. Individuals of "proper" social background can be bolstered by the security of a highly esteemed family status, but few Koreans in Japan are so blessed. Rather they are continually faced with the sense that others look down upon them. It is, therefore, psychologically easier for Koreans to explain failure than success. They do not share in group expectations of competence. On the contrary, they see before themselves, even if selectively, continuing examples of failure and degradation. Self-hatred deepens their sense of social and personal incompetence (chap. 13).

It is difficult for an individual to assert a sense of individual competence when he is so patently the member of a group that has little supportive, sustaining tradition. The minority individual who has unusual competence has to depend for status much more on his independent capacities than do members of, in this instance, the majority Japanese who inherit psychological support simply by being born into the majority.

Responsibility and Obligation

Part of being socialized into a responsible membership in any society is the internalizing of a moral code. In addition to proscriptions of behavior, a moral code includes obligations and expectations. In Japan the internalization of the moral code is put in terms of assuming obligations for repayment to parents, responsibility to the group, and loyalty to the nation. The Korean minority is ambivalent about being governed in good conscience by standards and proscriptions to which they, as "innately inferior" to Japanese, are not assumed to be capable of adhering.

Animosity and resentment over discrimination in one sense frees the individual from assuming the internalized standards of the majority. One dilemma of identity for a Korean has to do with whether he feels he should attempt to meet the social obligations assumed by ordinary Japanese. The situation of Han-il, the suicide cited previously (chap. 14), is a case in point. The individual is torn by possible internalized guilt in two respects: first, a guilt-ridden ambivalence about being or not being "Japanese" and its attendant expectations; second, guilt over not meeting maternal expectations combined with the knowledge that one's discreditable behavior reflects on the mother's adequacy and thereby hurts her. Although such a person feels guilty, he may also resent a parent who pushes him toward a course of behavior he is emotionally incapable of following.

For some Koreans, therefore, maintaining a Korean identity suggests maintaining some antagonistic posture that condones illegal or deviant marginal activity. To become "Japanese" is to assume a number of deprecatory attitudes and negative evaluations of Koreans. The individual is caught in a dilemma of integrity. He is caught by possible conscious or unconscious prejudices internalized as part of living in the larger society. One resolution of such a conflict is to resist passing, because to pass implies acceptance of Japanese judgments about his own people and their past.

In a negative direction, there are advantages to avoiding responsibility. In an ethnically pluralistic society, an individual may retain his minority to avoid certain obligations that are part of the role expectations of the majority. Conversely, one would expect some individuals from the majority to "drop out," identifying with a supposedly freer minority to indulge in behavioral patterns ordinarily forbidden. In the relationship of minority Koreans and Japanese this latter move is not often made. A few Japanese, however, do identify themselves as Koreans. In Arakawa Ward (chap. 10), we found an example of a Japanese boy who put a Korean button on his cap to intimidate his peers. To be considered "tough," some yakuza or gangster types use Korean speech mannerisms. Occasionally some lower-class Japanese prefer to live in Korean or Burakumin ghettos because they prefer such a life-style to living among their own group and its strictures. Such outsiders are tolerated in some instances and rejected in others. Koreans are usually suspicious of any outsider who seeks to gain acceptance among them.

In summary, the maintenance of a Korean identity invariably implies some conflict over assumption or avoidance of responsibility and guilt. To the degree in which the individual has introjected a negative self-image, he may find a great deal of internal conflict about ethical standards. To assume the same moral, ethical, and social obligations as the majority Japanese may be distasteful or burdensome to many Koreans. Conversely, the avoidance of responsibility may at times be made easier through blaming the negative attitudes of the majority for one's avoidance of any form of commitment.

Social Control: Dominance and Submission

To be a Korean in Japan is to come in conflict with the well-defined system of social hierarchy operative in Japanese society. One is placed "outside" and is subordinated without any compensatory reward. Koreans are not brought in to "belong." They are not treated in a positive sense with the paternalistic care that subordinates Japanese, to whom a sustaining hope is one of the payments of allegiance. Since the emotional gratification that makes power or control relationships tolerable is not forthcoming, Koreans can only resent subordination. Exercise of dominance and submission between Japanese and Koreans remains strictly instrumental, with none of the emotional lubrication that reduces friction. It is harder for the Korean to tolerate subordinate status and to view the Japanese as exercising his authority legitimately with constraint and concern for the
He feels much more put upon. Koreans tend to be very sensitiv
tive aspects of social control in their interpersonal relationsh
not apt to create illusions of gratitude for benevolence rece
ment or personal authority is perceived as exercised for the b
in power rather than for benevolent purposes.

Koreans are Confucianists within their own families. They expect the exercise of paternal authority. They avow male dominance in the family as part of the value of family life. Compared with Japanese, however, authority is more apt to be reinforced by physical punishment. Also, by and large we note that Korean women are less long-suffering and constrained by submissive role-behavior than are Japanese women. Although seen ideally as dutiful and responsible, they are also perceived as capable of aggressive, even violent, remonstration. As discussed previously (chap. 10) in regard to obligation and responsibility, Korean women allocated to lower social status are less concerned with maintaining status through the seemingly submissive role-behavior expected of high-status Japanese women. Expected role-behavior differs with status among Japanese women; for example, women from a fishing village are less constrained toward their husbands than are women from a farming village that prides itself on *samurai* ancestry. In general, however, Japanese women practice deferential behavior as part of the wifely role.[13]

De Vos's case-history material would seem to suggest that the use of physical punishment for control of children by both parents is more accepted among Koreans than among Japanese. This impression is not yet systematically sustained. Although in our previous intensive family studies in Tokyo we found instances among lower-class Japanese of the use of physical punishment, we could not characterize as normative, even among them, the employment of physical punishment as discipline. Lower-status Koreans are more given to the exercise of physical force between husband and wife and between parent and child. They are, therefore, more prone to direct expressions of aggressive attitudes, and their comportment contributes to their being perceived by Japanese as more aggressive in their interpersonal relationships.

Koreans in general are more accustomed socially to seeing expressions of aggression and are less upset by it than are Japanese. They do not feel that the direct expression of aggression in language or comportment results in an irrevocable breach, as do many Japanese. For some Koreans, the exercise of power entails a capacity to enforce one's will by physical force if necessary. Korean children in school are also more likely to assert themselves against their Japanese peers. Therefore they can more readily intimidate them. This difference in aggressive comportment is historically related to differences in class origins. The Korean migration to Japan (chap. 2) was comprised mostly of illiterate, impoverished, rural groups who would have been more likely to use force than words to settle disputes.

Koreans, finding themselves in a subordinate status, do not typically use long-range, devious, submissive tactics. They are more apt to lose patience, letting superiors know directly their true feelings or attitudes. This sometimes contributes to a confrontational atmosphere that disconcerts

Japanese. To summarize, Koreans are more apt to seek autonomy than to express loyalty. They are more apt to be perceived by Japanese as aggressive if not insubordinate.

Cooperation and Competition

Much has been written recently and is presently being studied about the nature of Japanese organizations, whether in business or in the government bureaucracy. It is apparent that the Japanese as a nation have been highly successful in competing economically with the industrial West. Their success results from various forms of internal cooperative structures that can unite to realize economic and social goals. The development of Korean industry is recent. It is difficult at present to judge, without intensive research, how Korean organizations operate and whether they are different from or similar to those found in Japan. We know that many upper-status Koreans in business and in education have been trained in Japanese settings. But we have gained the impression that patterns of interaction among Koreans, including the exercise of authority and the expression of loyalty by subordinates, may differ from that manifested by their Japanese counterparts.

Some cultural and historic organizational features continue their influence regardless of modern exigencies imposed by industrialization. It must be noted that Korean and Japanese organizational history is radically different in several respects. The Korean administrative system was modeled on that of the Chinese bureaucracy. In the premodern period it was centralized around the royal court structure, although not necessarily directly controlled by it. Officials sent out to local regions were usually alien to the region they were sent to govern. For the most part, no patterns of intercommunication or personal loyalty were developed between local subjects and their governors. This type of organization differed markedly from that of the Han feudatories of Tokugawa Japan, among whom loyalty to one's lord was espoused as a supreme virtue.

There was no Korean counterpart to the warrior class in feudal Japan. Korean officials, as with their Chinese counterparts, were totally devoid of military training or interest. As in China, the military was despised and was not trained to responsible governing. In contrast, Japan went into its modern period with a trained samurai class. Although officially abolished as a recognized group, the former samurai helped develop a modern bureaucracy, manned a system of compulsory education for all, and, as entrepreneurs, brought forms of samurai self-discipline into modern business activities. Through samurai influence on the system of compulsory education, Confucian ideology permeated the school system in the name of national unity and defense. The Confucianist hierarchy of relationships was basic to a nationalist ideology with strong military overtones.

A second feature of the premodern Japanese social class structure also lacked a counterpart in Korea. This was the influence of a burgeoning merchant-artisan-townsman culture, with its highly elaborated system of apprenticeships and sustaining mentorships exercised by masters over disciples. This stratum of Japanese society had its own ambience and its own aesthetics. Korean society, in contrast, consisted of a minuscule educated upper class and a large illiterate peasantry. There was no well-established, quasi-independent townsman tradition. Although the ideology of the upper class was Confucianist, it did not and could not set up vertical systems of loyalty and personal commitment of the kind constructed in Japan on both the samurai and the merchant levels. There were no comparable long-range apprenticeship programs nor forms of mentorship within age-graded bureaucratic structures.

Little wonder then, from a social-structural standpoint, that we do not find the same fierce sense of loyalty and the same intensive superior-subordinate relationship developed in Koreans as in Japanese. Koreans are not likely to subordinate themselves to group causes with the same degree of long-range altruism we sometimes find in the Japanese. Although Koreans can work together to mutual purpose, in many respects they seem much more individualistic than the Japanese and they define their goals in individual rather than collective terms.

There is considerable evidence that the modern occupational structures developed in Japanese industry are of relatively recent date, and that the concept of lifelong attachment to particular companies, either by workers or management, has been strengthened since the earlier period of industrialization at the turn of the century. Whatever the merits of the argument against direct structural continuity with the premodern past, the point is that Japanese society still had latent within it a potentially strong pattern of group loyalty that could be revised and developed by Japanese industry. It is questionable whether the psychological characteristics of people comfortable in this kind of life-career pattern are to be found with equal frequency or intensity among Koreans. Whatever the actuality, the Japanese for their part do not perceive Koreans as potentially loyal subordinates who will dedicate themselves to company enterprises. This perception may be in part a matter of prejudice, but it may also be based on the Korean's sense of individualism, which prevents him from making emotional commitments of the type implicitly expected by Japanese.

It has often been reported that Japanese social behavior depends on school ties and other intricate networks that are not easily broken without jeopardizing all future activities. Whereas the value of group behavior of this kind among Koreans in Korea has been reported, it is uncertain how widespread among Koreans of all classes is the application of cooperative, sustained group behavior.

Japanese are age-graded within organizations to avoid competition. There is a similar sense of age-grading in Koreans; informally at least, it is also apparent in interpersonal relationships. Koreans, however, are less obviously concerned with meticulous attention to deference behavior in their relationships both outside and inside the group. They are more easily relaxed in groups of mixed status. Minority Koreans have a greater sense of unpredictability about the possible behavior of others. Japanese are apt to be working within institutional and personal networks so binding that the individual's behavior is highly predictable. In this sense, Japanese can afford to trust each other in their group operations, whereas Koreans are not as bound and hence, not as predictable.

In contrast, there are many instances of Koreans coming together under crisis situations of political protest (chaps. 5 and 6). But we note that these situations are not so much examples of instrumental cooperation as they are emotional expressions of an aroused sense of identity. It is when this sense of belonging is actualized that Koreans respond by concerted action. Japanese, as part of their collective identity, can apply a steady, cooperative intensity toward the long-range maintenance of economic and political relationships and thereby are very often successful in the accomplishment of mutual ends.

In summary, Koreans in Japan expect to reach their own occupational goals without the assistance of a group. For them, group goals are not a substitute for individual accomplishment. They therefore tend to be more individualistically competitive than cooperative. Nevertheless, there is among them vehement support for Korean accomplishments and pride in those of their membership who attain some prominence, especially when they do so in competition with Japanese. There is, for example, a highly developed sense of Korean competitiveness in sports.

Politically, we have said much already about the factionalization within Korean ethnic groups (see especially chap. 5). Not only is there distrust of other groups but there is distrust by members of a group of the aims and advantages taken by their leaders. Many Koreans are suspicious that their leadership functions for selfish benefit. What is the ordinary individual to do in these circumstances? An individual may feel that as a Korean he should assume responsibility within available organizations, but he may not find his convictions to be well represented by them. There are many reasons why it is easier for Koreans in Japan to unite in expressive ad hoc protests than to pursue sustained, affirmative programs of action.

As we have illustrated, the main forms taken by Korean voluntary associations are political, economic, and religious (chap. 10). Each of these groupings is heavily concerned with how one maintains one's ethnic identity in an overwhelmingly Japanese cultural ambience. The economic cooperatives are perhaps the most directly guided by simple economic motives, but they are joined almost exclusively by individuals of a similar political persuasion. As we have reported in chapter 1 and elsewhere, the religious groups have a history of courageous protest against Japanese domination. In their attempts to maintain a moderating function they are opposed, however, by those espousing a Marxist ideology.

EXPRESSIVE BEHAVIOR IN KOREAN IDENTITY

Observing trends in the United States, Daniel Bell[14] and others have remarked upon the fact that a strong reason for the resurgence of ethnicity within the United States is the fact that there is instrumental gain to be derived; namely, that ethnic groupings have become interest groups, and that ethnic identity can therefore be rewarding instrumentally, given the responsiveness of government. Glazer and Moynihan,[15] for example, see the rise of the welfare state as increasing the strategic efficacy of ethnic demands. This development may be particularly true in the United States, one would say quickly, but it does not seem to be equally true for the Koreans in Japan, although the generalization would hold for the former Eta or Burakumin, who are full citizens, and for the Okinawans, who are once again citizens fully under Japanese jurisdiction.

In effect, as far as noncitizen Koreans are concerned, it would seem best to pass and to deny one's ethnic background. The Japanese, by mechanisms of denial, would be willing to forget origins if Koreans would manage their outer appearance well and would not make intermarriages that expose their foreign background. Nonetheless, it is obvious that such passing is psychologically difficult for Koreans. Given this difficulty, then, we would assume that Koreans have become aware that group action is more efficacious than individual action in overcoming discrimination. Whether one argues simply in instrumental terms or in terms of individual or group interest, the conclusion is reached that ethnicity has become more salient because, as Daniel Bell has stated, "it can combine to some degree an instrumental interest with an affective tie."

It is thereby incumbent on us, using our psychocultural form of analysis, to reexamine and analyze in detail so called affective ties or primordial feelings and their components, to better understand their composition and the sources of the need for Korean ethnic identity within the psychological structure of the individual. One especially notes in the discussion of expressive variables how harmony, affiliation, nurturance, and appreciation—or their negative counterparts in discord, isolation, deprivation, and disparagement—are often inextricably intertwined with one another as well as with instrumental motives. This will be apparent in our presentation in the following sections. We must continually return to the problems of discord, deprivation, and disparagement, no matter what principal theme we pursue.

Harmony vs. Discord

In the Confucian ideology, the greatest social virtue to pursue and the greatest social satisfaction to experience is to live in a state of interpersonal harmony. In the Confucian system more is discussed concerning harmony between individuals of unequal status than concerning patterns of affiliative friendship. The harmony of the family demands the subordination of the wife to the husband and of the younger to the older. The harmony of the nation is achieved through mutual responsibility of the governed and the governors.

The opposite of harmony is discord and the open expression of aggression. Confucianism was the principal "religion of government," if one may use this expression, in China, Korea, and Japan. Actual practice differed widely in these countries, not only in the political area but in the behavior of families. Confucianism in Korean could be readily afforded only by those of wealthier status. It is questionable whether the poor, illiterate peasants were convinced that Confucianist principles really benefited them in their governance by an alienated elite who took pride in speaking or writing in an alien tongue. This alienation of the Korean elite was not too different from that now witnessed in India, where the intellectual elite are still oriented to a foreign culture, priding themselves on their English speech, in effect being cut off in perception as well as in the language of their daily newspapers from the plight of the ordinary villager. Such extreme class alienation also existed between the Russian aristocracy and the serfs under the czars.

Within the family itself in Korea, there was, when it could be afforded, an attempt to assert the patriarchal aspects of Confucianism, emphasizing the superior status of the father. Koreans in general have always emphasized family harmony as the ideal for all group relationships. Ideally, at least, one should mute feelings of conflict and contention, avoiding their display within the family. Hostilities are best displayed outside rather than within the family group.

It is true for Koreans as well as for other groups that sometimes the ideals espoused are little exercised in actuality. The history of the Koreans in Japan shows much of the within-group political discord, as well as many examples of mutual antagonism, hostility, and resentment expressed by family members toward one another. The many voluntary organizations available to Koreans have been a source of emotional satisfaction, of a sense of harmony, but they have also been a means of expressing dissension. The instrumental goals of group cooperation to which they are supposedly dedicated sometimes become secondary to discordant expressive needs.

Individuals can find considerable emotional support as well as mobilization of energy by joining a professional or worker's group. Church membership has been useful as a means of expressing cohesion and a sense of belonging. But the division of the homeland and the consequent divisive political climate has made Korean groups dissipate much of their potential energy on internal discord rather than on the development of plans that could become instrumentally productive. Suspicion and wariness character- ize internal group processes; there is constant concern over the presence of spies. Some leaders, acutely aware of this divisiveness, take great pains to avoid internal criticism of fellow members, but the leadership role remains a difficult one.

To summarize, Koreans in Japan, past as well as present, generally find their need for harmony dissipated by deep and abiding discords, inher- ited hostilities, and traditions of divisiveness. Political groups manifest long-standing splits between North and South, between progovernment and antigovernment groupings, between Christian and non-Christian. Whereas many Koreans with considerable justification blame these cleavages on the fact that they are pawns in a power game in which the chief players are the Soviet Union and China, the United States and Japan, they must face the fact that discordant factionalism is also caused by the seeking of personal gain on the part of particular Koreans.

Social movements rising from within a minority group, such as the Koreans, often attempt to unite the group to achieve a new sense of har- mony within. The most expedient mechanism for achieving internal har- mony is to find some means of deflecting socially disruptive behavior onto outside individuals or groups. For example, the North Korean groups and their schools have sought to further their internal group solidarity by expressing discord toward those "less virtuous" in the Korean community. This is a well-researched mechanism in social psychology. Displacement of internal tensions onto an outside enemy is basic to ethnocentrism wherever it operates. But it is indeed an unfortunate destiny of many minority groups to embody in their subordinate social traditions forms of discord that are more internally expressed than externally displaced.

A dominant majority benefits more from displacement of discord by scapegoating, since it can do so without fear of retribution from the scape- goated minority. We have documented in chapter 1 how at the time of the earthquake in 1923 Koreans became victimized as scapegoats in Japan. The ease with which Koreans were seen as a criminal, disruptive element within Japanese society was obvious in journals and newspapers of the 1920s as well as in word-of-mouth accounts of the disorders that followed. The Japa- nese could think better of themselves if a crime could be attributed to Kore- ans. It gave them a sense of compensatory superiority to have within their society a disparaged minority to whom criminality and political radicalism could be attributed. It is ironic that in the world arena the Japanese, in turn, were experiencing the implicit disparagement underlying the United States policy barring the entry of Orientals despite the so-called Gentleman's Agreement of 1924. Only since World War II have racist attitudes toward the Japanese been absent from American foreign policy and its immigration laws.

Koreans today, both at home and in Japan, to attain internal harmony often have recourse to labeling the Japanese collectively as the enemy. It is easier to deflect hatred onto all Japanese rather than to distinguish those who are indeed prejudiced from those who are accepting and potentially helpful. Hence Koreans sometimes behave with anger and hostility toward all Japanese, irrespective of their personal guilt or innocence. This reciprocal stereotypic attitude of hatred contributes to acts of animosity on both sides.

Most Korean groups exercise particularly heavy sanctions against group members who take Japanese citizenship. Since the Japanese also reject them, naturalized citizens of Korean origin have set up their own group, the Seiwa Club, a name that can be roughly translated as "the realization of harmony." Naturalization is a form of avoiding passing by openly acknowledging one's Korean background and at the same time asserting one's Japanese citizenship. Finding themselves in a fairly precarious position and generally isolated, naturalized Korean-Japanese hope to make their position more acceptable or tolerated by others.

Perhaps the greatest problem that we have noted is how disruptive the circumstances of discrimination have been to the harmonious functioning of the Korean family. The destruction of the male's occupational prowess, the wounding of his sense of dignity, results in spasmodic acts of compensatory masculinity at home. It also results in disparagement of the husband by his wife within the home setting. Confucianist values, in which the wife ideally plays a subordinate role to the head of the house and sees to it that the children are obedient to those in authority, are not well exercised in many Korean homes. This leads to a sense of worthlessness about their family on the part of growing children. The family relationships themselves become bonds of aggressive displacement, of mute frustration, and of inescapable ignominy. The family is not a haven but a place of alienation. As noted above in respect to achievement motivation, many youths express their feelings in some form of delinquent behavior that eventuates in a criminal career, as with Kim Hi-lo (chap. 11).

Affiliation vs. Isolation

A sense of belonging can be expressed through one's identity with a group. It is a means of finding one's harmonious place in an entity larger than oneself. The need for affiliation, however, can also be directed more toward the satisfaction to be gained from intimacy and close contact between specific individuals, either in bonds of friendship or in heterosexual attachments.

Being alone, isolated or alienated, is intolerable for most human beings. Total social isolation without face-to-face contacts and communication afforded by some form of group membership or intimate personal contact is a difficult state to maintain. Marginality and apartness are sources of inner agony and tension. General ethnic group membership may supply the forms of contact and affiliation necessary for day-to-day living. But some individuals may feel such a strong need for personal autonomy and independence that they find themselves capable of doing without sustained social contact. They search out their own goals and are willing to become distant and uncommitted to others. For Koreans in Japan, resolving the need for affiliation is related to whether or not an individual chooses to pass, leaving his own family and childhood friendships behind in seeking an individual route of social mobility in Japanese society.

Individuals who seek to leave a group are subject to various forms of sanctioning. The principal threat, of course, is that of ostracism and rejection. A group that in turn feels rejected by a former member can become even physically destructive toward a perceived deserter or traitor. For some, the threat of isolation or of aggressive rejection can be a very heavy sanction that keeps them within the group.

A sense of intimacy is first fostered within the primary family. We have noted elsewhere that the Japanese family may provide a deep sense of psychological security without supplying intimate companionship to any of its members. Indeed, in his studies comparing modern Japanese and American marriages, Blood notes that one significant difference between the reasons given for marriage in Japan and the United States is the greater emphasis Americans place on companionship as a priority in choosing a mate.[16] Regardless of the priority given to direct companionate types of intimacy and contact, the Japanese family affords other forms of warmth and a sense of belonging for the individual. With Korean-Japanese, however, our psychological material collected thus far emphasizes a very strong sense of alienation in contrast with the family concerns found in Japanese records. Our small Korean sample tested to date is significantly different from its Japanese counterpart. One may infer that the Korean family in Japan often provides less expressive gratification, not only in intimacy but in harmony, self-respect, and nurturance.

Korean children seem to do relatively poorly in school for similar reasons found to operate in some American minorities, such as among blacks or Mexican-Americans. Individuals do not identify or internalize standards and expectations set for them by members of the external majority. Instead the peer group becomes the principal source of affiliative gratification, discouraging acquiescence and conformity to the school as an institution. The peer group also becomes the arena for demonstration of prowess and competence, the source of appreciative judgment.

We must also note impressionistically that Korean-Japanese youth in many instances are stronger in their disregard of family or adult authority simply because there is less gratification to be gained from interdependent family relationships. Affiliation is sought from peer group relationships that are frequently delinquency oriented and antagonistic toward social authorities, including teachers and others functioning in Japanese administrative agencies. These attitudes of protective association and antagonism toward the outside are sometimes perpetuated into adulthood.

Korean-Japanese seem to seek out individual affiliations in marriage. Although their Confucian tradition emphasizes family role patterns rather than intimate companionship, they seem today less prone to concern themselves with family considerations. One notes that among younger Koreans, just as among younger Japanese, there is a greater desire for closeness and intimacy in the marital bond. Indeed, romantic love today often transcends the social barriers set up between Koreans and Japanese. Such marriages can compound problems of identity on the part of the Korean partner. He or she is faced with the necessity to affirm or deny Korean affiliations outside of marriage and at the same time to maintain solidarity with his or her mate. There are numerous instances of difficulties arising in mixed marriages owing to external pressures of family or internal problems of divided loyalty. In turn, mixed marriages produce children who have their own identity problems, who must decide on their principal allegiances and the principal groups from which they will seek out companions.

Nurturance vs. Deprivation

There would seem to be considerable difference between Koreans and Japanese in the exercise of dependency gratification. Japanese mothers, in our impression, tend to hover over their children, providing a more intense kind of nurturance. Korean mothers are not so apt to be self-sacrificing, nor do they seem to *amaeru*, that is, they do not readily attempt instrumental dependency.[17] We have as yet no strong demonstrable evidence to back these impressions beyond the lack of stories of self-sacrificing mothers. As workers, Koreans seem less likely to anticipate gratification through patron-client, or *oyabun-kobun*, relationships.[18] Our impression that Japanese are more socialized than Koreans to interdependency in both their family and occupational relationships needs further investigation.

Significant emotional support for one's ethnic identity comes from the set of implicit expectations focused on giving and receiving. One needs a sense of being able to turn somewhere for help and comfort in times of stress or tribulation. Conversely, for some individuals a sense of belonging implies a responsibility or a need to nurture those of one's own group who are less fortunate or who are young and inexperienced. Nurturance is transmitted cross-generationally in many cultures. The transmission of care flows from the older to the younger generation and, in turn, the aged supposedly become the responsibility of the family or the group. Many of the legal problems concerning the Korean minority are related to the underlying fact that many Japanese do not feel a social compunction to care for "foreign" Koreans. A sense of responsibility for nurturance expressed among Japanese does not readily extend beyond ethnic boundaries. The Japanese admit that the Koreans have "human rights," but Korean legal status makes it uncertain whether these rights include general welfare or simply emergency aid in times of dire need.

The Japanese sense of paternalism found in occupational settings, in which there is also a sense of mentorship, is not as readily extended to younger Korean workers. Labor unions have both instrumental and expressive functions. They may be simply interest groups or they may impart to those who belong a sense of interdependency and brotherhood, a sense of nurturance and affiliation, and a sense of mutual care. Neither the instrumental nor the expressive functions of Japanese labor unions, however, are very effective for Koreans, given their lack of legal status. While the more militant, politically oriented unions are more likely to take up the causes of minorities than are the prevailing company unions, Koreans are generally seen as competitors rather than as people in need of assistance.

In general, private welfare agencies are fairly rare in Japan and religious organizations play only a minor role. In the United States some ethnic minorities have pioneered such agencies. The American Jews, for example, from a very early period have set up professional agencies to care for their distressed members. These agencies very often have extended public service to others outside the Jewish group and the same has been true for Catholic charities.

Programs that are politically oriented may use welfare as a means of gaining loyalty. The Ch'ongnyŏn and the Mindan, as voluntary organizations, are supposedly set up to provide nurturant functions within the Korean community. Their political objectives and interests usually take priority, however, and their funds are only in small part directed to people in need within the Korean community.

Minority groups who have experienced several generations of social deprivation may seek to exploit whatever welfare agencies are set up. This has been true for the Burakumin but not for the Koreans, since the latter are legally barred from public welfare benefits. Although the Japanese government has been pressured successfully by the formerly outcaste Burakumin to ameliorate housing and school deficiencies, Koreans have no such leverage with government agencies.

Appreciation vs. Disparagement

Ultimately, perhaps, the issue of social acceptance and dignity is the principal concern of any ethnic minority. As we have discussed throughout this volume, the Japanese, themselves sensitive to appreciation or deprecation from outsiders, generally have been deprecatory and derogatory toward Koreans. They cannot accept different Korean customs; they cannot even accept Korean eating habits. The poverty to which Koreans have been historically subjected is used to classify them as inherently uncouth and uncivilized. In this respect, direct parallels to race relations in the United States are very apparent. The Japanese cannot accept some aspects of the freer interpersonal expressions, both positive and aggressive, that Koreans manifest. These go against the greater degree of self-constraint exercised by the Japanese. This self-constraint has been particularly apparent in the society from the time of the annexation of Korea through the prewar militaristic period, and it has been maintained by many into the postwar era.

It is difficult for any majority group to accord equal value to the behavioral patterns of others which may stimulate tension in themselves. Only a very open, self-possessed individual who arrives at his own behavior out of choice rather than out of severely internalized constraints can accord acceptance to others behaving differently from himself. The Japanese have great difficulty in feeling comfortable in cultural settings other than their own. This discomfort is not limited to their contacts with Koreans but includes contacts with other peoples throughout eastern and southeastern Asia. The Japanese have been quick to disparage and derogate what is different from their own expectations. Their sense of uniqueness, their susceptibility to criticism, and their need for approval are the opposite sides of a readiness to disparage and disapprove of others.

In short, Koreans have been vulnerable to scapegoating because their behavior is thought to be not thoroughly "Japanese." Their anomalous status within Japanese society continues. The deviant behavior of some is used by many Japanese as supportive evidence to maintain a massive deprecatory attitude toward all. One need not belabor the point that Koreans are deprecated not because they eat garlic or have a higher delinquency and crime rate but because they are vulnerable objects of projection and displacement.

This brings up the crucial problem that some members of a disparaged ethnic minority are subject to self-hatred and self-disparagement. Wagatsuma and De Vos have written at length on this topic, beginning with their discussion of self-hatred among the Japanese Burakumin (1966). De Vos is currently investigating alternative modes of psychological coping involved in a narrowed defensive maintenance of an ethnic identity that may lead to forms of nonlearning in school by members of given ethnic minorities.[19] Wagatsuma, in chapters 13 and 14 of this volume, illustrates attempts to handle the deep sense of shame aroused in youth over their minority background. He points up the vulnerability to self-contempt that may become the fate of some who cannot manage to overcome the pejorative attitudes of majority peers toward minority youth. No theoretical statements can better express these processes at work than the actual writings and comments of those who must deal with their own damaged self-esteem. Some amelioration is perhaps possible through using the institution of the school to teach and instill ethnic pride. This subject has been discussed in this volume by Lee in chapter 8, Rohlen in chapter 9, and Wagatsuma in chapter 13. Their perspectives differ in each instance, and further brief comment is perhaps appropriate.

School can perform the vital function of creating both personal and social awareness of the historical circumstances shaping one's ethnic background. As has been noted in the previous chapters, school can be of some influence in changing the social attitudes of the majority toward a minority, but there is no present consensus among Korean parents about whether a child should use its Korean name in public. What is gained by a firm insistence on a Korean identity in these schools may be lost through inability of its graduates to adapt economically if not socially to life in Japan.

Irreconcilable instrumental and expressive difficulties are involved in using educational policies to resolve the complex issues of minority identity. Emphasis on immediate, practical, instrumental adaptation may sacrifice pride, the validity of being "Korean," and one's sense of self-worth. Conversely, a too rigid insistence that being "Korean" resides in objective criteria, such as language proficiency or dress, may be impractical for Koreans who plan to continue to live in Japan. Furthermore, it represents acceptance of the adversary view of those Japanese who equate Japanese ethnicity with Japanese citizenship.

This adversary position permits no latitude for maintaining self-esteem in being both a Japanese citizen and of Korean ethnic origin. In a modern, industrial state—whether it be France, the United States, or Japan —this equation of citizenship and ancestry is no longer tenable. No modern solution is possible in maintaining a narrow, defensive ethnicity through contrastive separation that diminishes or incapacitates the individual. The individual cannot adapt or adjust through systematic denial of another culture. The minority group cannot escape considerable damage from such prevention of cultural assimilation. A defensive minority identity, by its very nature, is maladaptive in a complex modern society. If Korean identity in Japan can be maintained only through attending a Korean language school, which handicaps the individual in the formal Japanese school system, then the individual becomes subject to continuous conflict, both external and internal. Conversely, if the Japanese school system derogates the assumption that it is legitimate and dignified to be Korean in ancestry, then the child perhaps has no alternative but to resist education at a cost to his sense of personal worth. The fact is that most children of Korean ancestry growing up in Japan will not speak Korean as their native tongue. They will speak Japanese. Nonetheless, there should be no need for them to renounce their heritage by denying their Korean name or by derogating their cultural tradition, a tradition in which, as citizens of Japan, they no longer participate directly.

Historical perspective demands some way of developing a sense of ethnicity that takes pride in more than one heritage. Intermarriage occurs in any multi-ethnic state, raising questions of identity for the children of parents of different ethnic backgrounds. In a racist society certain ethnic groups are considered inferior. Intermarriages between the dominant and the inferior groups are deemed contaminatory, and the children of such liaisons are identified with their less acceptable minority heritage. In situations of conflict, children faced with the need to choose between parental heritages will sometimes opt for the minority identity, seeking to protect the heritage of the demeaned parent out of a sense of honor and personal integrity. But in situations imputing nothing pejorative to either ancestry, a child will happily identify with a more complex heritage. When the school teaches the cultural history and language of both, the child acknowledges both of his ancestral backgrounds without conflict over the expediency or the integrity of being one or the other.

If a tenable educational policy is to be expressed within a national state, it must acknowledge that its citizenry should share in the majority culture to the point of adapting through formal education the language skills necessary to operate successfully. Conversely, no multi-ethnic state can afford to emphasize one cultural heritage as superior to another. History needs to be retaught in a more complex way. It is to be hoped that such will be the further policy of education in the Japanese system. The Japanese cannot sustain the illusion of separate origin. Their cultural heritage is interwoven with that of Korea, past and present.

The present legally anomalous status of Koreans in Japan makes any assuagement of social disparagement a difficult task. Prevalent pejorative attitudes make it incumbent upon Koreans to resist assimilation. Only when their past cultural background is accorded respect and they are given the right to be of Korean background can the Korean-Japanese accept the historical fact that they are destined to function as citizens of Japan in future generations.

Pleasure vs. Suffering

Emphasis on acute social problems may sometimes present a distorted picture. Suffice it to say that there is a great deal of enjoyment possible for Koreans in Japan from Japanese and Korean art forms, from dramatic and literary expression in song and dance, and from the culinary accomplishments possible within Korean dietary habits. Like any genuine traditional culture, the Korean culture evidences a sense of vitality and affords much human satisfaction to its members.

But many Koreans in Japan are culturally "Japanese." They enjoy most of the Japanese world of entertainment and are, themselves, often accomplished professionals in bringing such entertainment to others. Only in the realm of food habits have they sustained singularity in their cultural background. Most read only Japanese literature and see Japanese movies, despite their somewhat quixotic hope that Korean culture can be maintained whole in a foreign setting.

Acculturation in this sense is a natural occurrence for minority groups everywhere. Many minorities in the United States, for example, have sought without much success to cling to linguistics or other distinctions. Despite a continuity in ethnic identity and a lack of total social assimilation, for the most part individuals acculturate to the content of the majority culture. They maintain from their past heritage certain emblematic features to sustain a sense of continuity with their ancestry. But as members of an ethnic minority, it is ot often possible for them to maintain a truly substantial cultural heritage (see De Vos and Romanucci-Ross, *Ethnic Identity*, 1975). Attempts at ethnic education, such as those by the Koreans in Japan, are eventually doomed to failure (chap. 8). There is no alternative, given the course of time, to becoming Korean-Japanese. It is for this reason that a multi-ethnic concept of Japanese citizenship would seem to offer the most viable solution.

Japanese traditionally have transmuted an inherent sense of suffering into the virtue of endurance. Suffering, instrumentalized toward the attainment of goals, becomes an expressive experience and, as such, becomes almost an end in itself, indicative of a sense of purpose and an identification with the highest goals. Koreans, in contrast, have not adjudged suffering to be a virtue. Suffering has indeed been a reality, but it has been something to be sloughed off as quickly as possible. Rather than having emphasized a sense of necessary endurance, with all its philosophic implications, Koreans have developed a pragmatic sense of necessary survival. They have been themselves tempered by hardships, but they have made no virtue of it.

The Japanese have also given recognition, through the Buddhism initially brought from Korea, to a deep sense of human compassion. They have developed a universalist belief not only that all people are doomed to suffer but that all are worthy of compassion. Shōtoku Taishi, the early humanitarian Japanese prince (who himself was partially of Korean ancestry), personifies the three virtues of the ideal Japanese judicial system. The three virtues are depicted on large murals within the chambers of the Japanese Supreme Court: justice, with Prince Shōtoku in judgment; courage, with Prince Shōtoku in the hunt; and compassion, with the young infant, Prince Shōtoku, in his mother's arms. It is to be hoped that these representations will become actualized in resolving the case of citizenship for the Koreans in Japan. And beyond the formality of citizenship, it is to be hoped that true acceptance will be accorded to the fact that Japanese, like those who comprise other great cultures, comprise a blend of humanity—not a group unique in genetic heritage.

It must be emphasized that the authors and others who have helped and cooperated in the writing of the present book have not been harassed in researching and presenting this uncomfortable history of ethnic discrimination. In telling the story of the present imperfections in the functioning of modern Japanese society, our freedom to tell the story is a measure of the fact that democracy *is* working in Japan and that amelioration of prejudice is possible. Although the Japanese themselves are highly sensitive to negative judgments from outside, they are at present an open society that permits open criticism of its failings. The authors are appreciative of the fact that critical social science research can be conducted only in a free atmosphere. We are optimistic that an open disclosure of the problems we have described can lead to interest in rectifying the situation, not only because Japanese are sensitive to outsiders' knowledge of their society but because of a genuine expressive need on the part of many to broaden human rights within their own society.

NOTES

1: KOREANS AND JAPANESE: The Formation of Ethnic Consciousness

1. Edward Kidder, *Prehistoric Japanese Arts: Jōmon Pottery* (Palo Alto: Kodansha International, 1968), p. 75.

2. W. Robertson-Smith, *The Religion of the Semites* (London: Adam and Charles Black, 1907).

3. Gari Ledyard gives a perceptive summary of this period in "Galloping Along with the Horseriders: Looking for the Founders of Japan," *Journal of Japanese Studies* 2 (Spring 1976): 217-254.

4. Tsuda Sōkichi "Kogo Shui no kenkyū: Fu, Jōdai no be ni tsuite no kō," *Shingaku Zasshi* 9 (1928): 1-32; 10 (1928): 15-18; 11 (1928): 63-84; 12 (1928): 57-78. See also, "Jōdai no be ni t suite no hokō," *Shingaku Zasshi* 11, no. 1 (1929): 64-90; 11, no. 2 (1929): 33-52; 11, no. 4 (1929): 40-65. Felicia Bock (personal communication) has also drawn our attention to Nakada Kaoru, *Kodai Nikkan Kōshō Dampenkō* [A Study of Ancient Japan-Korea Relations] (Tokyo: Sobunsha, 1956). Nakada has correlated passages in the Nihon Shoki as to personal and place names in Yamato and Korea before development of the centralized Yamato state.

5. Cornelius Kiley, "State and Dynasty in Archaic Yamato," *Journal of Asian Studies*, 33 (Nov. 1973): 48. A change of names in the eighth and ninth centuries obscured possible foreign origin.

6. Ibid., p. 30.

7. Ledyard, "Galloping Along with the Horseriders," p. 217.

8. Tamura Echō, "Kudara Shiragi to Asuka no Bukkyō" [Paekche-Shilla and Askuka Buddhism], *Han*, 1 (1972): 2-31.

9. Kiley, "State and Dynasty in Archaic Yamato," pp. 48-50.

10. G. B. Sansom, *Japan: A Short Cultural History* (New York: Appleton-Century-Crofts, 1962), pp. 66-67, 71.

11. Richard J. Miller, *Ancient Japanese Nobility: The Kabane Ranking Systems* (Berkeley and Los Angeles: University of California Press, 1974). Miller also draws attention to the large group of families of foreign origin: the Uji, classified as "Shōgun." Appendix 1, p. 189 (personal communication, Felicia Bock).

12. Ibid., p. 144.

13. Ibid., p. 146.

14. Ledyard suggests that many of the ears were those of Chinese soldiers fighting against the Japanese (personal communication).

15. Yoshi S. Kuno, *Japanese Expansion on the Asian Continent* (Berkeley and Los Angeles: University of California Press, 1937), p. 175 ff.

16. Kim Ha-tai, "The Transmission of Neo-Confucianism to Japan by Kang Hang—a Prisoner of War," *Transactions of the Korean Branch of the Royal Asiatic Society*, 37 (1961).

17. Yi Ki-Paek, *Han'guksa shillon* [A New Thesis of Korean History] (Seoul: Ilchogak, 1977), pp. 254-255; and Ch'oe Yŏng-hui, *Imjin waenan chung ŭi sahoe tongt'ae* [The Social Conditions during the Imjin War] (Seoul: Korean Studies Institute, 1975). See also Chindan Hakhoe, ed., *Han'guk sa* [Korean History], 3 (Seoul: Ulya munwhasa, 1962), pp. 676-679.

18. Ibid.

19. Kim, "The Transmission of Neo-Confucianism to Japan," p. 93.

20. Ibid., p. 100.

21. Abe Yoshio, *Nihon Shushigaku to Chōsen* [Japanese Neo-Confucianism and Korea] (Tokyo: Tokyo University Press, 1965); and by the same author, "Nihon jukyō no hatten to Yi T'oegye" [The Development of Confucianism in Japan and Yi T'oegye], *Han*, 1:8 (1972): 3-27.

22. Yi, *Han'guksa shillon*, p. 255. See also Chindan Hakhoe, *Han'guksa*.

23. Gregory Henderson, *Korea: The Politics of the Vortex* (Cambridge, Mass.: Harvard University Press, 1968), p. 61.

24. Ibid., p. 67.

25. Ibid., p. 70.

26. The following excerpts are from Kan Dŏk-sang and Kŭm Byŏng-dong, eds., *Kantō Daishinsai to Chōsenjin* [Kantō Earthquake and the Koreans], Gendai Shiryō Series, 6 (Tokyo: Misuzu Shobō, 1963). This is the authoritative compilation of reports and documents on the events taking place at the time of the earthquake. Newspaper reports are excerpted, as are documents from public agencies.

27. Ibid., see chapter 10; see also pp. 159-162.

28. Ibid., see chapters 5, 6, 7, 8, and 9.

29. Ibid., see other testimonies and accounts of witnesses in chapter 12.

30. Ibid., pp. 39-43.

31. Ibid., see also testimonies in chapter 12.

2: THE COLONIAL EXPERIENCE—1910-1945

1. Paul Weiss, *Nationality and Statelessness in International Law* (London: Stevens, 1956).

2. Hoon K. Lee, *Land Utilization and Rural Economy in Korea* (Chicago: University of Chicago Press, 1936), pp. 283-284.

3. Yi Yu-hwan, *Zainichi Kankokujin gojūnenshi* [A Fifty Year History of Koreans in Japan] (Tokyo: Shinju Bussan Co., 1960), p. 18.

4. Andrew Gradijdanzev, *Modern Korea* (New York: John Day, 1944), pp. 75-79; Irene Taeuber, *The Population of Japan* (Princeton: Princeton University Press, 1958), p. 188; *Chōsen keizai nempō* [Economic Annual for Chōsen] (Tokyo: Kaizōsha Publishing Co., 1939), p. 445 ff.

5. Joung Yole Rew, "A Study of the Government-General of Korea with an Emphasis of the Period between 1919 and 1931" (Ph.D. dissertation, American University, 1962), p. 127.

6. Lee, *Land Utilization*, p. 274.

7. Gradjdanzev, *Modern Korea*, pp. 105-122.

8. Pak Kyŏng-sik, *Chōsenjin kyōseirenkō no kiroku* [A Record of Involuntary Korean Migration] (Tokyo: Miraisha, 1965). See chapter 2.

9. Ryoichi Ishii, *Population Pressure and Economic Life in Japan* (London: Stevens, 1937), p. 207.

10. Harada Shuichi, *Labour Conditions in Japan* (New York: Columbia University Press, 1928), pp. 103-104.

11. Ibid., p. 104.

12. Edward W. Wagner, *The Korean Minority in Japan: 1904-1950* (New York: Institute of Pacific Relations, 1951), pp. 11, 17-18. See also Richard H. Mitchell, *The Korean Minority in Japan* (Berkeley and Los Angeles: University of California Press, 1967).

13. Osaka City, Social Welfare Investigation Department, "Honshi ni okeru Chōsenjin no seikei" [The Living Conditions of the Koreans in Osaka] (Osaka: 1931), pp. 24-25; and Tokyo-fu, Social Welfare Department, "Zaikyō Chōsenjin rōdōsha no genjō" [The Current Situation of the Korean Laborers in Tokyo] (Tokyo: 1936), pp. 162-163.

14. Chŏn Chun, *Choch'ongnyŏn yŏnku* [A Study of Ch'ongnyŏn], 1 (Seoul: Koryŏ University Press, 1972), pp. 74-76.

15. The Welfare Department, Tokyo-fu, *Zaikyō Chōsenjin rōdōsha no genjō* [The Current Conditions of the Korean Laborers in Tokyo] (Tokyo: 1936), pp. 78-79.

16. Kamekichi Takahashi, *Nippon sangyō rōdōron* [Industrial Labor in Japan] (Tokyo: Chigura Co., 1937), p. 448.

17. Hatada Takashi, *Nihonjin no Chōsenjin kan* [Japanese View of Koreans] (Tokyo: Keiso shobō, 1969), pp. 72-73, 79-80.

18. *Japanese Yearbook* (Tokyo: 1921, 1922), p. 586.

19. Gregory Henderson, *Korea: The Politics of the Vortex* (Cambridge, Mass.: Harvard University Press, 1968), pp. 99-101.

20. Chŏn Chun, *Choch'ongnyŏn yŏnku*, pp. 19-20.

21. Ibid., p. 21.

22. Wagner, *Korean Minority*, p. 16; Takahashi, *Nippon Sangyō*, p. 452.

23. Wagner, *Korean Minority*, p. 18.

24. Chang Hyŏk-chu, "Chōsenjin shūraku o yuku" [A Visit to a Korean Ghetto], *Kaizō* (July, 1937), pp. 46-55.

25. The most scholarly analysis of this subject is that by Chong-sik Lee, *The Politics of Korean Nationalism* (Berkeley and Los Angeles: University of California Press, 1963).

26. Kim Tu-yong, *Nihon ni okeru Hanchōsen minzokushi* [A History of Anti-Nationalists in Japan] (Tokyo: Kyodo shobo, 1948).

27. Wagner, *Korean Minority*, p. 15 ff.

28. Ibid., p. 16.

29. Ibid., p. 17.

30. Hōmukenshūsho, Ministry of Justice, *Zainichi Chōsenjin shogū to suii to genjō* [The Development of the State of Koreans in Japan and the Current Situation] (Tokyo: Japanese Ministry of Justice, 1955), pp. 44-45 (hereafter cited as *Hōmukenshūsho, 1955*). Chŏn Chun, *Ch'ongnyŏn yŏnku*, pp. 115-130.

31. *Hōmukenshūsho, 1955*, p. 19.

32. Ibid.

33. Wagner, *Korean Minority*, pp. 31-33.

34. Office of Strategic Services, *United States Strategic Bombing Survey* (Washington, D.C.: 1947), p. 243 ff.

35. Wagner, *Korean Minority*, p. 32.

36. Ibid., p. 33 ff.

37. Ibid., p. 39.

38. *Hōmukenshūsho, 1955*, pp. 47-52.

39. After the government of the Republic of Korea was officially proclaimed, Chail Chosŏnnin Kŏryumindan was renamed as Chail Han'guk'in Kŏryumindan in 1948.

3: THE PERIOD OF REPATRIATION—1945-1949

1. The Korean Resident Association (Mindan) in Japan later informed the Military Government in Korea that there were about 2.4 million Koreans in Japan when the war ended. See William J. Gane, *Repatriation: From 25 September 1945 to 31 December 1945* (Seoul: United States Military Government in Korea, 1947), p. 14.

2. At this meeting, the Japanese officials appeared to be more concerned with how to bring home the Japanese citizens from Korea, Manchuria, and elsewhere. See Morita Yoshio, *Chōsen shūsen no kiroku: Beiso ryōgun no shinchu to Nihonjin no hikiage* [The Record of Ending the War in Korea: The Occupation of the U.S.-Soviet Forces and Japanese Repatriation] (Tokyo: Gannandō, 1965), p. 130.

3. Policies were outlined in brief in the Supreme Command for the Allied Powers directive, "Policies Governing Repatriation of Japanese Nationals in Conquered Territory," *Directives*, SCAPIN-148, AG 091 (16 Oct. 1945). Reception centers for outgoing Korean repatriates were to include Maizuru, Shimonoseki, Sensaki, Kagoshima, Kure, Hakata, Moji, and Hakodate. See "Reception Centers in Japan for Processing Repatriates," *Directives*, SCAPIN-142, AG 370.05 (15 Oct. 1945). More comprehensive and detailed instructions may be found in "Repatriation of Non-Japanese from Japan," *Directives*, SCAPIN-224, AG 370.5 (1 Nov. 1945). Many volumes compiled by SCAP concerning SCAPIN directives were issued to the Japanese Imperial government; (hereafter cited as *Directives*).

4. "Repatriation Reception Centers," *Directives*, SCAPIN-154, AG 370.05 (8 Nov. 1945).

5. For further details, see "Control over Exports and Imports of Gold, Silver, Security and Financial Instruments," *Directives*, SCAPIN-44, AG 091.31 (22 Sept. 1945); and "Supplemental Instructions Relating to Import and Export Controls," *Directives*, SCAPIN-127, AG 091.31 (12 Oct. 1945). These financial restrictions were incorporated in *Directives*, SCAPIN-224, AG 370.5 (1 Nov. 1945).

6. "Supplementary Instructions Relating to Import and Export Controls," *Directives*, SCAPIN-532, AG 091.714 (2 Jan. 1946).

7. "Repatriation," *Directives*, SCAPIN-882, AG 370.05, annex VI (16 Mar. 1946).

8. "Repatriation," *Directives*, SCAPIN-882/1, AG 370.05 (27 Mar. 1946).

9. "Repatriation," *Directives*, SCAPIN-882, AG 370.05, annex I (16 Mar. 1946).

10. Supreme Commander for the Allied Powers, *Summation of Non-Military Activities in Japan*, no. 11 (August 1946): 226; (hereafter cited as *Summation*). According to Wagner, not all the Koreans wanted to return to Japan; some wanted to enroll in school, and others wanted to visit relatives. See Edward Wagner, *The Korean Minority in Japan, 1904-1950* (New York: Institute of Pacific Relations, 1951), p. 49.

11. "Registration of Koreans, Chinese, Ryukyuans, and Formosans," *Directives*, SCAPIN-746, AG 053 (17 Feb. 1946); and Wagner, *Korean Minority*, p. 46.

12. For the complete repatriation plan, see "Repatriation," *Directives*, SCAPIN-927, AG 370.05 (7 May 1946), and SCAPIN-927/2, annex III (30 June 1946).

13. Although the official Korean repatriation program was terminated on 15 December 1946, it was resumed again in January 1947 on a smaller scale because of Korean demands and was continued until just before the outbreak of the Korean War. See Wagner, *Korean Minority*, pp. 47-50; and Shinozaki Heiji, *Zainichi Chōsenjin undō* [The Korean Movement in Japan] (Tokyo: Reibunsha, 1955), pp. 42-43.

14. Naimushō, Tokubetsu Kōtō Keisatsu [Home Affairs Ministry, the Special High Police Bureau], *Nendobetsu Chōsenjin chiihō ihan genkyō shirabe sonota* [Yearly Statistics of Violations of Peace Preservation Law by Koreans, 1944-45], Japanese Army and Navy Archives Series (1868-1945); Microfilm R1510 (R222 F93357), pp. 93,676-93,677.

15. Ibid.

16. United States Strategic Bombing Survey, *Effects of Strategic Bombing on Japanese Morale* (Washington, D.C., June 1947), p. 250; Wagner, *Korean Minority*, pp. 38-39.

17. Shinozaki, *Zainichi Chōsenjin*, pp. 45-46. See also Fuse Tatsuji et al., "Dantai kiseirei no inbō o tsuku" [Expose the Plot Behind the Enactment of the Organization Control Law], *Minshu Chōsen*, no. 5 (May 1950): 37-38.

18. Roger Swearingen and Paul Langer, *Red Flag in Japan* (Cambridge, Mass.: Harvard University Press, 1952), p. 88.

19. "Removal of Restrictions on Political, Civil, and Religious Liberties," *Directives*, SCAPIN-93 (4 Oct. 1945).

20. Concerning his alleged activities during the prewar period, see Kim Ch'ŏnhae *Okchung sibonyŏn* [Fifteen Years in Prison] (Tokyo: Minshu Chōsensha, 1946); and Kim Chŏng-myŏng, comp., *Chōsen dokuritsu undō: Kyōsanshugi undō hen* [The Korean Independence Movement: The Communist Movement], 4, 5 (Tokyo: Harashobō, 1966, 1967).

21. Nakanishi Inosuke, "Nihon tennō sei no datō to tōyō minzoku no minshu dōmei: Chōsenjin Renmei he no yōsei" [The Overthrow of the Emperor System and a Democratic League for Asian Races: An Appeal to Choryŏn], *Minshu Chōsen*, no. 7 (July 1946): 24-25.

22. Their statement was later published in complete form under the title, "Jinmin ni utafu" [An Appeal to the People], *Akahata*, 20 October 1945.

23. "Tōsō no atarashi hoshin ni tsuite—Shinjōsei wa wareware ni nanio yōkyū shite iruka" [One the New Line of Struggle: What the New Situation Demands of Us], *Akahata*, 20 October 1945.

24. Koyama Hirotake, *Sengo Nihon Kyōsantō shi* [A History of the Postwar Japanese Communist Party] (Tokyo: Hogashoten, 1966), pp. 13-15; and Yaginuma Masaji, *Nihon Kyōsantō undō shi* [A History of the Japanese Communist Party Movement] (Tokyo: Keibunkaku, 1953), pp. 2-3.

25. Koyama, *Nihon Kyōsantō*, p. 12.

26. SCAP issued a directive dated 9 December 1945 stating that all costs of the repatriations were to be borne by the Japanese government. It made further clarification on 31 January 1946 stating that reimbursement was to be made retroactive to 14 October 1945 to those who had paid their own train fares to the embarkation areas. The legal claims were made by the Choryŏn with proper powers of attorney. See Wagner, *Korean Minority*, p. 53; and "Repatriation of Non-Japanese from Japan," *Directives*, SCAPIN-295, AG 370.5 (17 Nov. 1945); "Railway Fares Charged to Koreans," *Directives*, SCAPIN-685, AG 555.1 (31 Jan. 1946).

27. See "Basic Initial Post-Surrender Directive to Supreme Commander for the Occupation and Control of Japan," J.C.S. 1380/8 (3 Nov. 1945), Report of Government Section, Supreme Commander for the Allied Powers, *Political Reorientation of Japan, September 1945 to September 1948* (Grosse Pointe, Mich.: Scholarly Press, 1968), 2:432.

28. For example, on 3 January 1946, when a Korean was jailed by the Japanese police for an unknown reason, a group of some eighty Koreans armed themselves with clubs and pistols, stormed the police station, and forcibly obtained the release of the Korean. See *Summation*, no. 4 (Jan. 1946): 34.

29. Ibid., p. 37.

30. "Payment of Bonus to Japanese Soldiers of Korean Descent," *Directives*, SCAPIN-113, AG 240 (9 Oct. 1945).

31. "Release from Prison and Repatriation of Korean Nationals," *Directives*, SCAPIN-1181, AG 014.33 (10 Sept. 1946).

32. "Control of Population Movements," *Directives*, SCAPIN-563, AG 091 (8 Jan. 1946); and "Suppression of Illegal Entry into Japan," *Directives*, SCAPIN-1735-A (16 July 1946).

33. SCAP informed the Japanese government that "Koreans, Formosans and Chinese nationals who elect to remain in Japan rather than to accept repatriation will be guaranteed the same rights, privileges and opportunities in employment as are extended to the Japanese nationals in comparable circumstances." See "Employment Policies," *Directives*, SCAPIN-360, AG 230.14 (28 Nov. 1945).

34. Kim Tu-yong, "Nihon ni okeru Chōsenjin mondai" [Korean Problems in Japan], *Zen-ei*, no. 1 (Feb. 1946): 15-16.

35. Suffrage for Koreans in Japan was suspended by Law no. 42, amendment to the Election Law for the House of Representatives, on 17 December 1945, which prohibited any Koreans from participating in Japan's first postwar election, to be held on 10 April 1946. *Kanppō*, Extra Issue, 17 December 1945, p. 1. The extent of SCAP's involvement in suspending the Korean suffrage is unclear.

36. Kim Tu-yong, *Zenei*, no. 1 (feb. 1946): 15-16.

37. Ibid., p. 18.

38. Im Hun, "Zainihon Chōsenjin Renmei to sono tainichi taido" [Choryŏn and Its Posture Toward Japan], *Minshu Chōsen*, no. 4 (April 1946): 16-20.

39. Ibid., p. 20.

40. The pamphlet entitled *Chōsen no kyōdai shokun he* [To Korean Brethren] (Tokyo: Nihon Kyōsantō Shuppanbu, 1946) was suppressed by SCAP censorship and has never been made public. But the confiscated pamphlet, in the form of galley proof, is in the possession of the East Asian Collection, University of Maryland Library.

41. Ibid., p. 38.

42. Ibid., p. 44.

43. Ibid., p. 45.

44. Ibid.

45. Wagner, *Korean Minority*, pp. 60-61; and David Conde, "The Korean Minority in Japan," *Far Eastern Survey*, 16 (26 Feb. 1946): 42.

46. A full text of his speech translated into English is in Japanese House of Representatives, *Proceedings: 90th Session of the Imperial Diet*, no. 30 (19 Aug. 1946): 4-5. A typographical error is found in the text: "Kashii Saburō" should be read as "Shiikuma Saburō." See also Conde, "Korean Minority," pp. 42-43, and Wagner, *Korean Minority*, p. 61.

47. See Choryŏn's official statements concerning Shiikuma Saburō's remarks, in *Kokusai Shimbun*, 30 September and 1 October 1946.

48. For further details on Pak Yŏl's legal case, see Morinaga Eisaburō, "Pak Yŏl, Kaneko Fumiko jiken" [Pak Yŏl, and Kaneko Fumiko Case], *Hōritsu Jihō*, 35, no. 3 (March 1963), pp. 57-63; and ibid., no. 4 (April 1963), pp. 60-67.

49. Chŏng Chŏl, *Mindan* (Tokyo: Yōyōsha, 1967), pp. 35-37; Pak Hi-chŏl, "Daikanminkoku Kyoryū Mindan ron" [A Discourse on the Korean Resident Association in Japan], *Minshu Chōsen*, no. 7 (July 1950), pp. 65-67; Shinozaki Heiji, *Zainichi Chōsenjin*, p. 51 (see n. 14, above); and Chang Hyŏk-chu, "Chōsenjin no naimaku" [The Inside Story of Koreans], *Shinchō*, no. 12 (Dec. 1949): 108-109.

50. For a complete text of the Moscow Agreement, see the U.S. State Department, *Moscow Meeting of Foreign Ministers, 16-26 December 1945* (Washington, D.C., Govt. Printing Office, 1946), pp. 14-16.

51. Wŏn Yong-dŏk, "Shintakutoji to minzoku tōitsu sensen" [The Trusteeship and National Unification Front], *Minshu Chōsen*, no. 4 (April 1946): 5-6.

52. According to the Japanese police record, the Choryŏn's membership at the time of dissolution was estimated at 350,000, whereas Kŏndong had 7,000 and Kŏnch'ŏng about 20,000 members during their peak periods. See Shinozaki, *Zainichi Chōsenjin*, pp. 69, 111, 115. But in ctober 1947 the Choryŏn claimed to have a membership of 614,198, with 48 local chapters throughout Japan. See *Chōren Chūō Jihō*, 17 October 1947.

53. For a complete text of the Mindan Declaration, see *Kokusai Shimbun*, 12 October 1946.

54. For the full text of the "Appeal to the Japanese People" see *Kokusai Shimbun*, 28 October 1946.

55. Pak Yŏl, "Nihon kokumin ni yosu" [An Appeal to the Japanese People], *Bunkyō Shimbun* (April 1948).

56. Pak Yŏl, "Nihon wa teki ka mikata ka" [Is Japan Our Foe or Friend?], *Kyoto Taimusu*, 20 November 1948.

57. For instance, see Chŏng T'ae-sŏng, *Ningen Pak Yŏl* [Pak Yŏl as a Man] (Tokyo: Shin Chōsen Kenetsu Dōmei, 1946); and by the same author, *Dokuritsu shidōsha Pak Yŏl* [Pak Yŏl as a Leader of the Independence Movement] (Tokyo: Shin Chōsen Kensetsu Dōmei, 1946). See also *Pak Yŏl*, Shin Chōsen kaumei ron [A Treatise of Revolution for a New Korea] (Tokyo: Chūō Shuppansha, 1949); and Yamakawa Tadao, *Chōsen wa dōnaruka* [What Will Happen to Korea?] (Tokyo: Jōhōsha, 1948).

58. It was reported that Pak Yŏl once asked President Syngman Rhee of South Korea to appoint him as Korean Ambassador to Japan. See Pak, "Kyoryū Mindan," p. 72; and Chang, "Chōsenjin," p. 109.

59. *Bunkyō Shimbun*, 8 March 1948; and Chŏng, *Mindan*, pp. 39-40, 50 ff.

50. Pak, "Kyoryū Mindan," pp. 70-71.

61. Chong, *Mindan*, pp. 51-52.

62. Pak, "Kyoryū Mindan," p. 69; and *Kokusai Nichinichi Shimbun* 27 July 1949.

4: KOREANS UNDER SCAP—AN ERA OF UNREST AND REPRESSION

1. For example, see *Akahata*, 22 November 1945; 22 December 1945; and 28 May 1946. See also Yaginuma Masaji, *Nihon Kyōsantō undō shi* [A History of the Japanese Communist Movement] (Tokyo: Keibunkaku, 1953), p. 3.

2. The dissolution statement made by the Japanese Bureau of the Korean Communist party was carried by *Akahata*, no. 61, 23 December 1931. See also Kim Chŏng-myŏng, comp., *Chōsen dokuritsu undō: Kyōsanshugi undō hen* [The Korean Independence Movement: The Communist Movement] (Tokyo: Harashobō, 1967), 5:689-690.

3. "Chōsen ni okeru kakumei undō no hatten to puroretariato no nimmu" [The Development of the Revolutionary Movement in Korea and the Task of the Proletariat], *Akahata*, 20 August 1932; and 30 August 1932.

4. Kim, *Chōsen dokuritsu*, 4:212-213; and Tsunobe Senji, *Chōsen minzoku dokuritsu undō hishi* [Hidden History of the Korean Independence Movement] (Tokyo: Nikkan rōdō tsūshisha, 1959), pp. 336-339.

5. *Akahata*, 22 January 1946.

6. "Daigokai Tōtaikai Sengen" [Manifesto of the Fifth Party Congress], *Zenei*, 1, no. 4 (April 1946): 16-17.

7. Nosaka Sanzō, "Taikai sengen ni tsuite" [Concerning the Party Manifesto], *Zen-ei*, 1, no. 4 (April 1946): 18-19.

8. Nakanishi Inosuke, "Nihon tennō no datō to tōyō minzoku no minshu dōmei: Chōsenjin Remmei he no yōsei" [The Overthrow of the Emperor System and the Democratic League for the Asian Races: An Appeal to the Choryōn], *Minshu Chōsen*, no. 7 (July 1947): 28-29.

9. Supreme Commander for the Allied Powers, *Summation of Non-Military Activities in Japan*, no. 8 (May 1946): 4-5 (hereafter cited as *Summation*).

10. "Exercise of Criminal Jurisdiction," *Directives*, SCAPIN-75, AG 015 (19 Feb. 1946); and "Misconduct Committed by Koreans," *Directives*, SCAPIN-1111/A, AG 250.1 (29 April 1946).

11. According to Japanese police, "violent acts" constitutes such activities as mob violence, assault and battery, robbery, fraud and extortion, assault on police officers, disputes and brawls among Koreans, non-negotiable demands to the Japanese authorities, and illegal occupancy of public hearings. See chapter 7, Shinozaki Heiji, *Zainichi Chōsenjin undō* [The Korean Movement in Japan] (Tokyo: Reibunsha, 1955).

12. David Conde, "The Korean Minority in Japan," *Far Eastern Survey*, 16 (Feb. 1947): 45. This article was reprinted in the *Korean Survey* (Dec. 1959), pp. 3-21. The picture is photocopied from the *Korean Survey*.

13. It was organized by the combined efforts of the Japanese and Korean lawyers in Japan. The most noted member was Fuse Tatsuji, a champion of civil rights and a lawyer, who led the famous Jiyū Hōsōdan [The Liberal Judicial Group], a civil libertarian group. Fuse served as a legal counsel, without fee, to many Korean political prisoners in the Japanese trial courts. See also Kim Il-myŏng, "Zainichi Chōsenjin to Jiyū Hōsōdan" [The Koreans in Japan and the Liberal Judicial Group], *Koria Hyōron*, 10, nos. 93 and 94 (Dec. 1968 and Jan. 1969): 19-31, 44-48. Concerning Fuse Tatsuji and his civil-rights movement in Japan, see Morinaga Eisaburō, "Jinken yōgo undōshijō no sentatsu—Fuse Tatsuji" [The Pioneer in the History of the Movement for the Protection of Human Rights—Fuse Tatsuji], *Hōgaku Semina* (Dec. 1956), pp. 44-48; and Hirano Yoshitarō, "Jinken o mamotta hitobito—Fuse Tatsuji" [The People Who Protected Human Rights—Fuse Tatsuji], *Hōgaku Semina* (Nov. 1959), pp. 56-61.

14. "Definition of United Nations' Nationals, Neutral Nations, and Enemy Nations," *Directives*, SCAPIN-217, AG 312.4 (31 Oct. 1945).

15. "Ration for United Nations' Nationals, Neutral Nationals, and Stateless Persons," *Directives*, SCAPIN-1094, AG 430 (30 July 1946); and SCAPIN-1841, under the same subject as above (8 Jan. 1948).

16. *Nippon Times* (21 Nov. 1946).

17. See "Circular Notice Concerning Nationality and Family Registration Pursuant to the Coming into Force of the Treaty of Peace," Civil Affairs, A. no. 438, issued by the Director of the Civil Affairs Bureau of the Ministry of Justice on 19 April 1952. See also Satō Shigemoto, "Chōsenjin no kokuseki ni tsuite" [Concerning the Korean Nationality], *Minji Geppō*, no. 5 (May 1967): 14-19; and Hashimoto Yūtaka, "Heiwa jōyaku to Chōsenjin no kokuseki" [The Peace Treaty and the Korean Nationality], *Minji Kenshū*, no. 57 (Jan. 1962): 33-34. For discussion from the international law point of view, see Tameika Yoshio, *International Law*, no. 2 (1958): 55-65.

18. For this specific provision, see "Applicability of Taxes to Non-Japanese Nationals," *Directives*, SCAPIN-4938/A, AG 012.2 (29 Nov. 1947); and "Applicability of Ordinary Taxes to Non-Japanese Nationals," *Directives*, SCAPIN-1826/A (25 July 1946).

NOTES TO PAGES 78-85

19. *Chōren Chūō Jihō*, 5 December 1947.

20. Edward Wagner, *The Korean Minority in Japan, 1904-1950* (New York: Institute of Pacific Relations, 1951), pp. 64-66.

21. Ibid.

22. Hōmubu [Ministry of Justice], *Nihon ni zai jūsuru Hinihonjin no hōritsujō no chii ni tsuite* [Concerning the Legal Status of Non-Japanese Residing in Japan], *Horitsu shiryō*, no. 308 (Dec. 1949).

23. Shinozaki, *Zainichi Chōsenjin undō*, pp. 136-138; and Wagner, *Korean Minority*, pp. 66-67.

24. Counter Measure Committee on Korean Education, *Kobe Chōsenjin kyōiku mondai no shinsō* [The Truth About Educational Problems of Koreans in Kobe] (22 May 1948) (hereafter cited as *Chōsenjin kyōiku mondai*).

25. *Summation*, no. 31 (April 1948): 303.

26. Wagner, *Korean Minority*, pp. 69-70.

27. *Summation*, no. 31 (April 1948): 303.

28. *Chōsenjin kyōiku mondai*, 23 May 1948, p. 1; Wagner, *Korean Minority*, p. 70; and Shinozaki, *Zainichi Chōsenjin undō*, pp. 162-163.

29. U.S. Army Military Government in Korea, *South Korean Interim Government Activities*, no. 30 (Mar. 1948): 12; and Wagner, *Korean Minority*, p. 71.

30. *Chōsenjin kyōiku mondai*, 23 May 1948, p. 1.

31. Ibid., p. 2; and *Summation*, no. 31 (April 1948); p. 55. More detailed and authentic accounts of the incident were written by a Kobe historian, Ochiai Shigenobu, *in* "Kōbe Chōsenjin gakkō sogi no gaikyō" [The Korean School Dispute in Kobe], *Rekishi to Kōbe*, no. 4 (1953); 73-77; and "Kōbe Chōsenjin jiken shokuhatten: Shōwa nijūsannen no Chōsenjin gakkō heisa o meguru Kōbe no sōran jiken" [The Cause of the Korean Incident in Kobe: The Korean Riot Incident in Kobe Concerning the Korean School Case in 1948], *Hyōgo Shigaku*, no. 28 (1961): 133-140.

32. *Chōsenjin kyōiku mondai*, 23 May 1948, p. 2; Wagner, *Korean Minority*, p. 72; and Ochiai, "Kōbe Chōsenjin gakkō," pp. 74-77.

33. *Nippon Times*, 28 April 1948. Because of his public statement, there was an uproar among Koreans, who accused the General of being "irresponsible" and "ignorant" of the fundamental issues involved. See Ch'oe Sŏn, "A Reply to General Eichelberger's Statement," *Bunkyō Shimbun*, 3 May 1948.

34. *Chōren Chūō Jihō*, 14 May 1948.

35. Ibid., 26 October 1948.

36. *Chosŏn ui byŏl*, 15 June 1948, p. 1.

37. Kim Tu-yong, "Chōsenjin undō wa tenkan shitsutsuaru" [The Korean Movement is Changing], *Zen-ei* (1 Mar. 1947): 38.

38. Ibid., p. 39.

39. Kim Tu-yong, "Chōsenjin undō no tadashii hatten no tameni" [Toward Correct Development of the Korean Movement], *Zen-ei*, no. 16 (1 May 1947): 18.

40. *Chōren Chūō Jihō*, 6 November, and 29 December 1948.

41. *Akahata*, 9 September, and 13 September 1949.

42. The estimated value of the Choryŏn's property confiscated by the Japanese police was 25 million yen in 1949. But Wagner, *Korean Minority*, p. 87, quoting from the *Nippon Times*, 11 November 1949, stated that the confiscated value was more than 70 million yen. The civil suit claiming illegal seizure of the Choryŏn's property was finally settled by the Tokyo Local Civil Court Division in March 1959, when 42,461.52 yen was awarded to the Ch'ongnyŏn, the organization that had succeeded the Choryŏn. See *Naigai Shuho*, no. 9 (8 Apr. 1959), 5-6.

43. *New York Times*, 29 July 1949, p. 4; and *Nippon Times*, 23 October 1949, p. 1.

44. Nosaka's view was published under the title of "Seiken he no tōsō to kokkai katsudō" [The Struggle for Political Power and Diet Activities], *Zen-ei* (April 1949): 1-11.

45. "Concerning the Situation in Japan," *For a Lasting Peace, For People's Democracy!* (6 Jan. 1950), p. 2. It was reprinted in *Nihon Kyōsantō gojūnen mondai shiryō shū* [A Collection of Documents Concerning the Japanese Communist Party], 1 (1950): 1-3; (hereafter cited as *Nikkyō gojūnen mondai*).

46. *Jen Min Jih Pao,* 17 January 1950. It was also reprinted in *Nikkyō gojūnen mondai,* 1 (1950): 9-11.

47. The blame was placed on Nosaka, who had been a JCP strategist and who admitted the errors in his thinking. His confession was published under the title, "My Self-Criticism," *Akahata,* 6 February 1950.

48. Actual lines of policy disagreement within the JCP were complex. They were confused by a web of factional struggles over the leadership. For further details, see Koyama Hirotake, *Sengo Nihon Kyōsantō shi* [A History of the Postwar Japanese Communist Party] (Tokyo: Hōgashoten, 1966), pp. 62-63; and Robert Scalapino, *The Japanese Communist Movement, 1920-1966* (Berkeley and Los Angeles: University of California Press, 1967), pp. 91-96.

49. Shinozaki, *Zainichi Chōsenjin undō,* pp. 233-235; and Hōmu Kenshūsho, comp., *Zainichi Hokusenkei Senjin dantai shiryōshū* [A Collection of Data Concerning the North Korean Organizations in Japan] (Tokyo: Ministry of Justice, 1952), pp. 49-50 (hereafter cited as *Hokusenkei dantai*).

50. Not until the Fourth Party Conference was held underground on 25 February 1951 did the JCP officially adopt the strategy of an armed struggle. But the rationale for the arms struggle had already been published in two articles appearing in the illegal JCP underground journal, *Naigai Hyōron:* the first was in no 4 (12 Oct. 1950), entitled "Kyōsanshugisha to aikokusha no atarashii nimmu: Chikara niwa chikara o motte tatakae" [The New Task of Communists and patriots: Struggle Against Power with Power]; and the second was in no. 5 (24 Jan. 1951), entitled "Naze buryoku kakumei ga mondai ni naranakattaka" [Why Has Armed Revolution Not Become the Issue of Our Party?].

51. *Hokusenkei dantai,* pp. 234-243.

52. For underground JCP's instructions to Chobang'ui regarding the need for armed struggle, see ibid., pp. 55-56, 449-458.

53. Ibid., and Tamagi Motoi, "Nihon Kyōsanto no Zainichi Chōsenjin shidō" [The JCP's Guidance of the Koreans in Japan], *Koria Hyōron* (Aug. 1961), p. 6. Soon after the Korean War broke out, the Chobang'ui was organized by young Korean radicals as an underground paramilitary unit.

54. Tamagi Motoi, "Nihon Kyōsantō," p. 13. For the complete text of the resolutions adopted at the Fourth and Fifth National Conferences of the JCP, see *Nihon Kyōsantō daiyonkai daigokai zenkoku kyōgikai ketteishū* [The Collected Resolutions of the Fourth and Fifth National Congresses of the JCP] (Tokyo: Sinyō-sha, 1952).

55. Tokuda Kyūichi, "On the 30th Anniversary of the Communist Party of Japan," *Akahata,* 15 July 1952.

56. For further details, see Tamagi, "Nihon Kyōsanto," pp. 14-15; and Hiroyama Shirō, "Minsen no kaisan to Zainihon Chōsenjin Sōrengōkai no kessei ni tsuite" [The Dissolution of Minchon and the Formation of the General Federation of Koreans in Japan], *Kōan Jōhō,* no. 22 (July 1955): 5-7.

57. "Zainichi Chōsenjin undō ni tsuite" [Concerning the Korean Movement in Japan], *Zen-ei,* no. 92 (May 1954): 40-44.

58. See "Nam Il Hokusen Gaisō no Nihonseifu ni taisuru tainichi kankei ni

kansuru senmei ni tsuite" [Concerning the Statement of Nam Il, Foreign Minister of North Korea], *Kōan Jōhō*, no. 21 (June 1955): 53-54.

59. Han Dŏk-su's speech was later published under the title of *Zainichi Chōsenjin undō no tenkan ni tsuite* [Concerning the Change of the Korean Movement in Japan] (Tokyo: Gakuyū shobō, 1955). His fundamental thesis had been published in 1952 under a pseudonym, Paek Su-bong, *Aekuk chinyŏng ŭi sŭnwha wa kangwha lŭl wihayŏ* (n.p., Ch'ongnyŏn chung'wang hakwŏn, 1952).

5: THE POLITICS OF REPATRIATION

1. Republic of Korea, Ministry of Foreign Affairs, *Oemu hengchŏng ŭi shimnyŏn* [Ten Years of Administration of Foreign Affairs] (Seoul, 1959), p. 29 (hereafter cited as *Oemu hengchŏng*).
2. The English text of Rhee's proclamation is reprinted in Tamura Kosaku, "The Rhee Line and International Law," *Contemporary Japan*, 22, nos. 7-9 (1953): 389-390. The Rhee Line was similar to the MacArthur Line, which had restricted the Japanese fishing fleet within this limit during the early days of the Allied occupation. The MacArthur Line ceased to exist when Japan regained her sovereignty in 1952, but it was immediately replaced by the Clark Line, established by General Mark Clark on 28 September 1952, as Supreme Commander of the United Nations Forces in Korea. General Clark himself stated that the zone was "strictly a wartime measure designed to safeguard the Koreans' and our line of communication and to bar the Korean coast to enemy agents and contraband." See Mark W. Clark, *From the Danube to the Yalu* (New York: Harper, 1954), p. 154.
3. For the protest note, see Japanese Foreign Affairs Ministry, *"Rhee Line" Problem* (Tokyo: 1961), pp. 16-17.
4. Mura Tsueno, "Rhee Line," *Japan Quarterly*, 4, no. 1 (Jan.-Mar. 1959): 26; and also Kaigai Jijō Chōsasho, comp., *Chōsen yōran* [A Handbook on Korea] (Tokyo: Musashi shobō, 1960), pp. 71-72. It is to be noted that the Japanese fishermen were seized not by the Korean authorities alone but by the Soviet Union and the People's Republic of China on similar charges. On this point, see *Japan Report*, 2, no. 1 (15 June 1956): 6.
5. The essence of Kubota's remarks were: (1) he questioned the legality of Korea's independence without final conclusion of a treaty with Japan; (2) in regard to Korea's demand for repatriations, Kubota stated that Korea could claim nothing from Japan because Korea had benefited more than it was harmed as a result of colonization. For details of Kubota's statement, see *Korean Survey*, 2, no. 10 (Dec. 1953): 13; and *Oemu hengchŏng*, p. 16.
6. Douglas H. Mendel, *The Japanese People and Foreign Policy* (Berkeley and Los Angeles: University of California Press, 1961), pp. 172-173.
7. For further details, see chapter 2 of Nakazono Eisuke, *Zainichi Chōsenjin: Nanajūnen dai Nihon no genten* [Koreans in Japan: The Focal Point of Japan in 1970s] (Tokyo: Zaikaitenbō shinsha, 1970). See also a special issue on the Ōmura prison camp, "In the Name of Human Beings' Dignity," *Atarashii Chōsen* (May 1955), pp. 15-19; "An Appeal to the World," ibid., pp. 21-25; and "Is There Such a Thing in the Society of Mankind?" ibid., pp. 25-26.
8. This was superseded by the Alien Registration Law of 1952, on the eve of the signing of the Japanese Peace Treaty. The content remained substantially the same. See Law no. 125, enacted 28 April 1952.
9. Kim So-un, *Ajiano yontō senshitsu* [The Fourth Class Cabin in Asia], quoted in Pak Chae-il, *Zainichi Chōsenjin ni kansuru sōgō chōsa kenkyū* [A General

Study of the Koreans in Japan] (Tokyo: Shin kigensha, 1957), p. 159.

10. "Statement of the Foreign Minister of the DPRK in Protest Against Persecution of the Korean Nationals in Japan," *On the Question of 600,000 Koreans in Japan* (P'yŏngyang: Foreign Language Publishing House, 1959), pp. 21-23. Nam Il's statement in Japanese was carried by *Zen-ei*, no. 98 (Nov. 1954): 16-17.

11. Kang No-hyang, *Chaeil Taep'yobu* [The Korean Mission in Japan] (Seoul: Tong'a P.R. yŏnkusŏ, 1966), pp. 16, 51-52.

12. Chŏng Chŏl, *Mindan* (Tokyo: Yŏyŏsha, 1967), pp. 56-57.

13. Ibid., pp. 58-59, 64. See also Kang, *Chaeil Taep'yobu*, pp. 204-210.

14. Concerning numerous incidents, see Chŏng, *Mindan*, pp. 25, 35-36, 64-65; and Kang, *Chaeil Taep'yobu*, pp. 172, 175, 178-179, 290.

15. "Nam Il Hokusen Gaisŏ no Nihon seifu ni taisuru tanichi kankei ni kansuru senmei ni tsuite" [Concerning the Statement of Nam Il, Foreign Minister of North Korea], *Kōan Jōhō*, no. 21 (June 1955): 53-54.

16. Ibid. See also Kiwon Chung, "Japanese-North Korean Relations Today," *Asian Survey*, 4, no. 4 (April 1964): 789-790.

17. "Zainichi Chōsenjin no genjō to Hokusen kikan mondai" [The Condition of Koreans in Japan and the Problem of Repatriation to North Korea], *Chōsa Geppō*, no. 40 (April 1959): 8 (hereafter cited as *Kikan Mondai*).

18. For the text, see Chōsen jijō kenkyūkai, ed., *Chōsen no keizai* [The Korean Economy] (Tokyo: Tokyo keizai shimpōsha, 1956), pp. 201-202; see also Kiwon, "Japanese-North Korean Relations Today," p. 792.

19. *Oemu hengchŏng*, pp. 171-172.

20. Ibid., p. 173.

21. Tamagi Motoi, "Nihon Kyōsanto no zainichi Chōsenjin Shidō" [The JCP's Guidance of the Koreans in Japan], *Koria Hyōron*, 5, no. 8 (Aug. 1961): 15.

22. *Kikan Mondai*, p. 8.

23. Ibid.

24. The DPRK has been remitting Korean Education Assistance Funds to the Ch'ongnyŏn regularly until the present time, although one amount decreased sharply in 1974. See chapter 9.

25. The Association for the Protection of Human Rights of the Koreans in Japan, *Kikoku kyōtei no enchō to kikoku jigyō no hoshō no tameni* [For the Extension of the Repatriation Agreement and Its Assurance for Further Repatriation] (Tokyo: Zainichi Chōsenjin no jinken o mamoru kai, 1967), pp. 25-26; and Fujishima Udai, "Chōsenjin kikoku to Nihonjin no mōten" [Korean Repatriation and the Blindspot of the Japanese], *Sekai*, no. 166 (Oct. 1959): 191.

26. *Kikan Mondai*, p. 9, and Fujishima, "Chōsenjin Kikoku," p. 191.

27. *On the Question of 600,000 Koreans in Japan*, pp. 10-11.

28. "Letter to Our Compatriots in Japan," document, *New Korea*, no. 31 (Oct. 1958): 27.

29. *On the Question of 600,000 Koreans in Japan*, pp. 13-16.

30. *Kikan Mondai*, p. 10.

31. Ibid., pp. 10-11; and Fujishima, *Chōsenjin Kikoku*, p. 194. See also "Hokusen kikoku undō no tembō" [The Prospects of the Repatriation Movement in North Korea], *Koria Hyōron*, 3, no. 1 (Jan. 1959): 44-45 (hereafter cited as "Hokusen kikoku undō no tenbō").

32. Hatada Takashi, "Zainichi Chōsenjin no kikoku to Nihonjin no kyōryoku" [The Repatriation of Koreans in Japan and Japanese Cooperation], *Koria Hyōron*, 3, no. 2 (Feb. 1959): 28-29.

33. Some of these articles were "Zainichi Chōsenjin rokujūman no genjitsu" [The Reality of 600,000 Koreans in Japan], *Chūō Kōron*, no. 847 (Dec. 1959); and "Kikoku to han Nihonjin" [Repatriation and the Half-Japanese], "Chōsenjin kikoku

to Nihonjin no mōten" [Korean Repatriation and the Blindspot of the Japanese], and "Kawaranu yūjo o" [Unchanging Friendship], *Sekai*, no. 166 (Oct. 1959); and "Chōsen kikoku o habamu mono" [Those Who Obstruct Repatriation to Korea], *Sekai*, no. 167 (Nov. 1959). Rōdōsha Ruporutaju Shūdan, comp., *Nihonjin no mita Zainichi Chōsenjin* [The Koreans in Japan Seen by the Japanese] (Tokyo: Nihon kikanshi tsūshinsha, 1959).

34. Japan, Ministry of Foreign Affairs, *Waga gaikō no kinkyō* [The Current Situation Concerning Our Foreign Relations], no. 4 (June 1959): 72-73.

35. Ibid.

36. The agreement was effective for only one year and three months after signing but was subject to renewal. It was renewed seven times before repatriation was officially terminated in 1967.

37. *Kikan Mondai*, p. 3.

38. Republic of Korea, Foreign Affairs Ministry, *Speeches and Statements by Foreign Minister Chung W. Cho* (Seoul: Foreign Affairs Ministry, 1959), pp. 84-85.

39. *Oemu hengchŏng*, pp. 173-174.

40. *Voice of Korea*, 16, no. 248 (31 Mar. 1959): 3; and *New York Times*, 15, 17, and 22 February 1959.

41. Republic of Korea, Foreign Affairs Ministry, *Republic of Korea Bulletin*, no. 18 (June 1959): 15-16.

42. *Voice of Korea*, 17, no. 260 (Aug. 1960): 3; and *New York Times*, 18 June 1959.

43. *New York Times*, 26 June 1959.

44. "Hokusen kikoku undō no tenbō," *Koria Hyōron*, p. 40.

45. Kōan Chōsachō [The Public Safety Investigation Bureau], comp., *Naigai jōsei no gaikyō to tenbō* [The Current Situation and Perspectives on Internal and External Affairs] (Tokyo: Kōanchō, n.d.), pp. 87-89.

46. Chŏng, *Mindan*, pp. 56-57.

47. A full text of the statement made by the Mindan is reprinted in ibid., p. 198.

6: ORGANIZATIONAL DIVISION AND CONFLICT: Ch'ongnyŏn and Mindan

1. Changsoo Lee, "The State-War-Navy Coordinating Committee and Joint Chiefs of Staff: A Reassessment of Its Decision on the Thirty-Eighth Parallel," *Korea Observer*, 3, no. 3 (Autumn 1977): 232-247.

2. After World War II, for example, the United States and West Germany established legal precedents in granting an option to "ex-colonial" subjects to retain their former nationality when the two western nations relinquished control over former territories. But the laws applied only to those already settled in the parent state at the time of the cession of territory. For further details, see Paul Weis, *Nationality and Statelessness in International Law* (London: Stevens, 1956).

3. Chŏn Chun, *Choch'ongnyŏn* (Seoul: Korea University Press, 1972), 1:538-539.

4. For details, see "Chōsensōren katsudō hōshin" [The Action Policy of Ch'ongnyŏn], *Atarashii Chōsen*, no. 9 (Sept. 1955): 6-9; and Hiroyama Shirō, "Minsen no kaisan to Zainihon Chōsenjin Sōrengōkai no kessei no kessei ni tsuite" [The Dissolution of the Minchon and Concerning the Founding of the General Federation of Korean Residents in Japan], *Kōan Jōhō*, no. 22 (July 1955): 10-11.

5. "Hokusen Saikō Jinmin Kaigi no daigiin senkyo to Chōsensōren" [The Election of the DPRK's Supreme People's Congress and the Ch'ongnyŏn], *Gaiji Tokuhō*, 12, no. 11 (Nov. 1964): 14-16.

6. Yŏn Chŏng, "Hadaka no Chōsensōren," [The Naked Ch'ongnyŏn], *Gunji Kenkyū* (Dec. 1974), pp. 22-25.

7. Chŏn, *Choch'ongnyŏn*, 2:442.

8. "Nitchō shinzen undō no hatten no tameni" [To Launch the Campaign for the Promotion of Friendly Relations Between Japan and the DPRK], *Kōan Jōhō*, no. 27 (Dec. 1955): 59.

9. Ibid.

10. For further details, see Tanaka Naokichi, *Nihon o ugokasu Nikkan kankei* [The ROK-Japan Relations Which Stir Japan] (Tokyo: Bunkyō Shoin, 1963), pp. 191-194, 195 ff.; and JCP Central Committee, comp., *Nikkan jōyaku to Nihon Kyōsantō* [The JCP and the ROK-Japan Treaty] (Tokyo: JCP Central Committee, 1965), pp. 57-68. See also Andō Hikotarō et al., *Nichi-Chō-Chū sankoku jinmin rentai no rekishi to riron* [A Treatise and History Concerning the Unity of Peoples of Japan-Korea-China] (Tokyo: Nihon Chōsen Kenkyusho, 1964), pp. 135-146; Ōhira Zengō, *Ajia Gaikō to Nikkan Kankei* [Asian Diplomacy and ROK-Japan Relations] (Tokyo: Yushindō, 1965), pp. 27-46; and Hatada Shigeo and Kawagoe Keizō, *Chōsen mondai to Nihon* [Japan and the Question of Korea] (Tokyo: Shin Nihon Shuppansha, 1968), pp. 157-171.

11. For these points, see several articles in the special issue, "Hanil hwedam ŭi p'amyŏlchŏk t'akyŏl" [The Ruinous Conclusion of the ROK-Japan Talks], *Sasangge*, no. 6 (June 1965): 50-117.

12. The objectives of the South Korean government in normalizing relations with Japan were well analyzed in the report published by the Office of the Prime Minister's Secretariat, *Nikkan jōyaku teikei o megura naigai no dōkō* (The Internal and External Situation Concerning the Conclusion of the ROK-Japan Normalization Treaty] (Tokyo: Naikaku kanbō Naikaku Chōsashitsu, 1966), pp. 7-9, 50 (hereafter cited as *Naigai no dōkō*).

13. "Nikkan jōyaku hijun soshi seiryoku no dōkō" [The Move Concerning the Forces Against Approval of the ROK-Japan Treaty], *Nikkan Mondai Jōhō*, no. 3 (Sept. 1965): 13-14. This periodical was published weekly by the Public Information Committee of the Liberal Democratic party especially for the consumption of LDP members during the campaign.

14. Ibid., no. 11 (Oct. 1965): 12; and *Naigai no dōkō*, pp. 51, 73.

15. *Nikkan Mondai Jōhō*, no. 3 (Sept. 1965): 50-51.

16. *Naigai no dōkō*, pp. 75-76; and "Hoteki chii o meguru dōyō [Unrest Related to the Question of Legal Status], *Asahi Janaru*, 7, no. 42 (10 Oct. 1965): 86.

17. *Naigai no dōkō*, p. 51.

18. Chŏng, *Mindan* (Tokyo: Yōyōsha, 1967), pp. 88-89; and *Nikkan Mondai Jōhō*, no. 3 (Sept. 1965): 19.

19. For further details on these demonstrations, see "Nikkan jōyaku hijun hantai undō no sōkatsu" [A Summary of the Campaign Against the ROK-Japan Treaty], *Chōsa Geppō*, no. 123 (March 1966): 34-50; "Nikkan jōyaku hijun o meguru uyoku kankei dantai no dōkō" [The Movement of Right-Wing Activities Concerning the ROK-Japan Treaty], *Kōan Jōhō*, no. 148 (Jan. 1966): 96-103; Gotō Naoshi, "Nikkan kaidan to handō ideologi no dōkō" [The ROK-Japan Talks and the Movement of Reactionary Ideology], *Bunka Hyōron*, no. 17 (April 1963): 54-62; and "Nikkan jōyaku hijun soshi tōsō no gaikyō to sono tokuchō" [Characteristics and General Situation of the Campaign Against the ROK-Japan Treaty], *Kōan Jōhō*, no. 146 (Nov. 1965): 29-35 (hereafter cited as *Nikkan jōyaku hijun soshi*).

20. *Naigai no dōkō*, p. 76.

21. *Nikkan jōyaku hijun soshi*, p. 69.

22. *Naigai no dōkō*, pp. 15-16.

23. Ibid., p. 20.

24. *Nikkan jōyaku hijun soshi,* p. 32.

25. Ibid., pp. 72-73, and *Naigai no dōkō,* pp. 16-21.

26. Hans S. Baerwald, "Nikkan Kokkai: The Japan-Korean Treaty Diet," in *Cases in Comparative Politics: Asia,* ed. by Lucian W. Pye (Boston: Little Brown, 1970), pp. 19-45.

27. "Nitchō gōsaku eiga *Ch'ŏllima* no jōei undō ni tsuite" [Concerning the Campaign for the Shwoing of the Japan-DPRK Joint Cinema Production *Ch'ŏllima*], *Kōan Jōhō,* no. 140 (May 1965): 40-47.

28. Tamagi Notoi, "Nihon Kyōsantō to Kitachōsen no tairitsu" [The JCP and DPRK Conflict], *Koria Hyōron,* no. 144 (Aug. 1973): 2-13.

29. *Nodong Shinmun,* 2 November 1970.

30. Kim Il-Sung, "Kakumei to kensetsu no dōtei" [A Route to Revolution and Reconstruction], *Sekai* (Feb. 1976): 186-197.

31. Kim Il-Sung, "Chōsen no heiwa to tōitsu" [The Peace in Korea and Unification], *Sekai* (June 1976): 120-135.

32. Kukche Munchae Yŏnkuso, ed., *Bukhan Chōnsō* [Collections on North Korea] (Seoul: Institute for East-Asian Studies, 1974), 3:166-167.

33. Tōitsu Chōsen Shinbun, comp., *Kim Byŏng-sik jiken* [The Kim Byong-sik Incident] (Tokyo: Tōitsu Chōsen Shinbun, 1973).

34. *Korean Central News,* 24 November and 12 December 1975.

35. *Tōitsu Nippō,* 30 September and 1 October 1975, and *Korean Central News,* 2 October and 6 October 1975.

36. Chŏng, *Mindan,* pp. 56-57. A full text of the Mindan statement denouncing the Rhee government is found on p. 198.

37. Korean Educators Association in Japan, eds. *Minchok shimp'ochium Bokosō* [Proceedings of the Ethnic Studies Symposium] (Nagoya: Korean Educators Assoc., 1976).

38. On the close collaboration between South Korean and Japanese Diet members in lobbying activities, see Satō Tasuya, "Nikkan riken no kōzō no jinmyaku" [The Structure of Japanese-South Korean Economic Interests and People], *Gendai no me* (June 1977), pp. 90-99; and Nomura Keiichirō, "Nihon ni okeru Bokuseiken no yujin tachi" [The Friends of the Park Regime in Japan], *Sekai* (Jan. 1977): 176-187.

7: THE LEGAL STATUS OF KOREANS IN JAPAN

1. Judicial Research and Training Institute, eds., *Zainichi Chōsenjin shogū no suii to genjō* [The Current Situation and Changes in the Legal Treatment of Koreans in Japan], Research Series, 43, no. 3 (Tokyo: Ministry of Justice, 1955): 27-31.

2. Supreme Commander for the Allied Powers, "Basic Initial Post-Surrender Directive to Supreme Commander for the Occupation and Control of Japan," J.C.S. 1380/8 (3 Nov. 1945), Report of Government Section. Reprinted in *Political Reorientation of Japan, September 1945, to September 1948* (Grosse Pointe, Mich.: Scholarly Press, 1968), 2:432.

3. For example, on 3 January 1946, when a Korean was jailed by the Japanese police for an unknown reason, a group of some eighty Koreans armed themselves with clubs and pistols, stormed the police station, and forcibly obtained the release of the Korean. See Supreme Commander for the Allied Powers, *Summation of Non-Military Activities in Japan, no.* 4 (Jan. 1946): 34.

4. Supreme Commander for the Allied Powers, "Definition of United Nations Nationals, Neutral Nations, and Enemy Nationals," *Directives,* SCAPIN-217, AG 312.4 (31 Oct. 1945) (Tokyo: SCAP headquarters). This is one of the many volumes

compiled by SCAP concerning SCAPIN directives issued to the Japanese Imperial government.

5. "Ration for United Nations Nationals and Stateless Persons," *Directives,* SCAPIN-1094, AG 430 (30 July 1946), and SCAPIN-1841 under the same subject (8 Jan. 1948).

6. SCAP press release, 19 November 1946.

7. *Nippon Times,* 21 November 1946.

8. It was later reaffirmed by Law no. 11, the Election Law of the House of Councillors, enacted on 24 February 1947, and Law no. 67, the Prefectural Home Rule Law, enacted on 17 April 1947.

9. See "Circular Notice Concerning Nationality and Family Registration Pursuant to the Effectiveness of the Peace Treaty," *Civil Affairs,* no. A-438, issued by the Director of the Civil Affairs Bureau of the Ministry of Justice on 19 April 1952. Regarding the legality, see Satō Shigemoto, "Chōsenjin no kokuseki ni tsuite" [Concerning Korean Nationality], *Minji Geppō,* no. 5 (May 1967): 14-19.

10. This was superseded by the new Alien Registration Law of 1952, on the eve of the signing of the San Francisco Peace Treaty. But the content remained substantially the same as the old one. See Law no. 125, enacted 28 April 1952.

11. Changsoo Lee, "Chōsōren: An Analysis of the Korean Communist Movement in Japan," *Journal of Korean Affairs,* 3, no. 2 (July 1973).

12. The Omura camp was built in December 1950, exclusively to accommodate those who violated the Immigration Control Law and the Alien Registration Law. Since a majority of violators were Koreans, the camp was known as a "Korean prison" in Japan. The treatment given to the prisoners was so notoriously inhumane that many prison riots took place. For further details, see chapter 2 in Nakazone Eisuke, *Zainichi Chōsenjin: Nanajūnendai Nihon no genten* [Koreans in Japan: The Focal Point of Japan in 1970s] (Tokyo: Zaikaitenbō shinsha, 1970), entitled "The Quiet Ōmura Camp." See also a special issue on the Ōmura camp, "In the Name of Human Beings' Dignity," *Atarashii Chōsen* (May 1955), pp. 15-19, and "An Appeal to the World," ibid., pp. 21-25, and "Is There Such a Thing in the Society of Mankind?" ibid., pp. 25-26.

13. When Japan annexed Taiwan in 1895 and Sakhalin in 1905, freedom to select their nationality was provided for the natives. For further details, see Egawa Hidebumi et al., *Kokuseikihō* [Nationality Law] (Tokyo: Yūhikaku, 1951), pp. 37, 98. But freedom of choice was not given to Koreans when Japan annexed Korea in 1910.

14. This refers to the "Disposition of the Laws and Orders Related to the Ministry of Foreign Affairs by the Acceptance of the Potsdam Declaration," Law no. 126, Art. 2, par. 6. No sooner had the San Francisco Peace Treaty become effective than a law was passed by the Japanese Diet to confirm, modify, or repeal the existing laws under SCAP authority.

15. For a complete text of the document written in Korean, Japanese, and English, see Ministry of Foreign Affairs, *Documents on the Statuses of Korean Residents in Japan,* Consular Materials 74/2 (Seoul: Ministry of Foreign Affairs) (hereafter cited as *Documents,* 74/2).

16. Ibid., pp. 45-46. On this point, see par. *a* of the Record of Discussion in "Agreed Minutes Regarding the Agreement on the Legal Status and the Treatment of the Nationals of the Republic of Korea Residing in Japan, Between Japan and the Republic of Korea" (hereafter cited as "Agreed Minutes").

17. Miyazaki Hideki, "Zainichi Chōsenjin no hōteki chii" [The Legal Status of Koreans in Japan], *Juristo,* no. 327 (Dec. 1965): 24, and Akiba Jun'ichi, "Iwayuru hōteki chii kyōteijō no eijū kyoka shinsei hōhō ni kansuru mondaiten" [Problems

Concerning the Application Procedure for Permanent Residence by Treaty Agreement on Legal Status], *Kokusaihō Gaikō Zasshi*, no. 64 (Mar. 1966): 422-430.

18. Ogawa Masaaki, "Zainichi Kankokujin no hōteki chii taigū kyōtei" [The Agreement on Legal Status and the Treatment of Koreans in Japan], *Hōritsu Jihō*, 37, no. 10 (Sept. 1965): 28.

19. See, *Documents*, 74/2, p. 42, "Agreed Minutes," Art. 3, par. 3.

20. For a list of all social welfare benefits to which aliens are not entitled in Japan, see a document compiled by the Mindan, *Taigū mondai ni kansuru shiryō* [Data Concerning the Legal Treatment of Koreans in Japan] (July 1971).

21. Ministry of Reconstruction Circular no. 932, dated 12 November 1954, issued in the name of the Director of Public Housing, quoted *in* Ogawa Masaaki, "Zainninchi Kankokujin," pp. 30-31.

22. Pak Kyŏng-sik, *Chōsenjin kyōsei renkō no kiroku* [The Record of Forcibly Conscripted Koreans] (Tokyo: Miraisha, 1965), pp. 62-63.

23. Ikegami Tsutomu, *Hōteki chii nihyaku no shitsumon* [Two Hundred Questions Concerning Legal Status] (Tokyo: Kyōbunsha, 1965), pp. 167-168.

24. *Documents*, 74/2, "Agreed Minutes," re Art. 4, par. 4(*ii*).

25. *Tōitsu Nippō*, 29 September 1978.

26. Ibid., 5 November 1975.

27. Regarding the experiences narrated by some naturalized Koreans in Japan, see Honda Masaharu, "Seiwa Kurabu o tazunete" [A Visit to Seiwa Club], *Madang*, no. 2 (1973): 134-136.

28. After his dramatic suicide by self-immolation at the nearby Waseda campus, his diary was published posthumously by his surviving brother. Yamamura Masaaki, *Inochi no moe tsukirutomo* [Even If My Life Ends in Flame] (Tokyo: Yamato shobō, 1971), pp. 24-25.

29. For a theoretical discussion of the concept of ethnic identity, see George De Vos, "Ethnic Pluralism: Conflict and Accommodation," *in* George De Vos et al., eds., *Ethnic Identity: Cultural Communities and Change* (Palo Alto: Mayfield, 1975).

30. Wagatsuma Hiroshi et al., *Henken no kōzō: Nihonjin no jinshukan* [The Formation of Prejudice: The Japanese Perception of Race] (Tokyo: Nihon Hōsō Shuppankai, 1972), chapter 5.

31. For further discussion, see Changsoo Lee, "Ethnic Discrimination and Conflict: The case of the Korean Minority in Japan," *in* Willem A. Veenhoven et al., eds., *Case Studies on Human Rights and Fundamental Freedoms: A World Survey* (The Hague: Martinus Nijhoff, 1976), 4:280-284. And also The Committee to Support Pak, ed., *Minzoku sabetsu* [Ethnic Discrimination] (Tokyo: Akishobō, 1974).

32. *Han'guk Ilbo*, 24 March 1977.

8: ETHNIC EDUCATION AND NATIONAL POLITICS

1. Professor Aoyanagi wrote three books concerning the Japanese colonial administration in Korea: namely, *Sōtaku seiji* [Politics of the Colonial Government] (Keijō: Chōsen kenkyūkai, 1918); *Sōtoku seji shiron* [A Treatise on the History of Colonial Government Administration] (Keijō: Keijō shinbunsha, 1928); and *Chōsen tōchi ron* [A Treatise on the Governing of Korea] (Keijō: Chōsen kenkyūkai, 1932).

2. Aoyanagi, *Sōtoku seiji shiron*, pp. 246-251.

3. Ibid., pp. 253-254. Similar objections were also raised by Yanaibara Tadao and Soejima Michimasa. Their alternative proposal was to provide autonomous rule under direct supervision of the Japanese Imperial government. On this point, see

Hatada Takashi, "Nihonjin no Chōsenjin kan" [Japanese Views of Koreans], *in* Nihon Chōsen kenkyūsho, ed., *Nihon to Chōsen* [Japan and Korea] (Tokyo: Keiso shobō, 1965), pp. 8-10.

4. For a study of Japanese assimilation policies in Taiwan and Korea, see Chen I-te, "Japanese Colonialism in Korea and Formosa: A Comparison of Its Effects upon the Development of Nationalism" (Ph.D. dissertation, University of Pennsylvania, 1968), pp. 71-85.

5. Fujishima Udai and Ozawa Yūsaku, *Minzoku kyōiku* [Ethnic Education] (Tokyo: Aogi shoten, 1966), pp. 18-21.

6. For further details, see Itō Yūten, *Senman no kōa kyōiku* [Education for Rising Asia in Korea and Manchuria] (Tokyo: Meguro shoten, 1942), pp. 8-9.

7. Kim Hong-o, *Chōsen dōhō wa kataru* [Korean Compatriots Speak Out] (Nagoya: Kyōwa gōjōkai, 1931); Yi Kwang-su, *Naisen ittai zuisōroku* [Essays on Japan-Korea as a Single Entity] (n.p., 1941); and Kang Ch'ang-ki, *Naisen ittai ron* [A Treatise on Japan and Korea as a Single Entity] (Tokyo: Kokumin hyōronsha, 1939).

8. For further details on the Kyōwa project, see Kyōwakai, ed., *Kyōwa sōsho* [Collected Works Related to the Kyōwa Project] (Tokyo: Kyōwakai, 1940-1943), a series of sixteen papers and reports by various writers.

9. Quoted in Yi Tong-jun, *Nihon ni iru Chōsen no kodomo* [Korean Children in Japan] (Tokyo: Shunjūsha, 1956), pp. 66-67.

10. Ibid., pp. 68-69.

11. Tokyo Liaison Office, USAMGIK, to OFA USAMGI, *Weekly Report*, 19-25 October 1947, and Fujishima and Osawa, *Minzoku kyōiku*, p. 51.

12. Supreme Commander for the Allied Powers, *Summation of Non-Military Activities in Japan*, no. 31 (April 1948): 303, and Yi, *Chōsen no kodomo*, p. 72.

13. Edward W. Wagner, *Korean Minority in Japan, 1904-1950* (New York: Institute of Pacific Relations, 1951), p. 70, and Yi, *Chōsen no kodomo*, pp. 67-77.

14. The protests centered in Kobe and are commonly known in Japan as the "Hanshin Incident of 1948." Detailed and accurate accounts of the incident were written by Ochiai Shigenobu, a well-known Kobe historian, in "Kōbe Chōsenjin gakkō sōgi no gaikyō" [The Korean School Dispute in Kobe], *Rekishi to Kōbe*, no. 4 (1953): 73-77, and "Kobe Chosenjin jiken shokuhatten: Shōwa Nijūsannen no Chō-senjin gakkō heissa o meguru Kōbe no sōranjiken" [Cause of the Korean Incident in Kobe: The Korean Riot Incident in Kobe Related to the Korean School Closure Case in 1948], *Hyōgo Shigaku*, no. 28 (1961): 133-140. See also Fujishima and Ozawa, *Minzoku kyōiku*, pp. 58-67.

15. *Chōren Chūō Jihō*, 14 May 1948.

16. Kajii Noboru, *Chōsenjin gakkō no Nihonjin kyōshi* [Japanese Teachers in Korean Schools] (Tokyo: Nihon Chōsen kenkyūsho, 1966), p. 18.

17. Yi, *Chōsen no kodomo*, p. 94.

18. Ibid., p. 106; Fujishima and Ozawa, *Minzoku kyōiku*, pp. 78-79; and Kajii, *Nihonjin kyōshi*, p. 124.

19. The six additional restrictions were: (1) no political education was allowed that might be prejudicial to Japanese government policy; (2) Korean ethnic studies were to be taught only as extracurricular subjects; (3) no student was to be admitted beyond a school's administrative capacity [a reiteration of the national govern-ment's first restriction]; (4) no student was allowed to circulate petitions; (5) classes were to be conducted only by authorized teaching staff; and (6) no outsiders were allowed to attend faculty and staff meetings.

20. *Zainichi Hokusenkei Chōsenjin no minshu minzoku no kyōiku no jitsujō* [The Current Situation Concerning the Democratic Ethnic Education of the Pro-North Koreans in Japan] (n.p., 1968), pp. 24-25. This pamphlet carried neither the

name of the author nor the publisher; nonetheless, it appears to be an authoritative report concerning the Ch'ongnyŏn's educational programs and activities in Japan. Judging from its scope and contents, it seems to have been prepared as a staff research paper only for official consumption by Japanese authorities. It is in the possession of the East Asia Collection, University of Maryland (call no. East Asia CS836 Z3), p. 15 (hereafter cited as *Minzoku kyōiku*).

21. On this point, see pamphlets published by the Mindan, *Zainichi Kankokujin kyōiku* [Korean Education in Japan], no. 1 (Dec. 1965), and no. 2 (Jan. 1967). See also Nagoya Hanguk Hakkyo, ed., *Minchok kyoyuk shimpochiŭm bokosŏ* [A Report on Ethnic Studies Symposium] (Nagoya, 1976), p. 30 (hereafter cited as *Bokosŏ*).

22. Fujishima and Ozawa, *Minzoku kyōiku*, p. 137.

23. Ibid., pp. 27-31.

24. Ibid., p. 33.

25. Ibid., pp. 40-41.

26. Ibid., p. 33.

27. Ibid., p. 97; and Soshinkai, *Chōsen Daigaku no enkaku to genjō* [Origin of Chosŏn University and the Current Situation] (n.p., Soshinkai, 1962), p. 1; and "Chōsen Daigaku no shunkō o meguru himitsu shiryō" [Confidential Information Concerning Completion of Chosŏn University], *Naigai Shūhō*, no. 18 (July 1959): 3 (hereafter cited as *Chōsen Daigaku no shiryō*).

28. According to the Agricultural Land Law, any transaction involving farmland or a conversion of farmland to other than agricultural purposes is subject to approval by the Agricultural Committee in each local government. On this point, see Arts. 3, 4, and 10 of the Agricultural Land law, no. 299, enacted 15 July 1952.

29. *Chōsen Daigaku no shiryō*, p. 4.

30. Ibid., pp. 4-5; and Soshinkai, *Chōsen Daigaku no enkaku*, pp. 1-2 and 10-11.

31. *Chōsen Daigaku no shiryō*, p. 5; and *Naigai Shūhō*, no. 43 (18 Mar. 1969): 3.

32. It is not known how many foreign students are enrolled in the university. In 1978 the student enrollment was reportedly about 1,500 with over 100 teaching faculty members. Chosŏn University has expanded to a four-year college composed of four academic divisions, two academic departments, a two-year teachers' college, and a graduate school. For further details, see *Minzoku kyōiku*, pp. 98-103; and Chosŏn Taehak'kyo, comp., *Chōsen Daigaku o mite* [Seeing Chosŏn University] (Tokyo: Chosŏn Taihakkyo, 1967).

33. *Minzoku kyōiku*, pp. 100-101.

34. For instance, see the statements made by various Japanese officials in the Ministry of Education and published in Zainichi Chōsenjin Chūō Kyōiku Iinkai, *Zainichi Chōsenjin shitei no minshushugiteki minzoku kyōiku ni taisuru Nihonseifu tōkyoku no futō na shochi* [Improper Actions Taken by Japanese Government Authorities against Democratic Ethnic Education for Korean Children in Japan] (Tokyo: Zainichi Chōsenjin Chūō Iinkai, 1964), pp. 4-5, 7-9, 26-29.

35. Art. 83, pars. 1, 2, and 3 of the School Education Law. According to Art. 83, "Institutions other than those mentioned in Article 1 which give education... similar to school education shall be classified as miscellaneous schools." The schools mentioned in Art. 1 refer to elementary and secondary schools, universities, schools for the blind and deaf, etc. Therefore, "miscellaneous schools" are not considered as regular schools but as schools that provide training in special vocational skills or trades, such as beauty schools, dress-design schools, and barber schools.

36. See Ministry of Education Circular 210, issued 28 December 1965, to all prefectural governors concerning Korean schools. The full text of this circular is re-

printed in Fujishima and Ozawa, *Minzoku kyōiku*, pp. 266-268. (See n. 5, above.)

37. *Nodong Shinmun*, 20 April 1966.

38. Art. 82, par. 15, of the "Foreigners' School System Bill."

39. The legal questions discussed by participants in the symposium were subsequently published in Ogawa Masaaki, Etō Yoshihirō, Yamazaki Masahide, and Kobakura Masatake, "Gaikokujin gakkō seido" [The Foreigners' School System], *Horitsu Jihō*, 39, no. 2 (Feb. 1967): 32-58.

40. Ibid., p. 48.

41. Ibid., pp. 51-52.

42. "Chōsen Daigakkō ninka mondai o meguru uyoku dantai no dōkō" [Right-wing Activities on the Question of Chosŏn University Accreditation], *Kōan Jōhō*, no. 169 (Oct. 1967): 80 (hereafter cited as *Chōsen Daigakkō ninka mondai*, no. 169).

43. See Ministry of Education Circular 210. Later the Ministry of Education repeatedly warned the Tokyo governor not to grant accreditation to Chosŏn University. See *Asahi Shimbun*, 23 August 1967.

44. The congratulatory messages were not entirely from university presidents in the Communist world but included some from the non-Communist countries, such as from Cambridge, Stanford, and Yale universities. For details, see Chosŏn Taehak'kyo, comp., *Chōsen Daigaku o mite*, pp. 127-131.

45. For summaries of the round-table discussions and names of the participants, including conversations with Ōkochi Kazuo, president of Tokyo University, see ibid., pp. 11-36, 40-41, 50 ff.

46. The texts of both resolutions are reprinted in ibid., pp. 173-178.

47. *Chōsen Daigakkō ninka mondai*, no. 169: 80.

48. According to Art. 84, par. 4 of the School Education Law of 1947, the prefectural governor is required to consult with the Private School Council, which is composed of prominent educators in the locality. But its recommendation is not legally binding.

49. *Chōsen Daigakkō ninka mondai*, no. 169: 78-79.

50. Seven of the nine candidates in the gubernatorial election had been from right-wing groups. See "Tokyo Chiji senkyo o meguru uyoku dantai no dōkō" [Activities of Right-wing Groups in the Tokyo Gubernatorial Election], *Kōan Jōhō*, no. 164 (May 1967): 73-80.

51. Igarashi Akira, "Chōsen Daigaku ninka sokushin shomeisha no kai" [Petition Signers' Association to Expedite the Accreditation of Chosŏn University], *Chōsen Kenkyū*, no. 61 (May 1967): 36-37; and also Chosŏn Taehakkyo, comp., *Chōsen Daigakkō no ninka mondai ni kansuru shiryō* [Data Concerning Chosŏn University Accreditation], no. 1 (Tokyo: Chosŏn Taehakkyo, 1967): 7.

52. "Chōsen Daigaku ninka mondai o meguru ugoki" [Activities Concerning Chosŏn University Accreditation], *Naigai Tokuhō* (Oct. 1967), pp. 5-8, and "Chōsen Daigakkō ninka ni taisuru Monbushō no kainyū wa hōteki konkyo ga nai" [The Ministry of Education Has No Legal Basis to Intervene in Chosŏn University Accreditation], *Akahata*, 9 September 1967.

53. Liberal Democratic Party, *Chosŏn Daigaku o naze ninka dekinaika* [Why Cannot Chosŏn University Be Accredited?] (Tokyo: Jimintō, 1967), pp. 1-11.

54. The full text of the council's report is reproduced in Arikura Ryōkichi, et al., "Chōsen Daigakkō setchi ninka ni kansuru tōshinsho no gyōseihōteki bunseki" [Analysis of the Report Concerning Chosŏn University Accreditation from the Administrative law Point of View], *Hōritsu Jihō*, 40, no. 6 (May 1968): 87-93 (hereafter cited as *Tōshinsho bunseki*).

55. In Japan, private colleges and universities often use words like *gakuin* or

juku rather than *daigakkō* to distinguish themselves from public universities, even if they provide the same level of education, e.g. Aoyama Gakuin or Keiō Juku.
56. *Tōshinsho bunseki*, pp. 87-93.

9: EDUCATION—POLICIES AND PROSPECTS

1. I spent most of March and April 1977 in Osaka and Kobe pursuing the question of the education of Koreans living in Japan utilizing interviews and school visits as well as collecting what documentation I could. In 1974-1975 I spent a year in five high schools in Kobe studying Japanese secondary education. I would like to thank Professor Toru Umakoshi of Hiroshima University for his generous assistance in locating materials.
2. Osawa Yūsaku, *Zainichi Chōsenjin Kyōikuron* (Tokyo: Toki Shobō, 1973). Sō Yŏng-dal, "Kankokukei Shokōjin no Gendai," *Sanzenri*, no. 8 (Winter 1976): 58-64.
3. A shortage of public high schools, coupled with the termination of compulsory education with ninth grade has resulted in a situation in which the academically less able junior high school graduates in Japan must choose between (a) employment, (b) public vocational schools, and (c) private high schools offering a college-prep curriculum.
4. Sō, *Kankokukei Shokōjin.*
5. Surveys by Chōsen Shōgakkai (i.e., Chōsen Shōgakkai, *Bokura ni totte Minzoku to wa.* In *Aozora*, no. 20 (June 1975) of students in high-school Korean clubs reveal, by and large, minimal Korean language ability among students attending Japanese schools. Ch'ongnyŏn school students I encountered spoke Japanese together on their way to school.
6. According to a survey reported in *Shinro Hoshō*, no. 7 (1976), and Hyogo-ken Shinrō Hoshō Kyōgikai, *Shinrō Hoshō*, nos. 2-3 (1975).
7. Osaka Kyōiku Iinkai (1976) statistics (unpublished).
8. Ibid.
9. Information comes from interviews in a particular public elementary school in Ikuno-ku, Osaka.
10. In Kobe, office of education officials and teachers of the schools in question were quite explicit on this question.
11. *Hyogo-ken Keisatsu Hakusho* (1971, 1972, and 1973) as provided in an interview at Prefectural Police Headquarters in April 1977. See also Hiroshi Wagatsuma, *Hikō Shōnen no Jirei Kenkyū* (Tokyo: Seishin Shobō, 1973).
12. These statistics come from the Shinrō Hoshō Kyōgikai which is an organization that collects and publishes statistics and reports on the educational achievements of minorities in the prefecture. This organization appears to be semiofficial as it has prefectural government office space. It focuses largely on the Burakumin problem and is supported by much volunteer work from interested teachers. The statistics it collects on minorities in education are the most thorough I have found in Japan. The Ministry of Education, by comparison, offers little statistical material of value in this area.
13. Hyogo-ken Shinrō Hoshō Kyōgikai, *Shinrō Hoshō*, nos. 4-8 (1976).
14. See The Committee to Support Pak, ed., *Minzoku Sabetsu: Hitachi Shūshoku Sabetsu Kyūdan* (Tokyo: Aki Shobō, 1974) for an account of the alleged discrimination against a Korean at Hitachi.
15. See Sakamoto Izumi, *Nihon Gakkō ni okeru Chōsenjin Jidō no Kyōiku no Mondai*, Research Bulletin, Faculty of Education, Ōita University, 4, no. 1 (1971);

Kōritsu Chōsenjin Gakkō no Jishuko Ikon no Mondai: Osaka-shi Nishimasato Chūgakko no baai o chūshin ni shite (pt. 1), Research Bulletin, Faculty of Education, Ōita University, 3, no. 4 (1969); *Kōritsu Chōsenjin Gakkō no Jishiko Ikan no Mondai: Osaka-shi Nishiimasato Chūgakko no baai o chūshin ni shite* (pt. 2), Research Bulletin, Faculty of Education, Ōita University, 3, no. 5 (1969); and Kajii Noboru, *Chōsenjin Gakkō no Nihonjin Kyōshi* (Tokyo: Toki Shobō, 1974).

16. These are the conclusions of Sakamoto, *Kōritsu Chōsenjin*, 1969, 1970, 1971.

17. Published materials on this school system are few and strongly colored by the authors' political biases. I have attempted to treat the Ch'ongnyŏn school system objectively, but much closer observation and some unbiased means of checking Ch'ongnyŏn school statistics is necessary before any solid facts can be established. Accounts can be found in Osawa, *Zainichi Chōsenjin*, 1973; Sakamoto, *Kōritsu Chōsenjin*, 1969, 1970, 1971; and Kajii, *Gakkō no Nihonjin*, 1974.

18. Chŏn Chun, *Chosenren: sono saikin no katsudō* (Tokyo: Warudo Sensho, 1976), and interviews with non-Ch'ongnyŏn members in Osaka.

19. Hyogo-ken Shinrō Hoshō Kyōgikai communication. This figure roughly approximates the percentage of Japanese schools in the area with more than a handful of Korean students.

20. Quoted from the discussion of this and related issues in an article titled "Zadankai" in *Sanzenri*, no. 8 (1976).

11: ON BOTH SIDES OF JAPANESE JUSTICE

1. Kim Hi-lo's testimony during his trial was published by the Committee to Help Kim Hi-lo, *Kim Hi-lo no hōteki chinjutsu* [The Court Testimony of Kim Hi-lo] (Tokyo: Sanichi shobō, 1970).

2. See George De Vos and Hiroshi Wagatsuma, *Japan's Invisible Race* (Berkeley and Los Angeles: University of California Press, 1966) and *The Heritage of Endurance* (n.d.).

3. For further details of Pak's case, see Committee to Support Pak, eds., *Minzoku sabetsu* [The Ethnic Discrimination] (Tokyo: Akishobō, 1974).

4. *Han'guk Ilbo* [Korean Daily Press], 24 March 1977.

12: PUBLIC FIGURES IN POPULAR CULTURE: Identity Problems of Minority Heroes

1. The term *gaijin* is almost always used to label "foreigners" on a racial rather than a legal basis. Thus, even Japanese may be called gaijin if they happen to be white, black, or racially mixed. In nonspecific contexts, however, the word tends to connote "white person" [*hakujin*] or "Westerner" [*seiyōjin*]. In pejorative contexts, it closely resembles the English word "gook" [Oriental] in the sense that it is used as a sweeping racial label without reference to nationality and with derogatory connotations.

2. Rikidōzan Mitsuhiro, *Karate choppu sekai o yuku: Rikidōzan jiden* [The Karate Chop World: The Autobiography of Rikidōzan] (Tokyo: Beesubooru Magajin Sha, 1962), p. 1. Ono Banboku (1890-1964) was an influential rural faction leader and vice-president of the politically conservative Liberal Democratic party. He was the commissioner of Japanese professional wrestling at the time of Rikidōzan's

death, and he served as chairman of the wrestler's funeral committee. It is possible that by "proxy," Ōno meant to imply that Rikidōzan was Korean.

3. Chin Shunshin [Ch'en Shun-ch'en], *Nihonjin to Chūgokujin: "Dōbun dōshu" to omoikomu kiken* [Japanese and Chinese: The Danger of Believing "Same Script, Same Race"] (Tokyo: Shodensha, 1971), p. 169. It is not clear that Chin is aware of Rikidōzan's ancestry.

4. Ōshima Yukio, *Harimoto Isao: Fukutsu no tōkon* [Harimoto Isao: Dauntless Fighting Spirit] (Tokyo: Suponichi Shuppan, 1976), p. 190.

5. Ibid., pp. 191-193.

6. Of the three major national dailies commanding general readerships, two reported in obituaries that Rikidōzan was born in Nagasaki prefecture. Only one wrote, without elaboration, that the deceased wrestler was born in Korea but that his *honseki* [domicile register] was in Ōmura city of Nagasaki prefecture. If true, then Rikidōzan was Japanese at the time of his death, for had he been Korean his honseki would have been in Korea, not Japan.

7. *Shūkan gendai*, 6, no. 1 (1 Jan. 1964): 46.

8. Important Rikidōzan biographies, in addition to the autobiography already cited (n. 2), include: Gunji Nobuo. *Rikidōzan, Endō Kōkichi: Puro resu oja* [Rikidōzan and Endō Kōkichi: Professional Wrestling Champions] (Tokyo: Tsuru Shobō, 1954); Kajiwara Ikki. *Rikidōzan to Nihon no puroresu shi* [Rikidōzan and the History of Japanese Professional Wrestling] (Tokyo: Akebono Shuppan, 1971); Kaneda Tatsuo. *Ōja Rikidōzan: Sekai senshuken o waga ude ni* [Champion Rikidōzan: The World Title in Our Arms] (Tokyo: Kindai Shuppan Sha, 1955); Mitsuhashi Kazuo. *Rikidōzan monogatari, Puro resura* [The Story of Rikidōzan, Professional Wrestler] (Tokyo: Muromachi Shobō, 1954); Supootsu Nippon Shinbun Tokyo Honsha, comp., *Rikidōzan: Hana no shōgai* [Rikidōzan: The Life of a Flower] (Tokyo: Supootsu Nippon Shinbun Sha, 1964). Enjoying a wider audience than all these biographies combined, and occasionally still shown in small rerun theaters, is the 1955 Nikkatsu film *Dotō no otoko: Rikidōzan monogatari* [The Man of Angry Waves: The Story of Rikidōzan], directed by Morinaga Kentarō. The 84-minute feature movie dramatizes the standard Rikidōzan nativity myth, and it even features the wrestler himself in documentary clips and studio shots. The film takes its title from an *enka* [popular ballad] first sung by Misora Hibari, the most popular songstress of postwar Japan, and one of the many enka singers who is sometimes rumored to be of Korean ancestry (see references in n. 37). "Dotō no otoko" (surging masculinity) was the theme song of the movie. It was natural that Misora sing in the film, for she rivalled Rikidōzan for viewer ratings in the neophyte television industry. For additional comments on this film and its pairing of Rikidōzan and Misora, see Mori Akihide, *Naze enka na no ka: Onpu mo yomezu gitaa mo hikenai sedai no jikkan-teki enka kō* [Why Enka?: Reflections on the Truly Felt Enka of a Generation that neither Read Notes nor Played Guitars] (Tokyo: Keimei Shobō, 1980), pp. 105-114.

9. Ali claimed in an interview with a Japanese sports writer, published in Japanese, that Inoki called him "nigger" (Nigaa [Kuronbo]) at a press conference in New York. As a rule, Japanese in Japan are not likely to be as sensitive to the word "Jap" as Japanese who reside in North America or Europe. But even Japanese who reside outside Japan may not be as sensitive to the term as North Americans and Europeans of Japanese ancestry. The highly regarded Japanese fashion designer Takada Kenzō, for example, established his Paris reputation with the trademark JAP, and when it appeared in his New York boutique, Japanese Americans protested, although in vain.

10. The same newspaper that reported in its obituary that Rikidōzan was born

in Korea (n. 6) reported that he said, "Negro go home" [*Niguro goo hoomu*] when he mounted the stage. Featured that evening at the New Latin Quarter was a group of black performers, and it was their show that he interrupted. Rikidōzan researcher Ushijima Hidehiko (see references in n. 15), however, reports that the gangster who stabbed Rikidōzan was someone the wrestler had punched on a previous occasion, and that the intoxicated wrestler had been shouting "Negro go home! Son of a bitch!" before he was stabbed.

11. *Shūkan shinchō*, 8, no. 32, ser. 410 (30 Dec. 1963): 98.

12. *Gongu*, in eight parts, from 4, no. 9, ser. 49 (Sept. 1971), through 5, no. 4, ser. 56 (April 1972).

13. *Shūkan bunshun*, 14, no. 44, ser. 699 (6 Nov. 1972): 164-166.

14. *Gongu*, 11, no. 7, ser. 153 (June 1978): 88-90.

15. Ushijima Hidehiko, " 'Hinomaru' no otoko: Rikidōzan no Shōwa hishi", [The Man of the "Rising Sun Flag": The Secret Shōwa History of Rikidōzan], *Ushio*, no. 219 (Aug. 1977): 110-149; and Ushijima Hidehiko, "Cha no ma no eiyū: Riki- dōzan no hikari to kage" [Living-room Hero: The Lights and Shadows of Riki- dōzan], *Ushio*, no. 220 (Sept. 1977): 264-283.

16. For many poignant anecdotes of Korean reactions to the deprivation of their ethnic names, see Richard Kim, *Lost Names: Scenes From a Korean Boyhood* (New York: Praeger, 1970); and Kim Il-myön, "Chōsenjin no 'Nihonmei': Nihon tōchika no Nihonmei shiyō no yurai to 'Sōshi kaimei' " [Koreans and "Japanese Names": The "Sōshi Kaimei" Order and the Origin of the Use of Japanese Names Under Japanese Rule], *Tenbō*, no. 208 (April 1976): 34-54. The latter source gives an account of Korean poet Kim So-un, who responded to the Sōshi Kaimei [Create Family Name, Change Personal Name] order by adopting the name Tetsu Jinpei, which he intended to mean something like "I don't give a damn that I've lost my gold!" The Chinese character for Tetsu [iron] consists of two parts which mean "gold lost" (i.e., iron is metal without gold), alluding to the fact that he had lost his ethnic name Kim [gold]. See also reference in n. 27.

17. The Japanization of Korean athletes and performers through adoption is a fairly common practice. Another well-known example is ace spiker Shirai Takako, who led Japan's women's volleyball team to a silver medal in the Munich Summer Olympics in 1972, and to a gold medal in the Montreal Summer Olympics in 1976. Shirai became a volleyball star as a Korean Nisei, but she had to become "Japanese" in both nationality and name before she could play in international competition on the All-Japan team. Both conditions were met when the coach of a company team she had played for adopted her as his daughter.

18. The Sino-Korean family name "Kim" is retained as the Sino-Japanese "Kin" in the personal name "Kintarō." This is one of the many ways that people of Korean ancestry in Japan embed their Korean names in their Japanese passing names.

19. Ōshima, *Harimoto Isao*, p. 191.

20. See n. 8 for Kajiwara's Rikidōzan biography. Kajiwara's principal genres of macho melodrama are professional sports, the martial arts, and the underworld. He was once indicted, along with his publishers, by a group of Japan-resident Kore- ans for stereotyping Koreans in *yakuza* [gangster] roles in the script he wrote for a comic-book story set in postwar Japan. A reedition of the comic book left the story intact but rendered stereotyped, Korean-accented Japanese dialogue in unaccented standard speech, and crypticized some overtly discriminatory ethnic labels. For Kajiwara's own account of the macho genres he favors, and his role in their develop- ment in postwar Japanese popular culture, see his "Gekiga ichidai" [First Generation Action Caricature], serialized weekly in the Sunday edition of *Mainichi shinbun* beginning 4 September 1977. Articles relating to Rikidōzan begin from installment no. 9 (30 Oct. 1977).

21. *Choosen* (an exaggerated form of *Chōsen* [Korea]) is a derogatory term for either Korea or Korean, and so *Chōsen ni kaere* means "Go back to Korea!"

22. There is an extensive literature on Ch'oe's case, which he appealed to the high court in late 1977 after losing in the district court. For the most important references, see his own book on the case, *Namae to jinken* [Personal Names and Human Rights] (Tokyo: Sakai Shoten, 1979).

23. Andrew Horvat, *Soredemo watashi wa Nihonjin ni naritai: Yudaya no me ga toraeta Nippon* [Still, I Want To Become Japanese: Japan as Caught by a Jewish Eye] (Tokyo: Nisshin Hōdō, 1976), pp. 142-143. The text, in Japanese, was translated by Toyoda Kōji from an apparently unpublished English manuscript.

24. *Step News* (Tokyo), no. 162 (June 1979): 4.

25. William Wetherall and George De Vos, "Ethnic Minorities in Japan," *in* Veenhoven et al., eds., *Case Studies on Human Rights and Fundamental Freedoms: A World Survey* (The Hague: Martinus Nijhoff, 1975) 1:333-375.

26. Figures (percents are mine) are from a copy of hand-written, internal-use statistics obtained through informant.

27. For a reasonably adequate discussion of the problem of passing names for Koreans in Japan, see Kim Il-myŏn, *Chōsenjin ga naze "Nihonmei" o nanoru no ka: Minzoku ishiki to sabetsu* [Why Do Koreans Use "Japanese Names?": Ethnic Awareness and Discrimination] (Tokyo: San'ichi Shobō, 1978). See also Kim, *Lost Names*.

28. Daekyun Chung, "Japan-born Koreans in the U.S.: Their Experiences in Japan and the U.S." (M.A. Thesis, Asian-American Studies, University of California at Los Angeles, 1978); and Chung Daekyun [Chŏng Taegyun] " 'Jiyū e no tōsō' ka: Atarashii Zainichi-Chōsenjin-ron e no shikaku" ["Escape to Freedom?": A Perspective for a New View of Koreans in Japan], *Chōsen kenkyū*, no. 189 (May 1979): 1-68 (entire contents).

29. The *Japan Times*, 3 February 1980, p. 9. See also Daekyun Chung's cogent rebuttal (printed without editorial comment and without any change in the paper's discriminatory advertising practices) on p. 12 of the 16 February issue.

30. Ōshima, *Harimoto Isao*, pp. 174-178.

31. For Takamiyama's interesting views of ethnicity in Japan, and for revealing insights into his own ethnic adjustments, see Takamiyama Daigorō, *Washi no sumō jinsei* [My Sumō Life] (Tokyo: Asahi Evening News, 1979), translated by Mushiake Aromu from an apparently unpublished English manuscript. His English autobiography, written with John Wheeler, *Takamiyama: The World of Sumō* (Tokyo: Kōdansha International, 1973) also touches upon the problems of cultural shock and ethnic identity, but not as comprehensively as in the more recent Japanese autobiography.

32. *Terebi gaido*, 15, no. 49 (3 Dec. 1976): 174.

33. *Terebi gaido*, 16, no. 35 (2 Sept. 1977): 9.

34. Itsuki and a score of equally popular singers are followed by rumors that their musical flowers stem from Korean roots, and that their Japanese "soul" should be spelled "Seoul." See also n. 8 and references in n. 37.

35. Koga Masao, *Uta wa waga tomo waga kokoro: Koga Masao jiden* [Songs are My Friends and My Soul: The Autobiography of Koga Masao] (Tokyo: Ushio Shuppan Sha, 1977), pp. 51-73. See also Mori, *Naze enka*, pp. 115-124.

36. See, for example, *Asahi shinbun*, 3 March 1977 (evening ed.), p. 3. It is significant that this article specifically notes that Miyako Harumi has a Korean [*Kankokujin*] father. Yi Sŏng-ae's enka challenge was also widely reported in the Japanese-language Korean press in Japan. See, for example, *Tōitsu nippō* [T'ong'il ilbo], 29 April 1977.

37. Akasaka Kishi (pseudonym), "Naze Kankokujin tarento ga maruhi na no ka!: Geino tabuu o kiru!" [Why Are the Ethnic Identities of Korean Entertainers

Kept Secret?: Breaking Taboos in the Performing Arts!], *Masukomi hyōron*, 2, no. 12 (Dec. 1976): 18. This article invited a strong rebuttal from Okaniwa Noboru, in " 'Uwasa' to iu terorizumu: Geinō o meguru 'mo hitotsu no isha' ni tsuite" [The Terrorism of "Rumor": On "One More Consolation" of the Performing Arts], *Gendai no me*, 18, no. 2, ser. 103 (Feb. 1977): 118-127. Akasaka responded to Okaniwa in a follow-up "Naze" article in *Masukomi hyōron*, 3, no. 3 (Mar. 1977): 24-31, which invited a second rebuttal from Okaniwa in *Gendai no me*, 18, no. 6, ser. 110 (June 1977): 276-285.

In 1979, an editor of *Masukomi hyōron* [Mass Media Critique] left the magazine and started publishing the look-alike competitor *Uwasa no shinsō* [The Truth About Rumors]. An unsigned article in 1, no. 6, ser. 6 (Sept. 1979): 9 of the latter reported that Mienoumi, a sumō wrestler who had just been made a Yokozuna [Grand Champion], the highest rank in national sumō, was a naturalized citizen, and that his parents were Koreans. The article criticized the fact that these details were conspicuously missing from Japanese mass media accounts of the wrestler's life, although the Korean community press gave considerable coverage to Mienoumi's "ethnic" achievement. The following issue (Oct. 1979) featured a lengthy article by Kaneyama Toshiaki (pseudonym?) entitled "Naze, Kankoku/Chōsenjin no tarento no 'kokuseki' ga tabuu na no ka!" [Why are the "Nationalities" of Korean Talents Taboo?!]. The author of the article cites the case of "Englishman Lafcadio Hearn" who is said to have taken the name Koizumi Yakumo as a means of endearing himself to the people of Japan and easing his entrance into Japanese society. He then reiterates that Mienoumi had naturalized, and that he is presently known as Ishiyama Gorō, but that his *honmyo* [true name, legal name] is Yi. But Lafcadio Hearn became a Japanese citizen, after which he was no longer "Englishman Lafcadio Hearn" but "Japanese Koizumi Yakumo." Similarly, if Mienoumi naturalized, then he is as Japanese as any member of the Imperial Family. And if he naturalized as Ishiyama, then his honmyo is Ishiyama, not Yi. Thus the author of this article, like the authors of similar "rumor" expose, would seem to be under the spell of taboos that are even more indelible than those which he would eradicate.

38. Harimoto Isao [Chang Hun], *Batto hitosuji: Harimoto Isao jiden* [Straight Bat: The Autobiography of Harimoto Isao] (Tokyo: Kōdansha, 1976), p. 200.

39. The movie, based on Ōshima's biography, *Harimoto Isao: Fukutsu no tōkon*, was directed by Yi Sang-on of Ryōnbang Yonghwa film company. It stars Kim Ae-gyŏng as Harimoto's mother, Yi Kang-yŏng as young Harimoto, and Yi Tong-jin as Harimoto the "Korean hero" of Japanese baseball. The film was shot on a shoestring budget, and the producer economized by making use of Koreans in Japan who volunteered to serve as extras. Harimoto himself coached Yi Tong-jin in the idiosyncracies of the Harimoto style, and he made a special appearance in the film.

40. Ōshima, *Harimoto Isao*, p. 197.

41. Yamamura Masaaki, *Inochi moetsukiru tomo: Yamamura Masaaki ikō shū* [Even If My Life Ends in Flame: Collected Posthumous Manuscripts of Yamamura Masaaki] (Tokyo: Yamato Shobō, 1971), pp. 3, 34. The title alludes to the manner in which Yamamura committed suicide, immolation by fire.

42. Wani was an immigrant from the Korean state of Paekche who came to Japan around the end of the fourth century A.D. about the time of Emperor Ōjin, who also may have been Korean. Ōjin's identity and reign dates, and thus the time that Wani came to Japan, are disputed. For a discussion of the dispute in English, see Gari Ledyard, "Galloping Along With The Horseriders: Looking for the Founders of Japan," *The Journal of Japanese Studies*, 1, no. 2 (Spring 1975): 217-254.

43. Watanabe Shōichi, *Nihongo no kokoro* [The Soul of the Japanese Language] (Tokyo: Kōdansha, 1974), pp. 105-106.

44. Ibid., pp. 8, 11-12. For a comprehensive critical review of Watanabe's

thesis that so-called *Yamato kotoba* (words believed by many Japanese to be purely "Japanese" in origin, and which are part and parcel of classical *waka*) continue to transmit the racial spirit of the Japanese language as it evolved in the pristine past, see Roy Andrew Miller, *The Japanese Language in Contemporary Japan: Some Sociolinguistic Observations* (Washington, D.C.: American Enterprise Institute for Public Policy Research, 1977), and his related articles in *The Journal of Japanese Studies*.

45. Ibid., p. 106. Karafuto-born, Japan-resident, Korean novelist Yi Hoe-sŏng won the coveted Akutagawa Prize in 1971, along with Okinawa-born novelist Azuma Mineo. I [Yi] is known in Sino-Japanese as Ri Kaisei.

46. Watanabe Shōichi, *Rekishi no yomikata: Ashita o yoken suru "Nihonshi no hōsoku"* [How To Read History: "Principles of Japanese History" That Foresee Tomorrow] (Tokyo: Shodensha, 1979), pp. 69-70.

47. Watanabe Shōichi and Gregory Clark, "Mottomo kōkateki-na gakushūhō o sagutte miru" [Searching for More Effective Ways to Learn (English)], *English Journal*, 9, no. 1, ser. 100 (Jan. 1979): 66.

48. Tsunoda Tadanobu, *Nihonjin no nō: Nō no hataraki to tōsei no bunka* [The Brain of Japanese People: The Functions of the Brain and East/West Culture] (Tokyo: Taishūkan Shoten, 1978). For a general critique of this book in English, see Makita Kiyoshi's review in *Journal of Japanese Studies*, 5, no. 2 (Summer 1979): 439-450.

49. Tsunoda, *Nihonjin no nō*, p. 317.

50. Ibid., pp. 58-60, 135-137.

51. Second-baseman Johnson, a former Atlanta Braves golden glover, broke the "color line" of the Central League Yomiuri Giants in 1975 as the first "quota foreigner" to join the team. Left-fielder Harimoto was acquired the following year from the Pacific League Nippon Ham Fighters, formerly the Tōei Flyers, and a second American, pitcher Clyde Wright, was added to the roster. Johnson and Harimoto joined first-baseman Oh Sadaharu to give Giants' manager Nagashima Shigeo the power he needed to field a pennant-contending team and restore the ever-popular Tokyo-based Giants to their former glory. Harimoto was traded to Lotte Orions for the 1980 season. Oh retired from active play at the end of the 1980 season when Nagashima resigned. Giants' pitcher Niiura Hisao is also known as Kim I-ryung, and Nagashima himself, rivalled by Harimoto and Oh in major batting records, is pursued by doubts about the "purity" of his ethnic ancestry (see, for example, Ishida Kenzō, "Nagashima Shigeo o osotta 'Kokuseki mondai' no uwasa o tsuiseki suru!" [Chasing the "Nationality Problem" Rumors that have Assailed Nagashima Shigeo], *Uwasa no shinsō*, 1, no. 9, ser. 9 (Dec. 1979): 16-22. Oh Sadaharu is a Chinese national, born and raised in Japan. His father is a Chekiang-born Chinese immigrant, and his mother is of Japanese ancestry. The Mandarin Chinese reading of Oh Sadaharu is Wang Chen-chih, and Oh's mailbox name is C. C. Wang. When he broke Hank Aaron's home run record in 1977, he was given the first *Kokumin Eiyū* [(Japanese) People's Honor] award by Prime Minister Fukuda Takeo. When Fukuda initiated the award and nominated Oh as its first recipient, he was criticized by those who felt that a foreigner should not receive such an award. For a readable and generally reliable discussion of ethnic problems in Japanese baseball, see Robert Whiting, *The Chrysanthemum and the Bat: Baseball Samurai Style* (New York: Dodd, Mead, 1977).

52. Sakamoto Uichirō, *Gansō to Nihonjin: Anata no senzo wa nanizoku ka* [Facial Physiognomy of Japanese: What Ethnicity Were Your Ancestors?] (Tokyo: Saimaru Shuppan Kai, 1976), p. 10.

53. Ibid., p. 21.

54. Ibid., p. 22.

55. Michael Berger, *The Business of Understanding Japan and the United States in Today's World* (as seen through *The Japanese Film*, a PBS television series produced by KQED, San Francisco) (Berkeley: Pacific Film Archives in cooperation with the Japan Society of New York, 1974), p. 6. Berger is actually very familiar with the problems that he inadvertently failed to mention. It is also of interest to note that he refers (p. 14) to the "hidden wish" of some Asian-Japanese "to have the yellow color of their skin changed into white."

56. For a thoroughly researched and sensitive field report on color discrimination in Japanese society, see Nathan Strong's doctoral dissertation, "Patterns of Social Interaction and Psychological Accommodation Among Japan's *Konketsuji* Population" (University of California at Berkeley, Anthropology and Education, 1978). See also Hiroshi Wagatsuma, "The Social Perception of Skin Color in Japan," *Daedalus*, 96, no. 2 (Spring 1967): 407-443.

57. All periods of Japanese history have witnessed ethnic conflict along Japan's northern, southern, and western frontiers. Run-ins between Yamato peoples and Ainu or other northern groups are well attested, as is the friction between main-islanders and the peoples of the Okinawan islands. The animosity engendered by the Japanese-dominated pirates who preyed upon East Asian seaports is also well known. Two failed invasions of the Korean peninsula at the end of the 16th century left scars still visible in present-day Japan/Korea relations.

As for confrontation nearer the inner sanctums of Japanese society, one of the most overlooked documents is the *Shinsen shōji roku* (815), an aristocratic peerage of clans with titles of nobility residing in the inner provinces centering on the Heian capital in present-day Kyoto. Some 326 (28%) of the 1182 clans listed in this register were of immigrant origin. The majority of these immigrant-origin clans resided in the capital itself, where they dominated the right district of the Chinese-style divided city. The sun-deity clans, and other clans of nonimmigrant origin, dominated the left district. Residential patterns in early Japan were clearly status related, and status was clearly a matter of ancestral proximity to the Imperial family and indigenous gods, with groups of immigrant origin or unknown ancestry at the bottom. See Richard Miller, *Ancient Japanese Nobility: The Kabane Ranking System* (Berkeley and Los Angeles: University of California Press, 1974), especially statistics on p. 190.

58. The Japanese sense of being "different" extends also to the manner in which some majorities tend to view ethnic and other minority group problems in Japan. To the extent that Japan is regarded as a homogeneous country, minorities are not supposed to exist. If their existence is acknowledged, their numbers are deemed insignificant. Some majorities prefer the word *kubetsu* (differentiation) to *sabetsu* (discrimination). *Kubetsu* implies that the treatment accorded minorities in Japan is not derivative of the malicious racial philosophies said to be found in other countries but not in Japan, where some would profess to have a corner on "human sensitivity" [*kokoro*].

While some journalistic and publishing enterprises devote considerable attention to minority problems, others—including some of the largest—regard the subject taboo. Some mainline presses are known to censor Japanese translations of the works of foreign scholars to give their majority readers the impression that Japan is being seen from abroad as they prefer that it be seen: with no ethnic minorities beneath the cherry blossoms. Surprisingly—or perhaps not surprisingly—some of this censorship is the result of pressure from minority group factions that cannot tolerate views of minority problems that differ from their own ideologically dogmatic views.

A recent example of such censorship is the case of the Japanese translation of Edwin Reischauer's best-seller *The Japanese* (Cambridge, Mass.: Harvard University Press, 1977), translated by interpreter cum scholar-critic Kunihiro Masao, and published in 1979 by Bungei Shunjū, one of Japan's largest and most distinguished publishing companies. Kunihiro claims in his epilogue that the translation is complete and accurate, but he makes no mention of the fact that Reischauer's half-page discussion of outcastes, historically called *eta* and presently known as *Burakumin*, was entirely expurgated. Although a half-page section on Korean minorities in Japan survived, some briefer references to both Koreans and Burakumin were either deleted or altered. Bungei Shunjū has had trouble with radical Burakumin-affiliated groups in the past, and Reischauer's understanding of minority problems in Japan is not without flaws. All but one of the many references to eta in James Clavell's *Shogun* were cut from the original Japanese translation. But the publishers were forced to recall the translation in March 1981. The following month, an entirely expurgated edition was issued sans all mentions of eta.

13. PROBLEMS OF SELF-IDENTITY AMONG KOREAN YOUTH IN JAPAN

1. The writer of this chapter is very grateful to Professor Changsoo Lee for his valuable suggestions and advice for completing this chapter and to Ms. Taimie Bryant of the Department of Anthropology at UCLA for her able editorial work.

2. For the formation of negative self-images, see George De Vos and Hiroshi Wagatsuma, eds., *Japan's Invisible Race: Caste in Culture and Personality* (Berkeley and Los Angeles: University of California Press, 1966), pp. 228-240. See also H. Wagatsuma, "Mixed Blood Children in Japan: An Exploratory Study," *Journal of Asian Affairs*, 2, no. 2 (1976): 9-17; H. Wagatsuma, "Identity Problems of Black Japanese Youths: An Essay," in Robert I. Rotberg, ed., *Mixing of People: Problems of Identity and Ethnicity* (Stamford, Conn.: Greylock, 1977), chap. 6; Calvin C. Hernton, *Sex and Racism in America* (New York: Doubleday, 1965); William H. Grier and Price M. Cobbs, *Black Rage* (New York: Basic Books, 1968).

3. Ushio Henshūbu, "Nihonjin ni yoru jinshu sabetsu: chōsenjin kara konketsuji made higaisha hyakunin no shōgen" [Racial discrimination by the Japanese: the testimonies of one-hundred victims ranging from Koreans to mixed-blood children], *Ushio*, no. 150 (Feb. 1972): 89-173.

4. For a study of the Burakumin, the ex-untouchable class in Japan, see George A. De Vos and Hiroshi Wagatsuma, eds., *Japan's Invisible Race* (Berkeley and Los Angeles: University of California Press, 1966). See also H. Wagatsuma, "Political Problems of a Minority Group in Japan: Recent Conflicts in Buraku Liberation Movements," in William A. Veenhoven and Winifred Crum Ewing, eds., *Case Studies on Human Rights and Fundamental Freedom: A World Survey* (The Hague: Martinus Mihjoff, 1976) 3:243-273.

5. *Han'guk Ilbo*, 24 March 1977.

6. Lee Hoe-sŏng, *Warera Seishun no Tōjō nite* [The Way of our Youth] (Tokyo: Kōdansha, 1973), pp. 1-100.

7. Ibid.

8. Ibid.

9. Ibid., pp. 171-229.

10. A number of highly successful popular singers, believed to be Koreans, are passing as Japanese. For a detailed discussion of these and others in the entertainment world see chapter 12 of this book.

11. Lee Hoe-sŏng, *Warera seishun*.

12. O Im-chun, *Chōsenjin no naka no nippon* [Japan Inside a Korean] (Tokyo: Sanshōdō, 1971), pp. 29-32.

13. Kim Hak-yŏng, "Manazashi no Kabe" [The Wall of Eyesights], *Bungei,* November 1969.

14. *Han'guk Ilbo,* 24 March 1977.

15. Yamamura Masaaki, *Inochi Moe Tsukiru Tomo* [Even If My Life Ends in Flame] (Tokyo: Yamato Shoten, 1971).

16. Chŏng Su-ryŏng, "Me ni mieru ai to mienai kokkyō" [Love that is visible and the border that is invisible], *Madang,* no. 6 (Summer 1975): 24-32.

17. Harold Isaacs, *Idols of the Tribe* (New York: Harper and Row, 1975), chap. 5.

18. Madang Henshū Bu, "Chiisana ashioto ga kikoeru" [We hear little foot steps], *Madang,* no. 5 (Spring 1975): 40-49.

19. Uchiyama Kazuo, "Waga ko ga watakushi o kaeta" [My own child has changed me], *Madang,* no. 5 (Spring 1975).

20. Kim Young-hae, "Honmyō o nanoru kora" [Children announcing their real names], *Madang,* no. 5 (Spring 1975): 29-37.

21. *Tōitsu Nippō,* 28 May 1977.

22. Ibid., 2 March, 2 April, 14 April, 1977.

23. "Zainichi Nisei no Seikatsu to Iken" [Life and Opinion of the Japan-born Koreans], *Sanzenri,* 8 (Winter 1976): 46-57.

24. Kim Yang-ki, "Jōhatsu shita hanayome" [An evaporated bride], *Madang,* no. 6 (Summer 1975): 10-23.

25. Ibid., p. 10.

26. Ibid., p. 11.

27. Ibid., p. 23.

14: NEGATIVE SELF-IDENTITY IN A DELINQUENT KOREAN YOUTH

1. The major portion of this chapter was originally published in Japanese as Yuzuru Sasaki, "Hikō ya Shinna Asobi no hateni Jisatsu shita Chōsenjin Shōnen no Jirei" [The Case of a Korean Juvenile Who Committed Suicide After Delinquent Acts and "Thinner Play"] *in* Hiroshi Wagatsuma, ed., *Hikō Shōnen no Jirei Kenkyū* [Case Studies of Juvenile Delinquents] (Tokyo: Seishin Shobō, 1973), chap. 5. For completion of the present chapter we are grateful to George De Vos, who contributed valuable thoughts.

2. George De Vos and Hiroshi Wagatsuma, "Socialization, Self-Perception, and Burakumin Status" and "Group Solidarity and Individual Mobility" *in* De Vos and Wagatsuma, eds., *Japan's Invisible Race* (Berkeley and Los Angeles: University of California Press, 1966), chaps. 11 and 12; H. Wagatsuma, "Mixed Blood Children in Japan: An Exploratory Study," *Journal of Asian Affairs,* 2, no. 2 (1976): 9-17; H. Wagatsuma, "Identity Problems of Black Japanese Youths: An Essay" *in* Robert Rotberg, ed., *Mixing of People: Problems of Identity and Ethnicity* (Stamford, Conn.: Greylock, 1978), chap. 6.

3. A *nagaya,* or long house, is a long, single building with a number of very small residential units. Very often each unit does not have its own toilet, so residents use a communal lavatory separate from the building. Such long houses were very common for low-income people during the feudal period and also in modern Japan until very recently.

4. For the relationships between police and community in Japan, see David H. Bayley, *Forces of Order: Police Behavior in Japan and the States* (Berkeley and Los Angeles: University of California Press, 1976).

5. S. and E. Glueck, *Unraveling Juvenile Delinquency* (Cambridge, Mass.: Harvard University Press, 1950).

6. L. E. Hewitt and R. L. Jenkins, *Fundamental Patterns of Maladjustment* (Springfield, Ill.: State of Illinois, 1946). These authors found, in so-called socialized delinquents, negligent parental patterns such as the mother's lack of interest in home-keeping, lack of regularity in the home routine, lack of supervision, a tendency to lax discipline, and periodic overly harsh discipline on the part of one or both parents. Sometimes the mother attempted to protect the child from the father's physical attacks. Often more than one of the children in the family became delinquent. This pattern was found to be associated with families living in deteriorated urban areas. Hewitt and Jenkins found that there was no simple correlation between the three parental attitudinal categories of (a) rejection, (b) neglect, and (c) repressive discipline and the delinquent behavioral categories. Nevertheless, they concluded that severe and active parental rejection, especially in the early years, produced a type of "antisocial aggressive" delinquency based on faulty internalization and a lack of capacity to have feeling for others. In contrast, neglect owing to inadequate or disorganized parents tended to orient the child toward some social form of delinquency.

15: CONCLUSIONS—THE MAINTENANCE OF A KOREAN ETHNIC IDENTITY IN JAPAN

1. Hiroshi Wagatsuma and George A. De Vos, *Heritage of Endurance* (n.d.).

2. Ibid.

3. Nathan Glazer and Daniel P. Moynahan, *Ethnicity: Theory and Experience* (Cambridge, Mass.: Harvard University Press, 1975).

4. Ralf Dahrendorf, "On the Origin of Inequality among Men," *in* Andre Beteille, ed., *Social Inequality* (Baltimore: Penguin Books, 1969); *in* Glazer and Moynihan, *Ethnicity*, pp. 12-13.

5. Ibid., p. 15.

6. Ralf Dahrendorf, *Class and Class Conflict in Industrial Society* (Stanford: Stanford University Press, 1959).

7. Glazer and Moynahan, *Ethnicity*, p. 25.

8. Daniel Bell, "Ethnicity and Social Changes," *in* Glazer and Moynihan, *Ethnicity*, pp. 141-174.

9. George A. De Vos, ed., *Socialization for Achievement: Essays on the Cultural Psychology of the Japanese* (Berkeley and Los Angeles: University of California Press, 1973).

10. Henry A. Murray, *Explorations in Personality* (New York: Oxford University Press, 1938).

11. Robert K. Merton, *Social Theory and Social Structure* (Glencoe: Fredd Press, 1957).

12. George A. De Vos and Hiroshi Wagatsuma, eds., *Japan's Invisible Race* (Berkeley and Los Angeles: University of California Press, 1966).

13. Ibid., pp. 228-230.

14. Bell, "Ethnicity and Social Changes," *in* Glazer and Moynihan, *Ethnicity*, pp. 160-171.

15. Ibid., pp. 9-10.

16. Robert O. Blood, *Love Marriage and Arranged Marriage* (New York: Free Press, 1967).

17. Takeo Doi, "Amaeru: A Key Concept for Understanding Japanese Per-

sonality Structure," in *Japanese Culture: Its Development and Characteristics* (Chicago: Aldine, 1962).

18. J. W. Bennett and Iwao Ishino, *Paternalism in the Japanese Economy: Anthropological Studies of Oyabun-Kobun Patterns* (Minneapolis: University of Minnesota Press, 1963).

19. George De Vos and Lola Romanucci-Ross, eds., *Ethnic Identity* (Palo Alto: Mayfield, 1975).

SELECTED BIBLIOGRAPHY

DOCUMENTS AND OFFICIAL PUBLICATIONS

English

Gane, William J. *Repatriation: From 25 September 1945 to 31 December 1945.* Seoul: United States Military Government in Korea, 1947.

Japan, House of Representatives. *Proceedings: The 90th Session of the Imperial Diet,* no. 30, 19 August 1946.

On the Question of 600,000 Koreans in Japan. P'yongyang: Foreign Languages Publishing House, 1959.

Supreme Commanders for the Allied Powers. *Directives.* Tokyo: SCAP Headquarters.

SCAPIN-44, AG 091.3 "Control over Exports and Imports of Gold, Silver, Security and Financial Instrument," 22 September 1945.

SCAPIN-93, "Removal of Restrictions on Political, Civil, and Religious Liberties," 4 October 1945.

SCAPIN-113, AG 240 "Payment of Bonus to Japanese Soldiers of Korean Descent," 9 October 1945.

SCAPIN-127, AG 091.3 "Supplemental Instructions Relating to Import and Export Controls," 12 October 1945.

SCAPIN-142, AG 370.05 "Reception Centers in Japan for Processing Repatriates," 15 October 1945.

SCAPIN-148, AG 091 "Policies Governing Repatriation of Japanese Nationals in Conquered Territory," 16 October 1945.

SCAPIN-154, AG 370.05 "Repatriation Reception Center," 8 November 1945.

SCAPIN-217, AG 312.4 "Definition of United Nations, Neutral Nations, and Enemy Nations," 31 October 1945.

SCAPIN-224, AG 370.1 "Repatriation of Non-Japanese from Japan," 1 November 1945.

SCAPIN-295, AG 370.5 "Repatriation of Non-Japanese from Japan," 17 November 1945.

SCAPIN-360, AG 230.14 "Employment Policies," 28 November 1945.

SCAPIN-532, AG 901.714 "Supplementary Instructions Relating to Import and Export Controls," 2 January 1946.

SCAPIN-563, AG 091 "Control of Population Movements" 8 January 1946.

SCAPIN-1735-A, "Suppression of Illegal Entry into Japan," 16 July 1946.

SCAPIN-685, AG 551.1 "Railway Fares Charged to Koreans," 31 January 1946.

SCAPIN-746, AG 053 "Registration of Koreans, Chinese, Ryukyuans and Formosans," 17 February 1946.
SCAPIN-882, AG 370.05 "Repatriation," Annex I, Annex VI, 16 March 1946.
SCAPIN-882.1, AG 370.5 "Repatriation," 27 March 1946.
SCAPIN-927, AG 370.05 "Repatriation," 7 May 1946.
SCAPIN-927/2, Annex III, 30 June 1946.
SCAPIN-1094, AG 430 "Ration for United Nations' Nationals, Neutral Nationals and Stateless Persons," 30 July 1946.
SCAPIN-1841 "Ration for United Nations' Nationals, Neutral Nationals and Stateless Persons, 8 January 1948.
SCAPIN-1111-A, AG 250.1 "Misconducts Committed by Koreans," 29 April 1946.
SCAPIN-1181, AG 014.33 "Release from Prison and Repatriation of Korean Nationals," 10 September 1946.
SCAPIN-4938 A, AG 012.2 "Applicability of Taxes to Non-Japanese Nationals," 29 November 1947.
SCAPIN-1826 A, "Applicability of Ordinary Taxes to Non-Japanese Nationals," 25 July 1946.
————. Political Reorientation of Japan, September 1945 to September 1948. Vol. II. Grosse Pointe, Michigan: Scholarly Press, 1968.
————. Summation of Non-Military Activities in Japan. Tokyo: SCAP, 1945-1948.

Japanese

Keisatsuchō, Keibikyoku [Police Department, Security Bureau]. Sayoku undō [The Left-wing Movement]. Tokyo: 1968.
Kōan Chōsachō [The Public Safety Investigation Bureau], comp. Naigai jōsei no gaikō to tenbō [The Current Situation and Perspective of the Internal and External Affairs]. Tokyo: Kōanchō, 1963.
————. "Nikkan jōyaku hijun hantai undō no sōkatsu" [A Summary of the Campaign Against the ROK-Japan Treaty]. Chōsa Geppō, no. 123, March 1966.
————. "Zainichi Chōsenjin no genjō to Hokusen kikan mondai" [The Conditions of the Koreans in Japan and the Problem of the Repatriation to North Korea]. Chōsa Geppō, no. 40, April 1959.
Naikaku Kanbō Naikaku Chōsashitsu [The Office of the Prime Minister's Secretariat]. Jōyaku teikei o meguru naigai no dōkō [The Internal and External Situations in Related to the Conclusion of the ROK-Japan Normalization Treaty]. Tokyo: 1966.
Naimushō, Tokubetsu Kōtō Keisatsu [The Home Affairs Ministry, the Special Higher Police Bureau]. Nendobetsu Chōsenjin chiihō ihan genkyō shirabe sonota [Yearly Statistics of Violations of Peace Preservation Law by Koreans: 1944-45]. Japanese Army and Navy Archives Series, 1868-1945; Microfilm T1510 (R222 F93357).
————. "Nikkan jōyaku hijun soshi seiryoku no dōkō" [The Movement Concerning the Forces against the Approval of the ROK-Japan Treaty]. Nikkan Mondai Jōhō, no. 3, September 1965.
Tatsumi, Nobuo. Zainichi Kankokujin no Hōteki Chii Kyōtei to Shutsunyūkoku Kanri Tokubetsūhō Kaisetsu [The Treaty Concerning the Legal Status of Koreans in Japan and Commentary on the Special Immigration Law]. Immigration Office. Ministry of Justice, 1966.

Korean

Korea. Ministry of Foreign Affairs. Oemu hangchōng ūi shipnyōn [The Ten Years of the Administration of Foreign Affairs]. Seoul: 1959.

BOOKS

English

Beckmann, George M. and Okubo Genji. *The Japanese Communist Party 1922-1945.* Stanford: Stanford University Press, 1969.
Kurzman, Dan. *Kishi and Japan.* New York: Ivan Obolensky, Inc., 1960.
Mitchell, Richard H. *The Korean Minority in Japan.* Berkeley and Los Angeles: University of California Press, 1967.
Scalapino, Robert A. *The Japanese Communist Movement: 1920-1966.* Berkeley and Los Angeles: University of California Press, 1967.
Swearigen, Roger and Langer, Paul. *Red Flag in Japan.* Cambridge, Mass.: Harvard University Press, 1952.
Wagner, Edward W. *The Korean Minority in Japan: 1904-1950.* New York: Institute of Pacific Relations, 1951.

Japanese

Andō, Hikotarō et al. *Nichi-Chō-Chū sankoku jinmin rentai no rekishi to riron* [A Treatise and History Concerning the Unity of Peoples of Japan-Korea-China]. Tokyo: Nihon Chōsen Kenkyūsho, 1964.
Chŏng, Chŏl. *Mindan.* Tokyo: Yōyōsha, 1967.
Chŏng, T'ae-sŏng. *Ningen Pak Yŏl* [Pak Yŏl as a Man]. Tokyo: Shin Chōsen Kensetsu Dōmei, 1946.
———. *Dokuritsu shidōsha Pak Yŏl* [Pak Yŏl, as a Leader for Independence]. Tokyo: Shin Chōsen Kensetsu Dōmei, 1946.
Chōsen Daigakukkō, comp. *Chōsen Daigaku o mite* [Seeing the Chosŏn University]. Tokyo: Chōsen Daigakukkō, 1967.
Fujishima, Udai and Ozawa Yūsaku. *Minsoku kyōiku* [The Ethnic Education]. Tokyo: Aogi Shoten, 1966.
Han, Dŏk-su. *Zainichi Chōsenjin undō no tenkan ni tsuite* [Concerning a Change of the Korean Movement in Japan]. Tokyo: Gakuyū shobō, 1955. [An earlier version was published in 1952 under a pseudonym, Paek Su-bong, *Aeguk chinyŏng ŭi sunwha wa kangwha lŭl wihayŏ* (n.p. 1952).]
Harimoto Isao, *Batto hitosuji: Harimoto Isao jiden* [Straight Bat: the Autobiography of Harimoto Isao]. Tokyo: Kōdansha, 1976.
Hatada, Takashi. *Nihonjin no Chōsenjin kan* [Japanese Views on Koreans]. Tokyo: Keiso Shobō, 1969.
Ikegami, Tsutomu. *Hōteki chii nihyaku no shitsumon* [Two Hundred Questions Concerning the Legal Status]. Tokyo: Kyōbunsha, 1965.
Inoue, Hideo and Ueda Masaaki, eds. *Nihon to Chōsen no nisennen* [Two Thousand Years of Korea and Japan]. Tokyo: Taihei Shuppansha, 1969.
Kajii, Noboru. *Chōsenjin gakkō no Nihonjin kyōshi* [The Japanese Teachers in the Korean School]. Tokyo: Nihon Chōsen Kenkyūsho, 1966.
Kajiwara Ikki, *Rikidōzan to Nihon no proresu shi* [Rikidōzan and a History of Japanese Professional Wrestling]. Tokyo: Akebono Shuppan, 1971.
Kaneda Tatsuo, *Ōja Rikidōzan: Sekai senshuken o waga udeni* [Champion Rikidōzan: The World Title in Our Arms]. Tokyo: Kindai Shuppansha, 1955.
Kang, Dŏk-san and Kŭm Byŏng-tong, eds. *Kantō Daishinsai to Chōsenjin* [The Kantō Earthquake and the Koreans]. Gendaishi Shiryō Series. Vol. VI. Tokyo: Mimizu Shobō, 1963.
Kim, Chŏng-myŏng, comp. *Chōsen dokuritsu undō: Kyōsanshugi undō hen* [The Korean Independence Movement: The Communist Movement]. Vols. VI and V. Tokyo: Harashobō, 1966 and 1967.

Kim Hi-lo's Trial Countermeasure Committee, ed. *Kim Hi-lo no hōtei chinjutsu* [Kim Hi-lo's Court Testimony]. Tokyo: San'ichi shobō, 1972.

Koyama, Hirotake. *Sengo Nihon Kyōsantō shi* [A History of the Postwar Japanese Communist Party]. Tokyo: Hōgashoten, 1966.

Kwǒn, Il. *Sokoku he no nengan* [My Desire for the Fatherland]. Tokyo: Matsuzawa Shoten, 1959.

Minzoku Kyōiku Hensū Iinkai, comp. *Zainichi Chōsenjin no kyōiku ni tsuite* [Concerning the Korean Education in Japan]. Tokyo: Minzoku Kyōiku Henshū Iinkai, 1965.

Morita, Yoshio. *Chōsen shūsen no kiroku: Beiso ryōgun no shinchū to Nihonjin no hikiage* [The Record of Ending the War in Korea: The Advancement of the US-Soviet Union Troops and the Japanese Repatriation]. Tokyo: Gannandō, 1965.

Nakazono, Eisuke. *Zainichi Chōsenjin: Nanajūnen dai nihon no genten* [The Koreans in Japan: The 1970's Focal Point of Japan]. Tokyo: Zaikaitenbō shinsha, 1970.

Nihon Kyōnsantō, comp. *Nichikan Jōyaku to Nihon Kyōsantō* [The JCP and the ROK-Japan Treaty]. Tokyo: The JCP Central Committee, 1965.

———. *Nihon Kyōsantō gojūnen mondai shiryō shū* [A Collection of Documents Concerning the Japanese Communist Incident of 1950]. 3 vols. Tokyo: The JCP Central Committee, 1953.

Ōshima Yukio, *Harimoto Isao: Fukutsu no tōkon* [Harimoto Isao: Dauntless Fighting Spirit]. Tokyo: Suponichi Shuppan, 1976.

Ozawa, Yūsaku, *Zainichi Chōsenjin kyōiku ron* [A Treatise Concerning Education of Koreans in Japan]. Tokyo: Akishobō, 1974.

Pak, Che-il. *Zainichi Chōsenjin ni kansuru sōgō chōsa kenkyū* [A General Survey Study of Koreans in Japan]. Tokyo: Shin Kigensha, 1957.

Pak, Kyǒng-sik. *Chōsenjin kyōsei renkō no kiroku* [The Record of the Forcibly Taken Laborers]. Tokyo: Miraisha, 1965.

———, ed. *Zainichi Chōsenjin kankei shiryō shūsei* [Collection of Data Concerning Koreans in Japan]. 5 vols. Tokyo: San-ichi shobō, 1975-1976.

Pak, Yǒl. *Shin Chōsen Kakumei ron* [A Treatise of Revolution for a New Korea]. Tokyo: Chūō Shuppansha, 1949.

Rikidōzan Mitsuhiro, *Karate choppu sekai o yuku: Rikidōzan jiden* [The Karate Chop World: the Autobiography of Rikidozan]. Tokyo: Beensubooru Magazinsha, 1962.

Satō, Katsumi, ed. *Zainichi Chōsenjin: Sono sabetsu to shogū no hensen* [The Koreans in Japan: Changes in Discrimination and Treatment]. Tokyo: Dōseisha, 1974.

———, ed. *Zainichi Chōsenjin no shomondai* [Various Problems of the Koreans in Japan]. Tokyo: Dōseisha, 1974.

Shakai Undō Chōsakai, comp. *Sayoku Jiten* [The Left-wing Dictionary]. Tokyo: Musashi Shobō, 1961.

Shinozaki, Heiji. *Zainichi Chōsenjin undō* [The Korean Movement in Japan]. Tokyo: Reibunsha, 1955.

Soshinkai. *Chōsen Daigaku no enkaku no genjo* [The Origin of the Chosǒn University and the Current Situation]. n.p.: Soshinkai, 1962.

The Committee to Support Pak, ed. *Minzoku sabetsu: Hitachi shūshoku sabetsu kyūdan* [Ethnic Discrimination: Denunciation against the Hitachi Discriminatory Employment Practice]. Tokyo: Aki shobō, 1974.

Tōitsu Chōsenshimbun tokushūhan, comp. *Kim Byǒng-sik jiken: sono jinsō to haikei* [Kim Byong-sik Incident: Its Truth and Background]. Tokyo: Tōitsu shimbunsha, 1973.

Tōitsu Hyōronsha, ed., *Tōitsuhyōron* (April 1977). Tokyo: Tōitsu Hyōronsha, 1977.

Tsukahara, Bison. *Bikaihō buraku* [Unliberated Villages]. Tokyo: Yūsankaku, 1969.

Tsuobe, Senji. *Chōsen Minzoku tokuritsu undō hishi* [The Hidden History of the Korean Independence Movement]. Tokyo: Nikkan Rōdō Tsūshinsha, 1959.

Yaginuma, Masaji. *Nihon Kyōsantō undō shi* [A History of the Japanese Communist Party Movement]. Tokyo: Keibunkakaku, 1953.

Yamura Masaaki, *Inochi moetsukiru tomo: Yamamura Masaaki ikō shū* [Even If My Life Ends in Flame: Collected Posthumous Manuscripts of Yamamura Masaaki]. Tokyo: Yamato shobō, 1971.

Yi, Yuwhan. *Zainichi Kankokujin gojūnen shi* [A Fifty-year History of Koreans in Japan]. Tokyo: Shinju Bussan Co., 1960.

————. *Zainichi Kankokujin rokujūman* [600,000 Koreans in Japan]. Tokyo: Yōyōsha, 1971.

Yi, Tong-jun. *Nihon ni iru Chōsen no kodomo* [The Korean Children in Japan]. Tokyo: Shunjūsha, 1956.

Zainichi Chōsenjin no Jinken o Mamoru Kai, comp. *Kikoku kyōtei no enchō to kikoku jigyō no hoshō no tameni* [For the Extension of the Repatriation Agreement and Its Assurance for the Further Repatriation]. Tokyo: Zainichi Chōsenjin no Jinken o Mamoru Kai, 1967.

————, comp. *Zainichi Chōsenjin no hōteki chii* [The Legal Status of Koreans in Japan]. Tokyo: Zainichi Chōsenjin no Jinken o Mamorukai, 1965.

————, comp. *Zainichi Chōsenjin no minshushugiteki minzoku kyōiku* [The Democratic Ethnic Education for the Koreans in Japan]. Tokyo: Zainichi Chōsenjin no Jinken o Mamoru Kai, 1965.

Korean

Chŏn, Chun. *Choch'ongnyŏn yonku* [A Study of the Federation of Korean Residents in Japan]. 2 vols. Seoul: Korea University Press, 1972.

Kang, No-hyang. *Cheil Taep'yobu* [The Korean Mission in Japan]. Seoul: Tong-a P.R. Yŏnkuso, 1966.

Kim, Ch'ŏn-hae. *Okchung sip'onyŏn* [The 17 Years in Prison]. Tokyo: Minshu Chōsensha, 1946.

Kim, Sang-hyŏn. *Cheil Hanguk'in* [Korean Residents in Japan]. Seoul: Dankok Haksul Yŏnkuwŏn, 1969.

Kŭktong Munchae Yŏnkuso, comp. *Pukhan Chŏnsŏ* [Collected Works on North Korea]. 3 vols. Seoul: Kŭktong Munchae Yŏnkuso, 1974.

Wŏn, Yong-sŏk. *Han'il hwaedam shipsa'nyŏn* [The Fourteen Years of ROK-Japanese Talk]. Seoul: Samhwa Ch'ulp'ansa, 1965.

ARTICLES

English

Conde, David. "The Korean Minority in Japan." *Far Eastern Survey*. Vol. XVI. 26 February 1946.

Lee, Changsoo. "Ethnic Discrimination and Conflict: The Case of the Korean Minority in Japan," *in* Willem A. Veenhoven, ed., Vol. IV of *Case Studies on Human Rights and Fundamental Freedoms: a World Survey*. The Hague: Martinus Nijhoff, 1976.

Smythe, Hugh. "A Note of Racialism in Japan," *American Sociological Review*, XVI, no. 6 (1951).

Tameike, Yoshio. "Nationality of Formosans and Koreans," *The Japanese Annual of International Law*, no. 2 (1958).

Japanese

Akiba, Jun-ichi. "Iwayuru hōtekichii kyōteijo no eijūkyoka shinsei hōhō ni kansuru mondaiten" [Problems with the Method of Applying Permanent Residence in Accordance with the So-called Agreement on the Legal Status], *Kokusaihō Gaikō Zasshi*, no. 64 (March 1966).

Arikura, Ryōkichi et al. "Chōsen Daigakō setsuchi ninka ni kansuru tōshinsho no gyōseihōteki bunseki" [Analysis of the Report Concerning Chosŏn University Accreditation from the Administrative Law Point of View], *Hōritsu Jihō*, 40, no. 6 (May 1968).

Chang, Hyŏk-chu. "Chōsenjin no naimaku" [The Inside Story of Koreans], *Shinchō*, no. 12 (December 1949).

Chang, Tu-sik. "Kikokuto Han-Nihonjin" [Half-Japanese and the Repatriation], *Sekai*, no. 10 (October 1959).

Chŏn, Chun. "Chōsensōren" [Ch'ongnyŏn], *Jiju*, no. 5 (May 1970).

"Chōsen Daigakō ninka mondai o meguru wyuoku dantai no dōkō" [The right-wing group activities concerning the question of the Chosŏn University accreditation], *Kōan Jōhō*, no. 169 (October 1967).

Fujishima, Udai et al. "Zainichi Chōsenjin rokujūman no genjitsu" [The Reality of 600,000 Koreans in Japan], *Chūō Kōron*, no. 12 (December 1958).

Fuse, Tatsuji et al. "Dantai Kiseiri no inbō o tsuku" [Expose the Plot Behind the Organization Control Law], *Minshu Chōsen*, no. 5 (May 1950).

Hashimoto, Yūtaka. "Heiwajōyaku to Chōsenjin no kokuseki" [The Peace Treaty and the Korean Nationality], *Minji Kenshū*, no. 57 (January 1962).

Hatada, Takashi. "Zainichi Chōsenjin no kikoku to Nihonjin no Kyōryoku" [The Repatriation of Koreans in Japan and the Japanese Cooperation], *Koria Hyōron*, III, no. 2 (February 1959).

Hirano, Yoshitarō. "Jinken o mamotta hitobito—Fuse Tatsuji" [The People Who Defended the Civil Rights—Fuse Tatsuji], *Hōgaku Semina*, no. 12 (November 1959).

Hiroyama, Shirō. "Minsen no kaisan to Zanihon Chōsenjin Sōrengōkai no ketsusei ni tsuite" [The Dissolution of the Minsen and Concerning the Creation of the Ch'ongnyŏn], *Kōan Jōhō*, no. 22 (July 1955).

———. "Hokusen kikoku mondai no tenbō" [The Prospects for the Repatriation Movement], *Koria Hyōron*, III, no. 1 (January 1959).

———. "Hokusen Saiko Jinmin Kaigi no daigiin senkyo to Chōsensōren" [The Election of the DPRK's Supreme People's Congress and the Ch'ongnyŏn], *Gaiji Tokuhō*, 12, no. 11 (November 1964).

Im, Hun. "Zainihon no jinshuteki henken" [The Japanese Racial Prejudice], *Sekai*, no. 10 (October 1963).

Kim, Il-myŏn. "Zainichi Chōsenjin to Jiyū Hōsōdan" [The Koreans in Japan and the Liberal Judicial Group], *Koria Hyōron*, X, no. 93 (December 1969); and no. 94 (January 1969).

Kim, Tu-yong. "Chōsenjin undō no tadashii hatten no tameni" [Toward Correct Development of the Korean Movement], *Zen-ei*, no. 16 (May 1947).

———. "Chōsenjin undō wa tenkan shitsutsuaru" [The Korean Movement is Changing], *Zen-ei*, no. 14 (1 March 1947).

———. "Nihon ni okeru Chōsenjin mondai" [The Korean Problems in Japan], *Zen-ei*, no. 1 (February 1946).

Morinaga, Eisaburō. "Pak Yŏl, Kaneko Fumiko jiken" [Pak Yŏl and Kaneko Fumiko Case], *Horitsu Jihō*, 35, no. 3 (March 1963); and no. 4 (April 1963).

———. "Jinken yōgo undōshijō no sentatsu—Fuse Tatsuji" [The Pioneer in the History of the Civil Rights Movement—Fuse Tatsuji], *Hōgaku Semina* (December 1956).

Nakanishi, Inosuke. "Nihon tennōsei no datō to tōyō minzoku no minshu dōmei: Chōsenjin Renmei heno yōsei" [The Overthrow of the Emperor Systems and a Democratic League for Asian Races: An Appeal to the Choryōn], *Minshu Chōsen*, no. 7 (July 1946).

"Nam Il Hokusen Gaisō no Nihon seifu ni taisuru tainichi kankei ni kansuru seimeini tsuite" [Concerning the Statement of Nam Il, Foreign Minister of North Korea], *Kōan Jōhō*, no. 21 (June 1955).

"Nikkan jōyaku hijun o meguru uyoku kankei dantai no dōkō" [The Movement of the Right-wing Activities Concerning the ROK-Japan Treaty], *Kōan Jōhō*, no. 148 (January 1966).

"Nitchō gōsaku eiga 'Ch'ollima' no jōei undō ni tsuite" [Concerning the Campaign for the Showing of the Japan-DPRK Joint Cinema Production 'Ch'ollima'], *Kōan Jōhō*, no. 140 (May 1965).

Ochiai, Shigenobu. "Kōbe Chōsenjin Gakkōsōgi no Gaikyō" [The School Dispute Concerning Koreans in Kōbe], *Rekishi to Kōbe*, no. 4 (1963).

———. "Kōbe Chōsenjin Jiken Shokuhatten: Shōwa Nijūsannen no Chōsenjin Gakkō Heisa o meguru Kōbe no Sōran jiken" [The Incident of the Koreans in Kōbe: The Korean Riot Incident in Kōbe Concerning the Korean School Case in 1948], *Hyōgo Shigaku*, no. 28 (1961).

Ogawa, Masaaki. "Zainichi Kankokujin no hōtekichii taigū kyōtei" [The Agreement on the Legal Status and the Treatment of the Koreans in Japan], *Hōritsu Jihō*, 37, no. 10 (September 1965).

Ogawa, Masaaki, Etō Yoshihirō, Yamazaki Masahide, and Kobakura Masatake. "Gaikokujin gakkō seido" [The Foreigners' School Systems], *Hōritsu Jihō*, 39, no. 2 (February 1967).

Pak, Hi-Chōl. "Taikanminkoku Kyoryū Mindan ron" [A Discourse on the Korean Resident Association in Japan], *Mishu Chōsen*, no. 7 (July 1950).

Pak, Yōl. "Nihon kokumin ni yosu" [An Appeal to the Japanese People], *Bunkyō Shimbun* (April 1948).

———. "Nihon wa teki ka mikata ka" [Is Japan our Foe or Ally?], *Kyōto Taimusu*, 20 November 1948.

Satō, Shigemoto. "Chōsenjin no Kokuseki ni tsuite" [Concerning the Korean Nationality], *Minji Geppō* (May 1967).

Tamagi, Motoi. "Nihon Kyosantō no Zainichi Chōsenjin shidō" [The JCP's Guidance on the Koreans in Japan], *Koria Hyōron*, April 1961; June 1961; August 1961.

Ushijima Hidehiko, " 'Hinomaru' no otoko: Rikidōzan no Shōwa hishi" [The Man of the "Rising Sun Flag": the Secret Shōwa History of Rikidōzan], *Ushio*, no. 219 (August 1977).

———. "Cha no ma no eiyū: Rikidōzan no hikari no kage [Living-room Hero: the Lights and Shadows of Rikidōzan], *Ushio*, no. 220 (September 1977).

Won, Yong-dōk. "Shintakutōji to minzoku tōitsu sensen" [The Trusteeship and National Unification Front], *Minshu Chōsen*, no. 4 (April 1946).

"Zainichi Chōsenjin undō ni tsuite" [Concerning Korean Movement in Japan], *Zen-ei*, no. 92 (May 1954).

Korean

"Choguk üi changnae lül tobak hachi malla" [Don't try to Gamble with the Future of the Fatherland], *Sasangge*, no. 5 (May 1965).

Chōn, Chun. "Ilbon kyokwasō e nat'anan Hanguk kwan" [The Japanese Views on Koreans Reflected on the School Text Books], *Sasangge*, no. 5 (May 1965).

Pak, Chun-kyu. "Kulyok üi oekyo lül iōkalyōnunka?" [Carrying on the Humiliating Diplomacy?], *Sasangge*, no. 4 (April 1965).

YEARBOOKS

Asahi Nenkan, 1960-.
Pukhan Ch'onggam, 1945-68.
Tōitsu Chōsen Nankan, 1964; 1965-66; 1967-68.

NEWSPAPERS

Asahi Shimbun, Tokyo, Japan.
Chōren Chūō Jihō, Tokyo, Japan, 1946-49.
Chosön Sibo, Tokyo, Japan.
Nodong Shinmun, P'yongyang, North Korea.
Tōitsu Nippō, Tokyo, Japan.
Tong-A Ilbo, Seoul, Korea.

INDEX